J. NIXON
AUGUST 1980.

ECONOMETRICS

ECONOMICS HANDBOOK SERIES

Burns SOCIAL SECURITY AND PUBLIC POLICY
Carlson ECONOMIC SECURITY IN THE UNITED STATES
Fisher THE IDENTIFICATION PROBLEM IN ECONOMETRICS
Hansen A GUIDE TO KEYNES
Hansen A SURVEY OF GENERAL EQUILIBRIUM SYSTEMS
Hansen THE AMERICAN ECONOMY
Hansen MONETARY THEORY AND FISCAL POLICY
Harris THE ECONOMICS OF HARVARD
Harrod THE BRITISH ECONOMY
Henderson and Quandt MICROECONOMIC THEORY
Hirsch THE ECONOMICS OF STATE AND LOCAL GOVERNMENT
Hirsch URBAN ECONOMIC ANALYSIS
Hoover THE LOCATION OF ECONOMIC ACTIVITY
Jones AN INTRODUCTION TO MODERN THEORIES OF ECONOMIC GROWTH
Johnston STATISTICAL COST ANALYSIS
Kindleberger and Herrick ECONOMIC DEVELOPMENT
Lebergott MANPOWER IN ECONOMIC GROWTH
Maddala ECONOMETRICS
McKean PUBLIC SPENDING
Nourse REGIONAL ECONOMICS
Ott, Ott, and Yoo MACROECONOMIC THEORY
Phelps FISCAL NEUTRALITY TOWARD ECONOMIC GROWTH
Quirk and Saposnik INTRODUCTION TO GENERAL EQUILIBRIUM THEORY AND WELFARE ECONOMICS
Taylor A HISTORY OF ECONOMIC THOUGHT
Theil, Boot, and Kloek OPERATIONS RESEARCH AND QUANTITATIVE ECONOMICS
Tinbergen and Bos MATHEMATICAL MODELS OF ECONOMIC GROWTH
Vickers THE THEORY OF THE FIRM: PRODUCTION, CAPITAL, AND FINANCE
Walton and McKersie A BEHAVIORAL THEORY OF LABOR NEGOTIATIONS

ECONOMETRICS

G. S. Maddala
University of Florida

INTERNATIONAL STUDENT EDITION

McGRAW-HILL KOGAKUSHA, LTD.
Tokyo Auckland Beirut Bogota Düsseldorf Johannesburg
Lisbon London Lucerne Madrid Mexico New Delhi Panama
Paris San Juan São Paulo Singapore Sydney

ECONOMETRICS

INTERNATIONAL STUDENT EDITION

This book was set in Times Roman by Computype, Inc. The editors were J. S. Dietrich and Michael Gardner; the production supervisor was Charles Hess. The drawings were done by Vantage Art, Inc.

Library of Congress Cataloging in Publication Data

Maddala, G S date
Econometrics.

(Economics handbook series)
Includes index.
1. Econometrics. I. Title.
HB139.M35 330'.01'82 76-26042
ISBN 0-07-039412-1

TOSHO PRINTING CO., LTD. TOKYO, JAPAN

CONTENTS

PREFACE

Many students at universities and applied econometricians in government and industry have expressed the opinion that most of the books in econometrics now available concentrate on theory and a limited number of topics. Thus they have to consult different books for different purposes. They felt a need for a comprehensive book with an empirical bias. The present book has been written with these people in mind. It was written entirely during 1974–75 and has not had the benefit of being tried in an actual teaching environment; otherwise, the text might have taken a different form.

Though I have learnt a lot from the work of all the respected econometricians in the profession (and thanking them all would make a long preface), the practical orientation of the book is due to the influence of Art Goldberger, Zvi Griliches, and Marc Nerlove, the first of whom I had contact with mainly through papers. Also my association with Jaques Dréze (since reading his pioneering paper of 1962) and Arnold Zellner has convinced me that every student in econometrics needs an exposure to the Bayesian approach. None of these people, however, have read any part of the book and so cannot be blamed for any shortcomings.

I would like to thank my students David Grether, Kajal Lahiri, and Forrest Nelson who went through the book and suggested some corrections. I would also like to thank Ken Gaver and Walter Oi at the University of Rochester for going through the manuscript. None of them are responsible for any remaining errors.

The book started out with undergraduates in mind and ended up at the graduate level. However, there is a steady progression in the level and the beginning portions can be used by undergraduates, whereas the book as a whole can be used by graduate students as well as applied econometricians in government and industry.

Part two of the book "Introduction to Probability and Statistical Inference" is perhaps very short, but elaborating on it would have made the book much too long. I thought of deleting it completely but finally felt that it is useful to have the review, even if it is cursory.

One objective throughout has been to minimize the algebraic detail. Some purists in theory might find portions of the book not sufficiently rigorous, but I had to do this purposefully. Proofs of theorems have been relegated to appendices. Matrix notation occurs only in the last chapters and the Appendixes. Also, at several places in the book the maximum-likelihood method is described, but the derivation of (asymptotic) standard errors is not presented because explicit presentation of the matrix of second derivatives in each and every case would merely clutter up the book with unnecessary notation. Readers can refer to Sec. 9.10 and work out the necessary first and second derivatives in each case.

The last chapter on Bayesian inference in econometrics may appear unsatisfactory to some "Bayesians." My purpose in including it was to emphasize the similarities between the classical and Bayesian approaches. Further, it gives a review of the area for those who do not want to spend time (initially) reading specialized books in the field. Likewise, some readers might find the discussion on limited and qualitative variables in Chap. 9 very brief. Again the purpose has been to expose readers to the main problems in this area. Since the field is vast, doing full justice to all the problems would have made the book unusually long.

Appendixes A, B, and C contain almost all the material in matrix notation that is often covered in graduate courses in econometrics at many universities. The exercises in Appendix D are drawn from some econometrics examinations at Chicago, Florida, Rochester, Stanford, and Yale.

I would like to thank Marjorie Adams, Martha Colburn, Carroll Cornwall, Susan Groth, and Janet Wood at the University of Rochester for their careful typing of the manuscript.

Finally, I would like to thank my wife, Kameswari, my daughter, Tara, and my son, Vivek, for their encouragement toward the completion of this book.

G. S. Maddala

PART ONE

INTRODUCTION

CHAPTER

ONE

DATA, VARIABLES, AND MODELS

Econometrics consists of an application of statistical methods to economic data. However, some special problems associated with economic data and economic relationships necessitate a separate discussion of these methods. In this book we will be illustrating these problems with reference to economic models and economic data. Before we proceed, we need to discuss briefly the special problems peculiar to economics. These can be classified under the headings:

1. Data
2. Relationships
3. Variables
4. Functional forms

1-1 DATA

The data we observe in economics are of two types: cross-section data and time-series data. In cross-section data we have observations on individual units at a point of time, e.g., data on consumer income and expenditures on food for a set of families, data on teacher salaries and characteristics, data on labor-force participation, or wages and characteristics of workers. These data are usually collected by some sample surveys. Hence before using these data, one should examine the type of survey conducted. Another type of cross-section data that is often used is a cross section of states or of regions. There have been many studies on demand functions, production functions, and cost functions in which the individual observations are aggregates over states. In fact there are several cross-country, cross-section studies in which the individual observations are the aggregates for different countries. This is perhaps stretching the definition of a cross section too far.

In time-series data we have observations over a period of time, e.g., quarterly data on GNP or monthly data on industrial production or employment. Economics involves a lot of time-series data relative to other fields. However, these time-series are often very short, and most of the series move up and down together. Hence there are severe problems in inferring cause and effect. In econometrics most theoretical developments have been in devising methods of handling time-series data, and often what one finds is an application of these sophisticated techniques to scanty data. Sometimes we find attempts to increase the number of observations, e.g., by using monthly series rather than quarterly series. But these create special problems, and moreover the monthly series is often obtained by an interpolation of the quarterly series. Another device used to increase the number of observations is considering a combination of cross-section and time-series data, e.g., if we have data on sales, profits, and investment for a number of companies over a number of years or if we have data on gasoline consumption, number of cars, population, income, etc., for a number of states over a number of years.

1-2 RELATIONSHIPS

The relationships we investigate in economics are of three types:

1. Single-equation
2. Multiple-equation
3. Simultaneous

In single-equation relationships there is a *dependent* or "determined" variable which is determined by one or more *independent* or "determining" variables; e.g., when we say consumption depends on income Y, wealth W, and rate of interest r, we write $C = f(Y, W, r)$. Here C is the dependent variable and Y, W, and r are the independent variables. If we are considering a family with given income, wealth, and market rate of interest, this relationship can be used to determine how the consumption C of the family changes in response to changes in these variables. Similarly, when we say quantity demanded depends on price, we can write $Q = f(P)$. Here Q is the dependent variable and P the independent variable. If we are faced with an individual customer faced with a given price, this equation can be used to determine how the quantity he purchases Q changes with changes in the market pnce P.

In multiple-equation relationships we have a set of equations. For example, let C_A, C_D, C_{ND}, and C_S denote, respectively, consumer expenditures on automobiles, on other durables, on nondurables, and on services. Each of these could be a function of income and wealth. But the way they depend on these variables could be different. Hence, instead of studying the relationship between total consumer expenditures and income and wealth, we would gain more knowledge by studying the relationship between C_A, C_D, C_{ND}, and C_S and income and wealth. We now have a four-equation system. In such cases sometimes we can treat each of these equations separately as in a single-equation relationship. But sometimes we have to treat them together.

In simultaneous-equation relationships, two or more variables are determined "simultaneously" by a number of determining variables. In the above examples, though Y is "given" for the individual family, for the economy as a whole we cannot treat Y as being "given." We have to treat both C and Y as being determined simultaneously by some policy variables and technological and sociological conditions. Similarly, price can be treated as "given" for the individual customer, but if we are considering the market as a whole, we have to consider both price and quantity as being determined simultaneously by demand and supply conditions and other variables. In this case we have a two-equation system like

$$Q = f(P,X) \qquad \text{demand relationship}$$

$$Q = g(P,Z) \qquad \text{supply relationship}$$

These two equations together determine Q and P, given the determining variables X and Z. For example, X could be income and Z could be weather. Simultaneous-equation relationships are also multiple-equation relationships. But there is an essential difference in the way the variables are interconnected. These differences will be clear when we discuss these problems in subsequent chapters.

1-3 VARIABLES

A common terminology used in econometrics for dependent and independent variables is *endogenous* and *exogenous* variables, respectively. Endogenous variables are those determined within the economic system, and exogenous variables are those given from outside the system. In a broad sense almost all variables are endogenous and the only exogenous variables one can think of are weather, cyclones, etc. However, in any problem this is a matter of approximation. While studying the demand for gasoline by households, we can treat the quantity demanded as endogenous and income and price as exogenous, arguing that the household does not have control over these. Similarly, for some purposes we can treat government expenditures and taxes as exogenous. However, as we lengthen the time period of our observations, these variables will also become endogenous. In general, the greater the level of aggregation—whether it be over time periods or over individual cross-section units—the more exogenous variables will have to be treated as endogenous.

Endogenous variables can further be classified as target and nontarget variables. Target variables are those we like to influence. Nontarget variables are those we do not care about; e.g., employment and price level may be target variables. Similarly, exogenous variables can be classified as instruments and noninstruments. An instrument is an exogenous variable that is specifically manipulated so as to achieve some targets. Government expenditures, taxes, and subsidies are examples of instruments.

1-4 FUNCTIONAL FORMS

Economic theory may tell us that quantity demanded is a function of price, but it may not tell us the functional form of the relationship; e.g., is the relationship of the form:

Linear: $Q = \alpha + \beta P$
Log-linear: $\log Q = \alpha + \beta \log P$
or semilog: $\log Q = \alpha + \beta P$
or: $Q = \alpha + \beta \log P$?

This is something we decide on the basis of the observed data. The observed data on Q and P can be graphed to see what the relation looks like. If the observations are as in Fig. 1-1, a linear relationship is appropriate. If they are as in Fig. 1-2, we need a curvilinear relationship to describe the data. In this case we can plot $\log Q$ against $\log P$, $\log Q$ against P, and $\log P$ against Q and see which of these is approximately linear. However, this is a very simplistic description of what should be done. Often there may be cases where none of these simple functional forms work well. For example, consider the adoption of a new product. Usually, it has been observed that such phenomena are described by a process as in Fig. 1-3. The rate of adoption is slow in the beginning stages; then it picks up, and finally it tapers off. In such cases one can describe

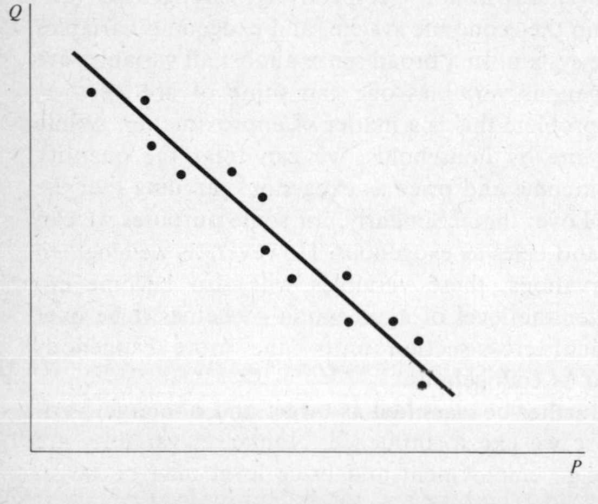

Figure 1-1 Linear relationship.

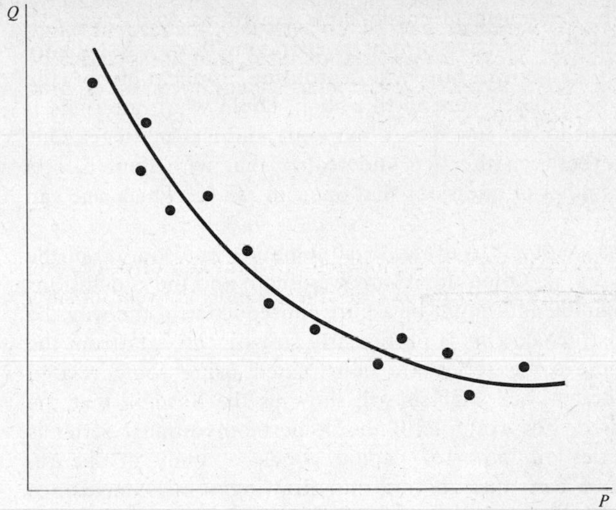

Figure 1-2 Curvilinear relationship.

the data by what is called a *logistic function*. It is given by

$$P = \frac{c}{1 + ae^{-bt}} \qquad (a > 0,\ b > 0,\ c > 0)$$

Here, P is the proportion of households who have adopted the product at time t and c is the ceiling of this proportion. As $t \to \infty$, $P \to c$. The higher the value of b, the higher the rate of approach of P to the ceiling c.

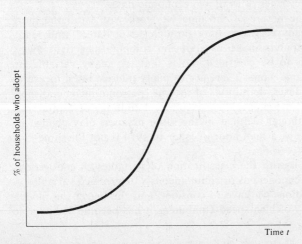

Figure 1-3 Logistic curve.

Regarding each of the factors mentioned—data, equations, variables, and functional forms—it is true that we have to rely on economic theory, but theory does not give us much guidance, nor will a routine application of the econometric methods to be outlined here in this book. Often what one finds is too much technique applied to too few data ("more art and less matter"). One must maintain a balance between the two and realize that with limited data there are only a limited number of questions that one can ask for which one can get reasonable answers.

One of the first things we ought to examine is the nature and sources of the data with which we are working. Often the results we obtain and the conclusions we draw may have no meaning and might be a pure consequence of the way the basic data have been constructed. This is particularly so with the data from the developing countries where some series are constructed using some related series. If we are smart enough, our analysis will show us the formula that the data-producing agency used. For example, if the domestic-investment series is constructed from the series on imported capital goods, a study of the relationship between the two can mislead one into drawing some conclusions about cause and effect, when in fact what we might have is the formula used by the data-producing agency in the construction of the series. Usually, for many of the developing countries, there are a few basic series like foreign-trade statistics that are the most reliable and most readily available; the other series are all constructed from these. Elaborate models have been constructed from a large number of such "manufactured" series of data for the developing countries, and the models of the United States based on monthly data possibly fall in the same category. These exercises are not fruitless, but one should be aware of the way the data have been constructed. It would be useful if every quantitative study discussed the way the data were obtained and listed the data used. Morgenstern[1] discusses some of the deficiencies of available economic data.

An examination of the nature of the data we work with is all the more important today when ready access to data through "data banks" and ready access to high-speed computers make us start the computations right away. Another problem one has to be careful about is that too many variables in economics go under the same name. There are so many interest rates, measures of money supply, price indexes, definitions of income (personal income, disposable income, "permanent" income, relative income), definitions of capital, etc. Also, the same variable, though defined in the same manner, may change its characteristics over time; e.g., a man-hour of labor in 1974 is not the same as a man-hour of labor in 1904.

Yet another problem is with the classification of variables as endogenous and exogenous. The more endogenous or simultaneously determined variables in our model, the more equations we have to consider, and the bigger the model. Again, with the availability of high-speed computers, it has become fashionable

[1] Oscar Morgenstern, "On the Accuracy of Economic Observations," Princeton University Press, Princeton, N.J., 1963.

to formulate big models ("the bigger the better"). Often it is much better to have a simple model than an intricate and elaborate model, because the data we have may permit answers to only a limited number of questions. Economic theory by itself will not be of too much guidance in this respect, because from the strictly theoretical point of view there are really very few exogenous variables and almost all variables are endogenous. Thus, one has to use one's judgment regarding the purpose of the investigation and the data available to decide which variables to treat as exogenous and which as endogenous.

Finally, and this is where statistics and econometrics come in, the relationships we consider will not be exact. This is due to all the errors we make in observations and in the specification of the relationships. Hence, some uncertainty is involved in the quantitative results we obtain. This uncertainty is expressed in terms of probabilities. Our inferences are, by nature, "uncertain" inferences and come under what is termed "statistical inference."

The plan of the book is as follows: Part 2 gives an introduction to probability and statistical inference. Part 3 outlines some elementary econometric methods. In Part 4 we consider these methods in greater detail.

PART TWO

INTRODUCTION TO PROBABILITY AND STATISTICAL INFERENCE

CHAPTER

TWO

PROBABILITY

2-1 DEFINITION OF PROBABILITY

The term *probability* is used to give a quantitative measure to the uncertainty associated with our statements. The earliest definition of probability was in terms of a long-run relative frequency. For example, suppose we have a box containing 10 balls: 5 red, 3 white, and 2 black. Suppose we draw a ball out of the box without looking at it and the balls are well mixed so that there is no reason for any particular ball to be favored. We are not certain about the color of the ball we pick, but we can express our uncertainty quantitatively by saying that the probability of picking a red ball is $\frac{5}{10}$, the probability of picking a white ball is $\frac{3}{10}$, and the probability of picking a black ball is $\frac{2}{10}$. What these statements mean is that if we conduct the experiment of mixing the box well, drawing a ball without looking at it (and replacing it before the next draw) a large number of times, then in approximately 50 percent of the cases we will find that the ball we have drawn is red, in approximately 30 percent of the cases it will be white, and in the remaining cases it will be black; this approximation will be closer to .5, .3, and .2, respectively, the larger the number of trials we repeat.

A number of technical terms are used in connection with the above experiment. The experiment of mixing and drawing a ball at random is called a *random experiment*. The result of drawing a ball and looking at it is called an *outcome*. The set of all possible outcomes is called the *sample space*. Each member of the sample space is called a *sample point*. In the above example there are 10 sample points: 5 corresponding to the outcome that the ball is red, 3 corresponding to the outcome that the ball is white, and 2 corresponding to the outcome that the ball is black. A subset of the sample space is called an *event*. Here we can consider the following events:

Event A: The ball drawn is red.
Event B: The ball drawn is white.
Event C: The ball drawn is black.
Event D: The ball drawn is white or black.
Event E: The ball drawn is red or white, etc.

Events A, B, and C are *mutually exclusive*, because if one occurs, the other does not. They are also *exhaustive*, because they exhaust all the possibilities. Events A and E are not mutually exclusive. The probability of an event A is defined as equal to: The number of sample points in A divided by the number of sample points in the entire sample space. We will henceforth denote this as $P(A)$. Thus, in the above example $P(A) = \frac{5}{10}$, $P(B) = \frac{3}{10}$, $P(C) = \frac{2}{10}$, $P(D) = \frac{5}{10}$, $P(E) = \frac{8}{10}$.

In the above example, event D is said to be the *union* of events B and C and similarly event E is the union of events A and B. We write D as $B + C$ or $B \cup C$. In this case we note that since B and C are mutually exclusive, $P(D) = P(B \cup C) = P(B) + P(C)$.

Probabilities must satisfy many conditions, but it has been found that if the following three conditions (called *axioms*) are satisfied, the other conditions that one would want to require are also satisfied:

1. If Ω is the sample space, $P(\Omega) = 1$.
2. $0 \leqslant P(E) \leqslant 1$ for every event E.
3. $P(E_1 \cup E_2 \cup E_3 \ldots) = P(E_1) + P(E_2) + P(E_3) + \cdots$ for every sequence of mutually exclusive events $E_1, E_2, E_3, \ldots$.

2-2 JOINT PROBABILITY, CONDITIONAL PROBABILITY, AND INDEPENDENCE

Sometimes we are interested in the joint occurrence of two events E_1 and E_2. We denote by $P(E_1 \cap E_2)$ or $P(E_1E_2)$ the probability of the *joint* occurrence of the two events E_1 and E_2. In the example we are considering $P(A \cap B) = 0$ because A and B cannot occur simultaneously. $P(A \cap E) = P(A)$ because the joint occurrence of A and E means that the red ball is drawn. Here A is said to be a *subset* of E. $P(D \cap \mathrm{E}) = P(B)$ because we know that both D and E occurring means that the ball drawn is white. Figure 2-1 describes the situation

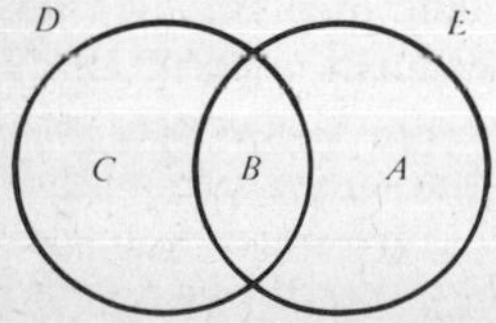

Figure 2-1 Probabilities in terms of sets.

figuratively. The set of points corresponding to the events A, B, C are so marked there. $D = B \cup C$, $E = B \cup A$, and $D \cap E = B$.

Sometimes we restrict our attention to a subset of the entire sample space and treat this as our new sample space; e.g., in our example suppose we are told that the ball drawn is either red or white and we are asked the probability that it is red. In this case our sample space consists of the subset of 8 points corresponding to the outcomes that the ball is red or white. The required probability is therefore $\frac{5}{8}$. We denote this probability by $P(A \mid E)$, and this is the *conditional probability* of A given that E has occurred. The definition of conditional probability is the following: Let E_1 and E_2 be two events in the sample space. Then the conditional probability of E_1 given E_2, denoted by $P(E_1 \mid E_2)$, is equal to

$$\frac{P(E_1 \cap E_2)}{P(E_2)} \quad \text{or} \quad \frac{P(E_1 E_2)}{P(E_2)}$$

provided $P(E_2)$ is not zero.

Two events E_1 and E_2 are said to be *independent* if the conditional and unconditional probabilities are equal, that is,

$$P(E_1 \mid E_2) = P(E_1) \quad \text{or} \quad P(E_2 \mid E_1) = P(E_2)$$

Since
$$P(E_1 \mid E_2) = \frac{P(E_1 E_2)}{P(E_2)} = P(E_1)$$

we have $P(E_1 E_2) = P(E_1) \cdot P(E_2)$

2-3 SUBJECTIVE PROBABILITY

The interpretation of probability as a long-run relative frequency is only one of the interpretations. It was originally developed to describe certain games of chance where plays (such as throwing dice, dealing cards, or spinning roulettes) are indeed repeated a large number of times under almost identical conditions. In some physical sciences there are situations in which one repeats experiments under identical conditions. In social sciences, however, where controlled experimentation is not possible, this notion of long-run frequency is rather difficult to accept.

One other interpretation of probability is in terms of *degrees of belief*. We often say: "The chances are one in ten that I will get this job," or "There is a 50 percent probability that it will rain this afternoon." These are probability statements, but they do not describe any long-run relative frequencies. The probabilities here are personalistic or subjective. In this approach a probability is interpreted as a degree of belief or a quantified judgment of the individual. However, we can give an objective interpretation to these subjective probabilities in terms of betting odds. Suppose you say that the probability that the Miami Dolphins will win is $\frac{2}{3}$. Consider now a bet wherein you are given \$1 if the Dolphins win and you pay $2 if the Dolphins lose. Your probability indicates that this is a "fair" bet, and you should be indifferent whether you take the bet or not. If you are not willing to take the bet, your subjective probability that the Miami Dolphins will win is $< \frac{2}{3}$, and if you are too anxious to take the bet, your subjective probability is $> \frac{2}{3}$. An alternative way of quantifying this subjective judgment is the following: Consider a box in which there are 3 balls—2 red and 1 white—the balls being identical in all respects except color. The box is thoroughly mixed and a ball is drawn without looking. Consider the following two lotteries:

Lottery A: You get $100 if the ball drawn is red.
You get $0 if the ball drawn is white.
Lottery B: You get $100 if the Miami Dolphins win.
You get $0 if the Miami Dolphins lose.

You are asked to choose between lottery A and lottery B. If you are indifferent between the two lotteries, your subjective probability that the Dolphins will win is $\frac{2}{3}$. If you prefer lottery A, your probability is $< \frac{2}{3}$, and if you prefer lottery B, your probability is $> \frac{2}{3}$.

Thus, using some betting situations and lotteries, we can give quantitative measures to subjective probabilities. It can be shown that if a person behaves in accordance with certain axioms of "coherence" and "consistency," these subjective probabilities satisfy all the rules of (frequency) probabilities stated earlier. There are several statements of the axioms of consistency. Two of these axioms are the axiom of transitivity and the axiom of substitutability. The axiom of transitivity says that if you prefer X to Y and Y to Z, you must prefer X to Z. The axiom of substitutability says that if you are indifferent between X and Y, then X can be substituted for Y as a prize in a lottery or as a stake in a bet; e.g., if you are indifferent between receiving $100 cash or $100 worth of gas coupons, the $100 worth of gas coupons can be substituted for the $100 cash in lottery A or lottery B considered earlier.

Subjective probabilities vary from person to person, but in this case one has to put greater emphasis on the subjective probabilities of "experts." Almost all decisions we make in economics do *not* depend on outcomes of repetitive experiments. A firm deciding on raising prices has to make the decision on the basis of some probabilities about what the competitive firms will do, but these probabilities are necessarily subjective and have no relative long-run frequency interpretation. However, these subjective probabilities themselves will be derived from previous experience in the same industry or in similar cases in other related industries or situations. Thus, there is a "frequency" basis to these probabilities too, but it all depends on whether the firm believes this particular situation to be very special or to fall in the same class as the previous cases. As still another example, suppose you are asked about the probability that one Mr. X will get into a car accident during the next year, and you know that the frequency of accidents of people in that age group is $\frac{1}{10}$. Then if you know nothing more, your subjective probability would be $\frac{1}{10}$. But if you know a lot more about this person's past driving record—say that he got into two accidents last year and one the year before—then you would increase your subjective probability substantially. Then the fact that the frequency of accidents in that age group is $\frac{1}{10}$ is of not too much value. We might also have information that Mr. X drives a red car and the frequency of accidents for red cars. We might also have the information that Mr. X wears glasses and the frequency of accidents among people wearing glasses. The question is one of attaching weights to all these factors, and this is again a subjective choice.

In any case, since the calculus of probabilities is the same whether the interpretation of probability is in terms of long-run relative frequency or subjective degrees of belief, we will first proceed with the algebraic aspects of probability theory. The interpretation of our results, of course, will depend on what meaning we attach to the term "probability," and this we can discuss later.

2-4 BAYES' THEOREM

Bayes' theorem is based on the definition of conditional probability given earlier. Let A and B be two events. Then by the definition of conditional probability we have

$$P(A \mid B) = \frac{P(AB)}{P(B)} \qquad \text{and} \qquad P(B \mid A) = \frac{P(AB)}{P(A)}$$

Hence,

$$P(A \mid B) = \frac{P(B \mid A) \cdot P(A)}{P(B)}$$

Now substitute H (hypothesis about the model that generated the data) for A and D (observed data) for B. Then we have

$$P(H \mid D) = \frac{P(D \mid H) \cdot P(H)}{P(D)}$$

Here $P(D \mid H)$ is the probability of observing the data given that H is true. This is usually called the *likelihood*. $P(H)$ is our probability that H is true *before* observing the data (usually called the *prior probability*). $P(H \mid D)$ is the probability that H is true *after* observing the data (usually called the *posterior probability*). $P(D)$ is the unconditional probability of observing the data (whether H is true or not). Often $P(D)$ is difficult to compute. Hence we write the above relation as

$$P(H \mid D) \propto P(D \mid H) \cdot P(H)$$

That is: Posterior probability varies with likelihood times prior probability.

This is a simple version of Bayes' theorem. It first appeared in his text published in 1763, which was reprinted in 1940 and 1958. Reverend Thomas Bayes was a part-time mathematician. As a theorem, Bayes' theorem is unquestionably valid. The controversy is about how and in what circumstances it should be used.

If we have two hypotheses H_1 and H_2, then

$$P(H_1 \mid D) = \frac{P(D \mid H_1) \cdot P(H_1)}{P(D)} \quad \text{and} \quad P(H_2 \mid D) = \frac{P(D \mid H_2) \cdot P(H_2)}{P(D)}$$

Hence,

$$\frac{P(H_1 \mid D)}{P(H_2 \mid D)} = \frac{P(D \mid H_1)}{P(D \mid H_2)} \cdot \frac{P(H_1)}{P(H_2)}$$

The left-hand side is called the *posterior odds*. The first term on the right-hand side is called the *likelihood ratio,* and the second term on the right-hand side is called the *prior odds*. Thus, we have: Posterior odds equals likelihood ratio times prior odds. Consider, for example, two urns—the first has 1 red ball and 4 white balls and the second has 2 red balls and 2 white balls. An urn is chosen at random and a ball is picked. It turns out to be white. What is the probability that the first urn was chosen? Let H_1 denote the hypothesis that we chose the first urn. Let H_2 denote the hypothesis that we chose the second urn. Let D be the data; i.e., the ball is white. We have

$$P(H_1) = P(H_2) = \tfrac{1}{2}$$

Also,

$$P(D \mid H_1) = \tfrac{4}{5} \quad \text{and} \quad P(D \mid H_2) = \tfrac{1}{2}$$

Hence,

$$\frac{P(H_1 \mid D)}{P(H_2 \mid D)} = \frac{8}{5}$$

Therefore,

$$P(H_1 \mid D) = \tfrac{8}{13} \quad \text{and} \quad P(H_2 \mid D) = \tfrac{5}{13}$$

The required probability is therefore $\frac{8}{13}$. Here the prior-odds ratio is 1 and the posterior-odds ratio is $\frac{8}{5}$.

Exercises

1. From the group tabulated in Table 2-1 a person is selected at random. What is the probability of the following events:

A: The person is white.
B: The person is black.
C: The person is male.
D: The person is female.
E: The person's earnings are between \$6,000 and \$9,999.

Also find the probabilities of the following events:

AD, BC, $AD + BC$, $AE + BE$, $ACE + BDE$

Are the following sets of events independent?

(i) A and E
(ii) A, C, and E
(iii) B and D
(iv) AE and BE

Table 2-1 Education pays . . . or does it?

Total money income (includes full and part-time workers, 25 and over, Mar. 1971)	Years of schooling						
	Total	7 or less	8	9–11	12	13–15	16 or more
White males with income (1,000)	45,937	5,531	6,110	7,073	14,568	5,410	7,246
Percent	100.0	100.0	100.0	100.0	100.0	100.0	100.0
Loss to $2,999	14.0	40.7	24.9	13.6	6.7	6.9	5.1
$3,000 to $5,999	18.2	30.4	29.4	20.9	14.7	11.7	8.5
$6,000 to $7,999	16.1	14.1	17.0	19.9	19.0	13.9	8.7
$8,000 to $9,999	15.9	7.4	13.6	19.6	20.3	17.2	11.0
$10,000 to $14,999	23.3	5.8	11.9	20.6	29.8	31.9	29.3
$15,000 and over	12.6	1.4	3.3	5.4	9.6	18.4	37.4
Mean income	$9,185	$4,651	$6,143	$7,902	$9,389	$11,081	$14,640
Black males with income (1,000)	4,382	1,490	419	972	1,025	264	211
Percent	100.0	100.0	100.0	100.0	100.0	100.0	100.0
Loss to $2,999	28.1	47.7	32.4	18.8	15.2	15.8	6.9
$3,000 to $5,999	31.9	32.0	38.4	36.6	31.0	19.6	16.1
$6,000 to $7,999	17.9	12.5	18.2	20.9	24.4	13.6	15.7
$8,000 to $9,999	11.7	5.4	6.4	14.1	16.3	24.6	17.6
$10,000 to $14,999	8.6	2.1	3.6	8.9	12.7	21.9	27.3
$15,000 and over	1.8	0.3	1.0	0.7	1.6	4.5	16.4
Mean income	$5,429	$3,671	$4,633	$5,704	$6,523	$7,579	$10,155
Mean income, full-time males (65.9% of total)	$10,697	$6,431	$7,947	$8,917	$10,080	$12,111	$15,946
White females with income (1,000)	34,272	4,021	4,467	5,581	12,901	3,744	3,558
Percent	100.0	100.0	100.0	100.0	100.0	100.0	100.0
Loss to $2,999	53.5	79.5	70.7	58.0	45.7	44.7	32.1
$3,000 to $5,999	27.4	17.6	23.7	31.0	33.4	25.8	17.9
$6,000 to $7,999	10.1	1.9	3.8	7.5	13.0	15.8	14.7
$8,000 to $9,999	4.8	0.4	1.1	2.4	4.9	7.0	15.7
$10,000 to $14,999	3.3	0.4	0.5	0.8	2.5	4.7	15.2
$15,000 and over	0.9	0.2	0.2	0.3	0.5	2.0	4.2
Mean income	$3,559	$1,947	$2,360	$2,938	$3,752	$4,334	$6,340
Black females with income (1,000)	4,492	1,276	469	1,117	1,110	294	226
Percent	100.0	100.0	100.0	100.0	100.0	100.0	100.0
Loss to $2,999	60.3	86.9	75.0	59.2	41.3	31.3	13.6
$3,000 to $5,999	27.2	11.7	21.9	34.0	40.4	34.6	18.3
$6,000 to $7,999	7.3	1.1	1.4	5.4	12.2	19.9	21.5
$8,000 to $9,999	3.1	0.1	1.8	0.7	4.0	8.2	22.9
$10,000 to $14,999	2.2	0.2	—	0.7	2.0	6.0	22.2
$15,000 and over	0.1	—	—	—	—	—	1.6
Mean income	$2,945	$1,629	$2,088	$2,717	$3,706	$4,692	$7,284
Mean income, full-time females (33.1% of total)	$6,046	$3,831	$4,277	$4,868	$5,820	$6,950	$8,940

Source: Bureau of the Census.

Percentages may not add to 100.0 due to rounding;—represents zero or rounds to zero.

Explanation: The tables above demonstrate that while income tends to rise with educational attainment, it rises far less for women and blacks than for white men. For every year of schooling, the black man tends to gain less than his white counterpart. (Black women appear to improve their incomes in comparison with white women, but this is probably because more black women tend to work full-time.)

Looking at the mean incomes for full-time workers, we can see that all women tend to make only a little more than half the earnings of men with the same educational attainments.

Are the following sets of events mutually exclusive?

(i) A and C
(ii) A and B
(iii) CE and DE
(iv) D and E

2. A five-question multiple-choice examination is given with four choices for each question. If a student guesses all his answers, what is your probability of his getting all of them correct, two correct, and all wrong? If the student is guessing, what is your most probable score for him? If the position of the correct answer has been selected at random and independently for each question and the student picks up the first alternative for each question, what is your probability that he will get two questions right, all right, and all wrong? Again, what is your most probable score for him? If you find that two students sitting next to each other have the same answers and you know that one of them is a good student and the other one is not and possibly resorts to guessing, how will you determine whether the latter has copied or not?

3. In a family of 5 children, which of the following patterns is the most probable?

(i) 2 boys, 1 girl, 2 boys
(ii) 4 boys, 1 girl
(iii) Boy, girl, boy, girl, boy
(iv) 4 girls, 1 boy

4. From the group in Table 2-1 a person is selected at random.

(i) If you are told that it is a black male, what is your probability that he has 12 years of schooling and earns $12,000? If it is a white male, what is the corresponding probability?
(ii) If you are told that the person has 12 years of schooling and earns $12,000, what is the probability that it is a male? What is the probability that it is a black female?

5. Comment on the title and the "explanation" given at the bottom of Table 2-1.

CHAPTER

THREE

RANDOM VARIABLES AND PROBABILITY DISTRIBUTIONS

3-1 RANDOM VARIABLES

A variable X is said to be a *random variable* (rv) if for every real number a there exists a probability $P(X \leqslant a)$ that X takes on a value less than or equal to a, for example, the income of an American family. We shall denote random variables by capital letters X, Y, Z, etc. We shall use small letters x, y, z, etc., to denote particular values of the random variables. Thus, $P(X = x)$ is the probability that the random variable X takes the value x. $P(x_1 \leqslant X \leqslant x_2)$ is the probability that the random variable X takes values between x_1 and x_2, both inclusive.

If the random variable X can assume only a particular finite or countably infinite set of values, it is said to be a *discrete* random variable. For example, if you throw a die, the outcome X is a random variable which can assume only the values 1, 2, 3, 4, 5, and 6. A random variable is said to be *continuous* if for every pair of values a and b such that $P(X \leqslant a) < P(X \leqslant b)$ it is true that $P(a < X < b) > 0$. An example of a continuous random variable is the height of a person.

3-2 PROBABILITY DISTRIBUTION

A table or a formula listing all possible values that a discrete random variable can take, together with the associated probabilities, is called a *discrete probability distribution.* For example, if we throw a fair die, the outcome X is a random variable with the following probability distribution:

X	Probability
1	$\frac{1}{6}$
2	$\frac{1}{6}$
3	$\frac{1}{6}$
4	$\frac{1}{6}$
5	$\frac{1}{6}$
6	$\frac{1}{6}$

For continuous variables the probability distribution is called a *probability density function*. The function $f(x)$ is called a probability density function for the continuous random variable X if the total area bounded by the x axis and the area under the curve between any two ordinates $X = a$ and $X = b$ gives the probability that X lies between a and b; that is,

$$P(a \leqslant X \leqslant b) = \int_a^b f(x)\,dx$$

In general, for a continuous random variable the occurrence of any *exact* value of X may be regarded as having a zero probability. Hence probabilities are discussed only for intervals—not for any specific values. A continuous random variable is merely an idealization; e.g., the random variable height of an American is theoretically continuous, but actual measurements will be at discrete intervals depending on the accuracy of the measuring instrument. However, we will use continuous probability distributions because their mathematical theory is simpler. Suppose we measure heights at intervals of 1 inch. Then we can prepare a frequency distribution, i.e., the number of people in each interval—the intervals being in distances of 1 inch. Dividing the number of people in each interval by the total number, we get the probability distribution. We can draw a graph wherein we erect a rectangle over each class interval where the height is proportional to the probability. This is called a *histogram*. We can pass a curve through the midpoints of the top of each rectangle. This would be the

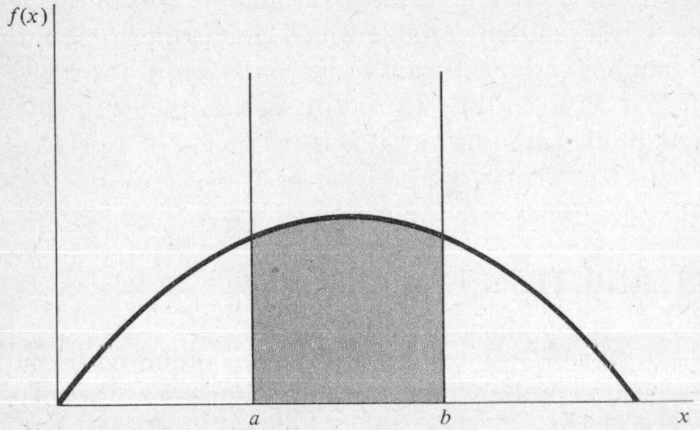

Figure 3-1 A frequency function.

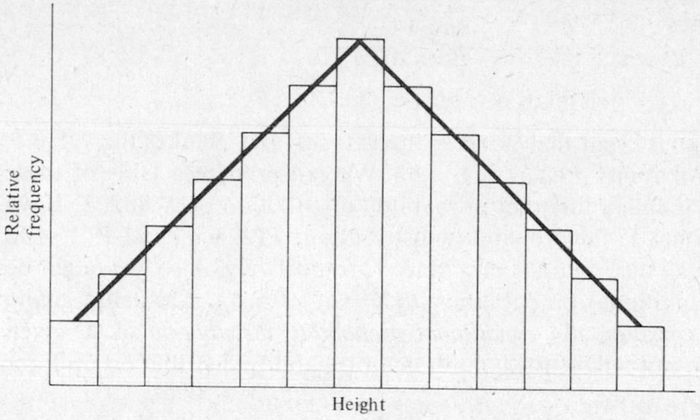

Figure 3-2 A histogram.

probability density function $f(x)$ of the random variable X—the height. The smaller the interval of measurement the closer will the probability density function we obtain be to the true probability density function.

3-3 CUMULATIVE DISTRIBUTION FUNCTION

The probability that the random variable X takes on a value at or below a number a is often written as $F(a) = P(X \leqslant a)$. The function $F(x)$ represents for different values of x the cumulative probabilities and hence is called the *cumulative distribution function*. A cumulative distribution function satisfies the following properties:

1. $0 \leqslant F(x) \leqslant 1$
2. If $a < b$, $F(a) \leqslant F(b)$
3. $F(\infty) = 1$, $F(-\infty) = 0$

If X is discrete,

$$F(a) = P(X \leqslant a) = \sum_{x \leqslant a} P(X = x)$$

If X is continuous,

$$F(a) = P(X \leqslant a) = \int_{-\infty}^{a} f(x)\, dx$$

3-4 JOINT PROBABILITY DENSITY FUNCTION

We are often interested in not just one random variable but in the relationship between education and income, between height and weight, etc. Suppose we have two discrete random variables

$$X, \text{ which takes } m \text{ values } a_1, a_2, \ldots, a_m$$
$$Y, \text{ which takes } n \text{ values } b_1, b_2, \ldots, b_n$$

We can talk of the joint event that X takes the value a_i and Y takes the value b_j and consider the probability $P(X = a_i, Y = b_j)$. We can prepare a table of these mn values, and this is called the joint probability distribution of X and Y. If we consider only X or only Y, the probability distributions $P(X = a_i)$ and $P(Y = b_j)$ are called the *marginal* distributions of X and Y, respectively. Also, we might be interested in the conditional probabilities $P(X = a_i \mid Y = b_j)$. The table giving these probabilities is called the *conditional probability distribution* of X given $Y = b_j$. Similarly, we can talk of the conditional probability distribution of Y for any given value of X.

For continuous random variables we consider the joint probability density function $f(x,y)$, which has the following properties:

1. $f(x,y) \geqslant 0$ for all real x, y
2. $\int_{-\infty}^{\infty} \int_{-\infty}^{\infty} f(x,y)\, dx\, dy = 1$
3. $P(a \leqslant X \leqslant b, c \leqslant Y \leqslant d) = \int_c^d [\int_a^b f(x,y)\, dx]\, dy$

The marginal densities are:

$$f(x) = \int_{-\infty}^{\infty} f(x,y)\, dy \qquad \text{and} \qquad f(y) = \int_{-\infty}^{\infty} f(x,y)\, dx$$

The conditional densities are:

$$f(x \mid Y = y) = \frac{f(x,y)}{f(y)} \qquad \text{and} \qquad f(y \mid X = x) = \frac{f(x,y)}{f(x)}$$

The extension of these formulas to the case of several variables is analogous.

Independence. Two discrete random variables X and Y are said to be independent if and only if $P(X = a, Y = b) = P(X = a) \cdot P(Y = b)$ for all possible values of a and b. For continuous variables the condition is $f(x,y) = f(x) \cdot f(y)$ for all x and y.

3-5 PROPERTIES OF PROBABILITY DISTRIBUTIONS

There are some summary measures in terms of which we can summarize the behavior of probability distributions. The most common of these are the average called *expected value* and dispersion about the average called the *variance*.

If X is a discrete random variable with the probability distribution:

x	x_1	x_2	$\cdots$	x_n
$P(X = x)$	P_1	P_2		P_n

then the expected value of X denoted by $E(X)$ is

$$E(X) = \sum_{i=1}^{n} x_i \cdot P_i$$

The expected value of a new random variable $g(X)$ is

$$E[g(X)] = \sum_{i=1}^{n} g(x_i) \cdot P_i$$

In the case of a continuous random variable with probability density function $f(x)$ these expressions are

$$E(X) = \int_{-\infty}^{\infty} xf(x)\, dx$$

$$E[g(X)] = \int_{-\infty}^{\infty} g(x) \cdot f(x)\, dx$$

Laws of expectation

1. If a and b are constants,
$$E(aX + b) = aE(X) + b$$
2. The expectation of the sum of two functions $g(X)$ and $h(X)$ is the sum of the expectations, that is,
$$E[g(X) + h(X)] = E[g(X)] + E[h(X)]$$
3. If X and Y are two random variables,
$$E(X + Y) = E(X) + E(Y)$$
4. If X and Y are two *independent* random variables,
$$E(XY) = E(X) \cdot E(Y)$$

In addition to the expected value, there are other ways of describing the average behavior of the probability distribution. Two such measures are the *median* and the *mode*. The median is that value of the random variable for which the cumulative probability is half; that is, m is said to be the median if $F(m) = .5$. The mode is the peak of the probability distribution or probability density function. If there is only one peak, the distribution is said to be *unimodal*. Otherwise it is *multimodal*. If there are two modes, we call it *bimodal*. Figure 3-3 illustrates unimodal and bimodal distributions. The bimodal distribution[1] has two peaks—x_1 and x_2—the former a local maximum of $f(x)$ and the

[1] Sometimes the mode may not exist, as in the case of a "uniform" distribution where $f(x)$ is constant over the entire range of x.

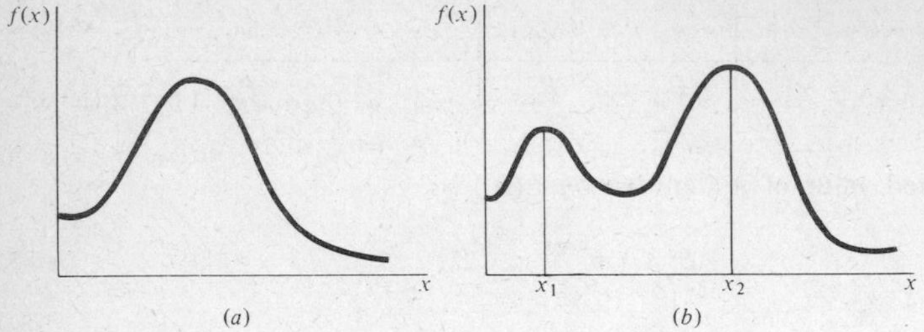

Figure 3-3 (*a*) Unimodal distribution; (*b*) bimodal distributions.

latter a global maximum. For distributions of this sort the expected value or the median are likely to be poor descriptions of the average.

Variance. If X is a random variable with expected value μ, that is, $E(X) = \mu$, then the variance is defined to be $\sigma^2 = V(X) = E(X - \mu)^2$. The quantity σ is called the *standard deviation* of the random variable X. Since

$$E(X - \mu)^2 = E(X^2 - 2\mu X + \mu^2) = E(X^2) - 2\mu E(X) + \mu^2 = E(X^2) - 2\mu^2 + \mu^2$$

we have
$$V(X) = E(X^2) - [E(X)]^2$$

Laws of variance. (try to prove these)

1. If X is a random variable and b is a constant,
$$V(X + b) = V(X)$$
2. If X is a random variable and a and b are constants,
$$V(aX + b) = a^2V(X)$$
3. If X and Y are *independent* random variables,
$$V(X + Y) = V(X) + V(Y)$$
and if a and b are constants
$$V(aX + bY) = a^2V(X) + b^2V(Y)$$
Hence
$$V(X - Y) = V(X) + V(Y)$$

3-6 MOMENTS

In addition to the mean and variance there are other measures for summarizing the characteristics of probability distributions. This is in terms of higher-order "moments." *Moments* are simply the expectations of different powers of the random variables X.

$E(X^r)$ is called the rth moment. The first moment is the mean μ. $E[(X-\mu)^r]$ is called the rth central moment. The first *central moment* is obviously zero, and the second *central moment* is the variance.

3-7 CONDITIONAL EXPECTATION AND VARIANCE

Sometimes we would be interested in the moments of the conditional distribution of X given $Y = y$.

$$E(X \mid Y = y) = \sum_x xp(x \mid y) \qquad \text{in the discrete case}$$

$$= \int_{-\infty}^{\infty} xf(x \mid y)\, dx \qquad \text{in the continuous case}$$

If X and Y are independent, we have

$$E(X \mid y) = E(X) \qquad \text{since} \qquad p(x \mid y) = p(x)$$

The conditional variance is defined as

$$V(X \mid y) = E(X^2 \mid y) - [E(X \mid y)]^2$$

Both $E(X \mid y)$ and $V(X \mid y)$ will in general be functions of y. We have the following important result relating conditional and unconditional variances of the random variable X:

$$V(X) = EV(X \mid y) + VE(X \mid y)$$

That is: The unconditional variance of X equals the expectation of its conditional variance plus the variance of its conditional expectation. (Prove it.)

3-8 MOMENTS OF JOINT DISTRIBUTION

If X and Y are two random variables, we can consider the joint moments $E(X^rY^s)$ or the joint central moments $E[(X-\mu_x)^r(Y-\mu_y)^s]$ where $\mu_x = E(X)$ and $\mu_y = E(Y)$. $E[(X-\mu_x)(Y-\mu_y)]$ is called the *covariance* between X and Y and is denoted by cov (X, Y). We have cov $(XY) = E(XY) - \mu_x\mu_y$.

If X and Y are *independent*, then $E(XY) = E(X) \cdot E(Y)$ and hence cov $(X, Y) = 0$. Note that the converse need not be true; i.e., if cov $(X, Y) = 0$, it need not be true that X and Y are independent. For instance, consider the discrete distribution of X and Y defined by the following table of probabilities:

y \ x	3	4	5
2	.2	0	.2
4	0	.2	0
6	.2	0	.2

We have $E(X) = 4$, $E(Y) = 4$, and $E(X, Y) = 16$. Hence $\text{cov}(X, Y) = 0$. But X and Y are not independent.

Covariance between X and Y measures how X and Y move together, but it is dependent on units of measurement. To remedy this, we divide it by the product of the standard deviations of X and Y. This is called the *correlation coefficient* between X and Y and is denoted by ρ_{xy}. We have

$$\rho_{XY} = \frac{\text{cov}(X, Y)}{\sqrt{V(X) \cdot V(Y)}}$$

It can be shown that

$$-1 \leqslant \rho_{XY} \leqslant +1$$

3-9 SOME COMMONLY USED PROBABILITY DISTRIBUTIONS

If we are given the probability distribution of a random variable X, we can determine the probability that X lies in an interval (a,b). There are some probability distributions for which these probabilities have been tabulated, and which are considered suitable descriptions for a wide variety of phenomena. Some of these like the binomial, normal, χ^2, t, and F distributions will be considered here.[1] There is the question of whether these are really suitable to describe the behavior of economic variables. We will postpone this discussion for the present. Actually what we may need is slight modifications of these distributions.

Among the distributions mentioned above the binomial is a discrete distribution and the others are continuous distributions. In actual practice, given the limitations of our measuring devices, our observations will be discrete. But the continuous distribution is only a convenient approximation and often not a bad one; e.g., even if we measure incomes in round dollars, if we have data on a large number of people, we can represent the observed distribution of incomes by a continuous distribution.

Binomial Distribution

Suppose the probability of a success in an experiment is p and the probability of a failure is q. $(p + q = 1.)$ Consider a sequence of n independent trials. Let X be the number of successes. Then

$$P(X = r) = \binom{n}{r} p^r q^{n-r} \qquad r = 0, 1, 2, \ldots, n$$

[This is because the probability of obtaining any particular combination of r successes and $(n - r)$ failures is $p^r q^{n-r}$ and $\binom{n}{r}$ such combinations are possible.]

[1] Some other distributions are discussed in Chap. 18.

Table 3-1

r	$P(r)$ for $p = .5$	$P(r)$ for $p = .1$
0	$\binom{4}{0}(.5)^0(.5)^4 =$ .0625	$\binom{4}{0}(.1)^0(.9)^4 =$ .6561
1	$\binom{4}{1}(.5)^1(.5)^3 =$ .2500	$\binom{4}{1}(.1)^1(.9)^3 =$ .2916
2	$\binom{4}{2}(.5)^2(.5)^2 =$ .3750	$\binom{4}{2}(.1)^2(.9)^2 =$ .0486
3	$\binom{4}{3}(.5)^3(.5)^1 =$ .2500	$\binom{4}{3}(.1)^3(.9)^1 =$ 0036
4	$\binom{4}{4}(.5)^4(.5)^0 =$ .0625	$\binom{4}{4}(.1)^4(.9)^0 =$ .0001
	Total = 1.0000	Total = 1.0000

Here

$$\binom{n}{r} = \frac{n!}{(n-r)!r!}$$

Since these probabilities are successive terms in the binomial expansion of $(p+q)^n$, the above probability distribution is called the binomial distribution. As an illustration of how the probabilities look, suppose $n = 4$. Then the probability distributions for $p = .5$ and $p = .1$ are given as in Table 3-1. The binomial distribution can be used in cases where the probability p is constant from trial to trial. This will be so if we are drawing samples from a large population or if we draw samples with replacement; i.e., an item drawn is replaced before the next drawing. The mean and variance of the binomial distribution are given by $E(X) = np$ and $V(X) = npq$. There are several uses of the binomial distribution—the most important being in quality control. Suppose there is a production process for which the manufacturer wants to maintain a certain degree of control by saying that he does not want to have more than 5 percent defectives. He occasionally draws samples and counts the number of defectives. Suppose he draws a sample of size 20 and finds 2 defective items. Then using the binomial distribution, with $p = .05$, he can calculate the probability of getting 2 or more defectives by chance. From this he can decide whether the process is under control or not. Another example of the use of the binomial distribution is in the analysis of brand loyalty. Actually, another distribution called the *negative binomial* has been extensively applied in marketing. The negative binomial[1] is defined by

$$P(X = r)\binom{r-1}{k-1} p^k q^{r-k} \qquad k \geqslant 1,\ r \geqslant k$$

The Normal Distribution

This is a bell-shaped continuous distribution, which is the most extensively used

[1] See, for example, A.S.C. Ehrenberg, "Repeat Buying—Theory and Applications," North-Holland Publishing Co., Amsterdam, 1972.

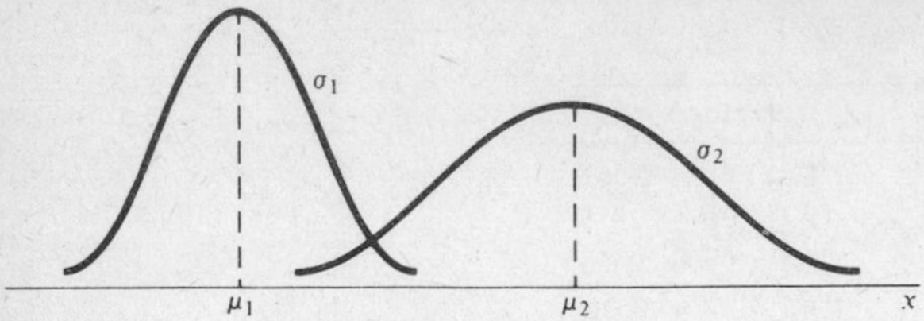

Figure 3-4 Normal curves with $\mu_1 \neq \mu_2$ and $\sigma_1 < \sigma_2$.

in statistical applications in a wide variety of fields. Its probability density function is given by

$$f(x) = \frac{1}{\sigma\sqrt{2\pi}} \exp\left[-\frac{(x-\mu)^2}{2\sigma^2} \right]$$

Its mean is μ and variance σ^2. If x has the normal distribution with mean μ and variance σ^2, we will henceforth denote this compactly as $x \sim N(\mu, \sigma^2)$. The frequency curves for the normal distribution are shown in Fig. 3-4. Extensive tables have been prepared for this probability distribution.

Many variables in practical life follow the normal distribution. One example is heights of all women in the United States. Some people feel that many variables in economics do not follow the normal distribution. However, we will discuss these other distributions later, and for the present we will assume that the normal distribution is a valid approximation.

For the normal distribution with the mean μ and variance σ^2 we note (from the tables of the standard normal distribution given at the end of this book) that approximately:

31%	observations are $> \mu + 0.5\sigma$ and $< \mu - 0.5\sigma$
16%	observations are $> \mu + 1.0\sigma$ and $< \mu - 1.0\sigma$
6.7%	observations are $> \mu + 1.5\sigma$ and $< \mu - 1.5\sigma$
2.3%	observations are $> \mu + 2.0\sigma$ and $< \mu - 2.0\sigma$
1%	observations are $> \mu + 2.5\sigma$ and $< \mu - 2.5\sigma$

So, if μ is normally distributed with mean 2.0 and variance 9.0, we can say that the probability that μ will lie between $2 \pm 2(3.0)$ is .95, that is, $P[-4 \leqslant \mu \leqslant 8]$

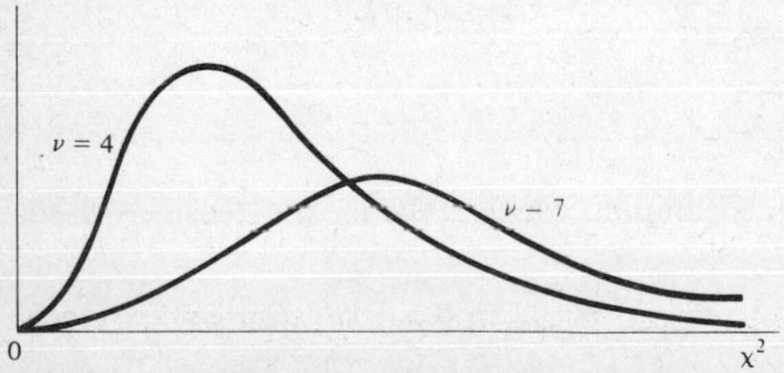

Figure 3-5 Chi-square curves for $\nu = 4$ and $\nu = 7$.

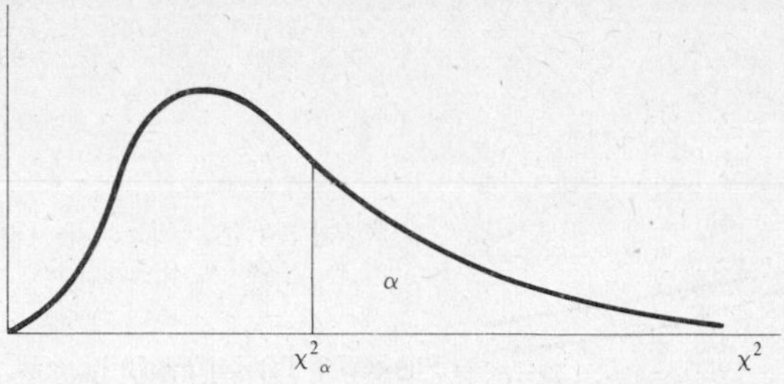

Figure 3-6 Tabulated values of the chi-square distribution.

= 0.95. We can make similar statements that μ lies between specific values by looking at the probabilities in the standard normal tables.

In addition to the normal distribution, there are other probability distributions which we will be using frequently. These are the χ^2, t, and F distributions tabulated at the end of this book. These distributions are derived from the normal distribution, and are defined as follows:

χ^2 **distributions.** If $x_1, x_2, \ldots, x_n$ are independent normal variables with mean 0 and variance 1, that is, x_i is $IN(0,1)$, $i = 1, 2, \ldots, n$, then

$$Z = \sum_1^n x_i^2$$

is said to have the χ^2-distribution degrees of freedom n, and we will write this as $Z \sim \chi_n^2$. If $x_i \sim IN(0,\sigma^2)$, then

$$Z = \sum_1^n \frac{x_i^2}{\sigma^2} \sim \chi_n^2 \qquad \text{or} \qquad \sum_1^n x_i^2 \sim \chi_n^2(\sigma^2)$$

An important property of the normal distribution is that *any* linear function of normally distributed variables is also normally distributed. This is true whether the variables are independent or correlated. If

$$x_1 \sim N(\mu_1, \sigma_1^2)$$

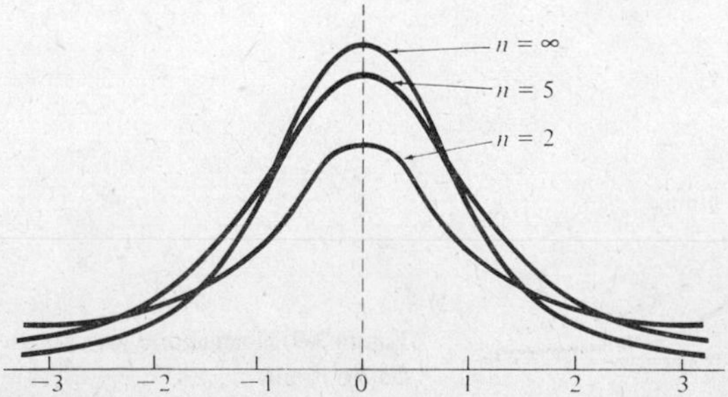

Figure 3-7 t-distribution curves for $n = 2, 5$, and ∞.

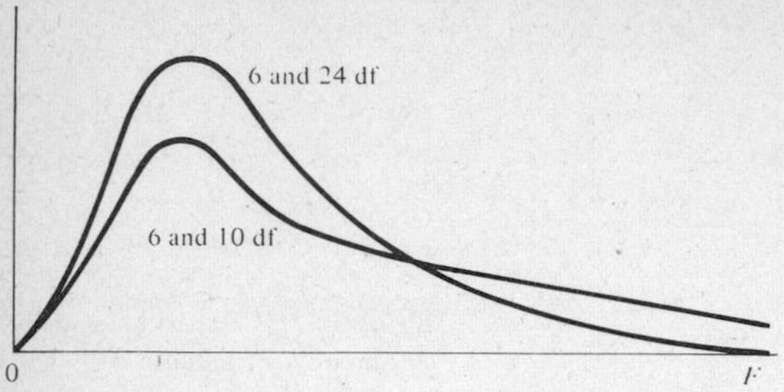

Figure 3-8 Typical F distributions.

and
$$x_2 \sim N(\mu_2, \sigma_2^2)$$
and the correlation between x_1 and x_2 is ρ, then
$$a_1 x_1 + a_2 x_2 \sim N(a_1\mu_1 + a_2\mu_2, a_1^2\sigma_1^2 + a_2^2\sigma_2^2 + 2a_1 a_2 \rho\sigma_1\sigma_2).$$
In particular,
$$x_1 + x_2 \sim N(\mu_1 + \mu_2, \sigma_1^2 + \sigma_2^2 + 2\rho\sigma_1\sigma_2)$$
and
$$x_1 - x_2 \sim N(\mu_1 - \mu_2, \sigma_1^2 + \sigma_2^2 - 2\rho\sigma_1\sigma_2)$$

(Prove these results.) The χ^2 distribution also has a similar "additive property" but much more restrictive. If $Z_1 \sim \chi^2_{n_1}$ and $Z_2 \sim \chi^2_{n_2}$ and Z_1 and Z_2 are *independent*, then $Z_1 + Z_2 \sim \chi^2_{n_1+n_2}$. We need independence and we can consider only simple additions, *not* general linear combinations. Even this limited property is very useful in practical applications. There are many distributions for which this restricted additive property does not hold.

***t* distribution.** If $x \sim N(0, \sigma^2)$ and $y \sim \chi^2_n(\sigma^2)$ and x and y are independent random variables, then $Z = x/\sqrt{y/n}$ has a t-distribution degrees of freedom (df) n. We write this $Z \sim t_n$. The t distribution is a symmetric probability distribution like the normal distribution but is flatter than the normal and has

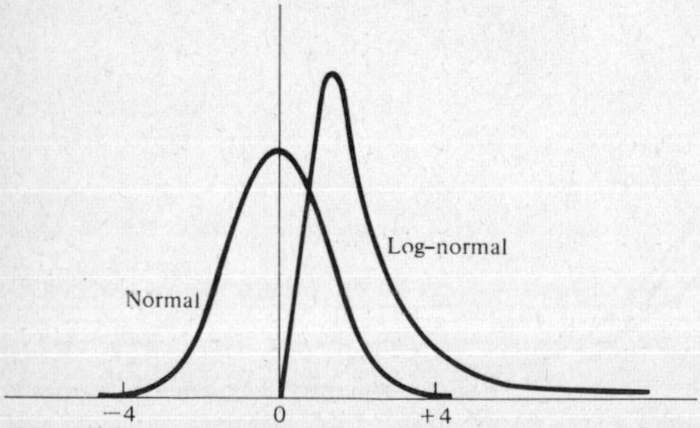

Figure 3-9 Normal and lognormal distributions.

longer tails. As the degrees of freedom n approach infinity, the t distribution approaches the normal distribution.

F distribution. If $Z_1 \sim \chi^2_{n_1}(\sigma^2)$ and $Z_2 \sim \chi^2_{n_2}(\sigma^2)$ and Z_1 and Z_2 are independent, then $y = (Z_1/n_1)/(Z_2/n_2)$ has an F-distribution degrees of freedom n_1 and n_2. We write this as $y \sim F_{n_1,n_2}$. In addition to the normal distribution and the derived distributions like χ^2, t, and F that are commonly used, there is one distribution that has several applications in economics: the lognormal distribution.

The Lognormal Distribution[1]

The random variable x is said to have the lognormal distribution if $\log_e x$ has the normal distribution. Suppose $y = \log x$ is $N(\mu, \sigma^2)$. Then $x = e^y$ has the lognormal distribution. Its mean and variance are given by

$$E(x) = E(e^y) = e^{\mu + (1/2)\sigma^2}$$

$$V(x) = V(e^y) = e^{2\mu + \sigma^2}(e^{\sigma^2} - 1)$$

The frequency curves of the normal and lognormal distributions are shown in Fig. 3-9. Since many variables in economics cannot take negative values and also do not have symmetric distributions as the normal, the lognormal distribution may be more appropriate in some economic applications than the normal. However, the distributions derived from the lognormal are not easily tractable as in the case of the normal distribution. Hence we will continue to make the assumption of normality.

Exercises

1. Suppose that X represents the monthly sales of a product and that the probability distribution of X is as follows:

x	$P(X = x)$
800	.05
900	.10
1000	.25
1100	.35
1200	.10
1300	.10
1400	.05

[1] See J. Aitchison and J. A. C. Brown, "The Lognormal Distribution with Special Reference to Its Uses in Economics," Cambridge University Press, New York, 1969.

Find $P(X \leqslant 1200)$, $P(900 \leqslant X \leqslant 1300)$, $E(X)$, and $V(X)$. If the net profit resulting from sales X is given by $Y = 2X - 1000$, find the expectation and variance of Y.

2. Suppose the variable X in No. 1 represents the sales of hot dogs at a football stand. Suppose the hot-dog vendor pays 30¢ per hot dog and sells it for 45¢. Thus, for every hot dog sold, he makes a profit of 15¢ and for every hot dog left unsold he loses 30¢. What is the expected value and variance of his profit if the number of hot dogs he initially orders is (*a*) 1100; (*b*) 1200; (*c*) 1300? If he wants to maximize expected profits, how many hot dogs should he order?

3. The density of a continuous random variable X is given by

$$f(x) = \begin{cases} kx(2-x) & 0 \leqslant x \leqslant 2 \\ 0 & \text{otherwise} \end{cases}$$

(*a*) Find k and graph the density function.
(*b*) Find $P(\frac{1}{2} < x < \frac{3}{2})$, $P(-\frac{1}{2} < x < \frac{1}{2})$, $P(1 < x < 3)$.
(*c*) Find the cumulative distribution function and graph it.
(*d*) Find $E(X), E(X^2), V(X), E(X^3)$.

4. Answer no. 3 when $f(x)$ is defined as follows:

$$f(x) = \begin{cases} kx & \text{for } 0 \leqslant x \leqslant 1 \\ k(2-x) & \text{for } 1 \leqslant x \leqslant 2 \\ 0 & \text{elsewhere} \end{cases}$$

5. Suppose the joint probability distribution of X and Y is represented by the following table:

x \ y	2	4	6
1	.2	0	.2
2	0	.2	0
3	.2	0	.2

(*a*) Are X and Y independent? Explain.
(*b*) Find the marginal distributions of X and Y.
(*c*) Find the conditional distribution of Y given that $X = 1$ and hence $E(Y \mid X = 1)$ and $V(Y \mid X = 1)$.
(*d*) Find $E(X), E(Y), E(X^2), E(Y^2), E(XY), E(2X + 3Y), \text{cov}(X, Y), \rho_{XY}, V(X + Y), V(2X - 3Y)$.
(*e*) How will you verify the result:

$$V(Y) = EV(Y \mid X) + VE(Y \mid X)$$

6. For the probability distribution tabulated in no. 5, leaving the entries in the first row the same, change the entries in the other two rows so that X and Y are independent.

7. Suppose X and Y are continuous random variables with the following joint probability density function:

$$f(x,y) = \begin{cases} k(x+y) & \text{for } 0 \leqslant x \leqslant 1, 0 \leqslant y \leqslant 2 \\ 0 & \text{otherwise} \end{cases}$$

(*a*) Find $k, E(X), E(Y), V(X), V(Y), \text{cov}(X,Y), \rho_{XY}$. Are X and Y independent?
(*b*) Find $P(0 \leqslant X \leqslant \frac{1}{2}, 0 \leqslant Y \leqslant 1)$.
(*c*) Find the marginal densities of X and Y.
(*d*) Find the conditional density of X given $Y = \frac{1}{2}$ and hence $E(X \mid Y = \frac{1}{2})$ and $V(X \mid Y = \frac{1}{2})$.

8. Answer no. 7 if $f(x,y)$ is defined as follows:

$$f(x,y) = \begin{cases} k(1-x)(2-y) & \text{for } 0 \leqslant x \leqslant 1, 0 \leqslant y \leqslant 2 \\ 0 & \text{otherwise} \end{cases}$$

9. Reading the N, t, χ^2, and F tables:

(*a*) Given that X is $N(2,9)$, find $P[-2 < X < +3]$.

(*b*) If $X \sim t_{20}$, find x_1 and x_2 such that

$$P(X < x_1) = .95$$

$$P(-x_1 < X < x_1) = .90$$

$$P(x_1 < X < x_2) = .90$$

Note that in the last case we can have several sets of values for x_1 and x_2. Find three sets of values from the tables.

(*c*) If $X \sim \chi^2_{10}$, find a value x_1 such that

$$P(X < x_1) = .95$$

$$P(X > x_1) = .95$$

Find two values x_1 and x_2 such that

$$P(x_1 < X < x_2) = .90$$

Note again that there can be several sets of values for x_1 and x_2. Find three such sets of values from the tables.

(*d*) If $X \sim F_{2,20}$, find x_1 such that

$$P(X > x_1) = .05$$

$$P(X > x_1) = .01$$

Can you find the value of x_1 if you are told that

$$P(X > x_1) = .50?$$

(*e*) Answer the same questions as in (*d*) if $X \sim F_{6,28}$

10. Given that $y = \log_e x$ is normal with mean 2 and variance 4, find the mean and variance of x. (Note that x has the lognormal distribution.)

CHAPTER

FOUR

CLASSICAL STATISTICAL INFERENCE

4-1 INTRODUCTION

The probability distributions considered in the preceding chapter serve as theoretical models from which our observations are obtained. Our assumption is that there is an unknown process that generates the data we have. This process can be described by a probability distribution, which in turn will be characterized by some unknown parameters; e.g., the binomial distribution has two parameters n and p; the normal has two parameters μ and σ^2. Our problem is to make inferences about these parameters on the basis of the observations. These inferences will be in the form of giving point estimates, interval estimates, testing of some suggested hypotheses, etc. Suppose the probability distribution involves a parameter θ, and we have a sample of size n, namely, $y_1, y_2, \ldots, y_n$ from this probability distribution. In *point estimation* we construct a function $t(y_1, y_2, \ldots, y_n)$ of these observations and say that t is our estimate (guess) of θ. The common terminology here is to call $t(y_1, y_2, \ldots, y_n)$ an *estimator* and its value in a *particular* sample an *estimate*. Thus, an estimator is a random variable, and an estimate is a particular value of this random variable. In *interval estimation* we construct two functions $t_1(y_1, y_2, \ldots, y_n)$ and $t_2(y_1, y_2, \ldots, y_n)$ and say that θ will lie between t_1 and t_2 (with a certain probability). In *hypothesis testing* we suggest a hypothesis about θ (for example, $\theta = 6.2$), and we either accept or reject this hypothesis on the basis of the data.

In practice what we need to know is how to construct the point estimator t, the interval estimator (t_1, t_2), and the rules for acceptance or rejection of a hypothesis. In the so-called "classical inference" all these are based on *sampling distributions*. Any function $g(y_1, y_2, \ldots, y_n)$ of the sample observations is called a *statistic*, and the probability distribution of this statistic is called its sampling distribution. For example, the sample mean $\bar{y}$ is a statistic and its probability distribution is called the sampling distribution of $\bar{y}$. This gives us information about the behavior of $\bar{y}$ in repeated samples of size n from this population. If $y_1, y_2, \ldots, y_n$ is a sample from a normal distribution with mean μ and variance σ^2, it can be shown that the sampling distribution of the sample mean $\bar{y}$ is also normal with mean μ and variance σ^2/n. Further, if $s^2 = [1/(n-1)]\sum(y_i - \bar{y})^2$, then $[(n-1)s^2/\sigma^2]$ has a χ^2-distribution degrees of freedom $(n-1)$ and $[\sqrt{n}\,(\bar{y} - \mu)]/s$ has a t-distribution degrees of freedom $(n-1)$. These sampling distributions can be used to make inferences about μ and σ^2. In the classical theory the properties of estimators and all other inferences are discussed in terms of their sampling distributions.

4-2 PROPERTIES OF ESTIMATORS

An estimator t is said to be *unbiased* for θ if its *expected value* or mean, to be denoted by $E(t)$, is equal to θ; i.e., the mean of the sampling distribution of t is θ. What this says is that if we calculate t for each sample and repeat this process infinitely many times, then the average of all these estimates will be equal to θ. If $E(t) \neq \theta$, our estimates are not equal to the true value even on the average, and we refer to $E(t) - \theta$ as the *bias*. If this is positive, t is said to be upward-biased and if this is negative, t is said to be downward-biased. Unbiasedness is a desirable property, but it is not desirable at any cost. Suppose we have two estimators t_1 and t_2. t_1 can assume values far from θ and yet have its mean equal to θ, whereas t_2 always ranges close to θ but has its mean slightly away from θ. Their probability distributions are as shown in Fig. 4-1. Then we might prefer t_2 to t_1, because it has smaller variance even though it is biased. If the variance of the estimator is large, we can have some unlucky samples where our estimate is far from the true value. Thus the second property we want in our estimators is that they have small variance. Obviously, it is a relative concept. Sometimes we confine ourselves to unbiased estimators and choose among them the one that has minimum variance. Such an estimator would be called MVUE (minimum-variance unbiased estimator). If we confine ourselves to *linear estimators*, where $t(y_1, y_2, \ldots, y_n)$ is a linear function, that is, $t = c_1 y_1 + c_2 y_2 + \ldots + c_n y_n$ where $c_1, c_2, \ldots, c_n$ are constants, and seek among these the unbiased estimator which has minimum variance, then we call it BLUE (best linear unbiased estimator). Often, we might be willing to tolerate a small degree of bias if we can get a reduction in the variance. Thus, instead of looking at unbiased estimators first and then picking the one that has minimum variance among this class, we might choose an estimator that has minimum mean square error (MSE) where MSE = (bias)^2 + variance. The MSE criterion gives equal weight to (bias)^2 and variance. Instead we might give them weights W_1 and W_2

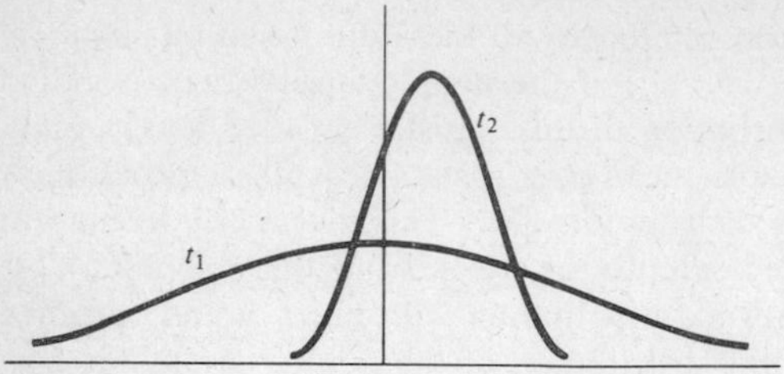

Figure 4-1 Sampling distributions of two estimators t_1 and t_2.

and minimize W_1 (bias)^2 + W_2 (variance). Strictly speaking, instead of doing something *ad hoc* like this, we should specify a loss function that gives the loss in using $t(y_1,y_2, \ldots, y_n)$ as an estimator for θ and choose t so as to minimize expected loss. This decision-theoretic approach will be discussed in the next chapter.

Often, it might not be possible to obtain estimators that have any desirable properties in small samples. In such cases, it is customary to look at some desirable properties in large samples. These are called *asymptotic* properties. Three such properties that are mentioned often are consistency, asymptotic unbiasedness, and asymptotic efficiency.

Suppose for each sample size n we construct the estimator t_n. The sequence of estimators t_n is said to form a consistent sequence if, given any positive numbers δ and ε, however small, we can find a sample size N such that for all $n > N$

$$P\left[|t_n - \theta| < \delta\right] > 1 - \varepsilon$$

i.e., by increasing the sample size n, the estimator t_n can be made to lie arbitrarily close to the true value θ, with probability arbitrarily close to 1. This is also denoted by $\text{plim}_{n\to\infty} t_n = \theta$ (plim means probability limit).

In practice we shall drop the subscript n on t_n and also drop the words "sequence of estimators" and merely say "t is a consistent estimator for θ."

An estimator is said to be *asymptotically unbiased* for θ if the mean of its limiting distribution (as $n \to \infty$) is equal to θ. An estimator is said to be *asymptotically efficient* if it is consistent and the variance of its limiting distribution is smaller than the variance of the limiting distribution of any other consistent estimator.

Another concept that is of great importance in the theory of estimation is that of *sufficiency*. A statistic t is said to be sufficient for the parameter θ if it contains all the information available in the data about the value of θ. A more formal definition is that if t' is any other statistic, the conditional distribution of t' given t does not involve θ. An example is the sample mean $\bar{y}$ for a normal population with mean μ; that is, in order to estimate μ, we do not need the individual observations $y_1,y_2, \ldots, y_n$. It is sufficient if we are given $\bar{y}$ and the sample size n. Sufficient estimators do not always exist, but when they do they are very important.

4-3 METHODS OF POINT ESTIMATION

We have discussed above some desirable properties of estimators. We will discuss now some methods of estimation. We will consider here only two methods: the method of moments and the method of maximum likelihood. There are two other commonly used methods: the least-squares method and the method of minimum χ^2. But we will consider these in subsequent chapters as the occasion arises.

1. *Method of moments*: In this method we equate the sample moments to the corresponding population moments and solve for the parameters; e.g., for samples from a Poisson distribution with parameter λ, we calculate the sample mean, and this gives us the estimate of λ. In the case of a normal distribution with mean μ and variance σ^2 we equate the sample mean and variance, respectively, to these parameters. In the case of the uniform distribution with parameters a and b, the mean is $(b + a)/2$ and variance $(b - a)^2/12$. Suppose the sample mean is 5 and variance is 3. Then we solve the equations $(b + a)/2 = 5$, $(b - a)^2/12 = 3$. Hence we get $b = 8$, $a = 2$. The method of moments is easy to apply, but there is no guarantee that the estimators have good properties. Hence the method is not often used. However, in many cases, it gives estimators identical to those given by the other methods.

2. *Method of maximum likelihood (ML)*: Let $L(y_1, y_2, \ldots, y_n \mid \theta)$ be the joint probability density of the sample observations when the true parameter value is θ. This is clearly a function of $y_1\ y_2, \ldots, y_n$ and θ. As a function of the sample observations it is called a joint probability density function of y_1, $y_2, \ldots, y_n$. As a function of the parameter θ it is called the *likelihood function* for θ. The method of ML says: Choose that value of θ for which $L(\theta)$ is maximum. In effect what this method says is: If you are faced with several values of θ, each of which might be the true value, your best guess is that value which would have made the sample actually observed have the highest probability. Intuitively this method makes sense.

ML estimators have an *invariance* property. If t is a ML estimator of θ, then t^2 is a ML estimator of θ^2, $a + bt$ is a ML estimator of $a + b\theta$, etc. Also under very general conditions ML estimators have many of the desirable properties discussed earlier (these conditions and proofs can be found in any advanced textbooks in statistics). Further, as Bayes' theorem (see Chap. 2) and Bayesian methods (to be discussed in the next chapter) make use of the likelihood function, the ML estimator is of interest by itself (as the maximum of the likelihood function) irrespective of the properties of its sampling distribution. This is because, given the sample observations, the likelihood function completely summarizes all the information in the sample about θ. Whenever possible, we would like to consider what the entire likelihood function looks like and not just its maximum. For example, in Fig. 4-2 we consider three different shapes for the likelihood function. In cases (b) and (c) the ML estimate θ^* does

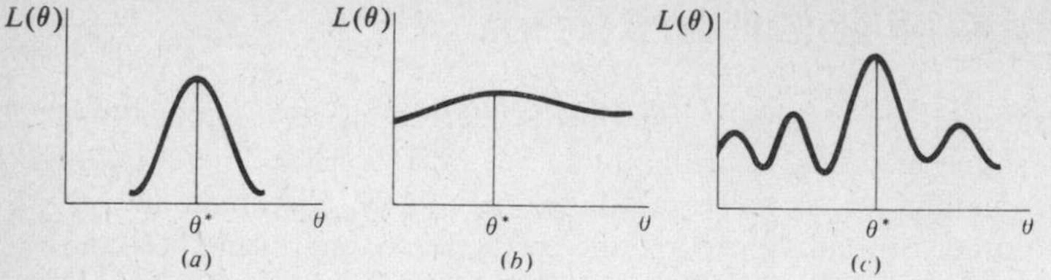

Figure 4-2 (*a*) A sharp likelihood function; (*b*) a flat likelihood function; (*c*) a multimodal likelihood function.

not convey as much information on θ as in case (*a*). In more complicated cases (i.e., with many parameters) we cannot plot the entire likelihood function, and hence we have to be satisfied studying its behavior at the maximum. An example: Let $y_1, y_2, \ldots, y_n$ be independent observations from a normal distribution with mean μ and variance σ^2.

The likelihood function is (since $y_1, y_2, \ldots, y_n$ are independent)

$$L = \prod_{i=1}^{n} \frac{1}{\sigma\sqrt{2\pi}} \exp\left[-\frac{1}{2\sigma^2}(y_i - \mu)^2 \right]$$

$$= \frac{1}{(\sqrt{2\pi}\,)^n \sigma^n} \exp\left[-\frac{1}{2\sigma^2} \sum (y_i - \mu)^2 \right]$$

Hence

$$\log L = -\frac{n}{2}\log 2\pi - n \log \sigma - \frac{1}{2\sigma^2} \sum (y_i - \mu)^2$$

Instead of maximizing L, we can maximize $\log L$, since it is easier to work with. For a maximum we have to have the first derivatives of $\log L$ with respect to μ and σ equal to zero.

$$\frac{\partial \log L}{\partial \mu} = 0 \qquad \text{gives} \qquad \sum (y_i - \mu) = 0$$

Hence $\hat{\mu} = \bar{y}$. (Henceforth we will use the symbol ˆ over a parameter to define an estimator for that parameter.)

$$\frac{\partial \log L}{\partial \sigma} = 0 \qquad \text{gives} \qquad \frac{n}{\sigma} + \frac{1}{\sigma^3} \sum (y_i - \mu)^2 = 0$$

or

$$\hat{\sigma}^2 = \frac{1}{n} \sum (y_i - \hat{\mu})^2 = \frac{1}{n} \sum (y_i - \bar{y})^2$$

One can verify that these estimates give the maximum for $\log L$ by examining the second derivatives.

4-4 INTERVAL ESTIMATION

In interval estimation we construct two statistics $t_1(y_1, y_2, \ldots, y_n)$ and $t_2(y_1, y_2, \ldots, y_n)$ such that

$$P(t_1 \leqslant \theta \leqslant t_2) = g \qquad \text{a given probability} \tag{4-1}$$

g is called the *confidence coefficient*, and the interval (t_1, t_2) is called a *confidence interval*. However, since θ is a parameter (or a constant though unknown), either it lies between t_1 and t_2 or it does not. If it lies between t_1 and t_2, the probability is 1; if it does not, it is zero. In either case the probability cannot be g. What the probability given in (4-1) implies is that if we use the formulas $t_1(y_1, y_2, \ldots, y_n)$ and $t_2(y_1, y_2, \ldots, y_n)$ repeatedly with different samples and in each case we construct the confidence interval using these formulas, then in 100 g percent of all the cases (samples) the interval given will include the true value. Thus, the probability statement is *not* about θ but about samples.

As an illustration of how to use sampling distributions to construct confidence intervals suppose that $y_1, y_2, \ldots, y_n$ are independent observations from a normal distribution with mean μ and variance σ^2. Define

$$\bar{y} = \frac{1}{n} \sum y_i \qquad \text{and} \qquad s^2 = \frac{1}{n-1} \sum (y_i - \bar{y})^2$$

Then $[(n-1)s^2/\sigma^2]$ has a χ^2-distribution degrees of freedom $(n-1)$ and $[\sqrt{n}\,(\bar{y}-\mu)]/s$ has a t-distribution degrees of freedom $(n-1)$. (The detailed derivations of these results are omitted here.)

If the sample size n is equal to 20 so that degrees of freedom $= n - 1 = 19$, we can refer to the χ^2 tables with degrees of freedom 19 and say that

$$P\left(\frac{19s^2}{\sigma^2} > 32.852\right) = .025 \tag{4-2}$$

or

$$P\left(10.117 < \frac{19s^2}{\sigma^2} < 30.144\right) = .90 \tag{4-3}$$

Also referring to the t tables with degrees of freedom 19 we find that

$$P\left[-2.093 \leqslant \frac{\sqrt{n}\,(\bar{y}-\mu)}{s} \leqslant 2.093\right] = .95 \tag{4-4}$$

From Eq. (4-3) we have

$$P\left(\frac{19s^2}{30.144} < \sigma^2 < \frac{19s^2}{10.117}\right) = .90$$

or if $s^2 = 9.0$ we have roughly

$$P(5.7 < \sigma^2 < 16.9) = .90 \tag{4-5}$$

Similarly, if $\bar{y} = 5$ and $s = 3$ we have, from Eq. (4-4),

$$P\left[-2.1 \leqslant \frac{4.5(5-\mu)}{3} \leqslant 2.1\right] = .95$$

or

$$P\left(-\frac{6.3}{4.5} \leqslant 5-\mu \leqslant \frac{6.3}{4.5}\right) = .95$$

or

$$P(3.6 \leqslant \mu \leqslant 6.4) = .95 \tag{4-6}$$

Equations (4-5) and (4-6) give confidence intervals for σ^2 and μ, respectively. Obviously, there are several ways of constructing confidence intervals with the same confidence coefficient. The "best" confidence interval is the one with minimum expected length. There is also a relationship between confidence intervals and tests of hypotheses which we will now discuss.

4-5 TESTING OF HYPOTHESES

A statistical hypothesis is a hypothesis concerning one or more of the parameters in the probability distribution. If the hypothesis completely specifies the distribution, it is called a *simple* hypothesis. Otherwise it is called a *composite* hypothesis. For example, consider a normal distribution with mean μ and variance σ^2. A hypothesis $\mu = 1$, $\sigma = 2$ is a simple hypothesis. A hypothesis $\mu = 2$, σ unspecified is composite. So is a hypothesis $\mu > 2$, $\sigma = 1$. Usually we specify a hypothesis H_0 and an alternative H_1; for example,

H_0: $\mu = 1$, $\sigma = 2$

H_1: $\mu = 2$, $\sigma = 4$

is a case where both H_0 and H_1 are simple. If

H_0: $\mu = 1$, $\sigma = 2$

H_1: $\mu \neq 1$, $\sigma \neq 2$

then H_0 is simple and H_1 a composite hypothesis which is merely a negation of H_0. Usually, H_0 is called a *null hypothesis*.

In testing H_0 against H_1, we are liable to commit two types of errors: We may wrongly reject H_0 when it is true. This is called the type I error. We may wrongly accept H_0 when H_1 is true. This is called the type II error.

Define: α = type I error = $P(\text{reject } H_0 \mid H_0 \text{ is true})$
β = type II error = $P(\text{accept } H_0 \mid H_1 \text{ is true})$

The usual procedure that is suggested is to choose the test so as to fix α at a certain level and minimize β. α is called the *significance level* and $(1-\beta)$ is called the *power* of the test. This, in brief, is the Neyman-Pearson approach

(1933) to testing hypotheses. One basic criticism of this approach is that this amounts to an asymmetric treatment of the hypotheses H_0 and H_1, and not all situations justify such treatment. Further, no explicit consideration is given to the relative losses due to type I and type II errors. These objections can be met by a decision-theoretic approach to the problem, which we shall discuss in the next chapter.

4-6 UNBIASEDNESS, CONSISTENCY, AND EFFICIENCY OF TESTS[1]

As in the theory of estimation, we shall be concerned with several properties of tests like unbiasedness, consistency, and efficiency, and asymptotic efficiency. A test is said to be *unbiased* if the power of the test is not less than the level of significance. If this condition is not satisfied, alternatives will exist under which acceptance of the hypothesis is more likely than in some cases when the hypothesis is true. A test is said to be *consistent* if the power of the test tends to 1 as n, the sample size, tends to infinity. This term was introduced by Wald and Wolfowitz in 1940. A test which is not consistent does not enable us to detect the alternative with certainty if it is true, even as n tends to infinity.

The concept of efficiency of tests is more problematical than the corresponding concept in estimation. If we consider two tests with the same type I error, then for each alternative, we can take the ratio of the powers as a measure of the efficiency (or alternatively, the ratio of the required sample sizes to attain the same power at the common significance level). But this measure does not lead to an unambiguous choice if the power functions cross, as is usually the case. Further, these measures depend on three factors—the level of significance chosen, the sample size, and the distance between the null and alternative hypotheses. There does not seem to be any satisfactory summary measure for finite samples. Hence attention is usually concentrated on asymptotic efficiency. At the asymptotic level, since consistency is a desirable property, it is not possible to use the limiting value of the power function as a criterion for distinguishing between tests because this limiting value is always unity. Hence the measures of asymptotic efficiency are usually based on the local behavior of the power curves at $\theta = \theta_0$ in large samples.

4-7 THE LIKELIHOOD-RATIO (LR) TEST

Most of the tests in common use can be derived from an important principle due to Neyman and Pearson (1928) called the likelihood-ratio principle. The LR tests play a role in the theory of testing similar to that of the maximum-

[1] The following discussion may be rather cryptic but is not difficult to follow. It is included to make the reader aware of these concepts.

likelihood method in the theory of estimation. Simply stated, the likelihood ratio is

$$\lambda = \frac{\max L(\theta) \text{ over values of } \theta \text{ specified by } H_0}{\max L(\theta) \text{ over all values of } \theta}$$

where $L(\theta)$ is the likelihood function. Clearly λ lies between 0 and 1 because the denominator, which is an unrestricted maximum of $L(\theta)$, has to be $\geqslant$ the numerator, which is a restricted maximum of $L(\theta)$. We reject H_0 if $\lambda \leqslant c_\alpha$ where c_α is a constant defined so that the type I error is α.

The intuitive argument for the test is as follows: If we are comparing the "plausibility" of one value of θ against another, given a sample $(y_1, y_2, \ldots, y_n)$, we would be choosing that value of θ which gives the likelihood a larger value. If we cannot find an appreciably larger value of the likelihood function by searching through the values of θ other than those specified by H_0, then we can reason that the most plausible value of θ belongs to the set specified by H_0. Hence we accept H_0.

The LR test has several important properties. It is unbiased and consistent. Further, $-2 \log_e \lambda$ has, in large samples, a χ^2-distribution degrees of freedom r where r is the number of parameters for which H_0 specifies given values. For example, we consider a normal distribution with mean μ and variance σ^2 and H_0: $\mu = 2$, σ^2 unspecified and H_1: $\mu \neq 2$, σ^2 unspecified, and if $L(\mu, \sigma^2)$ is the likelihood function, then

$$\lambda = \frac{\max\limits_{\sigma^2} L(2, \sigma^2)}{\max\limits_{\mu, \sigma^2} L(\mu, \sigma^2)}$$

and $-2 \log_e \lambda$ has a χ^2-distribution degrees of freedom 1 in large samples. Most of the tests we commonly use can be derived by the use of the LR method.

4-8 RELATIONSHIP BETWEEN CONFIDENCE-INTERVAL PROCEDURES AND TESTS OF HYPOTHESES[1]

Consider the previous example of a sample of size 20 from a normal population with mean μ and variance σ^2. Suppose as before that the sample mean $\bar{y} = 5$ and sample variance $s^2 = 9$. We saw that the 95 percent confidence interval for μ was (3.6,6.4); see Eq. (4-6). Suppose now we consider the problem of testing H_0: $\mu = 7$ against H_1: $\mu \neq 7$. The appropriate likelihood-ratio test can be shown to be the t test. If we use a significance level of 5 percent, the test says that we should reject the hypothesis H_0 if $[\sqrt{n}\,(\bar{y} - 7)/s] > 2.093$, where 2.093 is

[1] The relationship explained here is for tests of hypotheses about parameter values. There are other tests like tests of goodness of fit, tests of independence in contingency tables, etc., for which there is no confidence-interval counterpart. These we discuss later.

the point in the t tables for degrees of freedom 19 such that $P(-2.093 < t < 2.093) = .95$ or $P(|t| > 2.093) = .05$. In the above example $[\sqrt{n}\,(\bar{y}-7)]/s = -3$, and hence we reject H_0. In fact we will be rejecting H_0 at the 5 percent significance level whenever H_0 specifies μ to lie outside the 95 percent confidence interval (3.6,6.4).

The above example is a case of what is known as a *two-tailed test*. If H_0: $\mu \geqslant 7$, and H_1: $\mu < 7$, then we use a *one-sided test*. Again we compute the test statistic $t = [\sqrt{n}\,(\bar{y}-7)]/s$, but this time it is too low values of t that lead us to reject the null hypothesis. From the t tables with 19 degrees of freedom we find that $P[t < -1.73] = .05$. Hence we reject H_0 if the calculated $t < -1.73$. Here it is -3, and hence we reject H_0. The corresponding 95 percent confidence interval is given by

$$P\left[-1.73 < \frac{\sqrt{n}\,(\bar{y}-\mu)}{s}\right] = .95$$

that is,

$$P\left[-1.73 < \frac{\sqrt{20}\,(5-\mu)}{s}\right] = .95$$

Or

$$P(\mu < 6.15) = .95$$

The region for μ given by H_0 is outside this *one-sided* confidence region. Hence we reject H_0. These examples illustrate the close relationship that exists between confidence intervals and tests of significance.

4-9 SOME COMMENTS ON SIGNIFICANCE LEVELS

Often in applied work it is customary to say that something is "significant" or "not significant" without explaining what this means. When we say in the above example that the t value of -3 is significant at the 5 percent level, what we mean is that under the hypothesis H_0, the probability of obtaining a value of the computed t as small as this is < 5 percent. Hence either we conclude that we have an extremely improbable sample or else H_0 is not true. We take the latter course of action. At what level do we consider that an improbable event has occurred? When the probability is 5, 10, or 20 percent? This is quite arbitrary, and as mentioned earlier it cannot be decided without an explicit consideration of the losses involved in each decision. The most commonly used significance level is 5 percent, but this is purely arbitrary. Another point to note is that often H_0 is taken to specify the parameter value to be zero (the computer programs all print out the t values on this assumption). In many cases this may be a meaningless hypothesis to test; e.g., it is meaningless to test the hypothesis that the marginal propensity to consume is zero. In many economic applications it would be more informative if we report confidence intervals rather than saying that particular coefficient is "significant" or "not significant." Reporting results in this form should be avoided. There are many examples in economic literature (particularly when numerous estimates are made) where we are presented a summary table of the estimates, some of which have a single asterisk and others a double asterisk, and then there is a footnote explaining that a single asterisk denotes "significant at the 5 percent level" and a double asterisk denotes "significant at the 1 percent level." Such tables are meaningful only in those cases where all we are interested in is rejecting a "null hypothesis." But even in this case one cannot get a summary picture by counting the estimates with the asterisks.

4-10 TESTS OF GOODNESS OF FIT

We have till now discussed tests for parameters. There are some tests which are not based on any parameters. In such cases there is no counterpart to the tests in terms of confidence intervals as illustrated earlier. One category of such tests is the "goodness of fit" tests. If we postulate a theoretical probability distribution underlying our data, it would be convenient to compare how well this distribution fits the data we have. This is done by comparing the theoretical (or expected) frequencies with the observed frequencies. Suppose we group the data into k groups and E_i and O_i are, respectively, the expected and observed frequencies in the ith group. Then,

$$\chi^2 = \sum_{i=1}^{k} \frac{(O_i - E_i)^2}{E_i}$$

has a χ^2-distribution degrees of freedom $(k - 1)$. If the value of this statistic is large, we conclude that the postulated theoretical distribution does not fit the data well. To give a simple illustration, suppose a die is rolled 120 times. Suppose the observed frequencies are:

i	1	2	3	4	5	6
O_i	15	24	17	16	23	25

The question we want to decide is whether the die is loaded or not. If the die is fair, the expected frequencies are all 20. Hence

$$\chi^2 = \tfrac{1}{20}|(20 - 15)^2 + (20 - 24)^2 + (20 - 17)^2 + \dots|$$
$$= \tfrac{1}{20}|25 + 16 + 9 + 16 + 9 + 25| = 5.0$$

From the χ^2 tables with 5 degrees of freedom we see that the 10 percent probability point is 9.24. Hence the probability of getting a χ^2 value 5.0 or greater is definitely greater than 10 percent (possibly it is > 30 percent, but the tables are not detailed enough to infer the precise probability). Hence we do not reject the hypothesis that the die is fair.

Table 4-1

		Level of schooling			
		Low	Medium	High	Total
Income	Low	70	10	20	100
	Medium	20	40	20	80
	High	10	10	50	70
	Total	100	60	90	250

4-11 TESTS OF INDEPENDENCE IN CONTINGENCY TABLES

Another test we will sometimes use is to test independence among variables when the data are qualitative rather than quantitative. Suppose we have data on the level of schooling and the level of income for 250 people. These data are presented in Table 4-1, which is known as a two-way contingency table. If there is independence in the attributes level of schooling and level of income, then the theoretical frequencies will be the product of the marginal totals divided by the grand total. For example, in the first row of Table 4-1, the expected frequencies are

$$\frac{100 \times 100}{250} = 40 \qquad \frac{100 \times 60}{250} = 24 \qquad \frac{100 \times 90}{250} = 36 \qquad \text{etc.}$$

The theoretical frequencies in the next rows are 32, 19.2, 28.8 and 28, 16.8, 25.2. The χ^2 value is 106.2. In the case of a contingency table with r rows and c columns, the degrees of freedom for the χ^2 test is $(r-1)(c-1)$. (This is because if we fill $r-1$ rows and $c-1$ columns, the remaining entries are automatically determined by the marginal row and column totals.) In this case for 4 degrees of freedom the 1 percent value of χ^2 from tables is 13.28. Obviously, the value 106.2 we obtained is very high. Hence we reject the hypothesis that there is independence between the two variables. (Of course, in the above example even a rough inspection of the figures in Table 4-1 would have led us to infer that the two variables are correlated.)

4-12 COMBINING INDEPENDENT TESTS

Often in econometric work we have several pieces of evidence on the basis of which we would like to decide whether some hypothesis is valid or not. For example, suppose the question we are interested in is whether unionism affects wages or not. Sometimes in such problems the results from several studies are reported and the number of studies are counted in which the relevant coefficients are significant. However, the null hypothesis (in this example the hypothesis that unionism has no effects on wages) is rejected (or not rejected) at different levels of probabilities in the different studies. Hence a simple counting rule is not the proper way of summarizing the evidence. One way of combining the different tests is to calculate the probabilities p_i for each case of obtaining a coefficient as high as the one obtained assuming the null hypothesis to be true. (Usually, if this probability is $>.05$, we say the coefficient is "significant" and if it is $>.01$, we say the coefficient is "highly significant.") Then if there are k tests, $\lambda = \sum_{i=1}^{k}(-2 \log_e p_i)$ has a χ^2-distribution degrees of freedom $2k$. This statistic can be used for an overall rejection or acceptance of the null hypothesis on the basis of the k independent tests.[1]

Exercises

1. Consider a business firm. The amount of cash inflow in a week is a random variable x. The amount of cash outflow in a week is a random variable y. Given the following data on x and y and assuming both x and y to be normally distributed, obtain the maximum-likelihood estimates of the means and variances of x and y. Are these estimates unbiased? Are they consistent?

x	y	x	y
42	25	28	39
65	37	61	27
76	83	75	38
92	36	83	27
37	73	60	78
47	23	93	20
27	97	86	68
23	36	68	72
63	70	53	60
40	51	87	65
70	39	63	80
82	36	47	62
90	82	52	36
68	30	38	43
82	72	90	57

2. For the data in no. 1 obtain unbiased estimates of the means and variances of x and y. Also obtain 95 percent confidence limits for these four parameters.

3. If μx, μy, σ_x^2, σ_y^2, respectively, denote the mean of x, mean of y, variance of x, and variance of y, test the following hypotheses at the 5 percent level of significance:

(i) H_0: $\mu x = 40$ vs. H_1: $\mu x \neq 40$
(ii) H_0: $\mu x = 40$ vs. H_1: $\mu x > 40$
(iii) H_0: $\mu x = 40$ vs. H_1: $\mu x < 40$
(iv) H_0: $\sigma_x^2 = 49$ vs. H_1: $\sigma_x^2 \neq 49$
(v) H_0: $\sigma_x^2 = 49$ vs. H_1: $\sigma_x^2 > 49$
(vi) H_0: $\mu x = 40$, $\sigma_x^2 = 49$ vs. H_1: $\mu x \neq 40$, $\sigma_x^2 = 49$
(vii) H_0: $\mu x = 40$, $\sigma_x^2 = 49$ vs. H_1: $\mu x \neq 40$, $\sigma_x^2 \neq 49$
(viii) H_0: $\mu x = 40$, $\sigma_x^2 = 49$ vs. H_1: $\mu x = 40$, $\sigma_x^2 \neq 49$

Explain in each case the relationship of the test with the construction of a corresponding confidence interval.

[1] This test is called Pearson's p_λ test. See C. R. Rao, "Advanced Statistical Methods in Biometric Research," p. 44, John Wiley & Sons, Inc., New York, 1952.

4. For the data in no. 1, how will you test the hypothesis $\mu x = \mu y$ if

(i) x and y are independent.
(ii) x and y are not independent.

5. If, in no. 4, x is distributed as

$$f(x) = ae^{-bx} \qquad x \geqslant 0$$

and y is distributed as

$$g(y) = ce^{-dy} \qquad y \geqslant 0$$

obtain the maximum-likelihood estimates of the parameters a, b, c, and d. Are these estimates unbiased? Are they consistent? Can you find unbiased estimates for these parameters?

6. For the data in Table (2-1) apply goodness of fit tests to check whether the data are normally distributed with the following parameters:

(*a*) White males total: Mean = 9,185, standard deviation = 3,800
(*b*) White males with 12 years of schooling: Mean = 9,389, standard deviation = 3,000
(*c*) Black males with 16 or more years of schooling: Mean = 10,155, standard deviation = 3,500

What are your conclusions? What problems will you encounter in applying similar tests to other subgroups in that table (say black females with 8 years of schooling)?

7. Take the data in Table 2-1. Define

Income < \$6,000 as low income
\$6,000 to \$15,000 as medium income
and > \$15,000 as high income
Also < 11 years of schooling as low level
11 to 15 years of schooling as medium
and 16 or more years of schooling as high

Using the contingency tables, test for independence between level of income and level of schooling for white males, black males, white females, and black females separately. Also combine the results of these tests, using the procedure described in Sec. 4-12.

CHAPTER

FIVE

BAYESIAN INFERENCE AND DECISION THEORY

5-1 INTRODUCTION TO BAYESIAN INFERENCE

The basis of all Bayesian inference is Bayes' theorem, discussed in Chap. 2, which says: Posterior probability varies with likelihood × prior probability. The basic idea is very simple. We have some prior notions about the parameter θ. Based on the sample information as embodied in the likelihood function, we revise our opinions about θ. These revised opinions are incorporated in the posterior distribution. As an example, suppose a marketing manager is interested in λ, the proportion of consumers that will buy a particular product. He has some subjective feelings about λ which can be described by the prior-probability distribution in Table 5-1. Now from a random sample of 5 consumers 2 have said that they will buy the product. The likelihoods of obtaining 2 acceptances out of 5 for different values of λ are given by $\binom{5}{2}\lambda^2(1-\lambda)^3$. In Table 5-1 we show these likelihoods and the posterior probabilities—the probabilities that this manager has after observing the sample results. The posterior probabilities are obtained by dividing the entries in the fourth column by the sum—since the posterior probabilities have to sum to 1. That is,

$$\text{Posterior probability} = \frac{\text{likelihood} \times \text{prior probability}}{\Sigma(\text{likelihood} \times \text{prior probability})}$$

This division is called *normalization*. For continuous distributions we write

$$f(\theta \mid y) = \frac{L(y \mid \theta)\cdot h(\theta)}{\int L(y \mid \theta)\cdot h(\theta)d\theta} \tag{5-1}$$

Table 5-1

λ	Prior probability	Likelihood	Prior × likelihood	Posterior probability
.1	.2	.0729	.01458	.0762
.2	.5	.2048	.10240	.5355
.4	.2	.3456	.06912	.3615
.8	.1	.0512	.00512	.0268
		Sum =	.19122	1.0

$f(\theta \mid y)$ is the posterior distribution of θ given the sample observations y, $L(y \mid \theta)$ is the likelihood function, $h(\theta)$ is the prior probability density function, and $\int L(y \mid \theta) \cdot h(\theta)\, d\theta$ is the "normalization factor." The form of $L(y \mid \theta)$ will depend on the probability distribution assumed, e.g., normal, beta, gamma. Often $h(\theta)$ is chosen in such a way that the integral $\int L(y \mid \theta) \cdot h(\theta)\, d\theta$ can be easily performed and the functional form of the posterior distribution $f(\theta \mid y)$ is the same as that of $h(\theta)$. Such a prior distribution $h(\theta)$ is called a *conjugate prior*. The advantage with the conjugate prior is that every time a new sample is observed, the revision of opinions about θ can be performed by the same analytical procedure. That is, $f(\theta \mid y)$, being of the same form as $h(\theta)$, can be used as the new prior for analyzing the new sample information and the formulas derived earlier can be used to get the new posterior. A large number of such conjugate priors are discussed in Raiffa and Schlaifer.[1]

Often we do not have any prior notions about θ. In this case what is suggested is that we use a *diffuse* or *noninformative* prior. The term "diffuse" is more appropriate than "noninformative" because these priors are really noninformative only in a relative sense. The prior assumed is uniform over an unspecified range as shown in Fig. 5-1. Such priors are also called "improper" because the probabilities do not sum to one. Such priors have been advocated by Jeffreys,[2] and hence they are also known as Jeffreys' priors. For the normal distribution with mean μ and variance σ^2 the Jeffreys priors are

$$\begin{aligned} h(\mu) &\propto \text{constant} \qquad -\infty < \mu < \infty \\ h(\sigma) &\propto \frac{1}{\sigma} \qquad 0 < \sigma < \infty \end{aligned} \tag{5-2}$$

If the sample is very large or if the prior is diffuse, the posterior distribution will be just proportional to the likelihood function. Hence the mode of the posterior distribution will be the maximum-likelihood estimate, and if the likelihood function is symmetric, the mean of the posterior distribution will also be the ML estimate.

[1] H. Raiffa and R. Schlaifer, "Applied Statistical Decision Theory," Harvard Business School, Division of Research, Boston, 1961.

[2] H. Jeffreys, "Theory of Probability," 3d ed., Oxford University Press, Fair Lawn, N.J., 1961.

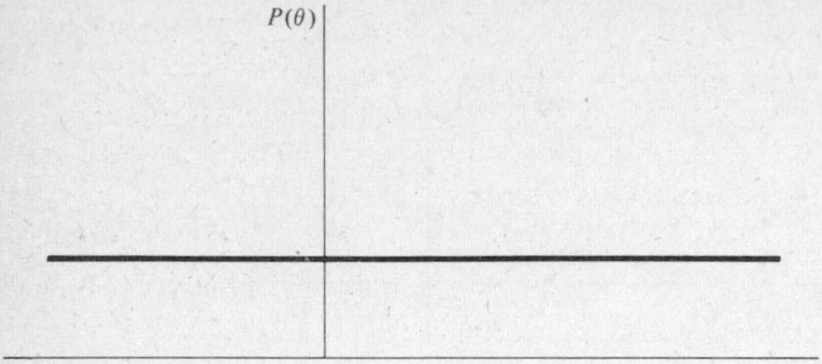

Figure 5-1 Diffuse prior.

As in classical inference, one can consider in Bayesian inference point estimation, interval estimation, and tests of significance. All these are based on the posterior distribution. Which point estimator we use will depend on the loss function; e.g., if the loss function is quadratic, the optimal point estimator is the mean of the posterior distribution. Regarding interval estimation, given the posterior distribution for θ we can find two numbers a and b such that $P(a < \theta < b) =$ any specified number between 0 and 1 (as shown in Fig. 5-2). (Often we choose a and b so as to minimize the distance between them.) As for tests of hypotheses we should note that for a continuous distribution, the probability that θ assumes any *particular* value is zero. Hence we cannot test hypotheses like H_0: $\theta = \theta_0$ against H_1: $\theta \neq \theta_0$. If H_0 specifies that $a < \theta < b$ and H_1 specifies that $c < \theta < d$, then all we have to do is compute from the posterior distribution the probabilities that θ lies between these two intervals. The important point to note is that in the classical methods H_0 and H_1 are treated asymmetrically. In the Bayesian methods they are treated symmetrically.

The above discussion suggests that the Bayesian methods are very straightforward and easy to understand and apply. From the practical point of view most of the controversies between the Bayesian and the classical groups—particularly in econometrics—are semantic. If the samples are large or the priors are diffuse, they should both give us the same answers; e.g., the confidence intervals that are usually presented are almost the same as the corresponding Bayesian intervals (though the meaning attached to them is different). There is a problem in giving a Bayesian interpretation to the tests of significance, but as

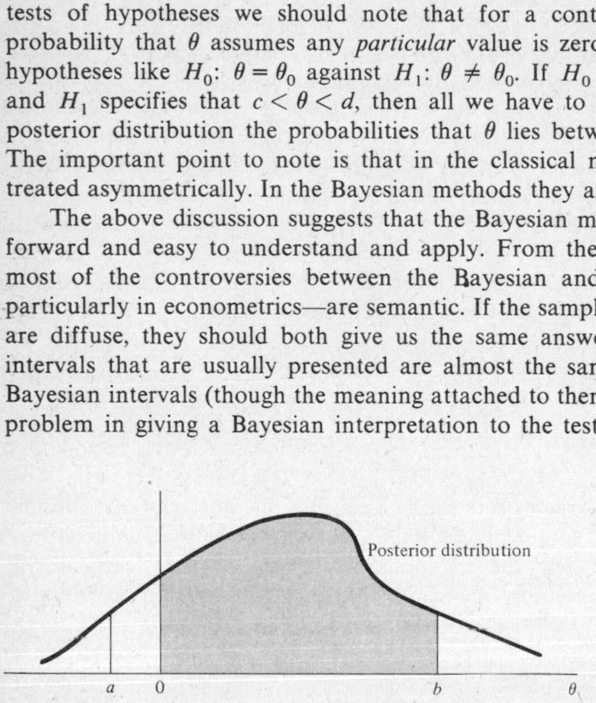

Figure 5-2 Bayesian intervals.

mentioned earlier econometricians should report confidence intervals rather than reporting results saying "significant" or "not significant."

In most economic applications, compared with the problems concerning the adequacy and nature of the data and specification errors in model formulation, the controversy over the Bayesian vs. the classical methods is often of minor importance. In this book we will be discussing the methods in the subsequent chapters in the classical framework given in Chap. 4. We will do this because most econometric practice is in that tradition. Also, though there is likely to be a lot of subjective prior information in the case of many decision problems at the level of the individual firm and hence the Bayesian methods are the most appropriate ones to use, there is not likely to be the same sort of prior information in the case of the models we consider—market-demand functions, industry-cost functions, and production functions, etc. Often, information like the fact that the demand function has a negative slope, that the marginal propensity to consume is < 1, etc., is cited by some Bayesians as prior information in these models that classical econometricians ignore. There is a point in this argument, though we should not push it too far. Suppose we estimate a demand function and find its slope to be positive. This suggests that we should examine our data more closely or that there are some specification errors which we should examine. On the other hand, a procedure that is constrained to yield only negative slopes might not reveal such deficiencies in the data or model specification. Where we have full confidence in the quality of the data we use, and the specification of the model, the prior information mentioned above should be incorporated. This is rarely the case in most econometric work, and thus the Bayesian methods, though theoretically sound, cannot be applied automatically. In Chap. 18 we give an outline of Bayesian econometric methods.

5-2 STATISTICAL DECISION THEORY

We have till now discussed sampling distributions, classical estimation, hypothesis testing, and Bayesian methods. The purpose of all these methods is inferential—to make inferences about some population from which our sample is drawn. Classical statistics prescribes inferential techniques based on sample information alone. In Bayesian methods we have an additional ingredient: the prior distribution. This is combined with the likelihood function which represents the sample information. In decision theory we are interested in taking an action rather than just making an inference about a population. Of course, many inferential procedures are also decisions; e.g., choosing a point estimate is a decision, accepting or rejecting a hypothesis is a decision. But the main ingredient of decision theory that we have not discussed yet is the *loss function*. If we assume a prior distribution too, we have Bayesian decision theory; otherwise it is part of classical decision theory.

In decision theory, we start with a loss function $L(d,\theta)$ which represents the loss resulting from decision d when θ is the true state of nature. The decision will be a function of the sample observations $(y_1,y_2, \ldots, y_n)$; so let us denote it by $d(y_1,y_2, \ldots, y_n)$. Our objective is to choose the function which is good in some sense, i.e., minimizes loss in some way.

For a given decision function $d(y_1,y_2, \ldots, y_n)$ we can define the *risk* $R(d,\theta)$ as the *expected loss*

$$R(d,\theta) = E\{L[d(y_1,y_2, \ldots, y_n) - \theta]\} \tag{5-3}$$

the expectation being the mean for all samples of size n. Now we may want to choose d so that $R(d,\theta)$ is minimum whatever the state of nature θ. However, such uniformly minimum-risk decision functions do not usually exist. For example, suppose the loss function is quadratic. $L(d,\theta) = (d - \theta)^2$ and d is the decision to use $\hat{\theta}(y_1,y_2, \ldots, y_n)$ as an estimator for θ. Then $R(\hat{\theta},\theta) = E(\hat{\theta} - \theta)^2$, i.e., the mean square error of $\hat{\theta}$. Hence the problem of choosing a uniformly minimum-risk decision function is to find an estimator $\hat{\theta}$ which has minimum mean square error. Unfortunately, this is not possible in general, because for any given θ, say θ_0, we can always find an estimator whose mean square error is equal to zero *for this particular value of* θ. Thus, to have *uniformly in* θ minimum mean square error, we must have zero mean square error for *every* θ, and this is not possible.

Since uniformly minimum-risk decision functions do not exist, some suggestions have been made in the literature. One criterion is the minimax criterion suggested by Wald. For each d, look at $\max_\theta R(d,\theta)$. Then choose that d which minimizes this maximum risk. This criterion corresponds to extremely cautious behavior and hence it is not of much use in practice. Another possibility is to restrict the class of decisions and hope that there is a uniformly minimum-risk decision function in that class. For example, since a minimum mean-square-error estimator cannot be found, restrict attention to unbiased estimators and then try to find a minimum-variance unbiased estimator. This approach can be used for particular problems.

A third possibility is not to find the best decision function but to eliminate bad ones. This is the idea behind *admissibility*. Suppose we have two decision functions d_1 and d_2 such that $R(d_1,\theta) \leqslant R(d_2,\theta)$ for all θ and $R(d_1,\theta) < R(d_2,\theta)$ for some θ. Then d_1 is said to dominate d_2 because d_1 is at least as good as d_2 for all θ and strictly better for some θ. Any procedure that is strictly dominated by another is said to be *inadmissible*. Any one which is not strictly dominated by another is admissible. However, this criterion is useful only for weeding out bad decisions. The problem of choosing among admissible decisions still remains.

Finally, if we admit a prior distribution for θ, difficulties disappear. What we now do is choose a d that minimizes expected risk or *Bayes' risk*, i.e., choose d so as to minimize $E_\theta[R(d,\theta)] = \int R(d,\theta)P(\theta)\,d\theta$, where $P(\theta)$ is the prior distribution of θ. Of course, the answer will depend on the prior $P(\theta)$, and two individuals with different priors will make different decisions. Yet another possibility in the Bayesian method is just to minimize expected loss rather than expected risk, i.e., minimize $\int L(d,\theta)P(\theta)\,d\theta$. In this case, we do not bother

Table 5-2*

		States of nature			
		θ_1	θ_2		θ_k
	d_1				
Decisions	d_2				
	d_m				

* The entries in the table are $L(d_i,\theta_j)$ or $R(d_i,\theta_j)$ depending on whether we are dealing with loss functions or risk functions, respectively.

about what happens to $L(d,\theta)$ in repeated samples—which is what we do when we consider the risk function $R(d,\theta)$.

Diagrammatically, one can explain the situation with reference to Table 5-2. For each decision d_i and state of nature θ_j we have a loss function $L(d_i,\theta_j)$ and a risk function $R(d_i,\theta_j)$ where $R(d_i,\theta_j)$ is the mean (over repeated samples) of $L(d_i,\theta_j)$..

In the minimax method where we minimize maximum risk, we go through each row of Table 5-2 and pick the value that is maximum. Then we see for which d we have the minimum of these values and choose that decision. The same procedure can be used for the loss function rather than the risk function. Then that would be a minimax loss solution. In the Bayesian method we take weighted averages of each row in Table 5-2 of the risk function, the weights being the prior probabilities. Then we choose that decision d for which this weighted average is minimum.[1]

5-3 ILLUSTRATION OF THE USE OF LOSS FUNCTIONS

Since dealing with risk functions involves taking expectations over possible sample outcomes, we will first illustrate the principles with reference to loss functions rather than risk functions.

Suppose a retailer has a choice of ordering 100, 200, or 500 items. The costs of the orders are, respectively, $200, $250, and $350. He also has a choice of not ordering anything at all, for which the cost is 0. Suppose the sale price of each

[1] There is some ambiguity in the literature as to what is meant by Bayesian decisions, whether they refer to those which minimize expected risk or expected loss. It does not really matter so long as one clearly states whether one is minimizing expected risk or expected loss and also notes that if expected risk is finite, expected loss is finite but that the converse need not be true. Thornber discusses the difference between the two and the use of minimum-expected-loss estimators in econometric applications. See H. Thornber, "Applications of Decision Theory to Econometrics," unpublished doctoral dissertation, University of Chicago, 1966.

Table 5-3 States of nature

		50	100	200	300	400	500
Decisions	0	0	0	0	0	0	0
	100	− 50	100	100	100	100	100
	200	− 100	50	350	350	350	350
	500	− 200	− 50	250	550	850	1150

item is $3, and that the states of nature (the demand in the market) can take the values of 50, 100, 200, 300, 400, or 500. There are thus 6 states of nature and 4 decisions: to order 0, 100, 200, or 500. The profits the retailer makes (losses are shown with a negative sign) are shown in Table 5-3. If the retailer were to minimize his maximum loss, he would choose not to order anything. This is, of course, the most pessimistic solution. Suppose his prior probabilities for the 6 states of nature are .5, .2, .2, .05, .04, and .01, respectively. Then his expected profits EP for the 4 decisions are:

$$EP(d_1) = 0$$
$$EP(d_2) = .5(-50) + .5(100) = 25$$
$$EP(d_3) = .5(-100) + .2(50) + .3(350) = 65$$
$$EP(d_4) = .5(-200) + .2(-50) + .2(250) + .05(550) + .04(850) + .01(1150) = 13$$

Thus he would be ordering 200 items. (He maximizes expected profit or equivalently minimizes expected loss.) In the above example we assumed a fixed price (which is perhaps a meaningful assumption in examples like sales of hamburgers at carnivals). However, one can generalize the above situation to a case where each state of nature is described by a demand function and we have prior probabilities on the different demand functions.

5-4 ILLUSTRATION OF THE USE OF RISK FUNCTIONS

We will illustrate the use of risk functions with the following simple example: Suppose we have two independent observations x_1, x_2 from a normal population with mean θ and variance 1. Our decision is to choose $c_1x_1 + c_2x_2$ as an estimator for θ. For different values of c_1 and c_2 we have different decision functions. Choosing the optimal decision function amounts to choosing the optimal values of c_1 and c_2. Let the loss function be a quadratic function $L = (c_1x_1 + c_2x_2 - \theta)^2$; i.e., we are penalized equally for underestimating and overestimating θ. To complete the picture we also need a prior distribution. Suppose we believe that all values of θ between 0 and 1 have equal probability.

The risk function is $E(c_1x_1 + c_2x_2 - \theta)^2 = c_1^2E(x_1^2) + c_2^2E(x_2^2) + 2c_1c_2E(x_1x_2) + \theta^2 - 2c_1\theta E(x_1) - 2c_2\theta E(x_2)$. Since $E(x^2) = V(x) + [E(x)]^2 = 1 +$

θ^2 and $E(x_1x_2) = \theta^2$, we get the risk function $= (c_1^2 + c_2^2) + \theta^2(c_1 + c_2 - 1)^2$.

The expected risk, or Bayes' risk, is the integral of this expression from 0 to 1. Thus Bayes' risk $= (c_1^2 + c_2)^2 + \frac{1}{3}(c_1 + c_2 - 1)^2$. Minimizing this, we get $c_1 = \frac{1}{5}$ and $c_2 = \frac{1}{5}$. Thus the estimator that minimizes Bayes' risk is $\frac{1}{5}(x_1 + x_2)$, which is less than half the sample mean.

If our prior probability is that θ lies between 0 and 1000 and all values are equiprobable, then Bayes' risk equals

$$c_1^2 + c_2^2 + \frac{10^9}{3}(c_1 + c_2 - 1)^2$$

Minimizing this gives $c_1 = \frac{1}{2}, c_2 = \frac{1}{2}$. Thus the estimator that minimizes Bayes' risk is $\frac{1}{2}(x_1 + x_2)$, or the sample mean.

If we minimize the maximum risk for θ in the range (0,1), we have to minimize $(c_1^2 + c_2^2) + (c_1 + c_2 - 1)^2$, and this gives $c_1 = \frac{1}{3}, c_2 = \frac{1}{3}$. Thus our minimax estimator is less than the sample mean in this case.

On the other hand if we minimize the maximum risk for θ in the range (0,2) we have to minimize $c_1^2 + c_2^2 + 4(c_1 + c_2 - 1)^2$, and this gives $c_1 = \frac{4}{9}, c_2 = \frac{4}{9}$.

The above two examples illustrate the use of loss functions and risk functions. More detailed discussion can be found in any book on decision theory.

Exercises

1. Consider the loss function specified in the accompanying table. Suppose the prior distribution θ is given by $P(\theta_1) = \frac{1}{8}, P(\theta_2) = \frac{3}{8}, P(\theta_3) = \frac{1}{4}$, and $P(\theta_4) = \frac{1}{4}$ There are three decisions: d_1, d_2, and d_3 What is the Bayesian decision?

	θ_1	θ_2	θ_3	θ_4
d_1	1	2	4	2
d_2	3	1	5	3
d_3	4	3	1	1

2. Consider the loss function specified in the accompanying table. Suppose the prior distribution of θ is given by $P(\theta_1) = P(\theta_2) = P(\theta_3) = P(\theta_4)$. What is the Bayesian decision?

	θ_1	θ_2	θ_3	θ_4
d_1	5	1	1	2
d_2	7	0	2	3
d_3	8	2	−2	1

3. Show that a Bayesian decision for the loss function in no. 2 is also a Bayesian decision for the loss function in no. 1 no matter what the prior distribution of θ is.

4. A newsdealer must order in the morning a supply of newspapers which he will try to sell that evening. Let N be the number of papers he orders and let X be the number of customers who wish to buy that evening. Suppose that the newsdealer can buy papers at 10¢ each and can sell them at 15¢ each (no price cutting or returns allowed). The profit for the dealer depends on both N and X as follows:

$$P(N,X) = \begin{matrix} 15X - 10N & \text{if } X < N \\ 15N - 10N & \text{if } X \geqslant N \end{matrix}$$

Suppose X is not known in the morning when N must be selected. Suppose, however, that the dealer considers X to be a random variable uniformly distributed between 50 and 150. That is, X has a continuous density function.

$$f(x) = \tfrac{1}{100} \qquad 50 \leqslant x \leqslant 150$$

Calculate, for given N less than 150, the expected profit $E[P(N,X)]$. What value of N maximizes the expected profit?

5. In no. 4 suppose that there are three states of the world described by three uniform distributions for X in the ranges 0 to 150, 50 to 200, 100 to 250. Suppose we consider three decisions: to order 50, 100, or 150. Tabulate for the three states of the world and the three decisions the expected loss (which is the negative of the expected profit). What is the minimax decision for this problem? Suppose that the newsdealer has equal prior beliefs about the three probability distributions. Which of the three values of N will he choose?

6. Suppose that a firm wants to decide whether or not to market a product. There are two states of the world described by weak demand and strong demand. Suppose the loss function is given by

	θ_1	θ_2
d_1	0	L_1
d_2	L_2	0

where θ_1 denotes weak demand
θ_2 denotes strong demand
d_1 denotes the decision not to market the product
d_2 denotes the decision to market

Suppose the prior feelings of the firm about the states of the world are given by $P(\theta_1) = \alpha$ and $P(\theta_2) = 1 - \alpha$. Let X denote a random variable defined by

$X = 1$ if a customer buys the product

$X = 0$ if a customer does not buy

Suppose the conditional distributions of X under the two states of the world are given by

$$P(X = 1 \mid \theta_1) = \tfrac{1}{4} \qquad P(X = 0 \mid \theta_1) = \tfrac{3}{4}$$

$$P(X = 1 \mid \theta_2) = \tfrac{4}{5} \qquad P(X = 0 \mid \theta_2) = \tfrac{1}{5}$$

That is, under weak demand, probability of purchase is only $\frac{1}{4}$, whereas under strong demand it is $\frac{4}{5}$. The firm can test market the product to revise its prior about the state of demand (θ_1 and θ_2).

(*a*) Before any test marketing, what will be the Bayesian decision of the firm if $L_1 = L_2$?

(*b*) Suppose the firm tries the product on one customer and the customer buys it. What is the posterior distribution (or revised prior) about the state of demand? What is the Bayesian decision now, assuming $L_1 = L_2$?

(*c*) Assume $\alpha = \frac{1}{2}$ so that initially the firm starts with equal prior beliefs that the demand is weak or strong. Suppose the product is tried on 5 customers and the values of X observed are 1,1,0,1,0. What is the posterior value of α? Assuming $L_1 = L_2$, what is the Bayesian decision of the firm? What is the value to the firm of the sample information (test marketing) in this case?

7. In no. 6 suppose that there are two groups of customers for whom the conditional probabilities of purchase, given the states of the world, are as follows:

Group 1: $P(X=1 \mid \theta_1) = \frac{1}{2}$ $\quad P(X=0 \mid \theta_1) = \frac{1}{2}$

$P(X=1 \mid \theta_2) = \frac{2}{3}$ $\quad P(X=0 \mid \theta_2) = \frac{1}{3}$

Group 2: $P(X=1 \mid \theta_1) = \frac{1}{2}$ $\quad P(X=0 \mid \theta_1) = \frac{1}{2}$

$P(X=1 \mid \theta_2) = \frac{3}{4}$ $\quad P(X=0 \mid \theta_2) = \frac{1}{4}$

Suppose that the problem is to test market the product in group 1 or group 2 and that the costs are the same. Show that whatever the values of α, L_1, and L_2, the firm should choose group 2 rather than group 1 for test-marketing purposes.

PART THREE

INTRODUCTION TO ECONOMETRIC METHODS

CHAPTER

SIX

DESCRIPTIVE MEASURES

Given any set of data, the first thing one does is to get some descriptive summary measures. The descriptive measures we will consider are: measures of central tendency and dispersion, and the correlation coefficient. Because the data we get are often in grouped form, we will also discuss some pitfalls in inference from grouped data.

6-1 MEASURES OF CENTRAL TENDENCY AND DISPERSION

Suppose we are given the following observations on quantities purchased of a certain good by 20 individuals: 10.0, 6.6, 7.0, 10.2, 9.0, 5.8, 8.0, 12.6, 13.0, 14.0, 6.0, 13.4, 16.8, 7.3, 2.9, 11.2, 13.6, 3.8, 17.6, 11.2. How can we summarize these data? A rough summary would be to give an average and an indication of how the observations deviate from the average. The former is called a measure of central tendency and the latter a measure of dispersion. For a measure of central tendency we can use the *mean*, which is the arithmetic average of the observations. In the above example the mean = 200.0/20 = 10.0. Another measure is the *median*, which is the "middlemost" observation. For finding this, we order the observations in increasing order of magnitude: 2.9, 3.8, 5.8, 6.0, 6.6, 7.0, 7.3, 8.0, 9.0, 10.0, 10.2, 11.2, 11.2, 12.6, 13.0, 13.4, 13.6, 14.0, 16.8, 17.6. If there are an odd number of observations, it is easy to pick the middle one. Here the number of observations is even. So we average the 10th and 11th observations, i.e., (10.0 + 10.2)/2 = 10.1. So, the median = 10.1.

For dispersion, or a measure of the spread of observations, we can look at the *range*, which is the difference between the largest and smallest observations.

Here it is 17.6 − 2.9 = 14.7. Another measure is the *mean deviation*, which is the average of absolute deviations from the mean. The absolute deviations in this case are 0.0, 0.6, 3.0, 0.2, 1.0, 4.2, 2.0, 2.6, 3.0, 4.0, 4.0, 3.4, 6.8, 2.7, 7.1, 1.2, 3.6, 6.2, 7.6, 1.2. The average of these is 64.4/20 = 3.22. Another measure is the *standard deviation*, which is the square root of the average of squared deviations from the mean. Here it is

$$\sqrt{\frac{1}{20}\left[(0.0)^2 + (0.6)^2 + \cdots + (1.2)^2\right]}$$

$$= \sqrt{\frac{1}{20}\left[\begin{matrix}(.36 + 9.0 + .04 + 1.0 + 17.64 + 4.0 + 5.26 + 9.0 + 16.0 + 11.56 \\ + 46.24 + 7.29 + 50.41 + 1.44 + 12.96 + 38.44 + 57.76 + 1.44)\end{matrix}\right]}$$

$$= \sqrt{\frac{1}{20}(305.84)} = \sqrt{15.292} \approx 3.91$$

Another measure of dispersion is the *semi-interquartile range*. Just as the median divides the set of observations into two groups, the *quartiles* divide them into four groups. In the above case we can roughly take the 5th, 10th, and 15th observations as the three quartiles. The semi-interquartile range is half the difference between the third and first quartiles. Here it is (13.0 − 6.6)/2 = 3.2. There are three quartiles—the second is the median. Just as the quartiles divide the observations into 4 groups, the *deciles* divide them into 10 groups and the *percentiles* divide them into 100 groups. There are nine deciles—the fifth is the median. There are 99 percentiles—the fiftieth is the median.

If the number of observations is very large, it is convenient to operate with grouped data. Suppose we have 100 observations and suppose the observations range from 3.0 to 19.0. Then we can group them into those falling between 3.0 and 5.0, between 5.0 and 7.0, etc. We can find the number falling in each group and prepare a table like Table 6-1, called a *frequency distribution*.

For computing the median and the quartiles we look at the cumulative frequency—which gives the number of observations below the upper end of the

Table 6-1

Range	Frequency	Cumulative frequency
3.0–5.0	5	5
5.0–7.0	12	17
7.0–9.0	15	32
9.0–11.0	27	59
11.0–13.0	20	79
13.0–15.0	16	95
15.0–17.0	4	99
17.0–19.0	1	100
Total	100	

range of that group. There are 5 observations below 5.0, 17 observations below 7.0, etc. Since the total number of observations is 100, the quartiles are those values below which there are 25, 50, and 75 observations, respectively. Assuming that the observations in each group are evenly spread out in that group, we get the three quartiles Q_1, Q_2, and Q_3 as

$$Q_1 = 7.0 + \left(\frac{2.0}{15}\right)8 = 8.066$$

$$Q_2 = 9.0 + \left(\frac{2.0}{27}\right)18 = 10.33$$

$$Q_3 = 11.0 + \left(\frac{2.0}{20}\right)16 = 12.60$$

The semi-interquartile range is $(Q_3 - Q_1)/2 = 2.267$. [The argument in these calculations is as follows: To get Q_1 we need to go up to 25 observations. We know that there are 17 observations below 7.0. The next group has 15 observations, and these are spread out at "distance" 2.0/15 from each other. Hence to get 8 more observations we need to go (2.0/15)8, and that will give us the location of the 25th observation. The argument for Q_2 and Q_3 is similar.]

For computing the mean, mean deviation, standard deviation, etc., we regard each observation in a group as having a value equal to the midpoint of the range, e.g., 5 observations having a value 4.0, 12 having a value 6.0, etc. The calculations can be set forth as shown in Table 6-2, where

$$\text{Mean} = \frac{1028}{100} = 10.28$$

$$\text{Standard deviation (sd)} = \sqrt{\frac{11{,}536}{100} - (10.28)^2}$$

$$= \sqrt{115.36 - 105.68} = \sqrt{9.68} \approx 3.11$$

$$\text{Mean deviation (md)} = \frac{249.04}{100} = 2.49$$

Table 6-2

(Mid)x	f	xf	x^2	x^2f	$\lvert x - \bar{x}\rvert$	$\lvert x - \bar{x}\rvert \cdot f$
4.0	5	20	16	80	6.28	31.40
6.0	12	72	36	432	4.28	51.36
8.0	15	120	64	960	2.28	34.20
10.0	27	270	100	2,700	.28	7.56
12.0	20	240	144	2,880	1.72	34.40
14.0	16	224	196	3,136	3.72	59.52
16.0	4	64	256	1,024	5.72	22.88
18.0	1	18	324	324	7.72	7.72
		1028		11,536		249.04

The explanation of the formula used for calculating standard deviation is as follows.

The symbol $\sum$ denotes summation over a number of observations. $\sum_1^3$ is summation from observation 1 to observation 3, etc. Let us denote the ith group by the subscript i. f_i is the frequency in the ith group and x_i the value of each observation in the ith group ($i = 1,2, \ldots, 8$). Each observation in the ith group is assumed to have the same value x_i. Since f_i observations all have a value x_i, the mean $\bar{x}$ is defined as

$$\bar{x} = \frac{1}{N} \sum_{i=1}^{8} x_i \cdot f_i$$

where $N = \sum_{i=1}^{8} f_i$. The standard deviation by definition equals

$$\sqrt{\frac{1}{N} \Sigma f_i (x_i - \bar{x})^2}$$

since f_i observations all have the same deviation $x_i - \bar{x}$. Now, we can write $(x_i - \bar{x})^2$ as $x_i^2 - 2x_i\bar{x} + \bar{x}^2$. Hence

$$\Sigma f_i (x_i - \bar{x})^2 = \Sigma f_i x_i^2 - 2\Sigma f_i x_i \bar{x} + \Sigma f_i \bar{x}^2$$

But $\sum f_i = N$ and $\sum f_i x_i = N\bar{x}$. Hence

$$\begin{aligned} \Sigma f_i (x_i - \bar{x})^2 &= \Sigma f_i x_i^2 - 2N\bar{x}^2 + N\bar{x}^2 \\ &= \Sigma f_i x_i^2 - N\bar{x}^2 \end{aligned}$$

Hence

$$\text{sd} = \sqrt{\frac{1}{N} (\Sigma f_i x_i^2 - N\bar{x}^2)} = \sqrt{\left(\frac{1}{N} \Sigma f_i x_i^2\right) - \bar{x}^2}$$

which is the formula used above. The formula for mean deviation is

$$\text{md} = \frac{1}{N} \Sigma f_i \mid x_i - \bar{x} \mid$$

the vertical lines denoting the fact that we take the absolute value of the deviation.

6-2 PITFALLS IN INFERENCE FROM GROUPED DATA

Grouping of data is not always in the form of a frequency distribution. Sometimes what we have is the value of another variable Y for given grouping by the variable X; e.g., X may be age group and Y the average income. Sometimes there is no single characteristic by which grouping of data can be done. In this case one can be led to different conclusions depending upon whether grouping is done with respect to one characteristic or another. For example, the Census Bureau publishes data on labor productivity by size of firm.

Table 6-3 Classification of firms by value of product

Value of product, thousands of $	Value of product per establishment	Wage earners per establishment	Value of product per wage earner
5–19	$ 11,235	3.13	$ 3,591
20–49	32,167	7.78	4,135
50–99	71,066	15.29	4,649
100–249	158,628	31.08	5,103
250–499	354,120	64.23	5,513
500–999	701,923	119.25	5,886
1000–2499	1,524,304	240.35	6,354
2500–4999	3,437,122	449.17	7,652
5000 and over	15,017,720	1335.25	11,247

Now size can be measured in terms of number of workers employed or value of output produced or amount of capital invested. Similarly, in studies of agricultural productivity, we can classify farms by acreage or output or capital or labor input. A clear example of how different conclusions on productivity emerge from the same data depending on the classification adopted is given in Johnston.[1] Tables 6-3 and 6-4 show that value of product and number of wage earners per establishment both increase steadily up the size groups on each basis of classification, but product per wage earner shows two markedly different patterns. This suggests that the cause of the paradox must be related to the two different bases of classification.

The best procedure in such cases is to analyze the original data and not make any inferences from the grouped data. The censuses (of manufactures, of mineral industries, etc.) give many tables in which such grouping by size is done. One has to be cautious while drawing inferences from such grouped data. Some

Table 6-4 Classification by number of wage earners

No. of wage earners per establishment	Value of product per establishment	Wage earners per establishment	Value of product per wage earner
1–5	$ 26,939	2.67	$10,074
6–20	83,615	11.07	7,552
21–50	219,042	32.34	6,772
51–100	461,855	71.25	6,482
101–250	1,022,245	155.70	6,437
251–500	2,230,629	347.38	6,421
501–1000	4,946,892	685.15	7,220
1001–2500	12,499,101	1478.13	8,456
2501 and over	37,094,179	4684.84	7,918

[1] See J. Johnston, "Statistical Cost Analysis," p. 114, McGraw-Hill Book Company, New York, 1960. Tables 6-3 and 6-4 are from Johnston's book.

Table 6-5 Data for Indian agriculture

State	T	K	L	w'	Π	V
West Bengal	12.15	127.33	402.41	1.54	923.28	1,811.56
	16.96	116.00	628.37	1.61	772.36	2,403.23
	.64	7.44	39.05	1.60	187.78	129.41
	1.81	14.84	97.96	1.49	373.03	352.59
	3.11	25.19	173.10	1.59	555.87	547.05
	4.47	33.30	213.58	1.53	1,948.21	809.07
	6.18	41.59	321.42	1.45	813.20	1,158.13
	8.15	37.89	323.80	1.54	955.08	1,401.80
Madras	11.81	86.21	336.58	.54	1,653.61	907.01
	17.35	93.69	395.58	.56	2,215.54	1,174.59
	22.97	103.36	560.41	.62	2,248.45	1,683.70
	43.78	205.76	897.49	.55	5,838.73	3,607.47
	1.16	39.60	179.35	.62	426.00	354.04
	3.66	37.69	229.85	.52	716.90	751.03
	6.02	67.42	276.92	.56	2,045.88	947.55
	8.83	98.89	342.60	.56	763.14	1,190.28
Madhya Pradesh	12.44	9.57	294.70	1.08	1,709.28	1,479.12
	17.19	11.86	403.45	1.00	6,718.47	1,693.21
	24.25	14.55	470.21	1.11	40.53	2,616.57
	34.77	31.64	756.25	1.04	144.37	3,689.10
	45.17	41.10	1,084.08	1.11	157.86	4,458.28
	93.36	82.15	1,831.72	1.15	334.62	10,017.53
	2.95	3.42	101.13	.94	513.87	422.73
	7.38	8.63	190.40	1.06	729.34	849.44
Uttar Pradesh	12.00	78.00	602.40	1.06	7.57	2,448.00
	16.90	95.99	765.57	1.06	320.98	3,380.00
	27.58	148.93	1,073.14	1.01	384.68	5,653.90
	3.33	31.00	209.16	1.01	411.48	922.41
	7.68	64.97	432.84	.98	227.80	1,843.20
Punjab	14.50	19.57	450.22	1.51	448.19	2,463.55
	28.45	20.48	701.86	1.38	124.41	4,056.97
	81.19	30.85	1,484.96	1.92	391.14	12,957.92
	3.98	8.95	158.96	1.33	129.43	702.47
	7.45	7.37	270.88	1.40	377.94	1,270.22

T = cultivable land per farm in acres
K = interest on fixed capital
L = labor days employed per farm
w' = money wage rate
Π = profit, i.e., total revenue less total variable costs
V = revenue per farm in rupees

other problems associated with the analysis of grouped data are discussed in Chap. 12.

Another common pitfall is the estimation of production functions and cost functions on the basis of grouped data. Again one would obtain different conclusions depending upon whether the grouping is done with respect to any of the inputs or the output. An example of such analysis on the basis of grouped data is an otherwise excellent paper by Lau and Yotoupolos.[1] The data used are presented in Table 6-5. They are based on cost-accounting records of 2962 holdings in six states in India and cover the period 1955–1957. All the data, however, are reported in terms of averages of farms of a given size; i.e., the classification is by land input. Lau and Yotoupolos conclude from their analysis that the smaller farms have higher profits. We will discuss this study in Chap. 12.

6-3 CORRELATION COEFFICIENT

Often we find that many economic variables move together, e.g., quantity demanded and price, air travel and income, consumption and income. Given data on two variables X and Y, we can first plot them on a graph. This is called a scatter diagram (Fig. 6-1). If there is a close relationship between the two variables, the points will tend to bunch together. Otherwise, they will be scattered all around.

Given n observations on X and Y, namely,

$$x_1, x_2, x_3, \ldots, x_n \quad \text{and} \quad y_1, y_2, y_3, \ldots, y_n$$

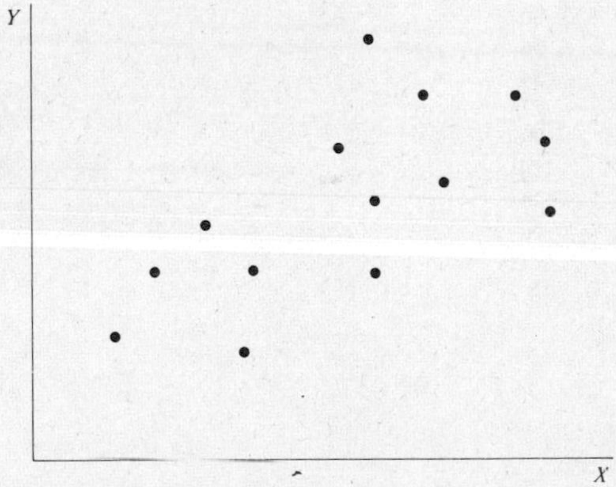

Figure 6-1 A scatter diagram.

[1] L. Lau and P. A. Yotoupolos, A Test for Relative Efficiency and Application to Indian Agriculture, *American Economic Review*, March 1971.

we can compute the following descriptive statistics:

$$\bar{x} = \frac{1}{n} \sum x_i, \text{ the mean of } x \qquad \bar{y} = \frac{1}{n} \sum y_i, \text{ the mean of } y$$

$S_{xx} = \sum(x_i - \bar{x})^2 = \sum x_i^2 - n\bar{x}^2$, the sum of squares of deviations of the values of x from their mean.

$V_{xx} = S_{xx}/n$ is called the variance of x; $\sqrt{V_{xx}}$ is called the standard deviation of x. Similarly, $S_{yy} = \sum(y_i - \bar{y})^2 = \sum y_i^2 - n\bar{y}^2$ is the sum of squares of deviations of the values of y from their mean.

$V_{yy} = S_{yy}/n$ is called the *variance* of y.

$\sqrt{V_{yy}}$ is called the *standard deviation* of y.

$S_{xy} = \sum(x_i - \bar{x})(y_i - \bar{y}) = \sum x_i y_i - n\bar{x}\bar{y}$ is the sum of products of the two deviations.

$V_{xy} = S_{xy}/n$ is called the *covariance* between x and y.

If high values of x are accompanied by high values of y and low values of x with low values of y, then S_{xy} will be positive because both the deviations $x_i - \bar{x}$

Table 6-6

x	y	x^2	y^2	xy
10	12	100	144	120
7	11	49	121	77
10	14	100	196	140
4	6	16	36	24
8	10	64	100	80
8	7	64	49	56
6	9	36	81	54
7	11	49	121	77
9	10	81	100	90
11	10	121	100	110
80	100	680	1048	828

$$\bar{x} = \frac{80}{10} = 8$$

$$\bar{y} = \frac{100}{10} = 10$$

$$S_{xx} = 680 - 10(8)^2 = 680 - 640 = 40$$

$$S_{xy} = 828 - 10(8)(10) = 828 - 800 = 28$$

$$S_{yy} = 1068 - 10(10)^2 = 1068 - 1000 = 68$$

$$r_{xy} = \frac{28}{\sqrt{40 \times 68}} \approx \frac{28}{52} \approx .54 \qquad \text{or} \qquad r_{xy}^2 = .29$$

and $y_i - \bar{y}$ will be either positive or negative so that their product is positive. If high values of x correspond to low values of y and vice versa, S_{xy} will be negative.

The correlation coefficient r_{xy} is defined as

$$r_{xy} = \frac{S_{xy}}{\sqrt{S_{xx}S_{yy}}} = \frac{V_{xy}}{\sqrt{V_{xx}V_{yy}}}$$

where r_{xy} is positive if S_{xy} is positive *and* r_{xy} is negative if S_{xy} is negative.

As an illustration, consider the data presented in Table 6-6. Note that r_{xy}^2 is always less than (or at most equal to) 1. This can be proved as follows: Given any two sets of n numbers each, $a_1, a_2, \ldots, a_n$ and $b_1, b_2, \ldots, b_n$, we can show that

$$(a_1^2 + a_2^2 + \cdots + a_n^2)(b_1^2 + b_2^2 + \cdots + b_n^2) \geqslant (a_1b_1 + a_2b_2 + \cdots + a_nb_n)^2$$

This is shown by noting that after multiplying out and canceling the appropriate terms we find that $(\sum a_i^2)(\sum b_i^2) - (\sum a_i b_i)^2$ is equal to the sum of squares of terms like $(a_i b_j - a_j b_i)$. These are always $\geqslant 0$. They are equal to zero if $a_i/b_i = a_j/b_j$. Now substitute

$$a_i = x_i - \bar{x}$$

$$b_i = y_i - \bar{y}$$

Then we have $S_{xx}S_{yy} \geqslant S_{xy}^2$, or

$$\frac{S_{xy}^2}{S_{xx}S_{yy}} \leqslant 1$$

That is, $r_{xy}^2 \leqslant 1$.

Rank Correlation

Sometimes when we feel that we cannot have too much confidence in the absolute magnitude of the variables x and y but that we can trust the relative ranking of these numbers, we compute what is known as the rank-correlation coefficient. What we do is rank the observations in increasing (or decreasing) order and replace the values of x and y by their ranks. Then we compute the correlation coefficient as before. (Note that $S_{xx} = S_{yy}$ in this case.)

Exercises

1. Table 6-7 gives educational attainment by race and sex for U.S. population with age 14 years and over in March 1971. Calculate the median years of schooling for white males, white females, males from the other races, and females from the other races. Also compute the semi-interquartile range in each case.

Table 6-7 Educational attainment by race and sex

Numbers of persons in thousands

Years of schooling	Whites		Negro and other races	
	Males	Females	Males	Females
5	848	820	258	297
6 and 7	4,291	4,074	900	981
8	8,603	8,724	922	1,057
9	4,311	4,837	703	882
10	4,839	5,636	706	891
11	3,765	4,297	688	783
12	18,780	25,755	1,764	2,315
13	3,231	3,227	258	312
14	3,490	3,434	264	262
15	1,520	1,367	90	108
16	4,605	3,914	241	267
17 and over	3,483	1,491	159	121
Total	61,766	67,576	6,953	8,276

2. In Table 6-8 the corresponding figures are given for the U.S. population 25 years and over. Repeat the calculations as in no. 1. What conclusions do you draw from these calculations?

Table 6-8 Educational attainment by race and sex

Population 25 years and over

Years of schooling	Whites		Negro and other races	
	Males	Females	Male	Female
5	772	792	234	270
6 and 7	3,058	3,118	621	757
8	6,474	6,722	544	668
9	2,307	2,736	305	527
10	2,912	3,671	380	522
11	1,984	2,450	375	432
12	14,754	20,427	1,254	1,594
13	1,960	2,109	125	167
14	2,551	2,560	161	161
15	954	926	48	61
16	4,006	3,234	206	220
17 and over	3,291	1,385	150	119
Total	45,023	50,130	4,403	5,498

3. Given the following data on X_1, X_2, and X_3, compute the means, variances, covariances, and correlation coefficients:

$$X_1 = \text{currency} + \text{demand deposits}$$

$$X_2 = X_1 + \text{time deposits at commercial banks}$$

$$X_3 = X_2 + \text{deposits at nonbank savings institutions}$$

		X_1	X_2	X_3
1971	Aug.	228.0	454.5	697.6
	Sept.	227.6	455.6	701.2
	Oct.	227.7	458.3	706.5
	Nov.	227.7	460.8	711.6
	Dec.	228.2	464.7	718.1
1972	Jan.	228.8	469.9	727.3
	Feb.	231.2	475.5	737.4
	Mar.	233.5	480.1	745.9
	Apr.	235.0	483.0	752.7
	May	235.5	486.1	758.8
	June	236.6	490.4	766.1
	July	239.4	495.0	774.8
	Aug.	240.4	498.1	781.5

4. For the data in Table 6-5 compute the means, variances, and covariances of all the variables.

5. Examine the data in Table 6-5 closely, and enumerate all the things you find unusual about the data.

CHAPTER

SEVEN

SIMPLE LINEAR REGRESSION

7-1 INTRODUCTION

A frequent objective in research is the specification of a functional relationship between two variables such as $y = f(x)$. Here y is called the *dependent* variable and x the *independent* variable. We cannot expect a perfect explanation, and hence we write $y = f(x) + u$, where u is a random variable called *residual* or *error*. This is called a *regression equation* of y on x. The error arises from measurement errors in y or imperfections in the specification of the function $f(x)$. For example, there may be many other variables beyond x that influence y, but we have left them out.

Since u is a random variable, y is also a random variable. We will assume for the present that the "independent" variable x is nonrandom. We will relax this assumption later (see Sec. 9-4). We will also assume $f(x)$ to be a linear function, that is, $f(x) = \alpha + \beta x$. This assumption will also be relaxed later. Suppose we have n observations on y and x. Then we have

$$y_i = \alpha + \beta x_i + u_i \qquad i = 1,2, \ldots, n \tag{7-1}$$

We will be estimating the parameters α and β in Eq. (7-1) by what is known as the "method of least squares," i.e., choose $\hat{\alpha}$ and $\hat{\beta}$ as estimators of α and β, respectively, so that

$$Q = \sum_{i=1}^{n} (y_i - \hat{\alpha} - \hat{\beta} x_i)^2 \tag{7-2}$$

is a minimum. The intuitive idea behind this procedure can be described figuratively with reference to Fig. 7-1, which gives a graph of the points (y_i, x_i).

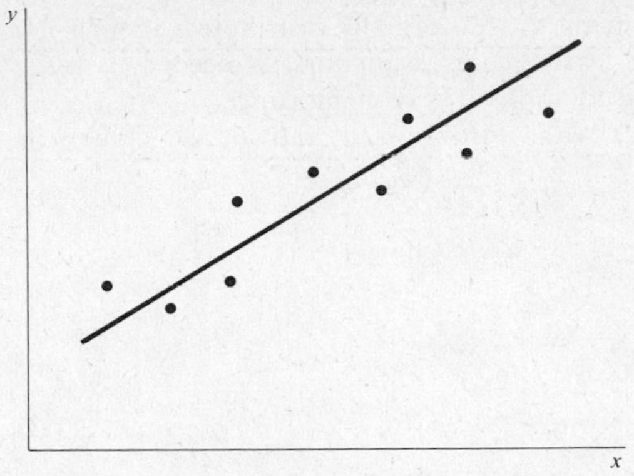

Figure 7-1 A linear regression.

We pass the regression line through the points in such a way that it is "as close as possible" to the scatter of points. The question is what is meant by "close." The procedure of minimizing Q in Eq. (7-2) implies that we minimize the sum of squares of vertical distances of the points from the line. Of course, we can define closeness in alternative ways, e.g., minimizing the sum of squares of horizontal or perpendicular distances, or minimizing the sum of absolute distances. These methods merely determine the algebraic procedure. Which procedure we adopt will depend on the assumptions we make about the residuals u_i in Eq. (7-1). The least-squares estimators obtained by minimizing Q in (7-2) have desirable properties under the following assumptions about u_i.

1. Zero mean: $E(u_i) = 0$ for all i.
2. Common variance: $V(u_i) = \sigma^2$ for all i.
3. Independence: that is, u_i and u_j are independent for any i and j $(i \neq j)$.
4. Independence of x_j: that is, u_i and x_j are independent for *all* i and j. This automatically follows if x_j are considered nonrandom variables.

Under these assumptions, it can be shown that the least-squares estimators of α and β are minimum-variance unbiased linear estimators. This property is often denoted as BLUE (best linear unbiased estimator). That is, if we confine ourselves to the class of linear estimators that are also unbiased, the least-squares estimators have minimum variance. (A linear estimator is a linear function of the form $c_1 y_1 + c_2 y_2 + \cdots + c_n y_n$, where c_i are constants.) These properties are proved in Appendix B. For the present it is sufficient to note that these properties do not depend on any assumptions about the form of the probability distribution of u_i. However, often we will make the following assumption:

5. Normality: In conjunction with assumptions 1, 2, and 3, this implies that $u_i \sim IN(0, \sigma^2)$.

The assumption that the residuals u_i are normally distributed, though not needed for the optimality of the least-squares estimators, is needed to make confidence-interval statements and to apply tests of significance.

To minimize Q in Eq. (7-2) with respect to α and β, we equate its derivatives with respect to α and β to zero. We get

$$\frac{\partial Q}{\partial \hat{\alpha}} = 0 \Rightarrow \sum 2(y_i - \hat{\alpha} - \hat{\beta}x_i)(-1) = 0$$

or

$$\sum y_i = n\hat{\alpha} + \hat{\beta} \sum x_i$$

or

$$\bar{y} = \hat{\alpha} + \hat{\beta}\bar{x} \tag{7-3}$$

$$\frac{\partial Q}{\partial \hat{\beta}} = 0 \Rightarrow \sum 2(y_i - \hat{\alpha} - \hat{\beta}x_i)(-x_i) = 0$$

or

$$\sum y_i x_i = \hat{\alpha} \sum x_i + \hat{\beta} \sum x_i^2 \tag{7-4}$$

Equations (7-3) and (7-4) are called the "*normal equations.*" Substituting the value of α from (7-3) into (7-4), we get

$$\begin{aligned} \sum y_i x_i &= \sum x_i(\bar{y} - \hat{\beta}\bar{x}) + \hat{\beta} \sum x_i^2 \\ &= n\bar{x}(\bar{y} - \hat{\beta}\bar{x}) + \hat{\beta} \sum x_i^2 \end{aligned} \tag{7-5}$$

Let us define, as in the preceding chapter,

$$S_{yy} = \sum (y_i - \bar{y})^2 = \sum y_i^2 - n\bar{y}^2$$

$$S_{xy} = \sum (x_i - \bar{x})(y_i - \bar{y}) = \sum x_i y_i - n\bar{x}\bar{y}$$

and

$$S_{xx} = \sum (x_i - \bar{x})^2 = \sum x_i^2 - n\bar{x}^2$$

Then (7-5) can be written as $\hat{\beta}S_{xx} = S_{xy}$

or

$$\hat{\beta} = \frac{S_{xy}}{S_{xx}} \tag{7-6}$$

Hence the least-squares estimators for α and β are

$$\hat{\beta} = \frac{S_{xy}}{S_{xx}} \qquad \hat{\alpha} = \bar{y} - \hat{\beta}\bar{x} \tag{7-7}$$

The estimated residuals are $\hat{u}_i = y_i - \hat{\alpha} - \hat{\beta} x_i$. The two normal equations show that these residuals satisfy the restrictions $\sum \hat{u}_i = 0$ and $\sum x_i \hat{u}_i = 0$. The residual sum of squares (to be denoted by RSS) is given by

$$\begin{aligned}
\text{RSS} &= \sum (y_i - \hat{\alpha} - \hat{\beta} x_i)^2 \\
&= \sum \left[y_i - \bar{y} - \hat{\beta}(x_i - \bar{x}) \right]^2 \\
&= \sum (y_i - \bar{y})^2 + \hat{\beta}^2 \sum (x_i - \bar{x})^2 - 2\hat{\beta} \sum (y_i - \bar{y})(x_i - \bar{x}) \\
&= S_{yy} + \hat{\beta}^2 S_{xx} - 2\hat{\beta} S_{xy} \\
&= S_{yy} + \left(\frac{S_{xy}}{S_{xx}} \right)^2 S_{xx} - 2\left(\frac{S_{xy}}{S_{xx}} \right) S_{xy} \\
&= S_{yy} - \frac{S_{xy}^2}{S_{xx}}
\end{aligned}$$

This can also be written as $S_{yy} - \hat{\beta} S_{xy}$. S_{yy} is a measure of the total variation in y, $\hat{\beta} S_{xy}$ is the amount "explained" by x, and $S_{yy} - \hat{\beta} S_{xy}$ is a measure of the residual variation. The proportion of the total variation explained is

$$\frac{\hat{\beta} S_{xy}}{S_{yy}} = \frac{S_{xy}^2}{S_{xx} S_{yy}} = r_{xy}^2$$

Thus r_{xy}^2 is the proportion of the variation in y explained by x and $(1 - r_{xy}^2)$ is the proportion left unexplained. If r_{xy}^2 is high, then x is a good "explanatory" variable for y.

In summary: Regression coefficients are

$$\hat{\beta} = \frac{S_{xy}}{S_{xx}} \qquad \hat{\alpha} = \bar{y} - \hat{\beta} \bar{x}$$

$$\text{RSS} = S_{yy} - \frac{S_{xy}^2}{S_{xx}} = S_{yy} - \hat{\beta} S_{xy} = S_{yy}(1 - r_{xy}^2)$$

$$r_{xy}^2 = \frac{S_{xy}^2}{S_{xx} S_{yy}} = \frac{\hat{\beta} S_{xy}}{S_{yy}}$$

We can also consider the regression of x on y. This will be the case if x is the dependent variable and y the independent variable. We can write the regression equation as

$$x_i = \alpha' + \beta' y_i + v_i$$

where v_i are the residuals that satisfy the same sort of assumptions as the u_i before. Interchanging x and y in the formulas obtained above, we get

$$\hat{\beta}' = \frac{S_{xy}}{S_{yy}} \qquad \hat{\alpha}' = \bar{x} - \hat{\beta}'\bar{y} \tag{7-8}$$

$$\text{RSS}' = S_{xx} - \frac{S_{xy}^2}{S_{yy}}$$

Note that $\hat{\beta}\hat{\beta}' = r_{xy}^2$. Hence if r_{xy}^2 is close to 1, the two regression lines will be close to each other.

As an illustration consider the data given in Table 6-6. We have

$$\hat{\beta} = \frac{S_{xy}}{S_{xx}} = \frac{28}{40} = 0.7$$

$$\hat{\alpha} = \bar{y} - \hat{\beta}\bar{x} = 10.0 - 0.7(8.0) = 4.4$$

Hence the regression of y on x is given by

$$y = 4.4 + 0.7x$$

$$\hat{\beta}' = \frac{S_{xy}}{S_{yy}} = \frac{28}{68} \approx 0.42$$

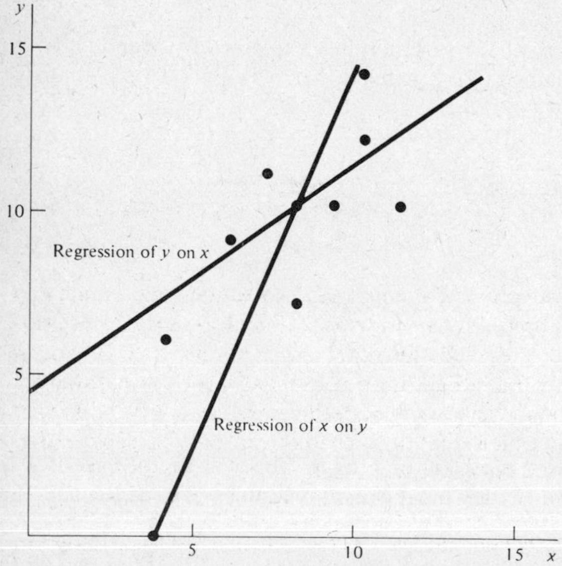

Figure 7-2 Regression lines for regression of y on x and x on y.

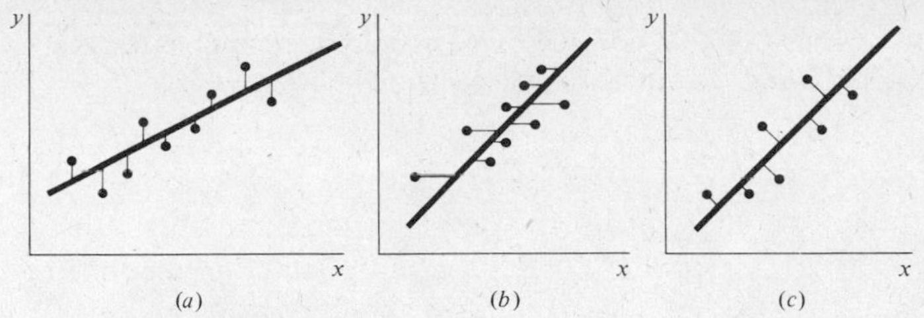

Figure 7-3 (*a*) Regression of y on x; (*b*) regression of x on y; (*c*) orthogonal regression.

and $$\hat{\alpha}' = 8.0 - 10(0.42) = 3.8$$

Hence the regression of x on y is given by

$$x = 3.8 + .42y$$

These two regression lines are presented in Fig. 7-2. The procedure used in the two regressions is illustrated in Fig. 7-3. In calculating the regression of y on x, we pass a line through the observed points so as to minimize the sum of squares of the vertical distances of the points from the line, as in Fig. 7-3(*a*). For the regression of x on y, we minimize the sum of squares of the horizontal distances—as shown in Fig. 7-3(*b*). We can also think of passing a line in such a way that we minimize the sum of squares of the *perpendicular* distances. This is called the *orthogonal regression*. Also in each of the above cases we can minimize the sum of absolute distances rather than the sum of squares of distances.[1] However, because these methods involve complicated calculations, we will not discuss them here. Further, in those cases where they are appropriate, one can think of some transformations of the variables to which the least-squares methods can be applied.[2]

7-2 STATISTICAL INFERENCE IN THE LINEAR-REGRESSION MODEL

To obtain the least-squares estimators of α and β, we do not need to assume any particular probability distribution for the residuals u_i. The least-squares estimators have optimal properties, provided the other assumptions 1, 2, 3, and 4 mentioned earlier are satisfied. But to get interval estimates for the parameters and to test any hypotheses about them, we need to assume that u_i have a normal distribution. Under the assumption that $u_i \sim IN(0,\sigma^2)$ it can be shown that (proofs are given in Appendix B for a general case):

[1] These estimators, known as LAR (least absolute residual) estimators, are discussed in Sec. 13-10.

[2] See Sec. 13-11 on data transformations.

1. $\hat{\alpha}$ has a normal distribution with mean α and variance

$$V(\hat{\alpha}) = \sigma^2\left(\frac{1}{n} + \frac{\bar{x}^2}{S_{xx}}\right)$$

2. $\hat{\beta}$ has a normal distribution with mean β and variance $V(\hat{\beta}) = \sigma^2/S_{xx}$. Also $\text{cov}(\hat{\alpha},\hat{\beta}) = \sigma^2(-\bar{x}/S_{xx})$.
3. If $\text{RSS} = S_{yy} - (S_{xy}^2/S_{xx})$ then RSS/σ^2 has a χ^2-distribution degrees of freedom $(n-2)$ and $\hat{\sigma}^2 = \text{RSS}/(n-2)$ is an unbiased estimator for σ^2.
4. If we substitute $\hat{\sigma}^2$ for σ^2 in $V(\hat{\alpha})$ and $V(\hat{\beta})$ given in 1 and 2, we get the estimated variances. The square roots of these estimated variances are called the *standard errors* (to be denoted henceforth by SE) of $\hat{\alpha}$ and $\hat{\beta}$, respectively. Then $(\hat{\alpha} - \alpha)/\text{SE}(\hat{\alpha})$ and $(\hat{\beta} - \beta)/\text{SE}(\hat{\beta})$ have each a t-distribution degrees of freedom $(n-2)$. These distributions can be used to make confidence-interval statements for α, β, and σ^2 the three unknown parameters in the model.

To illustrate these procedures, consider the data in Table 6-6:

$$V(\hat{\alpha}) = \sigma^2\left(\frac{1}{n} + \frac{\bar{x}^2}{S_{xx}}\right) = \sigma^2\left(\frac{1}{10} + \frac{64}{40}\right) = 1.7\sigma^2$$

$$V(\hat{\beta}) = \frac{\sigma^2}{S_{xx}} = \frac{\sigma^2}{40} = .025\sigma^2$$

$$\hat{\sigma}^2 = \frac{S_{yy} - S_{xy}^2/S_{xx}}{n-2} = \frac{68 - (28)^2/40}{8} = 6.05$$

$$\text{SE}(\hat{\alpha}) = \sqrt{(1.7)(6.05)} = 3.21$$

$$\text{SE}(\hat{\beta}) = \sqrt{(.025)(6.05)} = .389$$

It is customary to report the standard errors of the coefficients in parentheses below the coefficients. (Sometimes the t ratios are reported instead of the standard errors.) Thus, our regression equation in this example is

$$\underset{}{Y} = \underset{(3.2)}{4.4} + \underset{(.39)}{.70}\, x \qquad r^2 = .29$$

From the tables of the χ^2-distribution degrees of freedom 8, we find that the probability of obtaining a value < 2.18 is .025 and of getting a value > 17.53 is .025. Hence

$$P\left(2.18 < \frac{8\hat{\sigma}^2}{\sigma^2} < 17.53\right) = .95$$

and since $\hat{\sigma}^2 = 6.05$, we have

$$P\left(\frac{48.4}{17.53} < \sigma^2 < \frac{48.4}{2.18}\right) = .95$$

or

$$P(2.761 < \sigma^2 < 22.202) = .95$$

This is a 95 percent confidence interval for σ^2. As can be easily seen, it is very wide. Similarly, from the tables of the t distribution with 8 degrees of freedom we get

$$P\left[-1.86 < \frac{\alpha - \hat{\alpha}}{\mathrm{SE}(\hat{\alpha})} < 1.86\right] = .95$$

and

$$P\left[-1.86 < \frac{\beta - \hat{\beta}}{\mathrm{SE}(\hat{\beta})} < 1.86\right] = .95$$

These give the following confidence intervals for α and β:

$$P(1.552 < \alpha < 10.352) = .95$$

$$P(.025 < \beta < 1.425) = .95$$

We can construct different intervals with different probabilities by a similar procedure. Also, we used two-sided confidence intervals in the above illustrations, but we can as well construct one-sided confidence intervals if we so desire; i.e., we find $\sigma_0^2, \alpha_0, \beta_0$ such that $P(\sigma^2 > \sigma_0^2)$, $P(\alpha > \alpha_0)$, $P(\beta > \beta_0)$, or $P[\beta < \beta_0]$ are specified probabilities.

Turning next to the problem of testing hypotheses, suppose we want to test the hypothesis that the true value of β is 1.5. We know that $(\hat{\beta} - \beta)/\mathrm{SE}(\hat{\beta})$ has a t distribution of degrees of freedom 8. If the true value of β is 1.5, the value of this expression is approximately -2.0. Looking at the tables of the t distribution, we find that for 8 degrees of freedom the probability of obtaining a t value of -2.0 or less is smaller than 5 percent; i.e., if the true value of β is 1.5, we would have obtained a value of $\hat{\beta} = 0.7$ or less by pure chance in less than 5 percent of the samples. Hence, either the true value of β is not 1.5 or an improbable event has occurred. In statistics we reject the improbable. Hence, we reject the hypothesis that the true value of β is 1.5. Instead of specifying $\beta = 1.5$, if we had specified it as 1.0, the t value would now be $-.75$, and the probability of obtaining a t value as small as this or smaller through pure chance is greater than 20 percent. If we think this is also "improbable," we should reject the hypothesis that $\beta = 1.0$. But we cannot consider 20 percent as too small a probability. (It is customary to use 5 percent as the cutoff point, but there is nothing holy about this number.)

7-3 PREDICTION

The regression equation $y = \hat{\alpha} + \hat{\beta}x$ is used for predicting y for given values of x, and the equation $x = \hat{\alpha}' + \hat{\beta}'y$ is used to predict the values of x for given values of y. We will illustrate prediction procedures with reference to the prediction of y given x. Let x_F be a future value of x. Then we predict the corresponding value of y by

$$\hat{y}_F = \hat{\alpha} + \hat{\beta}x_F \tag{7-9}$$

The true value of y_F is given by

$$y_F = \alpha + \beta x_F + u_F$$

Hence the prediction error is

$$\hat{y}_F - y_F = (\hat{\alpha} - \alpha) + (\hat{\beta} - \beta)x_F - u_F$$

Since $E(\hat{\alpha} - \alpha) = 0$, $E(\hat{\beta} - \beta) = 0$, and $E(u_F) = 0$, we have $E(\hat{y}_F - y_F) = 0$ or $E(\hat{y}_F) = y_F$. Thus the predictor given by Eq. (7-9) is unbiased. Variance of the prediction error

$$V(\hat{y}_F - y_F) = V(\hat{\alpha} - \alpha) + x_F^2 V(\hat{\beta} - \beta) + 2x_F \operatorname{cov}(\hat{\alpha} - \alpha, \hat{\beta} - \beta) + V(u_F)$$

$$= \sigma^2\left(\frac{1}{n} + \frac{\bar{x}^2}{S_{xx}}\right) + \sigma^2 \frac{x_F^2}{S_{xx}} - 2x_F\sigma^2 \frac{\bar{x}}{S_{xx}} + \sigma^2$$

$$= \sigma^2\left[1 + \frac{1}{n} + \frac{(x_F - \bar{x})^2}{S_{xx}}\right]$$

Thus the variance increases the further away the value of x_F is from $\bar{x}$, the mean of the observations on the basis of which $\hat{\alpha}$ and $\hat{\beta}$ have been computed.

Since σ^2 is not known, we estimate it by

$$\hat{\sigma}^2 = \frac{\text{RSS}}{n-2}$$

Hence

$$\text{SE of } \hat{y}_F = \sqrt{\frac{\text{RSS}}{n-2}\left[1 + \frac{1}{n} + \frac{(x_F - \bar{x})^2}{S_{xx}}\right]}$$

This can be used to construct confidence intervals for y_F.

For example, suppose we estimate the regression function on the basis of 12 observations as $y = -10.0 + .976x$. $\hat{\sigma}^2 = 0.01$, $\bar{x} = 200.0$, and $S_{xx} = 4000.00$.

Given $x_F = 250$, we predict y as 234.0.

$$\text{SE of } \hat{y}_F = \sqrt{.01\left[1 + \frac{1}{12} + \frac{2500}{4000}\right]} = .157$$

Thus the 95 percent confidence interval for y_F is

$$234 \pm 2.228(.157) = 234 \pm .35$$

that is, (233.65,234.35). $t = 2.228$ from t tables with 10 degrees of freedom.

7-4 LEAST-SQUARES AND ML METHODS

In Chap. 4 we outlined a method of estimation called the maximum-likelihood (ML) method. The least-squares method does not depend on the assumption of normality for the residuals u_i. But we make this assumption to facilitate the construction of confidence intervals and application of tests of significance. We will now show that if we make this assumption, the least-squares estimators are the same as the ML estimators.

To see this, consider the model

$$y_i = \alpha + \beta x_i + u_i \qquad u_i \sim IN(0,\sigma^2)$$

Given this assumption, the joint probability density of the u_i is (since they are independent)

$$\frac{1}{(\sqrt{2\pi}\,)^n \sigma^n} \exp\left(-\frac{1}{2\sigma^2}\sum u_i^2\right)$$

Hence the joint density of the y_i is

$$L = \frac{1}{(\sqrt{2\pi}\,)^n \sigma^n} \exp\left[-\frac{1}{2\sigma^2}\sum (y_i - \alpha - \beta x_i)^2\right]$$

As explained earlier, this joint density considered as a function of the parameters is called the likelihood function for these parameters.

$$\log L = -\frac{n}{2}\log 2\pi - n\log\sigma - \frac{1}{2\sigma^2}\sum (y_i - \alpha - \beta x_i)^2$$

Maximizing $\log L$ with respect to α and β amounts to minimizing $\sum (y_i - \alpha - \beta x_i)^2$, which is what the least-squares method does. Also,

$$\frac{\partial \log L}{\partial \sigma} - 0 \qquad \text{gives} \qquad -\frac{n}{\sigma} + \frac{1}{\sigma 3}\sum (y_i - \alpha - \beta x_i)^2 - 0$$

or

$$\hat{\sigma}^2 = \frac{1}{n}\sum (y_i - \alpha - \beta x_i)^2$$

Hence the ML estimators of α and β are the same as the least-squares estimators. But the estimator for σ^2 is $1/n$ (residual sum of squares), and this is different from the unbiased estimator suggested earlier. The ML estimators of α and β are unbiased, but the ML estimator for σ^2 is not unbiased.

7-5 ANALYSIS OF RESIDUALS

One of the most important and informative parts of our analysis in regression equations is the analysis of residuals. After we compute the regression equation, we should examine the residuals $y - \hat{y}$, where $\hat{y}$ is the estimate of y from the regression equation, that is, $\hat{y} = \hat{\alpha} + \hat{\beta}x$. This may tell us whether there are any peculiarities in our data, whether the functional form chosen is a wrong one, whether there are omitted variables, and whether the assumptions we made about the residuals u_i are valid or not. A detailed analysis of all these problems will be given in subsequent chapters. Here we will illustrate some of these problems.

Table 7-1 Total and per-capita disposable personal income and personal consumption expenditure, in current and 1958 prices, 1929–1970

Year	Disposable personal income				Personal consumption expenditures				Population
	Total (billions of dollars)		Per capita (dollars)		Total (billions of dollars)		Per capita (dollars)		
	Current prices	1958 prices	Current prices	1958 prices	Current prices	1958 prices	Current prices	1958 prices	(thousands)
1929	83.3	150.6	683	1,236	77.2	139.6	634	1,145	121,875
1930	74.5	139.0	605	1,128	69.9	130.4	567	1,059	123,188
1931	64.0	133.7	516	1,077	60.5	126.1	487	1,016	124,149
1932	48.7	115.1	390	921	48.6	114.8	389	919	124,949
1933	45.5	112.2	362	893	45.8	112.8	364	897	125,690
1934	52.4	120.4	414	952	51.3	118.1	406	934	126,485
1935	58.5	131.8	459	1,035	55.7	125.5	437	985	127,362
1936	66.3	148.4	518	1,158	61.9	138.4	483	1,080	128,181
1937	71.2	153.1	552	1,187	66.5	143.1	516	1,110	128,961
1938	65.5	143.6	504	1,105	63.9	140.2	492	1,079	129,969
1939	70.3	155.9	537	1,190	66.8	148.2	510	1,131	131,028
1940	75.7	166.3	573	1,259	70.8	155.7	536	1,178	132,122
1941	92.7	190.3	695	1,427	80.6	165.4	604	1,240	133,402
1942	116.9	213.4	867	1,582	88.5	161.4	656	1,197	134,860
1943	133.5	222.8	976	1,629	99.3	165.8	726	1,213	136,739
1944	146.3	231.6	1,057	1,673	108.3	171.4	782	1,238	138,397
1945	150.2	229.7	1,074	1,642	119.7	183.0	855	1,308	139,928
1946	160.0	227.0	1,132	1,606	143.4	203.5	1,014	1,439	141,389
1947	169.8	218.0	1,178	1,513	160.7	206.3	1,115	1,431	144,126
1948	189.1	229.8	1,290	1,567	173.6	210.8	1,184	1,438	146,631
1949	188.6	230.8	1,264	1,547	176.8	216.5	1,185	1,451	149,188
1950	206.9	249.6	1,364	1,646	191.0	230.5	1,259	1,520	151,684
1951	226.6	255.7	1,469	1,657	206.3	232.8	1,337	1,509	154,287
1952	238.3	263.3	1,518	1,678	216.7	239.4	1,381	1,525	156,954
1953	252.6	275.4	1,583	1,726	230.0	250.8	1,441	1,572	159,565
1954	257.4	278.3	1,585	1,714	236.5	255.7	1,456	1,575	162,391
1955	275.3	296.7	1,666	1,795	254.4	274.2	1,539	1,659	165,275
1956	293.2	309.3	1,743	1,839	266.7	281.4	1,585	1,673	168,221
1957	308.5	315.8	1,801	1,844	281.4	288.2	1,643	1,683	171,274
1958	318.8	318.8	1,831	1,831	290.1	290.1	1,686	1,666	174,141
1959	337.3	333.0	1,905	1,881	311.2	307.3	1,758	1,735	177,073
1960	350.0	340.2	1,937	1,883	325.2	316.1	1,800	1,749	180,684
1961	364.4	350.7	1,983	1,909	335.2	322.5	1,824	1,755	183,756
1962	385.3	367.3	2,064	1,968	355.1	338.4	1,902	1,813	186,656
1963	404.6	381.3	2,136	2,013	375.0	353.3	1,980	1,865	189,417
1964	438.1	407.9	2,280	2,123	401.2	373.7	2,088	1,945	192,120
1965	473.2	435.0	2,432	2,235	432.8	397.7	2,224	2,044	194,592
1966	511.9	458.9	2,599	2,331	466.3	418.1	2,368	2,123	196,907
1967	546.3	477.5	2,744	2.398	492.1	430.1	2,471	2,160	199,119
1968	591.2	499.0	2,939	2,480	535.8	452.3	2,663	2,248	201,177
1969	631.6	511.5	3,108	2,517	577.5	467.7	2,842	2,301	203,213
1970	684.7	529.7	3,333	2,579	616.8	477.2	3,003	2,323	205,395

Source: *Economic Report of the President,* 1972.

Suppose there are some outlying observations. Then these will tilt the regression line and produce a systematic pattern in the residuals. As an illustration, consider the data in Table 7-1.

If we estimate a regression equation of C on Y where C = consumer expenditures per capita (1958 prices) and Y = disposable income per capita (1958 prices), we find

$$C = 55.43 + \underset{(.0291)}{.8735}Y \qquad r^2 = .958$$

If we merely look at the r^2, we feel that the equation fitted is very good. However, the residuals are shown in Table 7-2. What we have is a string of positive residuals, then 6 negative residuals, and then a string of positive residuals. The residuals which are negative and very large in magnitude are for the war years. This suggests that we should be omitting the war years from the computations. The recomputed equation omitting 1942–1945 is shown in Table 7-3. (Actually, it looks as if we should have omitted even 1941 and 1946.) It should be noted that the recomputed equation does not show any marked difference in the slope coefficient β. It is the intercept α that has shifted upward. The scatter diagram looks as shown in Fig. 7-4. The observations for the war year produce a parallel shift in the regression equation. This sort of problem can also be handled by the dummy-variable method, which will be discussed in a subsequent chapter.

Sometimes such systematic patterns in residuals can be produced not by peculiarities in the data but by a wrong functional form; e.g., suppose the data points are as shown in Fig. 7-5(a) and (b). If we fit a straight line in these cases, we will find a systematic pattern in residuals: Fig. 7-5(a) first negative, then positive, then negative; Fig. 7-5(b) first positive, then negative, then positive.

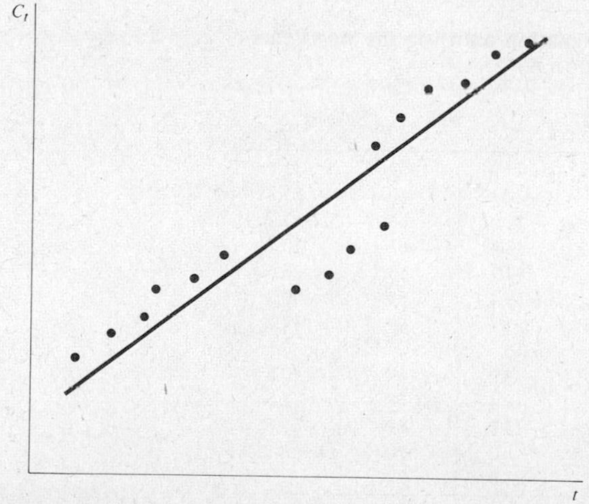

Figure 7-4 A case of outliers.

Table 7-2 Residuals for the consumption function estimated for 1929–1970

1929	9.8	1943	− 265.5	1957	16.7
30	18.2	44	− 278.9	58	11.1
31	19.7	45	− 181.8	59	36.4
32	59.0	46	− 19.4	60	48.7
33	61.4	47	53.9	61	31.9
34	46.9	48	13.7	62	38.4
35	25.4	49	44.2	63	51.1
36	12.9	50	26.7	64	35.0
37	17.6	51	6.1	65	36.2
38	58.2	52	3.7	66	31.3
39	36.0	53	8.8	67	9.8
40	22.7	54	22.3	68	26.2
41	− 62.0	55	35.5	69	46.9
42	− 240.4	56	11.1	70	14.7

Also, apart from the signs, there is in addition a systematic pattern in the absolute magnitudes.

For Fig. 7-5(a) a possible functional form is $y = \alpha + \beta \log x$ and for Fig. 7-5(b) it is $y = \alpha e^{\beta x}$. The estimation of these regression equations can be done after making suitable transformation of the variables. In Fig. 7-5(a) we redefine $\chi = \log x$ and fit a regression equation $y = \alpha + \beta\chi$. In Fig 7-5(b), we take logs of both sides to get $\log y = \log \alpha + \beta x$. Define the new variables $Y = \log y$ and $A = \log \alpha$. Then we fit the regression equation $Y = A + \beta x$. After we estimate A and β, we get $\hat{\alpha} = \text{antilog } \hat{A}$.[1] Other functional forms are possible; e.g., in Fig. 7-5(a) one can estimate a parabolic curve. This will be given by $y^2 = \alpha + \beta x$. In

Table 7-3 Residuals for the equation omitting the war years (1942–1945). Estimated equation is

$$C = 85.06 + \underset{(.0081)}{.87Y} \qquad R^2 = .997$$

1929	− 16.7	1946	− 44.9	1959	11.5
30	− 8.6	47	28.1	60	23.8
31	− 7.2	48	− 12.0	61	7.1
32	31.7	49	18.4	62	13.7
33	34.1	50	1.2	63	26.5
34	19.7	51	− 19.4	64	10.7
35	− 1.6	52	− 21.7	65	12.2
36	− 13.7	53	− 16.5	66	7.6
37	− 9.0	54	− 3.0	67	− 13.8
38	31.4	55	10.4	68	2.8
39	9.4	56	13.9	69	23.5
40	− 3.7	57	− 8.2	70	− 8.5
41	− 88.0	58	− 13.9		

[1] Note that $\hat{A}$ is an unbiased estimate of A. But $\hat{\alpha}$ is not an unbiased estimate of α.

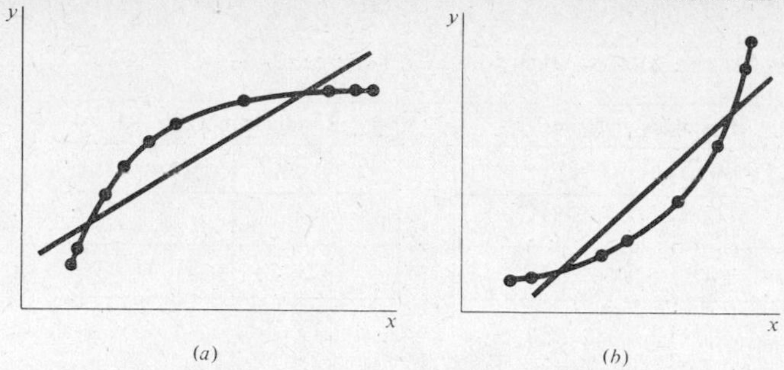

Figure 7-5 (*a*) y increasing more slowly than x; (*b*) y increasing faster than x.

this case we define $Y = y^2$ and fit a regression equation $Y = \alpha + \beta x$. Alternatively, we can consider $y = \alpha + \beta x + \gamma x^2$. But this falls under multiple regression, which will be discussed in the next chapter.

In summary, by making suitable transformations of the variables, the theory of simple regression outlined here can be used to estimate other functional forms. However, it is important to note that implicitly we are assuming that the residual is additive to the *transformed* equation; i.e., if we have $y = \alpha x^{\beta}$, we are assuming that the model is $\log y_i = \log \alpha + \beta \log x_i + u_i$. This implies that the residual enters the original equation in a multiplicative fashion; i.e., we assume $y_i = \alpha x_i^{\beta} \cdot u_i$ and not $y_i = \alpha x_i^{\beta} + u_i$. If we made the latter assumption, we have to estimate the parameters by what is known as the *nonlinear least-squares* method. This will be discussed in a subsequent chapter.

The pattern of residuals as in Table 7-2 can be summarized in a number of ways. One statistic often used is known as the *Durbin-Watson statistic*. This is defined as

$$\mathrm{DW} = \frac{\sum (\hat{u}_t - \hat{u}_{t-1})^2}{\sum \hat{u}_t^2}$$

where $\hat{u}_t$ is the residual for time period t. We can write DW as

$$\frac{\sum \hat{u}_t^2 + \sum \hat{u}_{t-1}^2 - 2\sum \hat{u}_t \hat{u}_{t-1}}{\sum \hat{u}_t^2}$$

Since $\sum \hat{u}_t^2$ and $\sum \hat{u}_{t-1}^2$ are approximately equal if the sample size is large, we have $\mathrm{DW} \approx 2(1 - \rho)$ where ρ is the correlation coefficient between $\hat{u}_t$ and $\hat{u}_{t-1}$. If $\rho = +1$, $\mathrm{DW} = 0$; if $\rho = 0$, $\mathrm{DW} = 2$; and if $\rho = -1$, $\mathrm{DW} = 4$. Hence if DW is close to 0 or 4, we know that the residuals $\hat{u}_t$ and $\hat{u}_{t-1}$ are highly correlated. In Table 7-2, $\mathrm{DW} = 0.33$ and in Table 7-3, $\mathrm{DW} = 1.36$. Probability tables for the DW statistic have been prepared, and these enable us to test whether $\rho = 0$ or not. Many regression-computing programs currently in use automatically compute the DW statistic along with the regression coefficients and r^2.

Table 7-4

	Residuals in Table 7-2		Residuals in Table 7-3	
	Positive at t	Negative at t	Positive at t	Negative at t
Positive at $t-1$	34	1	12	7
Negative at $t-1$	1	5	7	11

Though the DW statistic is often used to summarize the nature of the correlation between residuals, it sometimes gives a misleading story. Hence it is often desirable to examine the sign pattern of the residuals through what is known as a "contingency table." Table 7-4 is such a contingency table for the residuals in Tables 7-2 and 7-3. In the case of randomness one would expect the entries in the table to be evenly distributed in the 4 cells. Though in these examples, the contingency tables give the same picture as the DW statistic, sometimes this is not so. For instance, in the paper by Griliches et al.,[1] the DW statistic was 1.5 but the contingency table showed high positive correlation. It was

	Positive at t	Negative at t
Positive at $t-1$	13	5
Negative at $t-1$	5	16

The appropriate χ^2 test rejected the hypothesis of zero correlation. Thus the DW statistic can sometimes be misleading.

Another thing that might be noticed is that the magnitude of the residuals systematically increases with the value of x, as shown in Fig. 7-6. This indicates that the assumption $V(u_i) = \sigma^2$ for all i is not valid. This is the problem of "heteroscedasticity."

Another thing one could do, particularly if the number of observations is large, is to compute the third and fourth moments about the mean: μ_3 and μ_4, respectively. For the normal distribution $\mu_3 = 0$ and $\mu_4 = 3\mu_2^2$, where μ_2 is the second moment about the mean, or variance. These measures will indicate departures from normality. Sometimes an examination of the residuals will also suggest some variables that should have been included in the regression but were omitted initially through negligence.

In summary, an analysis of residuals should accompany every least-squares regression. This analysis may reveal whether:

1. There are outliers.
2. There are some omitted variables.

[1] Z. Griliches, G. S. Maddala, R. E. Lucas, and N. Wallace, Notes on Estimated Aggregate Quarterly Consumption Functions, *Econometrica*, July 1962.

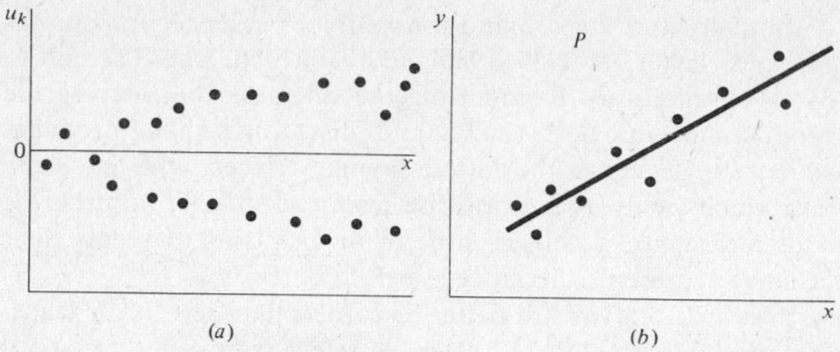

Figure 7-6 (*a*) Heteroscedastic residuals; (*b*) a case of an outlier.

3. The relationship is nonlinear instead of linear as assumed.
4. The u_i are correlated instead of independent as assumed.
5. The variance σ^2 of u_i is not constant.
6. The u_i are not normally distributed.

7-6 MODIFICATIONS OF THE SIMPLE LEAST-SQUARES METHOD

To tackle the above-mentioned problems, the simple least-squares method described above is modified in a number of ways. These problems are all discussed in greater detail in subsequent chapters. Here we will outline some of the solutions commonly used.

Outliers. An outlier is, roughly speaking, an observation that behaves differently from the rest of the observations (e.g., point P in Fig. 7-6*b* is an outlier). Sometimes we can give some reasons why these observations are behaving in the peculiar way. For instance, in the case of the data in Table 7-1, the behavior of the observations for 1941–1946 can be attributed to World War II. If there are outliers, the usual procedure is to omit them and reestimate the regression equation.

From the statistical point of view it makes a difference whether the so-called outliers are omitted before or after a preliminary analysis is made. If we estimate a regression equation, look at the residuals, then decide that some observations are outliers, and then estimate the equation omitting these observations, the standard errors and confidence intervals we report are no longer valid. On the other hand, if we do not discard these observations, even in view of some information we have on why they are out of the way, the results we get are not meaningful. Fisher[1] gives examples of the estimation of the quantitative structure of the United Kingdom wheat market 1867–1914, demand for aluminum

[1] F. M. Fisher, "A Priori Information and Time Series Analysis," North-Holland Publishing Company, Amsterdam, 1966.

ingot in the U.S. 1925–1940, and the demand for railroad passenger transportation between Boston and New York 1929–1940 and 1946–1956, where he had to discard some outlying observations. Recognizing the dilemma that leaving the observations in produces meaningless results and discarding them produces uncertain standard errors, he chose the latter, saying, "Faced with choosing between a procedure which yields, at best, precise results of little or no meaning and one which yields meaningful results of little or no precision, it seems clear that the latter alternative represents the more hopeful course."[1]

It is not always true that outliers are better discarded than left in. In fact it is possible that what we consider outliers give more relevant information about the relationship between x and y than the other observations considered by us "good" because they may correspond to something like a controlled experiment in the physical sciences. As an illustration, one can perhaps get more information on the price elasticity of demand for gasoline from observations during the "energy crisis" of 1973 than from the observations of the previous twenty years.

Another alternative that is often used is the method of minimizing the sum of absolute errors

$$\sum |y_i - a - bx_i|$$

rather than the sum of squared errors. This will ensure that extreme observations do not get an undue weight. This method, called the LAR (least absolute residual) method, is computationally complicated to discuss here. It is discussed in Sec. 13-10. The method is appropriate if there are many extreme observations and we have no strong a priori reason to discard any.

Omitted variables. If there is a systematic pattern in the residuals, this is possibly caused by some omitted variables. These variables are ignored because we cannot measure them, e.g., managerial input, quality changes in labor, etc., in production functions. In such situations, we may be able either to say something about the direction of the bias in the estimated coefficients or to use some substitute variables that capture the effects. These substitute variables are called *proxy variables*. Since these problems involve knowledge of multiple regression methods, they will be discussed in a subsequent chapter (Sec. 9-5).

Nonlinearity. As explained earlier, sometimes nonlinear relationships can be converted into linear relationships by transformations so long as we assume the residual to be additive in the transformed equation. Instances of this considered above are

$$y = \alpha e^{\beta x} \qquad \text{and} \qquad y^2 = \alpha + \beta x$$

Some nonlinearities can be taken care of by multiple regression, but this will be discussed later. An example of this is

$$y = \alpha + \beta x + \delta x^2 + u$$

[1] *Ibid.*, chap 1, Selective Estimation and the Dilemma of Objectivity, p. 13.

Some other nonlinearities can be handled by "search procedures." For instance, suppose we have the regression equation

$$y = \alpha + \frac{\beta}{x + c} + u$$

The estimates of α,β,c are obtained by minimizing

$$\sum \left(y_i - \alpha - \frac{\beta}{x_i + c} \right)^2$$

We can reduce this problem to one of simple least squares as follows: For each value of c, we define the variable $z_i = 1/(x_i + c)$ and estimate α and β by minimizing

$$\sum (y_i - \alpha - \beta z_i)^2$$

We look at the residual sum of squares in each case and choose that value of c for which the residual sum of squares is minimum. The corresponding estimates of α and β are the least-squares estimates of these parameters.

It might not always be possible to use the simple search procedure outlined here. For instance, if we have

$$y = \alpha_1 + \frac{\alpha_2}{(x + \alpha_3)^{\alpha_4}} + u$$

then we have to use a nonlinear minimization procedure to estimate the parameters α_1, α_2, α_3, and α_4

Residuals u_i are correlated.[1] If the residuals u_i are correlated among themselves (this correlation is called autocorrelation), one has to look for the pattern of this correlation. One statistic that is often used is the Durbin-Watson statistic defined earlier. If it is very low, the usual procedure is to estimate the regression equation in the first-difference form, i.e., regress $(y_t - y_{t-1})$ on $(x_t - x_{t-1})$. The implicit assumption is that the first differences of the residuals $(u_t - u_{t-1})$ are uncorrelated among themselves. For instance, if

$$y_t = \alpha + \beta x_t + u_t$$

is the regression equation, then

$$y_{t-1} = \alpha + \beta x_{t-1} + u_{t-1}$$

and we have by subtraction

$$(y_t - y_{t-1}) = \beta(x_t - x_{t-1}) + (u_t - u_{t-1})$$

If the residuals in this equation are independent, we can estimate the equation by ordinary least squares. However, since the constant term α disappears in subtraction, we should be estimating the regression equation with no constant

[1] More detailed discussion of this problem can be found in Chap. 12.

term. Often we find a constant term also included in regression equations with first differences. This procedure is valid only if there is a linear-trend term in the original equation. If the regression equation is

$$y_t = \alpha + \delta t + \beta x_t + u_t$$

then
$$y_{t-1} = \alpha + \delta(t-1) + \beta x_{t-1} + u_{t-1}$$

and on subtraction we get

$$(y_t - y_{t-1}) = \delta + \beta(x_t - x_{t-1}) + (u_t - u_{t-1})$$

which is an equation with the constant term δ.

Another important thing to note is that usually with time-series data one gets good R^2's when the regressions are estimated with the levels y_t and x_t but one gets poor R^2's if the regressions are estimated in first differences $(y_t - y_{t-1})$ and $(x_t - x_{t-1})$. Since usually a high R^2 is considered as proof of a strong relationship between the variables under investigation, there is a strong tendency to estimate the regression in terms of the levels rather than the first differences. This is sometimes called the "R^2 syndrome." However, if the Durbin-Watson statistic is very low, it often implies a misspecified equation, no matter what the value of the R^2 is. In such cases one should estimate the regression equation in first differences; and if the R^2 now is low, it is merely an indication that the variables y and x are not indeed related to each other, as the high R^2's obtained from the regressions of the levels might imply. Granger and Newbold[1] present some examples with artificially generated data where y, x, and the residual u are each highly autocorrelated series each generated independently so that there is no relationship between y and x, but the regression of y on x gives a high R^2 and a low Durbin-Watson statistic. When the regression is run in first differences, the R^2 is close to zero and the Durbin-Watson statistic is close to 2.0, thus demonstrating that the R^2 obtained earlier is spurious and that there is indeed no relationship between y and x. Thus regressions in first differences might often reveal the true nature of the relationship between y and x.

It is, of course, not always true that one should be estimating regression equations in first differences. In fact, if the Durbin-Watson statistic is greater than 1.2, which roughly implies that the correlation between u_t and u_{t-1} is less than $\frac{1}{2}(2.0 - 1.2)$, or 0.4, using first differences might actually increase the correlation between the resulting residuals $(u_t - u_{t-1})$ and $(u_{t-1} - u_{t-2})$. In such cases one should be using *quasi first differences* rather than first differences. For instance, if the Durbin-Watson statistic is 0.8, since this implies the correlation between u_t and u_{t-1} to be roughly $\frac{1}{2}(2.0 - 0.8)$, or 0.6, we should regress $(y_t - 0.6y_{t-1})$ on $(x_t - 0.6x_{t-1})$.

Finally, it should be emphasized that all this discussion of the Durbin-Watson statistic, first differences, and quasi first differences is relevant only if we believe that the residuals show first-order autocorrelation, that is, u_t and u_{t-1}

[1] C. W. J. Granger and P. Newbold, Spurious Regressions in Econometrics, *Journal of Econometrics*, vol. 2, no. 2, pp. 111–120, July 1974.

are correlated. Suppose we have quarterly data, then it is possible that the residuals in any quarter this year are most highly correlated with the residuals in the corresponding quarter last year rather than with the residuals in the preceding quarter, that is, u_t could be uncorrelated with u_{t-1} but it could be highly correlated with u_{t-4}. If this is the case, the Durbin-Watson statistic will fail to detect it. What we should be doing in this case is using a modified statistic defined as

$$\mathrm{DW}_4 = \frac{\sum \hat{u}_t \hat{u}_{t-4}}{\sum \hat{u}_t^2}$$

where $\hat{u}_t$ is the estimated residual for period t from the least-squares regression. Also, instead of using first differences and quasi first differences in the regressions, we should be using $(y_t - y_{t-4})$ and $(x_t - x_{t-4})$ or $(y_t - ry_{t-4})$ and $(x_t - rx_{t-4})$, where r is the estimated correlation between the residuals with a lag of four time periods, that is, u_t and u_{t-4}.

Heteroscedasticity.[1] As described earlier, this is a phenomenon where the residuals do not have a common variance. Often one can reduce these models to models where the residuals have a common variance either by a transformation of the variables or by deflation. For instance, suppose we have data on sales S_i and profits P_i for a number of firms large and small, and we want to estimate the regression equation

$$P_i = \alpha + \beta S_i + u_i$$

Then it is reasonable to assume that the residuals for the larger firms would have a higher variance than the residuals for the smaller firms. If we hypothesize that the variance of u_i is proportional to the square of sales S_i, that is, $\mathrm{var}(u_i) = \sigma^2 S_i^2$, then we can convert the above regression model to one where the residuals exhibit a constant variance σ^2 by dividing throughout by S_i. We then have

$$\frac{P_i}{S_i} = \alpha \frac{1}{S_i} + \beta + v_i$$

where the new residual

$$v_i = \frac{u_i}{S_i} \qquad \text{and} \qquad \mathrm{var}(v_i) = \frac{1}{S_i^2}\,\mathrm{var}(u_i) = \sigma^2$$

Thus, instead of regressing P_i on S_i, we should be regressing P_i/S_i on $1/S_i$. The constant term in this transformed equation measures the slope coefficient in the original equation, and the slope coefficient measures the constant term in the original equation.

[1] More detailed discussion of this problem can be found in Chap. 12.

If, on the other hand, $\mathrm{var}(u_i) = \sigma^2 S_i$, we have to divide the original equation throughout by $\sqrt{S_i}$, and we get

$$\frac{P_i}{\sqrt{S_i}} = \alpha \frac{1}{\sqrt{S_i}} + \beta \sqrt{S_i} + w_i$$

where $$w_i = \frac{u_i}{\sqrt{S_i}} \quad \text{and} \quad \mathrm{var}(w_i) = \frac{1}{S_i} \mathrm{var}(u_i) = \sigma^2$$

Thus we should be regressing $P/\sqrt{S_i}$ on $1/\sqrt{S_i}$ and $\sqrt{S_i}$ with no constant term in the regression equation.

Another procedure that is often used in such cases is to run the regression in logs, i.e., estimate

$$\log P_i = \alpha' + \beta' \log S_i + u_i$$

This way one takes care of the problem of giving undue weight to the large observations.

Thus the two commonly used solutions are deflation and log transformation. Which is better in any particular case depends on the hypothesized sources of heteroscedasticity and on whether one believes the variables and residuals to be additive or multiplicative.

Residuals not normally distributed. Finally, we come to the problem that the residuals may not be normally distributed. If the residuals are not normally distributed, the least-squares estimators are still best linear unbiased, but all the tests of significance we apply will not be valid. The problem of nonnormality and the solutions for it are discussed in detail in Sec. 13-9. But one important point to note here is that heteroscedasticity in the residuals often gives us the impression that the residuals are nonnormal. Thus solutions suggested above to tackle heteroscedasticity—deflation and transformations—may work also to produce residuals that are at least approximately normally distributed.

7-7 ANALYSIS OF STRUCTURAL SHIFTS

In the example of the consumption function we saw that the war years constituted some outlying observations. Since these observations correspond to a period of unusual behavior, we omit them from our analysis. Such might not be the case with other situations. If some shifts have occurred in the functions, we need to explain why these shifts have occurred. Only then can we forecast future shifts. As an example, consider the per-capita consumption and deflated prices of selected meats for the period 1948–1963. These are presented in Table 7-5. The scatter diagrams are shown in Fig. 7-7.[1] A glance at Fig. 7-7 shows abrupt

[1] The data are from Table 5-1, p. 39, and the figure is Fig. 5-1, p. 41, of Frederick V. Waugh, Demand and Price Analysis—Some Examples from Agriculture, U.S. Department of Agriculture Technical Bulletin 1316, Nov. 1964.

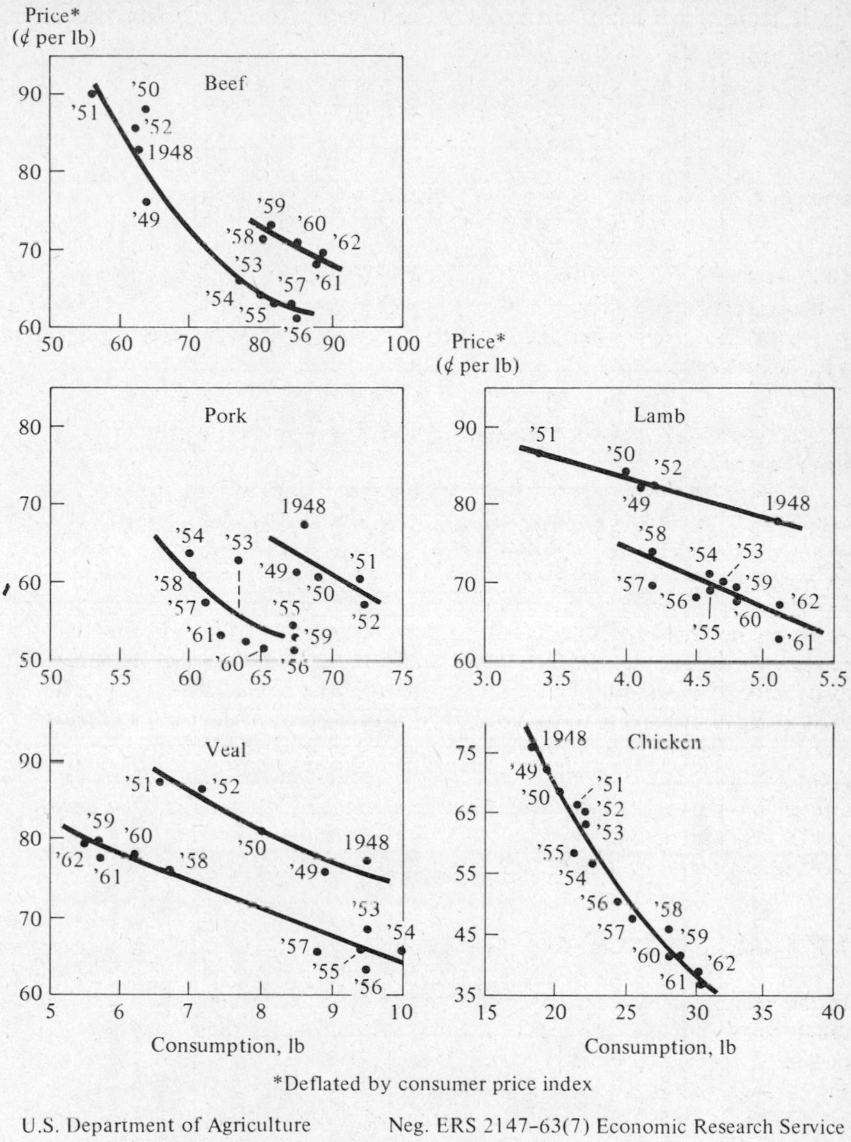

Figure 7-7 Scatter diagrams of consumption and deflated price.

Table 7-5 Per-capita consumption and deflated prices of selected meats, 1948–1963

	Beef		Pork		Lamb		Veal		Chicken	
Year	Consumption per capita,* lb	Price per pound,† cents	Consumption per capita,* lb	Price per pound,† cents	Consumption per capita,* lb	Price per pound,† cents	Consumption per capita,* lb	Price per pound,† cents	Consumption per capita,* lb	Price per pound,† cents
1948	63.1	82.9	67.8	67.6	5.1	77.8	9.5	77.1	18.3	75.4
1949	63.9	76.3	67.7	61.5	4.1	82.4	8.9	75.7	19.6	71.8
1950	63.4	88.3	69.2	60.4	4.0	84.2	8.0	81.1	20.6	68.0
1951	56.1	90.0	71.9	60.6	3.4	86.7	6.6	87.6	21.7	66.0
1952	62.2	85.4	72.4	57.3	4.2	86.2	7.2	86.3	22.1	65.0
1953	77.6	66.2	63.5	62.9	4.7	70.0	9.5	68.7	21.9	62.8
1954	80.1	64.1	60.0	63.7	4.6	71.0	10.0	65.8	22.8	56.4
1955	82.0	63.2	66.8	54.6	4.6	69.0	9.4	65.8	21.3	58.7
1956	85.4	60.9	67.3	51.4	4.5	68.3	9.5	63.6	24.4	50.4
1957	84.6	63.1	61.1	57.6	4.2	69.9	8.8	65.5	25.5	47.6
1958	80.5	72.0	60.2	60.5	4.2	74.1	6.7	76.1	28.2	45.8
1959	81.4	73.3	67.6	52.8	4.8	69.6	5.7	79.8	28.9	41.4
1960	85.2	70.4	65.2	51.6	4.8	67.6	6.2	77.8	28.2	41.4
1961	88.0	68.3	62.2	53.3	5.1	63.3	5.7	77.3	30.3	37.0
1962	89.1	69.8	64.0	52.9	5.1	67.1	5.5	79.5	30.2	38.6
1963‡	95.2	67.8	64.9	50.5	4.9	68.0	5.0	79.2	30.6	37.6

* Carcass weight equivalent.

† Divided by consumer price index (1957–1959 = 100).

‡ 1963 data are preliminary and were not used in the analysis.

shifts in the demand for beef, pork, lamb, and veal. Waugh tries to explain these shifts by changes in the quantities supplied of other meats and also by changes in consumer income. The relevant regressions will be presented in Chap. 9.

The important point to note in this example is that, unlike the case of the consumption function where we omitted the war years, we cannot throw away any observations. Unless we are able to explain and interpret the shifts that have occurred, there is not much point in analyzing these demand functions. Sometimes these shifts are labeled "structural shifts," but this is merely a confession that we do not know the reasons behind these shifts. As is well known, giving different names to ignorance does not dispel ignorance.[1] Since any further analysis of the shifts in the demand function will depend on the use of additional explanatory variables, we will discuss this problem after studying multiple regression.

7-8 ALTERNATIVE INTERPRETATIONS OF REGRESSION

Now that we have looked at some examples of the use of regression, we can turn to some controversial issues in interpretation. First, from the historical point of view, the term *regression* was first introduced by Francis Galton in a series of papers[2] to describe the relationship between the height of children and the height of parents. Galton noted that although tall parents had tall children and short parents had short children, the distribution of heights did not change from generation to generation. He also found that the mean heights of children for each of a set of given mid-parent heights[3] lay approximately on a straight line with a slope less than unity. He called the line a "regression" line because the fact that the slope is less than unity implies a tendency for the mean height of children born of parents of a given height to *regress* or move toward the population average height.

The term regression is not now used in this sense and has no implication about the slope or linearity.[4] But even now regression is used in two different ways. These might be called "bivariate" regression and "classical" or "least-

[1] There has been a similar criticism of studies that label shifts in the aggregate production function as due to "technical change." Since "technical change" is a phrase used to denote all those factors that contributed to the shifts in the production function, it does not convey any information. This is why measures of "technical change" in these studies have sometimes been called measures of "ignorance." A similar criticism has been made by Machlup about the term "structural disequilibrium." He argues that this term is an alternative expression for ignorance. See F. Machlup's paper in Merton H. Miller (ed.), "Essays in Semantics," Prentice-Hall Inc., Englewood Cliffs, N.J., 1963.

[2] The most famous of these papers is F. Galton, Family Likeness in Stature, *Proceedings of the Royal Society of London*, 1886, pp. 42–72.

[3] Since Galton found that the influences of the two parents were unequal, he multiplied the female height by 1.08 before computing the mid-parent height.

[4] As Anscombe said in 1967: "It is eighty years too late to complain about the term regression." See F. J. Anscombe, Topics in the Investigation of Least Squares (with discussion), *Journal of the Royal Statistical Society*, ser. B, 1967, pp. 1–52.

squares" regression. We discussed the latter earlier. We will now discuss the former. We have used (y_i,x_i) as the set of observed values. If both y_i and x_i are observations of the random variables Y and X, respectively, we have what is known as *bivariate regression*. If Y is a random variable and X is not (or vice versa), we have what is known as *least-squares regression*. In some cases bivariate regression is clearly not applicable. An example is when X is time measured in weeks, months, or years. In this case clearly X is not a random variable. On the other hand, there have been some questions about the applicability of the classical regression model in economics. For instance, Geary[1] asks: "Can anyone be happy about the classical regression model in economic applications, that Y on the one hand and X's on the other have so very different stochastic properties?"

In the case of bivariate regression we consider the conditional expectation of Y, that is, $E(Y \mid X = x)$. This is a function of x only. By varying x, we get different values of $E(Y \mid X = x)$. This function is known as the regression curve of Y on X. Similarly $E(X \mid Y = y)$ is a function of y only. This function is known as the regression curve of X on Y.

If X and Y are jointly normal with means μ_X and μ_Y, respectively, variances σ_X^2 and σ_Y^2, respectively, and correlation δ, then the conditional distributions are also normal. The conditional distribution of Y given $X = x$ is normal with mean $\mu_Y + (\delta\sigma_Y/\sigma_X)(x - \mu_X)$ and variance $\sigma_Y^2(1 - \delta^2)$. Note that this variance is independent of x. Similarly, the conditional distributión of X given $Y = y$ is normal with mean $\mu_X + (\delta\sigma_X/\sigma_Y)(y - \mu_Y)$ and variance $\sigma_X^2(1 - \delta^2)$. This variance is independent of y. Hence the regression of Y on X is

$$y = \mu_Y + \frac{\delta\sigma_Y}{\sigma_X}(x - \mu_X) \tag{7-10}$$

and the regression of X on Y is

$$x = \mu_X + \frac{\delta\sigma_X}{\sigma_Y}(y - \mu_Y) \tag{7-11}$$

Thus, when X and Y are normally distributed, the two regression curves are straight lines. If we denote the slopes of Eqs. (7-10) and (7-11), respectively, by β_1 and β_2, then clearly $\beta_1\beta_2 = \delta^2$. Also,

$$\beta_1 = \frac{\delta\sigma_Y}{\sigma_X} = \frac{\delta\sigma_X\sigma_Y}{\sigma_X^2} = \frac{\text{cov}(X,Y)}{\text{var}(X)}$$

$$\beta_2 = \frac{\delta\sigma_X}{\sigma_Y} = \frac{\text{cov}(X,Y)}{\text{var}(Y)}$$

Equations (7-10) and (7-11) are known as the "population regression functions." When we are given the sample values (y_i,x_i), $i = 1,2, \ldots, n$, then we estimate

[1] R. C. Geary, Some Remarks about Relations between Stochastic Variables: A Discussion Document, *Review of the International Statistical Institute*, 1963, pp. 163–181.

the population means, variances, and covariance by the sample means, variances, and covariance, respectively. (These are the maximum-likelihood estimators.)

$$\hat{\mu}_X = \bar{x} \qquad \hat{\mu}_Y = \bar{y} \qquad \hat{\sigma}_X^2 = \frac{S_{xx}}{n} \qquad \hat{\sigma}_Y^2 = \frac{S_{yy}}{n}$$

and $\operatorname{cov}(X,Y) = S_{xy}/n$. Substituting these in Eqs. (7-10) and (7-11), we get

$$y = \bar{y} + \frac{S_{xy}}{S_{xx}}(x - \bar{x}) = \hat{\alpha} + \hat{\beta}x$$

where $\hat{\alpha}$ and $\hat{\beta}$ are defined in (7-7) and

$$x = \bar{x} + \frac{S_{xy}}{S_{yy}}(y - \bar{y}) = \hat{\alpha}' + \hat{\beta}'y$$

where $\hat{\alpha}'$ and $\hat{\beta}'$ are defined in (7-8). Thus the formulas we derive are the same as before. What then is the difference? The main difference arises when we try to estimate the value of x that could have given rise to an observed y. In bivariate regression we obtain the predicted value from a regression of X on Y. In least-squares regression, since x_i, $i = 1,2, \ldots, n$, is a set of fixed numbers and Y is a random variable, this regression is meaningless. Hence we obtain the estimate of x for the given value of y from a regression of Y on X, not X on Y. As for the confidence limits for this predicted value, we obtain them by the use of a method due to Fieller, and the limits are called *tolerance* limits. These will be discussed in the next section. On the point of prediction and the uses of the two regressions there have been some controversies which we will summarize. But before we proceed, we need to clear up some terminology.

First, we often refer to Y as the dependent variable and X as the independent variable. In bivariate regression where the variables are not independent in the statistical sense, this terminology is still used, though it can be confusing. The terms dependent and independent merely denote the left-hand and right-hand variables, respectively. A better terminology is to call the left-hand variable *regressand* and the right-hand variable *regressor*. Wold[1] argues as follows:

> One difficulty is that the distinction between dependent and independent variables is in regression analysis used in two different meanings, none of which is the same as independence in the sense of probability theory. On the one hand the notions refer to variables involved in a unilateral causal dependence; alternative terms are here effect (= dependent) variable and cause or explanatory (= independent) variables. We see that this is a subject-matter distinction that has to be based on nonstatistical considerations. On the other hand the notions are used in a formal sense for the different variables in a regression relation, the left-hand variable being called dependent, the right-hand variables independent. To avoid ambiguity we shall never use the terms independent and dependent variable in regression analysis, but in the first situation speak of *cause* (or *explanatory*) and *effect* variables, in the second of *regressor* and *regressand.*

[1] Herman Wold, in association with Lars Jureen, "Demand Analysis—A Study in Econometrics," p. 33, John Wiley & Sons, Inc., New York, 1953.

> There is further the distinction between *random* variables in the sense of statistics and probability, and *nonrandom* variables in the usual mathematical sense. In regression analysis the regressand is always treated as random, but the regressors may be random or nonrandom in accordance with circumstances. Specifically, the controlled variables of an experiment are as a rule to be regarded as non-random variables subject to purposive variation, and so may also be the case with the stratified variables of non-experimental data, such as the income variable of family budget statistics. If we are dealing with non-experimental data that have not been stratified, such as the time-series data of economic statistics, the regressors will in general be treated as being random.

In the early 1940's there was a discussion between Ezekiel and Waugh on the issue of which regression to look at for prediction. Ezekiel[1] argued that if we have, say, two variables X_1 and X_2, whether our objective is to predict X_1 given X_2 or X_2 given X_1, the proper regression to look at is always the regression of the effect variable on the causal variable. Waugh,[2] on the other hand, argued that we should look at a regression of the predictand variable on the predictor variable regardless of the direction of causation. Ezekiel replied that in cases where we have definite nonstatistical knowledge of which variable is cause and which is effect, the reverse regression of the causal variable on the effect variable is generally of little significance and is likely to be used for illogical or incorrect conclusions.

The correct answer depends on the model we assume. In situations where the classical or least-squares regression model is appropriate, i.e., the X variable is treated as nonrandom, whether our objective is to predict Y given X or X given Y, we should always consider the regression of Y on X. This will be the appropriate model for experimental data and for growth curves where the X variable is time. Even with nonexperimental data, when we are considering a cause-and-effect relationship, it seems logical to consider the regression of the effect variable on the causal variable for both the prediction problems. As Wold remarks,[3] "Under the hypothesis of unilateral dependence the choice of the dependent variable will be strictly analogous to the case of experimental data." In other bivariate prediction problems, it is logical to take the variable to be predicted as the dependent variable.

When we have several variables, the discussion is the same. Instead of bivariate, we have to use the word multivariate. Wold calls the two approaches, least-squares and multivariate, the Gauss-Fisher and Galton-Yule specifications, respectively.[4] This is because the least-squares method is attributed to Gauss (1809), though the method was perhaps used earlier,[5] and was extensively used

[1] Mordecai Ezekiel, "Methods of Correlation Analysis," 2d ed., pp. 50–51, John Wiley & Sons, Inc., New York, 1941.

[2] Frederick V. Waugh, Choice of the Dependent Variable in Regression Analysis, *Journal of the American Statistical Association*, March 1943, pp. 210–213; Mordecai Ezekiel, Comments, *ibid*., pp. 214–216.

[3] Wold, *op.cit*., p. 32.

[4] Wold, *op.cit*., pp. 205–208.

[5] A history of least squares can be found in H. Seal, Studies in the History of Probability and Statistics, XV, The Historical Development of the Gauss Linear Model, *Biometrika*, 1967, pp. 1–24.

by R. A. Fisher; and the bivariate regression model was introduced by Galton and popularized by Yule.

Apart from the prediction problem, there are a few minor differences in the two regression models. In the least-squares model, as mentioned earlier, we need not make the assumption of normality for the residuals except for confidence-interval statements and tests of significance. The least-squares estimators have optimal properties whatever the probability distribution of the residuals, provided the other assumptions are satisfied. Also, the relationship is linear or not by assumption. In the bivariate (or multivariate) regression the conditional expectations need not be linear. But if we assume normality, they will necessarily be linear. Further, the sampling distributions of the estimators are somewhat different. This we will discuss later when we consider stochastic regressors.

Thus, though the algebra for obtaining the estimators is the same in both the cases for normal distribution, there are differences as far as prediction problems and sampling distributions of the estimators are concerned.

7-9 PREDICTION OF x GIVEN y IN LEAST-SQUARES REGRESSION: FIELLER'S METHOD

To simplify the algebra, we will write $x' = x - \bar{x}$ and $y' = y - \bar{y}$. The estimated regression equation is

$$y' = \hat{\beta}x' \tag{7-12}$$

We are given a future value of y, namely, y_f, and we are asked to estimate the value x_f that could have given rise to y_f and obtain a confidence interval for x_f. Define $y'_f = y_f - \bar{y}$ and $x'_f = x_f - \bar{x}$. Clearly the estimate of x'_f is given from Eq. (7-12) as

$$\hat{x}'_f = \frac{y'_f}{\hat{\beta}} \tag{7-13}$$

The main problem is with obtaining confidence limits for $\hat{x}_f$, because both y'_f and $\hat{\beta}$ are normally distributed. For this we will use a method due to Fieller.[1] Let θ represent $y'_f/\hat{\beta}$. Then the variable $y'_f - \hat{\beta}\theta$ is normally distributed with mean zero and variance

$$\sigma^2\left(1 + \frac{1}{n}\right) + \theta^2 \frac{\sigma^2}{S_{xx}} \tag{7-14}$$

[1] E. C. Fieller, A Fundamental Formula in the Statistics of Biological Assay and Some Applications, *Quarterly Journal of Pharmacy*, 1944, pp. 117–123. Fieller's method is also useful in deriving confidence intervals for estimates in simultaneous-equation models (see Chap. 11) and distributed-lag models (see Chap. 16).

[since $\text{var}(y'_f) = \text{var}(y_f - \bar{y}) = \sigma^2 + \sigma^2/n$ and $\text{cov}(y'_f, \hat{\beta}) = 0$]. Substituting the estimate $\hat{\sigma}^2$ derived earlier for σ^2 in Eq. (7-14), we get the estimated variance, and its square root is the standard error of $y'_f - \hat{\beta}\theta$. Hence

$$\frac{y'_f - \hat{\beta}\theta}{\sqrt{\hat{\sigma}^2(1 + 1/n + \theta^2/S_{xx})}}$$

has a t-distribution degrees of freedom $n - 2$. This can be used to construct a confidence interval for θ; for example, for a 95 percent confidence interval we find a value of t (from the t tables) with $n - 2$ degrees of freedom such that

$$P\left[\frac{\left(y'_f - \hat{\beta}\theta\right)^2}{\hat{\sigma}^2(1 + 1/n + \theta^2/S_{xx})} \leqslant t^2\right] = .95$$

To get the limits for θ, we solve the quadratic equation

$$\left(y'_f - \hat{\beta}\theta\right)^2 - t^2\hat{\sigma}^2\left(1 + \frac{1}{n} + \frac{\theta^2}{S_{xx}}\right) = 0 \qquad \text{(7-15)}$$

If θ_1 and θ_2 are the roots of this equation, these are the limits for $\hat{x}'_f$. The roots may turn out to be complex if $\hat{\beta}$ is not significantly different from zero. In this case we must conclude that any value $\hat{x}_f$ is acceptable. The limits obtained are often called *tolerance limits*, and the interval is called a *tolerance interval* rather than a confidence interval. Also it should be noted that the interval is not symmetric about $\hat{x}_f$.

As an example consider the regression equation based on 12 observations. The estimated equation is

$$y = -10.0 + .976x \qquad \bar{x} = 200.0 \qquad \bar{y} = 185.2 \qquad \hat{\sigma}^2 = .01 \qquad S_{xx} = 4000$$

Earlier we predicted y for a given value of $x = 250$. The prediction was $\hat{y} = 234$ and the 95 percent confidence interval was (233.65,234.35).

Consider now the prediction of x for $y = 234$. The point prediction is, of course, $\hat{x} = 250$. To get the tolerance interval for $\hat{x}$, we solve Eq. (7-15). Note that $y'_f = 234 - 185.2 = 48.8$ and $t = 2.228$ (from the t tables with 10 degrees of freedom). After simplifying, we get the tolerance interval (249.77,250.23), which is symmetric about $\hat{x} = 250$. However, this is because $\hat{\sigma}^2$ is very low and S_{xx} very high. If $\hat{\sigma}^2 = 5.0$ and $S_{xx} = 100$ (note that the r^2 in this case is still very high, .95), Eq. (7-15) simplifies to

$$.704\theta^2 - 95.26\theta + 2354.55 = 0$$

The two roots of this equation are $\theta_1 = 32.56$, $\theta_2 = 102.68$. Hence the tolerance interval for x is (232.56,302.68). Clearly, this is not symmetric about the point estimate $\hat{x} = 250$.

Exercises

1. Use ordinary least squares (OLS) to estimate the equation

$$y = \alpha + \beta x + u$$

where y – per-capita consumption
x = price per pound

Use the data in Table 7-5 for the years 1948–1962. Do this separately for beef, pork, lamb, veal, and chicken.

Calculate the standard errors r^2 and also 95 percent confidence intervals for α and β.

2. Repeat no. 1 but applying weighted least squares (WLS) on the assumption that

(i) $u_i \sim IN(0, \sigma^2 x_i^2)$

(ii) $u_i \sim IN(0, \sigma^2 x_i)$

3. Obtain the predicted values of y for 1963 in no. 1, using the reported values of x. Also obtain 95 percent confidence intervals for these predicted values.

4. In all the equations in no. 1 apply the Durbin-Watson test for first-order autocorrelation in the residuals.

5. Estimate the equation in no. 1 in first differences and quasi first differences (based on an estimated value of the first-order autocorrelation from the OLS residuals).

6. Explain the limitations of all the analysis done till now in view of what you see in Fig. 7-7.

CHAPTER

EIGHT

MULTIPLE REGRESSION

8-1 INTRODUCTION

In simple regression we study the relationship between a dependent variable y and an independent variable x. In multiple regression we study the relationship between y and a number of independent variables: $x_1, x_2, \ldots, x_k$. Often y is referred to as the "regressand" and $x_1, x_2, \ldots, x_k$ as the "regressors." The model we assume is

$$y_i = \alpha + \beta_1 x_{1i} + \beta_2 x_{2i} + \cdots + \beta_k x_{ki} + u_i \qquad i = 1,2, \ldots, n$$

The residuals u_i are again due to measurement errors in y and errors in the specification of the relationship between y and the x's. We make the same assumptions about the u_i as in the preceding chapter. Under these assumptions, the method of least squares gives estimators of $\alpha, \beta_1, \beta_2, \ldots, \beta_k$ that are unbiased and have minimum variance among the class of linear unbiased estimators. (Proofs are given in Appendix B.)

For illustrative purposes we will derive the estimating equations for three explanatory variables x_1, x_2, and x_3. We assume

$$y_i = \alpha + \beta_1 x_{1i} + \beta_2 x_{2i} + \beta_3 x_{3i} + u_i \qquad i = 1,2, \ldots, n \tag{8-1}$$

The least-squares method says that we should choose the estimators $\hat{\alpha}$, $\hat{\beta}_1$, $\hat{\beta}_2$, and $\hat{\beta}_3$ so as to minimize

$$Q = \sum (y_i - \hat{\alpha} - \hat{\beta}_1 x_{1i} - \hat{\beta}_2 x_{2i} - \hat{\beta}_2 x_{2i} - \hat{\beta}_3 x_{3i})^2$$

Differentiate Q with respect to $\hat{\alpha}$, $\hat{\beta}_1$, $\hat{\beta}_2$, and $\hat{\beta}_3$ and equate the derivatives to zero. We get

$$\frac{\partial Q}{\partial \hat{\alpha}} = 0 \rightarrow \sum 2(y_i - \hat{\alpha} - \hat{\beta}_1 x_{1i} - \hat{\beta}_2 x_{2i} - \hat{\beta}_3 x_{3i})(-1) = 0 \tag{8-2}$$

$$\frac{\partial Q}{\partial \hat{\beta}_1} = 0 \rightarrow \sum 2(y_i - \hat{\alpha} - \hat{\beta}_1 x_{1i} - \hat{\beta}_2 x_{2i} - \hat{\beta}_3 x_{3i})(-x_{1i}) = 0 \tag{8-3}$$

$$\frac{\partial Q}{\partial \hat{\beta}_2} = 0 \rightarrow \sum 2(y_i - \hat{\alpha} - \hat{\beta}_1 x_{1i} - \hat{\beta}_2 x_{2i} - \hat{\beta}_3 x_{3i})(-x_{2i}) = 0 \tag{8-4}$$

$$\frac{\partial Q}{\partial \hat{\beta}_3} = 0 \rightarrow \sum 2(y_i - \hat{\alpha} - \hat{\beta}_1 x_{1i} - \hat{\beta}_2 x_{2i} - \hat{\beta}_3 x_{3i})(-x_{3i}) = 0 \tag{8-5}$$

These four equations are called the "normal equations." They can be simplified as follows.

Equation (8-2) can be written as

$$\sum y_i = n\hat{\alpha} + \hat{\beta}_1 \sum x_{1i} + \hat{\beta}_2 \sum x_{2i} + \hat{\beta}_3 \sum x_{3i}$$

or

$$\bar{y} = \hat{\alpha} + \hat{\beta}_1 \bar{x}_1 + \hat{\beta}_2 \bar{x}_2 + \hat{\beta}_3 \bar{x}_3 \tag{8-6}$$

where $\bar{y} = \frac{1}{n} \sum y_i, \bar{x}_1 = \frac{1}{n} \sum x_{1i}, \bar{x}_2 = \frac{1}{n} \sum x_{2i}, \bar{x}_3 = \frac{1}{n} \sum x_{3i}$

Equation (8.3) can be written as

$$\sum x_{1i}\, y_i = \hat{\alpha} \sum x_{1i} + \hat{\beta}_1 \sum x_{1i}^2 + \hat{\beta}_2 \sum x_{1i} x_{2i} + \hat{\beta}_3 \sum x_{1i} x_{3i}$$

Substituting the value of $\hat{\alpha}$ from Eq. (8-6), we get

$$\sum x_{1i}\, y_i = n\bar{x}_1(\bar{y} - \hat{\beta}_1 \bar{x}_1 - \hat{\beta}_2 \bar{x}_2 - \hat{\beta}_3 \bar{x}_3) + \hat{\beta}_1 \sum x_{1i}^2 + \hat{\beta}_2 \sum x_{1i} x_{2i} + \hat{\beta}_3 \sum x_{1i} x_{3i} \tag{8-7}$$

Now let us define the following:

$$\begin{aligned}
S_{11} &= \sum x_{1i}^2 - n\bar{x}_1^2 & S_{1y} &= \sum x_{1i}\, y_i - n\bar{x}_1\, \bar{y} \\
S_{12} &= \sum x_{1i} x_{2i} - n\bar{x}_1 \bar{x}_2 & S_{2y} &= \sum x_{2i}\, y_i - n\bar{x}_2\, \bar{y} \\
S_{13} &= \sum x_{1i} x_{3i} - n\bar{x}_1 \bar{x}_3 & S_{3y} &= \sum x_{3i}\, y_i - n\bar{x}_3\, \bar{y} \\
S_{22} &= \sum x_{2i}^2 - n\bar{x}_2^2 & S_{yy} &= \sum y_i^2 - n\bar{y}^2 \\
S_{23} &= \sum x_{2i} x_{3i} - n\bar{x}_2 \bar{x}_3 & & \\
S_{33} &= \sum x_{3i}^2 - n\bar{x}_3^2 & &
\end{aligned} \tag{8-8}$$

Then Eq. (8-7) can be written as

$$S_{1y} = \hat{\beta}_1 S_{11} + \hat{\beta}_2 S_{12} + \hat{\beta}_3 S_{13} \tag{8-9}$$

By similar simplifications Eqs. (8-4) and (8-5) can be written as

$$S_{2y} = \hat{\beta}_1 S_{12} + \hat{\beta}_2 S_{22} + \hat{\beta}_3 S_{23} \tag{8-10}$$

$$S_{3y} = \hat{\beta}_1 S_{13} + \hat{\beta}_2 S_{23} + \hat{\beta}_3 S_{33} \tag{8-11}$$

Now we solve Eqs. (8-9), (8-10), and (8-11) for $\hat{\beta}_1$, $\hat{\beta}_2$, and $\hat{\beta}_3$. Then we substitute these values in (8-6) and get an estimate of $\hat{\alpha}$. The computational procedure would be:

1. First obtain all the means: $\bar{x}_1, \bar{x}_2, \bar{x}_3, y$.
2. Then obtain all the sums of squares and sums of products: $\sum x_{1i}^2, \sum x_{1i} x_{2i}$, etc.
3. Then obtain $S_{11}, S_{12}, \ldots,$ etc., and solve Eqs. (8-9), (8-10), and (8-11) to get $\hat{\beta}_1, \hat{\beta}_2, \hat{\beta}_3$.
4. Substituting these values in (8-6), we get

$$\hat{\alpha} = \bar{y} - \hat{\beta}_1 \bar{x}_1 - \hat{\beta}_2 \bar{x}_2 - \hat{\beta}_3 \bar{x}_3 \tag{8-12}$$

The solution of Eqs. (8-9), (8-10), and (8-11) has to be done by successive elimination. This can be done systematically on the desk calculator using what is known as the Doolittle method.[1] However, many packaged programs are available for use on the computers, and so we will not go through these methods here.

In simple regression the residual sum of squares was defined as $S_{yy} - \hat{\beta}_1 S_{xy}$ and r_{xy}^2 was defined as $\hat{\beta}_1 S_{xy}/S_{yy}$. The analogous expressions in multiple regression are

$$\text{RSS} = S_{yy} - \hat{\beta}_1 S_{1y} - \hat{\beta}_2 S_{2y} - \hat{\beta}_3 S_{3y} \tag{8-13}$$

and

$$R^2_{y \cdot x_1 x_2 x_3} = \frac{\hat{\beta}_1 S_{1y} + \hat{\beta}_2 S_{2y} + \hat{\beta}_3 S_{3y}}{S_{yy}} \tag{8-14}$$

We use the notation $y \cdot x_1 x_2 x_3$ in multiple correlation—the variable before the dot is the explained variable and the variables after the dot are the explanatory variables.

The formulas derived above can be written more compactly in matrix

[1] See P. S. Dwyer, "Linear Computations," John Wiley & Sons, Inc., New York, 1960. Also R. L. Anderson and T. A. Bancroft, "Statistical Theory in Research," McGraw-Hill Book Company, New York, 1952.

notation.[1] Also the analogy between simple and multiple regression can be more easily seen if we follow this notation. Define

$$\mathbf{S}_{xx} = \begin{bmatrix} S_{11} & S_{12} & S_{13} \\ S_{12} & S_{22} & S_{23} \\ S_{13} & S_{23} & S_{33} \end{bmatrix}$$

$$\mathbf{S}_{xy} = \begin{bmatrix} S_{1y} \\ S_{2y} \\ S_{3y} \end{bmatrix} \quad \text{and} \quad \hat{\boldsymbol{\beta}} = \begin{bmatrix} \hat{\beta}_1 \\ \hat{\beta}_2 \\ \hat{\beta}_3 \end{bmatrix}$$

Then Eqs. (8-9), (8-10), and (8-11) can be written as

$$\mathbf{S}_{xx}\hat{\boldsymbol{\beta}} = \mathbf{S}_{xy} \tag{8-15}$$

We assume that there are no linear dependencies among the x's. Then $\mathbf{S}_{xx}$ is a nonsingular matrix and its inverse exists.

Premultiplying both sides of Eq. (8-15) by $\mathbf{S}_{xx}^{-1}$, we get

$$\mathbf{I}\hat{\boldsymbol{\beta}} = \mathbf{S}_{xx}^{-1}\mathbf{S}_{xy}$$

Hence

$$\hat{\boldsymbol{\beta}} = \mathbf{S}_{xx}^{-1}\mathbf{S}_{xy}.$$

This equation is analogous to the equation obtained in simple regression. Also, if we denote

$$\bar{\mathbf{x}} = \begin{bmatrix} \bar{x}_1 \\ \bar{x}_2 \\ \bar{x}_3 \end{bmatrix}$$

then Eqs. (8-12), (8-13), and (8-14) can be written as

$$\hat{\alpha} = \bar{y} - \hat{\boldsymbol{\beta}}'\bar{\mathbf{x}}$$

$$\text{RSS} = S_{yy} - \hat{\boldsymbol{\beta}}'\mathbf{S}_{xy}$$

$$R^2_{y \cdot x_1 x_2 x_3} = \frac{\hat{\boldsymbol{\beta}}'\mathbf{S}_{xy}}{S_{yy}}$$

These formulas are analogous to the formulas given for simple regression.

Also if $\sigma^2\mathbf{C}$ is the matrix of variances and covariances of $\hat{\beta}_1$, $\hat{\beta}_2$, and $\hat{\beta}_3$, then $\sigma^2\mathbf{C} = \sigma^2\mathbf{S}_{xx}^{-1}$. This is also analogous to the formula for variance of $\hat{\beta}$ derived in simple regression. The advantage with the matrix notation is that we can write the formulas compactly whatever the number of regressors (we derived the

[1] See Appendix A for an introduction to matrix algebra.

formulas for three variables for simplicity). If we have k regressors, $\mathbf{S}_{xx}$ and $\mathbf{C}$ are $k \times k$ matrices and $\hat{\boldsymbol{\beta}}$, $\mathbf{S}_{xy}$, $\bar{\mathbf{x}}$ are k vectors.

8-2 REGRESSION WITH NO CONSTANT TERM

Sometimes we want to estimate the regression Eq. (8-1) with the constant term α excluded. This is also called regression through the origin because if the x's are all zero, y is also equal to zero. We will be considering this model if the equation derived from economic theory does not involve a constant term or, as we shall see later, we make suitable transformations of the variables and end up with an equation with no constant term.

The normal equations will be the same as before except that Eqs. (8-2) and (8-6) will not be there. Since there is no constant term, there will be no "mean corrections." The expressions in Eq. (8-8) will all be defined without "mean corrections," for example,

$$S_{11} = \sum x_{1i}^2 \qquad \text{and not} \qquad \sum x_{1i}^2 - n\bar{x}_1^2$$

$$S_{12} = \sum x_{1i}x_{2i} \qquad \text{and not} \qquad \sum x_{1i}x_{2i} - n\bar{x}_1\bar{x}_2 \qquad \text{etc.}$$

After these changes are made, $\hat{\beta} = S_{xx}^{-1}S_{xy}$ as before. Formulas (8-13) and (8-14) still hold good with the redefinitions of S_{1y}, S_{2y}, S_{3y}, and S_{yy}.

Many computer regression routines allow the option of including or excluding the constant term. However, most of them do not give the correct R^2, in the latter option. Sometimes these reported R^2's are even negative. The reason is that the R^2 is computed from the equation $R^2 = 1 - \text{RSS}/S_{yy}$, and if the residual sum of squares RSS is computed from a regression with no constant term and S_{yy} is computed adjusting for its mean, then it can happen that $\text{RSS} > S_{yy}$. Thus R^2 will be negative. Even if R^2 is not negative, it can be very small, and it is desirable to check the computer programs in such cases and see how the R^2 is computed before trying to interpret the results. Some other programs compute R^2 as $1 - \text{RSS}/\sum y_i^2$. This gives very high R^2 if $\bar{y}$ is very high.[1]

8-3 PARTIAL CORRELATIONS AND MULTIPLE CORRELATION

If we have an explained variable y and three explanatory variables x_1, x_2, x_3, then $r_{yx_1}^2$, $r_{yx_2}^2$, and $r_{yx_3}^2$, respectively, measure the proportion of the variance in y that x_1 *alone*, x_2 *alone*, and x_3 *alone* explain. On the other hand, $R_{y \cdot x_1x_2x_3}^2$ measures the proportion of the variance in y that x_1, x_2, x_3 *together* explain. We would also want to know something else. For example, how much does x_2 explain *after* x_1 is included? How much does x_3 explain after x_1 and x_2 are included? These are measured by the *partial* correlation coefficients. $r_{yx_2 \cdot x_1}^2$ measures the correlation between y and x_2 after x_1 has been allowed its effect. (The variables after the

[1] David Grether pointed out to me that the program at Yale did this, and often students would report that they got a "better fit" without an intercept term than with it. The moral is that one has to be careful.

dot are the variables already included.) After x_1 is included, the unexplained variation in y is $S_{yy}(1 - r^2_{yx_1})$, and $r^2_{yx_2 \cdot x_1}$ measures the proportion of this residual variation that x_2 explains. Similarly, $r^2_{yx_3 x_1 x_2}$ measures the proportion of the residual variation in y that x_3 explains—the residual being what is left unexplained after x_1 and x_2 are included. With three explanatory variables we have the following partial correlations: $r^2_{yx_1 \cdot x_2}$, $r^2_{yx_1 \cdot x_3}$, $r^2_{yx_2 \cdot x_1}$, $r^2_{yx_2 \cdot x_3}$, $r^2_{yx_3 \cdot x_1}$, and $r^2_{yx_3 \cdot x_2}$. These are called partial correlations of the *first order*. Then we have the following partial correlations of the *second order:*

$$r^2_{yx_1 \cdot x_2 x_3} \quad r^2_{yx_2 \cdot x_1 x_3} \quad r^2_{yx_3 \cdot x_1 x_2}$$

Always the variables after the dot are the variables already included. The usual convention is to denote simple and partial correlations by small r and multiple correlations by capital R, for example, $R^2_{y \cdot x_1 x_2}$, $R^2_{y \cdot x_1 x_3}$, $R^2_{y \cdot x_2 x_3}$, $R^2_{y \cdot x_1 x_2 x_3}$, etc.

Partial correlations are very important in deciding whether or not to include more explanatory variables; for example, $r^2_{yx_2}$ may be very high but $r^2_{yx_2 \cdot x_1}$ may be very low. What this says is, if x_2 alone is used to explain y, it can do a good job. But after x_1 is included, x_2 does not help any more in explaining y; that is, x_1 has done the job of x_2. In this case there is no use including the variable x_2.

Suppose we are given two explanatory variables x_1 and x_2 and we are asked to choose one or both. The best procedure would be first to look at $r^2_{yx_1}$ and $r^2_{yx_2}$, then include the one that has the higher correlation. If x_1 is first chosen, we next look at $r^2_{yx_2 \cdot x_1}$ and include x_2 only if this is high. If x_2 is chosen first, we decide about x_1 after looking at $r^2_{yx_1 \cdot x_2}$. Sometimes we may just decide to use a combination of x_1 and x_2 instead of the two variables separately. For example, suppose x_1 and x_2 are amount of skilled labor and unskilled labor, respectively, and y is output. Suppose $r^2_{yx_1}$ and $r^2_{yx_2}$ are both high but $r^2_{yx_1 \cdot x_2}$ and $r^2_{yx_2 \cdot x_1}$ are both very low. Then what this suggests is that the separation of total labor into two components—skilled and unskilled—does not help us much in explaining output. So, we might as well use $x_1 + x_2$ or total labor as the explanatory variable.

In some cases the order in which variables are included is automatically determined. For example, suppose we want to explain y in terms of a polynomial in x, that is, $y = a + b_1 x + b_2 x^2 + b_3 x^3 + b_4 x^4 +$ etc. This is a multiple regression with $x_1 = x$, $x_2 = x^2$, $x_3 = x^3$, $x_4 = x^4$, etc. Here, of course, we will include x_1 first, x_2 next, x_3 next, and so on, and stop at the point where the contribution of the next variable is negligible.

8-4 RELATIONSHIP AMONG SIMPLE, PARTIAL, AND MULTIPLE CORRELATION COEFFICIENTS

Suppose we have two explanatory variables x_1 and x_2.

$S_{yy}(1 - R^2_{y \cdot x_1 x_2})$ is the residual sum of squares (RSS) after x_1 and x_2 are both included.

$S_{yy}\left(1 - r^2_{yx_1}\right)$ is the RSS after only x_1 is included.

$r^2_{yx_2\cdot x_1}$ is the proportion of this residual explained by x_2. Hence the unexplained residual after x_2 also is included is

$$\left(1 - r^2_{yx_2\cdot x_1}\right)S_{yy}\left(1 - r^2_{yx_1}\right)$$

But this is $S_{yy}(1 - R^2_{y\cdot x_1x_2})$. Therefore,

$$1 - R^2_{y\cdot x_1x_2} = \left(1 - r^2_{yx_1}\right)\left(1 - r^2_{yx_2\cdot x_1}\right)$$

Similarly if we have three explanatory variables,

$$1 - R^2_{y\cdot x_1x_2x_3} = \left(1 - r^2_{yx_1}\right)\left(1 - r^2_{yx_2\cdot x_1}\right)\left(1 - r^2_{yx_3\cdot x_1x_2}\right)$$

and if we have four explanatory variables,

$$1 - R^2_{y\cdot x_1x_2x_3x_4} = \left(1 - r^2_{yx_1}\right)\left(1 - r^2_{yx_2\cdot x_1}\right)\left(1 - r^2_{yx_3\cdot x_1x_2}\right)\left(1 - r^2_{yx_4\cdot x_1x_2x_3}\right)$$

Note that the subscripts 1,2,3,4 can be interchanged in any order. That is, for the order 3,4,1,2 we have

$$1 - R^2_{y\cdot x_1x_2x_3x_4} = \left(1 - r^2_{yx_3}\right)\left(1 - r^2_{yx_4\cdot x_3}\right)\left(1 - r^2_{yx_1\cdot x_3x_4}\right)\left(1 - r^2_{yx_2\cdot x_1x_3x_4}\right)$$

8-5 STATISTICAL INFERENCE IN THE MULTIPLE REGRESSION MODEL

Again, as in the simple regression case we do not need to assume that the residuals u_i are normally distributed to derive the least-squares estimators. However, to obtain any confidence intervals or to apply any tests of significance, we do need to make the assumption of normality. Also when we make this assumption, the least-squares estimators of the regression parameters can be, as before, shown to be identical to the ML estimators.

Under the assumptions made about the u_i that $u_i \sim IN(0,\sigma^2)$ it can be shown (proofs are in Appendix B) that:

1. The least-squares estimator $\hat{\boldsymbol{\beta}} = \mathbf{S}_{xx}^{-1}\mathbf{S}_{xy}$ is normally distributed with mean $\boldsymbol{\beta}$ and covariance matrix $\sigma^2\mathbf{S}_{xx}^{-1}$. We will write this as $\hat{\beta}_i \sim N(\beta_i, c_{ii}\sigma^2)$ and $\text{cov}\,(\hat{\beta}_i, \hat{\beta}_j) = c_{ij}\sigma^2$, where c_{ij} is the (i,j)th element in $\mathbf{C} = \mathbf{S}_{xx}^{-1}$.
2. If the residual sum of squares RSS is defined as $\text{RSS} = S_{yy} - \hat{\boldsymbol{\beta}}'\mathbf{S}_{xy}$, then RSS/σ^2 has a χ^2-distribution degrees of freedom $(n - k - 1)$ and $\hat{\sigma}^2 = \text{RSS}/(n - k - 1)$ is an unbiased estimator for σ^2.
3. With $\hat{\sigma}^2$ defined as in 2, $t_i = (\hat{\beta}_i - \beta_i)/\sqrt{c_{ii}}\,\hat{\sigma}$ has a t-distribution degrees of freedom $(n - k - 1)$ for each i.

   Also, the partial correlation between y and x_i (after including all the other x's) is given by

$$r^2_{yx_i\cdot(\text{other variables})} = \frac{t_i^2}{t_i^2 + (n - k - 1)}$$

where t_i is calculated substituting $\beta_i = 0$.[1] The t distributions and the χ^2 distribution can be used to make confidence-interval statements or to apply tests of significance as in the simple regression case. Note also that t_i^2 has an F-distribution degrees of freedom $1, n-k-1$. Sometimes it is easier to talk in terms of F ratios rather than t ratios.

4. For tests of significance and confidence-interval statements in the case of an individual coefficient, we use the t ratios. When we consider more than two coefficients together, we use the F ratio. In this case we have confidence regions rather than intervals. For example, suppose we consider β_1 and β_2. Then

$$F = \frac{1}{2(c_{11}c_{22} - c_{12}^2)\hat{\sigma}^2}\left[c_{22}(\hat{\beta}_1 - \beta_1)^2 - 2c_{12}(\hat{\beta}_1 - \beta_1)(\hat{\beta}_2 - \beta_2) + c_{11}(\hat{\beta}_2 - \beta_2)^2\right]$$

has an F-distribution degrees of freedom $2, n-k-1$. From the F tables we can find a value F_0 such that $P(F < F_0) = .95$ (say). Then the 95 percent confidence region for β_1 and β_2 is given by $F \leqslant F_0$. What we get is an ellipse centered at $(\hat{\beta}_1, \hat{\beta}_2)$ as shown in Fig. 8-1. It is important to note that the 95 percent confidence interval for β_1 (or β_2) cannot be obtained simply by taking the limits of β_1 (or β_2) from this ellipse.

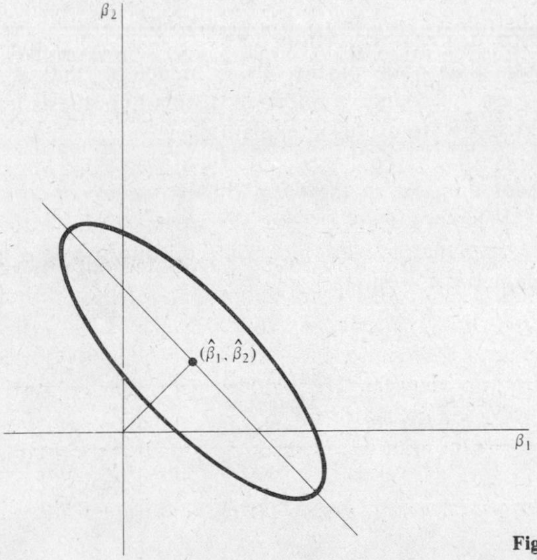

Figure 8-1 A confidence region.

[1] This formula, also often compactly written as $r^2 = t^2/(t^2 + \mathrm{df})$, is very useful in practice.

The above F ratio can be used to test any hypothesis about β_1 and β_2. What we do is substitute the given values of β_1 and β_2 in F and then find the probability of obtaining a value of F as high as or higher than the observed value. If this probability is small, we reject the hypothesis.

The F test can also be derived in a different way. We will just describe the procedure (the proof can be found in Appendix B). We first compute the residual sum of squares as usual. Call this URSS (unrestricted residual sum of squares). Next we compute the residual sum of squares with the specified values of β_1 and β_2 substituted. If these are β_1^*, β_2^*, we regress $y - \beta_1^* x_1 - \beta_2^* x_2$ on all the x's except x_1 and x_2. Call this residual sum of squares RRSS (restricted residual sum of squares). Obviously RRSS > URSS because the restricted minimum is greater than the unrestricted minimum. Then

$$F = \frac{(\text{RRSS} - \text{URSS})/2}{\text{URSS}/(n-k-1)}$$

has an F-distribution degrees of freedom 2, $n - k - 1$.

5. In the special case the hypothesis is

$$\beta_1 = \beta_2 = \cdots = \beta_k = 0$$

we have URSS $= S_{yy}(1 - R^2)$ as derived before and RRSS $= S_{yy}$.

Hence the test is given by

$$F = \frac{\left[S_{yy} - S_{yy}(1-R^2)\right]/k}{\left[S_{yy}(1-R^2)\right]/(n-k-1)} = \frac{R^2}{1-R^2}\,\frac{n-k-1}{k}$$

which has an F-distribution degrees of freedom k, $n - k - 1$. What this test does is test the hypothesis that none of the x's influence y; that is, the regression Eq. (8-1) is useless. Of course, a rejection of this hypothesis leaves us with the question: Which x's are useful in explaining y?

It is customary to present this test in the form of an *analysis-of-variance* table as shown in Table 8-1. What we do is analyze the variance of y into two components: that due to the explanatory variables x's (i.e., due to regression) and that which is left unexplained (i.e., residual).

Table 8-1

Source of variation	Sum of squares (SS)	Degrees of freedom (df)	Mean square = (SS/df)	F
Regression	$R^2 S_{yy}$	k	$R^2 S_{yy}/k = \text{MS}_1$	$F = \dfrac{\text{MS}_1}{\text{MS}_2}$
Residual	$(1 - R^2)S_{yy}$	$n - k - 1$	$(1 - R^2)S_{yy}/(n - k - 1) = \text{MS}_2$	
Total	S_{yy}	$n - 1$		

8-6 ILLUSTRATIONS

Consumption function. Consider the data in Table 7-1 excluding the war years. Instead of regressing per-capita consumer expenditures (in 1958 prices) on per-capita disposable income (in 1958 prices), we can run a regression of total consumer expenditures (in 1958 prices) on total disposable income (in 1958 prices) and population. We get

$$C = -28.2356 + \underset{(.0246)}{.8139Y} + \underset{(.000109)}{.000364N}$$

$$R^2 = .999 \qquad \text{DW} = 1.39$$

The variables Y and N together explain 99.9 percent of the variation in C. The residuals do not exhibit any conspicuously systematic pattern. Since the number of observations is $n = 38$, we apply the t and χ^2 tests with degrees of freedom $38 - 2 - 1 = 35$. Using the t tables for 35 degrees of freedom we find that the 95 percent confidence interval for the coefficient of Y is $.814 \pm 2.03(.0246)$ and for the coefficient of N is $.000364 \pm 2.03(.000109)$. These intervals are, respectively, (.764,.864) and (.000143,.000585). Thus, if one specifies the hypothesis that the marginal propensity to consume (holding N constant) is 0.9, then this hypothesis would be rejected at the 5 percent level. If

$$t_1 = \frac{.8139}{.0246} = 33.085 \qquad \text{and} \qquad t_2 = \frac{.000364}{.000109} = 3.339$$

then the partial correlations are given by

$$r^2_{CY \cdot N} = \frac{t_1^2}{t_1^2 + 35} = .976 \qquad r^2_{CN \cdot Y} = \frac{t_2^2}{t_2^2 + 35} = .242$$

Since we know $R^2_{C \cdot YN}$, we can also calculate the simple correlations r^2_{CY} and r^2_{CN}. (Actually the computer program gives these, but they are not reported here.) We have

$$\left(1 - R^2_{C \cdot YN}\right) = \left(1 - r^2_{CY}\right)\left(1 - r^2_{CN \cdot Y}\right)$$

or $(1 - .999) = (1 - r^2_{CY})(1 - .242)$. Hence $r^2_{CY} = .999$. Similarly,

$$\left(1 - R^2_{C \cdot YN}\right) = \left(1 - r^2_{CN}\right)\left(1 - r^2_{CY \cdot N}\right)$$

or

$$(1 - .999) = \left(1 - r^2_{CY}\right)(1 - .976)$$

Hence $r^2_{CN} = .958$. Thus, though C and N are both highly correlated, the correlation between C and N after removing the effect of Y is considerably smaller. The r^2 falls from .958 to .242.

One question that is worth asking at this stage is whether to use population N as an extra variable as in this example or to use it as a deflator as in the example considered in the preceding chapter. That is, do we estimate the equation

$$\frac{C}{N} = \alpha + \beta \frac{Y}{N} + u \tag{8-16}$$

or

$$C = \alpha + \beta_1 Y + \beta_2 N + u \tag{8-17}$$

A similar question also arises regarding prices. Do we treat the price index as a deflator or as an additional explanatory variable? The answers to these questions are not easy, and we have to consider several factors like how the aggregate consumption functions we are considering are derived, what economic theory says about the consumption behavior of the microunits, what the behavior of residuals is, and which function is stable over time. We will be discussing such factors as we go on. For the present we will see the nature of the problems that arise.

Let us first discuss the question of the population variable N. Suppose the consumption functions of the N individual units are given by

$$c_j = \alpha + \beta y_j + w_j \qquad j = 1,2, \ldots, N$$

Suppose the residuals w_j are mutually independent and have a common variance λ^2. The parameters α, β, and λ^2 are the same for all individuals. Summing over j, we get the aggregate consumption function:

$$\sum c_j = \sum \alpha + \beta \sum y_j + \sum w_j$$

$$C = \alpha N + \beta Y + W \qquad \text{where} \qquad \text{var}(W) = N \cdot \lambda^2 \tag{8-18}$$

Suppose we divide throughout by N. We get

$$\frac{C}{N} = \alpha + \beta \cdot \frac{Y}{N} + \frac{W}{N} \qquad \text{and} \qquad \text{var}\left(\frac{W}{N}\right) = \frac{1}{N^2}\,\text{var}(W) = \frac{\lambda^2}{N} \tag{8-19}$$

Thus we end up with equations of the form Eqs. (8-16) and (8-17); but comparing (8-19) with (8-16), we see that the error variance is not constant but proportional to $1/N$. Similarly, comparing Eqs. (8-18) with (8-17), we see that there is no constant term and again the error variance is not constant but is proportional to N. Both the Eqs. (8-18) and (8-19) can be transformed to an equation with constant residual variance. The resulting equation is

$$\frac{C}{\sqrt{N}} = \alpha\sqrt{N} + \beta \cdot \frac{Y}{\sqrt{N}} + u \tag{8-20}$$

where $u = W/\sqrt{N}$ has a constant variance λ^2.

Thus, if we start with the theory of microbehavior that is outlined above, we end up with an aggregate consumption function of the form Eq. (8-20) which is neither of the functions we have estimated. Equation (8-20) says that we should be estimating a regression of $C/\sqrt{N}$ on $\sqrt{N}$ and $Y/\sqrt{N}$ *without a constant term.* This is not to say that estimating Eq. (8-20) is the right thing to do and estimating (8-16) and (8-17) as we have done is wrong. Several other factors are involved beyond the one we have discussed here. What we have illustrated is a set of restrictive microbehavioral equations that when aggregated give us an idea of how to treat N in the aggregated consumption function. We will be discussing these points in greater detail when we come to the problem of aggregation.

Regarding the treatment of the price index, the crucial question is whether there is money illusion or not. If there is no money illusion, we should just estimate a regression equation of real consumer expenditures on real disposable income.

Demand for food. As another example, consider the data in Table 8-2 giving data on per-capita food consumption, price of food, and per-capita income.[1] Waugh estimates the following demand functions:

For 1927–1941:

$$\log q = 1.98 - \underset{(.05)}{0.24} \log p + \underset{(.02)}{0.24} \log y \qquad R^2 = .907 \tag{8-21}$$

1948–1962:

$$\log q = 2.19 - \underset{(.15)}{0.24} \log p + \underset{(.05)}{0.14} \log y \qquad R^2 = .874 \tag{8-22}$$

For both periods combined, he estimates another equation that allows for interaction between price and income. The equation is

$$\log q = 3.49 - \underset{(.37)}{1.00} \log p - \underset{(.41)}{.72} \log y + \underset{(.21)}{0.49} \log p \cdot \log y \qquad R^2 = .977 \tag{8-23}$$

The income coefficient now has a low t value, and the sign also appears to be wrong at first sight. However, we will see that we get positive income elasticities. The elasticities from Eq. (8-23) are given by

$$E_{qy} = \frac{d \log q}{d \log y} = -0.72 + .49 \log p$$

This ranges from .202 to .271 in the range of values for $\log p$ in Table 8-2. The price elasticity is given by

$$E_{qp} = \frac{d \log q}{d \log p} = -1.00 + .049 \log y$$

Thus, as income increases, demand for food becomes more price inelastic. For the range of values for $\log y$ in Table 8-2, E_{qp} ranges from .196 to .004.

Because of the high intercorrelations between $\log p$ and $\log y$ it is not usually possible to estimate the interaction term. Cramer[2] estimates the interac-

[1] The data are from Frederick V. Waugh, Demand and Price Analysis—Some Examples from Agriculture, *U.S. Department of Agriculture Technical Bulletin* 1316, November 1964, p. 16. The value of y for 1955 has been corrected to 96.5 from 86.5 in that table.

[2] J. S. Cramer, Interaction of Income and Price in Consumer Demand, *International Economic Review*, June 1973. One can argue for other interaction terms involving higher powers of $\log y$ and $\log p$. However, what we need is a simple model that captures the idea that the price elasticity might vary with income. Equation (8-23) does this in a simple way.

Table 8-2 Indexes of food consumption, food price, and consumer income

1957–1959 = 100			
Year	Food consumption per capita (q)	Food price* (p)	Consumer income† (y)
1927	88.9	91.7	57.7
1928	88.9	92.0	59.3
1929	89.1	93.1	62.0
1930	88.7	90.9	56.3
1931	88.0	82.3	52.7
1932	85.9	76.3	44.4
1933	86.0	78.3	43.8
1934	87.1	84.3	47.8
1935	85.4	88.1	52.1
1936	88.5	88.0	58.0
1937	88.4	88.4	59.8
1938	88.6	83.5	55.9
1939	91.7	82.4	60.3
1940	93.3	83.0	64.1
1941	95.1	86.2	73.7
(World War II years excluded)			
1948	96.7	105.3	82.1
1949	96.7	102.0	83.1
1950	98.0	102.4	88.6
1951	96.1	105.4	88.3
1952	98.1	105.0	89.1
1953	99.1	102.6	92.1
1954	99.1	101.9	91.7
1955	99.8	100.8	96.5
1956	101.5	100.0	99.8
1957	99.9	99.8	99.9
1958	99.1	101.2	98.4
1959	101.0	98.8	101.8
1960	100.7	98.4	101.8
1961	100.8	98.8	103.1
1962	101.0	98.4	105.5
1963‡	101.8	98.4	107.9

* Retail prices of Bureau of Labor Statistics, deflated by dividing by Consumer Price Index.

† Per-capita disposable income, deflated by dividing by Consumer Price Index.

‡ 1963 data are preliminary. They were not used on the analysis.

tion term from cross-section data for 13 commodities. The data are from the British National Food Survey covering 2000 households. They cover 40 consecutive quarterly surveys for the years 1960–1969, and 6 income classes. Thus there are 240 observations. Some typical equations where the interaction terms are significant are:

Butter: $\log q = \text{constant} - \underset{(.054)}{.259} \log p + \underset{(.017)}{.246} \log y + \underset{(.15)}{.55} \log p \cdot \log y$

Carrots: $\log q = \text{constant} - \underset{(.048)}{.379} \log p + \underset{(.044)}{.156} \log y + \underset{(.13)}{.51} \log p \cdot \log y$

Tea: $\log q = \text{constant} + \underset{(.033)}{.239} \log p - \underset{(.016)}{.355} \log y + \underset{(.13)}{.63} \log p \cdot \log y$

The equation for tea has a wrong sign for the price coefficient. The coefficient for $\log y$ also appears wrong, unless tea is considered an inferior or a Giffen good, but we cannot tell whether income elasticity is positive or negative unless we know the range of $\log p$ [as in Eq. (8-23)]. Anyway, the equation shows that some very important variable (perhaps the price of coffee) has been omitted. The equation for tea is an instructive example of coefficients that are "very significant" but have the wrong signs, thus indicating serious errors of specification.

Hospital costs. As yet another example, consider the analysis of hospital costs by case mix by Feldstein.[1] The data are for 177 hospitals. The dependent variable is average cost per case. The independent variables are proportions of cases treated in each category. There are nine categories: M = medical, P = pediatrics, S = general surgery, E = ENT, T = traumatic and orthopedic surgery, OS = other surgery, G = gynecology, Ob = obstetrics, Other = miscellaneous others. The regression coefficients, their standard errors, t values, partial r^2's, simple r^2's, and average cost per case are given in Table 8-3. Also an analysis-of-variance table like Table 8-1 is presented in Table 8-4 for illustrative purposes.

The 1 percent value of F for degrees of freedom 8168 from the F tables is 2.51. Thus the value of 9.33 is highly significant. All this means is that the

Table 8-3 Hospital cost regressions

Variable	Regression coefficient	SE	t ratio	Partial r^2	Simple r^2	Average cost per case
M	44.97	18.89	2.38	.0326	.1423	114.48
P	− 44.54	28.51	− 1.56	.0143	.0074	24.97
S	− 36.81	14.88	− 2.47	.0350	.0343	32.70
E	− 54.26	16.52	− 3.28	.0612	.0947	15.25
T	− 29.82	17.18	− 1.74	.0177	.0062	39.69
OS	28.51	20.27	1.41	.0117	.0478	98.02
G	− 10.79	21.47	− 0.50	.0015	.0099	58.72
Ob	− 34.63	16.34	− 2.12	.0261	.0011	34.88
Other	0					69.51
Constant	69.51					

$R^2 = .3076$.

[1] M. S. Feldstein, "Economic Analysis for Health Service Industry," Chap. 1, North-Holland Publishing Co., Amsterdam, 1967.

Table 8-4 Analysis of variance

Source	Sum of squares	df	Mean square	F
Regression	10,357	8	1294.625	9.33
Residual	23,311	168	138.756	
Total	33,668	176		

case-mix variables are important in explaining the variation in average cost per case between the hospitals. The coefficients in Table 8-3 need some explanation. The t values are just the coefficients divided by the respective standard errors. The partial r^2's are obtained by the formula

$$r^2 = \frac{t^2}{t^2 + \text{df}}$$

Thus, for the variable M,

$$\text{Partial } r^2 = \frac{(2.38)^2}{(2.38)^2 + 168} = .0326$$

The simple r^2 is just the square of the correlation of average cost per case and the proportion of the cases in that category. The two are presented together to illustrate how the partial r^2's can be lower or higher than the simple r^2's.

The regression coefficients in this example have to be interpreted in a different way. In the usual case, each regression coefficient measures the change in the dependent variable y for unit increase in that independent variable, *holding other variables constant*. In this example, since the independent variables are proportions in that category, an increase in one variable holding other variables constant does not make sense (in fact it is impossible to do it). The proper interpretation of the coefficients in this case is this: Put the value of $M = 1$, all others 0. Then the estimated value of the dependent variable = (constant + coefficient of M) = 69.51 + 44.97 = 114.48. This is the average cost of treating a case in M. Similarly constant + coefficient of P = 69.51 − 44.54 = 24.97 is the average cost of treating a case in P. Finally putting $M, P, \ldots, Ob$ all = 0, we get the constant term = 69.51 as the average cost of treating a case in the "others" category. These coefficients are all presented in the last column of Table 8-3. What the regression equation enables us to estimate in this case is the average cost of treating a case in each category. The standard errors of these estimates can be calculated as $\text{SE}(\hat{\alpha} + \hat{\beta}_i)$ if we know the covariance between the constant term $\hat{\alpha}$ and the other regression coefficient $\hat{\beta}$.[1]

This example illustrates how to interpret a multiple regression equation in which the independent variables are proportions.

[1] Since the figures presented by Feldstein do not enable us to compute these, we have not computed them.

8-7 BETA COEFFICIENTS

Some regression programs also present what are known as *beta coefficients*.[1] The argument is that the regression coefficients we have considered till now depend on the units of measurement of the variables and that they can be made more comparable by expressing each variable in terms of its own standard deviation. Ezekiel says that for comparison between problems where the standard deviations are much different, the beta coefficients may have value.

Consider the regression equation we discussed earlier

$$y = \hat{\alpha} + \hat{\beta}_1 x_1 + \hat{\beta}_2 x_2 + \hat{\beta}_3 x_3$$

If σ_1, σ_2, σ_3, and σ_y are the standard deviations of x_1, x_2, x_3, and y, respectively, and if the estimates of the regression coefficients when the variables are all defined in terms of standard-deviation units are α^*, β_1^*, β_2^*, and β_3^*, we have

$$\frac{y}{\sigma_y} = \alpha^* + \beta_1^* \frac{x_1}{\sigma_1} + \beta_2^* \frac{x_2}{\sigma_2} + \beta_3^* \frac{x_3}{\sigma_3}$$

or

$$y = \alpha^* \sigma_y + \left(\beta_1^* \frac{\sigma_y}{\sigma_1} \right) x_1 + \frac{\beta_2^* \sigma_y}{\sigma_2} x_2 + \frac{\beta_3^* \sigma_y}{\sigma_3} x_3$$

Comparing the two equations, we find that the relationship between the usual regression estimates and the beta coefficients is given by

$$\hat{\alpha} = \alpha^* \sigma_y \qquad \hat{\beta}_1 = \beta_1^* \frac{\sigma_y}{\sigma_1} \qquad \hat{\beta}_2 = \beta_2^* \frac{\sigma_y}{\sigma_2} \qquad \text{and} \qquad \hat{\beta}_3 = \beta_3^* \frac{\sigma_y}{\sigma_3}$$

What the usual regression coefficients measure is the change in the explained variable for unit change in each explanatory variable (holding other variables constant). What the beta coefficients measure is the change in the explained variable (in standard-deviation units) for unit change in each explanatory variable (in standard-deviation units) holding other variables constant. In simple regression the beta coefficient is identical to the correlation coefficient because $\beta^* = \hat{\beta}(\sigma_x/\sigma_y) =$ correlation coefficient r_{xy}. However, in multiple regression there is no relationship between the beta coefficients and the simple- or partial-correlation coefficients. Hence, often not much use is made of the beta coefficients.

8-8 PREDICTION

The formulas for prediction in multiple regression are similar to those in the case of simple regression, except that to compute the standard error of the predicted value we now need the covariance matrix of all the regression coefficients. Since

[1] M. Ezekiel, "Methods of Correlation Analysis," 2d ed., p. 217, John Wiley & Sons, Inc., New York, 1941, for a discussion of beta coefficients.

the formula can be more compactly written in matrix notation, it is presented in Appendix B.

One important point to note is that even if the R^2 for the estimated regression equation is very high, it does not necessarily follow that the predictions we get of future values will be good. The accuracy of predictions will depend on the stability of the coefficients between the period used for estimation and the period used for prediction. One classic example of where R^2's could be high but subsequent predictions poor is equations that study the determination of stock prices. Given any particular period, it is not inconceivable that we could find variables that will explain the stock price index with a high R^2. However, this relationship is often useless for predictive purposes.

Sometimes, even the "independent" variables themselves are forecast values. In this case one has to take account of their variance in computing the variance of the predicted value of y.[1]

8-9 DEGREES OF FREEDOM AND $\bar{R}^2$

If we have n observations and estimate four regression parameters as in Eq. (8-1), we can see from the normal equations (8-2) to (8-5) that the estimated residuals $\hat{u}_i$ satisfy four linear restrictions

$$\sum \hat{u}_i = 0$$

$$\sum x_{1i}\hat{u}_i = 0$$

$$\sum x_{2i}\hat{u}_i = 0 \qquad (8\text{-}24)$$

and $$\sum x_{3i}\hat{u}_i = 0$$

or in essence there are only $(n-4)$ residuals free to vary, because, given the values of any $(n-4)$ residuals, the remaining four can be found by solving Eqs. (8-24). This point we express by saying that there are $(n-4)$ degrees of freedom. The estimate of the residual variance $\hat{\sigma}^2$ is equal to $\sum \hat{u}_i^2/(n-4)$ or the residual sum of squares RSS divided by the degrees of freedom. As we increase the number of explanatory variables, both the numerator and the denominator of $\hat{\sigma}^2$ decrease. What happens to $\hat{\sigma}^2$ will depend on the proportional decreases in the numerator and the denominator. Thus there will come a point when $\hat{\sigma}^2$ will actually start increasing as we keep adding additional explanatory variables. It is often suggested that we should choose that set of explanatory variables for which $\hat{\sigma}^2$ is minimum. We will discuss the rationale behind this procedure later. (In the limiting case, when the number of constants estimated is equal to the number of observations, we get $\hat{\sigma}^2 = 0/0$.)

[1] See M. S. Feldstein, The Error of Forecast in Econometric Models When the Forecast-Period Exogenous Variables Are Stochastic, *Econometrica*, Jan. 1971.

This is also the reason why, in multiple regression problems, it is customary to report what is known as *adjusted* R^2, denoted by $\bar{R}^2$. The measure R^2 defined earlier keeps on increasing (till it reaches 1.0) as we add extra explanatory variables and thus does not take account of the degrees-of-freedom problem. $\bar{R}^2$ is simply R^2 adjusted for degrees of freedom. It is defined by the relation

$$1 - \bar{R}^2 = \frac{n-1}{n-k-1}(1 - R^2) \tag{8-25}$$

where k is the number of regressors. We subtract $(k + 1)$ from n because we estimate a constant term in addition to the coefficients of these k regressors. We can write (8-25) as

$$\frac{(1 - \bar{R}^2)S_{yy}}{n-1} = \frac{(1 - R^2)S_{yy}}{n-k-1} = \hat{\sigma}^2 \tag{8-26}$$

Since S_{yy} and n are constant, as we increase the number of regressors included in the equation, $\hat{\sigma}^2$ and $(1 - \bar{R}^2)$ move in the same direction as $\hat{\sigma}^2$ and $\bar{R}^2$ move in the opposite direction. Thus the set of variables that gives minimum $\hat{\sigma}^2$ is also the set that maximizes $\bar{R}^2$.

Also, from Eq. (8-25) we can easily see that if $R^2 < k/(n-1)$, $1 - R^2 > (n-k-1)/(n-1)$ and hence $1 - \bar{R}^2 > 1$. Thus $\bar{R}^2$ is negative! For example, with 2 explanatory variables and 21 observations, if $R^2 < .1$, $\bar{R}^2$ will be negative.

There is a relationship between the t tests and F tests outlined earlier and $\bar{R}^2$. If the t ratio for the coefficient of any variable is less than 1, then dropping that variable will increase $\bar{R}^2$. More generally, if the F ratio for any set of variables is less than 1, then dropping this set of variables from the regression equation will increase $\bar{R}^2$. Since the single-variable case is a special case of the many-variable case, we will prove the latter result. Equation (8-26) shows the relationship between $\bar{R}^2$ and $\hat{\sigma}^2$. So, instead of asking the question of whether dropping the variables will increase $\bar{R}^2$, we can as well ask the question of whether $\hat{\sigma}^2$ will decrease.

Let $\hat{\sigma}_1^2$ be the estimate of σ^2 when we drop r regressors. Then

$$\hat{\sigma}_1^2 = \frac{\text{restricted residual sum of squares}}{n - (k - r) - 1}$$

Since the unrestricted residual sum of squares is $(n - k - 1)\hat{\sigma}^2$, the F test outlined earlier is given by

$$F = \frac{\left[(n - k + r - 1)\hat{\sigma}_1^2 - (n - k - 1)\hat{\sigma}^2\right]/r}{\left[(n - k - 1)\hat{\sigma}^2\right]/(n - k - 1)}$$

It can be readily verified that $\hat{\sigma}_1^2 \lesseqgtr \hat{\sigma}^2$ according as $F \lesseqgtr 1$.

It should be noted that it can happen that all the t ratios in an equation are less than 1 but the F ratio is greater than 1. In this case, because all the t ratios are less than 1, it does not mean we can increase $\bar{R}^2$ by dropping *all* the variables. Once we drop one of the variables, the other t ratios will change. Also, the reverse may be the case. It is possible that all t ratios are greater than 1, but some F ratios for combinations of the variables are less than 1. In this case, though by dropping any one of the variables we cannot increase $\bar{R}^2$, by dropping a set of variables we can increase $\bar{R}^2$. Thus, if all t ratios are greater than 1, this does not necessarily mean that one cannot increase $\bar{R}^2$ by deleting any variables.

8-10 RELATIONSHIPS BETWEEN t AND F RATIOS IN REGRESSION ANALYSIS

There is a wide variety of relationships between the t and F ratios used in regression analysis. These have been summarized by Geary and Leser,[1] who enumerate the following situations:

1. R^2 and all β_i significant
2. R^2 and some but not all β_i significant
3. R^2 but none of the β_i significant
4. All β_i significant but not R^2
5. Some β_i significant, but not all, nor R^2
6. Neither R^2 nor any β_i significant

Case 6 is easy to dismiss because the regression equation is obviously useless. Case 1 does not present a problem unless some coefficients have signs opposite to what we expect on the basis of economic theory. Case 2 is common, particularly if we have a large number of variables. Here the problem is to decide which of the nonsignificant variables to drop. Several computer programs are now available that do this systematically. We will discuss these later. Case 5 is still more problematical. If R^2 is not significant, we would be inclined to drop the equation. But if some coefficients are significant, we would be tempted to include them and drop the rest. Then the resulting R^2 could be significant, too. There is one important point we should bear in mind with this procedure. If we search over a large number of variables, we are often bound to hit on a few that produce significant coefficients.[2] But if we use this "search" procedure, we cannot use the usual t and F tables. What the appropriate t and F values should be is not known—all we can say is that they are higher than the tabulated values

[1] R. C. Geary and C. E. V. Leser, Significance Tests in Multiple Regression, *The American Statistician*, February 1968. See also the discussion in Elliot M. Cramer, Significance Tests and Tests of Models in Multiple Regression, *The American Statistician*, October 1972.

[2] See A. Ando and G. M. Kaufman, Evaluation of an Ad Hoc Procedure for Estimating Parameters of Some Linear Models, *Review of Economics and Statistics*, August 1966. They start with a randomly generated series for both the dependent variable y and the independent variable x's, and find that it is possible to get a "highly significant" correlation between y and an x by searching over a sufficient number of x's.

and perhaps much higher if we found the "significant" variables after searching over a large number of variables. Often such search procedures are used and the significant equation found is reported as though it were the first one tried. Sometimes the investigator is honest in admitting that he tried several alternatives which "did not work out well." What is still wrong in this case is that the t ratios are reported as usual and interpreted as usual.

Case 3 occurs often in econometric applications and is referred to as *multicollinearity*. The problem is that though the explanatory variables as a group can explain the dependent variable well, the effect of each variable separately cannot be estimated with any reasonable degree of precision. This problem occurs usually in cases where the explanatory variables are highly intercorrelated, but it can also occur if there are many explanatory variables, all weakly correlated, both among themselves and with the explained variable. The latter case often occurs in equations with a large number of "dummy" variables, which we will be discussing later. Geary and Leser give an example of a regression of prices of 14 makes of cars regressed on 6 attributes. The t values were 0.2, 2.0, -0.4, 0.7, and 2.2, respectively, nonsignificant (for 8 degrees of freedom) at the 5 percent level. The R^2 was .88, which for F with degrees of freedom 6 and 8 is significant at the 1 percent level. They then deleted all variables but the second (engine power) and the sixth (interior comfort). The R^2 was then .87 and both the t values were highly significant. Geary and Leser say that taking into account the fact that variables 2 and 6 were arrived at after searching over 6 variables, one should use higher values than the tabled ones to assess the significance of the coefficients. But even allowing for this, they say the equation can be deemed satisfactory. In this example we can easily calculate $\bar{R}^2$ as .79 with all 6 variables and .85 with variables 2 and 6.

Finally, coming to case 4, this is not commonly observed in econometric work. With two explanatory variables x_1 and x_2, this can occur in some cases where the correlations r_{y1} and r_{y2} are small and r_{12} is negative. For example, let the correlation matrix between y, x_1, and x_2 be

	y	x_1	x_2
y	1	.1	.1
x_1	.1	1	$-.5$
x_2	.1	$-.5$	1

In this case the partial correlations will be given by

$$r^2_{y1\cdot2} = r^2_{y2\cdot1} = .023$$

and the multiple correlation coefficient is given by $R^2 = .0327$. If we have 175 observations, noting that $t^2/(t^2 + \text{df}) = \text{partial } r^2$, we see that each of the t ratios is 2.01, which for 172 degrees of freedom is significant at the five percent level. The F test for R^2 is

$$F = \frac{.0327}{1 - .0327} \times \frac{172}{2} = 2.91$$

which for degrees of freedom 2 and 172 is not significant at the 5 percent level. Of course, one can argue in this case that the regression equation is useless anyway. Also, the tabulated 5 percent value of F for degrees of freedom 2 and 172 is 3.0, which is only slightly above the value of F we obtained. In any case the example illustrates how one can get each individual coefficient significant but the regression equation as a whole not significant.

The point in all this discussion is that in multiple regression equations one has to be careful in drawing conclusions from individual t ratios. In particular this is so for analyzing the effect on $\bar{R}^2$ of deletion or addition of sets of variables. Often, in applied work it is customary to run a "stepwise" regression where explanatory variables are entered into the equation sequentially and to stop at a point where $\bar{R}^2$ stops increasing. The rationale behind the procedure of choosing the set of variables that maximize $\bar{R}^2$ is discussed in Appendix B (section on Specification Errors). But the important point to note is that one cannot maximize $\bar{R}^2$ by a stepwise procedure that looks at only the t ratios at each stage. Suppose in a regression equation after including four variables the inclusion of any *one* of the remaining variables reduces $\bar{R}^2$. So we do not add any more variables. The discussion above shows that this reasoning is wrong. It might be possible that the addition of two variables instead of one will increase $\bar{R}^2$.

Finally, an equation with a higher $\bar{R}^2$ is not necessarily better than an equation with a lower $\bar{R}^2$. One should also look at whether the coefficients have the right signs and whether they make sense. The examples in the successive sections and chapters will illustrate all these points.

8-11 SELECTION OF VARIABLES IN MULTIPLE REGRESSION

In practice, though we specify that y depends on $x_1, x_2, \ldots, x_k$, not all the coefficients of these variables can be estimated with any reasonable precision. Hence we have to consider which variables to include and which to exclude. Some procedures have been developed for systematically adding and deleting variables, and we will discuss these. It should be noted that the procedures do not all give the same final answers. The procedures are:

1. All possible regressions
2. Backward-elimination or step-down procedures
3. Forward-selection or step-up procedures
4. Stepwise regression
5. Optimum regression (using procedure 1 in conjunction with procedure 4).

1. *All possible regressions.* In this procedure we compute all the possible regressions and choose the one with maximum $\bar{R}^2$ or the one with minimum $\hat{\sigma}^2$. The problem is that unless the number of regressors is small, the total number of regressions to be run is enormous (it is $2^k - 1$, where k is the number of

regressors). Beale, Kendall, and Mann[1] discuss methods of doing this efficiently. By their method one can handle < 20 variables easily. The computer time builds up rapidly if the number of regressors is > 20.

2. *Backward elimination.* Here we first estimate the equation with all the variables in and progressively eliminate variables with partial-correlation coefficients or the t ratios or F ratios ($F = t^2$) less than a specified value. Suppose we decide to eliminate a variable if its F value is < 1.0 (this increases $\bar{R}^2$, as noted earlier). After eliminating this variable, we rerun the regression and repeat the procedure. Sometimes (with economic data perhaps quite often) there may be many coefficients with F values < 1.0. In this case we eliminate the one with the smallest F value, or apply F tests for combinations of coefficients. With most economic data, where multicollinearity is a serious problem, this procedure of backward elimination does not work well. The reason is that if we start with an equation with all the variables in, there can be many variables with nonsignificant F ratios and the backward-elimination procedure might eliminate the most important variable in the very first step. This is also the reason why this procedure often gives an equation with a larger residual sum of squares than the equation with the same number of variables found in forward selection.

3. *Forward selection.* This procedure involves much less computational effort than the backward-elimination procedure. We first select the explanatory variable, say x_4, that has the highest simple correlation with the dependent variable y. Then we look at the partial-correlation coefficients of y with the other variables after including x_4, that is, $r^2_{yx_1 \cdot x_4}$, $r^2_{yx_2 \cdot x_4}$, etc., and select the variable that has the highest partial-correlation coefficient—say it is x_2. Next we look at the partial-correlation coefficients $r^2_{yx_1 \cdot x_2 x_4}$, $r^2_{yx_3 \cdot x_2 x_4}$, etc., and select the variable with the highest partial-correlation coefficient, and so on. We continue as long as the $\bar{R}^2$ increases or as long as the F value associated with the new variable to be introduced is greater than a specified value. This procedure is used with some modifications in the next procedure.

4. *The stepwise-regression procedure.* The procedure of forward selection has one drawback. A variable which may have been the best single variable at an early stage may be superfluous at a later stage. For example, in the above procedure, though x_4 was the best variable at the first step, it may be superfluous after the inclusion of x_2 and x_5. What the stepwise procedure does in this case is the following: It starts with x_4. Then it enters x_2 using the forward-selection procedure. After x_2 is entered, it looks at x_4 and decides whether to retain it or not—by looking at the F value for x_4. If it is retained, it enters the next variable, say x_5, by the forward-selection procedure. After x_5 is entered, it looks again at the F values for the variables already in, x_2 and x_4, and deletes any variable that is superfluous. Thus, at each stage, the forward-selection procedure is used to

[1] See E. M. L. Beale, M. G. Kendall, and D. W. Mann, The Discarding of Variables in Multivariate Analysis, *Biometrika*, 1967, pp. 357–366. Also E. M. L. Beale, Selecting an Optimum Subset, in J. Abadie (ed.), "Integer and Non-linear Programming," North-Holland Publishing Company, Amsterdam, 1970.

decide which variable to include and the backward-elimination procedure is used to decide which variable to eliminate. Usually we are required to specify two F values, the F value which determines the addition of variables and the F value which determines which variables to delete.

The procedure due to Efroymson[1] is one of the commonly used stepwise routines in economics. A program that incorporates this with some other features used in econometrics is the BMD 34 program from the University of Chicago (this is an adaptation of a BMD program from UCLA Biomedical Computer Programs).

5. *Optimum regression.* The stepwise procedure does not guarantee that the set of variables finally arrived at are optimal—say in the sense of minimizing the residual sum of squares for that number of explanatory variables. What one can do is rerun all possible regressions with the number of regressors given in the final step of the stepwise-regression program.

All these regression-selection procedures can be easily misused. It is too easy to let the computer pick up variables. What one should do is exercise some judgment in the initial selection of variables, and also examine at each stage whether the equation estimated makes sense. This involves an examination of the signs and magnitudes of the coefficients and an analysis of the residuals.

One factor is missing in all these procedures for selection of variables in multiple regression. This is that the objectives are not clearly stated. Lindley[2] discusses this problem with clearly stated objectives in the framework of decision theory using a Bayesian approach. Though it is not exactly clear how his results can be used in econometric applications, since the basic element in his analysis is the cost of observation, the paper is interesting because it argues that the solution to the problem of selection of variables in multiple regression depends on whether the purpose is to use the regression equation for prediction or for control (of the regressors to set a fixed value of y). To consider the simplest case where the regressors are independent and the cost c_i of observing each x_i is additive, Lindley argues that in the prediction problem x_i should be observed if and only if

$$\left[E(\hat{\beta}_i)\right]^2 \operatorname{var}(x_i) \geqslant c_i$$

and that in the control problem x_i should be observed if and only if

$$E(\hat{\beta}_i^2) \operatorname{var}(x_i) > c_i$$

Thus the decision of whether or not to include a variable depends only on the magnitude, not the precision, of the corresponding regression coefficient in the case of the prediction problem, and depends on the precision in the case of the control problem. Though these results are interesting, one main reason why

[1] M. A. Efroymson, Multiple Regression Analysis, in A. Ralston and H. S. Wilf (eds.), "Mathematical Methods for Digital Computers," John Wiley & Sons, Inc., New York, 1960.

[2] D. V. Lindley, The Choice of Variables in Multiple Regression, *Journal of the Royal Statistical Society*, ser. B, 1968, pp. 31–66.

these criteria are not of much use in econometric work, at least with published data, is that the costs c_i are almost zero. Thus Lindley's criteria would result in the conclusion that we should include all the variables.

There is also one more important point to bear in mind. This is that the stepwise procedures invalidate the usual statistical tests of significance. If we start with a model and then estimate it with the data on hand, the confidence intervals and tests have the specified probabilities. However, when we apply repeated tests to the same data and let the data decide what model is reasonable, it is not clear what probabilities to attach to the confidence-interval statements and tests made on the model finally arrived at. This is why stepwise procedures are regarded with some suspicion by many statisticians, though the condemnation is not universal. For instance, Anscombe[1] says:

> Curiously enough some statisticians seem to regard successive testing as improper and unmentionable. I have heard experienced men assert that "stepwise regression" was "utterly invalid." This attitude springs from the idea that all statistical analysis should be based on a definite set of assumptions or "model" taken as "given" and so held absolutely, without verification. There is an associated idea that significance tests are procedures for making decisions or forming opinions and we, therefore, ought not to confuse ourselves by using more than one procedure at once. . . . I have argued elsewhere that significance tests are forms of evidence. We are at liberty to collect all the pieces of evidence that we can use.

Thus, in spite of its limitations, stepwise regression, provided it is not used mechanically (letting the computer pick up what it likes), is a very useful tool.

8-12 A NOTE ON REPORTING RESULTS

Often in empirical work though the methodology is described adequately, the data are not described carefully nor are the results presented in a comprehensive fashion. This is because of an excessive weight given by the econometric profession to the development of sophisticated techniques and too little attention paid to the data on which the techniques are used. Thomas[2] gives a good discussion of how the current empirical work is being presented and how the principles suggested by Frisch for the presentation of empirical results are not followed. In his editorial for the first issue of *Econometrica*, Frisch[3] said, "In statistical and other numerical work presented in *Econometrica*, the original data will, as a rule, be published, unless their volume is excessive. This is important in order to stimulate criticism, control and further studies. The aim will be to present this kind of paper in a condensed form. Brief precise descriptions of (1)

[1] F. J. Anscombe, Topics in the Investigation of Linear Relations Fitted by the Method of Least Squares (with discussion), *Journal of the Royal Statistical Society*, ser. B, 1967, pp. 1–52.

[2] J. J. Thomas, The Reporting of Empirical Work in Economics, *Applied Statistics*, 1967, pp. 172–176.

[3] R. Frisch, Editorial, *Econometrica*, 1933.

the theoretical setting, (2) the data, (3) the method, and (4) the results are essential."

Thomas examined 9 leading journals in 1965 and found that of the 425 articles published, 145 contained empirical work. Of these 145 articles, 34 had specific references to official sources giving page and table, 54 had vague references to official sources, 26 specific references to another author's work, 14 vague references to another author's work, 18 had references to author's own data, 5 references to unpublished data by another agency, and in 13 papers no references were given at all. Also he found that of these 145 articles, 70 were based on multiple regression of which 69 presented t ratios or standard errors, 44 gave R^2, 18 gave $\bar{R}^2$, and 18 gave SEE.[1] Among the 40 time-series studies, only 15 reported any test statistics for serial correlation.

Exercises

1. The following are data pertaining to the demand for and supply of food in the United States, 1922–1941:

Year	Q_D	P_D	Y	Q_S	P_S	t
1922	98.6	100.2	87.4	108.5	99.1	1
1923	101.2	101.6	97.6	110.1	99.1	2
1924	102.4	100.5	96.7	110.4	98.9	3
1925	100.9	106.0	98.2	104.3	110.8	4
1926	102.3	108.7	99.8	107.2	108.2	5
1927	101.5	106.7	100.5	105.8	105.6	6
1928	101.6	106.7	103.2	107.8	109.8	7
1929	101.6	108.2	107.8	103.4	108.7	8
1930	99.8	105.5	96.6	102.7	100.6	9
1931	100.3	95.6	88.9	104.1	81.0	10
1932	97.6	88.6	75.1	99.2	68.6	11
1933	97.2	91.0	76.9	99.7	70.9	12
1934	97.3	97.9	84.6	102.0	81.4	13
1935	96.0	102.3	90.6	94.3	102.3	14
1936	99.2	102.2	103.1	97.7	105.0	15
1937	100.3	102.5	105.1	101.1	110.5	16
1938	100.3	97.0	96.4	102.3	92.5	17
1939	104.1	95.8	104.4	104.4	89.3	18
1940	105.3	96.4	110.7	108.5	93.0	19
1941	107.6	100.3	127.1	111.3	106.6	20

Source: M. A. Girschick and T. Haarelmo, Statistical Analysis of the Demand for Food, *Econometrica*, April 1947.

Q_D = food consumption per capita
Q_S = food production per capita
P_D = food prices at retail level/cost of living index
Y = disposable income/cost of living index
P_S – prices received by farmers for food/cost of living
t = time

[1] SEE is the square root of $\hat{\sigma}^2$, where $\hat{\sigma}^2$ = the residual sum of squares divided by the degrees of freedom.

(*a*) Estimate the following demand functions:

(i) $Q_D = \alpha + \beta P_D$
(ii) $Q_D = \alpha + \beta Y$
(iii) $Q_D = \alpha + \beta_1 P_D + \beta_2 Y$
(iv) $Q_D = \alpha + \beta_1 P_D + \beta_2 Y + \beta_3 t$

(*b*) Also estimate the following supply functions:

(i) $Q_S = \alpha' + \beta' P_S$
(ii) $Q_S = \alpha' + \beta'[P_S + (P_S)_{-1}]/2$
(iii) $Q_S = \alpha' + \beta_1'(P_S)_{-1} + \beta_2'(Q_S)_{-1}$

(*c*) What can you say about the major determinants of the demand for and supply of food in the United States during the years 1922–1941 on the basis of these results?
(*d*) Gather similar data for the period 1947–1972 and discuss any structural changes that might have taken place during the post World War II period as compared with the interwar years.

2. Table 8-5 gives data on gasoline consumption in the United States from 1947 to 1969. Estimate the price and income elasticity of demand for gasoline. Formulate the appropriate equations to

Table 8-5

Year	K	C	M	P_g	P_T	Pop.	L	Y
1947	9732	30.87	14.95	97.0	.538	145	59.3	1513
48	9573	33.39	14.96	100.8	.564	147	60.6	1567
49	9395	36.35	14.92	105.4	.633	150	61.3	1547
50	9015	40.33	14.40	104.3	.678	152	62.2	1646
51	9187	42.68	14.50	98.0	.694	155	62.0	1657
52	9361	43.82	14.27	97.3	.723	158	62.1	1678
53	9370	46.46	14.39	100.0	.765	160	63.0	1726
54	9308	48.41	14.57	101.4	.814	163	63.6	1714
55	9359	52.09	14.53	101.8	.840	166	65.0	1795
56	9348	54.25	14.36	103.3	.860	170	66.6	1839
57	9391	56.38	14.40	103.2	.862	172	66.9	1844
58	9494	57.39	14.30	98.5	.879	175	67.6	1831
59	9529	60.13	14.30	98.1	.897	178	68.4	1881
60	9446	62.26	14.28	98.6	.913	181	69.6	1883
61	9456	63.87	14.38	96.4	.944	184	70.5	1909
62	9441	66.64	14.37	95.0	.965	187	70.6	1968
63	9240	69.84	14.26	93.2	.965	189	71.8	2013
64	9286	72.97	14.25	91.8	.970	192	73.1	2123
65	9286	76.63	14.15	92.6	.972	194	74.5	2235
66	9384	80.11	14.10	92.7	.979	196	75.8	2331
67	9399	82.37	14.05	93.1	1.000	199	77.3	2398
68	9488	85.79	13.91	90.8	1.004	201	78.7	2480
69	9633	89.16	13.75	89.0	1.026	203	80.7	2517

K = miles traveled per car per year
C = number of cars in millions
M = miles per gallon
P_g = retail gasoline price index deflated by consumer price index (1953 = 100)
P_T = price of public transport (1967 = 100)
Pop. = population in millions
L = labor force in millions
Y = per-capita disposable income in 1958 prices

estimate discussing how you will treat the variables population and labor force. What are the major determinants of miles traveled? (Most of the data are from the American Petroleum Institute, *Petroleum Facts and Figures*.)

3. You are given data on the following variables:[1]

H_g = per-capita gross rate of nonfarm residential construction in constant dollars
H = End-of-year per-capita nonfarm housing stock in constant dollars
y_p = Friedman's measure of permanent income
Y_c = per-capita current real income
p = index of residential construction costs in real terms
R = National Industrial Conference Board Rent Index in real terms
r = average quality of new dwellings
N = average size of household
m = an index of relative building-material prices
U = relative wages of unskilled construction workers
s = ratio of wages of skilled to unskilled workers

Construct a demand function and a supply function for residential housing. What do you think will be the determining factors for the quality of new housing? Also, what will determine the rent?

The following equations were fitted with the data on the above variables for the interwar years. Interpret each as depicting the demand factors or supply factors or both and discuss whether the equation makes sense and is a "good" equation.

(*a*) $$H_g = -\underset{(.589)}{2.49p} + \underset{(.092)}{.438y_p} - \underset{(4.47)}{8.34r} - \underset{(.070)}{.282h} \qquad R^2 = .621$$

(*b*) $$H = -\underset{(1.45)}{4.66p} + \underset{(.219)}{.820y_p} - \underset{(11.4)}{24.7r} \qquad R^2 = .448$$

(*c*) $$H_g = -\underset{(1.38)}{1.11p} - \underset{(62.0)}{50.1m} + \underset{(3.71)}{1.92U} + \underset{(10.1)}{.48s} \qquad R^2 = .100$$

(*d*) $$p = -\underset{(.053)}{.043H_g} - \underset{(.124)}{.034m} + \underset{(4.3)}{21.6U} + \underset{(13.7)}{54.9s} \qquad R^2 = .804$$

(*e*) $$\frac{H_g}{H} = \underset{(.046)}{.255}\frac{R}{p} - \underset{(.00451)}{.00608r} \qquad R^2 = .714$$

(*f*) $$R = -\underset{(.0414)}{.0875H} + \underset{(.043)}{.121y_p} \qquad R^2 = .302$$

(*g*) $$H_n = -\underset{(17.7)}{59.1p} + \underset{(.62)}{4.09y_p} - \underset{(146)}{510r} + \underset{(802)}{385N} \qquad R^2 = .723$$

4. Suppose you are asked to estimate the income elasticity of demand for (*a*) clothing, (*b*) automobiles, (*c*) baby-sitters. What are the data you would look for in each case? Derive the function you would be estimating. What are the basic differences among the three cases?

5. Consider the following equations estimated to study the effect of property taxes and local public expenditures on property values.[2] The dependent variable is Y = median value of owner-occupied housing. The explanatory variables are:

T = effective property tax rate
E = educational expenditures per pupil
Z = municipal spending per capita on other functions (police, fire protection, streets, health, libraries, parks, etc.)

[1] From R. M. Muth, Demand for Non-Farm Housing, in A. C. Harberger (ed.), "Demand for Durable Goods," Chicago, 1960.

[2] The Effects of Property Taxes and Local Public Spending on Property Values, comment by H. O. Pollakowski, reply by W. E. Oates, *Journal of Political Economy*, July–August 1973.

M = adjusted linear distance in miles to nearest major downtown area
R = median number of rooms per house
N = percent of new houses (built since 1950)
Y = median family income
P = percent of population with family incomes under $3000
B = percent of units with more than one bathroom

The equations estimated are:

	C	$\log T$	$\log E$	$\log M$	R	N	Y	P	B	$\log Z$	R^2
I	− 23	− 9.1	1.4	0.73	3.8	.036	1.8	.14			.97
	(14)	(3.4)	(2.1)	(0.50)	(1.4)	(.013)	(.50)	(.11)			
II	− 49	− 8.0	4.3		8.0	.058					.93
	(18)	(4.5)	(2.8)		(.70)	(.016)					
III	− 59	− 3.8	8.4		4.8	.022			.096		.95
	(16)	(4.3)	(3.0)		(1.6)	(.021)			(.042)		
IV	− 21	− 3.6	3.3	− 1.4	1.7	.052	1.5	.30			.93
	(8.5)	(.88)	(1.5)	(.29)	(.42)	(.013)	(.17)	(.083)			
V	− 53	− 4.2	8.8	− 1.5	3.9	.083					.81
	(12)	(1.4)	(2.3)	(.47)	(.50)	(.018)					
VI	26	− 4.2	3.6	− 1.2	1.4	.06	1.5	.30		1.5	.94
	(8.7)	(.91)	(1.5)	(.28)	(.44)	(.014)	(.17)	(.097)		(.79)	

The first three equations are based on 19 cities in the bay area. What more can you conclude from these equations than that rich people live in costly houses, that these houses have more rooms and more bathrooms? The last three equations are estimated on the basis of 53 communities in the New York metropolitan area. What do you conclude from these results? Do you think having more disaggregated data will help? If so, what sort of disaggregated data will you look for and how will you analyze them?

CHAPTER

NINE

DUMMY VARIABLES, LAGGED VARIABLES, AND NONLINEARITIES IN MULTIPLE REGRESSION

9-1 INTRODUCTION

In the preceding chapter we discussed the estimation of a multiple regression equation, tests of significance for the regression coefficients, $\bar{R}^2$, and selection of variables. In this chapter we will discuss some special kinds of variables occurring in multiple regression equations and the problems caused by them. These are:

1. Dummy explanatory variables
2. Lagged dependent variables as explanatory variables
3. Stochastic explanatory variables
4. Omission of relevant and inclusion of irrelevant variables
5. Proxy variables for explanatory variables
6. Limited and dummy dependent variables

Further, some of these models result in nonlinear relationships, and we will also discuss problems of nonlinear optimization, nonlinear least squares, and the maximum-likelihood approach.

9-2 DUMMY VARIABLES

Sometimes there will be some explanatory variables in our regression equation that are only qualitative, e.g., presence or absence of college education, racial differences, sex differences. In such cases one often takes account of these effects by the dummy-variable method. The implicit assumption is that the regression lines for the different groups differ only in the intercept term but have the same slope coefficients. For example, suppose the relationship between income Y and years of schooling X for two groups is as shown in Fig. 9-1. The dots are the observations for group 1 and the circles are observations for group 2. Then it is clear that the slopes of the regression lines for both groups are roughly the same but the intercepts are different. Hence the regression equations we fit will be

$$y = \alpha_1 + \beta x + u \qquad \text{for the first group}$$
$$y = \alpha_2 + \beta x + u \qquad \text{for the second group}$$

These equations can be combined into a single equation

$$y = \alpha_1 + (\alpha_2 - \alpha_1)D + \beta x + u \tag{9-1}$$

where $D = 1$ for group 2
$= 0$ for group 1

This is the dummy variable we are talking of. The coefficient of the dummy variable measures the differences in the two intercept terms.

Again, for the data on consumption function presented in Table 7-1, we saw that the observations for the war years 1942–1945 had to be dropped. If we believe that the consumption function had a parallel downward shift during those years, we can include the war years in our regression equation and estimate the equation

$$C = \alpha_1 + (\alpha_2 - \alpha_1)D + \beta Y$$

where $D = 1$ for the war years 1942–1945
$= 0$ for the others

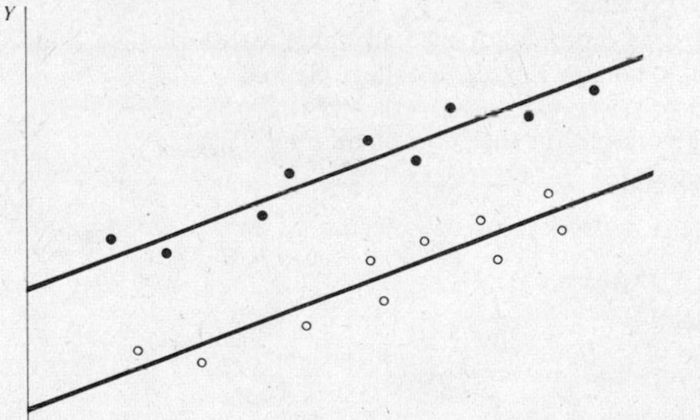

Figure 9-1 Regression lines with a common slope and different intercepts.

If we believe that the consumption function had parallel shifts during the war years and the postwar years, we define two dummies:

$$\begin{aligned} D_1 &= 1 \text{ for the war years 1942–1945} \\ &= 0 \text{ for others} \\ D_2 &= 1 \text{ for the postwar years 1946–1970} \\ &= 0 \text{ for others} \end{aligned}$$

If there is a constant term in the regression equation, the number of dummies defined should always be one less than the number of groupings by that category because the constant term is the intercept for the base group and the coefficients of the dummy variables measure differences in intercepts, as can be seen from Eq. (9-1). In the above illustration the constant term measures the intercept for the prewar years, the coefficient of D_1 measures the differences in the intercepts between the prewar and war years, and the coefficient of D_2 measures the differences in the intercepts between the prewar and postwar years. If we do not introduce a constant term in the regression equation, we can define a dummy for each group, and in this case the coefficients of the dummy variables measure the intercepts for the respective groups. If we include both the constant term and three dummies, we will be introducing *perfect* multicollinearity, and the regression program will not run (this is often referred to as the "dummy-variable trap"), though if one uses a stepwise-regression program, one of the dummies will be automatically eliminated.

As yet another example, suppose we have data on consumption C and income Y for a number of households. In addition we have data on:

1. S: the sex of the head of the household
2. A: age of the head of the household, which is given in three categories: < 25 years, 25–50 years, and > 50 years
3. E: education of the head of household, also in three categories: $<$ high school, $\geq$ high school but $<$ college degree, $\geq$ college degree

We include these qualitative variables in the form of dummy variables:

$$\begin{aligned} D_1 &= 1 \text{ if sex is male} \\ &= 0 \text{ if female} \\ D_2 &= 1 \text{ if age} < 25 \text{ years} \\ &= 0 \text{ otherwise} \\ D_3 &= 1 \text{ if age between 25 } \textit{and} \text{ 50 years} \\ &= 0 \text{ otherwise} \\ D_4 &= 1 \text{ if } < \text{ high school degree} \\ &= 0 \text{ otherwise} \\ D_5 &= 1 \text{ if } \geq \text{ high school degree but } < \text{ college degree} \\ &= 0 \text{ otherwise} \end{aligned}$$

For each category the number of dummy variables is one less than the number of classifications.

Then we run the regression equation

$$C = \alpha + \beta Y + \gamma_1 D_1 + \gamma_2 D_2 + \gamma_3 D_3 + \gamma_4 D_4 + \gamma_5 D_5 + u$$

The assumption made in the dummy-variable method is that it is only the intercept that changes for each group but not the slope coefficients, i.e., coefficients of Y. For example, in the above case the intercept term is α for female head of household and $\alpha + \gamma_1$ for male head of household.

It is α if age is > 50 years

$\alpha + \gamma_2$ if age is < 25 years
$\alpha + \gamma_3$ if age is > 25 but < 50 years

It is α if education is $\geqslant$ college degree

$\alpha + \gamma_4$ if education $<$ high school degree
$\alpha + \gamma_5$ if education $\geqslant$ high school degree but $<$ college degree

Thus if the head of the household is male, with age 40 years and high school degree, the consumption function is $C = (\alpha + \gamma_1 + \gamma_3 + \gamma_5) + \beta Y$.

The dummy-variable method is also used if one has to take care of seasonal factors. For example, if we have quarterly data on C and Y, we fit the regression equation

$$C = \alpha + \beta Y + \lambda_1 D_1 + \lambda_2 D_2 + \lambda_3 D_3 + u$$

where D_1, D_2, and D_3 are seasonal dummies defined by

$$\begin{aligned} D_1 &= 1 \text{ for the first quarter} \\ &= 0 \text{ for others} \\ D_2 &= 1 \text{ for the second quarter} \\ &= 0 \text{ for others} \\ D_3 &= 1 \text{ for the third quarter} \\ &= 0 \text{ for others} \end{aligned}$$

If we have monthly data, we use 11 seasonal dummies:

$$\begin{aligned} D_1 &= 1 \text{ for January} \\ &= 0 \text{ for others} \\ D_2 &= 1 \text{ for February} \\ &= 0 \text{ for others} \qquad \text{etc.} \end{aligned}$$

Or, if we feel that, say, December (because of Christmas shopping) is the only month with strong seasonal effect, we use only one dummy variable:

$$\begin{aligned} D &= 1 \text{ for December} \\ &= 0 \text{ for other months} \end{aligned}$$

Dummy variables can also be used to allow for differences in slope coefficients. For example, if the regression equations are

$$
\begin{aligned}
& y_1 = \alpha_1 + \beta_1 x_1 + u_1 \qquad \text{for the first group} \\
\text{and} \qquad & y_2 = \alpha_2 + \beta_2 x_2 + u_2 \qquad \text{for the second group}
\end{aligned}
\tag{9-2}
$$

we can write these equations together as

$$
\begin{pmatrix} y_1 \\ y_2 \end{pmatrix} = \alpha_1 \begin{pmatrix} 1 \\ 1 \end{pmatrix} + (\alpha_2 - \alpha_1) \begin{pmatrix} 0 \\ 1 \end{pmatrix} + \beta_1 \begin{pmatrix} x_1 \\ x_2 \end{pmatrix} + (\beta_2 - \beta_1) \begin{pmatrix} 0 \\ x_2 \end{pmatrix} + \begin{pmatrix} u_1 \\ u_2 \end{pmatrix}
$$

or

$$
y = \alpha_1 + (\alpha_2 - \alpha_1) D_1 + \beta_1 x + (\beta_2 - \beta_1) D_2 + u \tag{9-3}
$$

where $D_1 = 0$ for all observations in the first group
$= 1$ for all observations in the second group
$D_2 = 0$ for all observations in the first group
$= x_2$, i.e., the respective observation of x in the second group

The coefficient of D_1 measures the differences in the intercept terms and the coefficient of D_2 measures the differences in slopes. Estimation of Eq. (9-3) amounts to estimating the two equations in (9-2) separately. If we delete D_2 from Eq. (9-3), this amounts to allowing for different intercepts but not different slopes; and if we delete D_1 from (9-3), it amounts to allowing for different slopes but not different intercepts.

Suppose we have data for three periods and in the second period only the intercept term changed and in the third period only the slope coefficient changed. Then the equations are

$$
\begin{aligned}
y_1 &= \alpha + \beta x_1 + u_1 \text{ for period 1} \\
y_2 &= \alpha' + \beta x_2 + u_2 \text{ for period 2} \\
y_3 &= \alpha' + \beta' x_3 + u_3 \text{ for period 3}
\end{aligned}
\tag{9-4}
$$

These three equations can be written as

$$
\begin{bmatrix} y_1 \\ y_2 \\ y_3 \end{bmatrix} = \alpha \begin{bmatrix} 1 \\ 1 \\ 1 \end{bmatrix} + (\alpha' - \alpha) \begin{bmatrix} 0 \\ 1 \\ 1 \end{bmatrix} + \beta \begin{bmatrix} x_1 \\ x_2 \\ x_3 \end{bmatrix} + (\beta' - \beta) \begin{bmatrix} 0 \\ 0 \\ x_3 \end{bmatrix} + \begin{bmatrix} u_1 \\ u_2 \\ u_3 \end{bmatrix}
$$

This can be written as

$$
y = \alpha + (\alpha' - \alpha) D_1 + \beta x + (\beta' - \beta) D_2 + u \tag{9-5}
$$

where $D_1 = 1$ for all observations in periods 2 and 3
$= 0$ for all observations in period 1
$D_2 = 0$ for all observations in periods 1 and 2
$= x_3$ or the respective value of x for all observations in period 3

The coefficient of D_1 measures the change in the intercept from period 1 to period 2, and the coefficient of D_2 measures the change in slope from period 2 to period 3.

Table 9-1

Coefficient of	1960	1959	1957
H	.119	.118	.117
	(.029)	(.029)	(.030)
W	.136	.238	.135
	(.046)	(.034)	(.010)
L	.015	−.016	.039
	(.017)	(.015)	(.013)
V	−.039	−.070	−.025
	(.025)	(.039)	(.023)
T	.058	.027	.028
	(.016)	(.019)	(.012)
A	.003	.063	.114
	(.040)	(.038)	(.025)
P	.225	.188	.078
	(.037)	(.041)	(.030)
B			.159
			(.026)
C	.048		
	(.039)		
R^2	.951	.934	.966

H = advertised brake horsepower in 100's
W = shipping weight in thousands of pounds
L = overall length in tens of inches
V = 1 if the car has a V-8 engine, = 0 if it has a six-cylinder engine
T = 1 if the car is hard top, = 0 if not
A = 1 if automatic transmission is "standard" (i.e., included in price), = 0 if not
P = 1 if power steering is "standard," = 0 if not
B = 1 if power brakes are "standard," = 0 if not
C = 1 if car is designated as a "compact," = 0 if not

Sometimes the dependent variable y is also a dummy variable. Suppose the variable y is whether or not a person has bought a car and we have several independent variables like income, wealth, and age of current automobile that determine y. In this case one can define y as a (0,1) variable and regress this on the independent variables. However, there are special problems with the assumptions made about the residuals and also the interpretation of the coefficients. Hence we will discuss this case in a later section on probit and logit analysis.

An example: In a study of the determinants of automobile prices, Griliches[1] regressed the logarithm of new U.S. passenger-car prices on various specifications. The results are shown in Table 9-1. Since the dependent variable is the logarithm of price, the regression coefficients can be interpreted as the estimated percentage change in the price to a unit change in a particular quality, *holding*

[1] Z. Griliches, "Hedonic Price Indexes for Automobiles: An Econometric Analysis of Quality Change," Government Price Statistics, Hearings, U.S. Congress, Joint Economics Committee, Government Printing Office, Washington, D.C., 1961.

other qualities constant. For example, the coefficient of H indicates that an increase in 10 units of horsepower, ceteris paribus, results in a 1.2 percent increase in price. However, some of the coefficients have to be interpreted with caution. For example, the coefficient of P in the equation for 1960 says that the presence of power steering as "standard equipment" led to a 22.5 percent higher price in 1960. In this case the variable P is obviously not measuring the effect of power steering alone but is measuring the effect of "luxuriousness" of the car. It is also picking up the effects of A and B. This explains why the coefficient of A is so low in 1960. In fact, A, P, and B together can perhaps be replaced by a single dummy that measures "luxuriousness." These variables appear to be highly intercorrelated. Another coefficient, at first sight puzzling, is the coefficient of V, which, though not significant, is consistently negative. Though a V-8 costs more than a six-cylinder engine on a "comparable" car, what this coefficient says is that, holding horsepower and other variables constant, a V-8 is cheaper by about 4 percent. Since the V-8's have higher horsepower, what this coefficient is saying is that higher horsepower can be achieved more cheaply if one shifts to V-8 than by using the six-cylinder engine. It measures the decline in price per horsepower as one shifts to V-8's even though the total expenditure on horsepower goes up. This example illustrates the use of dummy variable and the interpretation of seemingly wrong coefficients.

As another example consider the estimates of liquid-asset demand by manufacturing corporations. Vogel and Maddala[1] computed regressions of the form $\log C = \alpha + \beta \log S$ where C = cash and S = sales, on the basis of data from the Internal Revenue Service, "Statistics of Income," for the year 1960–1961. The data consisted of 16 industry subgroups and 14 size classes, size being measured by total assets. When the regression equations were estimated separately for each industry, the estimates of β ranged from .929 to 1.077. The R^2's were uniformly high, ranging from .985 to .998. Thus one might conclude sales elasticity of demand for cash is close to 1. Also, when the data were pooled and a single equation estimated for the entire set of 224 observations, the estimate of β was .992 and $R^2 = .987$. When industry dummies were added, the estimate of β was .995 and $R^2 = .992$. From the high R^2's and relatively constant estimate of β one might be reassured that the sales elasticity is very close to 1. However, when asset-size dummies were introduced, the estimate of β fell to .334 with R^2 of .996. Also, all asset-size dummies were highly significant. The situation is described in Fig. 9-2. That the sales elasticity is significantly less than 1 is also confirmed by other evidence. This example illustrates how one can be very easily misled by high R^2's and apparent constancy of the coefficients. It also illustrates how one can get misleading results from grouped data, as mentioned in Chap. 6. When grouping is only by one variable, as in this case, more meaningful results will be obtained by considering a rectangular array of data consisting of several cross sections and analyzing it by pooled regressions

[1] R. C. Vogel and G. S. Maddala, Cross-Section Estimates of Liquid Asset Demand by Manufacturing Corporations, *The Journal of Finance*, December 1967.

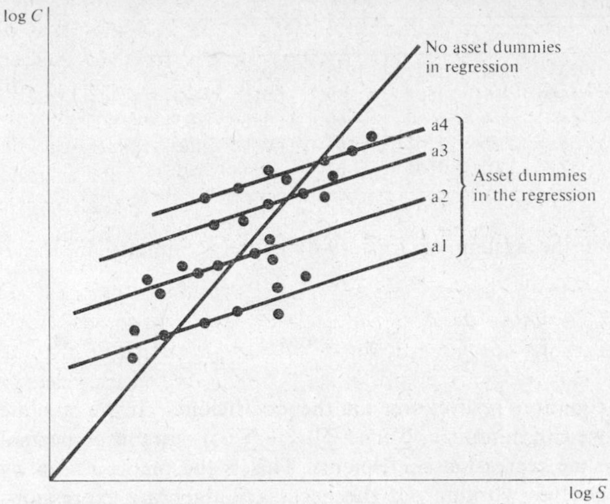

Figure 9-2 Bias due to omission of dummy variables.

and dummy variables. Some further examples of analysis from grouped data will be given later.

As mentioned earlier, dummy variables are not necessarily (0,1) variables. As an illustration, consider the joint estimation of the demand for beef, pork, and chicken on the basis of data presented in Table 7-5. Waugh estimates a set of demand functions of the form

$$\begin{aligned} P_1 &= \alpha_1 + \beta_{11}x_1 + \beta_{12}x_2 + \beta_{13}x_3 + \gamma_1 y + u_1 \\ P_2 &= \alpha_2 + \beta_{12}x_1 + \beta_{22}x_2 + \beta_{23}x_3 + \gamma_2 y + u_2 \\ P_3 &= \alpha_3 + \beta_{13}x_1 + \beta_{23}x_2 + \beta_{33}x_3 + \gamma_3 y + u_3 \end{aligned} \tag{9-6}$$

where P_1 = retail price of beef
P_2 = retail price of pork
P_3 = retail price of chicken
x_1 = consumption of beef per capita
x_2 = consumption of pork per capita
x_3 = consumption of chicken per capita
y = disposable income per capita

x_1, x_2, x_3 can be obtained from Table 7-5. The prices in Table 7-5 are, however, retail divided by a consumer price index. Hence we multiplied them by the consumer price index p to get p_1, p_2, and p_3. This index p and disposable income y are as follows:[1]

[1] There appears to be a misprint in the price of beef given in Table 7-5 for the year 1950 (on the basis of other information given in Waugh). We corrected this to 83.3 from 88.3.

	p	y		p	y		p	y
1948	.838	1291	1953	.932	1582	1958	1.007	1826
49	.830	1271	54	.936	1582	59	1.015	1904
50	.838	1369	55	.934	1660	60	1.031	1934
51	.906	1473	56	.947	1742	61	1.041	1980
52	.925	1520	57	.981	1804	62	1.054	2052

The special thing about the system of Eqs. (9-6) is the symmetry in the β coefficients. We have

$$\frac{dp_1}{dx_2} = \frac{dp_2}{dx_1} = \beta_{12} \qquad \frac{dp_1}{dx_3} = \frac{dp_3}{dx_1} = \beta_{13} \qquad \text{and} \qquad \frac{dp_2}{dx_3} = \frac{dp_3}{dx_2} = \beta_{23}$$

Thus, there are cross-equation restrictions on the coefficients. If we assume $V(u_1) = V(u_2) = V(u_3)$, we can minimize $(\sum u_1^2 + \sum u_2^2 + \sum u_3^2)$, obtain the normal equations, and estimate the regression coefficients. This is the method used by Waugh. This method involves working out the necessary algebraic expressions and programming things afresh. Instead we can use the standard regression programs by using the dummy-variable method. We can write Eqs. (9-6) as a single equation:

$$\begin{bmatrix} p_1 \\ p_2 \\ p_3 \end{bmatrix} = \alpha_1 \begin{bmatrix} 1 \\ 0 \\ 0 \end{bmatrix} + \alpha_2 \begin{bmatrix} 0 \\ 1 \\ 0 \end{bmatrix} + \alpha_3 \begin{bmatrix} 0 \\ 0 \\ 1 \end{bmatrix} + \beta_{11} \begin{bmatrix} x_1 \\ 0 \\ 0 \end{bmatrix} + \beta_{12} \begin{bmatrix} x_2 \\ x_1 \\ 0 \end{bmatrix}$$

$$+ \beta_{13} \begin{bmatrix} x_3 \\ 0 \\ x_1 \end{bmatrix} + \beta_{22} \begin{bmatrix} 0 \\ x_2 \\ 0 \end{bmatrix} + \beta_{23} \begin{bmatrix} 0 \\ x_3 \\ x_2 \end{bmatrix} + \beta_{33} \begin{bmatrix} 0 \\ 0 \\ x_3 \end{bmatrix}$$

$$+ \gamma_1 \begin{bmatrix} y \\ 0 \\ 0 \end{bmatrix} + \gamma_2 \begin{bmatrix} 0 \\ y \\ 0 \end{bmatrix} + \gamma_3 \begin{bmatrix} 0 \\ 0 \\ y \end{bmatrix} + \begin{bmatrix} u_1 \\ u_2 \\ u_3 \end{bmatrix}$$

We ran this equation with 45 observations and the 12 dummies (no constant term). The values of the dummy variables are easily generated; e.g., the set of observations for β_{12} consists of the 15 observations of x_2 followed by the 15 observations of x_1 and 15 zeros. The results (with t ratios in the parentheses) are[1]

$$p_1 = \underset{(12.00)}{118.98} - \underset{(14.55)}{1.534x_1} - \underset{(4.31)}{.474x_2} - \underset{(3.01)}{.445x_3} + \underset{(12.61)}{.0650y}$$

$$p_2 = \underset{(9.18)}{149.79} - \underset{(4.31)}{.474x_1} - \underset{(6.20)}{1.189x_2} - \underset{(1.54)}{.319x_3} + \underset{(2.83)}{.0162y}$$

$$p_3 = \underset{(7.36)}{131.06} - \underset{(3.01)}{.445x_1} - \underset{(1.54)}{.319x_2} - \underset{(4.32)}{2.389x_3} + \underset{(1.66)}{.0199y}$$

[1] The results are almost the same as those obtained by Waugh. Part of the difference could be that our program is in double precision.

There are some questions about the appropriateness of the specification of the system of demand functions adopted above. The purpose of the example, however, has been to illustrate the use of dummy-variable methods to estimate equations with cross-equation constraints on the coefficients.

9-3 LAGGED DEPENDENT VARIABLES

Sometimes the explanatory variables in our regression equation are lagged dependent variables. These arise in the following classes of models:

1. Distributed lag models
2. Partial-adjustment models
3. Models with expectations
4. Models with serially correlated residuals

We will discuss these briefly here. Detailed discussion will be found in subsequent chapters.

Distributed-Lag Models

Suppose we say that current consumption depends not only on current income but on the incomes of the past k periods. So we can write[1]

$$C_t = \beta_0 y_t + \beta_1 y_{t-1} + \cdots + \beta_k y_{t-k} \tag{9-7}$$

This is called a "distributed-lag" consumption function—distributed lag because the lag with which income affects consumption is distributed over a number of periods. However, because $y_t, y_{t-1}, y_{t-2}, \ldots$, etc., are very highly correlated, if we try to estimate this equation we will get poor estimates of the β's. Also, every time we add another lagged y, we have one less observation to estimate the regression equation. Thus, if we have 40 observations to start with and use 15 lagged y's, we have only 25 observations to work with and 15 coefficients to estimate. To solve this problem, Koyck[2] suggested the following: It is reasonable to assume that the β's successively diminish over time; e.g., our consumption this year will be 50 percent of this year's income, 25 percent of last year's, 10 percent of the previous year's, etc. Koyck suggested that we assume the β_i to decline geometrically, i.e., $\beta_1 = \lambda\beta_0$, $\beta_2 = \lambda^2\beta_0$, $\beta_3 = \lambda^3\beta_0$, etc., $0 < \lambda < 1$. The

[1] We will be purposely omitting the error term. If the error term is included, then, during the transformation of the equations we will be doing, the error term gets transformed into one with serial correlation. This creates problems which we need not get into here. These problems will be discussed later. Also, the notation for distributed-lag models gets considerably simpler if we use the lag operator L. This is done in Chap. 16, where we discuss these models in greater detail.

[2] L. M. Koyck, "Distributed Lags and Investment Analysis," North-Holland Publishing Company, Amsterdam, 1954.

smaller the value of λ the faster the decline and the smaller the lag between income and consumption. Making this assumption, we get

$$C_t = \beta_0 y_t + \beta_0 \lambda y_{t-1} + \beta_0 \lambda^2 y_{t-2} + \cdots + \text{etc.}$$

Hence
$$\lambda C_{t-1} = \beta_0 \lambda y_{t-1} + \beta_0 \lambda^2 y_{t-2} + \cdots + \text{etc.}$$

Hence by subtraction we have

$$C_t - \lambda C_{t-1} = \beta_0 y_t$$

or
$$C_t = \beta_0 Y_t + \lambda C_{t-1} \tag{9-8}$$

So, we estimate a regression equation of C_t on Y_t and C_{t-1}. This will give us estimates of β_0 and λ, and once we get these we can obtain all the β_i; e.g., for the data in Table 7-1 on consumption and income for the U.S. 1929–1970, we get

$$C_t = 5.2607 + .695 Y_t + .231 C_{t-1}$$

The relationship between consumption and income is

$$Y_t = \text{const.} + .695 Y_t + (.695)(.231) Y_{t-1} + .695(.231)^2 Y_{t-1} + \cdots + \text{etc.}$$

or
$$Y_t = \text{const.} + .695 Y_t + .161 Y_{t-1} + .037 Y_{t-2} + .008 Y_{t-3} + .002 Y_{t-4}$$

The other coefficients are smaller. The short-run marginal propensity to consume is .695. The long-run marginal propensity to consume = .695 + .161 + .037 + .008 + .002 = .903. Actually, you can obtain it as the sum of the infinite series

$$.695\left[1 + .231 + (.231)^2 + (.231)^3 + \cdots\right] = \frac{.695}{1 - .231} = \frac{.695}{.769} = .904$$

Partial-Adjustment Models

Suppose a firm anticipates some change in the demand for its product. In anticipation of that, it has to adjust its productive capacity or, say, capital stock K_t. But it cannot do this immediately.

Let K_t^* be the "desired" capital stock. Then $K_t^* - K_{t-1}$ is the "desired" change and $K_t - K_{t-1}$ is the actual change.

The partial-adjustment model says that the actual change is only a fraction of the desired change, i.e.,

$$K_t - K_{t-1} = \delta(K_t^* - K_{t-1}) \qquad \text{where} \qquad 0 < \delta \leqslant 1$$

Also, suppose the desired capital stock K_t^* is a function of sales S_t so that we have[1]

$$K_t^* = \alpha + \beta S_t \tag{9-9}$$

[1] Actually it should be expected sales in time period t, but if expectations are perfect, we can use actual sales S_t.

then combining these two equations we get

$$K_t - K_{t-1} = \delta(\alpha + \beta S_t - K_{t-1})$$

or

$$K_t = \alpha\delta + \beta\delta S_t + (1 - \delta)K_{t-1}$$

Thus we estimate a regression equation of K_t on S_t and K_{t-1}. If this equation is written as

$$K_t = \alpha_0 + \alpha_1 S_t + \alpha_2 K_{t-1} + u_t$$

where u_t is a residual, we have

$$\alpha_0 = \alpha\delta \qquad \alpha_1 = \beta\delta \qquad \text{and} \qquad \alpha_2 = (1 - \delta)$$

Hence $\hat{\delta} = 1 - \hat{\alpha}_2$
$\hat{\beta} = \hat{\alpha}_1/(1 - \hat{\alpha}_2)$
$\hat{\alpha} = \hat{\alpha}_0/(1 - \hat{\alpha}_2)$

We can think of a similar model for the consumption function.

Let C_t^* be desired consumption in period t and suppose that it is proportional to income Y_t in period t, that is,

$$C_t^* = \beta Y_t \tag{9-10}$$

Also let the actual change in consumption $(C_t - C_{t-1})$ be a fraction of the desired change $(C_t^* - C_{t-1})$, that is, $C_t - C_{t-1} = \delta(C_t^* - C_{t-1})$. These two equations together give

$$C_t - C_{t-1} = \delta(\beta Y_t - C_{t-1})$$

or

$$C_t = \beta\delta Y_t + (1 - \delta)C_{t-1} \tag{9-11}$$

Thus we estimate a regression equation of C_t on Y_t and C_{t-1}. If this equation is written as

$$C_t = \alpha_1 Y_t + \alpha_2 C_{t-1} + u_t$$

where u_t is the residual, then

$$\hat{\delta} = 1 - \hat{\alpha}_2$$

and

$$\hat{\beta} = \frac{\hat{\alpha}_1}{1 - \hat{\alpha}_2}$$

It is easily seen that Eq. (9-11) is indistinguishable from Eq. (9-8). Thus when we estimate a regression equation of C_t on Y_t and C_{t-1}, we cannot tell whether this is a consequence of a "partial-adjustment model" or a distributed-lag model.[1]

[1] However, instead of adding the residual to the "final" equations (9-8) and (9-11), if we start with the residuals in the basic behavioral equations like (9-7) and (9-10), then the final forms for the two models will have a different structure of residuals, and we can thus distinguish between them.

Models with Expectations

One of the familiar themes in the formation of expectations is that they depend on the past behavior of the variable. Many economic relations involve expectational variables, and since these variables are unobservable, we have to have some hypothesis as to how they are related to observable variables. A commonly used model for expectation formation is what is known as the "adaptive" expectations model. This says that you revise your expectations based on the most recent error. If Y_t^* is the expected income in period t,

$$Y_t^* - Y_{t-1}^* = \lambda(Y_{t-1} - Y_{t-1}^*) \qquad \text{where} \qquad 0 < \lambda < 1$$

or

$$Y_t^* = \lambda Y_{t-1} + (1 - \lambda)Y_{t-1}^*$$

What this says is, Y_{t-1}^* is what you expected for period $t - 1$. Y_{t-1} is what you actually observed. If what you observed is more than what you expected, you revise your expectations upward. In the opposite case you revise them downward. In either case your revision is only a fraction of the most recent error.

Suppose C_t depends on expected income Y_t^* and expectations are formed according to the adaptive-expectations model. Then we have

$$C_t = \beta Y_t^* \qquad \text{and} \qquad Y_t^* - (1 - \lambda)Y_{t-1}^* = \lambda Y_{t-1}$$

Hence

$$C_t - (1 - \lambda)C_{t-1} = \beta[Y_t^* - (1 - \lambda)Y_{t-1}^*]$$
$$= \beta\lambda Y_{t-1}$$

or

$$C_t = \beta\lambda Y_{t-1} + (1 - \lambda)C_{t-1} \tag{9-12}$$

To estimate β and λ, we regress C_t on Y_{t-1} and C_{t-1}. This is similar to the partial-adjustment model. But the interpretation of the coefficients is different. In actual practice it is hard to distinguish between an adaptive-expectations model and a partial-adjustment model.

Suppose we combine the two models. Let us go back to the earlier model of desired capital stock and expected sales, that is,

$$K_t - K_{t-1} = \delta(K_t^* - K_{t-1})$$

$K_t^* = \beta_0 + \beta_1 S_t^*$; that is, "desired" capital stock depends on "expected" sales and $S_t^* - S_{t-1}^* = \lambda(S_{t-1} - S_{t-1}^*)$; that is, expectations about sales are formed by the adaptive-expectations model. We now have

$$K_t = \beta_0\delta + (1 - \delta)K_{t-1} + \beta_1\delta S_t^*$$

Now multiply this equation throughout by $(1 - \lambda)$ and lag it one period. We have

$$(1 - \lambda)K_{t-1} = \beta_0\delta(1 - \lambda) + (1 - \delta)(1 - \lambda)K_{t-2} + \beta_1\delta(1 - \lambda)S_{t-1}^*$$

By subtraction and using the equation for S_t^* we get

$$K_t = \beta_0\delta\lambda + (1 - \delta + 1 - \lambda)K_{t-1} - (1 - \delta)(1 - \lambda)K_{t-2} + \beta_1\delta\lambda S_{t-1}$$

So, we have to regress K_t on K_{t-1}, K_{t-2}, and S_{t-1}. But there is an ambiguity about δ and λ because they occur symmetrically. Note, however, that we can determine β_0 and β_1 unambiguously.

In this case, if there are other variables in the K_t^* equation, we can determine both δ, the speed of adjustment, and λ, the reaction of expectations, unambiguously; e.g., suppose $K_t^* = \beta_0 + \beta_1 S_t^* + \beta_2 L_t$ where L_t is the amount of labor hired. Then we will get

$$K_t = \beta_0\delta\lambda + (1 - \delta + 1 - \lambda)K_{t-1} - (1-\delta)(1-\lambda)K_{t-2}$$
$$+ \beta_1\delta\lambda S_{t-1} + \delta\beta_2 L_t - \delta\beta_2(1-\lambda)L_{t-1}$$

Now we regress K_t on K_{t-1}, K_{t-2}, S_{t-1}, L_t, and L_{t-1}. From the coefficients of L_t and L_{t-1} we can determine uniquely λ. But once λ is known, we get two estimates for δ: one from the coefficient of K_{t-1} and another from the coefficient of K_{t-2}. Corresponding to each δ we get one set of estimates of β_0, β_1, and β_2 from the estimates of the constant term and the coefficients of S_{t-1} and L_t. Thus λ is "uniquely determined" but δ is "overdetermined." In this case what one does is to use the least-squares procedure but subject to the restrictions on the coefficients. Note that there are six coefficients in the equation but only five parameters to estimate: β_0, β_1, β_2, λ, and δ. Thus there is one restriction on the coefficients. Suppose we write the equation as

$$K_t = \alpha_1 + \alpha_2 K_{t-1} + \alpha_3 K_{t-2} + \alpha_4 S_{t-1} + \alpha_5 L_t + \alpha_6 L_{t-1}$$

Then
$$\lambda = 1 + \frac{\alpha_6}{\alpha_5}$$

The estimate of δ from the coefficient of K_{t-1} is

$$\delta = 2 - \alpha_2 - \lambda = 1 - \alpha_2 - \frac{\alpha_6}{\alpha_5}$$

The estimate of δ from the coefficient of K_{t-2} is

$$\delta = 1 + \frac{\alpha_3}{1-\lambda} = 1 - \frac{\alpha_3\alpha_5}{\alpha_6}$$

These two estimates should be equal. Hence the restriction is

$$1 - \alpha_2 - \frac{\alpha_6}{\alpha_5} = 1 - \frac{\alpha_3\alpha_5}{\alpha_6}$$

or
$$-\alpha_3\alpha_5^2 + \alpha_2\alpha_5\alpha_6 + \alpha_6^2 = 0$$

This is a nonlinear restriction. To get estimates of α_1, α_2, α_3, α_4, α_5, α_6, we minimize

$$\sum(K_t - \alpha_1 - \alpha_2 K_{t-1} - \alpha_3 K_{t-2} - \alpha_4 S_{t-1} - \alpha_5 L_t - \alpha_6 L_{t-1})^2$$

subject to the above nonlinear restriction. This is called the *nonlinear least-squares method.*[1]

[1] See Sec. 9-9 for further discussion of the nonlinear least-squares method.

Sometimes what is done is to use a two-step procedure. Note that, *given* λ, the equation to be estimated can be written as

$$K_t - (1-\lambda)K_{t-1} = \beta_0\delta\lambda + (1-\delta)[K_{t-1} - (1-\lambda)K_{t-2}] + \beta_1\delta\lambda S_{t-1} + \beta_2\delta[L_t - (1-\lambda)L_{t-1}]$$

Let

$$\bar{K}_t = K_t - (1-\lambda)K_{t-1}$$
$$\bar{L}_t = L_t - (1-\lambda)L_{t-1}$$

Then what we do is regress $\bar{K}_t$ on $\bar{K}_{t-1}$, S_{t-1}, and $\bar{L}_t$. The coefficient of $\bar{K}_{t-1}$ will give an estimate of $(1-\delta)$. Thus we can estimate δ. Hence we can get estimates of β_0, β_1, and β_2 from the estimates of the other coefficients. Thus what we could do is: First estimate the equation with no restrictions and get an estimate of λ. Use this to transform the variables to $\bar{K}_t$ and $\bar{L}_t$ and now regress $\bar{K}_t$ on $\bar{K}_{t-1}$, S_{t-1}, and $\bar{L}_t$ to get estimates (unique) of β_0, β_1, and β_2 and δ. This is called a *two-step procedure.*

An alternative method is: Choose different values of λ. Since we know that λ lies between 0 and 1, choose $\lambda = 0.0, 0.1, 0.2, \ldots, 1.0$ and for each value of λ run the regression of $\bar{K}_t$ on $\bar{K}_{t-1}$, S_{t-1}, and $\bar{L}_t$. Then the value of λ for which the residual sum of squares is minimum is the best estimate of λ and the corresponding estimates of δ, β_0, β_1, and β_2 are the best estimates of those parameters. This is called the *search method.* Actually, we can conduct the search first at intervals of 0.1 and after we have located the best value of λ we conduct a second search at intervals of 0.01. For example suppose the first round produced the best estimate of λ as 0.6. Then in the second round we search at values of $\lambda = .55, .56, \ldots, .65$ and pick the best value of λ.

Whenever we have a nonlinear equation to estimate which reduces to an ordinary linear equation given the value of one of the parameters, we can use the search procedure described above. The search procedure can, in principle, be used with simultaneous search over more than one parameter. However, it uses up a lot of computer time if we have more than two or three parameters.

Models with Serially Correlated Errors

Suppose we have the model

$$C_t = \beta Y_t + u_t$$

and the residuals u_t are not independent but follow the relationship $u_t = \rho u_{t-1} + e_t$ where e_t are independent with common variance σ^2. Then we have

$$C_t - \rho C_{t-1} = \beta(Y_t - \rho Y_{t-1}) + u_t - \rho u_{t-1}$$

or

$$C_t = \rho C_{t-1} + \beta Y_t - \beta\rho Y_{t-1} + e_t \tag{9-13}$$

Thus, we have to estimate a regression equation of C_t on Y_t, C_{t-1} and Y_{t-1}. But there is a restriction on the coefficients that

$$(\text{Coefficient of } Y_{t-1}) = -(\text{coefficient of } Y_t)(\text{coefficient of } C_{t-1})$$

Hence we have to estimate (9-13) by a nonlinear-least-squares method, or use a search procedure on ρ as described in the preceding section, or use a two-step procedure. The two-step procedure would be as follows: First estimate Eq. (9-13) with no restrictions. Get an estimate of ρ from the coefficient of C_{t-1}. Next use this estimate, say $\hat{\rho}$, to transform the data.

Define $$\overline{C}_t = C_t - \hat{\rho} C_{t-1}$$

and $$\overline{Y}_t = Y_t - \hat{\rho} Y_{t-1}$$

Now estimate a regression of $\overline{C}_t$ on $\overline{Y}_t$ to get an estimate of β.

Equation (9-13) is also similar to Eqs. (9-8) and (9-11) except for the fact that the former has an extra term Y_{t-1}. In fact, Griliches[1] has argued that often we might have a model with no lags but only serially correlated errors, but we might mistakenly think that we have a distributed-lag model or a partial-adjustment model. One way of checking this is to include the lagged value of the explanatory variable in the regression equation. If the coefficient of this variable is approximately equal to the product of the coefficient of the lagged dependent variable and the coefficient of the current value of the explanatory variable with the sign reversed, then we have a serial-correlation model rather than a distributed-lag model.[2] The example he considers is that of estimation of elasticity of substitution in U.S. manufacturing in 1958. The elasticity of substitution is obtained as the estimate of β in the regression equation

$$y = \alpha + \beta x + u$$

where y = log of value added per man-hour
x = log of wage rate per man-hour

The estimated equations were (based on 417 cross-sectional observations)

$$y_{58} = \alpha_1 + \underset{(.047)}{1.198}\, x_{58} \qquad R^2 = .606$$

The elasticity of substitution is thus ≈ 1.2. If we assume a partial-adjustment model we have

$$y_{58} = \alpha_2 + \underset{(.037)}{.233}\, x_{58} + \underset{(.024)}{.827}\, y_{57} \qquad R^2 = .890$$

By introducing the lagged value of y the R^2 increased considerably. The elasticity of substitution is now $\hat{\beta} = .233/1 - .827 \approx 1.35$. But the adjustment coefficient is $1 - .827 = .173$, which is implausibly low. On introducing x_{57} as an extra variable we have

$$y_{58} = \alpha_3 + \underset{(.089)}{1.056}\, x_{58} + \underset{(.022)}{.855}\, y_{57} - \underset{(.022)}{.900}\, x_{57} \qquad R^2 = .918$$

[1] Zvi Griliches, Distributed Lags: A Survey, *Econometrica*, January 1967, pp. 16–49.

[2] Griliches suggests a rough test. A formal discussion of this procedure can be found in K. M. Gaver and G. S. Maddala, "On Testing a Distributed Lag Model vs. a Serial Correlation Model, University of Rochester, September 1974.

This equation gives a better fit than the previous equation. Also (1.056)(.855) = .903, and this is very close to .900, which is the coefficient of x_{57} with sign reversed. Thus, what we have is a serial-correlation model rather than a partial-adjustment model. The elasticity of substitution is close to 1. (It is 1.056 with a standard error of .089.)

In summary, we have considered four different types of models that result in lagged dependent variables among the explanatory variables. It is often very difficult to distinguish among these models, but at the same time the distinctions are important, since the interpretations of the coefficients are very different, depending on the type of model considered.

9-4 STOCHASTIC EXPLANATORY VARIABLES

In the linear-regression model

$$y = \beta x + u$$

we have been assuming that the explanatory variable x is not a random variable. This assumption is rarely valid in econometrics where the observations are seldom generated by a controlled experiment. Also, in the case where the explanatory variables are lagged dependent variables, they cannot be considered as nonrandom.

If x is a random (or stochastic) variable, the derivation of exact finite sampling distributions becomes difficult and we often have to use asymptotic results; i.e., what we consider is the properties of estimators as the sample size grows very large. Presumably, the argument is that if the estimator does not have any desirable properties even in large samples, then it is not worth considering.

One property that is often considered is *consistency*. Suppose $\hat{\beta}_n$ is the estimator of β based on sample size n. Then the sequence of estimators $\hat{\beta}_n$ is called a *consistent* sequence if for any arbitrarily small positive numbers ε and η there is a sample size n_0 such that

$$P\left[|\hat{\beta}_n - \beta| < \varepsilon\right] > 1 - \eta \qquad \text{for all } n > n_0$$

i.e., by increasing the sample size n, the estimator $\hat{\beta}_n$ can be made to lie arbitrarily close to the true value β with probability arbitrarily close to 1. Briefly, we write this as plim $\hat{\beta}_n = \beta$ (plim is probability limit). In practice we often drop the subscript n on $\hat{\beta}_n$ and also drop the words "sequence of estimators" and merely say $\hat{\beta}$ is a consistent estimator for β.

A sufficient condition for $\hat{\beta}$ to be consistent is that the bias and the variance should both tend to zero as the sample size increases.[1] This condition is often useful to check in practice, but it should be noted that the condition is not

[1] Proof of this proposition can be found in any textbook on statistics. See S. S. Wilks, "Mathematical Statistics," John Wiley & Sons, Inc., New York, 1962.

necessary. There are also some relations in probability limits that are useful in proving consistency. These are

$$\text{plim}(c_1 y_1 + c_2 y_2) = c_1 \text{ plim}(y_1) + c_2 \text{ plim}(y_2)$$

where c_1 and c_2 are constants

$$\text{plim}(y_1 y_2) = \text{plim}(y_1) \text{ plim}(y_2)$$

$$\text{plim}\left(\frac{y_1}{y_2}\right) = \frac{\text{plim}(y_1)}{\text{plim}(y_2)} \qquad \text{provided plim}(y_2) \neq 0$$

Also if plim $y = c$ and $g(y)$ is a continuous function of y, then plim $g(y) = g(c)$.

Another concept that is commonly referred to is that of *limiting* distribution. If we consider a sequence of random variables $y_1, y_2, y_3, \ldots,$ with corresponding distribution functions $F_1, F_2, F_3, \ldots,$ this sequence is said to converge in distribution to a random variable y with distribution function F if $F_n(x)$ converges to $F(x)$ as $n \to \infty$ for all continuity points of $F(x)$. The distribution function $F(x)$ is called the *limiting distribution* of this sequence of random variables. It is shown in Fig. 9-3. It is not necessarily true that the moments of F are the limits of the moments of F_n as $n \to \infty$. In fact, often it is the case in econometrics that F_n does not have moments but F does. As an example, suppose x is a random variable with mean $\mu \neq 0$ and variance σ^2 and $P(x = 0) = c > 0$. Suppose a random sample $x_1, x_2, \ldots, x_n$ is drawn from this population and $\bar{x}_n$ is the sample mean based on a sample of size n. If we consider the sequence of random variables $y_n = 1/\bar{x}_n$, then $E(y_n)$ does not exist because there is a positive probability that $x_1 = x_2 = \cdots x_n = 0$ and thus $y_n = \infty$ when $\bar{x}_n = 0$. However, it can be shown that $\sqrt{n}\,(1/\bar{x}_n - 1/\mu)$ has a limiting distribution which is normal with mean zero and variance σ^2/μ^4 so that y_n is asymptotically normally distributed with mean $1/\mu$ and variance $\sigma^2/n\mu^4$. Because moments may not exist for F_n, it is customary to talk of moments of the limiting distribution F, when referring to asymptotic results.

There is, however, no uniformity among econometricians as to how some terms like asymptotic mean and asymptotic variances are defined. For instance, the term *asymptotic unbiasedness* is often defined as follows:

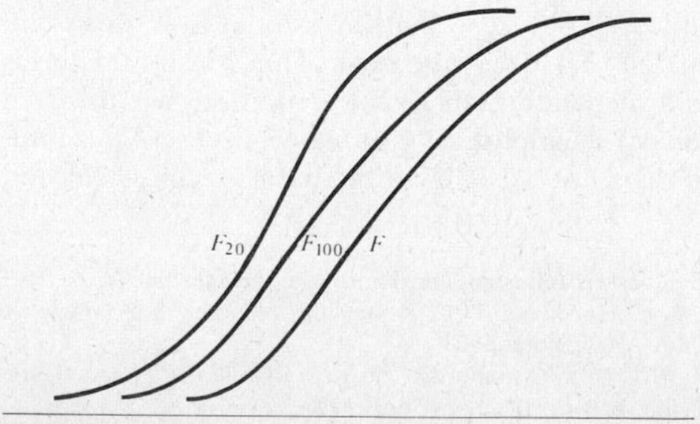

Figure 9-3 Distribution functions for different sample sizes.

If $\hat{\theta}_n$ is an estimator of θ based on a sample of size n, θ_n is called an asymptotically unbiased estimator of θ if $\lim_{n\to\infty} E(\hat{\theta}_n) = \theta$. This definition is not useful if $E(\hat{\theta}_n)$ does not exist.[1]

On the other hand, an alternative definition is the following:[2] $\hat{\theta}_n$ is an asymptotically unbiased estimator for θ if the mean of the limiting distribution of $\sqrt{n}\,(\hat{\theta}_n - \theta)$ is zero. The notation used here is to say $\hat{\theta}_n$ is asymptotically unbiased if

$$\mathrm{AE}(\hat{\theta}_n) = \theta \qquad (\mathrm{AE} = \text{asymptotic expectation})$$

The same is the case with the definition of asymptotic variance. It can be defined as

$$\lim_{n\to\infty} E\left[\sqrt{n}\,(\hat{\theta}_n - \theta)\right]^2 \qquad \text{if we consider limits of variances}$$

or $\mathrm{AE}\left[\sqrt{n}\,(\hat{\theta}_n - \theta)\right]^2$ if we consider variance of the limiting distribution. Note that since the variances of many estimators tend to zero as $n \to \infty$, in defining asymptotic variances we consider $\sqrt{n}\,(\hat{\theta}_n - \theta)$ so that the variances do not tend to zero as $n \to \infty$. Otherwise, it becomes difficult to compare two estimators on the basis of their asymptotic variances.[3]

Consistency and asymptotic unbiasedness are different, and the two definitions of asymptotic unbiasedness are also different. To show this we need examples where $\mathrm{plim}(\hat{\theta}_n)$, $\lim E(\hat{\theta}_n)$, and $\mathrm{AE}(\hat{\theta}_n)$ are different.

Suppose we have a sample of size n, $x_1, x_2, \ldots, x_n$ from a normal distribution with mean θ and variance 1. Consider $\hat{\theta}_n = \bar{x}$ as an estimator of θ. In this case we have $\mathrm{plim}(\hat{\theta}_n) = \lim E(\hat{\theta}_n) = \mathrm{AE}(\hat{\theta}_n) = \theta$. But suppose we consider

$$\hat{\theta}_n = \frac{1}{2}x_1 + \frac{1}{2n}\sum_{2}^{n} x_i$$

as an estimator of θ. Then

$$E(\hat{\theta}_n) = \frac{1}{2}\theta + \frac{n-1}{2n}\theta \qquad \text{so that } \lim_{n\to\infty} E(\hat{\theta}_n) = \theta$$

But $\mathrm{plim}(\hat{\theta}_n) = \frac{1}{2}x_1 + \frac{1}{2}\theta \neq \theta$. Thus we have an asymptotically unbiased estimator that is not consistent. As another example, consider $1/\bar{x}_n$ as an estimator of $1/\theta$. We have $\mathrm{plim}(1/\bar{x}_n) = 1/\theta$ so that the estimator is consistent. Also $\mathrm{AE}(1/\bar{x}_n) = 1/\theta$. But $\lim E(1/\bar{x}_n)$ does not exist. Thus the estimator is asymptotically unbiased or not depending on what definition we use. An estimator can be consistent but not asymptotically unbiased by the AE definition if the limiting distribution does not exist. If an estimator is consistent and

[1] This is the definition used by Goldberger, Johnston, and Kmenta in their textbooks.

[2] This is the definition used in W. C. Hood and T. C. Koopmans, "Studies in Econometric Method," p. 129, John Wiley & Sons, Inc., New York, 1953.

[3] Christ uses $c_n(\hat{\theta}_n - \theta)$, though $c_n = \sqrt{n}$ in most important cases. See C. Christ, "Econometric Models and Methods," p. 265, John Wiley & Sons, Inc., New York, 1966.

asymptotically normal, it is of course asymptotically unbiased (by the AE definition because the limiting distribution exists). Often in econometric literature the asymptotic variances and covariances of estimators are found by replacing AE by plim and evaluating plims. (The implicit assumption is that they are equal.)[1]

If we confine our attention to what are known as CAN (consistent, asymptotically normal) estimators, we can define asymptotic efficiency as follows: If an estimator $\hat{\theta}_n$ is a CAN estimator of θ, it is said to be *asymptotically efficient* if its variance is smaller than or as small as that of any other CAN estimator of θ.

With this preliminary discussion of asymptotic properties of estimators, we can now proceed to discuss the properties of least-squares estimators when the regressors are stochastic.

Properties of Least-Squares Estimators

Consider again the regression model

$$y_i = \beta x_i + u_i$$

where the u_i are independently and identically distributed random variables with mean 0 and variance σ^2. If x is a random variable, we have to specify something about its distribution. We will consider two cases.

(*a*) x and u are independent

(*b*) $\operatorname{plim}\left(\sum_{i=1}^{n} x_i u_i / n\right) = 0$

In case (*a*) the least-squares estimator is still unbiased.

To see this, note that

$$\hat{\beta} = \frac{\sum x_i y_i}{\sum x_i^2}$$

$$= \frac{\sum x_i(\beta x_i + u_i)}{\sum x_i^2}$$

$$= \beta + \frac{\sum x_i u_i}{\sum x_i^2}$$

[1] Johnston defines the asymptotic variances as limits of variances and says it is customary to replace lim E with plim in actual practice because plim is easier to evaluate. See J. Johnston, "Econometric Methods," 2d ed., pp. 270–273, McGraw-Hill Book Company, New York, 1972. However, replacing lim E with plim requires much stronger assumptions (which are rarely satisfied for many estimators considered in econometrics) than replacing AE with plim. We will assume that what we are referring to by asymptotic variance is $\text{AE}\left[\sqrt{n}\,(\hat{\theta}_n - \theta)\right]^2$.

But

$$E\left(\frac{\sum x_i u_i}{\sum x_i^2}\right) = E\left(\frac{x_1 u_1}{\sum x_i^2}\right) + E\left(\frac{x_2 u_2}{\sum x_i^2}\right) + \cdots + E\left(\frac{x_n u_n}{\sum x_i^2}\right)$$

$$= E\left(\frac{x_1}{\sum x_i^2}\right)E(u_1) + E\left(\frac{x_2}{\sum x_i^2}\right)E(u_2) + \cdots + E\left(\frac{x_n}{\sum x_i^2}\right)E(u_n)$$

because x_i are independent of u_i. Since $E(u_i) = 0$ for all i, the above expectation is zero. Thus $E(\hat{\beta}) = \beta$. However, variance of $\hat{\beta}$ is now $E(\sigma^2/\sum x_i^2)$ instead of $\sigma^2/\sum x_i^2$. Unless we know the distribution of x's, we cannot evaluate this expression. In practice one uses $\sigma^2/\sum x_i^2$ as the variance (conditional on the observed x's).

In case (*b*) where x and u are not independent but $\text{plim}(\sum x_i u_i/n) = 0$, we cannot prove unbiasedness but we can show consistency provided $\text{plim}(1/n) \sum x_i^2 \neq 0$, because

$$\begin{aligned}\text{plim } \hat{\beta} &= \beta + \text{plim} \frac{\sum x_i u_i}{\sum x_i^2} \\ &= \beta + \text{plim} \frac{\left[(1/n)\sum x_i u_i\right]}{\text{plim}\left[(1/n)\sum x_i^2\right]} \\ &= \beta \text{ by virtue of the assumptions made}\end{aligned}$$

One can also prove the properties of asymptotic normality and asymptotic efficiency of the least-squares estimators, but we will omit the proofs here.

In many situations the assumption $\text{plim}(\sum x_i u_i/n) = 0$ is not valid. In this case the least-squares estimators are not even consistent. There are four questions one can ask in this connection:

1. How do the correlations between the explanatory variables x and the residuals u arise?
2. How serious can this problem be?
3. What are the solutions to this problem?
4. How can we detect that the problem exists?

Regarding the first question, there are several sources, each of which we will be discussing later. Here we will list four sources. If the residuals u comprise some omitted variables and some of the omitted variables are correlated with the included explanatory variables x, then this can cause correlations between u and x. In another case x is measured with error so that instead of x we observe $X = x + e$. Then if the regression equation is $y = \beta x + u$, the equation in observed variables that we can estimate is

$$\begin{aligned} y &= \beta(X - e) + u \\ &= \beta X + (u - \beta e)\end{aligned}$$

Since $X = x + e$, in this case the residual $(u - \beta e)$ is correlated with the explanatory variable X. Yet another case is what is known as the simultaneous-equation model. Consider a demand-and-supply model. Suppose the demand function is

$$q = \alpha p + u$$

u refers to shifts in the demand function. Unless supply is perfectly elastic, shifts in the demand function will produce changes in price. Hence the residual u and the explanatory variable p will be correlated. Finally, there are models with lagged dependent variables as explanatory variables. In these models if the residuals are autocorrelated, we will have a correlation between the residuals and the explanatory variables. We will discuss this case below.

Regarding the second question, the answer depends on the particular problem, but we can mention here one general result. Consider the regression model

$$y_t = \beta x_t + u_t \qquad t = 1,2, \ldots, T$$

and suppose $\text{var}(x_t) = \sigma_x^2$, $\text{var}(u_t) = \sigma_u^2$, and the correlation between x_t and u_t is ρ. If $\hat{\beta}$ is the ordinary least-squares estimator of β,

$$\text{plim } \hat{\beta} = \beta + \frac{\text{plim}(1/T)\sum xu}{\text{plim}(1/T)\sum x^2}$$

$$= \beta + \frac{\text{cov}(x,u)}{\text{var}(x)} = \beta + \rho \frac{\sigma_u}{\sigma_x}$$

Hence, even if ρ is high, if σ_u/σ_x is small, the (asymptotic) bias is negligible.

This result was given the name "proximity theorem" by Wold. The result was generalized by Wold and Faxer[1] to the case of multiple regression. It shows that even if the correlations between the error and the explanatory variables are high, if the variance of the error is small relative to the variance of the systematic component, then this entails only a small bias in the ordinary least-squares estimators. This same result was proved by Fisher[2] for more complicated models.

Turning next to the third question, the solution will depend on what the problem is. If the problem is omitted variables, one has to reexamine the model. If the problem is one of simultaneous equations or serially correlated residuals and lagged dependent variables, methods of estimation other than ordinary least squares exist. These we will discuss subsequently. One "universal" solution that is suggested for this problem is one of what are known as "instrumental variables." An instrumental variable is one that is uncorrelated with the residual

[1] H. Wold and R. Faxer, On the Specification Error in Regression Analysis, *Annals of Mathematical Statistics*, March 1957.

[2] F. M. Fisher, On the Cost of Approximate Specification in Simultaneous Equation Estimation, *Econometrica*, April 1961.

and highly correlated with x(!). If z is such a variable, estimate $\hat{\beta}$ as $\sum yz/\sum xz$. Hence

$$\hat{\beta} = \frac{\sum(\beta x + u)z}{\sum xz} = \beta + \frac{\sum uz}{\sum xz}$$

$$\text{plim } \hat{\beta} = \beta + \frac{\text{plim}(1/T)\sum uz}{\text{plim}(1/T)\sum xz}$$

Since $\text{plim}(1/T)\sum uz = \text{cov}(u,z) = 0$ and $\text{plim}(1/T)\sum xz = \text{cov}(x,z) \neq 0$ by assumption, we have $\text{plim } \hat{\beta} = \beta$. Thus the method gives consistent estimates of the parameters. One relevant question that anyone would ask immediately is: Where do you get such a variable?

Finally, we come to the question of how to detect whether x and u are uncorrelated. Obviously, one cannot use the least-squares residuals $\hat{u}$ to test this hypothesis because they are by construction uncorrelated with the explanatory variable x. If, however, some instrumental variables are available, one can construct some tests to test the hypothesis that x and u are correlated. A number of such tests have been suggested by Wu,[1] and Revankar and Hartley.[2] It is difficult to explain these tests at this stage.

We will now discuss a model with the lagged dependent variable as an explanatory variable and the residuals u_t not independent but autocorrelated.

$$y_t = \alpha y_{t-1} + u_t$$
$$u_t = \rho u_{t-1} + e_t$$

where e_t are serially independent. The least-squares estimator of α is

$$\hat{\alpha} = \frac{\sum y_t y_{t-1}}{\sum y_{t-1}^2}$$

To evaluate its asymptotic bias, note that

$$y_t = (\alpha + \rho) y_{t-1} - \alpha\rho y_{t-2} + e_t$$

Now multiply both sides by y_{t-1} and sum with respect to t. We get

$$\sum y_t y_{t-1} = (\alpha + \rho)\sum y_{t-1}^2 - \alpha\rho \sum y_{t-1} y_{t-2} + \sum e_t y_{t-1}$$

or
$$\frac{\sum y_t y_{t-1}}{\sum y_{t-1}^2} = \alpha + \rho - \alpha\rho \frac{\sum y_{t-1} y_{t-2}}{\sum y_{t-1}^2} + \frac{\sum e_t y_{t-1}}{\sum y_{t-1}^2}$$

Now, in large samples $\sum y_{t-1} y_{t-2}/\sum y_{t-1}^2$ is approximately $\hat{\alpha}$. Hence, we have

$$\text{plim}(\hat{\alpha}) = (\alpha + \rho) - \alpha\rho\,\text{plim}(\hat{\alpha}) + \text{plim } \frac{\sum e_t y_{t-1}}{\sum y_{t-1}^2}$$

[1] De-Min Wu, Alternative Tests of Independence between Stochastic Regressors and Disturbances, *Econometrica*, 1973, pp. 733–750.

[2] N. S. Revankar and M. J. Hartley, An Independence Test and Conditional Unbiased Prediction in the Context of Simultaneous Equations Systems, *International Economic Review*, October 1973, pp. 625–631.

But $\text{plim}(1/n)\sum e_t y_{t-1} = 0$ because y_{t-1} depends only on $u_{t-1}, u_{t-2}, \ldots$, etc., and therefore e_{t-1}, e_{t-2}, etc., and e_t are serially independent. Hence

$$\text{plim}(\hat{\alpha}) = \frac{\alpha + \rho}{1 + \alpha\rho} = \alpha + \frac{\rho(1 - \alpha^2)}{1 + \alpha\rho}$$

Thus, the asymptotic bias in $\hat{\alpha}$ is $[\rho(1 - \alpha^2)]/(1 + \alpha\rho)$. We assume $|\alpha|$ and $|\rho|$ to be < 1 (otherwise the y_t and u_t series are unstable). Thus if ρ is positive, $\hat{\alpha}$ is upward-biased and if ρ is negative, $\hat{\alpha}$ is downward-biased.

If $\hat{u}_t = y_t - \hat{\alpha} y_{t-1}$ are the estimated residuals based on the OLS estimate $\hat{\alpha}$, and we compute $\hat{\rho}$ as

$$\hat{\rho} = \frac{\sum \hat{u}_t \hat{u}_{t-1}}{\sum \hat{u}_t^2}$$

then it can be shown by a similar reasoning that[1]

$$\text{plim}(\hat{\rho}) = \rho - \frac{\rho(1 - \alpha^2)}{1 + \alpha\rho}$$

Thus, the bias in $\hat{\rho}$ is equal in magnitude and opposite in sign to that in $\hat{\alpha}$. We note that

$$\text{plim}(\hat{\alpha} + \hat{\rho}) = \alpha + \rho$$

Malinvaud also shows that, instead of a model with only the lagged dependent variable, we also have an exogenous variable x_t so that the model is

$$y_t = \alpha y_{t-1} + \beta x_t + u_t$$
$$u_t = \rho u_{t-1} + e_t$$

Then the asymptotic bias in $\hat{\alpha}$, the least-squares estimator of α, is reduced in absolute value but does remain significant.[2]

These results on least-squares bias in models with lagged dependent variables (among regressors) and serially correlated residuals are very important because often ρ is positive and the upward bias in the estimate of α implies very long lags of adjustment, and the downward bias in the estimate of ρ implies that we cannot detect serial correlation by using the Durbin-Watson statistic.[3]

9-5 OMISSION OF RELEVANT AND INCLUSION OF IRRELEVANT VARIABLES

Though this topic falls in the category of specification errors, we will discuss this problem here because the results are needed in the discussion of other topics (like proxy variables).

[1] E. Malinvaud, "Statistical Methods of Econometrics," 2d rev. ed., pp. 556–557, North-Holland Publishing Company, Amsterdam, 1970.

[2] *Ibid*, pp. 559–561.

[3] See Z. Griliches, A Note on Serial Correlation Bias in Estimates of Distributed Lags, *Econometrica*, January 1961.

Suppose the "true" regression equation is

$$y = \beta_1 x_1 + \beta_2 x_2 + u$$

Instead, we estimate the equation $y = \beta_1 x_1 + V$.

The least-squares estimator of β_1 from the "omitted-variable" equation is

$$\begin{aligned}\hat{\beta}_1 &= \frac{\Sigma y x_1}{\Sigma x_1^2} \\ &= \frac{\Sigma x_1(\beta_1 x_1 + \beta_2 x_2 + u)}{\Sigma x_1^2} \\ &= \beta_1 + \beta_2 \frac{\Sigma x_1 x_2}{\Sigma x_1^2} + \frac{\Sigma x_1 u}{\Sigma x_1^2}\end{aligned}$$

Since the expected value of the last term is zero, we have

$$E(\hat{\beta}_1) = \beta_1 + \beta_2 b_{12}$$

where b_{12} is the regression coefficient in the "auxiliary" regression[1] of the excluded variable x_2 on the included variable x_1.

Thus, the bias equals the true coefficient of the omitted variable times the regression coefficient of the excluded variable on the included variable. If the x's are random variables, we consider plim instead of expectation, and we get a similar result about asymptotic bias.

If x_1 and x_2 are independent, the bias is zero, but this does not necessarily mean that we can omit the variable x_2. Since the residuals will now include x_2, the estimated variance of $\hat{\beta}_1$ will be upward-biased. This will result in conservative tests of significance for β_1.

These results can be readily extended to the case of several included and excluded variables. What we have to do is to estimate the auxiliary regressions of each of the excluded variables on all the included variables. In matrix notation we have:

If
$$\mathbf{y} = \mathbf{X}_1\boldsymbol{\beta}_1 + \mathbf{X}_2\boldsymbol{\beta}_2 + \mathbf{u}$$

and we estimate $\mathbf{y} = \mathbf{X}_1\boldsymbol{\beta}_1 + \mathbf{V}$, then

$$\begin{aligned}\hat{\boldsymbol{\beta}}_1 &= (\mathbf{X}_1'\mathbf{X}_1)^{-1}\mathbf{X}_1'\mathbf{y} \\ &= (\mathbf{X}_1'\mathbf{X}_1)^{-1}\mathbf{X}_1'(\mathbf{X}_1\boldsymbol{\beta}_1 + \mathbf{X}_2\boldsymbol{\beta}_2 + \mathbf{u})\end{aligned}$$

Hence
$$E(\hat{\boldsymbol{\beta}}_1) = \boldsymbol{\beta}_1 + \mathbf{P}\boldsymbol{\beta}_2$$

where $\mathbf{P} = (\mathbf{X}_1'\mathbf{X}_1)^{-1}\mathbf{X}_1'\mathbf{X}_2$ is the matrix of regression coefficients from the auxiliary regression of $\mathbf{X}_2$ on $\mathbf{X}_1$.

[1] Note that x_2 and x_1 are assumed to be nonstochastic. Thus the "auxiliary" regression is not a regression equation in the usual sense. It is used here merely as an interpretive device.

Consider now the case of inclusion of irrelevant variables. Suppose the true equation is

$$y = \beta_1 x_1 + u$$

but we estimate the equation

$$y = \beta_1 x_1 + \beta_2 x_2 + V$$

The least-squares estimates of β_1 and β_2 from the misspecified equation are

$$\hat{\beta}_1 = \frac{m_{22}m_{1y} - m_{12}m_{2y}}{m_{11}m_{22} - m_{12}^2}$$

and

$$\hat{\beta}_2 = \frac{m_{11}m_{2y} - m_{12}m_{1y}}{m_{11}m_{22} - m_{12}^2}$$

where $m_{11} = \sum x_1^2$, $m_{12} = \sum x_1 x_2$, etc. Now $E(m_{2y}) = \beta_1 m_{12}$ and $E(m_{1y}) = \beta_1 m_{11}$, since $y = \beta_1 x_1 + u$. Hence $E(m_{11}m_{2y} - m_{12}m_{1y}) = \beta_1 m_{11}m_{12} - \beta_1 m_{11}m_{12} = 0$. Thus $E(\hat{\beta}_2) = 0$. Also $E(\hat{\beta}_1) = \beta_1$.

Thus we get unbiased estimates of both the parameters. This result, coupled with the earlier results regarding the biases introduced by the omission of relevant variables, might lead one to believe that it is better to include variables in the regression equation (when in doubt) rather than exclude them. However, this is not so, because though the inclusion of irrelevant variables has no effect on the bias of the estimators, it does affect the variances.

If β^*_1 is the estimator of β_1 from the correct equation, then $\text{var}(\beta^*_1) = \sigma^2/m_{11}$. But

$$\text{var}(\hat{\beta}_1) = \frac{\sigma^2}{m_{11}(1 - r_{12}^2)}$$

where r_{12} is the correlation between x_1 and x_2. Thus $\text{var}(\hat{\beta}_1) \geqslant \text{var}(\beta^*_1)$, the equality holding for $r_{12} = 0$. Thus we will be getting unbiased but inefficient estimates by including the irrelevant variable. It can be shown, however, that the estimator for the residual variance we use is an unbiased estimator for σ^2. Thus, there is no further bias arising from the use of estimated variances from the misspecified equation.[1]

[1] This proposition is easy to prove in matrix notation:

Let

$\mathbf{y} = \mathbf{X}_1\boldsymbol{\beta}_1 + \mathbf{u}$ be the true equation

$\mathbf{y} = \mathbf{X}_1\boldsymbol{\beta}_1 + \mathbf{X}_2\boldsymbol{\beta}_2 + \mathbf{V} = \mathbf{X}\boldsymbol{\beta} + \mathbf{V}$ be the misspecified equation $\hat{\boldsymbol{\beta}} = (\mathbf{X}'\mathbf{X})^{-1}\mathbf{X}'\mathbf{y}$

Estimated residual $\hat{\mathbf{V}} = \mathbf{y} - \mathbf{X}\hat{\boldsymbol{\beta}} = [\mathbf{I} - \mathbf{X}(\mathbf{X}'\mathbf{X})^{-1}\mathbf{X}']\mathbf{y} = \mathbf{My}$(say). But $\mathbf{y} = \mathbf{X}_1\boldsymbol{\beta}_1 + \mathbf{u}$. Hence $\hat{\mathbf{V}} = \mathbf{MX}_1\boldsymbol{\beta} + \mathbf{Mu}$. But $\mathbf{MX}_1 = 0$. Hence $\hat{\mathbf{V}} = \mathbf{Mu}$. $\hat{\sigma}^2 = \hat{\mathbf{V}}'\hat{\mathbf{V}}/(n-k)$ where k is the dimension of $\mathbf{X}$.

$$E(\hat{\sigma}^2) = \frac{1}{n-k}E(\mathbf{u}'\mathbf{MU}) = \frac{(n-k)\sigma^2}{n-k} = \sigma^2$$

9-6 PROXY VARIABLES

Often the variables we measure are not really what we want to measure. It is customary to call the measured variable a "proxy" variable—it is a proxy for the true variable. For instance, in an investigation of the effect of education on income, what we want to measure is years of education. Instead we measure years of schooling, which is a proxy for years of education.

Sometimes the proxy variable is treated as just the true variable with a measurement error. An example of this is the "permanent income hypothesis" of Friedman where the true variable we want to use is "permanent income" Y_p. Instead we use the proxy "measured income" Y. It is assumed that $Y = Y_p + Y_t$, where Y_t, the "transitory income," is assumed to have the following properties

$$E(Y_t) = 0$$

$$\text{cov}(Y_t, Y_p) = 0$$

i.e., Y_t is an error term with zero mean and is uncorrelated with the true variable Y_p. Problems like this are often discussed under the title of "errors in variables models." We will discuss them in detail in a later chapter. Here we will outline the basic problems arising in such models.

Consider the regression model

$$y = \beta z + u$$

where, instead of the true variable z, we measure the proxy $p = z + e$.

In addition to the usual assumption $\text{cov}(u,z) = 0$, it is often assumed that $\text{cov}(e,z) = \text{cov}(e,u) = 0$, i.e., the measurement error e is uncorrelated with both the error in the regression equation u and the" true" value of the variable z. This assumption, though common in the errors-in-variables literature, may not be a valid one to make in most econometric applications. But the consequences of this are discussed in Chap. 13. For the present we will make this assumption.

We thus have the equation

$$\begin{aligned} y &= \beta(p - e) + u \\ &= \beta p + (u - \beta e) \end{aligned} \tag{9-14}$$

Application of ordinary least squares to (9-14) results in an inconsistent estimator for β, since the composite residual $(u - \beta e)$ is correlated with p. The least-squares estimator of β will be, in large samples[1]

$$\frac{\text{cov}(p,y)}{\text{var}(p)}$$

Since $\text{cov}(p,u - \beta e) = \text{cov}(z + e,u - \beta e) = -\beta\,\text{var}(e)$ we have $\text{cov}(p,y) = \beta\,\text{var}(p) - \beta\,\text{var}(e)$.

[1] In large samples the sample variances and covariances are approximately equal to the population variances and covariances.

Hence the least-squares estimator of β is, in large samples,

$$\beta - \beta \frac{\text{var } e}{\text{var } p} = \beta\left(1 - \frac{\text{var } e}{\text{var } p}\right)$$

Since var p = var z + var e, this expression can also be written as

$$\beta \frac{\text{var } z}{\text{var } z + \text{var } e}$$

Thus the least-squares estimator will underestimate β; the degree of underestimation will depend on the magnitude of the variance of the true variable z. This conclusion should not be taken too seriously in econometric work unless one believes in the restricted assumptions stated earlier.

One suggestion often made in the literature as an alternative to ordinary least squares is to use the "instrumental-variable method" described in Sec. 9-4. In actual practice, the method of instrumental variables is not easy to implement. The question is: Where do you get such a variable? Further, though instrumental-variable methods give estimators that have a smaller bias than the ordinary-least-squares estimator, they have a higher variance. Thus, even if one can, in theory, find instrumental variables, one should not always prefer this method to ordinary least squares.

Sometimes in multiple regression models it is not the coefficient of the proxy variable that we are interested in but the other coefficients. In such cases one question that is often asked is whether it is not better to omit the proxy variable altogether. To simplify matters, consider the two-regressor case

$$y = \beta x + \gamma z + u \tag{9-15}$$

where z is unobserved and x is observed. We make the usual assumption about x,z, and u. Suppose we have a proxy $p = z + e$ where e is uncorrelated with z and u. Then the question is: If we are interested in estimating β, are we better off dropping z altogether or using the proxy p instead of z?

Let us denote the population variances and covariances by m_{xx}, m_{xu}, m_{xz}, etc. We will assume that m_{xx}, m_{xz}, and m_{zz} are finite and $m_{xu} = m_{xe} = m_{zu} = m_{ze} = m_{ue} = 0$. Also denote by σ_u^2 the variance of u and by σ_e^2 the variance of e.

If we omit the variable z altogether from the regression equation, the estimator of β will be, in large samples, equal to

$$\frac{\text{cov}(yx)}{\text{var}(x)} = \beta + \gamma \frac{m_{xz}}{m_{xx}} \tag{9-16}$$

On the other hand, if we use p as a proxy for z in Eq. (9-15) and denote the estimator of β by $\hat{\beta}$, then $\hat{\beta}$ is, in large samples, equal to

$$\frac{m_{pp}m_{xy} - m_{xp}m_{py}}{m_{xx}m_{pp} - m_{xp}^2} \tag{9-17}$$

The denominator of Eq. (9-17) can be written as

$$D = \left(m_{xx}m_{zz} - m_{xz}^2\right) + \sigma_e^2 m_{xx}$$

$$= m_{xx}\left(m_{z\cdot x}^2 + \sigma_e^2\right) \qquad \text{where} \qquad m_{z\cdot x}^2 = m_{zz} - \frac{m_{xz}^2}{m_{xx}} \tag{9-18}$$

is the residual variance of z after removing the effect of x on z. It can be verified that Eq. (9-17) simplifies to

$$\beta + \gamma \frac{m_{xz}}{m_{xx}} \frac{\sigma_e^2}{m_{z\cdot x}^2 + \sigma_e^2}$$

Thus the bias in omitting the variable z is, from Eq. (9-16), $\gamma(m_{xz}/m_{xx})$. The bias from using the proxy p is $\gamma(m_{xz}/m_{xx})\,[\sigma_e^2/(m_{z\cdot x}^2 + \sigma_e^2)]$. Since the factor in the brackets is < 1, it follows that the bias is reduced by using the proxy. McCallum and Wickens[1] have argued on the basis of this result that it is desirable to use even a poor proxy.

This unqualified conclusion of McCallum and Wickens needs to be qualified on two counts. First, they considered only the bias aspect and ignored the variance. The variance of the estimator of β with z omitted will be less than the variance of the estimator of β with the proxy p included. Aigner[2] studies the mean square errors of the two estimators and arrives at the conclusion that the MSE of the estimator omitting z is smaller than the MSE of the estimator including the proxy p if

$$\frac{1-(1-\lambda n)\rho_{xz}^2}{1-(1-\lambda)\rho_{xz}^2}\,\frac{\lambda}{n} > \rho_{xz}^2 \tag{9-19}$$

where $\lambda = \sigma_e^2/(\sigma_e^2 + m_{zz})$ and ρ_{xz} is the correlation between x and z. (This condition is a sufficient, not a necessary, condition.) Aigner computes the regions where the use of the proxy variable is superior on the MSE criterion. He concludes that if λ is small, quite low values for ρ_{xz}^2 and n will suffice to guarantee superiority of the method.

The second major qualification is that the proxy variable does not always fall in the pure errors-in-variables case. Usually, the proxy variable is "some variable" that also depends on the same factors; i.e., p is of the form

$$p = \alpha x + \delta z + e$$

Since z, being unobserved, does not have any natural units of measurement, we will assume that $\delta = 1$, and we can write

$$p = \alpha x + z + e \tag{9-20}$$

[1] B. T. McCallum, Relative Asymptotic Bias from Errors of Omission and Measurement, *Econometrica*, July 1972, pp. 757–758. M. R. Wickens, A Note on the Use of Proxy Variables, *Econometrica*, July 1972, pp. 759–760.

[2] D. J. Aigner, MSE Dominance of Least Squares with Errors-of-Observation, *Journal of Econometrics*, vol. 2, no. 4, December 1974, pp. 365–372.

Also we will assume that m_{ue} is not zero. Under these assumptions it can be verified that Eq. (9-17) simplifies to

$$\beta - \frac{\gamma\alpha\left(m_{xx}m_{zz} - m_{xz}^2\right)}{D} + \frac{\gamma m_{xz}\sigma_e^2 - m_{ue}(\alpha m_{xx} + m_{xz})}{D} \tag{9-21}$$

The expression derived by McCallum and Wickens corresponds to the case $\alpha = 0$ and $m_{ue} = 0$, in which case (9-21) simplifies to

$$\beta + \gamma \frac{m_{xz}}{m_{xx}} \frac{\sigma_e^2}{\sigma_e^2 + m_{z \cdot x}^2}$$

The expression (9-21) shows that including the proxy p does not necessarily lead to smaller bias.

In any specific problem one can derive the appropriate conclusions from the expression in (9-21) after making the appropriate assumptions. However, we might analyze the expression a bit more. Suppose we assume $m_{ue} = 0$ but $\alpha \neq 0$. In this case

$$\text{plim}(\hat{\beta}) = \beta + \gamma\left[w\frac{m_{xz}}{m_{xx}} + (1 - w)(-\alpha)\right] \tag{9-22}$$

where $w = \sigma_e^2/(\sigma_e^2 + m_{z \cdot x}^2)$. Thus the question of the relative bias from the use of the proxy variable as compared with the omission of z depends upon whether $w(m_{xz}/m_{xx}) + (1 - w)(-\alpha)$ is smaller in absolute value than m_{xz}/m_{xx}. As can be seen, this weighted average can even be smaller than $w(m_{xz}/m_{xx})$ in some cases, thus reinforcing the conclusions of McCallum and Wickens (e.g., suppose $m_{xz}/m_{xx} = \alpha$).

One can easily work out the resulting expressions from Eq. (9-21) based on different assumptions. The important point to note is that except in cases where the proxies fall in the category of pure errors in variables, it does not follow that using even a poor proxy is better than using none at all.

Another kind of proxy often used is the dummy-variable type.[1] Suppose we do not observe z but we know when it is in different ranges. For example, "effective education" might be the variable. We do not know how to measure it, but we use dummies for the amount of education, e.g., grade school, high school, college.

For simplicity consider only a simple dummy p, which assumes values 1 and 0. Let Y_1, Z_1, and X_1 be the set of N_1 values for which $p = 1$ and Y_2, Z_2 and X_2 be the set of N_2 values for which $p = 0$. ($N_1 + N_2 = N$.) The observations are thus

y	x	z	p
Y_1	X_1	Z_1	1
Y_2	X_2	Z_2	0

[1] The following example was suggested to me by David M. Grether.

The variance of p is $m_{pp} = \lambda(1-\lambda)$ where $\lambda = N_1/N$. The covariances with the dummy variable p are given by

$$m_{xp} = \lambda(1-\lambda)(\bar{x}_1 - \bar{x}_2)$$
$$m_{py} = \lambda(1-\lambda)(\bar{y}_1 - \bar{y}_2)$$

where $\bar{x}_1, \bar{x}_2, \bar{y}_1, \bar{y}_2$ are the respective means of x and y in the two groups. Thus expression (9-17) simplifies to

$$\frac{\lambda(1-\lambda)m_{xy} - \lambda^2(1-\lambda)^2(\bar{x}_1 - \bar{x}_2)(\bar{y}_1 - \bar{y}_2)}{\lambda(1-\lambda)m_{xx} - \lambda^2(1-\lambda)^2(\bar{x}_1 - \bar{x}_2)^2}$$
$$= \frac{m_{xy} - \lambda(1-\lambda)(\bar{x}_1 - \bar{x}_2)(\bar{y}_1 - \bar{y}_2)}{m_{xx} - \lambda(1-\lambda)(\bar{x}_1 - \bar{x}_2)^2}$$
$$= \beta + \gamma\frac{m_{xz} - \lambda(1-\lambda)(\bar{x}_1 - \bar{x}_2)(\bar{z}_1 - \bar{z}_2)}{m_{xx} - \lambda(1-\lambda)(\bar{x}_1 - \bar{x}_2)^2} \tag{9-23}$$

Whether or not the use of the proxy variable will increase (or decrease) the bias will depend on whether the coefficient of γ in Eq. (9-23) is larger (or smaller) than m_{xz}/m_{xx} in absolute terms. Making different assumptions about the behavior of x and z, one can get different conclusions. One important point to note with the use of dummy variables as proxies is that, in general, the signs of simple-correlation coefficients are not invariant to order preserving transformations of one of the variables.[1] Thus, in the "effective education" example, suppose it is monotonic in the amount of schooling so we can use the years of schooling as a proxy variable. But it is quite possible that the correlation between education and x could have the opposite sign from the correlation between years of schooling and x.

9-7 LIMITED AND DUMMY DEPENDENT VARIABLES

Sometimes in multiple regression models we do not observe the dependent variable over the entire range. For instance, suppose the regression model is

$$y = \beta x + u$$

and we observe y only if $y > 0$. Thus our model is

$$\begin{aligned} y &= \beta x + u \qquad && \text{if } \beta x + u > 0 \quad \text{or } u > -\beta x \\ &= 0 && \text{otherwise} \end{aligned}$$

Here we cannot use just the observations for which $y > 0$ to estimate the regression equation by ordinary least squares because the residuals do not

[1] See D. M. Grether, Correlations with Ordinal Data, *Journal of Econometrics*, vol. 2, no. 3, September 1974, pp. 241–246.

satisfy the condition $E(u) = 0$ if we consider only those residuals such that $u > -\beta x$. If we make some specific assumption about the distribution of u, we can use the ML method to estimate the parameters. For instance, if we assume that u has a normal distribution with mean zero and variance σ^2, the joint distribution of the observations is

$$\prod_1 \frac{1}{\sigma\sqrt{2\pi}} \exp\left[-\frac{1}{2\sigma^2}(y_i - \beta x_i)^2\right] \prod_2 \left\{\int_{-\infty}^{0} \frac{1}{\sigma\sqrt{2\pi}} \exp\left[-\frac{1}{2\sigma^2}(y_j - \beta x_j)^2\right] dy_j\right\}$$

where the first term corresponds to those observations for which we observe y_i and the second term corresponds to these observations for which all we know is that y_j is less than or equal to zero. Compactly, we can write this expression as

$$L = \prod_1 \frac{1}{\sigma} f\left(\frac{y_i - \beta x_i}{\sigma}\right) \prod_2 F\left(\frac{-\beta x_j}{\sigma}\right) \tag{9-24}$$

where $f(\cdot)$ is the standard normal density and $F(\cdot)$ is the cumulative normal density. The ML estimates are obtained by maximizing L with respect to β and σ. This is a nonlinear problem and can be solved using the nonlinear-maximization routines described in the next section.

The earliest application in economics of this model was by Tobin,[1] who used it in the estimation of demand for automobiles. Suppose we have a group of consumers N_1 of whom bought a car and N_2 of whom did not. Suppose y is expenditures on the car and x is, say, income (both in logs). Then if we just use the observations on the people who bought the cars, we would get a biased estimate of the income elasticity of demand. Tobin suggested using all the observations and estimating the parameters by maximizing the likelihood function in Eq. (9-24).

This model is now commonly called the *tobit* (Tobin's probit or, more accurately, Tobin's normit) model. It should be noted that in Eq. (9-24) we do not have to use just the normal density, though Tobin used the normal density. We can use any other probability distribution for u. For instance, if we use the Sech^2 distribution

$$f(u) = \frac{e^u}{(1 + e^u)^2}\, du \qquad -\infty < u < \infty$$

the cumulative density of which is the logistic

$$F(u) = \frac{e^u}{1 + e^u}$$

then Eq. (9-24) will be

$$L = \prod_1 \frac{e^{\beta x_i}}{(1 + e^{\beta x_i})^2} \prod_2 \frac{e^{\beta x_j}}{1 + e^{\beta x_j}} \tag{9-25}$$

This would be the logit model for this problem.

[1] J. Tobin, Estimation of Relationships for Limited Dependent Variables, *Econometrica*, Jan. 1958, pp. 24–36.

There are now many extensions of this simple model that have found interesting practical applications. The special feature of all these models is that they give rise to likelihood functions which are mixtures of densities and cumulative densities as in Eq. (9-24).

In the preceding example, suppose that the dependent variable is a dummy variable. For instance, the variable y is defined as

$$\begin{aligned} y &= 1 \quad \text{if the person bought a car} \\ &= 0 \quad \text{otherwise} \end{aligned}$$

If we use the regression model

$$y = \beta x + u$$

then in this case the residual u can take on only two values $(1 - \beta x)$ and $(-\beta x)$. This produces both nonnormality and heteroscedasticity in the residuals.

Instead we can treat the problem in the following way: Suppose that the true regression model is $y = \beta x + u$.

But we do not observe y. We observe only a dummy variable which takes on values 1 if $\beta x + u > 0$ and 0 if $\beta x + u < 0$. Then the likelihood function for the model is

$$L = \prod_{y=1} F(-\beta x) \prod_{y=0} [1 - F(-\beta x)] \tag{9-26}$$

and making some appropriate assumptions about u, one maximizes this likelihood function. If u follows the Sech^2 distribution, the cumulative densities are logistic and the model is what is commonly known as the logit model. Again the problem of maximizing L is a nonlinear-maximization problem, and some standard routines described in the next section can be used.

Usually the problem we should be formulating is more complicated than this. What we have is a desired expenditure function and an actual expenditure function. We observe that the person buys a car if his desired expenditures are greater than or equal to the actual expenditures. If he does not buy, we know that his desired expenditures are less than the actual expenditures. Similarly, in a labor-market context, we have a reservation wage function and a market wage function. The person is in the labor force if the reservation wage is less than or equal to the market wage. The person is not in the labor force if the opposite is the case. Models of this kind all depend on limited and dummy dependent variables.

In the problem of the demand for automobiles suppose the equations

$$\begin{aligned} y^* &= \beta_1 x_1 + \beta_2 x_2 + u \\ y &= \gamma_1 x_1 + \gamma_2 x_3 + v \end{aligned} \tag{9-27}$$

respectively, describe the actual purchases y^* and the threshold purchases (in this case the price of the cheapest automobile acceptable to the household). For simplicity we are assuming two explanatory variables in each case with one overlapping explanatory variable x_1. We observe the actual expenditures y^* only if $y^* \geqslant y$. In this case we can define a dummy variable D as follows:

$$D = 1 \quad \text{if the person buys a car, i.e., if} \quad y^* \geqslant y$$
$$= 0 \quad \text{otherwise}$$

Also, $y^* \geqslant y \leftrightarrow \beta_1 x_1 + \beta_2 x_2 + u \geqslant \gamma_1 x_1 + \gamma_2 x_3 + v$ or $u - v \geqslant (\gamma_1 - \beta_1)x_1 - \beta_2 x_2 + \gamma_2 x_3$. Let $w = u - v$. Then

$$P(D = 1) = \int_z^\infty f(w)\, dw = 1 - F(z)$$

where
$$z = (\gamma_1 - \beta_1)x_1 - \beta_2 x_2 + \gamma_2 x_3 \tag{9-28}$$

If we do not use the observations on y^*, i.e., the actual expenditures, but use only the information on whether or not the individual has bought a car, we would be maximizing the likelihood function

$$L = \prod_1 [1 - F(z)] \prod_2 F(z) \tag{9-29}$$

where the first term corresponds to those observations for which $D = 1$ and the second term corresponds to those observations for which $D = 0$. Looking at Eq. (9-28), we can easily see that only $(\gamma_1 - \beta_1)$ is estimable but γ_1 and β_1 are not estimable separately. If we use the logistic distribution, Eq. (9-29) will be

$$L = \prod_1 \frac{1}{1 + e^z} \prod_2 \frac{e^z}{1 + e^z} \tag{9-30}$$

If we assume that w follows a normal distribution with mean 0 and variance σ^2, Eq. (9-29) will be

$$L = \prod_1 \int_{z/\sigma}^\infty f(t)dt \prod_2 \int_{-\infty}^{z/\sigma} f(t)dt \tag{9-31}$$

where $f(t)$ is the density function corresponding to the standard normal distribution. In this case it is easy to see that only $(\gamma_1 - \beta_1)/\sigma$, β_2/σ, and γ_2/σ are estimable. Since σ is not estimable, we might as well assume it to be 1 and get estimates of $(\gamma_1 - \beta_1)$, β_2, and γ_2. It is intuitively obvious that when we observe only the (0,1) dependent variable the scale parameter σ is not estimable.

Things are better if we use the information on y^*. For the set of observations for which $D = 1$ (i.e., for those who buy the car) we observe y^*. For those who do not buy, all we know is $w < z$. If $g(u,v)$ is the joint density of u and v, then for the observations $D = 1$, we have

$$y^* = \beta_1 x_1 + \beta_2 x_2 + u$$

and
$$u - [(\gamma_1 - \beta_1)x_1 - \beta_2 x_2 + \gamma_2 x_3] \geqslant v$$

or
$$v \leqslant y^* - \gamma_1 x_1 - \gamma_2 x_3$$

Hence the likelihood function in this case is

$$L = \prod_1 \int_{-\infty}^{y^* - \gamma_1 x_1 - \gamma_2 x_3} g(y^* - \beta_1 x_1 - \beta_2 x_2, v)dv \prod_2 F\left(\frac{z}{\sigma}\right) \tag{9-32}$$

where, again, the first term corresponds to those observations for which $D = 1$ and the second term to those for which $D = 0$.

Suppose u and v are independent and that both are normally distributed with means zero and variance σ_1^2 and σ_2^2, respectively. Then Eq. (9-32) can be written as

$$L = \prod_1 F\left(\frac{y^* - \gamma_1 x_1 - \gamma_2 x_3}{\sigma_2} \right) \frac{1}{\sigma_1} f\left(\frac{y^* - \beta_1 x_1 - \beta_2 x_2}{\sigma_1} \right)$$

$$\times \prod_2 F\left[\frac{(\gamma_1 - \beta_1)x_1 - \beta_2 x_2 + \gamma_2 x_3}{\sigma} \right] \tag{9-33}$$

where $\sigma^2 = \text{var}(u - v) = \sigma_1^2 + \sigma_2^2$, $f(\cdot)$ is the density function, and $F(\cdot)$ is the cumulative distribution function of the standard normal distribution. The observations on y^* now permit estimation of β_1 and γ_1 separately, and we can also get estimates of σ_1 and σ_2 by maximizing the likelihood function of Eq. (9-33). If we assume the covariance between u and v to the σ_{12} ($\neq 0$), it can be shown that σ_{12} is also estimable. On the other hand, if all the explanatory variables occur in the equations for both y^* and y in (9-27), then σ_{12} is not estimable. These problems of which parameters can be estimated and which cannot be estimated are discussed in Nelson.[1]

Cragg[2] discusses this problem, but he estimates two separate equations. One is an equation to explain the decision of whether or not to purchase a car and the other a decision of how much to spend *if* the decision is made to buy a car. The first equation is similar to a tobit model, and the second is an ordinary regression equation. If the variable y (expenditures on the car) is restricted to be positive, the regression equation is specified in terms of $\log y$ rather than y as the explanatory variable. Let us specify

$$P(y = 0) = P(\beta_1 x_1 + u < 0) = P(u < -\beta_1 x_1) \tag{9-34}$$

and $y = \beta_2 x_2 + v$ *if* $y \neq 0$. Assume that u and v are normally distributed with means 0 and variances σ_1^2 and σ_2^2, respectively. Then

$$P(y = 0) = F\left(-\frac{\beta_1 x_1}{\sigma_1} \right)$$

The likelihood function to be maximized is

$$L = \prod_{y=0} F\left(-\frac{\beta_1 x_1}{\sigma_1} \right) \prod_{y \neq 0} \left[1 - F\left(-\frac{\beta_1 x_1}{\sigma_1} \right) \right] \frac{1}{\sigma_2} f\left(\frac{y - \beta_2 x_2}{\sigma_2} \right) \tag{9-35}$$

where $f(\cdot)$ and $F(\cdot)$ are, respectively, the density function and the cumulative

[1] F. D. Nelson, "Censored Regression Models with Unobserved Stochastic Censoring Thresholds," Working Paper 63, Dec. 1974, National Bureau of Economic Research Computing Center, Cambridge, Mass.

[2] J. G. Cragg, Some Statistical Models for Limited Dependent Variables with Application to the Demand for Durable Goods, *Econometrica*, Sept. 1971, pp. 829–844.

distribution function for the standard normal. Obviously, only β_1 is estimable and we cannot get separate estimates of β_1 and σ_1.

Cragg considers several other versions of model (9-34), but the formulation of these models is similar to the one considered above. The formulation in (9-27) where the decisions of whether or not to purchase and how much to purchase are made simultaneously is, however, conceptually better than that of Cragg, which is a two-stage decision framework.

A similar formulation can be adopted for the labor-force participation problem. Let y^* be the reservation wage and y the market wage. Then we find that the individual participates in the labor force if $y \geqslant y^*$ and in this case we observe y. If $y < y^*$, all we observe is that the individual is not in the labor force. In this case we do not observe y. In either case we do not observe y^*. The analysis of this model is similar to that for the one on the demand for cars considered earlier except that we have to reverse some inequalities. In that model we observed y^* if $y^* \geqslant y$. In the labor-force participation model we observe y if $y^* \leqslant y$. This model was analyzed by Nelson[1] using some data analyzed earlier by Gronau.[2] The analysis was based on a random sample of 750 observations for urban white married women, spouse present, from the 1960 census 1/1000 sample. The variables were:

y = hourly wage rate (in dollars)
$E_1 = C_1$ = dummy variable (0,1) for age less than 30
$E_2 = C_2$ = dummy variable (0,1) for age greater than 49
$E_3 = C_3$ = dummy variable (0,1) for education less than high school
$E_4 = C_4$ = dummy variable (0,1) for education greater than high school
C_5 = family income (in \$10,000) net of wife's earnings
C_6 = husband's age (in years)
C_7 = dummy variable (0,1) for husband's education less than high school
C_8 = dummy variable (0,1) for husband's education greater than high school
C_9 = number of children less than 3 years of age
C_{10} = number of children 3 to 5 years of age
C_{11} = number of children 6 to 12 years of age
C_{12} = number of children greater than 12 years of age

If y^* is the reservation wage, the model is

$$y = f(E_1, E_2, E_3 E_4) + v$$
$$y^* = g(C_1, C_2, C_3, C_4, C_5, C_6, C_7, C_8, C_9, C_{10}, C_{11}, C_{12}) + u \tag{9-36}$$

[1] See Nelson, *op. cit.*

[2] R. Gronau, The Effect of Children on the Household's Value of Time, *Journal of Political Economy*, March 1973.

Table 9-2 Estimates of the value of a housewife's time

Variable	Coefficient	*t* ratio
Constant	−.4057	−1.443
C_1	.1518	.982
C_2	.1815	1.275
C_3	−.0235	−.204
C_4	.2166	1.731
C_5	.6817	5.939
C_6	.1141	1.878
C_7	−.0276	−.282
C_8	.0616	.596
C_9	.3681	3.397
C_{10}	.2004	2.690
C_{11}	.1479	2.330
C_{12}	−.0903	−1.488
Standard error	.4278	
Mean value of time	$2.61	
Constant	.2689	2.084
E_1	−.0772	−.704
E_2	−.0656	−.551
E_3	−.2400	−2.119
E_4	.2796	2.247
Standard error	.7287	
Mean potential wage	$1.26	

Since all the variables that appear in the determination of y also occur in the determination of y^*, Nelson assumes $\text{cov}(u, v) = 0$ in his estimation method. The results he obtains are in Table 9-2.

This problem was also analyzed by Heckman,[1] but in Heckman's model there is an extra variable, hours of work H. Equations (9-36) in his model are

$$y = f(E) + v$$
$$y^* = g(C, H) + u$$

If hours worked are perfectly flexible, working women adjust H so as to equate y to y^*. When a corner point solution is reached ($H = 0$), y^* exceeds y, both variables are unobserved, and the individual drops out of the labor force. The likelihood function to analyze Heckman's model is much more complicated than that for the model considered by Nelson. Since it involves knowledge of simultaneous-equation models (discussed in Chap. 11), we will not discuss this model here.

There are many other models that depend on the methods discussed here.

[1] J. Heckman, Shadow Prices, Market Wages and Labor Supply, *Econometrica*, July 1974, pp. 679–694.

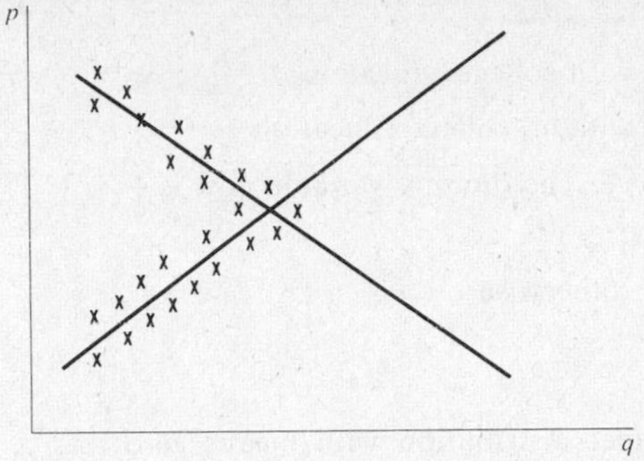

Figure 9-4 Disequilibrium-market model.

One set of such models is what are known as *disequilibrium-market models*. These are models where we have a demand function and a supply function but the market does not clear in each time period. We observe the quantity demanded (if there is excess supply) and the quantity supplied (if there is excess demand). The situation is as illustrated in Fig. 9-4. The observations are marked by crosses.

Models of this kind were first analyzed by Fair and Jaffee,[1] who used some variants of least-squares methods. The correct likelihood functions for the application of the ML method in these models are presented in Amemiya[2] and Maddala and Nelson.[3]

A further set of models is what is known as *dummy-endogenous-variable models*. Consider as an illustration the following simple example where the problem is to estimate the returns to college-going education. Suppose that we are given data on the variable y (income) for n individuals; n_1 of them have had college education and n_2 of them have not. We are interested in estimating the average increment in income due to going to college.[4] One simple solution is to regress y on a dummy variable D defined as

$$D = 1 \text{ if the individual has college education}$$
$$= 0 \qquad \text{otherwise}$$

The coefficient of D will measure the average increase in income due to going to college. If $\bar{y}_1$ is the mean income of those with college education and $\bar{y}_2$ the mean income of those without college education, this coefficient is nothing but $\bar{y}_1 - \bar{y}_2$.

However, suppose that all the individuals have the same opportunities available to them and that an individual goes to college if he thinks his income will be higher by having college education. Otherwise he does not.

[1] R. C. Fair and D. M. Jaffee, Methods of Estimation for Markets in Disequilibrium, *Econometrica*, 1972, pp. 497–514.

[2] T. Amemiya, A Note on a Fair and Jaffee Model, *Econometrica*, 1974, pp. 759–762.

[3] G. S. Maddala and F. D. Nelson, Maximum Likelihood Methods for Models of Markets in Disequilibrium, *Econometrica*, 1974, pp. 1013–1030.

[4] For simplicity we are avoiding the problems of costs of going to college, foregone earning, etc.

Let

$$y_1^* = \text{expected income with college education}$$
$$y_2^* = \text{expected income without college education}$$

The individual goes to college if $y_1^* > y_2^*$. The dummy variable now is

$$D = 1 \text{ if } y_1^* > y_2^*$$
$$= 0 \qquad \text{otherwise}$$

Suppose that $y_1^* = \alpha_1 + u_1$
$y_2^* = \alpha_2 + u_2$

and u_1 and u_2 have a bivariate normal distribution with means zero and a covariance matrix

$$\begin{bmatrix} \sigma_1^2 & \sigma_{12} \\ \sigma_{12} & \sigma_2^2 \end{bmatrix}$$

Our objective is to estimate α_1, α_2, σ_1^2, σ_2^2, and σ_{12}. The difference $\alpha_1 - \alpha_2$ now measures the average increase in income due to college education. Two assumptions are being made in the above formulation: first that people choose, second that they are right in their decisions. The first assumption is very reasonable. The second assumption can be defended on the grounds that it is hard to formulate a theory of systematic mistakes. The sample quantities we have are the means $\bar{y}_1$, $\bar{y}_2$, the variances s_1^2 and s_2^2, and the proportion $n_1/(n_1 + n_2)$ going to college. From these five sample quantities, we can estimate the five parameters α_1, α_2, σ_1^2, σ_2^2, and σ_{12} (details are not given here and are left as an exercise). However, there is one interesting feature of this model that is worth mentioning here. Since u_1 and u_2 are normally distributed, $u_1 - u_2$ is also normally distributed with variance $\sigma^2 = \sigma_1^2 + \sigma_2^2 - 2\sigma_{12}$. Probability that an individual goes to college is

$$P(y_1^* > y_2^*) = P(u_1 - u_2 > \alpha_2 - \alpha_1)$$
$$= 1 - \int_{-\infty}^{z} \frac{1}{\sqrt{2\pi}} e^{-t^2/2} dt \qquad \text{where} \qquad z = \frac{\alpha_2 - \alpha_1}{\sigma}$$

An estimate of this quantity is $n_1/(n_1 + n_2)$. Given this number, we can estimate z by looking at the tables of the cumulative normal distribution. Thus if $n_1 = n_2$, the estimate of z is zero or $\hat{\alpha}_2 = \hat{\alpha}_1$. Thus the incremental returns to college education are zero. This result is in marked contrast to the result we would obtain if we regarded the dummy variable D as exogenous rather than endogenous.

All the models considered in this section are highly nonlinear. To estimate the parameters by the maximum-likelihood method, we have to use some methods of nonlinear optimization. In the following sections we will briefly describe the methods of nonlinear optimization, the nonlinear least-squares method, and some important results one needs to know about the ML approach.

Since we cannot go into all the details here, our discussion will necessarily be brief. Details can be found in the references cited.[1]

9-8 METHODS OF NONLINEAR OPTIMIZATION

Often we have n observations $y_1, y_2, \ldots, y_n$, each of which depends on a set of m parameters $\Theta_1, \Theta_2, \ldots, \Theta_m$, so that we can write

$$y_j = f_j(\Theta_1, \Theta_2, \ldots, \Theta_m) \qquad j = 1, 2, \ldots, n$$

The functions f_j are not necessarily linear functions. We are required to obtain estimates of the parameters Θ_i which satisfy a criterion function. In the maximum-likelihood method we obtain those estimates that maximize the likelihood function. In the nonlinear-least-squares procedure we obtain the estimates that minimize the sum of squares

$$\sum_i [y_i - f_i(\Theta_1, \Theta_2, \ldots, \Theta_m)]^2$$

or maximize the negative of this expression. In either case, so far as the numerical techniques are concerned, we have the problem of maximizing a function of the form $F(x_1, x_2, \ldots, x_m)$ where x's are the parameters. The following are some numerical procedures for this maximization problem.

Cauchy's method. The earliest method is the steepest-ascent method suggested by Cauchy in 1847. In the simplest case of a function of two variables, we can consider the surface $Z = F(x_1, x_2)$ and ask the question: Which uphill direction is steepest? If F is differentiable and we take a small step from the point (x_1, x_2), expanding in Taylor series, we get approximately

$$F(x_1 + d_1, x_2 + d_2) - F(x_1, x_2) \approx d_1 g_1 + d_2 g_2$$

where $$g_1 = \frac{\partial F}{\partial x_1} \qquad \text{and} \qquad g_2 = \frac{\partial F}{\partial x_2}$$

The vector (g_1, g_2) is called the "gradient vector" at the point (x_1, x_2). Also

$$d_1 g_1 + d_2 g_2 = \sqrt{d_1^2 + d_2^2}\,\sqrt{g_1^2 + g_2^2}\,\cos\alpha$$

where α is the angle between the step (d_1, d_2) and the gradient vector at (x_1, x_2). Different directions at the step give different angles, but the steepest direction is one for which $\cos\alpha = 1$, i.e., for which $\alpha = 0$ or the direction of the gradient vector. In the general case of m parameters $(x_1, x_2, \ldots, x_m)$ let

$$g_i = \frac{\partial F}{\partial x_i} \qquad i = 1, 2, \ldots, m$$

[1] See also Y. Bard, "Non-Linear Parameter Estimation," Academic Press, Inc., New York, 1974.

A step of the steepest ascent is chosen in the direction $(g_1, g_2, \ldots, g_m)$. The length of the step is chosen so as to maximize the new value of F. This is done by choosing that value of λ which maximizes

$$\phi(\lambda) = F(x_1 + \lambda g_1, x_2 + \lambda g_2, \ldots, x_m + \lambda g_m)$$

The steepest-ascent method has been found to converge very slowly. Hence it is often best to use the other methods described below.

The Newton-Raphson method. Cauchy's method uses only the first derivatives g_i. The Newton-Raphson method depends on a Taylor-series expansion to the second order. Let

$$G_{ij} = \frac{\partial^2 F}{\partial x_i \partial x_j} \qquad i, j = 1,2, \ldots, m$$

Then the Taylor expansion to the second order gives

$$F(x_1 + d_1, x_2 + d_2, \ldots, x_m + d_m) - F(x_1, x_2, \ldots, x_m) \approx \sum_i d_i g_i + \sum_i \sum_j G_{ij} d_i d_j$$

At the maximum, the first derivatives are all zero, and hence if the quadratic approximation is exact, the point $(x_1 + d_1, x_2 + d_2, \ldots, x_m + d_m)$ is the required optimum only if

$$g_i + \sum_j G_{ij} d_j = 0 \qquad i = 1,2, \ldots, m$$

Thus, if

$$\mathbf{d} = \begin{bmatrix} d_1 \\ d_2 \\ d_m \end{bmatrix} \qquad \mathbf{g} = \begin{bmatrix} g_1 \\ g_2 \\ g_m \end{bmatrix} \qquad \text{and} \qquad \mathbf{G} = [G_{ij}]$$

then $\mathbf{d} = -\mathbf{G}^{-1}\mathbf{g}$. This technique is applied iteratively, changing the starting values of x_i at each stage to $x_i + d_i$ and computing $\mathbf{G}$ and $\mathbf{g}$ at the new values to get the new step. If the function F is quadratic, the quadratic approximation is exact and we get the maximum in a single step. If F is not quadratic but the starting point $(x_1, x_2, \ldots, x_m)$ is close to the maximum, the approximation is likely to be good and the iterative process can be expected to converge rapidly. If the starting value is far from the maximum, the Newton-Raphson method may not converge and can keep moving in the wrong direction. One well-known strategy to avoid going in the wrong direction is not to take the entire step d but to choose a value λ and take a step λd so that $\phi(\lambda) = F(x_1 + \lambda d_1, x_2 + \lambda d_2, \ldots, x_m + \lambda d_m)$ is maximum (as was done in the Cauchy method). This "extended Newton-Raphson method" has been found to be very successful in practice. If $\mathbf{G} = -\mathbf{I}$ where $\mathbf{I}$ is the identity matrix, then this "extended Newton-Raphson method" is the Cauchy method.

Quadratic hill-climbing method. The performance of the Newton-Raphson method can be poor if the initial values are far from the position of the maximum. Hence some modifications of this method have been suggested by Greenstadt, and Goldfeld, Quandt, and Trotter. The method suggested by the latter is known as the quadratic hill-climbing method. Greenstadt's method is the following: Suppose the matrix of second derivatives **G** at any iteration is not negative definite. We can write **G** as **PDP**′, where **P** is an orthogonal matrix and **D** is a diagonal matrix whose elements are the eigenvalues of **G**. Instead of **G**, Greenstadt suggests using $\mathbf{G}^* = \mathbf{P}\mathbf{D}^*\mathbf{P}'$, where $\mathbf{D}^*$ is a diagonal matrix obtained by changing the sign of the positive diagonal elements of **D**, leaving the negative elements as they are. This ensures that $\mathbf{G}^*$ is negative definite. Apparently, this method works well in practice. The quadratic hill-climbing method replaces **G** by $\mathbf{G} - \alpha\mathbf{I}$, where $\alpha \geqslant 0$ so that

$$\mathbf{d} = -(\mathbf{G} - \alpha\mathbf{I})^{-1}\mathbf{g}$$

If $\alpha = 0$, we have the Newton-Raphson method. If α is very large, the interpolation moves in the direction of the steepest-ascent method but with a very small step. Thus the quadratic hill-climbing method can be regarded as an interpolation between these two methods. The subtraction of $\alpha\mathbf{I}$ from **G** ensures that **G** is negative definite. Goldfeld, Quandt, and Trotter suggest a modification of the quadratic hill-climbing method in which **G** is replaced by $\mathbf{G} - \mathbf{Q}$, where **Q** is a positive-definite matrix,[1] so that

$$\mathbf{d} = -(\mathbf{G} - \mathbf{Q})^{-1}\mathbf{g}$$

Davidon-Fletcher-Powell method.[2] One major problem with the Newton-Raphson method and its refinements discussed above is that they require the matrix of second derivatives. To solve this problem, methods have been devised that take account of second-derivative terms but do not explicitly use the second derivatives. These methods have been found to work well in practice, though theoretical reasons for their good performance are not known. The methods also have been found to work well even if the initial value is poor and far away from the optimum. One method is the Fletcher-Reeves method, in which we choose the first step *d*, using the steepest-ascent method, and generate the successive steps as

$$\mathbf{d}_k = \mathbf{g}_k + \frac{\alpha_k}{\alpha_{k-1}}\mathbf{d}_{k-1}$$

where $\alpha_k = \mathbf{g}'_k\mathbf{g}_k$ and $\mathbf{g}_k$ is the gradient vector at step k. But by far the most popular of these methods is the Davidon-Fletcher-Powell (DFP) method.

Note that the Newton-Raphson method requires the inverse of the matrix of second derivatives $\mathbf{G}^{-1}$. Let **H** be an initial approximation to this so that

$$\mathbf{d} = -\mathbf{H}\mathbf{g}$$

[1] See S. M. Goldfeld and R. E. Quandt, "Nonlinear Methods in Econometrics," chap. 1, North-Holland Publishing Company, Amsterdam, 1972.

[2] R. Fletcher and M. J. D. Powell, A Rapidly Convergent Descent Method for Minimization, *Computer Journal*, 1963, pp. 163–168.

The idea of the DFP method is to calculate the change in the gradient to get a better approximation to **H**. The original suggestion of Davidon was to use the revised **H** as

$$\mathbf{H}^* = \mathbf{H} - \frac{1}{\gamma'\mathbf{d}}(\mathbf{dd}') - \frac{1}{\gamma'\mathbf{H}\gamma}\mathbf{H}\gamma\gamma'\mathbf{H}$$

where $\gamma = \mathbf{g}(x + d) - \mathbf{g}(x)$ is the calculated change in the gradient. Note that each of the matrices $\mathbf{dd}'$ and $\mathbf{H}\gamma\gamma'\mathbf{H}$ has rank 1. Another suggestion in the literature is to use

$$\mathbf{H}^* = \mathbf{H} - \frac{(\mathbf{d} + \mathbf{H}\gamma)(\mathbf{d} + \mathbf{H}\gamma)'}{(\gamma'\mathbf{d} + \gamma'\mathbf{H}\gamma)}$$

Note that the latter matrix in this expression has rank 1. In a subsequent paper,[1] Powell gives some further expressions for revising **H**.

9-9 NONLINEAR LEAST SQUARES

In nonlinear least squares we have a set of n observations $y_1, y_2, \ldots, y_n$ where

$$y_i = f_i(\theta_1, \theta_2, \ldots, \theta_m) + u_i$$

and we choose the parameters $\theta_1, \theta_2, \ldots, \theta_m$ so as to minimize

$$\sum_{i=1}^{n} [y_i - f_i(\theta_1, \theta_2, \ldots, \theta_m)]^2$$

The functions f_i will, of course, involve some explanatory variables in regression problems, but we need not consider them here. Written compactly in vector and matrix notation, we minimize

$$S(\theta) = [\mathbf{y} - \mathbf{f}(\theta)]'[\mathbf{y} - \mathbf{f}(\theta)]$$

Let **F** be an $n \times m$ matrix of partial derivatives

$$\frac{\partial f_i}{\partial \theta_j} \qquad i = 1,2, \ldots, n$$

$$j = 1,2, \ldots, m$$

The ith row of **F** gives the derivatives of f_i with respect to $\theta_1, \theta_2, \ldots, \theta_m$. Let $\mathbf{F}_0$ be the value of **F** evaluated at the initial value $\theta_0 = (\theta_{10}, \theta_{20}, \ldots, \theta_{m0})$.

The Gauss-Newton method. This method consists of taking a linear expansion of $\mathbf{f}(\boldsymbol{\theta})$ around $\boldsymbol{\theta}_0$ and then using ordinary least squares. We therefore minimize with respect to $\boldsymbol{\theta}$

$$[\mathbf{y} - \mathbf{f}(\boldsymbol{\theta}_0) - \mathbf{F}_0(\boldsymbol{\theta} - \boldsymbol{\theta}_0)]'[\mathbf{y} - \mathbf{f}(\boldsymbol{\theta}_0) - \mathbf{F}_0(\boldsymbol{\theta} - \boldsymbol{\theta}_0)]$$

[1] M. J. D. Powell, A New Algorithm for Unconstrained Optimization, in Rosen et al. (eds.), "Non-Linear Programming," Academic Press, Inc., New York, 1970.

This gives $\mathbf{F}_0'[\mathbf{y} - \mathbf{f}(\boldsymbol{\theta}_0) - \mathbf{F}_0(\boldsymbol{\theta} - \boldsymbol{\theta}_0)] = \mathbf{0}$. Or the change $\mathbf{d} = \boldsymbol{\theta} - \boldsymbol{\theta}_0$ is given by

$$\mathbf{d} = (\mathbf{F}_0'\mathbf{F}_0)^{-1}\mathbf{F}_0'[\mathbf{y} - \mathbf{f}(\boldsymbol{\theta}_0)]$$

This procedure is repeated with the new value as the starting value. As an illustration suppose the regression model is $y_i = \theta_1 + \theta_2 X_i^{\theta_3} + u_i$ and we minimize the sum of squares $\sum[y_i - \theta_1 - \theta_2 X_i^{\theta_3}]$. Here $f_i(\boldsymbol{\theta}) = \theta_1 + \theta_2 X_i^{\theta_3}$. The ith row of the matrix $\mathbf{F}$ is

$$\left[\frac{\partial f_i}{\partial \theta_j}\right] = \begin{bmatrix} 1 & X_i^{\theta_3} & \theta_2 X_i^{\theta_3} \log X_i \end{bmatrix}$$

Hence

$$\mathbf{F}'\mathbf{F} = \begin{bmatrix} n & \sum X_i^{\theta_3} & \sum \theta_2 X_i^{\theta_3} \log X_i \\ \sum X_i^{\theta_3} & \sum X_i^{2\theta_3} & \sum \theta_2 X_i^{2\theta_3} \log X_i \\ \sum \theta_2 X_i^{\theta_3} \log X_i & \sum \theta_2 X_i^{2\theta_3} \log X_i & \sum \theta_2^2 X_i^{2\theta_3} (\log X_i)^2 \end{bmatrix}$$

(All summations are from 1 to n.) Also

$$\mathbf{F}'[\mathbf{y} - \mathbf{f}(\boldsymbol{\theta})] = \begin{bmatrix} \sum(y_i - \theta_1 - \theta_2 X_i^{\theta_3}) \\ \sum X_i^{\theta_3}(y_i - \theta_1 - \theta_2 X_i^{\theta_3}) \\ \sum(\theta_2 X_i^{\theta_3} \log X_i)(y_i - \theta_1 - \theta_2 X_i^{\theta_3}) \end{bmatrix}$$

At each iteration we have to evaluate these two expressions at the starting values. The correction factor is given by $(\mathbf{F}'\mathbf{F})^{-1}\mathbf{F}'[\mathbf{y} - \mathbf{f}(\boldsymbol{\theta})]$. For the steepest-descent method, it should be noted that all we need is the gradient vector $S'(\boldsymbol{\theta})$, which is $\mathbf{F}'[\mathbf{y} - \mathbf{f}(\boldsymbol{\theta})]$. Thus for the Gauss-Newton method we have the extra computational effort involved in computing and inverting the matrix $\mathbf{F}'\mathbf{F}$.

Hartley[1] suggests a modification of the Gauss-Newton method where instead of taking the step d, we take the step λd, where λ is between 0 and 1 and $\text{SSE}(\theta_0 + \lambda d) \leqslant \text{SSE}(\theta_0)$, where SSE is the sum of squares of errors

$$\text{SSE}(\boldsymbol{\theta}_0) = [\mathbf{y} - \mathbf{f}(\boldsymbol{\theta}_0)]'[\mathbf{y} - \mathbf{f}(\boldsymbol{\theta}_0)]$$

The value of λ changes from iteration to iteration.

If we assume that the residuals u_i are independently and identically distributed with mean 0 and variance σ^2 and if $\hat{\boldsymbol{\theta}}$ is the final estimate of $\boldsymbol{\theta}$, then

$$\hat{\sigma}^2 = \frac{1}{n}\,\text{SSE}(\hat{\boldsymbol{\theta}})$$

and the nonlinear-least-squares estimator $\hat{\boldsymbol{\theta}}$ is approximately normally distributed with mean $\boldsymbol{\theta}$ and covariance matrix $\hat{\sigma}^2[\mathbf{F}(\hat{\boldsymbol{\theta}})'\mathbf{F}(\hat{\boldsymbol{\theta}})]^{-1}$.

[1] See H. O. Hartley, The Modified Gauss-Newton Method for the Fitting of Non-Linear Regression Functions by Least Squares, *Technometrics*, 1961, pp. 269–280. Also H. O. Hartley and A. Booker, Non-Linear Least Squares Estimation, *Annals of Mathematical Statistics*, 1965, pp. 638–650.

9-10 THE MAXIMUM-LIKELIHOOD APPROACH

Given a sample of n independent observations $(y_1, y_2, \ldots, y_n)$ from a density function $f(y,\theta)$ the joint density of the observations is

$$\prod_{i=1}^{n} f(y_i,\theta)$$

This function (regarded as a function of θ) is called the *likelihood function* of θ. Let us call it $L(\theta)$. The ML method of estimation involves choosing that value of θ (as an estimator for θ) for which $L(\theta)$ is maximum. Instead of maximizing the likelihood function $L(\theta)$, it is often found convenient to maximize the log of the likelihood function

$$\log L(\theta) = \sum_{i=1}^{n} \log f(y_i,\theta)$$

A necessary condition that $\log L$ is maximum at $\theta = \hat{\theta}$ is

$$\left.\frac{\partial \log L}{\partial \theta}\right]_{\theta=\hat{\theta}} = 0$$

The quantity $(\partial \log L)/\partial\theta$ is sometimes called the *efficient score* for θ and is denoted by $S(\theta)$. Thus the ML estimator is the value of θ for which the efficient score vanishes.

Also $E[-(\partial^2 \log L)/\partial\theta^2]$ is called the *information on θ in the sample.* It is denoted by $I(\theta)$. The equation

$$\frac{\partial \log L}{\partial \theta} = 0$$

is called the *likelihood equation*. Sometimes it can be solved easily. But often it is very nonlinear and has to be solved in an iterative fashion. For this purpose any of the methods suggested in Sec. 9-8 can be used. One other method closely related to the Newton-Raphson method is what is known as the *method of scoring.*[1] If θ_0 is a trial value of the estimate, then expanding $(\partial \log L)/\partial\theta$ and retaining only the first power of $\delta\theta = \theta - \theta_0$, we get

$$\frac{\partial \log L}{\partial \theta} \approx \frac{\partial \log L}{\partial \theta_0} + \delta\theta \frac{\partial^2 \log L}{\partial \theta_0^2}$$

In large samples we can substitute $-I(\theta_0)$ for $(\partial^2 \log L)/\partial\theta_0^2$. Hence we get, using the definition of $S(\theta)$,

$$\frac{\partial \log L}{\partial \theta} \approx S(\theta_0) - \delta\theta\, I(\theta_0)$$

[1] The difference between the Newton-Raphson method and the method of scoring is that the former depends on *observed* second derivatives and the latter depends on *expected values* of the second derivatives. There seems to be some evidence that the method of scoring, where feasible, is to be preferred.

At the maximum $(\partial \log L)/\partial\theta = 0$. Hence the correction $\delta\theta$ from the initial value θ_0 is $S(\theta_0)/I(\theta_0)$. As an illustration of the scoring method, consider the following regression model:

$$y_i = \frac{1}{x_i - \beta} + u_i$$

where u_i are $IN(0,1)$. We assume the variance of u_i to be unity, since we want to discuss the single-parameter case here. The log likelihood function is

$$\log L = \text{const} - 1/2 \sum \left(y_i - \frac{1}{x_i - \beta} \right)^2$$

$$\frac{\partial \log L}{\partial \beta} = S(\beta) = \sum \left(y_i - \frac{1}{x_i - \beta} \right) \frac{1}{(x_i - \beta)^2} = 0$$

is the likelihood equation. This is a nonlinear equation in β.

$$\frac{\partial^2 \log L}{\partial \beta^2} = \sum \left[\frac{2y_i}{(x_i - \beta)^3} - \frac{3}{(x_i - \beta)^4} \right]$$

Since

$$E(y_i) = \frac{1}{x_i - \beta}$$

we have

$$I(\beta) = E\left(\frac{-\partial^2 \log L}{\partial \beta^2} \right) = \sum \frac{1}{(x_i - \beta)^4}$$

Suppose we start with an initial value β_0. Then we calculate $S(\beta_0)$ and $I(\beta_0)$. The next value

$$\beta_1 = \beta_0 + \frac{S(\beta_0)}{I(\beta_0)}$$

We next calculate $S(\beta_1)$ and $I(\beta_1)$ and proceed with this iteration until convergence.

The expression $I(\beta)$ plays a central role in the theory of ML estimation. It has been proved[1] that, under fairly general conditions, the ML estimator is consistent and asymptotically normally distributed with variance $[I(\beta)]^{-1}$. Thus, in the above problem at the final step of the iteration we get an estimate of asymptotic variance of the ML estimator as $[I(\hat{\beta})]^{-1}$.

The quantity $[I(\beta)]^{-1}$ is also known as the information limit to the variance, or alternatively as the *Cramer-Rao lower bound* for the variance of the estimator $\hat{\beta}$. It is called the lower bound because it has been shown that under some

[1] There are several statements and proofs in the literature. See R. H. Norden, A Survey of Maximum Likelihood Estimation, *Review of the International Statistical Institute*, 1972, pp. 329–354.

general conditions if we consider any other estimator β^* for β that is consistent and uniformly asymptotically normally distributed (CUAN), then

$$V(\beta^*) \geqslant [I(\beta)]^{-1}$$

We need not go into the proofs of these propositions here. Details of this can be found in Rao.[1]

The method of scoring, like the Newton-Raphson method, requires the evaluation of the second derivatives; and in addition it also requires the expected values of the second derivatives. In actual practice, one can use some properties of the likelihood function and get away with only first derivatives. To see this, we note that we can write $I(\theta)$ as

$$I(\theta) = E\left(\frac{\partial \log L}{\partial \theta}\right)^2$$

This can be shown as follows: Since $L(y,\theta)$ is nothing but the joint density of the observations, we have $\int L(y,\theta)dy = 1$. (Here we have used y to denote the n observations $y_1, y_2, \ldots, y_n, dy$ to denote $dy_1, dy_2, \ldots, dy_n$, and the single integral sign to denote an n-fold integral.) Assuming that we can differentiate under the integral sign, we have

$$\int \frac{\partial L}{\partial \theta} dy = 0 \qquad \text{or} \qquad \int \left(\frac{1}{L}\frac{\partial L}{\partial \theta}\right) L\, dy = 0 \qquad \text{or} \qquad E\left(\frac{\partial \log L}{\partial \theta}\right) = 0$$

Consider now

$$\int \frac{\partial \log L}{\partial \theta} L\, dy = 0$$

Differentiate once again with respect to θ. We get

$$\int \left[\frac{\partial^2 \log L}{\partial \theta^2} + \left(\frac{\partial \log L}{\partial \theta}\right)^2\right] L\, dy = 0$$

or

$$E\left(-\frac{\partial^2 \log L}{\partial \theta^2}\right) = E\left(\frac{\partial \log L}{\partial \theta}\right)^2 = I(\theta)$$

Now

$$E\left(\frac{\partial \log L}{\partial \theta}\right)^2 = E\left[\sum_{i=1}^{n} \frac{\partial \log f(y_i,\theta)}{\partial \theta}\right]^2 = E(Q)$$

where

$$Q = \sum_{i=1}^{n}\left[\frac{\partial \log f(y_i,\theta)}{\partial \theta}\right]^2$$

[1] See C. R. Rao, "Linear Statistical Inference and Its Applications," John Wiley & Sons, Inc., New York, 1965. See chap. 5, sec. 5C, on Criteria of Estimation in Large Samples.

The expected values of all cross-product terms are zero since

$$E\left[\frac{\partial \log f(y_i,\theta)}{\partial\theta}\right]=0$$

In large samples we can substitute Q for $E(Q)$, and thus in the method of scoring we substitute Q for I. The expression Q can be evaluated only using the first-order derivatives. Thus, if we use some properties of the likelihood function, we can use an iterative process that makes use of the first derivatives only.[1] There are other methods like the Davidon-Fletcher-Powell method discussed in Sec. 9-8 that also make use of first derivatives only, but these are methods that have been suggested by numerical analysts for very general problems, whereas in econometric work most of our problems are based on the likelihood function and it is useful to exploit the properties of the likelihood function.

The generalization of these results to the case of many parameters is straightforward. Suppose there are r parameters $\theta_1,\theta_2,\ldots,\theta_r$. The vector of efficient scores $\mathbf{S}(\boldsymbol{\theta})$ has as its ith element $(\partial \log L)/\partial\theta_i$. The information matrix $\mathbf{I}(\boldsymbol{\theta})$ now is an $r\times r$ matrix whose (i,j)th element is $E[-(\partial^2 \log L)/\partial\theta_i\partial\theta_j]$. The scoring method now works as follows: For any initial $\boldsymbol{\theta}_0$ we construct $\mathbf{S}(\boldsymbol{\theta}_0)$ and $\mathbf{I}(\boldsymbol{\theta}_0)$. The new estimate $\boldsymbol{\theta}_1$ is given by $\boldsymbol{\theta}_1=\boldsymbol{\theta}_0+[\mathbf{I}(\boldsymbol{\theta}_0)]^{-1}\mathbf{S}(\boldsymbol{\theta}_0)$. The alternative procedure suggested by Berndt et al., which uses first derivatives only, is to construct

$$\mathbf{Q}(\boldsymbol{\theta})=\sum_{i=1}^{n}\left[\frac{\partial \log f(y_i,\boldsymbol{\theta})}{\partial\boldsymbol{\theta}}\right]\left[\frac{\partial \log f(y_i,\boldsymbol{\theta})}{\partial\boldsymbol{\theta}}\right]'$$

and the iterative procedure now is

$$\boldsymbol{\theta}_1=\boldsymbol{\theta}_0+\left[\mathbf{Q}(\boldsymbol{\theta}_0)\right]^{-1}\mathbf{S}(\boldsymbol{\theta}_0)$$

An estimate of the covariance matrix of the ML estimates is obtained in the two methods by $[\mathbf{I}(\hat{\boldsymbol{\theta}})]^{-1}$ or $[\mathbf{Q}(\hat{\boldsymbol{\theta}})]^{-1}$, respectively, where $\hat{\boldsymbol{\theta}}$ is the final (converged) value of $\boldsymbol{\theta}$, obtained by these iterative procedures.

For tests of significance one can use the asymptotic variances and covariances obtained from $[\mathbf{I}(\hat{\boldsymbol{\theta}})]^{-1}$ and use the normal tables if the test relates to a single parameter and the χ^2 tables if the test relates to several parameters. Actually, there are many asymptotic tests, all based on the ML estimation method. These are:

1. The likelihood ratio (LR) test discussed in Sec. 4-6. This is the most commonly discussed test and was suggested by Neyman and Pearson in 1928. Suppose there are k parameters in $\boldsymbol{\theta}$ and suppose that we can partition them into two sets $(\boldsymbol{\theta}_1,\boldsymbol{\theta}_2)$ consisting of r and $k-r$ parameters, respectively.

[1] This is the method suggested in E. R. Berndt, B. H. Hall, R. E. Hall, and J. A. Hausman, Estimation and Inference in Non-Linear Structural Models, *Annals of Economic and Social Measurement*, 1974, pp. 653–665.

Suppose the hypothesis to be tested is $\boldsymbol{\theta}_1 = \bar{\boldsymbol{\theta}}_1$. Then what we compute is the ML estimates without any restrictions on $\boldsymbol{\theta}$ and with the restrictions $\boldsymbol{\theta}_1 = \bar{\boldsymbol{\theta}}_1$. Let $\hat{\boldsymbol{\theta}}$ be the unrestricted and $\boldsymbol{\theta}^*$ the restricted ML estimator of $\boldsymbol{\theta}$, respectively. Define

$$\lambda = \frac{L(\boldsymbol{\theta}^*)}{L(\hat{\boldsymbol{\theta}})}$$

Then $-2 \log_e \lambda$ has (asymptotically) a χ^2-distribution degrees of freedom r. This method involves the computation of both the restricted and unrestricted ML estimates.

2. The Wald test. This was suggested by Abraham Wald in 1943. It depends on only the unrestricted ML estimates. From the covariance matrix $[\mathbf{I}(\hat{\boldsymbol{\theta}})]^{-1}$ we can obtain[1] the covariance matrix of the ML estimator of $\boldsymbol{\theta}_1$. Let this be denoted by $[\mathbf{V}(\hat{\boldsymbol{\theta}}_1)]^{-1}$. Then the Wald statistic is $W = (\hat{\boldsymbol{\theta}}_1 - \bar{\boldsymbol{\theta}}_1)'\mathbf{V}(\hat{\boldsymbol{\theta}}_1) \cdot (\hat{\boldsymbol{\theta}}_1 - \bar{\boldsymbol{\theta}}_1)$, and W has (asymptotically) a χ^2-distribution degrees of freedom r.
3. The Rao statistic. This was suggested by C. R. Rao in 1948. It depends on only the restricted ML estimates $\boldsymbol{\theta}^*$ and is related to the method of scoring. It is defined by $S = \mathbf{S}(\boldsymbol{\theta}^*)'[\mathbf{I}(\boldsymbol{\theta}^*)]^{-1}\mathbf{S}(\boldsymbol{\theta}^*)$, where $\mathbf{S}(\boldsymbol{\theta}^*)$ is the vector of efficient scores and $\mathbf{I}(\boldsymbol{\theta}^*)$ the information matrix (defined earlier), both evaluated at $\boldsymbol{\theta} = \boldsymbol{\theta}^*$. S/n has (asymptotically) a χ^2-distribution degrees of freedom r.
4. The lagrangian-multiplier test. This was suggested by Aitchison and Silvey in a set of papers in 1958–1960. Whereas the Wald test is based on the distribution of the unconstrained ML estimator $\hat{\boldsymbol{\theta}}$, the lagrangian-multiplier test is based on the distribution of the constrained ML estimator $\boldsymbol{\theta}^*$.

A recent account of the relations among the different test statistics can be found in Moran,[2] and some evidence of how in practice there can be conflict among the results yielded by the use of the different test statistics can be found in a paper by Berndt and Savin.[3] They show that (in their model) W $\geqslant$ LR $\geqslant$ LM, where W is the Wald statistic, LR is the likelihood-ratio test statistic, and LM is the lagrangian-multiplier test statistic. Thus two researchers employing the same body of data, the same estimation technique (ML), and the same significance level but different asymptotically equivalent testing procedures may reach conflicting decisions with regard to the truth of the null hypothesis.

The preceding discussion gives an overview of ML estimation and associated tests. For our purposes this is enough. More details can be found in the book by C. R. Rao. Also, in further chapters, we will not write down

[1] See Appendix A, section on inversion of partitioned matrices. For our discussion here we need not write the actual expression in terms of submatrices of $\mathbf{I}(\hat{\boldsymbol{\theta}})$.

[2] P. A. P. Moran, On Asymptotically Optimal Tests of Composite Hypotheses, *Biometrika*, 1970, pp. 47–55.

[3] E. R. Berndt and N. E. Savin, "Conflict among Criteria for Testing Hypotheses in the Multivariate Linear Regression Model," Discussion Paper, August 1975, University of British Columbia. Forthcoming in *Econometrica*.

explicitly the information matrix every time we discuss the ML method. This would merely increase the algebraic details.

Exercises

1. Suppose we have data on output y and labor input x for a set of N firms for T time periods. Let y_{it} and x_{it}, respectively, denote the output and input for the ith firm in the tth time period. Let

$$y_{it} = \alpha_i + \beta x_{it} + u_{it}$$

where α_i is a separate constant for each firm that accounts for all the firm-specific factors (assumed to be constant over time). Explain how you can estimate α_i and β by the dummy-variable method. Suppose you have data on 5000 firms for 5 time periods. Will you run a regression with 5000 explanatory variables?

2. Assume that a linear production function $Q = f(L,K)$ is relevant, where L is labor and K is capital, and that you are interested in the marginal productivity of labor. Unfortunately, however, you do not have observations on K. Therefore, you regress Q on L to obtain the slope estimate b_{QL}. What if anything can be said about $b_{QL \cdot K}$, the slope (partial regression coefficient) one would have obtained for Q on L in the presence of K? Present your assumptions and reasoning carefully.

3. "In the general linear regression model the right-hand variables are often called the *independent variables*, the columns of X are assumed to be *linearly independent*, and the errors u_i are assumed to be *independently distributed* random variables." The word "independent" is used in three different ways in the above sentence. Explain each use of the word. What roles do these three different concepts play in the theory of estimation in the linear model?

4. "A large part of econometric theory is concerned with discovering good estimation methods when the classical assumptions of the regression model are violated. The major conclusion seems to be that *consistent* estimators can be found, but these are likely to have large variances."

Illustrate this point by using the *errors-in-variables problem* as an example. What classical assumptions are violated? What estimation methods are proposed? *Why* are they likely to have large variances? (Answer concisely and without proofs.)

5. Consider the regression model

$$Y_t = \alpha Y_{t-1} + \beta X_t + U_t$$
$$U_t = \zeta U_{t-1} + e_t$$

where e_t are serially independent random variables. Let $\hat{\alpha}$ and $\hat{\beta}$ be the ordinary-least-squares (OLS) estimators of α and β. Find plim $\hat{\alpha}$ and plim $\hat{\beta}$. Make any additional assumptions that you need about X_t.

6. Consider the model

$$Y_t = \alpha Y_{t-1} + U_t$$
$$U_t = \zeta U_{t-1} + e_t$$

where e_t are serially independent. Let $\hat{\alpha}$ be the OLS estimator of α, $\hat{\zeta}$ the estimator for ζ based on the OLS residuals $\hat{U}_t$, and $\hat{d}$ the DW statistic estimated from the OLS residuals $\hat{U}_t$. Prove that

$$\text{plim}(\hat{\alpha} + \hat{\zeta}) = \alpha + \zeta$$

and

$$\text{plim } \hat{d} = 2\left[1 - \frac{\zeta\alpha(\alpha + \zeta)}{1 + \alpha\zeta}\right]$$

Comment on the practical implications of these results.

7. In our discussion of proxy variables, we talked of the consequences of inclusion or exclusion of the proxy variable on the estimation of the coefficient of the variable measured without error. Implicitly, we were assuming that this is the coefficient of major interest. What would you do if you are interested in the coefficient of the variable for which we are using a proxy? If different proxy variables are available, how would you choose between them? How would you combine them?

8. The following are data on Y and X:

Y	19	10	8	6	3	2	3	3	2	1	1
X	0	1	2	3	4	6	7	9	11	14	19

Estimate by the ML method the parameter θ in the model

$$Y_i = \frac{20}{X_i + \theta} + u_i$$

Plot the likelihood function for different values of θ, and locate the ML estimate graphically.

Also use the Newton-Raphson method and the method of scoring with the initial value $\theta = 0$. Check the convergence properties of the two methods.

9. For the regression model

$$Y = \alpha + \frac{\beta}{X + C} + U \qquad \text{where } U \sim IN(0,\sigma^2)$$

describe the (*a*) Newton-Raphson method, (*b*) Gauss-Newton method, and (*c*) method of scoring to estimate the parameters α, β, and C. Also describe some methods that can be used which depend on the evaluation of only the first derivatives of the likelihood function.

10. In Sec. 9-7 there is a discussion of an example where the fact that an individual has college education or not is treated not as an ordinary dummy variable but as a choice-determined variable. Show in that example that given the sample means and variances of those with and without college education and the proportion going to college, we can determine the population means, variances, and the correlation coefficient. Make use of the properties of the truncated normal distribution mentioned in the next exercise.

11. Consider the limited-dependent-variable model

$$\begin{aligned} Y_i &= \beta X_i + U_i \qquad \text{if } \beta X_i + U_i > 0 \\ &= 0 \qquad \text{otherwise} \end{aligned} \tag{9-37}$$

The problem with the application of the ordinary-least-squares method to Eq. (9-37) is that the residuals do not have a zero mean. In fact, the mean depends on X_i. However, we can find their expectation as follows: What we need is

$$E(U_i \mid U_i > -\beta X_i) = \sigma E\left(\frac{U_i}{\sigma} \mid \frac{U_i}{\sigma} > \frac{-\beta X_i}{\sigma}\right) \tag{9-38}$$

Note that U_i/σ has a standard normal distribution. Now the mean and variance of the truncated normal distribution are given by the following expressions:[1] Let z be $N(0,1)$. Let $f(z)$ be the density function and $F(t)$ the cumulative distribution function of the standard normal, so that $F(t) = \int_{-\infty}^{t} f(z)\,dz$. Then

$$E(z \mid z > \gamma) = \frac{f(\gamma)}{1 - F(\gamma)} = \mu \qquad \text{(say)}$$

and

$$V(z \mid z > \gamma) = 1 - \mu(\mu - \gamma)$$

Note that $f(\gamma)$ is the ordinate at the point $z = \gamma$ and $1 - F(\gamma)$ is the tail area $P(z > \gamma)$. Thus the mean of the truncated distribution $z > \gamma$ is equal to the ordinate at $z = \gamma$ divided by the tail area for $z > \gamma$.

Using these results obtain the expression for Eq. (9-38) and suggest least-squares methods for estimating (9-37).

[1] See A. C. Cohen, Jr., Estimating the Mean and Variance of Normal Populations from Singly and Doubly Truncated Samples, *Annals of Mathematical Statistics*, 1950, pp. 557–569.

CHAPTER

TEN

SOME FURTHER TOPICS IN MULTIPLE REGRESSION

In earlier chapters we talked briefly of multicollinearity and tests of hypotheses in multiple regression. Here we will discuss these problems in greater detail. Further, we will also discuss the problems of missing observations and aggregation.

10-1 MULTICOLLINEARITY

The term multicollinearity, introduced by Ragnar Frisch in his book on confluence analysis,[1] refers to a situation where the variables dealt with are subject to two or more relations. However, the term is now used in a more restricted sense. It refers to a situation where, because of strong interrelationships among the independent variables, it becomes difficult to disentangle their separate effects on the dependent variable. The question is how strong these interrelationships have to be to cause a problem. Thus, with multicollinearity, the problem is one not of existence or nonexistence but of how serious or problematical it is. The problems that Frisch was concerned about in his confluence analysis were mostly problems about errors in variables and unobservable variables and will be dealt with in chapters on these topics and simultaneous-equation models. Here we will be considering multicollinearity as it is currently interpreted in econometric work.

[1] R. Frisch, "Statistical Confluence Analysis by Means of Complete Regression Systems," University Institute of Economics, Oslo, Publication 5, 1934.

Consider the model

$$y = \beta_1 x_1 + \beta_2 x_2 + \beta_3 x_3 + u$$

If $x_3 = 2x_1 + 3x_2$, we have

$$\begin{aligned} y &= \beta_1 x_1 + \beta_2 x_2 + \beta_3(2x_1 + 3x_2) + u \\ &= (\beta_1 + 2\beta_3)x_1 + (\beta_2 + 3\beta_3)x_2 + u \end{aligned}$$

Hence we can estimate $\beta_1 + 2\beta_3$ and $\beta_2 + 2\beta_3$ but not $\beta_1, \beta_2, \beta_3$ separately. This is the case of "perfect" multicollinearity. In this case if we try to run a regression of y on x_1, x_2, x_3, we will find that the matrix S_{xx} will be singular because $|S_{xx}| = 0$. Hence we will not get unique solutions to the normal equations. In actual practice we seldom observe such perfect multicollinearity. But if S_{xx} is very close to singularity, what will happen is that even slight changes in the matrix (e.g., due to the addition or deletion of an observation) will produce large changes in the estimates of the regression coefficients. If S_{xx} is a singular matrix, $|S_{xx}| = 0$, but if S_{xx} is very close to being singular, we cannot detect it by just noting that $|S_{xx}|$is small — because $|S_{xx}|$ can be changed by changing the units of measurement of the x's. Hence what is usually done is to look at the determinant of the matrix of correlation coefficients, i.e., $|R_x|$.

As an illustration, consider the case where

$$S_{xx} = \begin{bmatrix} 200 & 150 \\ 150 & 113 \end{bmatrix} \quad \text{and} \quad S_{xy} = \begin{bmatrix} 350 \\ 263 \end{bmatrix}$$

so that the normal equations are

$$\begin{aligned} 200\beta_1 + 150\beta_2 &= 350 \\ 150\beta_1 + 113\beta_2 &= 263 \end{aligned}$$

The solution is $\hat{\beta}_1 = 1$, $\hat{\beta}_2 = 1$. Suppose we drop an observation and the new values are

$$S_{xx} = \begin{bmatrix} 199 & 149 \\ 149 & 112 \end{bmatrix} \quad \text{and} \quad S_{xy} = \begin{bmatrix} 347.5 \\ 261.5 \end{bmatrix}$$

Now solving the equations

$$\begin{aligned} 199\beta_1 + 149\beta_2 &= 347.5 \\ 149\beta_1 + 112\beta_2 &= 261.5 \end{aligned}$$

We get $\hat{\beta}_1 = -\frac{1}{2}$, $\hat{\beta}_2 = 3$. Thus very small changes in the elements of S_{xx} and S_{xy} produce drastic changes in the estimates of the regression coefficients β_1 and β_2. In this case multicollinearity is serious. It is easy to see that the correlation coefficient between the two regressors is given by

$$r_{12}^2 = \frac{(150)^2}{200 \times 113} = .995$$

which is very high. Also

$$|R_x| = \begin{bmatrix} 1 & r_{12} \\ r_{12} & 1 \end{bmatrix} = (1 - r_{12}^2) = .005$$

In the case of two explanatory variables we can suspect multicollinearity by looking at the correlation coefficient between the two variables. However, in the case of more than two variables, the simple correlations could all be low and yet multicollinearity could be very serious. For example, suppose we have 10 observations each on x_1, x_2, x_3 and the observations are

$$x_1: (1, 1, 1, 1, 1, 0, 0, 0, 0, 0)$$

$$x_2: (0, 0, 0, 0, 0, 1, 1, 1, 1, 1)$$

$$x_3: (1, 1, 1, 1, 1, 1, 1, 1, 1, 1)$$

Obviously $x_3 = x_1 + x_2$, and we have perfect multicollinearity. But we can easily compute the simple correlation coefficients and see that $r_{12} = -\frac{1}{3}$ and $r_{13} = r_{23} = 1/\sqrt{3} \approx .59$, which are not high. However, since $x_3 = x_1 + x_2$, we will have $R^2_{3.12} = 1$, and also it can be checked that $|R_x| = 0$, where R_x is the matrix of the correlation coefficients. Thus, in the case of more than two explanatory variables, what we should be looking at is the multiple correlation coefficients of each of the explanatory variables with others and $|R_x|$ (not just the simple correlation coefficients). Unfortunately, most multiple regression programs print out the matrix of the simple correlation coefficients but do not present the above-mentioned statistics.

Another symptom of multicollinearity is when the R^2 for the equation is high but the partial r^2's are low; e.g., with three variables, $R^2_{y\cdot x_1x_2x_3}$ can be very high but $r^2_{yx_1\cdot x_2x_3}$, $r^2_{yx_2\cdot x_1x_3}$, and $r^2_{yx_3\cdot x_1x_2}$ could all be very low. This will happen if x_1, x_2, and x_3 are highly intercorrelated. What this says is that after using two of these as explanatory variables, the third variable does not add much. Though this criterion is often used to decide whether multicollinearity is serious or not, it is a very stringent criterion. Sometimes, even if multicollinearity is serious, we find that the partial r^2's are not low (an example will be given later). What might happen in such cases is that some of the coefficients have the "wrong signs," or even if they have the right signs, their magnitudes may be meaningless. Still another indication would be that the estimates of the coefficients will change by a large magnitude with the deletion of a few observations (though some conventional tests for stability to be described in the next section may show the changes to be not statistically significant).

There are other rules of thumb that are followed in judging when multicollinearity is harmful. One such rule is the one suggested in Klein, which says, "Intercorrelation of variables is not necessarily a problem unless it is high relative to the overall degree of multiple correlation."[1] As is illustrated in the example given earlier, if there are more than two explanatory variables, it is not sufficient to look at simple correlations. Thus the term "intercorrelations" in this case should be interpreted as multiple correlation of each explanatory variable with the other explanatory variables. Thus, by Klein's rule multicollinearity would be regarded as a problem only if $R_y^2 < R_i^2$, where $R_y^2 = R^2_{y\cdot x_1x_2\cdots x_k}$ and

[1] See L. R. Klein, "An Introduction to Econometrics," p. 101, Prentice-Hall, Inc., Englewood Cliffs, N.J., 1962.

$R_i^2 = R^2_{x_i \cdot \text{other } x\text{'s}}$. However, it should be noted that even if $R_y^2 < R_i^2$ we can still have significant partial-correlation coefficients. For example, suppose the correlation matrix among y, x_1, and x_2 is

	y	x_1	x_2
y	1	.95	.95
x_1	.95	1	.97
x_2	.95	.97	1

Then it can be verified that $R_y^2 = .916$ and $r_{12}^2 = .941$. Thus $R_y^2 < r_{12}^2$. However, $r^2_{y1 \cdot 2} = r^2_{y2 \cdot 1} \approx .14$. If the number of observations is 60 or above, this will give t values for the regression coefficients > 3.

All the above-mentioned criteria are simply guides to detecting when multicollinearity is a problem. What criterion to apply in any particular case will depend on the nature of the problem. Sometimes it is easy to lay the blame for wrong signs for coefficients and implausible values of coefficients on multicollinearity when in fact the problem may have been a poor specification of the model.

Another statement often made is that even though multicollinearity is a problem for estimation of the regression coefficients, it is not a problem for prediction. Again this is true only if the interrelationship among the collinear variables is stable.

There are also some suggestions in the literature that one should apply some tests to decide whether multicollinearity is serious or not.[1] These tests are not very meaningful, because multicollinearity is a problem with the sample we have, not with any population. Farrar and Glauber suggest that we test whether $|R_x|$ is significantly different from 1 where R_x is the matrix of the correlations between the explanatory variables. However, $|R_x|$ will be equal to 1 if all the explanatory variables are independent. Multicollinearity is not a problem even if $|R_x|$ is significantly different from 1, because all this says is that the explanatory variables are not independent. It is a problem only if $|R_x|$ is close to zero. Haitovsky[2] pointed out this error and suggested testing whether $|R_x|$ is close to zero. However, even this test is not meaningful because, as mentioned earlier, our concern is with the behavior of the explanatory variables in the sample we have—not in any population from which they are drawn.

In summary, there are only some rough rules of thumb by which we can decide whether multicollinearity is serious or not. One has to use one's judgment in any particular problem. Before we discuss solutions to the problem, we will give some examples.

In Table 10-1 we present data on C, Y, and L for the period from the first quarter of 1952 to the second quarter of 1961. C is consumption expenditures

[1] D. E. Farrar and R. R. Glauber, Multicollinearity in Regression Analysis: The Problem Revisited, *Review of Economics and Statistics*, February 1967.

[2] Y. Haitovsky, Multicollinearity in Regression Analysis: Comment, *Review of Economics and Statistics*, November 1969.

Table 10-1

Year, quarter	C	Y	L	Year, quarter	C	Y	L
1952 I	220.0	238.1	182.7	1957 I	268.9	291.1	218.2
II	222.7	240.9	183.0	II	270.4	294.6	218.5
III	223.8	245.8	184.4	III	273.4	296.1	219.8
IV	230.2	248.8	187.0	IV	272.1	293.3	219.5
1953 I	234.0	253.3	189.4	1958 I	268.9	291.3	220.5
II	236.2	256.1	192.2	II	270.9	292.6	222.7
III	236.0	255.9	193.8	III	274.4	299.9	225.0
IV	234.1	255.9	194.8	IV	278.7	302.1	229.4
1954 I	233.4	254.4	197.3	1959 I	283.8	305.9	232.2
II	236.4	254.8	197.0	II	289.7	312.5	235.2
III	239.0	257.0	200.3	III	290.8	311.3	237.2
IV	243.2	260.9	204.2	IV	292.8	313.2	237.7
1955 I	248.7	263.0	207.6	1960 I	295.4	315.4	238.0
II	253.7	271.5	209.4	II	299.5	320.3	238.4
III	259.9	276.5	211.1	III	298.6	321.0	240.1
IV	261.8	281.4	213.2	IV	299.6	320.1	243.3
1956 I	263.2	282.0	214.1	1961 I	297.0	318.4	246.1
II	263.7	286.2	216.5	II	301.6	324.8	250.0
III	263.4	287.7	217.3				
IV	266.9	291.0	217.3				

(billions of 1954 dollars); Y is disposable income (billions of 1954 dollars); and L is liquid assets (billions of 1954 dollars at the end of the previous quarter.[1] Using the 38 observations, we obtain the following regression equations:

$$C = \underset{(-1.93)}{-7.160} + \underset{(73.25)}{.95213}\, Y \qquad r^2_{CY} = .9933 \tag{10-1}$$

$$C = \underset{(-3.25)}{-10.627} + \underset{(9.60)}{.68166}\, Y + \underset{(3.96)}{.37252}\, L \qquad R^2_{C \cdot YL} = .9953 \tag{10-2}$$

(Figures in parentheses are t ratios, not standard errors.) Looking at the t ratios and the fact that the coefficients have the right signs, we might conclude that multicollinearity is not a problem here. The regression of L on Y gives

$$L = \underset{(1.80)}{9.307} + \underset{(37.20)}{.72607}\, Y \qquad r^2_{LY} = .9758 \tag{10-3}$$

Thus, using Klein's rule of thumb, we have $r^2_{LY} < R^2_{C \cdot YL}$, and we might again be reassured that multicollinearity is not serious here. However, there are some interesting things to note. First, substituting the value of L in terms of Y from Eq. (10-3) into Eq. (10-2) and simplifying, we get Eq. (10-1) correct to four decimals! Thus, the relationship between L and Y is almost exact. Also, the coefficient of L in Eq. (10-2) has a magnitude that is hard to interpret. Though it has the right sign, taken literally it means that a billion dollar increase in the

[1] The data are from Z. Griliches et al., Notes on Estimated Aggregate Quarterly Consumption Functions, *Econometrica*, July 1962.

stock of consumer liquid assets leads to a *permanent* increase of 372 million dollars in the *annual rate* of consumer expenditures.[1] Yet another thing to see is how the coefficients change if we drop a few observations. Dropping the last two observations and using only the first 36 for estimation, we get the following results:

$$C = \underset{(-1.74)}{-6.980} + \underset{(67.04)}{.95145}\,Y \qquad r^2_{CY} = .9925 \tag{10-4}$$

$$C = \underset{(-3.71)}{-13.391} + \underset{(8.32)}{.63258}\,Y + \underset{(4.24)}{.45065}\,L \qquad r^2_{C \cdot YL} = .9951 \tag{10-5}$$

and

$$L = \underset{(2.69)}{14.255} + \underset{(37.80)}{.70758}\,Y \qquad r^2_{LY} = .9768 \tag{10-6}$$

Comparing Eq. (10-4) with (10-1) and Eq. (10-5) with Eq. (10-2), we see that the coefficients in the latter equation show far greater changes than those in the former equation. It might be argued that the differences are not "statistically significant," but in cases like this one should not put too much emphasis on "statistical significance." If the multicollinearity is higher still, even wider differences will be "statistically insignificant" (more on this point in the next section).

Finally, we might consider predicting C for the first two quarters of 1961 using Eqs. (10-4) and (10-5). The predictions are:

	Equation (10-4)	Equation (10-5)
1961 I	295.96	298.93
II	302.05	304.73

Thus the predictions from the equation including L are further off from the true values than the predictions from the equation excluding L.

The above example illustrates how we could come to different conclusions about the seriousness of the multicollinearity depending on what criterion we choose. If we just look at r^2_{LY}, we would conclude that multicollinearity is serious. If we look at the t ratios and see whether they are "significant" or not, of course we find them "highly significant," and hence we might conclude that multicollinearity is not serious. (As mentioned in Chap. 4, however, saying merely that a coefficient is "significant" is meaningless, because what we are saying in this case is that the marginal propensity to consume is significantly different from zero, which is hardly an interesting statement.) If we apply Klein's rule, since $R^2_{C \cdot YL} > r^2_{YL}$, we might again conclude that multicollinearity is not serious. However, if we try to interpret the values of the coefficients or examine how the coefficients change when we drop a few observations, we might conclude that multicollinearity is serious. There would be instances where

[1] There are several ways of rationalizing the coefficient of the liquid-asset variable. See Griliches et al. (*op. cit.*) for some interpretations.

we could unambiguously say that multicollinearity is a problem, e.g., when R^2 is high but the t ratios for the regression coefficients are all "insignificant." In econometric problems this is not an uncommon occurrence. But this is too stringent a test. As the above example illustrates, problems may exist even with "highly significant" t ratios.

Finally, it should be noted that if multicollinearity is high, it implies that the individual coefficients cannot be precisely estimated but there will be some linear functions of the coefficients that can be estimated with great precision. If these linear functions have no meaningful interpretation (e.g., 2 income elasticity + 3 price elasticity), this is a poor consolation. But sometimes we can give a meaningful interpretation to the linear functions of the coefficients. For example, consider the data in Table (10-1). Suppose we estimate a consumption function of the form

$$C_t = \beta_0 Y_t + \beta_1 Y_{t-1} + \cdots + \beta_k Y_{t-k} + u_t \tag{10-7}$$

Table 10-2 Distributed-lag regressions of consumption on income

Coefficient of	1	2	3	4	5	6
y_t	.931 (.002)	.654 (.168)	.782 (.166)	.782 (.148)	.709 (.154)	.736 (.165)
y_{t-1}		.279 (.169)	.123 (.223)	.177 (.209)	.228 (.209)	.182 (.224)
y_{t-2}			.027 (.163)	.303 (.205)	.302 (.206)	.271 (.215)
y_{t-3}				−.523 (.197)	−.461 (.202)	−.489 (.218)
y_{t-4}				.190 (.143)	.202 (.201)	.298 (.222)
y_{t-5}					−.229 (.194)	−.278 (.212)
y_{t-6}					.178 (.146)	.125 (.208)
y_{t-7}						−.110 (.215)
y_{t-8}						.200 (.161)
Sum of coefficients	.931	.933	.932	.929	.929	.935
SE of sum	.0022	.0025	.0029	.0032	.0042	.0045
DW statistic	.92	.66	.85	.91	.81	.87

The figures in parentheses are the standard errors.

The coefficients with t ratios greater than 2 are those of y_t and y_{t-3}. The fact that the latter coefficient always has a negative sign is an indication either that the true lag distribution is not that long or that the seasonal-adjustment procedures used have a strong distortionary effect on the data.

Here $\beta_0, \beta_1, \ldots, \beta_k$ are, respectively, the marginal propensities to consume during the current period out of current and past incomes, of one period back, two periods back, etc. The sum $\beta_0 + \beta_1 + \cdots + \beta_k$ is the long-run marginal propensity to consume. Equation (10-7) is known as a *distributed-lag* consumption function because the lag with which income affects consumption is "distributed" over $k + 1$ periods. Because Y_t, Y_{t-1}, Y_{t-2}, etc., are highly intercorrelated, we cannot estimate the individual β's with any precision. However, it can be easily seen that the sum of the β's can be estimated well, and in this case this sum has a meaningful interpretation. The regressions for different values of k, i.e., different lengths of lags, are presented in Table (10-2).[1]

10-2 SOLUTIONS TO MULTICOLLINEARITY

Till now we have discussed how to detect multicollinearity. The question is what to do when we do find that the problem exists. The solutions suggested are:

1. Dropping variables
2. Using extraneous estimates
3. Ridge regression
4. Using ratios or first differences
5. Using principal components
6. Getting more data

Dropping variables. The problem with multicollinearity is essentially lack of sufficient information in the sample to permit accurate estimation of the individual parameters. In some situations it may be the case that we are not interested in all the parameters. In such cases we can get estimators for the parameters we are interested in that have smaller mean square errors than the ordinary least-squares estimators; e.g., consider the case

$$y = \beta_1 x_1 + \beta_2 x_2 + u \tag{10-8}$$

and the problem is that x_1 and x_2 are very highly correlated. Suppose our main interest is in β_1. Then we can drop x_2 and estimate the equation

$$y = \beta_1 x_1 + u' \tag{10-9}$$

The estimator of β_1 obtained from (10-8), say $\hat{\beta}_1$, is the ordinary-least-squares (OLS) estimator. The estimator of β_1 obtained from (10-9), say β_1^*, is called the omitted-variable (OV) estimator. β_1^* is biased because of the omitted variable x_2, and $\hat{\beta}_1$ is unbiased. However, β_1^* has a smaller variance than $\hat{\beta}_1$. In fact it can be shown that the mean square error (MSE) = variance + (bias)^2 for the two estimators is in the ratio

$$\frac{\text{MSE } (\beta_1^*)}{\text{MSE } (\hat{\beta}_1)} = 1 + r_{12}^2\ (t_2^2 - 1) \tag{10-10}$$

[1] The results are from G. S. Maddala, "Some Notes on Discrimination between Different Distributed Lag Models," CORE Discussion Paper, June 1971.

where r_{12} is the correlation coefficient between x_1 and x_2 and $t_2 = \beta_2/[\text{var}(\hat{\beta}_2)]^{\frac{1}{2}}$ [this is the "true" t ratio for x_2 in Eq. (10-8)—not the "estimated" t ratio]. From Eq. (10-10) we see that β_1^* has a smaller mean square error than $\hat{\beta}_1$ if $|t_2| < 1$. Since t_2 is not known, what is usually done is to use the estimated value $\hat{t}_2$ from an estimation of (10-8). As an estimator of β_1 we can use the conditional-omitted-variable (COV) estimator, which is defined as

$$\tilde{\beta}_1 = \begin{cases} \hat{\beta}_1 \text{ the OLS estimator if } |\hat{t}_2| \geqslant 1 \\ \beta_1^* \text{ the OV estimator if } |\hat{t}_2| < 1 \end{cases}$$

Instead of 1, we can use any other dividing point for $\hat{t}_2$. The COV estimator was suggested first by Bancroft. Feldstein[1] studied its mean square error for different true values of t_2 and different dividing points based on $\hat{t}_2$.

Instead of using $\hat{\beta}_1$ or β_1^* depending on $\hat{t}_2$, we can consider a linear combination of both, namely, $\lambda\hat{\beta}_1 + (1 - \lambda)\beta^*_1$. This is called the weighted-average (WTD) estimator, and it has minimum mean square error if $\lambda = t_2^2/(1 + t_2^2)$. Again, since t_2 is not known, we have to use its estimated value. This estimator was first suggested by Huntsberger. Feldstein studied its mean square error for different true values of t_2.

The literature on COV and WTD estimators is interesting, but it should be noted that these solutions are purely statistical simplifications. As Feldstein points out, in practical applications even if these estimators are used, one should always present the OLS estimates and the associated covariance matrix to allow the reader to assess the effect of multicollinearity. In the example we used as an illustration earlier, since the t ratios are high, the COV estimator would be the OLS estimator, and the WTD estimator would also be almost the same. Clearly, this does not mean that we should do nothing but accept the OLS results.

Using extraneous estimates. This method was followed in early demand studies. It was found that in time-series data income and price were both highly correlated. Hence neither the price nor the income elasticity could be estimated well. What was done was to get an estimate of the income elasticity from budget studies (where prices did not vary much), use this estimate to "correct" the quantity series for income variation, and then estimate the price elasticity.[2] For example, if the equation to be estimated is

$$\log Q = \alpha + \beta_1 \log P + \beta_2 \log Y + u$$

first get $\hat{\beta}_2$ from budget studies and then regress $\log Q - \hat{\beta}_2 \log Y$ on $\log P$ to get estimates of α and β_1. Here $\hat{\beta}_2$ is known as the "extraneous" estimate. There are two main problems with this procedure. First, the fact that β_2 has been estimated should be taken into account in computing the variances of the

[1] M. S. Feldstein, Multicollinearity and the Mean Square Error of Alternative Estimators, *Econometrica*, March 1973. The references to Bancroft, Huntsberger, and other literature can also be obtained from this paper.

[2] For an example of this see J. Tobin, A Statistical Demand Function for Food in the U.S.A., *Journal of the Royal Statistical Society*, ser. A, pp. 113–41, 1950.

estimates of α and β_1 in the second step. In most practical applications this is not done, though it is easy to do.[1] Second, and this is the more important problem, the cross-section estimate of β_2 may be measuring something entirely different from what the time-series estimate is supposed to measure. As Meyer and Kuh argue,[2] the "extraneous" estimate can be really extraneous.

Ridge regression. This is a suggestion of Hoerl and Kennard.[3] The idea is that since the matrix S_{xx} is almost singular when multicollinearity is serious, what we should do is multiply each diagonal element by $(1 + d)$ where d is small. The question is How small? Hoerl and Kennard suggest starting with very small values of d (say .01) and increasing it till the resulting estimates of the regression parameters are "stable" or do not vary much. The ridge-regression procedure has been used in several fields but not much in econometric work, perhaps because it was not very successful. Some experiments with it in the estimation of distributed-lag models showed that the value of d that was found useful was indeed very small ($\leq .005$) with the data used which seem typical in econometric work. One problem with the ridge-regression method is that it is a purely statistical solution to the multicollinearity problem, and hence might not appeal to many economists.

Using ratios or first differences. This is a device often used in time-series analysis when a common trend is the source of multicollinearity. However, even if this is so, one has to take into account the fact that these transformations have adverse effects on the properties of the resulting residuals. If we take ratios, this introduces heteroscedasticity. If we take first differences, this introduces autocorrelation. For example, suppose the equation is

$$y_t = \alpha + \beta_1 x_{1t} + \beta_2 x_{2t} + u_t \tag{10-11}$$

Changing t to $t - 1$, we get

$$y_{t-1} = \alpha + \beta_1 x_{1,t-1} + \beta_2 x_{2,t-1} + u_{t-1} \tag{10-12}$$

By subtraction we get

$$\Delta y_t = \beta_1 \Delta x_{1t} + \beta_2 \Delta x_{2t} + \Delta u_t \tag{10-13}$$

where $\Delta y_t = y_t - y_{t-1}$, etc. Often, what is done is to estimate this equation in first differences by ordinary least squares. The multicollinearity is often less because Δx_{1t} and Δx_{2t} are not as highly correlated as x_{1t} and x_{2t} for most economic time series. However, if the residuals in (10-11) are independent to start with, the

[1] For further analysis with Tobin's data on demand for food, see G. S. Maddala, The Likelihood Approach to Pooling Cross-Section and Time-Series Data, *Econometrica*, 1971.

[2] John Meyer and Edwin Kuh, How Extraneous Are Extraneous Estimates? *Review of Economics and Statistics*, November 1957.

[3] A. E. Hoerl and R. W. Kennard, Ridge Regression: Biased Estimation for Non-Orthogonal Problems, *Technometrics*, 1970, pp. 55–82.

residuals in (10-13) are correlated. The problem is similar if we use ratios and instead of estimating (10-11) we estimate an equation of the form

$$\frac{y_t}{x_{1t}} = \beta_1 + \beta_2 \frac{x_{2t}}{x_{1t}} + \alpha \frac{1}{x_{1t}} + u'_t \tag{10-14}$$

Now the resulting residuals will be heteroscedastic.[1] Thus, unless some suitable assumptions are made about the residuals u_t in the original equation (10-11) so that these transformations produce independent and homoscedastic residuals in the transformed equations (10-13) and (10-14), one cannot justify these procedures of taking first differences or ratios just to "get rid of multicollinearity."

Using principal components. This is another purely statistical device that is often suggested as a solution to the multicollinearity problem. Suppose we have k explanatory variables. Then we can consider linear functions of these, say,

$$l_1 = a_1x_1 + a_2x_2 + \cdots + a_kx_k$$
$$l_2 = b_1x_1 + b_2x_2 + \cdots + b_kx_k \qquad \text{etc.}$$

Suppose we choose the a's so that variance of l_1 is maximized subject to the condition that $a_1^2 + a_2^2 + \cdots + a_k^2 = 1$ (called normalization condition). Then l_1 is said to be the first principal component. It is the linear function of the x's that has the highest variance (the normalization is required, because otherwise this variance can be increased indefinitely). Next, we can consider the linear function l_2 such that l_2 is uncorrelated with l_1 and has maximum variance subject to the condition $b_1^2 + b_2^2 + \cdots + b_k^2 = 1$. Then l_2 is said to be the second principal component. Following this procedure, we find k linear functions $l_1, l_2, \ldots, l_k$. It can be shown that

$$\text{var}(l_1) + \text{var}(l_2) + \cdots + \text{var}(l_k) = \text{var}(x_1) + \text{var}(x_2) + \cdots + \text{var}(x_k) \tag{10-15}$$

But unlike $x_1, x_2, \ldots, x_k$, which may be highly correlated, $l_1, l_2, \ldots, l_k$ are mutually orthogonal or uncorrelated. The suggestion often made is that instead of regressing y on $x_1, x_2, \ldots, x_k$, we regress y on $l_1, l_2, \ldots, l_k$. But if we do this and then substitute the values of the l's in terms of the x's, we finally get the same answers as before. So there is a point in using principal components only if we regress y on a subset of the l's. There are two problems in this. First, the first principal component l_1, though it picks up the major portion of the variances of the x's, need not necessarily be the one that is most correlated with y. In fact, there is no necessary relationship between the order of the principal components and the degree of their correlation with the dependent variable y. Second, often the linear combinations l_1, l_2, etc., have no meaningful economic interpretation. For example, what is the meaning of 2(income) + 3(price)? This is one of the most important drawbacks of principal components.

[1] There is also the problem of "spurious" correlation arising from the fact that $1/x_{1t}$ is used as an explanatory variable.

However, there are some uses for the principal-component method mainly in the exploratory stage of an investigation. For example, in Eq. (10-15) suppose var (l_1) is 80 percent of the total variation of all x's and var(l_1) + var(l_2) is 99 percent of the total. Then this says that there are in effect only two "latent" variables that account for all the variation in the x's. Thus the principal-component method will give us some guidance to the question: How many independent sources of variation are really there? This would be interesting to know if the number of explanatory variables is really large. In addition, if we can give an economic interpretation to the principal components, this is then very useful.

The method of principal components is thus of very limited use, and it can be (and has been) easily misused in econometric work. As a solution to the multicollinearity problem, though it is often suggested, its use is very limited.[1]

Getting more data. One solution to the multicollinearity problem that is often suggested is to "go and get more data." There is a point in this advice, but one should not take it too literally. What is relevant is not the number of observations but the informational content. For instance, if we have only annual data in the beginning, we might try to get quarterly data or monthly data or a combination of time-series and cross-section data. But these methods do not necessarily solve our problem of weak data. Sometimes we might be adding other sources of variation; e.g., going from yearly to monthly data introduces seasonality, and cross-section data introduce cross-sectional variation. Also one should check that the disaggregated data are not pure interpolations. For example, if the monthly series is an interpolation of the quarterly series, then by going to the monthly data we will have three times as many observations, but this is a merely deceptive increase.

10-3 TESTS OF LINEAR RESTRICTIONS

We outlined earlier how to test some hypotheses about individual coefficients in multiple regression. Sometimes we are interested in some hypotheses not about individual parameters but about linear functions of all the parameters. For example, in the estimation of a production function of the type (called Cobb-Douglas function) $X = AL^{\alpha}K^{\beta}$, where X is output, L is labor input, and K is capital input, if there are constant returns to scale, we should have $\alpha + \beta = 1$. Thus we might be interested in confidence intervals for the returns to scale parameter or testing the hypothesis that $\alpha + \beta = 1$. Similarly in the demand function $Q = Ap^{\alpha}\pi^{\beta}y^{\gamma}$, where Q is the quantity demanded, p is the price of the

[1] For those interested in using the method nevertheless, a good reference is S. James Press, "Applied Multivariate Analysis," chap. 9, Holt, Rinehart and Winston, Inc., New York, 1972. There are also two BMD programs in the BMD series of the UCLA computing center that compute principal components and do regressions on principal components.

good, π is an index of prices of all other goods, and y is income, if we multiply p, π, and y by the same factor, we expect Q to remain unchanged. Hence we might be interested in testing the hypothesis $\alpha + \beta + \gamma = 0$ or in obtaining confidence intervals for $\alpha + \beta + \gamma$. These are examples of linear restrictions on the parameters, or "linear hypotheses."

We mentioned earlier that if $\hat{\beta}$ is the vector of least-squares estimators of β, then $\hat{\beta}$ are jointly normally distributed with mean β and covariance matrix $\sigma^2 S_{xx}^{-1}$. If we denote this covariance matrix by $\sigma^2 C = \sigma^2[c_{ij}]$ so that $\text{var}(\hat{\beta}_i) = \sigma^2 \cdot c_{ii}$ and $\text{cov}(\hat{\beta}_i, \hat{\beta}_j) = \sigma^2 c_{ij}$, then, if we consider a linear function of the $\hat{\beta}$'s, say $\hat{L} = a_1\hat{\beta}_1 + a_2\hat{\beta}_2 + \cdots + a_k\hat{\beta}_k$, since any linear function of normally distributed variables is also normally distributed, we find that $\hat{L}$ is normally distributed with mean $L = a_1\beta_1 + a_2\beta_2 + \cdots + a_k\beta_k$ and variance $(a_1^2c_{11} + a_2^2c_{22} + \cdots + a_k^2c_{kk} + 2a_{12}c_1c_2 + 2a_{13}c_1c_3 + \cdots)\sigma^2$ or $(\sum_i\sum_j a_i\, a_j\, c_{ij})\sigma^2$. Again, substituting $\hat{\sigma}^2 = RSS/(n-k-1)$, for σ^2, we get the estimated variance of $\hat{L}$, and the square root of this is the standard error of $\hat{L}$ [to be denoted by $\text{SE}(\hat{L})$]. The ratio $(\hat{L} - L)/\text{SE}(\hat{L})$ has a t-distribution degrees of freedom $n - k - 1$. This can be used to test any hypothesis about L or to obtain confidence intervals for L. As an example, consider the data in Table 10-3.[1]

X = an index of gross domestic product in the United States in constant dollars
L_1 = labor-input index (this is number of persons adjusted for hours of work and educational level)
L_2 = persons engaged
K_1 = capital-input index (this is capital stock adjusted for rates of utilization)
K_2 = capital stock in constant dollars

The function we estimate is

$$\log X = \alpha + \beta_1 \log L + \beta_2 \log K + u$$

The estimated equation based on data for 1929–67 (39 observations) on X, L_1, and K_1 is

$$\log X = \underset{(-15.20)}{-3.8766} + \underset{(15.95)}{1.4106} \log L_1 + \underset{(8.24)}{.4162} \log K_1 \tag{10-16}$$

$R^2 = .9937$, SEE = .03755, and figures in parentheses are t ratios. SEE is $(\text{residual SS}/n - k - 1)^{\frac{1}{2}}$, that is, $\hat{\sigma}$.

$$S_{xx}^{-1} = \begin{pmatrix} 5.5461 & -3.0032 \\ -3.0032 & 1.8079 \end{pmatrix}$$

$$\hat{\beta}_1 + \hat{\beta}_2 = 1.4106 + .4162 = 1.8268$$

$$\text{var}(\hat{\beta}_1 + \hat{\beta}_2) = \sigma^2[5.5461 + 1.8079 - 2(3.0032)] = 1.3476\sigma^2$$

$$\text{SE}(\hat{\beta}_1 + \hat{\beta}_2) = \sqrt{1.3476} \cdot \hat{\sigma} = (1.161)(.03755) = .0436$$

[1] The data are from L. R. Christensen and D. W. Jorgenson, U.S. Real Product and Real Factor Input 1929–67, *Review of Income and Wealth*, March 1970.

Table 10-3

Year	X	L_1	L_2	K_1	K_2
1929	189.8	173.3	44.151	87.8	888.9
30	172.1	165.4	41.898	87.8	904.0
31	159.1	158.2	36.948	84.0	900.2
32	135.6	141.7	35.686	78.3	883.6
33	132.0	141.6	35.533	76.6	851.4
34	141.8	148.0	37.854	76.0	823.7
35	153.9	154.4	39.014	77.7	805.3
36	171.5	163.5	40.765	79.1	800.4
37	183.0	172.0	42.484	80.0	805.5
38	173.2	161.5	40.039	77.6	817.6
39	188.5	168.6	41.443	81.4	809.8
40	205.5	176.5	43.149	87.0	814.1
41	236.0	192.4	46.156	96.2	830.3
42	257.8	205.1	49.010	104.4	857.9
43	277.5	210.1	49.695	110.0	851.4
44	291.1	208.8	48.668	107.8	834.6
45	284.5	202.1	47.136	102.1	819.3
46	274.0	213.4	49.950	97.2	812.3
47	279.9	223.6	52.350	105.9	851.3
48	297.6	228.2	53.336	113.0	888.3
49	297.7	221.9	51.469	114.9	934.6
50	328.9	228.8	52.972	124.1	964.6
51	351.4	239.0	55.101	134.5	1021.4
52	360.4	241.7	55.385	139.7	1068.5
53	378.9	245.2	56.226	147.4	1100.3
54	375.8	237.4	54.387	148.9	1134.6
55	406.7	245.9	55.718	158.6	1163.2
56	416.3	251.6	56.770	167.1	1213.9
57	422.8	251.5	56.809	171.9	1255.5
58	418.4	245.1	55.023	173.1	1287.9
59	445.7	254.9	56.215	182.5	1305.8
60	457.3	259.6	56.743	189.0	1341.4
61	466.3	258.1	56.211	194.1	1373.9
62	495.3	264.6	57.078	202.3	1399.1
63	515.5	268.5	57.540	205.4	1436.7
64	544.1	275.4	58.508	215.9	1477.8
65	579.2	285.3	60.055	225.0	1524.4
66	615.6	297.4	62.130	236.2	1582.2
67	631.1	305.0	63.162	247.9	1645.3

Hence the 95 percent confidence limits for $\hat{\beta}_1 + \hat{\beta}_2$, the returns to scale parameter, are $1.8268 \pm 2.03(.0436)$, i.e., (1.7383, 1.9153). Here 2.03 is the 5 percent probability point in the t tables with 36 degrees of freedom. Thus, if we test the hypothesis of constant returns to scale, i.e., that $\beta_1 + \beta_2 = 1$, then we would reject it at the 5 percent level. We would also reject a hypothesis that $\beta_1 + \beta_2 = 2$ at the 5 percent level.

Note that in this example SE $(\hat{\beta}_1) = .0884$ and SE $(\hat{\beta}_2) = .0505$. Thus SE $(\hat{\beta}_1 + \hat{\beta}_2)$ is less than both these standard errors. This is because of the high negative correlation between $\hat{\beta}_1$ and $\hat{\beta}_2$. There is high positive correlation between log L and log K ($r^2 = .8995$). All the variables in Table 10-3 exhibit strong time trends. Regressing the variables on time t (measured from 1 to 39), we get

$$\log X = 4.8973 + \underset{(27.99)}{.03951}\, t \qquad R^2 = .9549$$

$$\log L = 4.9925 + \underset{(20.67)}{.01828}\, t \qquad R^2 = .9203$$

$$\log K_1 = 4.1712 + \underset{(24.25)}{.03238}\, t \qquad R^2 = .9408$$

However, regressing log X on log L_1 and log K_1 with a time trend, we get

$$\log X = \underset{(-5.92)}{-2.9036} + \underset{(13.33)}{1.2973} \log L_1 + \underset{(4.92)}{.3174} \log K_1 + \underset{(2.28)}{.0055}\, t$$

$R^2 = .9945$, SEE $= .03554$, and figures in parentheses are t ratios. The covariance matrix of $(\hat{\beta}_1, \hat{\beta}_2)$ is

$$\sigma^2 \begin{pmatrix} 7.5036 & -1.2969 \\ -1.2969 & 3.2954 \end{pmatrix}$$

Thus the 95 percent confidence interval for the returns to scale $\hat{\beta}_1 + \hat{\beta}_2$ is in this case $(1.2973 + .3174) \pm 2.03(.1018)$, i.e., (1.4080, 1.8214). There are several problems with the estimation of production-function parameters from such aggregate time-series data. Walters[1] reports some production functions from aggregate time-series data, some of which show increasing returns to scale (but most of the studies surveyed showed almost constant returns to scale). Walters' estimates for 1909–1949 for the United States were $\hat{\beta}_1 = .99$, $\hat{\beta}_2 = .23$ so that $\hat{\beta}_1 + \hat{\beta}_2 = 1.22$. Another study by Wall for United States manufacturing and mining gave $\hat{\beta}_1 = 1.34$, $\hat{\beta}_2 = .93$, $\hat{\beta}_1 + \hat{\beta}_2 = 2.27$, with a linear-trend term included.

The using of crude measures of labor and capital inputs L_2 and K_2 in Table 10-3 results in the following estimates:

$$\log X = \underset{(-21.58)}{-6.3749} + \underset{(20.82)}{2.0835} \log L_2 + \underset{(8.10)}{.5678} \log K_2 \qquad R^2 = .9830$$

$$\log X = \underset{(3.03)}{-2.4944} + \underset{(11.02)}{1.5236} \log L_2 + \underset{(3.56)}{.2836} \log K_2 + \underset{(4.91)}{.01367}\, t \qquad R^2 = .9899$$

These equations show still higher returns to scale than the previous equations.[2]

Often we may have a hypothesis that specifies not one but several linear restrictions. In this case the appropriate procedure is to estimate the regression equation with and without the restrictions and use the F test:

$$F = \frac{(\text{RRSS} - \text{URSS})/r}{\text{URSS}/(n - k - 1)}$$

[1] A. A. Walters, Production and Cost Functions—An Econometric Survey, *Econometrica*, January–April 1963.

[2] Some studies have tried to interpret the coefficient of t in the aggregate production functions as measuring the rate of technical progress. These studies are summarized in Walters' survey (*op. cit.*). It is also customary to impose constant returns to scale a priori and estimate the production function with a time trend on the argument that the production-function parameters cannot be estimated well owing to high multicollinearity among L, K, and t.

as an F variate with degrees of freedom r and $(n-k-1)$, where RRSS is the restricted residual sum of squares, URSS the unrestricted residual sum of squares, and r the number of linearly independent restrictions. A special case of this test is the test for stability of coefficients, often referred to in econometric literature as the Chow test.[1]

Suppose we have two sets of data of sizes n_1 and n_2 and the regression equation is

$$y = \alpha^{(1)} + \beta_1^{(1)}x_1 + \cdots + \beta_k^{(1)}x_k + u \qquad \text{for the first set} \tag{10-17}$$

$$y = \alpha^{(2)} + \beta_1^{(2)}x_1 + \cdots + \beta_k^{(2)}x_k + u \qquad \text{for the second set}$$

If

$$\alpha^{(1)} = \alpha^{(2)} \qquad \beta_1^{(1)} = \beta_1^{(2)} \qquad \ldots \qquad \beta_k^{(1)} = \beta_k^{(2)} \tag{10-18}$$

then we can estimate a common relationship for the entire data. But Eqs. (10-18) provide $k+1$ linear restrictions which we can test using the F test. To obtain the unrestricted residual sum of squares, we estimate each equation separately, get the residual sum of squares for each equation, and add them. This has degrees of freedom $(n_1-k-1)+(n_2-k-1)=(n_1+n_2-2k-2)$. To obtain the restricted residual sum of squares, we pool the data and estimate a single equation. This residual sum of squares has degrees of freedom (n_1+n_2-k-1). Then we apply the F test:

$$F = \frac{(\text{RRSS} - \text{URSS})/(k+1)}{\text{URSS}/(n_1+n_2-2k-2)}$$

which has an F distribution with degrees of freedom $(k+1)$, (n_1+n_2-2k-2). As an illustration, consider the production-function estimation with the data in Table 10-3. Suppose we estimate separately for the first 20 observations (1929–1948) and for the last 19 observations (1949–1967). We get the following results.

1929–1948:

$$\log X = \underset{(-11.36)}{-4.0576} + \underset{(7.74)}{1.6167}\log L_1 + \underset{(.96)}{.2197}\log K_1 \tag{10-19}$$

$R^2 = .9759$, SEE $= .04573$.

1949–1967:

$$\log X = \underset{(-2.19)}{-1.9564} + \underset{(3.35)}{.8336}\log L_1 + \underset{(7.86)}{.6631}\log K_1 \tag{10-20}$$

$R^2 = .9904$, SEE $= .02185$.

[1] G. C. Chow, Tests of Equality between Subsets of Coefficients in Two Linear Regressions, *Econometrica*, 1960, pp. 591–605. Though the test is referred to as the Chow test by econometricians, it was derived much earlier by C. R. Rao and others. See C. R. Rao, "Advanced Statistical Methods in Biometric Research," John Wiley & Sons, Inc., New York, 1952; O. Kempthorne, "The Design and Analysis of Experiments," John Wiley & Sons, Inc., New York, 1952; S. Kullback and H. M. Rosenblatt, On the Analysis of Multiple Regression in k Categories, *Biometrika*, 1957, pp. 67–83. In view of this, it is better not to attach any name to the test.

Suppose we want to test whether the production-function coefficients are stable during the two periods. Then URSS $= [(.04573)^2 17] + [(.02185)^2 16] = .04319$. This has 33 degrees of freedom. The restricted residual sum of squares is obtained from a regression for the entire data. This was obtained in Eq. (10-16). RRSS $= (.03755)^2 36 = .05076$. This has 36 degrees of freedom. Hence

$$F = \frac{(.05076 - .04319)/3}{.04319/33} = 1.93$$

which has an F-distribution degrees of freedom 3, 33. From the F tables the 5 percent significance point is 2.90. Thus the above value of F is not significant at the 5 percent level, and we do not reject the hypothesis that the relationship is stable.

Looking at the estimates in Eqs. (10-19) and (10-20), we would feel that the coefficients are not stable. Yet the test does not reject the hypothesis of stability. This is indeed surprising, and we would suspect that something is wrong with the test. However, this is not so. If there is high multicollinearity in the regressors, it is not unusual that what look to us like drastic differences in the coefficients turn out to be "statistically insignificant." In such cases one should try to solve the basic problem of multicollinearity and not get too excited about having found the differences "statistically insignificant," because from the practical point of view these differences are often "very significant."

Another problem that is often ignored in the use of tests for stability is the problem of heteroscedasticity, or unequal error variances. One basic assumption of the test, which unfortunately is often forgotten in empirical applications, is that the error variances in the different groups are equal. Toyoda[1] examines this problem in considerable detail, and though his conclusions are based on some approximations which have been found to be not too accurate, his results do indicate that the problem can be serious and is worth worrying about. Thus, before applying the test for stability, it would be useful to look at $\hat{\sigma}^2$ for each group. As an illustration, consider the consumption-function data (per capita in constant dollars) in Table 7-1. The estimated equations for the prewar and postwar periods are the following.

1929–1941:

$$C = \underset{(7.13)}{282.56} + \underset{(19.75)}{.69328}\, Y$$

$R^2 = .9726$, SEE = 18.119, RSS = 3611.39, degrees of freedom 11.

1946–1970:

$$C = \underset{(2.84)}{63.09} + \underset{(77.82)}{.88286}\, Y$$

$R^2 = .9962$, SEE = 17.936, RSS = 7399.05, degrees of freedom 23.

[1] Toshihisa Toyoda, Use of the Chow Test under Heteroscedasticity, *Econometrica*, May 1974, pp. 601–608. See also subsequent comments on the paper in *Econometrica*, 1976.

Thus $\hat{\sigma}^2$ is almost the same for both equations, and hence we can go ahead with our test. For the whole period:

$$C = \underset{(6.10)}{85.06} + \underset{(107.45)}{.87104}\,Y$$

$R^2 = .9969$, SEE $= 23.476$, RSS $= 19{,}839.62$, degrees of freedom 36.

Hence URSS $= 3611.39 + 7399.05 = 11{,}010.44$.

$$F = \frac{(19{,}839.62 - 11{,}010.44)/2}{11{,}010.44/34} = 13.63$$

which is significant at the 1 percent probability level. The 1 percent point in the F tables for degrees of freedom 2 and 34 is 5.3.

Sometimes the second set n_2 does not contain enough observations to estimate all the regression parameters (i.e., $n_2 < k + 1$). In this case Chow suggests the following test: Let RSS_1 be the residual sum of squares with n_1 observations. It has degrees of freedom $n_1 - k - 1$. Let RSS be the residual sum of squares with $n_1 + n_2$ observations. It has degrees of freedom $n_1 + n_2 - k - 1$. Then use the F test:

$$F = \frac{(\text{RSS} - \text{RSS}_1)/n_2}{\text{RSS}_1/(n_1 - k - 1)}$$

as an F variate with degrees of freedom n_2, $n_1 - k - 1$.

As an illustration, consider the estimation of the production function from the data in Table 10-3 with the first 37 observations. The estimates are

$$\log X = \underset{(-16.31)}{-3.9419} + \underset{(17.00)}{1.4442}\log L_1 + \underset{(7.85)}{.3922}\log K_1$$

$R^2 = .9938$, SEE $= .03538$, RSS $= .04256$.

We want to test whether the next two observations have been generated by the same model. To test this hypothesis, we estimate the equation with 39 observations. The estimated equation is given in Eq. (10-16), with residual sum of squares .05076. Hence, the F test is given by

$$F = \frac{(.05076 - .04256)/2}{.04256/34} = 3.28$$

The 5 percent F value for 2 and 34 degrees of freedom is 3.28. Hence this is just significant at the 5 percent level. We reject the hypothesis that the last two observations came from the same model as the first 37. The latter test, where $n_2 < k + 1$, is much weaker in detecting changes in structure than the earlier test, where there are enough observations to estimate the parameters from both the samples.

These tests for stability can also be applied for subsets of the coefficients rather than the entire set of coefficients. In this case the unrestricted residual sum of squares can be computed as before by running separate regressions for each group and then taking the sum of these residual sums of squares. The restricted residual sum of squares can be computed by using the dummy-variable method outlined earlier. Consider, for instance, the three equations in Eq. (9-4). These are the equations to estimate if the hypothesis is that the slope coefficient is the same between period 1 and period 2 and the intercept term is the same between period 2 and period 3. Thus the restricted residual sum of squares can be obtained from Eq. (9-5). If there are n_1, n_2, n_3 observations, respectively, in the three groups, this has $(n_1 + n_2 + n_3 - 4)$ degrees of freedom. The unrestricted residual sum of squares has $(n_1 - 2) + (n_2 - 2) + (n_3 - 2)$ degrees of freedom. The F test is given by

$$F = \frac{(\text{RRSS} - \text{URSS})/2}{\text{URSS}/(n_1 + n_2 + n_3 - 6)}$$

Both the unrestricted and restricted residual sums of squares can be obtained from the same dummy-variable regression if we introduce enough dummy variables. As an illustration, consider Eq. (9-2). Then estimating both equations separately is equivalent to estimating (9-3). A test[1] for the significance of D_1 tests whether the intercept terms are equal, a test for the significance of D_2 tests whether the slope coefficients are equal, and a test of the hypothesis that the coefficients of *both* D_1 and D_2 are zero is a test for the stability of the entire regression relationship. However (and this is particularly so if the number of regressors is greater than 1), we should be rather cautious in making inferences about stability and instability of the coefficients by looking at the t ratios of the dummy variables alone. As was pointed out in the earlier discussion on $\bar{R}^2$, it can happen that the t ratios for each of a set of coefficients are all insignificant and still the F ratios for the entire set of coefficients are significant. What one should do in any particular example is to use the F tests and then use the t tests on individual dummy variables only if they correspond to economically meaningful hypotheses.

10-4 MISSING OBSERVATIONS

In econometric work we often, though not always, face the problem that the data we work with are deficient in many ways. The problems are measurement errors, lack of correspondence between the theoretical quantities and empirical measures, nonexistence of series, gaps in records, multicollinearity, etc. We have discussed the last one. We will now discuss the case of missing data.

There are a variety of reasons why data may be missing. In some cases the desired series may just be unobservable. Another case is that in cross-section

[1] See D. Gujarathi, Use of Dummy Variables in Testing for Equality between Sets of Coefficients in Two Linear Regressions—A Note, *American Statistician*, February 1970. Gujarathi suggests using the dummy-variable method in preference to the Chow test, arguing that the Chow test might reject the hypothesis of stability but not let us know which particular coefficients are unstable, whereas the dummy-variable method will give us this information.

data where data are collected by surveys some respondents may not answer some questions or may not respond at all and thus there are gaps in the data or some observations may be completely missing. In time-series data gaps can occur because different series are recorded at different intervals—some annual, some quarterly, and some monthly. Since the reasons for the gaps in cross-section and time-series data are different, the solutions will also differ. But before we explain these differences we will first outline the several solutions suggested in the literature.

First, to fix ideas, let us consider the case of only two variables y and x with n_1 observations for which both x and y are observed, n_2 observations for which only x is observed, and n_3 observations for which only y is observed. Afifi and Elashoff[1] suggest several methods, but the main ones are as follows:

1. *Classical least squares*: Discard all the observations for which y or x is missing.
2. *Zero-order regression method*: Substitute for each missing value the mean of the corresponding variable. For example, in the above case calculate $\bar{x}$ from $n_1 + n_2$ observations and $\bar{y}$ from $n_1 + n_3$ observations, and substitute $\bar{x}$ for each of the n_3 missing x's and $\bar{y}$ for each of the n_2 missing y's.
3. *Modified zero-order regression method*: Instead of substituting $\bar{x}$ and $\bar{y}$, we substitute γ for each missing x and δ for each missing y where γ and δ are obtained by minimizing

$$\sum_1 (y_i - \alpha - \beta x_i)^2 + \sum_2 (\delta - \alpha - \beta x_i)^2 + \sum_3 (y_i - \alpha - \beta\gamma)^2$$

The first sum is over the n_1 observations for which we have both x and y, the second over the n_2 observations for which we have only x, and the third over the n_3 observations for which we have only y. This procedure can be set up in a dummy-variable regression. Write

$$\begin{bmatrix} y_1 \\ 0 \\ y_3 \end{bmatrix} = \alpha \begin{bmatrix} 1 \\ 1 \\ 1 \end{bmatrix} + \beta \begin{bmatrix} x_1 \\ x_2 \\ 0 \end{bmatrix} + \delta \begin{bmatrix} 0 \\ -1 \\ 0 \end{bmatrix} + \beta\gamma \begin{bmatrix} 0 \\ 0 \\ 1 \end{bmatrix} + \begin{bmatrix} u_1 \\ u_2 \\ u_3 \end{bmatrix}$$

That is, put $y = 0$ if it is not observed and $x = 0$ if it is not observed. Then estimate a regression equation of y on x, D_1, and D_2, where D_1 and D_2 are dummy variables defined as

$$\begin{aligned} D_1 &= -1 \text{ if } y \text{ is not observed} \\ &= 0 \qquad \text{otherwise} \\ D_2 &= 1 \text{ if } x \text{ is not observed} \\ &= 0 \qquad \text{otherwise} \end{aligned}$$

[1] A. A. Afifi and R. M. Elashoff, Missing Observations in Multivariate Statistics, *Journal of the American Statistical Association*, Part I, September 1966; Part II, March 1967; Parts III, IV, March 1969.

The implicit assumption in methods 2 and 3 is that all the missing values are equal.

4. *First-order regression method*: Compute the regression of y on x and x on y based on the n_1 observations for which we have data on both x and y. Estimate the missing y values from the former regression and the missing x values from the latter regression. Now estimate the regression equation from the completed sample.

5. *Modified first-order regression*:[1] This is a variant of the preceding method. It is simply to estimate the values of x for those observations for which y is observed as in method 4 and to discard those observations for which we have missing y's.

6. *Maximum-likelihood method*: We assume that the joint distribution of x and y is a bivariate normal distribution. Anderson[2] considered the case where we have $n_1 + n_2$ observations on x and n_1 observations on y. The basic idea in the estimation procedure is to note that the joint distribution can be written as

$$f(x,y) = f(y \mid x) \cdot f(x)$$

The mean and variance of x can be estimated from the $(n_1 + n_2)$ observations, and the parameters of the conditional distribution of y given x can be estimated only from n_1 observations. Thus the estimate $\hat{\beta}$ of the regression coefficient of y on x is obtained from only n_1 observations. The only difference is in the estimation of the mean and variance of y and the correlation coefficient between x and y. If $\bar{x}$ and $\hat{\sigma}_x^2$ are the estimates of the mean and variance of x from $n_1 + n_2$ observations and $\bar{x}^*$, $\bar{y}^*$, $\hat{\sigma}^{*2}_x$, $\hat{\sigma}^{*2}_y$, and $\hat{\beta}$ are, respectively, the ML estimates of the means, variances, and the regression coefficient of y on x from the complete sample of n_1 observations, then the ML estimates of μ_y, the mean of y, σ_y^2, the variance of y, and ρ, the correlation between x and y, are

$$\hat{\mu}_y = \bar{y}^* + \hat{\beta}(\bar{x} - \bar{x}^*)$$

$$\hat{\sigma}_y^2 = \hat{\sigma}^{*2}_y + \hat{\beta}^2(\hat{\sigma}_x^2 - \hat{\sigma}^{*2}_x)$$

and

$$\hat{\rho} = \hat{\beta}\ \hat{\sigma}_x/\hat{\sigma}_y$$

Thus the main differences between classical least squares and the ML method are in the estimates of these parameters—not in the estimate of the regression coefficient β. Since in econometric work our interest is usually in the regression coefficient of y on x, this method is not very helpful.

Afifi and Elashoff compare the relative biases and efficiencies of these methods in the estimation of the several parameters. Since our interest in econometric work is mainly in the regression parameters, we might look at these.

[1] Afifi and Elashoff call this a two-stage regression method, but since this term is used in a different context in econometrics, we have called it "modified first-order method."

[2] T. W. Anderson, Maximum Likelihood Estimates for a Multivariate Normal Distribution When Some Observations Are Missing, *Journal of the American Statistical Association*, June 1957.

Even so, it is hard to summarize all their conclusions. Stated briefly, their conclusion is that the least-squares estimators are generally worse than the others. That is, it is not desirable to throw away the observations for which y or x is missing. If ρ is large, say $|\rho| \geqslant .5$, then the modified first-order method is better than the first-order method, which in turn is better than the zero-order method. If ρ is small, the first-order method is better than the zero-order method, which in turn is better than the modified first-order method. How do these methods generalize to the case of several explanatory variables? The classical least-squares, the zero-order, and the modified zero-order methods can be generalized easily. The generalization of the ML method which is implicit in Anderson's paper is explicitly discussed in Afifi and Elashoff's second paper. But this applies only to a monotone sample; i.e., if y is observed for n_0 observations, x_1 for n_1 observations, x_2 for n_2 observations, x_3 for n_3 observations, etc., n_0 is a subset of n_1 which is a subset of n_2 which is a subset of n_3, etc. Thus the application of this method in econometric work is very limited.

This leaves us with the first-order regression methods. In the case of several variables, there are many regressions we can choose from which can be used to estimate the missing observations. For example consider the setup:

No. of observations	y	x	z
n_1	y_1	x_1	z_1
n_2	y_2	x_2	
n_3	y_3		z_3
n_4		x_4	z_4
n_5		x_5	
n_6			z_6
n_7	y_7		

We have n_1 complete observations. For n_2 observations z is missing, for n_3 observations x is missing, for n_4 observations y is missing, for n_5 observations y and z are missing, for n_6 observations y and x are missing, and for n_7 observations x and z are missing. There are two questions we might want to ask: (1) Do we estimate even the missing values of y? (2) In the estimation of the missing values of x, do we consider the regression of x on z only or the regression of x on z and y? The answers to both questions will depend on whether our model is the classical regression model or the multivariate regression model (the difference is discussed in Chap. 7). Since, in most econometric applications, we have the former in mind, it does not appear appropriate to consider estimation of the missing y values or the estimation of missing x values based on a regression of x on y. The procedure commonly used in econometric work is therefore to consider only the regressions among the independent variables to estimate the missing values among these variables. Thus, in the example we have, we use only $n_1 + n_2 + n_3$ observations, estimate regression equations of x on z and z on x based on $n_1 + n_4$ observations, and estimate z_2 and x_3 from these regressions.

Not much is known about the relative performance of these methods. Haitovsky[1] compared by a Monte Carlo study the classical least-squares and the zero-order method and found that the latter is worse than the former if the independent variables are even moderately correlated. Other studies have come to similar conclusions. Thus, if the correlations among the explanatory variables are even moderately high, one should not use the zero-order method. Also, on common-sense considerations we would expect that in this case the first-order regression methods should do better than the classical least-squares methods which discard all the observations with gaps in data.[2]

One important thing to note is that often the variances of the estimated regression coefficients based on the completed sample are presented as if the sample is the true sample; i.e., the fact that some sample observations are estimated is ignored. It is because of this that Kosobud[3] arrives at the conclusion that residual variances will be smaller with the first-order method than with the classical least squares where incomplete observations are dropped altogether. That this is not necessarily so is shown in the paper by Kelejian.

The methods we have discussed till now are for cross-section data. In time-series data both the problems and the methods are different. First, the missing observations will be missing in a systematic way. For example, we might have only annual data but not quarterly data or only quarterly data and not monthly data. Second, the problems of estimation of missing observations can be classified into three categories which Friedman[4] calls (1) interpolation, (2) distribution, and (3) extrapolation.[5] In interpolation our objective is to estimate intermediate values for a given series. For example, if we have comprehensive data every alternate year from the censuses of manufacturers and some other data that are less comprehensive but available annually, we use these to interpolate between the biennial data. That is, we are given Y_t and Y_{t+2} and X_t, X_{t+1}, and X_{t+2} and we are required to estimate Y_{t+1}. In distribution problems we have to distribute the total for one time unit among shorter time units; e.g., we might have comprehensive annual national income estimates, but less comprehensive estimates at the quarterly level. Using these, we want to distribute the comprehensive annual estimates among the four quarters; i.e., we are given $(Y_t + Y_{t+1} + Y_{t+2} + Y_{t+3})$ and X_t, X_{t+1}, X_{t+2}, and X_{t+3}. We are asked to

[1] Haitovsky, Missing Data in Regression Analysis, *Journal of the Royal Statistical Society*, ser. B, 1968, pp. 67–82.

[2] Kelejian studies the asymptotic efficiency of the first-order regression method as compared with classical least squares. See H. H. Kelejian, "Missing Observations in Multivariate Regression-Efficiency of a First Order Method," *The Journal of the American Statistical Association*, December 1969, pp. 1609–1616.

[3] R. Kosobud, A Note on a Problem Caused by Assignment of Missing Data in Sample Surveys, *Econometrica*, 1963, pp. 562–563.

[4] M. Friedman, The Interpolation of Time Series by Related Series, *The Journal of the American Statistical Association*, December 1962.

[5] The appropriate regression models for these three problems are discussed in G. C. Chow and An-loh Lin, Best Linear Unbiased Interpolation, Distribution and Extrapolation of Time Series by Related Series, *Review of Economics and Statistics*, 1971, pp. 372–375.

estimate Y_t, Y_{t+1}, Y_{t+2}, and Y_{t+3}. In extrapolation, we are given data Y_1, $Y_2, \ldots, Y_T$ and we are to estimate the observations Y_{T+1}, Y_{T+2}, etc.

In all these problems one can either use the same series or use a related series. For example, given Y_t and Y_{t+4}, one can use a linear interpolation formula to interpolate the intermediate values. If

$$T_y = \frac{Y_{t+4} - Y_t}{4}$$

then
$$\hat{Y}_{t+1} = Y_t + T_y$$
$$\hat{Y}_{t+2} = Y_t + 2T_y$$
and
$$\hat{Y}_{t+3} = Y_t + 3T_y$$

This is the most naive method similar to using the means for all missing values we considered in cross-section data. In the case of extrapolation elaborate models have been developed where future values of the series are forecast just on the basis of past values of the same series. These models, called ARIMA models, will be discussed at length under the title of Box-Jenkins methods in a later chapter. In the case of distribution, too, we can think of naive models as in the case of interpolation. One naive rule would be to distribute the annual totals equally among the four quarters. Another rule would be to distribute it so as to preserve the trend in the annual series.

However, often the estimation of missing observations im time series is done with the help of a related series. Consider the interpolation problem. We have first to select what related series we want to use and next what method of interpolation to use.

Let Y be the series to be interpolated and X the series to be used in interpolation. Suppose Y is observed at the beginning of each year and X at the beginning of each month. Our objective is to estimate the monthly data on Y. Let

$$T_x = \frac{X_{12} - X_0}{12} \qquad (10\text{-}21)$$

be the mean trend in X and

$$T_y = \frac{Y_{12} - Y_0}{12}$$

be the mean trend in Y. If we did not observe X and used a linear interpolation formula for Y, we would have estimated $Y_1, Y_2, \ldots, Y_{11}$ by

$$\hat{Y}_i = Y_0 + iT_y \qquad i = 1,2, \ldots, 11 \qquad (10\text{-}22)$$

However, since we observe X, if we can assume that the intrayear movements in X and Y are similar, we can use the errors committed in the linear interpolation of X to improve on the linear interpolation of Y. Thus the interpolated values of X would be

$$\hat{X}_i = X_0 + iT_x \qquad i = 1,2, \ldots, 11 \qquad (10\text{-}23)$$

The errors committed in the case of X by this procedure are $X_i - \hat{X}_i$. Hence the estimate of Y_i "corrected" for interpolation error is

$$Y_i^* = \hat{Y}_i + \frac{T_y}{T_x}(X_i - \hat{X}_i) \tag{10-24}$$

We multiply the error in X by T_y/T_x because we want to make an allowance for differences in the units of measurement for X and Y. Also instead of considering X and Y we can, if we think it is more appropriate, use log X and log Y in place of X and Y, respectively, and go through the procedures described in formulas (10-21) to (10-24).

Friedman[1] calls these methods "noncorrelation" methods of using related series and discusses several variants of these methods. If u and v are the errors $X - \hat{X}$ and $Y - \hat{Y}$, Friedman shows that using X as an interpolator gives a better estimate of the interpolated Y series than the straight-line interpolation method only if

$$\rho_{uv} > \frac{1}{2}\,\frac{\sigma_u}{\sigma_v}$$

where ρ_{uv} is the correlation between u and v and σ_u and σ_v are the standard deviations of u and v, respectively. Friedman argues that the important point to note is that it is the correlation between u and v that is relevant and not that between X and Y. The former may be quite low even though the latter may be quite high—because of high serial correlation between successive values of X and Y. Since this is difficult to judge by looking at the correlations between X and Y, it is often possible that the use of related series gives larger errors than straight-line interpolation.

We will be discussing problems in time-series analysis in a later chapter. The above discussion is meant to point out the differences in missing data problems between cross-section and time-series data. First, data will be missing in a specific order. Second, one has to take account of the time structure of the series with the missing observations and the related series. An assumption often made in all the statistical literature on analysis with missing data, that the successive observations are independent, is not a valid assumption. In fact it is the lack of independence that gives us mileage in the interpolation, distribution, and extrapolation problems.

10-5 AGGREGATION

There are several different questions that can be discussed under aggregation. All the problems in index-number construction are problems in aggregation. Here the problem is one of constructing an aggregate index of, say, different prices or quantities. These are problems of aggregation of variables. We will not go into these here.

[1] M. Friedman, *op. cit.*

By contrast there is a whole class of problems that relates to aggregation of relations. Here we study the correspondence between the parameters of the micro- and macrorelations. The questions asked are of the following types:

1. Given a certain microrelation, under what conditions can we justify estimation of a similar relation in macrovariables. For instance, suppose the individual consumption functions for N households are linear.

$$c_{it} = \alpha_i + \beta_i y_{it} + u_{it} \qquad i = 1,2, \ldots, N \tag{10-25}$$

When can we estimate an aggregate consumption function that is also linear?

$$C_t = \alpha + \beta\ Y_t + U_t \tag{10-26}$$

2. What are the conditions on the microvariables that will justify a certain type of macrorelation? For example, what do we have to assume about individual firm behavior so that the production function at the aggregate level is of the Cobb-Douglas or CES form?
3. What is the relationship between the parameters of the macrorelations and the parameters of the microrelations? This is the question studied by Theil.
4. What are the gains or losses by aggregation when we have access to both micro- and macrodata? This is the question raised by Grunfeld and Griliches, Orcutt, and others.

Regarding question 1, suppose we consider the consumption functions Eq. (10-25). If all the households have the same marginal propensity to consume so that $\beta_i = \beta$ for all i, it is obvious that we get the aggregate consumption function of the form Eq. (10-26). Here

$$C_t = \sum_i c_{it} \qquad \alpha = \sum_i \alpha_i \qquad Y_t = \sum_i y_{it} \qquad \text{and} \qquad U_t = \sum_i u_{it}$$

Another alternative is to assume that the distribution of income among the households is described by a stable linear function.

$$y_{it} = \gamma_i + \sigma_i Y_t + v_{it} \tag{10-27}$$

Then, substituting (10-27) in (10-25), we get

$$\sum_i c_{it} = \sum_i \alpha_i + \sum_i \beta_i(\gamma_i + \delta_i Y_t + v_{it}) + \sum_i u_{it}$$

which can be written in the form of Eq. (10-26), but now

$$\alpha = \sum_i (\alpha_i + \beta_i \gamma_i)$$

$$\beta = \sum_i \beta_i \delta_i$$

$$U_t = \sum_i (\beta_i v_{it} + u_{it})$$

Thus, again the estimation of linear consumption function at the aggregate level is justified.

As yet another example, suppose we consider the Cobb-Douglas production function (in log form)

$$\log x_{it} = \alpha_i \log l_{it} + \beta_i \log k_{it} + u_{it} \tag{10-28}$$

where x_{it}, l_{it}, k_{it} are, respectively, the output, labor input, and capital input for the ith firm. Under what conditions can we estimate an aggregate Cobb-Douglas function

$$\log X_t = \alpha \log L_t + \beta \log K_t + \gamma + u_t \tag{10-29}$$

Clearly, even if $\alpha_i = \alpha$ for all i and $\beta_i = \beta$ for all i, we cannot justify the estimation of (10-29) if we define the aggregates X_t, L_t, and K_t in the conventional way, that is,

$$X_t = \sum_i x_{it} \qquad L_t = \sum_i l_{it} \qquad \text{and} \qquad K_t = \sum_i k_{it}$$

What we need to justify Eq. (10-29) is to define the aggregates as

$$X_t = \prod_i x_{it} \qquad L_t = \prod_i l_{it} \qquad \text{and} \qquad K_t = \prod_i k_{it}$$

That is, we have to define the averages at the aggregate level as geometric averages rather than arithmetic averages. It should also be noted that again it is not necessary to have the elasticities α_i and β_i constant for all i. If we have stable stochastic relationships about the distribution of labor and capital inputs of the form

$$\begin{aligned} \log l_{it} &= \log A_i + \theta_i \log L_t + v_{it} \\ \log k_{it} &= \log B_i + \delta_i \log K_t + w_{it} \end{aligned} \tag{10-30}$$

then we can again estimate an aggregate production function of the form (10-29). We then have

$$\log X_t = \sum_i \log x_{it}$$

$$\alpha = \sum_i \alpha_i \theta_i$$

$$\beta = \sum_i \beta_i \delta_i$$

$$\gamma = \sum_i (\gamma_i + \alpha_i \log A_i + \beta_i \log \beta_i)$$

$$U_t = \sum_i (u_{it} + \alpha_i v_{it} + \beta_i w_{it})$$

Thus, a Cobb-Douglas function like Eq. (10-28) at the individual level, an appropriate definition of aggregates, and a specification of the distribution of inputs as in Eq. (10-30) result in a Cobb-Douglas production function at the aggregate level.

Regarding question 2, it appears to be a more sensible question to ask than question 1. Instead of asking, When can we have the same functional form for both the micro- and macrorelations? we ask, What assumptions about microbehavior give rise to a particular functional form at the aggregate level? The pioneering paper in this area is by Houthakker,[1] who considered microunits with fixed production coefficients and one fixed factor of production. He showed that if the input-output coefficients are Pareto-distributed, the resulting aggregate production function is Cobb-Douglas. Levhari[2] extended this result by showing that an aggregate constant elasticity of substitution (CES) production function results if the input-output coefficients have a generalized Pareto distribution. The Houthakker-Levhari results are thus limited to microspecifications with no input substitution.

Turning next to question 3, this problem is the one analyzed by Theil using the formula for specification errors.[3] To illustrate the simplest case, consider n individuals, and the microequations are

$$y_{it} = \alpha_i x_{it} + \beta_i z_{it} + u_{it} \tag{10-31}$$

The "true" aggregate relation is

$$y_t = \sum_{i=1}^{n} \alpha_i x_{it} + \sum_{i=1}^{n} \beta_i z_{it} + u_t \tag{10-32}$$

But the equation we estimate is

$$y_t = \alpha x_t + \beta z_t + u_t \tag{10-33}$$

There is thus a specification error. To calculate the specification bias, as discussed in the section on omitted variables, we have to compute the regression coefficients of all the excluded variables x_{it} and z_{it} on the included variables x_t and z_t.

Let these auxiliary regressions be

$$\begin{aligned} x_{it} &= b_{1i} x_t + c_{1i} z_t + v_{1i} \\ z_{it} &= b_{2i} x_t + c_{2i} z_t + v_{2i} \end{aligned} \tag{10-34}$$

Then if $\hat{\alpha}$ and $\hat{\beta}$ are the least-squares estimators of α and β in Eq. (10-33), we have

$$\begin{aligned} E(\hat{\alpha}) &= \sum_i \alpha_i b_{1i} + \sum_i \beta_i b_{2i} \\ E(\hat{\beta}) &= \sum_i \alpha_i c_{1i} + \sum_i \beta_i c_{2i} \end{aligned} \tag{10-35}$$

[1] H. S. Houthakker, The Pareto Distribution and the Cobb-Douglas Production Function in Activity Analysis, *Review of Economic Studies*, 1955–1956, pp. 27–31.

[2] D. Levhari, A Note on Houthakker's Aggregate Production Function in a Multifirm Industry, *Econometrica*, 1968, pp. 151–154.

[3] H. Theil, "Linear Aggregation of Economic Relations," North-Holland Publishing Company, Amsterdam, 1954.

Thus α depends not only on all the α_i but also on all the β_i; β is similar. The expected value of each estimated macroparameter is a weighted average of not only the corresponding microparameters but also the noncorresponding microparameters. These weights are obtained from the auxiliary regression Eqs. (10-34). Also, it should be noted that Eqs. (10-34) give some restrictions on the weights. Since

$$x_t = \sum_i x_{it} = \sum_i (b_{1i}x_t + c_{1i}z_t + v_{1i})$$

we get

$$\sum_i b_{1i} = 1 \qquad \sum_i c_{1i} = 0 \qquad \text{and} \qquad \sum_i v_{1i} = 0 \tag{10-36}$$

Similarly, since

$$z_t = \sum_i z_{it} = \sum_i (b_{2i}x_t + c_{2i}z_t + v_{2i})$$

we have

$$\sum_i b_{2i} = 0 \qquad \sum_i c_{2i} = 1 \qquad \text{and} \qquad \sum_i v_{2i} = 0 \tag{10-37}$$

Thus the sum of the weights for the corresponding parameters is equal to 1 and the sum of the weights for the noncorresponding parameters is zero.

If $\alpha_i = \alpha$ and $\beta_i = \beta$ for all i, it can be easily seen from Eqs. (10-36) and (10-37) that $E(\hat{\alpha}) = \alpha$ and $E(\hat{\beta}) = \beta$, as should be expected.

Also suppose Eqs. (10-31) are individual demand equations, y is log of quantity, x is log of price, and z is log of income so that the coefficients are price and income elasticities. Since price does not vary over individuals, x_{it} is constant for all i. In this case, in the first auxiliary equation in (10-34) we will have

$$c_{1i} = 0 \qquad \text{(since } x_{it} \text{ and } x_t \text{ are perfectly correlated)}$$

and

$$b_{1i} = \frac{1}{n} \qquad \left(\text{since } x_t = \sum_{i=1}^{n} x_{it}\right)$$

Hence from Eq. (10-35) we see that the expected value of the estimated macro income elasticity $\hat{\beta}$ depends only on the individual income elasticities β_i. However, the expected value of the estimated macro price elasticity α is a simple (unweighted) average of the individual price elasticities α_i plus a weighted average of the income elasticities β_i. Thus the macro price elasticity still depends on the micro income elasticities β_i. These are some of the important results obtained by Theil. He considers the cases of several variables and has also extended the results to simultaneous equations, but the resulting expressions are more complicated. We need not go through the details here. The major conclusion of all this work is that if we start with some microrelations and estimate a corresponding macrorelation, the expected values (in simultaneous-equation models, the probability limits) of the estimated macroparameters are weighted averages of *both* the corresponding and noncorresponding microparameters, the weights for the corresponding parameters summing to 1 and the weights for the noncorresponding parameters summing to 0.

Coming finally to question 4, there has been some controversy on the merits and demerits of aggregation. Orcutt has repeatedly argued that disaggregation always results in more information and that there is an information loss in aggregation. If the microrelations are all well specified and accurate microdata are available, this could well be true. However, if the microdata are subject to large errors (as compared with macrodata) and if microrelations are likely to be more poorly specified than macrorelations, there would be a gain in using the aggregate data rather than the disaggregated data. Grunfeld and Griliches[1] make the latter argument.

Grunfeld and Griliches give two examples of some relations between micro R^2's and macro R^2's. One of the examples they consider is that of Grunfeld's investment study. The R^2's were as follows:

Corporation	R^2
General Motors	.919
General Electric	.705
U.S. Steel	.471
Atlantic Refining	.680
Union Oil	.764
Diamond Match	.643
Goodyear Tire	.666
American Steel	.142
Aggregate for 8 corporations	.926
Composite for 8 corporations	.906

They note that the aggregate R^2 is higher than any individual R^2. They also note that if we try to predict the investment level for each firm separately from its regression, add these predicted values, get the predicted total investment, and compare the variance of this with the actual variance of total investment, we will get an implied "composite" R^2 and that this composite R^2 is .906, which is less than the R^2 for the aggregate. They therefore conclude that if our aim is merely to explain total investment, we would have gained nothing from disaggregation.

Of course, these conclusions have to be qualified in certain respects. The comparison between "aggregate" R^2 and "composite" R^2 may not be the best comparison of the relative merits of predicting from aggregate vs. disaggregated

[1] Y. Grunfeld and Z. Griliches, Is Aggregation Necessarily Bad? *Review of Economics and Statistics*, February 1960, pp. 1–13. A formal analysis of the case where aggregates are measured more accurately than the disaggregates is given in D. J. Aigner and S. M. Goldfeld, Estimation and Prediction from Aggregate Data When Aggregates Are Measured More Accurately than Their Components, *Econometrica*, January 1974, pp. 113–134. They show that in this case there is considerable scope for an analysis based on the macroequation to be superior to that based on the microequations.

data. What one has to ask is the best prediction that one can generate, given the microdata. In any case, if the microequatioms are all correctly specified and the microparameters are all different, there is an "aggregation error" arising from the use of a common regression coefficient. On the other hand, as Grunfeld and Griliches argue, if the aggregate variables are more important in determining the microdependent variables, there is a specification error in the microrelations, and this will be larger than the aggregation error.

Examples that come to conclusions exactly opposite to those of Grunfeld and Griliches are presented by Orcutt, Watts, and Edwards,[1] and Edwards and Orcutt,[2] who do some simulation experiments to show that the predictions they obtain from the disaggregated data are better (in fact enormously better) in terms of mean square error than those obtained from the aggregates. Aigner and Goldfeld[3] show that this superiority can be attributed to the special structure assumed and in any case the results can be derived analytically without any simulation. The illustrative example they consider is the following:

Let

$$y_1 = \beta x_1 + u_1$$
$$y_2 = \beta x_2 + u_2$$

be the two microequations. Let

$$\operatorname{var}(x_1) = \operatorname{var}(x_2) = \sigma_x^2 \qquad \operatorname{cov}(x_1, x_2) = \delta_x \sigma_x^2$$
$$\operatorname{var}(u_1) = \operatorname{var}(u_2) = \sigma_u^2 \qquad \operatorname{cov}(u_1, u_2) = \delta_u \sigma_u^2$$

Also, let $\hat{\beta}_1$ and $\hat{\beta}_2$ be the estimators of β from the two microequations. And let $\hat{\beta}$ be the estimator from the aggregate equation:

$$(y_1 + y_2) = \beta(x_1 + x_2) + (u_1 + u_2)$$

Then

$$\operatorname{var}(\hat{\beta}_1) = \operatorname{var}(\hat{\beta}_2) = \frac{\sigma_u^2}{N\sigma_x^2}$$

$$\operatorname{var}(\hat{\beta}) = \frac{\sigma_u^2(1 + \delta_u)}{N\sigma_x^2(1 + \delta_x)}$$

The estimator actually reported by Edwards and Orcutt corresponds to an average of $\hat{\beta}_1$ and $\hat{\beta}_2$. Call it $\hat{\beta}_A$. Since

$$\operatorname{cov}(\hat{\beta}_1, \hat{\beta}_2) = \frac{\delta_u \delta_x \sigma_u^2}{N\sigma_x^2}$$

[1] G. H. Orcutt, H. W. Watts, and J. B. Edwards, Data Aggregation and Information Loss, *American Economic Review*, 1968, pp. 773–787.

[2] J. B. Edwards and G. H. Orcutt, Should Aggregation Prior to Estimation Be the Rule?, *Review of Economics and Statistics*, November 1969, pp. 409–420.

[3] D. J. Aigner and S. M. Goldfeld, Simulation and Aggregation: A Reconsideration, *Review of Economics and Statistics*, 1973, pp. 114–118.

we have

$$\text{var}(\hat{\beta}_A) = \frac{\sigma_u^2}{2N\sigma_x^2}(1 + \delta_u\delta_x)$$

In this case, Edwards and Orcutt consider δ_A equal to zero (and δ_x is perhaps negative). Hence

$$\text{var}(\hat{\beta}_A) = \frac{\sigma_u^2}{2N\sigma_x^2} < \text{var}(\hat{\beta}) = \frac{\sigma_u^2}{N\sigma_x^2(1 + \delta_x)}$$

Table 10-4 Grunfeld's data

	G.M.			U.S. Steel			G.E.			Chrysler		
	I	F_{-1}	C_{-1}	I	F_{-1}	C_{-1}	I	F_{-1}	C_{-1}	I	F_{-1}	C_{-1}
1935	317.6	3078.5	2.8	209.9	1362.4	53.8	33.1	1170.6	97.8	40.29	417.5	10.5
36	391.8	4661.7	52.6	355.3	1807.1	50.5	45.0	2015.8	104.4	72.76	837.8	10.2
37	410.6	5387.1	156.9	469.9	2676.3	118.1	77.2	2803.3	118.0	66.26	883.9	34.7
38	257.7	2792.2	209.2	262.3	1801.9	260.2	44.6	2039.7	156.2	51.60	437.9	51.8
39	330.8	4313.2	203.4	230.4	1957.3	312.7	48.1	2256.2	172.6	52.41	679.7	64.3
40	461.2	4643.9	207.2	361.6	2202.9	254.2	74.4	2132.2	186.6	69.41	727.8	67.1
41	512.0	4551.2	255.2	472.8	2380.5	261.4	113.0	1834.1	220.9	68.35	643.6	75.2
42	448.0	3244.1	303.7	445.6	2168.6	298.7	91.9	1588.0	287.8	46.80	410.9	71.4
43	499.6	4053.7	264.1	361.6	1985.1	301.8	61.3	1749.4	319.9	47.40	588.4	67.1
44	547.5	4379.3	201.6	288.2	1813.9	279.1	56.8	1687.2	321.3	59.57	698.4	60.5
45	561.2	4840.9	265.0	258.7	1850.2	213.8	93.6	2007.7	319.6	88.78	846.4	54.6
46	688.1	4900.9	402.2	420.3	2067.7	232.6	159.9	2208.3	346.0	74.12	893.8	84.8
47	568.9	3526.5	761.5	420.5	1796.7	264.8	147.2	1656.7	456.4	62.68	579.0	96.8
48	529.2	3254.7	922.4	494.5	1625.8	306.9	146.3	1604.4	543.4	89.36	694.6	110.2
49	555.1	3700.2	1020.1	405.1	1667.0	351.1	98.3	1431.8	618.3	78.98	590.3	147.4
50	642.9	3755.6	1099.0	418.8	1677.4	357.8	93.5	1610.5	647.4	100.66	693.5	163.2
51	755.9	4833.0	1207.7	588.2	2289.5	342.1	135.2	1819.4	671.3	160.62	809.0	203.5
52	891.2	4924.9	1430.5	645.5	2159.4	444.2	157.3	2079.7	726.1	145.00	727.0	290.6
53	1304.4	6241.7	1777.3	641.0	2031.3	623.6	179.5	2371.6	800.3	174.93	1001.5	346.1
54	1486.7	5593.6	2226.3	459.3	2115.5	669.7	189.6	2759.9	888.9	172.49	703.2	414.9

I = gross investment* = additions to plant and equipment plus maintenance and repairs in millions of dollars deflated by P_1

F = value of the firm† = price of common and preferred shares at Dec. 31 (or average price of Dec. 31 and Jan. 31 of the following year) times number of common and preferred shares outstanding plus total book value of debt at Dec. 31 in millions of dollars deflated by P_2

C = stock of plant and equipment* = accumulated sum of net additions to plant and equipment deflated by P_1 minus depreciation allowance deflated by P_3 in these definitions

P_1 = implicit price deflator of producers' durable equipment (base 1947)‡

P_2 = implicit price deflator of GNP (base 1947)‡

P_3 = depreciation expense deflator = 10 year moving average of wholesale price index of metals and metal products (base 1947)§

* *Moody's Industrial Manual* and Annual Reports of Corporations.

† *Bank and Quotation Record* and *Moody's Industrial Manual.*

‡ *Survey of Current Business*, July 1956, July 1957.

§ *Historical Statistics of the U.S.*, 1789–1945, and *Economic Report of the President*, January 1957, p. 161.

Table 10-4 (*Continued*)

	Atlantic Richfield			I.B.M.			Union Oil		
	I	F_{-1}	C_{-1}	I	F_{-1}	C_{-1}	I	F_{-1}	C_{-1}
1935	39.68	157.7	183.2	20.36	197.0	6.5	24.43	138.0	100.2
36	50.73	167.9	204.0	25.98	210.3	15.8	23.21	200.1	125.0
37	74.24	192.9	236.0	25.94	223.1	27.7	32.78	210.1	142.4
38	53.51	156.7	291.7	27.53	216.7	39.2	32.54	161.2	165.1
39	42.65	191.4	323.1	24.60	286.4	48.6	26.65	161.7	194.8
40	46.48	185.5	344.0	28.54	298.0	52.5	33.71	145.1	222.9
41	61.40	199.6	367.7	43.41	276.9	61.5	43.50	110.6	252.1
42	39.67	189.5	407.2	42.81	272.6	80.5	34.46	98.1	276.3
43	62.24	151.2	426.6	27.84	287.4	94.4	44.28	108.8	300.3
44	52.32	187.7	470.0	32.60	330.3	92.6	70.80	118.2	318.2
45	63.21	214.7	499.2	39.03	324.4	92.3	44.12	126.5	336.2
46	59.37	232.9	534.6	50.17	401.9	94.2	48.98	156.7	351.2
47	58.02	249.0	566.6	51.85	407.4	111.4	48.51	119.4	373.6
48	70.34	224.5	595.3	64.03	409.2	127.4	50.00	129.1	389.4
49	67.42	237.3	631.4	68.16	482.2	149.3	50.59	134.8	406.7
50	55.74	240.1	662.3	77.34	673.8	164.4	42.53	140.8	429.5
51	80.30	327.3	683.9	95.30	676.9	177.2	64.77	179.0	450.6
52	85.40	359.4	729.3	99.49	702.0	200.0	72.68	178.1	466.9
53	81.90	398.4	774.3	127.52	793.5	211.5	73.86	186.8	486.2
54	81.43	365.7	804.9	135.72	927.3	238.7	89.51	192.7	511.3

	Westinghouse			Goodyear			Diamond Match		
	I	F_{-1}	C_{-1}	I	F_{-1}	C_{-1}	I	F_{-1}	C_{-1}
1935	12.93	191.5	1.8	26.63	290.6	162	2.54	70.91	4.50
36	25.90	516.0	.8	23.39	291.1	174	2.00	87.94	4.71
37	35.05	729.0	7.4	30.65	335.0	183	2.19	82.20	4.57
38	22.89	560.4	18.1	20.89	246.0	198	1.99	58.72	4.56
39	18.84	519.9	23.5	28.78	356.2	208	2.03	80.54	4.38
40	28.57	628.5	26.5	26.93	289.8	223	1.81	86.47	4.21
41	48.51	537.1	36.2	32.08	268.2	234	2.14	77.68	4.12
42	43.34	561.2	60.8	32.21	213.3	248	1.86	62.16	3.83
43	37.02	617.2	84.4	35.69	348.2	274	.93	62.24	3.58
44	37.81	626.7	91.2	62.47	374.2	282	1.18	61.82	3.41
45	39.27	737.2	92.4	52.32	387.2	316	1.36	65.85	3.31
46	53.46	760.5	86.0	56.95	347.4	302	2.24	69.54	3.23
47	55.56	581.4	111.1	54.32	291.9	333	3.81	64.97	3.90
48	49.56	662.3	130.6	40.53	297.2	359	5.66	68.00	5.38
49	32.04	583.8	141.8	32.54	276.9	370	4.21	71.24	7.39
50	32.24	635.2	136.7	43.48	274.6	376	3.42	69.05	8.74
51	54.38	723.8	129.7	56.49	339.9	391	4.67	83.04	9.07
52	71.78	864.1	145.5	65.98	474.8	414	6.00	74.42	9.93
53	90.08	1193.5	174.8	66.11	496.0	443	6.53	63.51	11.68
54	68.60	1188.9	213.5	49.34	474.5	468	5.12	58.12	14.33

Table 10-5 Micro- and Macroequations

Firm	Coefficient of					
	Constant	F_{-1}	C_{-1}	R^2	$\hat{\sigma}^2$	DW
G.M.	−149.8	0.12	0.37	.921	8424	.94
	(−1.42)	(4.62)	(10.0)			
U.S. Steel	−49.2	0.17	0.39	.471	9300	.95
	(−0.33)	(2.36)	(2.74)			
G.E.	−9.96	0.03	0.15	.705	777.5	1.07
	(−0.32)	(1.71)	(5.90)			
Chrysler	−6.19	0.08	0.32	.914	176.3	1.98
	(−0.46)	(3.90)	(10.96)			
Atlantic Richfield	26.13	0.13	0.01	.633	83.43	2.38
	(3.77)	(2.34)	(0.38)			
I.B.M.	−8.69	0.13	0.09	.952	65.32	1.76
	(−1.91)	(4.22)	(0.85)			
Union Oil	−4.50	0.09	0.12	.764	88.67	1.67
	(−0.40)	(1.33)	(7.25)			
Westinghouse	−0.51	0.05	0.09	.744	104.3	1.41
	(−0.06)	(3.37)	(1.65)			
Goodyear	−7.72	0.08	0.08	.666	82.79	1.30
	(−0.83)	(2.22)	(2.93)			
Diamond Match	0.16	0.005	0.44	.643	1.18	1.07
	(0.08)	(0.17)	(5.50)			
Macro	−327.7	0.10	0.26	.939		1.32
	(−1.69)	(4.94)	(10.62)			

Figures in parentheses are t ratios.

However, suppose $\delta_x = 0$ and $\delta_u = -0.8$. Then

$$\operatorname{var}(\hat{\beta}) = 0.2\frac{\sigma_u^2}{N\sigma_x^2} \qquad \text{and} \qquad \operatorname{var}(\hat{\beta}_A) = 0.5\frac{\sigma_u^2}{N\sigma_x^2}$$

Thus, $\operatorname{var}(\hat{\beta}_A) > \operatorname{var}(\hat{\beta})$, and we have the opposite result.

As Aigner and Goldfeld point out, though this simple example does not capture all the intricacies and detail of the models considered in the simulation experiments by Edwards and Orcutt, it does throw light on what sort of results to expect. It also points out that it is often desirable to derive some results analytically before simulating.

In Table 10-4 we reproduce the data for 10 firms.[1] (Some of these are different from the ones considered in the Grunfeld-Griliches paper.) The prediction from macro- and microequations is left as an exercise.

Table 10-5 presents the estimates for the individual equations and the aggregate equation. The F test described earlier to test for homogeneity of the coefficients gave an F ratio of 27.78 with degrees of freedom 27 and 170. Since this is significant at even the 1 percent level, we reject the hypothesis of

[1] The data are taken from J. C. G. Boot and G. M. DeWit, Investment Demand: An Empirical Contribution to the Aggregation Problem, *International Economic Review*, 1960, pp. 27–28.

Table 10-6 Correlations among Residuals

	1	2	3	4	5	6	7	8	9	10
1	1.00	−.26	.28	−.27	−.35	.12	.51	.16	.21	−.26
2		1.00	.43	.34	.21	.36	−.27	.61	.28	.70
3			1.00	−.07	−.01	.46	−.02	.73	.41	.56
4				1.00	.11	.20	−.12	.12	.07	.11
5					1.00	.16	.15	−.02	−.14	.10
6						1.00	.13	.52	−.17	.39
7							1.00	.14	.19	−.22
8								1.00	.52	.57
9									1.00	.26
10										1.00

homogeneity of the coefficients. Thus there will be an aggregation bias. Actually, the figures on $\hat{\sigma}^2$ show that there is considerable heteroscedasticity and thus the F test is not valid unless we correct for this. One crude way to do this is to use the estimated variances to homogenize the error variances. For example, since $\hat{\sigma}^2$ is 8424 for G.M. and 83.43 for Atlantic Richfield, we multiply each observation for the latter firm by 10. Then the error variance for this equation will be 8343. After doing this for every firm, we apply the F test again. This is left as an exercise. The differences in the coefficients in this example are so marked that we would be rejecting the hypothesis of homogeneity anyway.

The F test for homogeneity is not valid even in the presence of autocorrelated residuals, and the DW statistics in Table 10-5 also show significant autocorrelations. In principle one has to make corrections for this before applying the tests for homogeneity.

Apart from the DW statistics, the correlations across equations will give us some evidence of whether there are specification errors (due to omitted variables). These correlations are presented in Table 10-6 for the equations reported in Table 10-5. Eight of the correlations are greater than 0.5. When the aggregate "value of firm" was included as an extra variable (as a proxy for general economic conditions), its coefficient was not significant in any of the equations, it did not improve the DW statistics, and the correlations shown in Table 10-6 did not change much. For instance, the highest correlation .73 fell to .69. Thus, one has to look for better alternatives for the omitted variables. Further experimentation with the data is left as an exercise.

Exercises

1. Implicit in our discussion on missing observations there were two separate problems: (*a*) estimation of the parameters of the regression model when observations are missing and (*b*) interpolation of data for missing values. Discuss the similarities and differences between the solutions to these two problems in (i) cross-section data, (ii) time-series data.

Often data-producing agencies use interpolations and these data are used by investigators as if they were continuous series. In what ways should investigators take account of the fact that data are interpolated?

In what respects is a quarterly model better than an annual model and monthly model better than a quarterly model?[1] An example of an elaborate econometric model constructed from long time series interpolated from very few basic observations is the model by Narasimham.[2] At the end of his book data are presented on national income, consumption, investment, and so on for 1923–1948. For how many years do data really exist in each case? Comment on the usefulness of such models. (Present also some strong arguments in defense.)

2. Consider the three-variable regression model

$$y = \beta_1 X_1 + \beta_2 X_2 + u$$

where $u \sim IN(0,\sigma^2)$ and the X's are nonstochastic. Assume that all variables are measured as deviations from their sample means.

(*a*) It is desired to test the hypothesis that $\beta_1 = \beta_2$. Carefully describe, step by step, how you would perform the test on a given body of data. Be explicit, giving algebraic expressions whenever possible.

(*b*) Assuming that it is accepted that $\beta_1 = \beta_2$, how would you estimate β_1 and β_2 from a given body of data?

(*c*) Would you prefer to use two different samples for parts (*a*) and (*b*) rather than using the same sample for both testing and estimating? Why?

3. An economist thinks that aggregate output Q is related by a production function to capital input K, labor input L, and time t (the latter representing steady technological progress). Assuming a Cobb-Douglas production function with constant returns to scale, the economist tells his research assistant to use time-series data to fit a least-squares regression of the form

$$\ln \frac{Q}{L} = \gamma + \alpha t + \beta \ln \frac{K}{L} + u$$

The research assistant finds an estimate of α that is three times its standard error and an estimate of β that is roughly equal to its standard error. He also notes that the simple correlation coefficient between t and $\ln(K/L)$ is .9. The research assistant concludes that productivity is better explained by technical progress than by changes in factor inputs. The economist rejects this conclusion on the grounds that "the independent variables are collinear and therefore the regression is worthless."

(*a*) What do you think of this criticism?

(*b*) Write the production function in its nonlogarithmic form with Q a function of t, K, L, and u.

(*c*) If the error term u has mean zero and constant variance, will the production function in its nonlogarithmic form show homoscedasticity?

4. Consider the following two versions of the consumption functions:

(*a*) $c_t = \beta_0 + \beta_1 y_t + \beta_2 y_{t-1} + \epsilon_t$

(*b*) $c_t = \beta_0' + \beta_1' y_t + \beta_2' c_{t-1} + \epsilon_t'$

In order to choose which specification of the consumption function is most appropriate, it was proposed that you form a "hybrid" function:

(*c*) $c_t = \beta_0'' + \beta_1'' y_t + \beta_2'' y_{t-1} + \beta_3'' c_{t-1} + \epsilon_t''$

and separately test the hypotheses $H_1 : \beta_2 = 0$ and $H_2 : \beta_3 = 0$. Acceptance of H_1 would imply version (*b*), and acceptance of H_2 would imply version (*a*).

Equation (*c*) was estimated using OLS, with the following results:

$$\hat{c}_t = \underset{(-.60)}{-19.22} + \underset{(4.39)}{.4129}\, y_t - \underset{(-2.71)}{.2959}\, y_{t-1} + \underset{(11.78)}{.8941}\, c_{t-1}$$

where the values in parentheses are t values. The t values indicate that either hypothesis would be rejected at the 95 percent level.

[1] For an illustration of a monthly model see T. C. Liu, A Monthly Recursive Econometric Model of United States: A Test of Feasibility, *Review of Economics and Statistics*, 1969, pp. 1–13.

[2] N. V. A. Narasimham, "A Short-Term Planning Model for India," North-Holland Publishing Co., Amsterdam, 1956.

The zero-order correlation matrix for the regressors is as follows:

$$\begin{bmatrix} & y_t & y_{t-1} & c_{t-1} \\ y_t & 1 & .978 & .939 \\ y_{t-1} & & 1 & .952 \\ c_{t-1} & & & 1 \end{bmatrix}$$

What justification, if any, can you give for the approach? What methods would you propose for choosing between (*a*) and (*b*) as a specification? What surprises, if any, did you experience with the results from fitting equation (*c*)? What assumptions with regard to equation (*c*) are needed to justify the use of OLS? With these assumptions, what statistical properties do the estimators have?

5. In our discussion of aggregation problems we considered the problems of estimation and prediction from aggregate and disaggregate data. Often we find investigators constructing elaborate theoretical models based on microbehavior (at the firm or individual level) and then "testing" the validity of this theory or the superiority of this theory to other competing theories on the basis of aggregate data without any discussion of the aggregation problem. (This is particularly common in the case of the work connected with the microfoundations of macroeconomics.)

Give three examples of where the theory is formulated at the microlevel and the testing of the theory is done (*a*) (inappropriately) with macrodata or (*b*) (quite appropriately) with microdata.

CHAPTER

ELEVEN

INTRODUCTION TO SIMULTANEOUS-EQUATION MODELS

11-1 JOINTLY DEPENDENT VARIABLES AND IDENTIFICATION

In the usual regression model y is the dependent or determined variable and $x_1, x_2, \ldots,$ etc., are the independent or determining variables. The crucial assumption we make is that these variables are independent of the residual u. Sometimes, for example, in demand-and-supply models, this assumption is violated. (It is violated in the case of errors in variables too, as we noted earlier.) The error term in the demand function corresponds to shifts in the demand function, and unless supply is completely inelastic, a shift in the demand function changes both quantity and price. Thus if we write the demand function as

$$q = \alpha + \beta p + u$$

then p and u are correlated. The solution in this case is to bring the supply equation into the picture. Such models are known as *simultaneous-equation models*.

In simultaneous-equation models, there are a number of endogenous or jointly determined variables and a number of exogenous or determining variables. Consider the following model:

$$\begin{aligned} q &= a_1 + b_1 p + c_1 Y + u_1 && \text{demand function} \\ q &= a_2 + b_2 p + c_2 R + u_2 && \text{supply function} \qquad (11\text{-}1) \end{aligned}$$

q is quantity, p is price, Y is income, R is rainfall, and u_1 and u_2 are the disturbance terms. Here p and q are the jointly determined variables or endogenous variables and Y and R are the exogenous or determining variables. The exogenous variables are assumed to be uncorrelated with the residuals. They thus satisfy the usual requirements for regression analysis. We can therefore estimate a regression equation of q on Y and R, and p on Y and R by ordinary least squares. But if we estimate either one of the equations in (11-1), which are called *structural equations*, by ordinary least squares, we will get inconsistent estimators for the parameters, because the variable p is correlated with the residuals u_1 and u_2.

If we solve the two equations in (11-1) for q and p in terms of Y and R, we get

$$q = \frac{a_1 b_2 - a_2 b_1}{b_2 - b_1} + \frac{c_1 b_2}{b_2 - b_1} Y - \frac{c_2 b_1}{b_2 - b_1} R + \text{a residual}$$

$$p = \frac{a_1 - a_2}{b_2 - b_1} + \frac{c_1}{b_2 - b_1} Y - \frac{c_2}{b_2 - b_1} R + \text{a residual}$$

These equations are called the *reduced-form* equations. We can write them as

$$q = \pi_1 + \pi_2 Y + \pi_3 R + v_1$$
$$p = \pi_4 + \pi_5 Y + \pi_6 R + v_2$$

where $$\pi_1 = \frac{a_1 b_2 - a_2 b_1}{b_2 - b_1} \qquad \pi_2 = \frac{c_1 b_2}{b_2 - b_1} \qquad \text{etc.}$$

These equations can be estimated by ordinary least squares to obtain consistent estimates of the parameters. From these estimates we have to determine the coefficients of the structural equations, viz., a_1, b_1, c_1, a_2, b_2, and c_2. We get

$$\hat{b}_1 = \frac{\hat{\pi}_3}{\hat{\pi}_6} \qquad \hat{b}_2 = \frac{\hat{\pi}_2}{\hat{\pi}_5} \qquad \hat{c}_2 = -\hat{\pi}_6(\hat{b}_1 - \hat{b}_2)$$

$$\hat{c}_1 = \hat{\pi}_5(\hat{b}_1 - \hat{b}_2) \qquad \hat{a}_1 = \hat{\pi}_1 - \hat{b}_1 \hat{\pi}_4 \qquad \hat{a}_2 = \hat{\pi}_1 - \hat{b}_2 \hat{\pi}_4$$

This is what is known as the *indirect least-squares method*.[1]

It may not always be possible to get estimates of the structural coefficients from the estimates of the reduced form, and sometimes we might get multiple estimates and have the problem of choosing between them. For example, suppose we have the demand-and-supply model as (omitting the residuals for simplicity)

$$q = a_1 + b_1 p + c_1 Y \qquad \text{demand function}$$
$$q = a_2 + b_2 p \qquad \text{supply function}$$

[1] To obtain confidence intervals estimated by the indirect least squares method, we can use Fieller's method described in Chap. 7, Sec. 7-9.

Then the reduced form is

$$q = \frac{a_1 b_2 - a_2 b_1}{b_2 - b_1} + \frac{c_1 b_2}{b_2 - b_1} Y$$

$$p = \frac{a_1 - a_2}{b_2 - b_1} + \frac{c_1}{b_2 - b_1} Y$$

or

$$q = \pi_1 + \pi_2 Y$$

$$p = \pi_3 + \pi_4 Y$$

Note that $\hat{b}_2 = \hat{\pi}_2/\hat{\pi}_4$ and $\hat{a}_2 = \hat{\pi}_1 - \hat{b}_2\hat{\pi}_3$. But there is no way of getting estimates of a_1, b_1, and c_1. Thus the supply function is estimable but the demand function is not estimable. On the other hand, suppose that we have the model

$$q = a_1 + b_1 P \qquad \text{demand function}$$

$$q = a_2 + b_2 P + c_2 R \qquad \text{supply function}$$

Now the demand function would be estimable but the supply function is not.

Suppose that we have the system

$$q = a_1 + b_1 P + c_1 Y + d_1 R \qquad \text{demand function}$$

$$q = a_2 + b_2 P \qquad \text{supply function}$$

Rainfall affects demand and not supply (if there is more rain, people don't go shopping). The reduced-form equations are

$$q = \frac{a_1 b_2 - a_2 b_1}{b_2 - b_1} + \frac{c_1 b_2}{b_2 - b_1} Y + \frac{d_1 b_2}{b_2 - b_1} R$$

$$p = \frac{a_1 - a_2}{b_2 - b_1} + \frac{c_1}{b_2 - b_1} Y + \frac{d_1}{b_2 - b_1} R$$

or

$$q = \pi_1 + \pi_2 Y + \pi_3 R$$

$$p = \pi_4 + \pi_5 Y + \pi_6 R$$

Note that we now get two estimates of b_2. One is $\hat{b}_2 = \hat{\pi}_2/\hat{\pi}_5$ and the other is $\hat{b}_2 = \hat{\pi}_3/\hat{\pi}_6$, and these need not be equal. For each of these we get an estimate of a_2, viz., $\hat{a}_2 = \hat{\pi}_1 - \hat{b}_2\hat{\pi}_4$.

On the other hand, we get no estimates for the parameters of the demand function, viz., a_1, b_1, c_1, d_1. Here we say that the supply function is *overidentified* and the demand function is *underidentified*. When we get unique estimates for the parameters of an equation, we say that the equation is *exactly identified*. When we get multiple estimates, we say that the equation is *overidentified*. When we get no estimates, we say that the equation is underidentified. In all this discussion we are talking of getting estimates of the parameters of the structural equations from the estimates of the parameters of the reduced-form equations.

The above discussion of identification has been in terms of obtaining solutions for the parameters of the structural equations from the parameters of the reduced-form equations. An alternative way of looking at the identification problem is to see whether the equation under consideration can be distinguished from a linear combination of all equations. Consider, for example, the equations

$$q = a_1 + b_1 p + c_1 y + u \qquad \text{demand function} \qquad (11\text{-}2)$$

$$q = a_2 + b_2 p + v \qquad \text{supply function} \qquad (11\text{-}3)$$

Suppose we take a weighted average of both equations with weights w and $(1 - w)$. Then we get

$$\begin{aligned} q &= w(a_1 + b_1 p + c_1 y + u) + (1 - w)(a_2 + b_2 p + v) \\ &= a_1^* + b_1^* p + c_1^* y + u^* \end{aligned} \qquad (11\text{-}4)$$

where
$$\begin{aligned} a_1^* &= wa_1 + (1 - w)a_2 \\ b_1^* &= wb_1 + (1 - w)b_2 \\ c_1^* &= wc_1 \\ u^* &= wu + (1 - w)v \end{aligned}$$

Equation (11-4) is indistinguishable from Eq. (11-2). When we estimate the parameters of the demand function, we do not know whether we are getting estimates of a_1, b_1, and c_1 or a_1^*, b_1^*, and c_1^*. Thus we do not know whether we are getting estimates of the parameters of the demand function only or a mixture of the parameters of the demand-and-supply function. This we express by saying that the parameters of the demand function are not identified. Note that Eq. (11-4) does not look like the supply function (11-3) unless $w = 0$. There is no way of generating an equation that looks like the supply function by taking a weighted average of both equations with a nonzero weight for the demand function. Hence, when we estimate the supply function (11-3), we know for sure that the estimates we have are the estimates of the parameters of the supply function only. Thus the parameters of the supply function are identified.

When there are many equations, we need a more systematic way of checking this condition for identification. We do it the following way: For illustrative purposes consider the case of three endogenous variables y_1, y_2, y_3 and three exogenous variables z_1, z_2, z_3. Let us mark with an x if a variable occurs in the equation and a 0 if it does not. Suppose the system of equations is the following:

	y_1	y_2	y_3	z_1	z_2	z_3
Equation 1	x	0	x	x	0	x
Equation 2	x	0	0	x	0	x
Equation 3	0	x	x	x	x	0

The rule for identification of any equation is: Delete that particular row and pick up the columns corresponding to the elements that have zeros in that row. If we can form a matrix of rank $(G - 1)$, where G is the number of endogenous variables (or number of equations), from these columns, then the equation is identified, otherwise not.[1] This condition is referred to as the *rank condition*. This is a necessary and sufficient condition for identification. Clearly, to form a matrix of rank $(G-1)$ we should have at least $(G-1)$ columns. Thus there should be at least $(G-1)$ missing variables from the particular equation under consideration. This condition is often referred to as the *order condition*, which is only a necessary condition. The order condition is very easy to check—it is a simple counting rule. Often in econometric work the order condition is verified because it is easy to verify, but the rank condition is not. This is not a desirable practice. An equation is said to be overidentified if the number of missing variables is greater than $G-1$, exactly identified if the number of missing variables is equal to $G-1$, and underidentified if the number of missing variables is less than $(G-1)$. All this terminology refers to the order condition. The rank condition merely refers to whether an equation is identified (over or exactly) or not.

In the above-mentioned illustrative example, the number of equations G is 3. Hence $G-1$ is 2. The number of missing variables is 2 for the first equation, 3 for the second equation, and 2 for the third equation. Thus, by the order condition, the first and third equations are exactly identified and the second equation is overidentified.

Next consider the rank condition. For the first equation delete the first row and pick up the columns corresponding to the missing variables y_2 and z_2. The columns are

$$\begin{bmatrix} 0 & 0 \\ x & x \end{bmatrix}$$

The rank of this matrix is only 1 because the first row has both elements 0. Hence the equation is not identified. Though the order condition tells us that the equation is exactly identified, the rank condition shows that the equation is not identified. Consider the second equation. Deleting the second row and picking up the columns corresponding to the zero elements for y_2, y_3, and z_2, we get

$$\begin{bmatrix} 0 & x & 0 \\ x & x & x \end{bmatrix}$$

The rank of this matrix is 2. Hence the equation is identified. Similarly, for the third equation, the columns for y_1 and z_3 give

$$\begin{bmatrix} x & x \\ x & x \end{bmatrix}$$

The rank of this matrix is again 2. Hence the equation is identified.

In summary, only the second and third equations are estimable.[2] The parameters of the first equation are not estimable. There are, however, many

[1] This condition is an alternative way of expressing the fact that we cannot form an equation that looks like the equation under consideration by taking a linear combination of the other equations and adding it to this equation. It should also be noted that this condition is specific to linear models and for simple equations.

[2] Note that when we talk about the rank condition being satisfied we mean that it holds *almost everywhere*, i.e., it does not fail identically.

estimation methods for simultaneous-equation models that break down if the order condition is not satisfied but do give estimates of the parameters if the order condition is satisfied, even if the rank condition is not. We will be discussing these methods below. In this example, since the first equation is exactly identified by the order condition, we will be getting some estimates of the parameters if we use these methods. In that sense the parameters are "estimable." What the failure of the rank condition tells us is that these estimates we obtain cannot be interpreted as the estimates of the parameters of the first equation alone. They can be the estimates of some linear combinations of the parameters of all the three equations. This is what we mean by saying that the parameters of the first equation are not estimable.

11-2 IDENTIFICATION UNDER HOMOGENEOUS LINEAR RESTRICTIONS

Our discussion till now has been in terms of what are known as "exclusion restrictions"; i.e., some variables are included and some excluded. In actual practice we can have equations where the restrictions on the coefficients are general homogeneous linear restrictions. As an example consider again a model with three endogenous variables y_1, y_2, y_3 and three exogenous variables z_1, z_2, z_3. We can write the equation system in its most general form as

$$\beta_{11}y_1 + \beta_{12}y_2 + \beta_{13}y_3 + \gamma_{11}z_1 + \gamma_{12}z_2 + \gamma_{13}z_3 = u_1$$
$$\beta_{21}y_1 + \beta_{22}y_2 + \beta_{23}y_3 + \gamma_{21}z_1 + \gamma_{22}z_2 + \gamma_{23}z_3 = u_2$$
$$\beta_{31}y_1 + \beta_{32}y_2 + \beta_{33}y_3 + \gamma_{31}z_1 + \gamma_{32}z_2 + \gamma_{33}z_3 = u_3$$

If the first equation is

$$y_1 + \beta_{12}(y_2 - z_3) + \gamma_{11}(z_1 + z_2) = u_1$$

only one variable is missing from the equation. There is thus only one exclusion restriction $\beta_{13} = 0$. The other restrictions are homogeneous linear restrictions: $\gamma_{12} = \gamma_{11}$ and $\gamma_{13} = -\beta_{12}$ or $\gamma_{12} - \gamma_{11} = 0$ and $\beta_{12} + \gamma_{13} = 0$.

Fisher[1] derives conditions for identification in the presence of general linear homogeneous restrictions. Let there be G endogenous and K exogenous variables in the system. Let A be the $G \times (G + K)$ matrix of all the coefficients in the system and α_1 the first row. Express the restrictions on the first equation as $\alpha_1\phi = 0$. Then the (rank) condition for identification is $\rho(A\phi) = G - 1$ where $\rho(M)$ refers to the rank of the matrix M.

Note that $A\phi$ has G rows and as many columns as ϕ. Since the first row of $A\phi$ consists of all zeros (since $\alpha_1\phi = 0$), the rank of $A\phi$ can never be greater than $G - 1$. Also, in order that $\rho(A\phi)$ may be $G - 1$, there should be at least $G - 1$ columns in ϕ, i.e., at least $G - 1$ restrictions on the coefficient of the first equation. This is the order condition for identification we discussed earlier.

[1] F. M. Fisher, "The Identification Problem," McGraw-Hill Book Company, New York, 1966.

In the above example $G = 3$ so that $G - 1 = 2$.

$$\alpha_1 = [\beta_{11}\ \beta_{12}\ \beta_{13}\ \gamma_{11}\ \gamma_{12}\ \gamma_{13}]$$

The restrictions are

$$\beta_{13} = 0$$
$$-\gamma_{11} + \gamma_{12} = 0$$
$$\beta_{12} + \gamma_{13} = 0$$

and hence

$$\phi = \begin{bmatrix} 0 & 0 & 0 \\ 0 & 0 & 1 \\ 1 & 0 & 0 \\ 0 & -1 & 0 \\ 0 & 1 & 0 \\ 0 & 0 & 1 \end{bmatrix}$$

$$A\phi = \begin{bmatrix} 0 & 0 & 0 \\ \beta_{23} & -\gamma_{21} + \gamma_{22} & \beta_{22} + \gamma_{23} \\ \beta_{33} & -\gamma_{31} + \gamma_{32} & \beta_{32} + \gamma_{33} \end{bmatrix}$$

To find $\rho(A\phi)$, we need to know what restrictions there are on the coefficients of the other equations. Suppose $\beta_{23} = 0$, $-\gamma_{21} + \gamma_{22} = 0$, and $\beta_{22} + \gamma_{23} = 0$. Then $\rho(A\phi) = 1$ and the first equation is not identified even though by the order condition the equation is overidentified. This is similar to the case considered earlier in the discussion of exclusion restrictions.

If there are identities in the system, we can express the restrictions either for the original version of the model or for the derived version after eliminating the identities. The conclusions would be precisely the same, though in the case of large models considering the original version is easier. For instance, in a macro model with four endogenous variables C = consumption, I = investment, Y = income, r = rate of interest, if there is the income identity

$$Y = C + I + G$$

Where G = government expenditures (treated as exogenous), we can either consider the four-equation model or use the identity to eliminate C, I, or Y and treat the model as a three-equation model. In either case we will arrive at the same conclusions regarding identification.

11-3 IDENTIFICATION BY COVARIANCE RESTRICTIONS

In addition to restrictions on the coefficients, sometimes there may be restrictions on the covariances between the errors. Suppose we assume that the errors in Eqs. (11-2) and (11-3) are independent, i.e., $\mathrm{cov}(u, v) = 0$. Then Eq. (11-4) can be distinguished from Eq. (11-2) because the transformed equation (11-4) has a residual u^* which is correlated with the residual v in the supply equation. We have

$$\operatorname{cov}[u^*, v] = \operatorname{cov}[wu + (1-w)v, v] = (1-w)\sigma_v^2$$

Thus, even if $\operatorname{cov}(u,v) = 0$, $\operatorname{cov}(u^*,v) \neq 0$ unless $w = 1$. Thus it is not possible to generate an equation that has the same properties as Eq. (11-2) by combining Eqs. (11-2) and (11-3). Hence the demand function is identified. This is an example of how identification is achieved through "covariance restrictions."

To see how one can get estimates of the structural parameters from the estimates of the reduced-form parameters in this case, note that the reduced-form equations are

$$q = \pi_1 + \pi_2 y + w_1$$
$$p = \pi_3 + \pi_4 y + w_2$$

where $\pi_1 = \dfrac{a_1 b_2 - a_2 b_1}{b_2 - b_1}$ $\quad \pi_2 = \dfrac{c_1 b_2}{b_2 - b_1}$ $\quad w_1 = \dfrac{b_2 u - b_1 v}{b_2 - b_1}$

$$\pi_3 = \frac{a_1 - a_2}{b_2 - b_1} \qquad \pi_4 = \frac{c_1}{b_2 - b_1} \qquad w_2 = \frac{u - v}{b_2 - b_1}$$

As noted earlier, we can get estimates of b_2 and a_2 from the estimates of the reduced-form parameters, $\hat{b}_2 = \hat{\pi}_2/\hat{\pi}_4$ and $\hat{a}_2 = \hat{\pi}_1 - \hat{b}_2\hat{\pi}_3$. But we cannot get estimates of a_1, b_1, c_1. If $\operatorname{cov}(u,v) = 0$, we can use the information in the variances and covariances of w_1 and w_2 to get estimates of these parameters. Let $\operatorname{var}(u) = \sigma_u^2$, $\operatorname{var}(v) = \sigma_v^2$, and $\operatorname{cov}(u,v) = 0$. Then

$$\operatorname{var}(w_1) = \frac{1}{(b_2 - b_1)^2}(b_2^2\sigma_u^2 + b_1^2\sigma_v^2) = \sigma_{11} \quad \text{(say)}$$

$$\operatorname{var}(w_2) = \frac{1}{(b_2 - b_1)^2}(\sigma_u^2 + \sigma_v^2) = \sigma_{22} \quad \text{(say)}$$

$$\operatorname{cov}(w_1, w_2) = \frac{1}{(b_2 - b_1)^2}(b_2\sigma_u^2 + b_1\sigma_v^2) = \sigma_{12} \quad \text{(say)}$$

Hence $\dfrac{\sigma_{11}}{\sigma_{22}} = \dfrac{b_2^2 + b_1^2\lambda}{1 + \lambda}$ and $\dfrac{\sigma_{12}}{\sigma_{22}} = \dfrac{b_2 + b_1\lambda}{1 + \lambda}$

where $\lambda = \sigma_v^2/\sigma_u^2$. We can get estimates of σ_{11}, σ_{12}, and σ_{22} from the reduced-form residuals, and since we already have an estimate of b_2 we can solve the above two equations to get estimates of b_1 and λ. Substituting the estimates of a_2, b_2, and b_1 in $\hat{\pi}_3$, we get an estimate of a_1 and substituting the estimates of b_2 and b_1 in $\hat{\pi}_2$, we get an estimate of c_1. Also substituting the estimates of b_1, b_2, and λ in $\hat{\sigma}_{11}$, we get an estimate of σ_u^2. Thus all the parameters can be estimated if $\operatorname{cov}(u,v) = 0$.

Another form of restrictions on the variances and covariances is where we have some prior knowledge about the ratios of variances. Suppose we have a demand-and-supply model and we have reason to believe that the variance of the error in the supply equation is four times as large as the variance of the error in the demand equation. Such information also aids in the identification of parameters. This kind of information is not often used, and most empirical practice unfortunately relies on restrictions on the parameters in the equations to achieve identification.

General conditions for identification by covariance restrictions are rather complicated to be discussed here.[1] However, in actual practice such examples do occur, and in many cases one can devise an appropriate estimation method taking the special features of the model into account.[2]

11-4 SOME FURTHER PROBLEMS IN IDENTIFICATION

Till now we have treated only systems of equations which are linear and we considered only within-equation homogeneous linear restrictions. In many practical situations we have, among other problems, the complications of nonhomogeneous restrictions, nonlinearities, and cross-equation restrictions. We will briefly discuss these.

Nonhomogeneous restrictions are very common in econometric work. For example, suppose we have a Cobb-Douglas production function which can be written (in log form) as

$$\log Q = \alpha + \beta_1 \log K + \beta_2 \log L + u$$

If we impose constant returns to scale, we have the inhomogeneous restriction $\beta_1 + \beta_2 = 1$.

Earlier we wrote the set of restrictions on the first equation as $\alpha_1\phi = 0$. Now we write them as $\alpha_1\phi = \lambda$, where λ has at least one element nonzero and ϕ is a matrix of known constants. Also earlier the matrix $A\phi$ had the first row with all elements zero (because $\alpha_1\phi = 0$), and hence $\rho(A\phi) \leqslant G - 1$. The rank condition for identification was $\rho(A\phi) = G - 1$. Now the first row of $A\phi$ is λ and $\rho(A\phi) \leqslant G$. The rank condition in the presence of inhomogeneous restrictions[3] is

$$\rho(A\phi) = G$$

Another common problem is that of nonlinearities which can arise from either nonlinearities in the variables or nonlinearities in the restrictions. If the equations are linear in the endogenous variables but nonlinear in the exogenous variables, we have no new problems because we can redefine the exogenous variables suitably that would make the equations linear. Hence we will consider

[1] See Fisher, *ibid.*, chaps. 3 and 4.

[2] Such examples are given in A. S. Goldberger, Structural Equation Methods in the Social Sciences, *Econometrica*, 1972, pp. 979–1002, and Zvi Griliches, Errors in Variables and Other Unobservables, *Econometrica*, November, 1974, pp. 971–998.

[3] Note that this condition includes the normalization choice. It does not imply that we now really require more substantive information.

only equations which are nonlinear in the endogenous variables. As examples consider two demand-and-supply models with q and p as endogenous variables and a single exogenous variable z. The first set is

$$\log q = a_1 \log p + a_2 z + u_1 \qquad \text{demand function} \tag{11-5}$$

$$q = b_1 p + b_2 z + u_2 \qquad \text{supply function} \tag{11-6}$$

Here the demand function is log-linear in p and q and the supply function is linear in p and q. The second set of equations is

$$q = a_1 p + a_2 p^2 + a_3 z + u_1 \qquad \text{demand function} \tag{11-7}$$

$$q = b_1 p + b_2 z + u_2 \qquad \text{supply function} \tag{11-8}$$

Here the demand function is quadratic in p and the supply function is linear in p.

Fisher derives the conditions for identification in such systems provided there is at least one nonconstant exogenous variable, and some conditions (which are not very restrictive in practice) are satisfied. What we do, in the case of a model consisting of Eqs. (11-5) and (11-6), is to consider the system as consisting of five variables $\log q$, $\log p$, q, p, and z rather than the three variables q, p, and z. The matrix of coefficients is now

$$A = \begin{bmatrix} 1 & -a_1 & 0 & 0 & -a_2 \\ 0 & 0 & 1 & -b_1 & -b_2 \end{bmatrix}$$

The restriction matrix ϕ for the first equation is

$$\phi = \begin{bmatrix} 0 & 0 \\ 0 & 0 \\ 1 & 0 \\ 0 & 1 \\ 0 & 0 \end{bmatrix}$$

Hence
$$A\phi = \begin{bmatrix} 0 & 0 \\ 1 & -b_1 \end{bmatrix}$$

The condition Fisher derives for identification is the same as before with the linear systems, viz., that $\rho(A\phi) = G - 1$. Here the condition is satisfied for both equations. Hence both equations are identified. Thus, though q, p, and z all occur in both the equations, we can identify both equations because of the differences in functional forms. Similarly, in the case of the model given by Eqs. (11-7) and (11-8) we consider the system as consisting of four variables q, p, p^2, and z rather than q, p, and z. The matrix A is

$$A = \begin{bmatrix} 1 & -a_1 & -a_2 & -a_3 \\ 1 & -b_1 & 0 & -b_2 \end{bmatrix}$$

We can easily verify that the supply equation is identified but the demand equation is not. Here the nonlinearity in the demand function helps us identify the supply function.

In the case of nonlinearity in the restrictions rather than variables, Fisher discusses what is known as local and global identifiability and gives the necessary and sufficient conditions for this, which we cannot go into here.[1] For local identification, roughly speaking, what we do is expand the nonlinear restrictions around a set of values of the parameters and then discuss the identifiability around these values. Suppose we consider the first equation of the system and this equation has k parameters $(\beta_1, \beta_2, \ldots, \beta_k)$. Suppose there are J restrictions of the form $f_i(\beta_1 \beta_2 \cdots \beta_k) = 0 \quad i = 1, 2, \ldots, J$. Let ϕ be the matrix of the partial derivatives $\partial f_i / \partial \beta_j$ and ϕ_0 the value of this matrix at the set of values $(\beta_{10}, \beta_{20}, \ldots, \beta_{k0})$. Then the condition for local identification of this equation is $\rho(A\phi_0) = G - 1$. Note that when f_i are linear functions, ϕ_0 is a constant matrix. The condition is thus similar to the one derived earlier.

Finally, we come to cross-equation restrictions. Our discussion has all along been in terms of restrictions on within-equation parameters. Often there will be restrictions connecting parameters in the different equations. One common example of such restrictions is in case of systems of demand equations where there are restrictions on the sums of the elasticities from the different equations. As an illustration of how restrictions on the sum of the coefficients across equations can help in identification, consider the model

$$y_1 + a_1 y_2 + a_2 z = u_1 \tag{11-9}$$

$$b_1 y_1 + y_2 + b_2 z = u_2 \tag{11-10}$$

with the restriction $a_2 + b_2 = 0$. Suppose we add λ times the second equation to the first. We get

$$(1 + \lambda b_1) y_1 + (a_1 + \lambda) y_2 + (a_2 + \lambda b_2) z = u_1 + \lambda u_2$$

or

$$y_1 + a_1^* y_2 + a_2^* z = u_1^* \tag{11-11}$$

where

$$a_1^* = \frac{a_1 + \lambda}{1 + \lambda b_1} \qquad a_2^* = \frac{a_2 + \lambda b_2}{1 + \lambda b_1} \qquad \text{and} \qquad u_1^* = \frac{u_1 + \lambda u_2}{1 + \lambda b_1}$$

Equation (11-11) can be confused with Eq. (11-9) only if it satisfies the condition $a_2^* + b_2 = 0$

or

$$\frac{a_2 + \lambda b_2}{1 + \lambda b_1} + b_2 = 0$$

or

$$a_2 + b_2 + \lambda b_2 (1 + b_1) = 0$$

This gives $\lambda = 0$, since $a_2 + b_2 = 0$. Thus there is no way of adding a multiple of the second equation to the first and generating an equation that looks exactly like it, i.e., satisfies the condition that the sum of the coefficients of z is zero. Thus, even though Eqs. (11-9) and (11-10) are both underidentified without any further restrictions, both equations are identified with the cross-equation restriction $a_2 + b_2 = 0$.

[1] See Fisher, *op. cit.*, chap. 5.

In the presence of cross-equation constraints we have to consider the identification of the system as a whole (or at least blocks of equations) rather than each equation individually as we have done till now. The general conditions in this case have been derived by Wegge[1] and Rothenberg[2] and are somewhat complicated for the present discussion.

11-5 METHODS OF ESTIMATION

Different methods of estimation for simultaneous-equation models have been proposed in the literature. These can be classified under the category of single-equation methods (alternatively called limited-information methods) and system methods (alternatively called full-information methods). In single-equation methods we estimate each equation separately using only the information about the restrictions on the coefficients of that particular equation. The restrictions on the coefficients of the other equations are not used. They are (or should be) used to check the identifiability of the particular equation. But they are not used for estimation purposes. This is the reason these methods are called limited-information methods. In system methods we estimate all equations jointly using the restrictions on the parameters of all the equations as well as the variances and covariances of the residuals. This is the reason they are called full-information methods.

The most commonly used single-equation methods are ordinary least squares (OLS), indirect least squares (ILS), two-stage least squares (2SLS), and limited-information maximum likelihood (LIML). The OLS method does not give consistent estimates of the parameters because of the correlation between the residuals and the regressors, whereas the other methods give consistent estimates. This does not mean that the OLS method is useless. Sometimes it is possible (even for some underidentified models) to say something about the direction of the bias (asymptotic) of the OLS estimators, and this is useful. We will discuss this later under Least-Squares Bias. More importantly, it has been found that the OLS method is more robust against specification errors than many of the simultaneous-equation methods and also that the predictions from equations estimated by OLS often compare favorably with those obtained from equations estimated by the simultaneous-equation methods. In view of this it is fruitful to report OLS estimates of the structural equations (even if they are not consistent) along with those from the other methods that give consistent estimates.

In ILS, we estimate the reduced-form equations by OLS and then obtain estimates of the structual parameters from the estimates of the reduced-form parameters. As discussed earlier, if the equation under consideration is exactly

[1] L. Wegge, Identifiability Criteria for a System of Equations as a Whole, *Australian Journal of Statistics*, 1965.

[2] T. J. Rothenberg, Identification in Parametric Models, *Econometrica*, May, 1971, pp. 577–591.

identified (by the order condition), we get unique solutions with this method. If the equation is overidentified, we get multiple solutions. Because ILS gives multiple solutions, it is not discussed much in the literature. However, since all the estimation methods suggested for overidentified equations amount to taking weighted averages of these multiple solutions, it would be instructive to look at the ILS estimates so that we know how the averaging is done.

The 2SLS method is one way of weighting the multiple solutions. The method is as follows:

$$y_1 = \beta_{12}y_2 + \gamma_{11}z_1 + \gamma_{12}z_2 + u_1 \qquad (11\text{-}12)$$

$$y_2 = \beta_{21}y_1 + \gamma_{23}z_3 + \gamma_{24}z_4 + u_2 \qquad (11\text{-}13)$$

Here y_1, y_2 are the endogenous and z_1, z_2, z_3, z_4 the exogenous variables. Note that both equations are overidentified by the order condition. In 2SLS we first estimate the reduced-form equations by OLS. In this example this involves regressing each of y_1 and y_2 on z_1, z_2, z_3, z_4. We get $\hat{y}_1$ and $\hat{y}_2$, the estimated values of y_1 and y_2, respectively, from these reduced-form equations. In the second stage of 2SLS we regress y_1 on $\hat{y}_2$, z_1, z_2 and y_2 on $\hat{y}_1$, z_3, z_4. For the endogenous variables on the right-hand side of Eqs. (11-12) and (11-13) we substitute their estimated values from the reduced-form equations.

The basic idea in 2SLS is to substitute for the endogenous variables, which are correlated with the residuals, linear functions of all the exogenous variables. Since these variables are uncorrelated (in probability limit) with the residuals, this procedure will give consistent estimates for the parameters. The linear functions are chosen so that each is the most highly correlated with the endogenous variable it replaces. Thus these linear functions are the estimated values $\hat{y}_1$, $\hat{y}_2$ from the reduced-form equations. However, in this process the residual in the original equation is transformed to a residual with a different variance. For instance, let $y_2 = \hat{y}_2 + \hat{v}_2$, where $\hat{v}_2$ is the estimated residual from the reduced form. Then Eq. (11-12) can be written as

$$y_1 = \beta_{12}\hat{y}_2 + \gamma_{11}z_1 + \gamma_{12}z_2 + (u_1 + \beta_{12}\hat{v}_2) \qquad (11\text{-}12a)$$

Hence, after estimating the parameters β_{12}, γ_{11}, γ_{12} from this equation by the OLS method, we should be careful not to use the estimated standard errors from this equation. The correct standard errors (asymptotic) for the 2SLS estimates can be obtained by a simple adjustment which is explained later in an illustrative example.

The LIML method, which is also alternatively known as the least-variance-ratio (LVR) method, proceeds as follows: Write Eq. (11-12) as

$$y_1^* = y_1 - \beta_{12}y_2 = \gamma_{11}z_1 + \gamma_{12}z_2 + u_1 \qquad (11\text{-}12b)$$

For each β_{12} we can construct a y_1^*. Consider a regression of y_1^* on z_1 and z_2 only, and compute the residual sum of squares (which will be a function of β_{12}). Call it RSS_1. Now consider a regression of y_1^* on all the exogenous variables z_1, z_2, z_3, z_4, and compute the residual sum of squares. Call this RSS_2. What Eq. (11-12b) says is that z_3 and z_4 are not important in determining y_1^*. Thus the extra reduction in the residual sum of squares with the inclusion of z_3 and z_4 in a regression of y_1^* on z_1 and z_2 should be minimal. What the LVR method does is to choose β_{12} so that $(\text{RSS}_1 - \text{RSS}_2)/\text{RSS}_1$ is minimized or $\text{RSS}_1/\text{RSS}_2$ is minimized. After β_{12} is determined, the estimates of γ_{11} and γ_{12} are obtained by regressing y_1^* on z_1 and z_2. The procedure is similar for the second equation.

There is an important relationship between the LVR and the 2SLS methods. The 2SLS method can be shown to minimize the difference $\text{RSS}_1 - \text{RSS}_2$ rather than the ratio $\text{RSS}_1/\text{RSS}_2$. Another important result is that if the equation under consideration is exactly identified, the ILS, 2SLS, and LIML estimates of the parameters are identical.

11-6 INSTRUMENTAL-VARIABLE METHODS

In addition, we can also consider what is known as the instrumental-variable method. Earlier, we argued that if we have a regression equation where the "explanatory" variable is correlated with the residual, we cannot get consistent estimates for the parameters by using OLS but we can get consistent estimates by using the instrumental variable (IV) method. However, we saw that the basic problem here was finding the instrumental variables. In a simultaneous-equation model this is not a problem because the exogenous variables not in the equation can be used as instrumental variables. For instance, in Eq. (11-12) there is one variable y_2 that is occurring as an explanatory variable that is correlated with the residual u_1. Hence we need one instrumental variable. We can use either z_3 or z_4. If we use z_3, the equations we have to solve to get estimates of β_{12}, γ_{11}, γ_{12} are $\sum z_3 u_1 = 0$, $\sum z_1 u_1 = 0$, and $\sum z_2 u_1 = 0$. Written at length, these equations are

$$\sum z_3 y_1 = \beta_{12} \sum z_3 y_2 + \gamma_{11} \sum z_3 z_1 + \gamma_{12} \sum z_3 z_2$$

$$\sum z_1 y_1 = \beta_{12} \sum z_1 y_2 + \gamma_{11} \sum z_1^2 + \gamma_{12} \sum z_1 z_2$$

$$\sum z_2 y_1 = \beta_{12} \sum z_2 y_2 + \gamma_{11} \sum z_2 z_1 + \gamma_{12} \sum z_2^2$$

If we use z_4 as an instrumental variable, the equations we solve are $\sum z_4 u_1 = 0$, $\sum z_1 u_1 = 0$, and $\sum z_2 u_1 = 0$. In the OLS method, the equations we solve are $\sum y_2 u_1 = 0$, $\sum z_1 u_1 = 0$, and $\sum z_2 u_1 = 0$. It can be shown that the 2SLS method is also an instrumental-variable method, where $\hat{y}_2$ is used as the instrumental variable, $\hat{y}_2$ being obtained from a regression of y_2 on all the exogenous variables z_1, z_2, z_3, z_4. Thus the 2SLS estimates are the same as those obtained by solving the equations

$$\sum \hat{y}_2 u_1 = 0 \qquad \sum z_1 u_1 = 0 \qquad \text{and} \qquad \sum z_2 u_1 = 0 \tag{11-14}$$

To see this equivalence, note that since $y_2 = \hat{y}_2 + \hat{v}_2$, where $\hat{v}_2$ is the estimated residual from the reduced form, Eq. (11-12) can be written as

$$y_1 = \beta_{12}\hat{y}_2 + \gamma_{11} z_1 + \gamma_{12} z_2 + (u_1 + \beta_{12}\hat{v}_2)$$

The 2SLS estimates are obtained by estimating this equation by OLS. The estimating equations are

$$\sum \hat{y}_2(u_1 + \beta_{12}\hat{v}_2) = 0$$

$$\sum z_1(u_1 + \beta_{12}\hat{v}_2) = 0 \qquad (11\text{-}15)$$

$$\sum z_2(u_1 + \beta_{12}\hat{v}_2) = 0$$

But since the residual from a regression equation is uncorrelated with each of the regressors, we have $\sum \hat{y}_2\hat{v}_2 = 0$, $\sum z_1\hat{v}_2 = 0$, and $\sum z_2\hat{v}_2 = 0$. Hence Eqs. (11-15) reduce to $\sum \hat{y}_2 u_1 = 0$, $\sum z_1 u_1 = 0$, and $\sum z_2 u_1 = 0$, which are Eqs. (11-14) for the IV method.

In the above example, for the estimation of Eq. (11-12) we needed one instrumental variable. But we had two available instruments. This is because the equation is overidentified. In fact, one alternative way of looking at the order condition for identification is to check how many instrumental variables are needed and how many are available. The number of instrumental variables needed is the number of endogenous variables in the equation minus one (since one of the endogenous variables is the "dependent" variable). The number of instrumental variables available is the number of missing exogenous variables. Hence the equation is over-, exactly, or underidentified according as the number of missing exogenous variables is greater than, equal to, or less than the number of included endogenous variables minus one. Add the number of missing endogenous variables to both sides of this relationship. Then we get the rule that an equation is over-, exactly, or underidentified according as the number of missing variables in the equation is greater than, equal to, or less than the number of endogenous variables in the system minus one. This is the rule mentioned earlier.

In practice, it may be better to look at the number of instrumental variables needed and available than to count the number of missing variables, particularly if there are restrictions on the parameters. For example, consider a model with three endogenous variables y_1, y_2, y_3 and two exogenous variables z_1 and z_2. Suppose the first equation is

$$y_1 = \beta_{12}(y_2 + y_3) + \gamma_{11}z_1 + u_1$$

The number of missing variables is one which is less than the number of endogenous variables minus one. Thus, using the counting rule about missing variables blindly would lead us to conclude that the equation is underidentified. This is not so because y_2 and y_3 occur together (their coefficients are equal). What we need is only one instrument for $(y_2 + y_3)$, and for this we use z_2. Thus the equation is exactly identified. Suppose the equation is $y_1 = \beta_{12}y_2 + \beta_{13}(y_3 + z_1) + u$. Again the counting rule about missing variables is not appropriate. We need two instruments, one for y_2, another for $(y_3 + z_1)$. We can use z_1 and z_2 as the two instrumental variables. We have seen earlier how to check for the conditions for identification when there are general linear restrictions on the parameters.

If an equation is exactly identified, the IV method and the 2SLS method give identical results. For instance, suppose that the system given by Eqs. (11-12) and (11-13) excludes variable z_4. Now Eq. (11-12), which has only one missing exogenous variable z_3, is exactly identified. Thus only z_3 can be used as an instrumental variable for y_2. The equations to solve are

$$\sum z_3 u_1 = 0 \qquad \sum z_1 u_1 = 0 \qquad \sum z_2 u_1 = 0$$

On the other hand (as shown above), the 2SLS method amounts to getting estimates from the equations

$$\sum \hat{y}_2 u_1 = 0 \qquad \sum z_1 u_1 = 0 \qquad \sum z_2 u_1 = 0$$

But $\hat{y}_2 = c_1 z_1 + c_2 z_2 + c_3 z_3$, where c_1, c_2, c_3 are the regression coefficients in the regression of y_2 on z_1, z_2, and z_3 (the reduced-form equation). Hence

$$\sum \hat{y}_2 u_1 = 0$$

$$\Leftrightarrow c_1 \sum z_1 u_1 + c_2 \sum z_2 u_1 + c_3 \sum z_3 u_1 = 0$$

$$\Leftrightarrow \sum z_3 u_1 = 0 \qquad \text{because} \qquad \sum z_1 u_1 = 0 \qquad \text{and} \qquad \sum z_2 u_1 = 0$$

Thus the 2SLS method and the IV method, where z_3 is used as an instrumental variable, give identical estimates.

11-7 NORMALIZATION

One other problem we have to discuss is that of what is known as "normalization." The way we have written Eqs. (11-12) and (11-13), in the first equation y_1 has coefficient 1 and in the second equation y_2 has coefficient 1. Alternatively, we say that the first equation is "normalized" with respect to y_1 and the second with respect to y_2. Sometimes this is taken to mean that y_1 is the "dependent" variable in the first equation and y_2 is the dependent variable in the second equation. This is particularly so for the purpose of 2SLS estimation or any other method that depends on least squares. Strictly speaking, this goes contrary to the spirit of simultaneous equations because by definition y_1 and y_2 are jointly determined and we cannot label any single variable as the dependent variable in any equation. Of course, we will have to assume the coefficient of one of the variables as 1, i.e., normalize the equation with respect to one variable. This variable can be any variable in the equation, however, and also the normalized variable need not be considered as the dependent variable. Also, the methods of estimation used to estimate simultaneous-equation models should be such that the resulting estimates do not depend on what variable we choose for normalization. The early methods of estimation suggested, like the full-information maximum-likelihood and limited-information maximum-likelihood, satisfied this requirement. But the more popular methods like 2SLS and IV methods do not always satisfy this requirement and are not, strictly speaking, in the spirit of simultaneous equations. The 2SLS estimates do not depend on the choice of the variable for normalizing only if the equation is exactly identified. Otherwise the estimates will depend on what variable is chosen for normalization. In practice this normalization is determined by the way the economic theories are formulated. For instance, even in a macro model of income determination, though consumption C and income Y are considered jointly determined, we write the consumption function as

$$C = \alpha + \beta Y + u$$

and we do not write it as

$$Y = \gamma + \delta C + v$$

In the back of our minds there are still some causal relationships, and the way we write the consumption function we feel the causal relationship still runs from Y to C rather than C to Y.

In some extreme cases equations have been normalized with respect to exogenous variables and the two-stage least-squares method applied by regressing an exogenous variable on endogenous variables. For instance, Smith[1] considers the following model:

$$Y = C + I$$

$$C = a_0 + a_1 Y + a_2 T + u_2 \tag{11-16}$$

$$I = b_0 + b_1 Y_{-1} + b_2 r_{-1} + u_3 \tag{11-17}$$

$$M = h_0 + h_1 Y + h_2 r + u_4 \tag{11-18}$$

where Y = GNP

C = personal-consumption expenditures

I = gross private domestic investment + government expenditures + net foreign investment

T = federal personal taxes

M = demand deposits + currency in the hands of the public

r = rate of interest on AAA corporate bonds

Here Y, C, I, and r are endogenous variables. Smith says the data used were not deflated by the price level for two reasons: First, tax rates apply to income in current dollars, not constant dollars. Second, for stabilization goals variables in current prices are more relevant.

Using data for the United States for 1947–1960, Smith gets the following results by two-stage least squares:

$$Y = C + I$$

$$C = 15.66 + .67Y - .66T$$

$$I = 3.82 + .39Y_{-1} - 4.2r_{-1}$$

$$M = 86.17 + .21Y - 9.69r$$

Note that Eq. (11-18) has been estimated by regressing an exogenous variable M on endogenous variables Y and r. The results will be different if this equation is normalized with respect to r. (The details are left as an exercise.)

[1] Paul E. Smith, A Note on the Built-in Flexibility of the Individual Income Tax, *Econometrica*, October, 1963, pp. 704–711.

Sometimes the variable with respect to which the equation is normalized is not exactly exogenous but almost is. For instance, in Eq. (11-17) suppose that gross private domestic investment is very small compared with government expenditures and net foreign investment and the latter two are treated as exogenous. Then the variable I has a very large exogenous component. Something similar is the case with, for instance, the econometric models for India,[1] where investment functions have been fitted in exactly the same fashion as in the United States (with the same explanatory variables), though investment in India is almost all determined by governmental policies, and allocations can hardly be considered as endogenous and responsive to "the rate of interest."

In brief, if one is estimating simultaneous-equation models by least-squares methods, one should be careful about proper normalization of the equations and particularly avoid regressing an exogenous variable on endogenous variables.

11-8 AN ILLUSTRATIVE EXAMPLE—KLEIN'S MODEL 1

As an illustrative example consider the following model, which is commonly called Klein's[2] model 1. We will consider this model because it highlights many important problems and also because several estimators for this model are readily available in the literature. The model consists of a consumption function, an investment function, a demand-for-labor function, and three identities. The equations are

Consumption function: $C = \delta_1 P + \delta_2(W + W') + \delta_3 P_{-1} + \delta_4 + u_1$

Investment function: $I = \delta_5 P + \delta_6 P_{-1} + \delta_7 K_{-1} + \delta_8 + u_2$

Demand-for-labor function: $W = \delta_9(Y + T - W') + \delta_{10}(Y + T - W')_{-1} + \delta_{11} t + \delta_{12} + u_3$

Identity: $Y + T = C + I + G$

Identity: $Y = W + W' + P$

Identity: $K = K_{-1} + I$

The variables are:
C = consumer expenditures
I = investment expenditures
G = government expenditures
P = profits
W = private wage bill
W' = government wage bill
K = capital stock
T = taxes
t = time
Y = income net of taxes

[1] A survey of these models can be found in M. J. Desai, A Macro-Econometric Models for India—A Survey, *Sanhkya*, 1973.

[2] L. R. Klein, "Economic Fluctuations in the United States 1921–41," John Wiley & Sons, Inc., New York, 1950.

Table 11-1

Year	C	P	W	I	K_{-1}	X	W'	G	T
1920	39.8	12.7	28.8	2.7	180.1	44.9	2.2	2.4	3.4
21	41.9	12.4	25.5	−.2	182.8	45.6	2.7	3.9	7.7
22	45.0	16.9	29.3	1.9	182.6	50.1	2.9	3.2	3.9
23	49.2	18.4	34.1	5.2	184.5	57.2	2.9	2.8	4.7
24	50.6	19.4	33.9	3.0	189.7	57.1	3.1	3.5	3.8
25	52.6	20.1	35.4	5.1	192.7	61.0	3.2	3.3	5.5
26	55.1	19.6	37.4	5.6	197.8	64.0	3.3	3.3	7.0
27	56.2	19.8	37.9	4.2	203.4	64.4	3.6	4.0	6.7
28	57.3	21.1	39.2	3.0	207.6	64.5	3.7	4.2	4.2
29	57.8	21.7	41.3	5.1	210.6	67.0	4.0	4.1	4.0
1930	55.0	15.6	37.9	1.0	215.7	61.2	4.2	5.2	7.7
31	50.9	11.4	34.5	−3.4	216.7	53.4	4.8	5.9	7.5
32	45.6	7.0	29.0	−6.2	213.3	44.3	5.3	4.9	8.3
33	46.5	11.2	28.5	−5.1	207.1	45.1	5.6	3.7	5.4
34	48.7	12.3	30.6	−3.0	202.0	49.7	6.0	4.0	6.8
35	51.3	14.0	33.2	−1.3	199.0	54.4	6.1	4.4	7.2
36	57.7	17.6	36.8	2.1	197.7	62.7	7.4	2.9	8.3
37	58.7	17.3	41.0	2.0	199.8	65.0	6.7	4.3	6.7
38	57.5	15.3	38.2	−1.9	201.8	60.9	7.7	5.3	7.4
39	61.6	19.0	41.6	1.3	199.9	69.5	7.8	6.6	8.9
1940	65.0	21.1	45.0	3.3	201.2	75.7	8.0	7.4	9.6
41	69.7	23.5	53.3	4.9	204.5	88.4	8.5	13.8	11.6

Lagged values have a subscript of minus 1 (lagged for one period only). The data are presented in Table 11-1. The variable X in the table is $Y + T - W'$.

The endogenous variables are C, I, W, Y, P, and K. In this model, as in many models of this kind, lagged endogenous variables like P_{-1}, K_{-1}, Y_{-1}, etc., are treated as exogenous. It is customary to call exogenous and lagged endogenous variables together *predetermined* variables. However, series like Y and K are so highly autocorrelated that it is a very artificial subdivision of the variables to treat Y and K as endogenous and Y_{-1} and K_{-1} as exogenous. Unfortunately, this is a customary practice in many simultaneous-equation models and is not often questioned!

Since W is endogenous, $W + W'$ is also an endogenous variable. Similarly, since Y is endogenous, $Y + T - W'$ is also an endogenous variable. To use the 2SLS method, what we need are the estimates from the reduced-form equations for the endogenous variables on the right-hand side of the structural equations, viz., P, $W + W'$, and $Y + T - W'$. Thus we have to regress each of these variables on all the predetermined variables in the system. These are P_{-1}, K_{-1}, $(Y + T - W')_{-1}$, t, T, and G.

Though the OLS method is inappropriate for this model, we will nevertheless present the OLS estimates for comparison. For the 2SLS method, we first get the RFLS estimates of the equations for P, $W + W'$, and $Y + T - W'$. After getting the estimated values of these variables from these equations, we estimate the structural equations by OLS, using these estimated values of the endogenous variables rather than the true values. Because this procedure involves using OLS twice, it is called two-stage least squares (2SLS).[1] However, one should be careful *not* to use the estimated standard errors from the second stage in the 2SLS procedure as the standard errors to report. These can, however, be easily corrected. To see what the problem and the appropriate correction is, consider Eq. (11-2). Let $\text{var}(u_1) = \sigma_1^2$. Also let $\hat{y}_2$ be the estimate of y_2 from the RFLS. We can write $y_2 = \hat{y}_2 + \hat{v}_2$, where $\hat{v}_2$ is the estimated residual from the reduced form. Hence Eq. (11-2) can be written as

$$y_1 = \beta_{12}\hat{y}_2 + \gamma_{11}z_1 + \gamma_{12}z_2 + (u_1 + \beta_{12}\hat{v}_2)$$

In the second stage of the 2SLS procedure it is this equation that is estimated by OLS. Hence, if we obtain an estimate of the residual variance from this equation, we will be obtaining an estimate of the variance of $(u_1 + \beta_{12}\hat{v}_2)$, not of u_1. To get an estimate of the variance of u_1, let $\tilde{\beta}_{12}$, $\tilde{\gamma}_{11}$, and $\tilde{\gamma}_{12}$ be the 2SLS estimates. We substitute these in Eq. (11-2) and compute the estimated residuals

$$\tilde{u}_1 = y_1 - \tilde{\beta}_{12}y_2 - \tilde{\gamma}_{11}z_1 - \tilde{\gamma}_{12}z_2$$

Then $\tilde{\sigma}_1^2 = [1/(T-3)]\sum \tilde{u}_1^2$ is the estimate of σ_1^2 we should be using. The estimate we obtain from the second stage of the 2SLS procedure is

$$\hat{\sigma}_1^2 = \frac{1}{T-3} \sum \hat{u}_1^2$$

where $$\hat{u}_1 = y_1 - \tilde{\beta}_{12}\hat{y}_2 - \tilde{\gamma}_{11}z_1 - \tilde{\gamma}_{12}z_2$$

Thus, when we obtain the estimated standard errors by the usual procedures from the second stage of the 2SLS, all we have to do to correct them is to multiply each by $\tilde{\sigma}_1/\hat{\sigma}_1$, where $\tilde{\sigma}_1$ and $\hat{\sigma}_1$ are defined above.[2]

The standard errors and tests we have been talking about until now are asymptotic, but there are as yet no better alternatives for this procedure. Some alternative tests have been suggested in the literature, for instance, by Dhrymes[3] and Richardson and Rohr,[4] and these tests have even been built into some

[1] In actual practice we replace only the right-hand-side endogenous variables by their estimated values. But it can be shown that the 2SLS estimates obtained are exactly the same if we replace *all* (those on the left-hand side too) endogenous variables by their estimated values. Also, one need not, in practice, go through the several steps of computing RFLS estimates, getting estimated values of the endogenous variables, and then using OLS for structual equations. The whole procedure can be done in one step using the relevant matrices.

[2] In the definitions of $\tilde{\sigma}_1^2$ and $\hat{\sigma}_1^2$ we have used $(T-3)$ as the divisor (T is the number of observations and 3 is the number of parameters estimated). Unlike the case with regression models, there is no uniformity in practice as to what divisor to use. Arguing that the properties of 2SLS estimators are asymptotic anyway, some use T as a divisor and use the tables of the normal distribution rather than the t distribution to test the significance of individual coefficients. Adjusting for degrees of freedom and using t tables will usually be more conservative.

[3] P. J. Dhrymes, Alternative Asymptotic Tests of Significance and Related Aspects of 2SLS and 3SLS Estimated Parameters, *Review of Economic Studies*, 1969, pp. 213–226.

[4] D. H. Richardson and R. J. Rohr, The Distribution of a Structural t-Statistic for the Case of Two Included Endogenous Variables, *Journal of the American Statistical Association*, 1971, pp. 375–382.

regression packages.[1] But these tests ignore a lot of relevant sample information on residual variances and hence should not be used in practice. Maddala[2] provides some small-sample evidence on the bad performance of these tests as compared with that of the conventional asymptotic tests.

To see what information is ignored in these tests, consider the simpler regression model

$$y = \beta x + u \qquad \text{where } u \sim IN(0,\sigma^2)$$

The sample second moments are obtained from

$$\begin{bmatrix} \sum y^2 & \sum xy \\ & \sum x^2 \end{bmatrix}$$

To obtain the OLS estimator of β, since $\hat{\beta} = \sum xy/\sum x^2$, we do not need the information $\sum y^2$. However, the variance of $\hat{\beta}$ is $\sigma^2/\sum x^2$, and to get the standard error of $\hat{\beta}$ we need an estimate of σ^2, which is $\hat{\sigma}^2 = 1/(n-1)(\sum y^2 - \hat{\beta}\sum xy)$, where n is the sample size. Thus we use the information in $\sum y^2$.

In the 2SLS method the argument is analogous.[3] The sample information consists of

1. The variances and covariances of the included endogenous variables
2. The variances and covariances of all the exogenous variables in the system
3. The covariances between the included endogenous and all the exogenous variables

To obtain the 2SLS estimates, we need only the information contained in 2 and 3. But to apply the conventional (asymptotic) tests we also need the information in 1. The tests suggested by Dhrymes, and Richardson and Rohr, *do not* use this information at all. All you need is the information in 2 and 3. These tests are undefined if the equation is not overidentified. What this suggests, however, is that in simultaneous-equation models, if an equation is overidenti-

[1] See, for instance, the RAPE program (Regression Analysis Program for Economists) from Harvard, which incorporates the Dhrymes test. Unfortunately, many empirical workers have the mistaken impression that this test is a better test than the conventional tests.

[2] G. S. Maddala, Some Small Sample Evidence on Tests of Significance in Simultaneous Equations Models, *Econometrica*, September, 1974, pp. 841–851. In addition to the tests under discussion, Maddala also considers a test suggested earlier by Anderson and Rubin. The Anderson-Rubin test is an exact finite-sample test, but it can be used only in the case of two included endogenous variables.

[3] In matrix notation let $\mathbf{Y} = [y, \mathbf{Y}_1]$ be the matrix of observations on the included endogenous variables and $\mathbf{X}$ the matrix of observations on all the exogenous variables. The sample second moment matrix is $\begin{bmatrix} \mathbf{Y'Y} & \mathbf{Y'X} \\ & \mathbf{X'X} \end{bmatrix}$. For obtaining the 2SLS estimates all we need is the information $\mathbf{Y'X}$ and $\mathbf{X'X}$. But to get an estimate of the residual variance we also need the information $\mathbf{Y'Y}$. This is *not* the case with the tests suggested by Dhrymes and Richardson and Rohr. Even the estimate of the residual variance is obtained from $\mathbf{Y'X}$ and $\mathbf{X'X}$.

fied, one can get an estimate of the residual variance even if one is given only the information contained in 2 and 3. (This is obviously not possible in the simple regression model.) But this estimate of the residual variance is likely to be a poor estimate because it does not use any information on the variances and covariances of the endogenous variables.

A considerable amount of work has also been done on the small-sample distributions of simultaneous-equation estimators.[1] Though this work is admirable, the distributions derived are for small models, and further they involve some unknown parameters in the model. Hence it is not possible to use these distributions to derive any tests of significance. From this voluminous work, only one test has emerged. This is the test suggested by Richardson and Rohr, and its limitations have been discussed earlier.[2]

Another thing that has been found in the discussion of the finite-sample distributions is that sometimes the finite-sample variance of 2SLS estimators may be infinite.[3] This result, however, need not be alarming. What this implies is that the tails of the distribution are much thicker than is assumed in the asymptotic distribution (which always has a finite variance). Thus, when we assume a significance level of say 5%, the actual significance level is much higher than that. This may be one justification for using the t tables rather than the normal tables in practice, though strictly speaking, since we use the asymptotic distributions, we should be using the normal tables.

In Table 11-2 we present the ordinary-least-squares estimates of the structural equations and reduced-form equations as well as two-stage least-squares estimates of the structural equations, for the data in Table 11-1. What is noteworthy is that the 2SLS estimates of the parameters in the third equation are the same as the OLS estimates, though the standard errors are higher in the former case. In general, the standard errors for the 2SLS estimates are higher than those for the OLS estimates. This does not, however, mean that the OLS method is better. The standard errors we get for the OLS method are not the correct ones, whereas for the 2SLS method they are at least asymptotically the correct estimates. Also, if the reduced-form R^2's are very high so that the estimated values of the endogenous variables are the same as the actual values, the 2SLS estimates will be very close to the OLS estimates. In the example we are considering, even though the reduced-form R^2 for X is not very high, we find the 2SLS and OLS estimates of the parameters of the third equation very close. This is somewhat surprising.

[1] For a survey of this subject, see R. L. Basmann, Exact Finite Sample Distributions for Some Econometric Estimators and Test Statistics: A Survey and Appraisal, in M. D. Intrilligator and D. Kendrick (eds.), "Frontiers of Quantitative Economics," vol. II, North-Holland Publishing Company, Amsterdam, 1975.

[2] See the comment by G. S. Maddala on Basmann's paper.

[3] If the structural equation has two endogenous variables, the moments up to order r exist if $K_2 > r$, where K_2 is the number of excluded exogenous variables. Thus with one excluded exogenous variable even the mean of the 2SLS estimator does not exist and with two excluded exogenous variables the mean will exist but not the variance.

Table 11-2

OLS:

$$C = \underset{(1.203)}{16.237} + \underset{(.091)}{.193}P + \underset{(.040)}{.796}(W + W') + \underset{(.090)}{.089}P_{-1} \qquad \bar{R}^2 = .977 \qquad DW = 1.367$$

$$I = \underset{(5.465)}{10.125} + \underset{(.097)}{.479}P + \underset{(.100)}{.333}P_{-1} - \underset{(.026)}{.112}K_{-1} \qquad \bar{R}^2 = .919 \qquad DW = 1.810$$

$$W = \underset{(1.151)}{0.064} + \underset{(.032)}{.439}X + \underset{(.037)}{.146}X_{-1} + \underset{(.031)}{.130}t \qquad \bar{R}^2 = .932 \qquad DW = 2.244$$

Reduced-form:

$$P = \underset{(10.870)}{46.383} + \underset{(.444)}{.813}P_{-1} - \underset{(.067)}{.213}K_{-1} + \underset{(.252)}{.015}X_{-1} + \underset{(.154)}{.297}t - \underset{(.385)}{.926}T + \underset{(.373)}{.443}G$$

$$\bar{R}^2 = .753 \qquad DW = 1.854$$

$$W + W' = \underset{(8.787)}{40.278} + \underset{(.359)}{.823}P_{-1} - \underset{(.054)}{.144}K_{-1} + \underset{(.204)}{.115}X_{-1} + \underset{(.124)}{.881}t - \underset{(.311)}{.567}T + \underset{(.302)}{.859}G$$

$$\bar{R}^2 = .949 \qquad DW = 2.395$$

$$X = \underset{(18.860)}{78.281} + \underset{(.771)}{1.724}P_{-1} - \underset{(.110)}{.319}K_{-1} + \underset{(.438)}{.094}X_{-1} + \underset{(.267)}{.878}t - \underset{(.669)}{.565}T + \underset{(.648)}{1.317}G$$

$$\bar{R}^2 = .882 \qquad DW = 2.049$$

2SLS:

$$C = \underset{(1.464)}{16.543} + \underset{(.130)}{.019}P + \underset{(.044)}{.810}(W + W') + \underset{(.118)}{.214}P_{-1}$$

$$I = \underset{(8.361)}{20.284} + \underset{(.191)}{.149}P + \underset{(.180)}{.616}P_{-1} - \underset{(.040)}{.157}K_{-1}$$

$$W = \underset{(1.894)}{.065} + \underset{(.065)}{.438}X + \underset{(.070)}{.146}X_{-1} + \underset{(.053)}{.130}t$$

The interpretation of the OLS, RFLS, and 2SLS equations is left as an exercise.

11-9 LEAST-SQUARES BIAS[1]

Though we know that the simultaneity problem results in inconsistent estimators of the parameters when the structural equations are estimated by ordinary least squares, we may at least be able to say something about the direction of the (large-sample) bias. In many practical applications this would be a useful piece of information. Take, for instance, the case of a demand-and-supply model:

$$q_t = \beta p_t + u_t \qquad \text{demand function} \tag{11-19}$$

$$q_t = \alpha p_t + v_t \qquad \text{supply function} \tag{11-20}$$

[1] The discussion here is based on Jean Bronfenbrenner, Sources and Size of Least Squares Bias in a Two-Equation Model, in Hood and Koopmans (eds.), "Studies in Econometric Method," John Wiley & Sons, Inc., New York, 1953.

Let $\text{var}(u_t) = \sigma_u^2$, $\text{var}(v_t) = \sigma_v^2$, and $\text{cov}(u_t, v_t) = \sigma_{uv}$. q_t and p_t are deviations from their respective means. Since

$$\hat{\beta} = \frac{\sum p_t q_t}{\sum p_t^2} = \beta + \frac{(1/T)\sum p_t u_t}{(1/T)\sum p_t^2}$$

we have

$$\text{plim}\ \hat{\beta} = \beta + \frac{\text{plim}\left[(1/T)\sum p_t u_t\right]}{\text{plim}\left[(1/T)\sum p_t^2\right]}$$

Since

$$\beta p_t + u_t = \alpha p_t + v_t$$

or

$$p_t = \frac{v_t - u_t}{\beta - \alpha}$$

we have

$$\text{plim}\left(\frac{1}{T}\sum p_t u_t\right) = \text{cov}(p_t u_t) = \frac{1}{\beta - \alpha}\left(\sigma_{uv} - \sigma_u^2\right)$$

and

$$\text{plim}\left(\frac{1}{T}\sum p_t^2\right) = \text{var}(p_t) = \frac{1}{(\beta - \alpha)^2}\left(\sigma_v^2 + \sigma_u^2 - 2\sigma_{uv}\right)$$

Hence

$$\text{plim}\ \hat{\beta} = \beta + (\beta - \alpha)\frac{\sigma_{uv} - \sigma_u^2}{\sigma_v^2 + \sigma_u^2 - 2\sigma_{uv}} \tag{11-21}$$

Thus we cannot say anything about the direction of the bias unless we make some assumptions about σ_{uv}. However, if $\sigma_{uv} = 0$, we have

$$\text{plim}\ \hat{\beta} = \beta + (\beta - \alpha)\left(-\frac{\sigma_u^2}{\sigma_v^2 + \sigma_u^2}\right) \tag{11-21a}$$

Now β is expected to be negative and α positive. Thus the bias term is expected to be positive. Hence if we find, say, a price elasticity of demand of -0.8, the true price elasticity is < -0.8 (we are assuming that q and p are both measured in log form in the above equations so that the coefficients are elasticities).

We can show by a similar reasoning that if we estimate the supply function by ordinary least squares,

$$\hat{\alpha} = \frac{\sum p_t q_t}{\sum p_t^2}$$

$$= \alpha + \frac{\sum p_t v_t}{\sum p_t^2}$$

Hence
$$\text{plim } \hat{\alpha} = \alpha + (\beta - \alpha) \frac{\sigma_v^2 - \sigma_{uv}}{\sigma_v^2 + \sigma_u^2 - 2\sigma_{uv}} \tag{11-22}$$

If $\sigma_{uv} = 0$, we have
$$\text{plim}(\hat{\alpha}) = \alpha + (\beta - \alpha) \frac{\sigma_v^2}{\sigma_v^2 + \sigma_u^2} \tag{11-22a}$$

The bias is now negative since $(\beta - \alpha)$ is expected to be negative. Again, suppose the supply elasticity is estimated to be $+0.6$, we know that the supply elasticity is at least this high.

In the above example, it should be noted that when we regress q on p we do not know whether we are estimating the demand function or the supply function. However, if we regress q on p and obtain, say, an estimate of $+0.3$, we know that the supply elasticity is $0.3 +$ a positive number and the demand elasticity is $0.3 +$ a negative number. Thus the practically useful conclusion is that the supply elasticity is at least 0.3. On the other hand, if we had obtained this coefficient as -0.9, we know that the supply elasticity is $-0.9 +$ a positive number and that the demand elasticity is $-0.9 +$ a negative number. Thus the practically useful conclusion is that the demand elasticity is at least 0.9 in absolute value.

It can also be seen in the above example that
$$\text{plim}\left[\frac{\sum p_t q_t}{\sum p_t^2}\right] \to \beta \qquad \text{as } \sigma_u^2 \to 0$$

and
$$\to \alpha \qquad \text{as } \sigma_v^2 \to 0$$

Thus the regression coefficient of q on p will estimate the demand elasticity if the demand function is stable and the supply elasticity if the supply function is stable.

Figure 11-1 gives the case of a supply curve shifting and the demand curve not shifting. What we observe in practice are the points of intersection of the demand curve and the supply curve. As can be seen, the locus of these points of intersection traces out the demand curve in Fig. 11-1. In Fig. 11-2, where the supply curve is stable and the demand curve shifts, this locus determines the supply curve.[1]

Suppose that we have some a priori information on the relative magnitudes of the shifts in the demand-and-supply curve; i.e., we assume $\sigma_v^2 = k\sigma_u^2$, where k is known. Then
$$\text{plim}\left[\frac{\sum p_t q_t}{\sum p_t^2}\right] = \beta \frac{k}{k+1} + \frac{1}{k+1} \alpha \tag{11-23}$$

[1] This was the main conclusion of the article by E. J. Working, What Do Statistical Demand Curves Show? *Quarterly Journal of Economics*, February, 1927, reprinted in American Economics Association, "Readings in Price Theory," 1953, pp. 97–118.

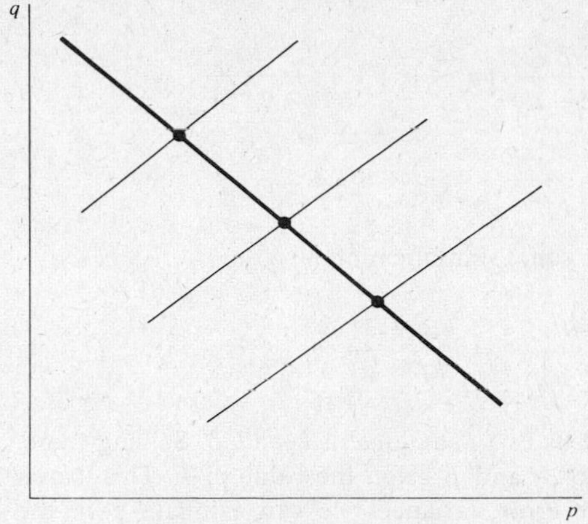

Figure 11-1 Stable demand and shifting supply.

Suppose we run the reverse regression, i.e., the regression of p_t on q_t, and take the reciprocal of this regression coefficient. It will be

$$\frac{\sum q_t^2}{\sum p_t q_t} = \frac{\sum (\beta p_t + u_t)^2}{\sum p_t(\beta p_t + u_t)}$$

If we assume that $\sigma_{uv} = 0$, since

$$\text{cov}(p_t u_t) = \frac{\sigma_u^2}{\alpha - \beta} \qquad \text{and} \qquad \text{var}(p_t) = \frac{1}{(\beta - \alpha)^2}(\sigma_v^2 + \sigma_u^2)$$

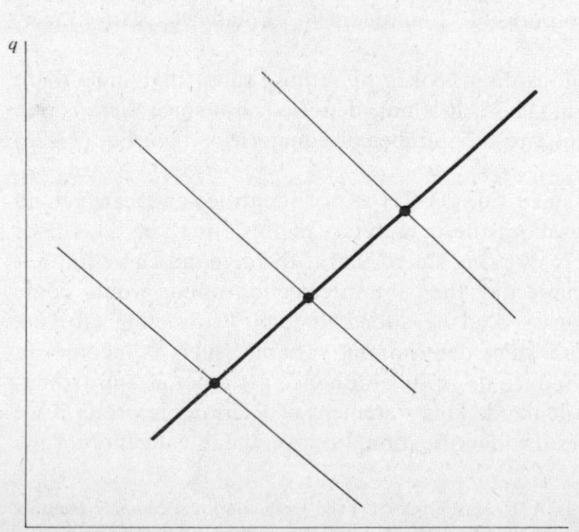

Figure 11-2 Stable supply and shifting demand.

we have

$$\operatorname{plim}\left(\frac{1}{T}\sum q_t^2\right) = \frac{\beta^2}{(\beta-\alpha)^2}(\sigma_v^2+\sigma_u^2)+\sigma_u^2+\frac{2\beta\sigma_u^2}{\alpha-\beta}$$

and

$$\operatorname{plim}\left(\frac{1}{T}\sum p_t q_t\right) = \frac{\beta}{(\beta-\alpha)^2}(\sigma_v^2+\sigma_u^2)+\frac{\sigma_u^2}{\alpha-\beta}$$

Substituting $\sigma_v^2 = k\sigma_u^2$, we get, after some simplification,

$$\operatorname{plim}\left[\frac{\sum q_t^2}{\sum p_t q_t}\right] = \frac{k\beta^2+\alpha^2}{k\beta+\alpha} \tag{11-24}$$

Thus Eqs. (11-23) and (11-24) give us two equations in α and β. Solving these, we could get consistent estimates of α and β given the value of k. This shows that if we know the ratios of the error variances we can estimate both the demand and the supply elasticities for the model given by Eqs. (11-19) and (11-20).

Suppose now that there is an exogenous variable x_t in the demand function so that the model is

$$q_t = \beta p_t + \gamma x_t + w_t \qquad \text{demand function} \tag{11-25}$$

$$q_t = \alpha p_t + v_t \qquad \text{supply function} \tag{11-26}$$

Since the definition of the exogenous variable is that it is uncorrelated with the residuals (or shift variables) w_t and v_t, we have

$$\operatorname{plim}\left[(1/T)\sum w_t x_t\right] = \operatorname{plim}\left[(1/T)\sum v_t x_t\right] = 0$$

Also, we will assume that $\operatorname{plim}[(1/T)\sum x_t^2] = \sigma_x^2$, a finite positive constant. This is often referred to as the assumption of "boundedness." Finally, let $\operatorname{var}(w_t) = \sigma_w^2$ and $\operatorname{cov}(w_t v_t) = \sigma_{wv}$.

We know, from the previous discussion on counting rules, that since there are no missing variables in Eq. (11-25) it is not identified. But since there is one missing variable in Eq. (11-26) and the number of equations is two, Eq. (11-26) is exactly identified.

It is often thought that since Eq. (11-25) is not identified, we can get no information from the sample about the parameters of this equation. This is of course not true.[1] Back in 1927, Working stated that if the demand curve did not shift much, but the supply curve did, then the intersection points would come close to tracing a demand curve. And he added that, by "correcting" for the influence of an additional important determining variable (such as income) in the demand curve, we could reduce its shifts and hence get a better approximation of the price elasticity of demand. This statement of Working is wrong if we follow the usual counting rules for identification, because the introduction of the

[1] The discussion here is based on A. C. Harberger, "On the Estimation of Economic Parameters," paper presented before the Econometric Society, Montreal, September, 1954 (mimeo).

variable x_t in the demand equation (11-25) helps to identify the supply equation (11-26), not the demand equation. However, to see what sense can be made of the statement by Working, let us evaluate the probability limits of the OLS estimators for the parameters in Eq. (11-25). The least-squares estimators are

$$\hat{\beta} = \frac{1}{D}\left[\left(\sum x_t^2\right)\left(\sum p_t q_t\right) - \left(\sum p_t x_t\right)\left(\sum x_t q_t\right)\right]$$

$$\hat{\gamma} = \frac{1}{D}\left[\left(\sum p_t^2\right)\left(\sum x_t q_t\right) - \left(\sum x_t p_t\right)\left(\sum p_t q_t\right)\right]$$

where

$$D = \left(\sum p_t^2\right)\left(\sum x_t^2\right) - \left(\sum p_t x_t\right)^2$$

Substituting the value of q_t, we get

$$\hat{\beta} = \beta + \frac{1}{D}\left[\left(\sum x_t^2\right)\left(\sum p_t w_t\right) - \left(\sum p_t x_t\right)\left(\sum x_t w_t\right)\right] \tag{11-27}$$

$$\hat{\gamma} = \gamma + \frac{1}{D}\left[\left(\sum p_t^2\right)\left(\sum x_t w_t\right) - \left(\sum p_t x_t\right)\left(\sum p_t w_t\right)\right] \tag{11-28}$$

We now have to evaluate the probability limits of each of these expressions.

First we note that $\text{plim}[(1/T)\sum x_t w_t] = 0$. Also from Eqs. (11-25) and (11-26) we get

$$\beta p_t + \gamma x_t + w_t = \alpha p_t + v_t$$

or

$$p_t = \frac{v_t - w_t}{\beta - \alpha} - \frac{\gamma x_t}{\beta - \alpha}$$

Hence

$$\text{plim}\left(\frac{1}{T}\sum p_t^2\right) = \text{var}(p_t) = \frac{1}{(\beta-\alpha)^2}\left(\sigma_v^2 + \sigma_w^2 - 2\sigma_{wv} + \gamma^2\sigma_x^2\right)$$

$$\text{plim}\left(\frac{1}{T}\sum p_t x_t\right) = -\frac{\gamma}{\beta-\alpha}\sigma_x^2$$

$$\text{plim}\left(\frac{1}{T}\sum p_t u_t\right) = \frac{1}{\beta-\alpha}\sigma_{wv} - \sigma_w^2$$

In Eqs. (11-27) and (11-28) we divide numerator and denominator throughout by T^2 and use the above plims. We get

$$\text{plim}\ \hat{\beta} = \beta + \frac{\left[\sigma_x^2/(\beta-\alpha)\right]\left(\sigma_{wv} - \sigma_w^2\right)}{\left[\sigma_x^2/(\beta-\alpha)^2\right]\left(\sigma_v^2 + \sigma_w^2 - 2\sigma_{wv} + \gamma^2\sigma_x^2\right) - \left[\gamma/(\beta-\alpha)\right]^2\sigma_x^4}$$

$$= \beta + (\beta - \alpha)\frac{\sigma_{wv} - \sigma_w^2}{\sigma_v^2 + \sigma_w^2 - 2\sigma_{wv}} \tag{11-29}$$

Comparing this with the expression (11-21), we see that the expression for the asymptotic bias appears to be the same as before. Though it appears to be the same, the magnitude of σ_w^2 will be less than that of σ_u^2 if x_t is a relevant explanatory variable. If indeed (11-25) is the true equation and we omit the relevant variable x_t and estimate Eq. (11-19), since $\sigma_u^2 = \sigma_w^2 + \gamma^2\sigma_x^2$, the bias will be

$$(\beta - \alpha)\frac{\sigma_{wv} - \sigma_w^2 - \gamma^2\sigma_x^2}{\sigma_v^2 + \sigma_w^2 + \gamma^2\sigma_x^2 - 2\sigma_{wv}}$$

Thus the bias would be larger in magnitude if σ_{wv} is negative or zero. Only if σ_{wv} is positive and the correlation coefficient r_{wv} is greater than the ratio σ_v/σ_w will introduction of the variable x_t fail to reduce the bias. Usually, since the demand function is better specified, we have $\sigma_v/\sigma_w > 1$, but even if it is < 1, it requires a fairly high r_{wv} to produce a situation where the addition of the variable x_t fails to reduce the least-squares bias.

Thus, as Working asserted, the introduction of other relevant explanatory variables (like income in the demand equation) could reduce the shifts and hence enable us to get a better approximation of the price elasticity of demand.

As mentioned earlier, the supply equation is identified in this case and we can get a consistent estimate of the supply elasticity by using some method like two-stage least squares. However, let us see what happens if we estimate the equation by ordinary least squares.

$$\hat{\alpha} = \frac{\sum p_t q_t}{\sum p_t^2} = \alpha + \frac{(1/T)\sum p_t v_t}{(1/T)\sum p_t^2}$$

$$\text{plim}\left(\frac{1}{T}\sum p_t v_t\right) = \text{cov}(p_t v_t) = \frac{1}{\beta - \alpha}(\sigma_v^2 - \sigma_{wv})$$

Hence $$\text{plim}\ \hat{\alpha} = \alpha + (\beta - \alpha)\frac{\sigma_v^2 - \sigma_{wv}}{\sigma_v^2 + \sigma_w^2 - 2\sigma_{wv} + \gamma^2\sigma_x^2}$$

When $\sigma_{wv} = 0$, this simplifies to

$$\text{plim}\ \hat{\alpha} = \alpha + (\beta - \alpha)\frac{\sigma_v^2}{\sigma_v^2 + \sigma_w^2 + \gamma^2\sigma_x^2}$$

Comparing this expression with (11-22*a*), we notice two things. First the asymptotic bias is always less when there is an exogenous variable, since we are dividing by a larger number. Also, earlier, the bias depended solely on the ratio of error variances σ_v^2/σ_u^2. Now it depends also on the magnitudes of these variances. If these are small relative to $\gamma^2\sigma_x^2$, the asymptotic bias of the least-squares estimator is negligible. This result is similar to the proximity theorem of Wold discussed earlier.

If we introduce another exogenous variable z in the supply function so that the model is

$$q = \beta p + \gamma x + w \qquad \text{demand function}$$
$$q = \alpha p + \delta z + v \qquad \text{supply function}$$

then we find by a similar reasoning (if we assume $\sigma_{wv} = 0$ for convenience)

$$\text{plim}\ \hat{\beta} = \beta + (\beta - \alpha)\frac{-\sigma_w^2}{\sigma_w^2 + \sigma_v^2 + \delta^2\sigma_z^2(1 - r_{xz}^2)}$$

and $$\operatorname{plim} \hat{\alpha} = \alpha + (\beta - \alpha) \frac{\sigma_v^2}{\sigma_w^2 + \sigma_v^2 + \gamma^2 \sigma_x^2 (1 - r_{xz}^2)}$$

Thus we find that the asymptotic bias in both $\hat{\beta}$ and $\hat{\alpha}$ is reduced by the presence of the exogenous variables. However, if r_{xz}^2 is very high, this improvement is reduced. The least-squares bias is really negligible if $\delta^2\sigma_z^2$ and $\gamma^2\sigma_x^2$ are high relative to σ_w^2 and σ_v^2 and r_{xz}^2 is low.

In simultaneous-equation models the classification of variables as endogenous and exogenous is often quite arbitrary. As mentioned earlier, often current values of some variables are treated as endogenous and lagged values of these same variables are treated as exogenous even when the current and lagged values are very highly correlated. In addition, some equations are regarded as identified (over- or exactly) and others as not identified by merely looking at how many variables are excluded from the equation, and the underidentified equations are often regarded as nonestimable. The above discussion illustrates that least-squares estimation of these equations can still be worthwhile, and in fact one should also use any prior information on the relative magnitudes of the shift variables to get some information on the parameter values. Also, instead of simply counting the number of exogenous variables, one should also look at how high their intercorrelations are.

As yet another example of how to study the least-squares bias, consider the Haavelmo model[1] (this is the simplest of the several models considered by Haavelmo)

$$c = \alpha y + \beta + u \qquad \text{consumption function}$$
$$y = c + i \qquad \text{income identity}$$

where i is investment treated as exogenous.

The reduced-form equations are

$$c = \frac{1}{1-\alpha}(\alpha i + \beta + u)$$

$$y = \frac{1}{1-\alpha}(i + \beta + u)$$

Let $\operatorname{var}(i) = \sigma_i^2$, $\operatorname{var}(u) = \sigma_u^2$. Also $\operatorname{cov}(i,u) = 0$ since i is exogenous. The least-squares estimator of β is

$$\hat{\alpha} = \frac{\sum (c - \bar{c})(y - \bar{y})}{\sum (y - \bar{y})^2}$$

$$\operatorname{plim} \hat{\alpha} = \frac{\operatorname{cov}(cy)}{\operatorname{var}(y)} = \frac{[1/(1-\alpha)^2](\alpha\sigma_i^2 + \sigma_u^2)}{[1/(1-\alpha)^2](\sigma_i^2 + \sigma_u^2)} = \frac{\alpha\sigma_i^2 + \sigma_u^2}{\sigma_i^2 + \sigma_u^2}$$

[1] T. Haavelmo, Methods of Measuring the Marginal Propensity to Consume, *Journal of the American Statistical Association*, March, 1947, pp. 105–122. (Also chap. IV in Hood and Koopmans (eds.), "Studies in Econometric Method," John Wiley & Sons, Inc., New York, 1953.)

Hence
$$\text{plim}\ \hat{\alpha} = \alpha + \frac{(1-\alpha)\sigma_u^2}{\sigma_i^2 + \sigma_u^2}$$

The asymptotic bias is positive since σ_u^2 and σ_i^2 are both > 0 and $(1-\alpha) > 0$. Thus the OLS estimate will overestimate the marginal propensity to consume. Again, if σ_i^2 is high relative to σ_u^2, the bias will be small.

Not all simultaneous-equation models result in bias by ordinary least squares. An important class of models is the recursive model. These are models in which the residuals from the different equations are independent of each other and the matrix of coefficients of the endogenous variables is triangular. For example, consider a model with three endogenous variables y_1, y_2, and y_3 and three exogenous variables z_1, z_2, and z_3 which has the following structure:

$$\begin{aligned} y_1 + \beta_{12}y_2 + \beta_{13}y_3 + \gamma_1 z_1 &= u_1 \\ y_2 + \beta_{23}y_3 + \gamma_2 z_2 &= u_2 \\ y_3 + \gamma_3 z_3 &= u_3 \end{aligned}$$

where u_1, u_2, u_3 are independent. Here the matrix of coefficients of the endogenous variables is

$$\begin{bmatrix} 1 & \beta_{12} & \beta_{13} \\ & 1 & \beta_{23} \\ & & 1 \end{bmatrix}$$

which is triangular. In such systems, each structural equation can be estimated by ordinary least squares.

Sometimes, even if the system of equations does not satisfy the conditions of a recursive system, at least some equations can be estimated by ordinary least squares. This is the case with the production-function model considered by Zellner, Kmenta, and Dreze.[1] They consider the estimation of the Cobb-Douglas production function.

$$\begin{aligned} \text{Let } X &= AL^{\alpha_1}K^{\alpha_2} \text{ be the production function} \\ \Pi &= pX - wL - rK \text{ be the profit function} \end{aligned} \tag{11-30}$$

Then the profit-maximizing conditions $\partial \Pi / \partial L = 0$ and $\partial \Pi / \partial K = 0$ give

$$\frac{X}{L} = \frac{w}{\alpha_1 p} \qquad \text{and} \qquad \frac{X}{K} = \frac{r}{\alpha_2 p} \tag{11-31}$$

Let $y_{1i} = \log X_i$, $y_{2i} = \log L_i$, and $y_{3i} = \log K_i$. Then Eqs. (11-30) and (11-31) can be written, after adding the error terms, as

$$\begin{aligned} y_{1i} - \alpha_1 y_{2i} - \alpha_2 y_{3i} &= \lambda_1 + v_{1i} \\ y_{1i} - y_{2i} &= \lambda_2 + v_{2i} \\ y_{1i} - y_{3i} &= \lambda_3 + v_{3i} \end{aligned} \tag{11-32}$$

[1] A. Zellner, J. Kmenta, and J. Dreze, Specification and Estimation of Cobb-Douglas Production Function Models, *Econometrica*, October, 1966, pp. 784–795.

where $\lambda_1 = \log A$, $\lambda_2 = \log(w/\alpha_1 p)$, $\lambda_3 = \log(r/\alpha_2 p)$, and v_{1i}, v_{2i}, and v_{3i} are the error terms.

Zellner, Kmenta, and Dreze argue that if there is an error term in the production function, output is stochastic and hence what the firm should be maximizing is not profits but expected profits. They then write Eq. (11-30) as

$$X_i = AL_i^{\alpha_1} K_i^{\alpha_2} e^{u_{1i}}$$

If u_{1i} are $IN(0, \sigma_1^2)$, then $E(e^{u_{1i}}) = e^{(1/2)\sigma_1^2}$. Hence $E(X_i) = AL_i^{\alpha_1} K_i^{\alpha_2} e^{(1/2)\sigma_1^2}$. Expected profits are now $E(\Pi) = pE(X) - wL - rK$, and Eqs. (11-31) become

$$\frac{X_i}{L_i} = \frac{w}{\alpha_1 p} e^{u_{1i} - (1/2)\sigma_1^2} \quad \text{and} \quad \frac{X_i}{K_i} = \frac{r}{\alpha_2 p} e^{u_{1i} - (1/2)\sigma_1^2} \tag{11-33}$$

Hence Eqs. (11-32) become

$$\begin{aligned} y_{1i} - \alpha_1 y_{2i} - \alpha_3 y_{3i} &= \lambda_1 + u_{1i} \\ y_{1i} - y_{2i} &= \lambda_2^1 + u_{1i} + u_{2i} \\ y_{1i} - y_{3i} &= \lambda_3^1 + u_{1i} + u_{3i} \end{aligned} \tag{11-34}$$

where

$$\lambda_2^1 = \log\left(\frac{w}{p\alpha_1}\right) - \frac{1}{2}\sigma_1^2$$

$$\lambda_3^1 = \log\left(\frac{r}{p\alpha_2}\right) \frac{1}{2}\sigma_1^2$$

u_{2i} and u_{3i} are the disturbances added to Eqs. (11-33) after taking logs.

Now the reduced form corresponding to Eqs. (11-34) is

$$\begin{aligned} y_{1i} &= k_1 + \frac{1}{1 - \alpha_1 - \alpha_2}\left[(1 - \alpha_1 - \alpha_2)u_{1i} - \alpha_1 u_{2i} - \alpha_2 u_{3i}\right] \\ y_{2i} &= k_2 + \frac{1}{1 - \alpha_1 - \alpha_2}\left[(\alpha_2 - 1)u_{2i} - \alpha_2 u_{3i}\right] \\ y_{3i} &= k_3 + \frac{1}{1 - \alpha_1 - \alpha_2}\left[-\alpha_1 u_{2i} + (\alpha_1 - 1)u_{3i}\right] \end{aligned} \tag{11-35}$$

It is reasonable to assume that u_{1i} are uncorrelated with u_{2i} and u_{3i} because the former are due to "acts of nature" like weather and the latter arise from "human errors." Under this assumption $\text{cov}(y_{2i}, u_{1i}) = \text{cov}(y_{3i}, u_{1i}) = 0$ because the reduced-form equations (11-35) show that y_{2i} and y_{3i} depend on u_{2i} and u_{3i} only. Hence ordinary least-squares estimation of the first equation (production function) in (11-34) yields consistent estimates of the parameters. Here is an example where there is no simultaneity bias in using the OLS method to estimate the production function. In this model we do not have a recursive system, but from the peculiar way the error terms entered the equations, we could show that in the first equation the included endogenous variables are uncorrelated with the residual in that equation.

Exercises

11-1 In the following model y variables are endogenous and x variables are exogenous:

$$y_1 = \alpha_1 y_2 + \alpha_2 x_1 + \alpha_3 x_2 + u_1$$
$$y_2 = \beta_1 y_1 + \beta_2 y_3 + \beta_3 x_2 + \beta_4 x_3 + u_2$$
$$y_3 = \gamma_1 y_1 + \gamma_2 x_2 + u_3$$

(*a*) Using the order condition (which asks whether the number of excluded exogenous variables is equal to, greater than, or less than the number of endogenous parameters in the equation), state whether the first equation is overidentified, underidentified, or exactly identified. What about the second and third equations?

(*b*) What single-equation method would you use to estimate the parameters of the first equation? The second equation? The third equation?

(*c*) Suppose that the above model describes some sector of the aggregate economy and that in some future year the government can control x_1. How could you use a previous sample to measure the effect a unit change in x_1 will have on the value of y_1?

11-2 Comment on the following statements:

(*a*) It's easy to get an equation identified. Just think of some exogenous variables that clearly do not belong in the equation and exclude them.

(*b*) Omitted variables and omitted equations are the two most common sources of nonsense estimates of demand elasticities.

(*c*) It is not appropriate to compare the R^2 from the equation estimated by 2SLS with the R^2 from the OLS equation. The R^2 from the OLS will always be smaller than the R^2 from 2SLS. (In discussing this statement, give also the correct procedure for computing R^2 from a 2SLS estimated equation.)

11-3 Two endogenous variables x and y are determined by the two-equation model.

$$y = \alpha x + u \tag{1}$$
$$x = \beta y + v \tag{2}$$

where u and v are independent, normally distributed random variables each with zero mean and with

$$\text{var}[u] = \sigma_1^2 \qquad \text{var}[v] = \sigma_2^2 \qquad \text{cov}[uv] = 0$$

(*a*) Solve for the reduced-form equations. (In this case, with no exogenous variables, only functions of u and v appear on the right-hand side.)

(*b*) Using the result from (*a*), find the probability limit of the least-squares estimator (based on a sample of size n).

$$\hat{\alpha} = \frac{\sum_{i=1}^{n} y_i x_i}{\sum_{i=1}^{n} x_i^2}$$

(*c*) Under what conditions will $\hat{\alpha}$ be a consistent estimator of α? What do these conditions mean intuitively?

(*d*) Suppose Eq. (2) is replaced by

$$x = \beta z + v \tag{2'}$$

where z is an exogenous variable. Under the same assumptions about the distribution of u and v as before, what is the probability limit of $\hat{\alpha}$ now?

11-4 Consider the model

$$y_1 + \beta_{12} y_2 + \gamma_1 z_1 = u_1$$
$$\beta_{21} y_1 + \gamma_2 z_2 = u_2$$

$\hat{\beta}_{12}$ is the OLS estimate of β_{12}. Show that

$$\text{plim } \hat{\beta}_{12} = \beta_{12} + \frac{(1 - \beta_{12}\beta_{21})(\beta_{21}\sigma_1^2 - \sigma_{12})}{\beta_{21}^2\sigma_1^2 - 2\beta_{21}\sigma_{12} + \sigma_2^2 + \gamma_2^2 m_{22}(1 - r_{12}^2)}$$

where $\sigma_1^2 = \text{var}(u_1)$

$\sigma_2^2 = \text{var}(u_2)$

$\sigma_{12} = \text{covar}(u_1 u_2)$

$m_{22} = \text{var}(z_2)$

r_{12} = correlation coefficient between z_1 and z_2

11-5 A major proposition of the monetary approach to the balance of payments is that a devaluation will be successful unless accompanied by an equiproportionate expansion in domestic credit.[1] A simple version of the monetary model can be represented as:

$$\frac{\Delta B}{M} = \beta_1 \frac{\Delta r}{r} + \beta_2 \Delta \frac{\Delta D}{M} + \mu \qquad (1)$$

where $\Delta B/M$, $\Delta r/r$, and $\Delta(\Delta D/M)$ are, respectively, the improvement in the balance of payments as a proportion of the money stock, the rate of devaluation, and the increase in the rate of growth of domestic credit expressed as a percentage of the money stock. The monetary approach suggests $\beta_1 = 1$ and $\beta_2 = -1$.[2]

However, if sterilization of the effects on the domestic money stock of balance of payments deficits takes place, we have, in addition:[3]

$$\Delta \frac{\Delta D}{M} = \alpha \frac{\Delta B}{M} + v \qquad (2)$$

where α, the sterilization coefficient, ranges from zero (no sterilization) to minus unity (complete neutralization). Answer the following:

(*a*) Solve for the asymptotic bias of the OLS estimates of β_1 and β_2 from Eq. (1) given that sterilization takes place according to Eq. (2).

(*b*) What are the biases in the special case where $\sigma_{v\mu} = 0$?

(*c*) Do special problems in estimation arise when neutralization is complete, that is, as $\alpha \to -1$?

(*d*) How will you test the hypothesis $\alpha = 0$?

11-6 It was for some time a widespread belief that the supply of food crops responds little or even negatively to price increases in less-developed countries.

(*a*) Discuss the possible reasons for perverse response to price in the supply of a commodity which is largely consumed by the producer and his family.

(*b*) On the basis of your theoretical discussion, develop a simultaneous-equations model for a single food crop consumed in large part by its producers. Assume there are no alternative crops, commercial or subsistence. In your system explain *at least* the following variables:

(i) Marketed surplus
(ii) Consumption by farm families
(iii) Price of the crop

[1] Johnson, H. G., "The Monetary Approach to Balance of Payments Theory," *Journal of Financial and Quantitative Studies*, March, 1972.

[2] Connolly, M. B., and Taylor, D. G., "Testing the Monetary Approach to Devaluation in Developing Countries," *Journal of Political Economy*, June, 1976.

[3] P. J. K. Kouri and M. G. Porter, "International Capital Flows and Portfolio Equilibrium," *Journal of Political Economy*, 1974, pp. 443–467. (See Appendix A. Note that there is an error there. The numerator of $\text{plim}(\hat{a}_2 - a_2)$ should be $-b_1^2\sigma_4^2 a_2$ in their notation.)

(iv) Inputs of factors other than labor and land (e.g., fertilizer, insecticides, etc.)
Be sure to indicate which variables are endogenous in your system and which are treated as exogenous. In the case of the latter, indicate the rationale for such treatment.

(*c*) Discuss the identifiability of the structural equations in your system. Which equations are overidentified, just identified, or underidentified on the basis of the *order conditions*?

(*d*) Indicate the nature of the various methods which might be employed to estimate the parameters of the structural equations in your system and, in broad outline, how each of them would work. Why would ordinary least-squares estimates of the parameters in the structural equations generally be unsatisfactory?

(*e*) Comment on the desirability of structural estimation in this context.

11-7 Consider the following model to study the formation of inflationary expectations and their interest-rate effects:[1]

$$p_t^* = \pi_t + u_{1t}$$
$$r_t = \alpha + \beta\pi_t + u_{2t}$$
$$\pi_t = \sum_{i=1}^{m} w_i\, p_{t-i} + u_{3t}$$

where p_t^* = expected rate of change of prices obtained from survey data

π_t = the true *unobservable* price expectation variable

p_t = the actual rate of change in prices

r_t = nominal rate of interest

Explain how you will estimate the parameters in this model.

[1] See K. Lahiri, "Inflationary Expectations: Their Formation and Interest Rate Effects," *The American Economic Review*, 1976, pp. 124–131.

PART FOUR

FURTHER DISCUSSION OF SELECTED TOPICS

CHAPTER

TWELVE

HETEROSCEDASTICITY AND AUTOCORRELATION

12-1 INTRODUCTION

To begin with, recall that the basic assumptions of our model have been that the relationship between y and x is linear and can be written as

$$y_i = \alpha + \beta x_i + u_i$$

and that the residuals u_i satisfy the following assumptions:

1. Zero mean $E(u_i) = 0$ for all i.
2. Homoscedasticity or same variance $V(u_i) = \sigma^2$ for all i.
3. Serial independence in the residuals: u_i and u_j are independent for all $i \neq j$.
4. u_i are normally distributed.
5. x_i are nonstochastic or nonrandom variables, and hence u_i are independent of x_j for all i and j.

In this chapter we will discuss what to do if assumptions 1, 2, and 3 are violated. In the next chapter we will discuss the violation of assumption 4 and the violation of assumption 5 due to errors in variables. As discussed earlier, assumption 5 can be violated owing to other causes too.

First, let us consider violation of assumption 1. If $E(u_i) = \theta$ the same for all i, there is no problem because we can absorb this in the constant term. The regression equation is $y_i = (\alpha + \theta) + \beta x_i + V_i$, where $V_i = u_i - \theta$ and $E(V_i) = 0$. If, however, $E(u_i) = \theta_i$, which is different for different observations, there is nothing we can do about it unless we have repeated observations or we make some strong assumptions about θ_i. For example, suppose we have data on output and labor input for N farms over T time periods so that our data are

$$y_{it} = \alpha + \beta x_{it} + u_{it} \qquad \begin{array}{l} i = 1,2, \ldots, N \\ t = 1,2, \ldots, T \end{array}$$

and $E(u_{it}) = \theta_i$ where θ_i can be regarded as the effect of all omitted physical inputs and managerial input. In this case, since we have T observations for each farm, we can estimate the θ_i by using a dummy-variable method. In fact, we can estimate $(N-1)$ of these constants, the Nth one being absorbed in the constant term. We define the dummy variables

$$D_i = 1 \text{ for the } i\text{th farm}$$
$$= 0 \text{ for the others} \qquad i = 1,2,\ldots,(N-1)$$

and regress y on x and the $(N-1)$ dummies D_i. More complicated versions of this model will be discussed in the chapter on pooling cross-section and time-series data (Chap. 14).

Usually the reason that the residuals have nonzero mean is that there are some omitted variables in the equation. If these omitted variables are not correlated with the included variables, the above type of analysis is valid and we can do something about these variables if they are constant and we have repeated observations. In the above example managerial input might be such a variable. However, if the omitted variable is capital input, we would expect it to be correlated with the labor input. Thus we have a case where the residual has not only a nonzero mean but is correlated with the regressor x. We considered this problem earlier in Chap. 9. What we are saying is that the true relation is

$$y_i = \beta x_i + \gamma z_i + V_i \qquad \text{where } E(V_i) = 0 \tag{12-1}$$

But we are estimating

$$y_i = \beta x_i + u_i \qquad \text{where } E(u_i) = \gamma z_i \neq 0 \tag{12-2}$$

The least-squares estimator of β from (12-2) is

$$\hat{\beta} = \frac{\sum x_i y_i}{\sum x_i^2} = \frac{\sum x_i(\beta x_i + \gamma z_i + V_i)}{\sum x_i^2}$$

substituting the value of y_i from Eq. (12-1). Since $E(\sum x_i V_i / \sum x_i^2) = 0$, we have

$$E(\hat{\beta}) = \beta + \gamma \frac{\sum x_i z_i}{\sum x_i^2} \tag{12-3}$$

But $\sum x_i z_i / \sum z_i^2$ is the regression coefficient from a regression of z on x. Thus $E(\hat{\beta})$ equals the true coefficient of x, the included variable plus the true coefficient of the omitted variable times the regression coefficient of the omitted variable on the included variable. Thus, the least-squares estimator is biased, and in some cases we may be able to tell the direction of the bias. For instance, if we are considering a regression of log output on log labor input, the omitted variable is log capital input, and we believe that farms with higher labor input are also farms with higher capital input, then the estimated labor elasticity will be biased upward because $E(\hat{\beta}) = \beta +$ a positive number. Similarly, if we are estimating the demand for television sets from time-series data and omit the income variable (income and price being negatively correlated over time), the estimated price elasticity will be biased upward in absolute value because $E(\hat{\beta}) = \beta +$ a negative quantity and β is expected to be negative.

12-2 HETEROSCEDASTICITY

The next assumption we come to is the assumption that the residuals have a common variance σ^2. This is known as homoscedasticity, and the violation of this assumption is known as heteroscedasticity. This is a problem that is encountered more often in cross-section data than in time-series data. Prais and Houthakker[1] found in their analysis of family budgets that the residuals from the regression had variance increasing with household income.

The consequences of heteroscedasticity are twofold. The estimates of the regression parameters are still unbiased but inefficient; and the estimates of the variances are biased. To see this, consider the very simple model with no constant term.

$$y_i = \beta x_i + u_i \qquad V(u_i) = \sigma_i^2 \tag{12-4}$$

The least-squares estimator is $\hat{\beta} = \sum x_i y_i / \sum x_i^2 = \beta + \sum x_i u_i / \sum x_i^2$. If the other assumptions about the residuals are satisfied, since $E(\sum x_i u_i / \sum x_i^2) = 0$, we have $E(\hat{\beta}) = \beta$. Thus $\hat{\beta}$ is unbiased.

$$V(\hat{\beta}) = V\left(\frac{x_1}{\sum x_i^2} u_1 + \frac{x_2}{\sum x_i^2} u_2 + \cdots + \frac{x_n}{\sum x_i^2} u_n \right)$$

$$= \frac{1}{\left(\sum x_i^2\right)^2} (x_1^2\sigma_1^2 + x_2^2\sigma_2^2 + \cdots + x_n^2\sigma_n^2) = \frac{\sum x_i^2\sigma_i^2}{\left(\sum x_i^2\right)^2} \tag{12-5}$$

Suppose we write $\sigma_i^2 = \sigma^2 z_i^2$, where z_i are known; i.e., we know the variances up to a multiplicative constant. Then by dividing (12-4) by z_i we have the model

$$\frac{y_i}{z_i} = \beta \frac{x_i}{z_i} + V_i$$

where $V_i = u_i / z_i$ has a constant variance σ^2. The weighted-least-squares estimator from this equation is

$$\beta^* = \frac{\sum (y_i/z_i)(x_i/z_i)}{\sum (x_i/z_i)^2}$$

$$= \beta + \frac{\sum [(x_i/z_i)V_i]}{\sum (x_i/z_i)^2}$$

and since the latter term has expectation zero, β^* is also unbiased.

$$V(\beta^*) = \frac{\sigma^2}{\sum (x_i/z_i)^2}$$

[1] S. J. Prais and H. S. Houthakker, "The Analysis of Family Budgets," pp. 55 ff., Cambridge University Press, New York, 1955.

Also
$$V(\hat{\beta}) = \sigma^2 \frac{\sum x_i^2 z_i^2}{\left(\sum x_i^2\right)^2}$$

from (12-5). Thus

$$\frac{V(\beta^*)}{V(\hat{\beta})} = \frac{\left(\sum x_i^2\right)^2}{\left[\sum (x_i^2/z_i^2)\right]\left(\sum x_i^2 z_i^2\right)}$$

This expression is of the form $(\sum a_i b_i)^2/\sum a_i^2 \sum b_i^2$, where $a_i = x_i z_i$ and $b_i = x_i/z_i$. Thus it is < 1 unless a_i and b_i are proportional, i.e., $x_i z_i$ and x_i/z_i are proportional or z_i^2 is constant, which is the case if the residuals are homoscedastic.

Thus the ordinary-least-squares (OLS) estimator is unbiased but less efficient (has higher variance) than the weighted-least-squares (WLS) estimator.

Also, if we ignored heteroscedasticity, we would be estimating the variance of the OLS estimator $\hat{\beta}$ by

$$\frac{\text{residual SS}}{n-1} \frac{1}{\sum x_i^2}$$

But
$$E(\text{residual SS}) = E\left[\sum (y_i - \hat{\beta} x_i)^2\right] = \sum \sigma_i^2 - \frac{\sum x_i^2 \sigma_i^2}{\sum x_i^2}$$

(after simplifications—details are omitted here, as they can be checked easily).

Note that if $\sigma_i^2 = \sigma^2$ for all i, this reduces to $(n-1)\sigma^2$. Thus we would be estimating the variance of $\hat{\beta}$ by an expression whose expected value is

$$\frac{\sum x_i^2 \sum \sigma_i^2 - \sum x_i^2 \sigma_i^2}{(n-1)\left(\sum x_i^2\right)^2}$$

whereas the true variance is

$$\frac{\sum x_i^2 \sigma_i^2}{\left(\sum x_i^2\right)^2}$$

Thus the estimated variances are also biased. If σ_i^2 and x_i^2 are positively correlated, as is often the case with most economic data, so that $\sum x_i^2 \sigma_i^2 > (1/n) \sum \sigma_i^2 \sum x_i^2$, the expected value of the estimated variance is smaller than the true variance. Thus we would be *underestimating* the true variance of the OLS estimator and getting shorter confidence intervals than the true ones. This also affects tests of hypotheses about the regression parameter β. The type I error will be higher than the assumed value.

What are the solutions to the heteroscedasticity problem? If the variances are known up to a multiplicative constant, there is no problem at all. If $V(u_i) = \sigma^2 z_i^2$, where z_i are known, we divide the equation throughout by z_i and use ordinary least squares. The only thing to remember is that if the original equation contained a constant term, i.e., $y_i = \alpha + \beta x_i + u_i$, the transformed equation will not have a constant term. It is

$$\frac{y_i}{z_i} = \alpha \frac{1}{z_i} + \beta \frac{x_i}{z_i} + V_i$$

where $V_i = u_i/z_i$. Thus we should be running a regression of y_i/z_i on $1/z_i$ and x_i/z_i with no constant term. One interesting case is where $V(u_i) = \sigma^2 x_i$ and $\alpha = 0$. In this case the transformed equation is

$$\frac{y_i}{\sqrt{x_i}} = \beta \frac{x_i}{\sqrt{x_i}} + V_i$$

Hence $$\beta^* = \frac{\sum (y_i x_i / x_i)}{\sum (\sqrt{x_i})^2} = \frac{\bar{y}}{\bar{x}}$$

i.e., the WLS estimator is just the ratio of the means.

Often we do not know the nature of heteroscedasticity. One particular model considered by Prais and Houthakker is that σ_i^2 is proportional to the square of the regression function; i.e., $\sigma_i^2 = \sigma^2(\alpha + \beta x_i)^2$. For this model one can consider a two-step procedure as follows: First estimate α and β by OLS. Let these estimators be $\hat{\alpha}$ and $\hat{\beta}$. Now use the WLS procedure as outlined earlier; i.e., regress $y_i/(\hat{\alpha} + \hat{\beta} x_i)$ on $1/(\hat{\alpha} + \hat{\beta} x_i)$ and $x_i/(\hat{\alpha} + \hat{\beta} x_i)$ with no constant term. This might be called the two-step WLS procedure. One can iterate this procedure further, i.e., use the new estimates of α and β and again use WLS and repeat until convergence. This we might call the iterated WLS procedure. If we make some specific assumptions about the distribution of the residuals, e.g., that they are normally distributed, then since $V(u_i) = \sigma^2(\alpha + \beta x_i)^2$ we can write the log-likelihood function as

$$\log L = -n \log \sigma - \sum \log(\alpha + \beta x_i) - \frac{1}{2\sigma^2} \sum \left(\frac{y_i - \alpha - \beta x_i}{\alpha + \beta x_i} \right)^2$$

One can maximize this by iterative procedures and obtain the maximum-likelihood estimates.[1]

[1] Amemiya discusses the maximum-likelihood estimation for this model when the residuals follow a normal, log-normal, and gamma distribution. He also compares the asymptotic efficiency of the WLS and ML estimators. When the residuals follow a normal or log-normal distribution, the WLS estimator is less efficient than the ML estimator. But when the residuals follow a gamma distribution, they are equally efficient. See T. Amemiya, Regression Analysis When Variance of Dependent Variable Is Proportional to Square of Its Expectation, *Journal of the American Statistical Association*, December, 1973.

A more general model is to assume that the variance σ_i^2 is equal to $(\gamma + \delta x_i)^2$. In this case, too, we can consider a WLS method, i.e., minimize

$$\sum_i \left(\frac{y_i - \alpha - \beta x_i}{\gamma + \delta x_i} \right)^2$$

or if the residuals can be assumed to follow a known distribution use the ML method. For example, if they follow a normal distribution we can write the log-likelihood function as

$$\log L = -\sum \log(\gamma + \delta x_i) - \frac{1}{2} \sum \left(\frac{y_i - \alpha - \beta x_i}{\gamma + \delta x_i} \right)^2$$

We can maximize this by an iterative procedure. Clearly, the WLS and the ML procedures are not the same. The ML procedure has been discussed by Rutemiller and Bowers.[1] In the WLS method one can use a two-step procedure as follows: Compute the OLS estimators of α and β. Get the estimated residuals and regress the absolute values of these residuals on x to get estimates of γ and δ. Then use WLS. One can iterate this procedure till convergence is attained.

Instead of assuming that $V(u_i) = (\gamma + \delta x_i)^2$, we can consider other alternative functions like $\gamma + \delta x_i$ or $\gamma + \delta / x_i$, etc. In each case a test for $\delta = 0$ is a test for homoscedasticity. This was in fact the procedure suggested by Glejser.[2] If $|e_i|$ is the absolute value of the estimated residual from least squares, Glejser suggested running the regression

$$|e_i| = \alpha + \beta x_i$$
$$|e_i| = \alpha + \beta / x_i$$
$$|e_i| = \alpha \quad \beta\sqrt{x_i} \qquad \text{etc.}$$

He argued on the basis of some sampling experiments that this test is generally more powerful than that of Goldfeld and Quandt.[3] The idea of the Goldfeld and Quandt test is to split the observations into two groups—one corresponding to large values of x and the other corresponding to small values of x—fit separate regressions for each, and then apply an F test to test the equality of residual variances. They suggest omitting some observations in the middle to increase our ability to discriminate between the two error variances. An alternative

[1] H. C. Rutemiller and D. A. Bowers, Estimation in a Heteroscedastic Regression Model, *Journal of the American Statistical Association*, June, 1968. Rutemiller and Bowers estimate the parameters α and β by OLS and take the square root of the estimate of the residual variance as an estimate of γ (initially $\hat{\delta} = 0$). They then compute the ML estimates by an iterative procedure starting from these initial values. They also suggest testing the hypothesis $\delta = 0$ by a likelihood-ratio test. Compute the maximum of the likelihood function for $\delta \neq 0$, say this is L_1; and compute the maximum for $\delta = 0$, say this is L_0. Then $-2 \log(L_0/L_1)$ has a χ^2-distribution degrees of freedom 1. In both the examples that they considered, the hypothesis $\delta = 0$ was rejected at the .1 percent level.

[2] H. Glejser, A New Test for Heteroscedasticity, *Journal of the American Statistical Association*, March, 1969.

[3] S. M. Goldfeld and R. E. Quandt, Some Tests for Homoscedasticity, *Journal of the American Statistical Association*, September, 1965.

test—a nonparametric one—is suggested in Johnston.[1] This is to compute the rank correlation between the absolute values of the residuals and the absolute values of x_i and test that this correlation is zero.

If the number of observations is large, one can use a likelihood-ratio test. Divide the residuals (estimated from the OLS regression) into k groups with n_i observations in the ith group, $\sum n_i = n$. Estimate the residual variances in each. Let these be $\hat{\sigma}_i^2$ and let the estimate obtained from the entire sample be $\hat{\sigma}^2$. Then if

$$\lambda = \frac{\prod_{i=1}^{k} (\hat{\sigma}_i)^{n_i}}{\hat{\sigma}^n} \tag{12-6}$$

$-2 \log \lambda$ has a χ^2-distribution degrees of freedom $k - 1$. If there is only one explanatory variable in the equation, the ordering of the residuals can be based on the absolute magnitude of this variable. But if there are two or more variables and no single explanatory variable can provide a satisfactory ordering, the predicted values of the dependent variable can be used.

Of course, with any of these tests for heteroscedasticity the question is always what to do after the tests. For either the Goldfeld-Quandt test or the Glejser tests, if one rejects the hypothesis of homoscedasticity, one has to go ahead and reestimate the parameters making the appropriate assumptions about the nature of heteroscedasticity. The performance of these two-step estimators in small samples as compared with the estimators that (wrongly) assume homoscedasticity is not known. The purpose in applying these tests is to avoid more complicated computations if the hypothesis of homoscedasticity is not rejected. But if computational simplicity is not an important criterion and if one has a moderate-sized sample, one can as well go ahead and make the appropriate assumptions about the nature of the heteroscedasticity and get both the ML estimates and the appropriate LR tests at the same time, as done by Rutemiller and Bowers.

Feldstein[2] used the LR test described in (12-6) for his hospital-cost regressions (described in Chap. 8). He divided the total number of observations into four groups of equal size, the residuals being ordered by the OLS predicted values of the dependent variable. The estimated residual variances were 71.47, 114.82, 102.81, and 239.34. He found that the value of $-2 \log \lambda$ was 18.265. The 1 percent value of χ^2 for degrees of freedom 3 is 11.34. Thus there are significant differences between the residual variances. Next he used WLS, weighting each observation in the group by $\hat{\sigma}_i^{-1}$. The weights for the four groups, normalized to make their average equal to 1, were 1.2599, .9940, 1.0504, .6885. The new error variances from the reestimated equations were almost equal: 106.34, 110.71,

[1] J. Johnston, "Econometric Methods," 2d ed., p. 219, McGraw-Hill Book Company, New York, 1972.

[2] M. S. Feldstein, "Economic Analysis for Health Service Efficiency," pp. 52–54, North-Holland Publishing Company, Amsterdam, 1967.

Table 12-1 Comparison of OLS and WLS estimates for hospital-cost regression

Case type	Average cost per case OLS	WLS
General medicine	114.48	111.81
Pediatrics	24.97	28.35
General surgery	32.70	35.07
ENT	15.25	15.58
Traumatic and orthopedic surgery	39.69	36.04
Other surgery	98.02	101.38
Gynecology	58.72	58.48
Obstetrics	34.88	34.50
Others	69.51	66.26

Source: M. S. Feldstein, "Economic Analysis for Health Service Efficiency," p. 54, North-Holland Publishing Company, Amsterdam, 1967.

114.99, and 117.06. However, the regression parameters did not change very much.[1] The results are shown in Table 12-1.

The assumption made in this example is that the error variances are different for the four different groups of observations, i.e.,

$$\begin{aligned} V(u_i) &= \sigma_1^2 \quad &&\text{for } i = 1,2,\ldots,n_1 \\ &= \sigma_2^2 \quad &&\text{for } i = n_1+1,\ldots,n_1+n_2 \\ &= \sigma_3^2 \quad &&\text{for } i = n_1+n_2+1,\ldots,n_1+n_2+n_3 \\ &= \sigma_4^2 \quad &&\text{for } i = n_1+n_2+n_3+1,\ldots,n \end{aligned}$$

For models like this, Rao[2] suggests an alternative method of estimating the residual variances called the MINQUE (minimum-norm quadratic unbiased estimation) method. However, our ultimate objective is to estimate the regression parameters based on the preliminary estimates of the variances, and not much is known about the performance of these estimates based on MINQUE estimates of variances as compared with the normally used procedure which Feldstein used in the above example. Perhaps it does not make that much difference.[3]

Lancaster[4] suggests the use of grouping methods in the case of heterosce-

[1] Though the point estimates did not change much, the standard errors could be different. Feldstein does not present them. Moreover, the standard errors would now be right, whereas in the OLS they would be biased.

[2] C. R. Rao, Estimation of Heteroscedastic Variances in Linear Models, *Journal of the American Statistical Association*, March, 1970.

[3] For some evidence on this in the context of an alternative heteroscedastic model see G. S. Maddala and T. D. Mount, A Comparative Study of Alternative Estimators for Variance Components Models, *Journal of the American Statistical Association*, June, 1973.

[4] Tony Lancaster, Grouping Estimators on Heteroscedastic Data, *Journal of the American Statistical Association*, March, 1968.

dastic models. These methods were suggested by Wald[1] and Bartlett[2] to estimate regression parameters in errors-in-variables models. The procedure is to use $\hat{\beta} = (\bar{y}_1 - \bar{y}_2)/(\bar{x}_1 - \bar{x}_2)$ as an estimate of the slope coefficient where the means of y and x are for the two exclusive groups consisting of n_1 and n_2 observations. In Wald's method $n_1 = n_2 = n/2$ and in Bartlett's method $n_1 = n_2 = n/3$ (the middle $n/3$ observations are omitted). Lancaster compares the efficiencies of these grouping estimators with the OLS estimator under the following assumptions:

$$A: \quad x \text{ follows a log-normal distribution}$$

$$B: \quad V(u_i) = \lambda x_i^P \qquad (\lambda > 0)$$

He studies the efficiencies for P ranging from -2 to $+2$. The general conclusion is that the Bartlett method of three groups is better than Wald's method of two groups and that the grouping estimators are more efficient than the OLS estimators for positive values of p and moderate variance of x. Lancaster argues that most economic data fall in this category, and thus, in addition to being computationally simple, the grouping estimator is more efficient than the OLS in the presence of heteroscedasticity of the type that is most common with economic data. The performance of the grouping estimator compared with the WLS and ML estimators is not known. The latter two are expected to be better, but computationally they are much more complicated.

12-3 HETEROSCEDASTICITY AND THE USE OF DEFLATORS

There are two remedies that are often suggested and used for heteroscedasticity. One is transforming the variables into logs, and the other is to deflate all variables by some measure of "size." The former method often does reduce the heteroscedasticity in the residual variances, though there are also other criteria by which one has to decide between the linear and the logarithmic forms. We will have to defer this discussion to a later stage.

Regarding deflation, as pointed out earlier (see Chap. 7, Sec. 7-6), if the original equation involves a constant term, one should not estimate a regression equation in just the deflated variables. One should be estimating an equation with the reciprocal of the deflator added as an extra variable and no constant term in the regression (unless the deflator also occurs in the original equation as an extra variable). Griliches[3] gives an example of the use of deflators to solve heteroscedasticity in the estimation of railroad-cost functions. The variables are C = total cost, M = miles of road, and X = output.

[1] A. Wald, The Fitting of Straight Lines if Both Variables Are Subject to Errors, *Annals of Mathematical Statistics*, 1940.

[2] M. S. Bartlett, Fitting a Straight Line When Both Variables Are Subject to Errors, *Biometrics*, 1949.

[3] Z. Griliches, Railroad Cost Analysis, *The Bell Journal of Economics and Management Science*, Spring, 1972.

If $C = aM + bX$, dividing by M gives $C/M = a + b(X/M)$. But if the true relation is $C = aM + bX + c$, deflation leads to $C/M = a + b(X/M) + c(1/M)$. For 97 observations using 1957–1969 averages as units, the regressions were

$$\frac{C}{M} = \underset{(6218)}{13{,}016} + \underset{(.871)}{6.431}\frac{X}{M} \qquad R^2 = .365$$

$$\frac{C}{M} = \underset{(5115)}{827} + \underset{(.682)}{6.439}\frac{X}{M} + \underset{(393{,}000)}{3{,}065{,}000}\frac{1}{M} \qquad R^2 = .614$$

$$C = \underset{(2.906)}{-1.884}M + \underset{(.375)}{6.613}X + \underset{(4730)}{3676} \qquad R^2 = .945$$

The coefficient c is significant in the second equation but not in the third, and the coefficient of a is not significant in either the second or third equation. From this Griliches concludes that there is no evidence that M belongs in the equation in any form. It appears in a significant form in the second equation only because the other variables were divided by it.

Some other equations estimated with the same data are the following:

$$C = \underset{(4524)}{2811} + \underset{(.18)}{6.39}X \qquad R^2 = .944$$

$$\frac{C}{\sqrt{M}} = \underset{(3713)}{3805}\frac{1}{\sqrt{M}} + \underset{(.51)}{6.06}\frac{X}{\sqrt{M}} \qquad R^2 = .826$$

The last equation is the appropriate one to estimate if $C = a + bX + u$ and $V(u) = M\sigma^2$.

One important thing to note is that the purpose in all these procedures of deflation is to get more efficient estimates of the parameters. But once those estimates have been obtained, one should make all inferences—calculation of the residuals, prediction of future values, calculation of elasticities at the means, etc., from the original equation—not the equation in the deflated variables.

Another point to note is that since the purpose of deflation is to get more efficient estimates, it is tempting to argue about the merits of the different procedures by looking at the standard errors of the coefficients. However, this is not correct, because in the presence of heteroscedasticity the standard errors themselves are biased, as we showed earlier. For instance, in the five equations presented above, the second and third are comparable and so are the fourth and fifth. In both cases if we look at the standard errors of the coefficient of X, the coefficient in the undeflated equation has a smaller standard error than the corresponding coefficient in the deflated equation. However, if the standard errors are biased, we have to be careful in making too much of these differences. An examination of the residuals will give a better picture.

In the preceding example we have considered miles M as a deflator and also as an explanatory variable. In this context we should mention some discussion in the literature on "spurious correlation" between ratios.[1] The argument simply is that even if we have two variables X and Y that are uncorrelated, if we deflate

[1] See E. Kuh and J. R. Meyer, Correlation and Regression Estimates When the Data Are Ratios, *Econometrica*, October, 1955, pp. 400–416.

both the variables by another variable Z, there could be a strong correlation between X/Z and Y/Z because of the common denominator Z. It is wrong to infer from this correlation that there exists a close relationship between X and Y. Of course, if our interest is in fact the relationship between X/Z and Y/Z, there is no reason why this correlation need be called "spurious." As Kuh and Meyer[1] point out, "The question of spurious correlation quite obviously does not arise when the hypothesis to be tested has initially been formulated in terms of ratios, for instance, in problems involving relative prices. Similarly, when a series such as money value of output is divided by a price index to obtain a 'constant dollar' estimate of output, no question of spurious correlation need arise. Thus, spurious correlation can only exist when a hypothesis pertains to undeflated variables and the data have been divided through by another series for reasons extraneous to but not in conflict with the hypothesis framed as an exact, i.e., nonstochastic relation."

However, even in cases where deflation is done for reasons of estimation, we should note that the problem of "spurious correlation" exists only if we start drawing inferences on the basis of correlation coefficients when we should not be doing so. For example, suppose the relationship we derive is of the form

$$Y = \alpha Z + \beta X + u \tag{12-7}$$

and we find that the residuals u are heteroscedastic with variance roughly proportional to Z^2. Then we should not hesitate to divide (12-7) throughout by Z and estimate the regression equation

$$\frac{Y}{Z} = \alpha + \beta \frac{X}{Z} + u' \tag{12-8}$$

where $u' = u/Z$ has a constant variance σ^2. The estimates of α, β, and σ^2 should be obtained from (12-8) and not from (12-7). Whether the correlation between Y/Z and X/Z is higher or lower than the correlation between Y and X is irrelevant. The important point to note is that we cannot argue whether (12-7) or (12-8) is a better equation to consider by looking at correlations. So long as we do not base our inferences on correlations, there is nothing wrong with deflation in this case. It should also be noted that if (12-7) is not homogeneous, i.e., it involves a constant term, we end up with an equation of the form

$$\frac{Y}{Z} = \gamma \frac{1}{Z} + \alpha + \beta \frac{X}{Z} + u'$$

which is different from (12-8). The equation will also be different if the variance of u is proportional not to Z^2 but to Z or some other function of Z.

In actual practice, deflation may increase or decrease the resulting correlation. The algebra is somewhat tedious, but with some simplifying assumptions Kuh and Meyer derive the conditions under which the correlation between X/Z and Y/Z is in fact less than that between X and Y. They show that, given certain simplifying assumptions, "the ratio correlation will be higher or lower

[1] *Ibid.*, p. 401.

than the numerator relationship depending on whether the ratio of the deflator's coefficient of variation to that of the deflated series is higher or lower than twice the correlation between the deflator and the deflated series."[1]

Though deflation is done also in time-series problems, it is done more commonly in cross-section studies. In these, large units of observation will commonly have large values and small units will have small values, so that the influence of size must somehow be eliminated. The common method used is to use a measure of size (gross fixed assets, total sales, etc.) as a deflator. However, as the above discussion shows, the question of whether to use these size variables as deflators or to use them as additional explanatory variables depends on the nature of heteroscedasticity in the residuals and whether the relationships are homogeneous (i.e., do not involve a constant term) or not. Kuh and Meyer give an example where deflation probably led to, rather than corrected for, heteroscedasticity (though the example is for a time-series study).

Sometimes, with time-series data, deflation is also done to "get rid of common trends." Here the problem is one of strong interrelationships between the explanatory variables because of a common trend. Again, deflation may not be the right solution to this problem. The problem is the "multicollinearity problem," which we discussed in Chap. 10.

In summary, often in econometric work, deflated or ratio variables are used. These are justified either by economic reasoning or by the statistical procedures of stabilizing the residual variances. One should bear in mind whether deflation can be justified on these grounds in the particular example considered. In any case, deflation may increase or decrease the resulting correlations, but this is beside the point. What one should avoid is drawing inferences solely on the basis of correlations, which are often not comparable.

12-4 HETEROSCEDASTICITY AND GROUPED DATA

Another case where error variances are expected to be unequal is when we have grouped data. In this case we have k groups with n_i observations in the ith group ($i = 1,2, \ldots, k$) and we use regressions based on group averages. That is, we estimate the equation

$$\bar{y}_i = \alpha + \beta \bar{x}_i + \bar{u}_i \tag{12-9}$$

Since $\operatorname{var}(\bar{u}_i) = \sigma^2/n_i$ if $\operatorname{var}(u_i) = \sigma^2$, we know the variances of the residuals in (12-9) up to a multiplicative constant σ^2. We can thus easily use the weighted-least-squares method. All we do is estimate the equation

$$\sqrt{n_i}\, \bar{y}_i = \alpha\sqrt{n_i} + \beta\sqrt{n_i}\, \bar{x}_i \tag{12-10}$$

by ordinary least squares (no constant term).

Cramer[2] studies the efficiency of least-squares estimators from the grouped and ungrouped data.

[1] *Ibid.*, p. 412.

[2] J. S. Cramer, Efficient Grouping, Regression and Correlation in Engel Curve Analysis, *Journal of the American Statistical Association*, March, 1964.

Let x_{ij} $(j = 1,2, \ldots, n_i)$ be the observations in the ith group, so that $\bar{x}_i = (1/n_i)\sum_j x_{ij}$ and the overall mean $\bar{x} = \sum n_i\bar{x}_i / \sum n_i$. The total sum of squares for x is $S_{xx} = \sum_j\sum_i(x_{ij} - \bar{x})^2$. This can be split into two components—between-group S_{xxB} and within-group S_{xxw}—where

$$S_{xxB} = \sum_i n_i(\bar{x}_i - \bar{x})^2 \qquad \text{and} \qquad S_{xxw} = \sum_i \sum_j (x_{ij} - \bar{x}_i)^2$$

If $\hat{\beta}$ is the estimator of β from ungrouped data and $\hat{\beta}_B$ is the estimator from group means,

$$V(\hat{\beta}) = \frac{\sigma^2}{S_{xx}} \qquad \text{and} \qquad V(\hat{\beta}_B) = \frac{\sigma^2}{S_{xxB}}$$

Hence
$$\frac{V(\hat{\beta})}{V(\hat{\beta}_B)} = \frac{S_{xxB}}{S_{xx}} = \frac{1}{1 + S_{xxw}/S_{xxB}}$$

Thus the estimator from grouped data is always less efficient than the estimator from ungrouped data. The loss of efficiency is minimized by minimizing the within-group variation and maximizing the between-group variation. If observations are grouped according to x, as is usually done, we will be minimizing the loss in efficiency.

Another thing to note is that R^2 will be generally much higher for the regression with grouped data than for the regression with ungrouped data.[1] To see this, let R_B^2 and R^2 be the R^2's from the grouped and ungrouped data. Then

$$R_B^2 = \hat{\beta}_B^2 \frac{S_{xxB}}{S_{yyB}}$$

$$R^2 = \hat{\beta}^2 \frac{S_{xx}}{S_{yy}}$$

Since $\hat{\beta}_B$ and $\hat{\beta}$ will be close to each other, we have

$$\frac{R_B^2}{R^2} \approx \frac{S_{xxB}/S_{xx}}{S_{yyB}/S_{yy}}$$

If grouping is done with respect to x so that S_{xxB}/S_{xx} is made as high as possible, this ratio will often be substantially greater than S_{yyB}/S_{yy}. Thus R_B^2 is greater than R^2.

The above discussion is for a single explanatory variable x and grouping by this variable. If grouping is by the explained variable y rather than the variable x, one gets very misleading results. This is also true when there are two or more explanatory variables and grouping is done by one of them. This is the case in the example on Indian agriculture quoted in Chap. 6. The problem here is not merely heteroscedasticity. Haitovsky[2] discusses extensively the problems with

[1] *Ibid.*

[2] Y. Haitovsky, "Regression Estimation from Grouped Observations," Hafner Publishing Company, Inc., New York, 1973. Kmenta considers two-way grouping in the case of two variables X and Y and shows that the regression estimates of Y on X are identical from the two-way grouping as

Table 12-2 Estimates from ungrouped and grouped data

Model	Intercept	Coeff. of Y	Coeff. of S	R^2	$\hat{\sigma}^2$
All data ($n = 1218$)	17.10	.7578 (.1398)	−.1778 (.0367)	.0347	5250
Two-way table ($n = 56$)	16.47	.7474 (.1203)	−.1624 (.0323)	.4969	3914
Y table ($n = 7$)	10.86	.5505 (1.6139)	.0382 (1.8752)	.7284	9027
S table ($n = 8$)	73.74	−.6532 (2.5391)	−.0931 (.1572)	.9098	1345
Houthakker method (GLS)	18.08	.7263 (.1259)	−.1719 (.0338)	.8139	4285
WLS ($n = 15$)	19.62	.7133 (.1320)	−.1698 (.0355)		
Haitovsky method	18.03	.7271 (.1033)	−.1718 (.0282)	.7704	4337

Figures in parentheses are standard errors.

Source: Y. Haitovsky, "Regression Estimation from Grouped Observations," Hafner Publishing Company, Inc., New York, 1973.

regression analysis from such grouped data. The calculations he makes from the different types of classifications are very interesting. Haitovsky considers data on 1218 households collected by Houthakker. The observations consist of P = net purchases of automobiles, Y = income, and S = value of the automobile stock held at the beginning of the year. The original observations were cross-classified by income into seven groups and by stock into eight groups. When we are given the grouped data, we are given the number of observations in the group and the mean values of P, Y, and S for that group. In the two-way classification we are given 56 such observations, in the Y classification we have 7 such observations, and in the S classification we have 8 such observations. In each of these cases, we can estimate a regression based on the mean values, and since the variance of the error term is known up to a multiplicative constant (it is proportional to $1/f$, where f is the number of observations in that group), we can use weighted least squares.

The interesting thing is that the estimates based on the Y or S classification alone are very poor. The results Haitovsky obtained are shown in Table 12-2. It is easy to see that the estimates obtained from the two-way table are well within one standard error of the estimates obtained from the complete data, but the

one-way grouping by X. See J. Kmenta, "Elements of Econometrics," pp. 330–335, The Macmillan Company, New York, 1971. But what Kmenta means by two-way grouping is entirely different. What he has is a frequency table by $\bar{X}$ and $\bar{Y}$, i.e., the number of observations corresponding to each pair $(\bar{X}, \bar{Y})$. What we mean here by two-way grouping and what Haitovsky discusses is that we have class ranges for X and Y and for each cell we are given the number of observations and the means of X and Y. This is the more common practical situation.

estimates from the one-way classifications are very poor. The estimates from the Y table and the S table have opposite signs, and none of the coefficients is significant. Though the R^2's are high, each individual coefficient has a very low t ratio, thus suggesting that there is high multicollinearity between the variables. Thus, given that we do not have all the individual observations, the next best thing is to have the original observations cross-classified simultaneously by *all* the explanatory variables. However, in actual practice data are not presented this way. What we have is one-way classification tables, each table classified by one explanatory variable as shown in Table 12-3. Given that the regression equations from each of these tables are very poor, the question is can we do anything better by using them together. Haitovsky describes two methods in this case, one due to Houthakker and the other due to himself.

In the Houthakker method we use all the means obtained from all the classifications; e.g., in the above example there are seven obtained from the Y classification and eight from the S classification. However, since the weighted average of the first seven observations is equal to the weighted average of the last eight observations (each giving the overall means for the data), we omit the last observation in the S classification to avoid linear dependency among the variables. Thus we use 14 observations for the estimation of the regression equation. If there are k explanatory variables, we do a similar thing. We drop the last observation for the classification corresponding to each explanatory variable except the first.

Consider the data in Table 12-3. The residuals for the first seven observations are independent but have variances $\sigma^2/86, \sigma^2/89, \ldots,$ etc., $\sigma^2/100$. Simi-

Table 12-3 Data grouped by each explanatory variable separately

		n	$\bar{P}$	$\bar{Y}$	$\bar{S}$
Y grouping	1	86	27.616	14.116	53.628
	2	89	29.753	24.079	50.393
	3	277	26.065	33.982	61.383
	4	259	36.896	43.680	69.884
	5	273	43.524	53.099	79.407
	6	134	59.351	62.276	84.694
	7	100	47.200	71.970	98.850
S grouping	1	195	50.395	39.431	7.569
	2	210	41.567	40.881	29.824
	3	227	37.930	44.000	46.159
	4	151	40.960	45.536	65.629
	5	118	35.449	46.169	90.805
	6	118	31.229	49.169	114.746
	7	119	29.958	47.748	144.874
	8	80	19.625	50.638	218.625
Total		1218	38.057	44.434	71.521

Source: Y. Haitovsky, "Regression Estimation from Grouped Observations," Hafner Publishing Company, Inc., New York, 1973.

Table 12-4 Effect of grouping on the simple regression coefficients

Method	b_{py}	b_{ps}	b_{ys}	b_{sy}	b_{yp}	b_{sp}
All observations	.581	−.128	.057	.824	.026	−0.083
Two-way grouping	.608	−.116	.062	.857	.421	−1.121
Y grouping	.583	.663	1.136	.841	1.250	1.054
S grouping	−2.037	−.130	.057	14.860	−.412	−6.879

Source: Y. Haitovsky, "Regression Estimation from Grouped Observations," p. 20, Hafner Publishing Company, Inc., New York, 1973.

larly, the residuals from the last eight observations are independent but have variances $\sigma^2/195, \sigma^2/210, \ldots$, etc., $\sigma^2/80$. However, the residuals from the first group and the second group are not independent of each other. Their covariance will depend upon how many observations are common to the ith Y group and the jth S group. Let n_{ij} be the number of such observations ($i = 1,2, \ldots, 7$ and $j = 1,2, \ldots, 8$). Also, let $n_{i.}$ be the total number of observations in the ith Y group and $n_{.j}$ the total number of observations in the jth S group. Then the covariance between the residuals for the ith Y group and the jth S group is $(n_{ij}/n_{i.}n_{.j})\sigma^2$. Thus we cannot use simple weighted least squares in this case—we have to use generalized least squares. Also, to obtain these covariances, we need the data on n_{ij}. Thus, in addition to the data presented in Table 12-3 we need a complete frequency table of the number of observations in the 56 groups to apply Houthakker's method. The results of this GLS estimation are presented in Table 12-2.

It might be of some interest to see what would happen if we applied the weighted-least-squares (WLS) method to the 15 observations in Table 12-3. This method takes into account only the differences in the variances and ignores the covariances. These results are also presented in Table 12-2. It is interesting that this regression gives better results than the regressions from the Y grouping alone or the S grouping alone.

Since Houthakker's method requires more data than those provided by one-way groupings as in Table 12-3, Haitovsky suggests a method that uses just these data. He first notes that the simple regression coefficients are well estimated if the grouping is by the explanatory variable. Table 12-4 shows the effects of grouping on the simple regression coefficients. If we take the Y grouping, except for b_{py} and b_{sy}, the other regression estimates are way off. Similarly, for the S grouping except for b_{ps} and b_{ys} the other estimates are way off. For the two-way grouping (by Y and S) the last two coefficients are way off.

The procedure Haitovsky suggests is the following: Let the equation to be estimated be $p = \beta_1 y + \beta_2 s + u$ (all variables are measured as derivations from the overall mean). If we estimate a regression of p on y only and b_{py} is the estimate of the regression coefficient, using formula (12-3) for omitted variables we get

$$E(b_{py}) = \beta_1 + \beta_2 \frac{\sum ys}{\sum y^2} \tag{12-11a}$$

Similarly, if we estimate a regression of p on s only and b_{ps} is the estimate of the regression coefficient, we get

$$E(b_{ps}) = \beta_2 + \beta_1 \frac{\sum ys}{\sum s^2} \tag{12-11b}$$

Haitovsky suggests using b_{py} and $\sum ys/\sum y^2$ from the data given by the Y grouping and b_{ps} and $\sum ys/\sum s^2$ from the data given by the S grouping and solving the equations for $\hat{\beta}_1$ and $\hat{\beta}_2$:

$$b_{py} = \hat{\beta}_1 + \hat{\beta}_2 \frac{\sum ys}{\sum y^2}$$

$$b_{ps} = \hat{\beta}_2 + \hat{\beta}_1 \frac{\sum ys}{\sum s^2}$$

to get unbiased estimates of β_1 and β_2. In the case of Table 12-3, Haitovsky gets $b_{py} = .58263$, $\sum ys/\sum y^2 = .84119$, and $b_{ps} = -.13034$, $\sum ys/\sum s^2 = .05698$. Thus, solving the equations,

$$.58263 = \beta_1 + .84119\beta_2$$

$$-.13034 = .05698\beta_1 + \beta_2$$

we get $\hat{\beta}_1 = .72713$ and $\hat{\beta}_2 = -.17177$. These are the estimates reported in Table 12-2. The standard errors of these estimates depend on the standard errors of b_{py} and b_{ps}. The derivation is omitted here. It can be found in Haitovsky (pp. 31–36).

In summary, if we are given data which are grouped by the explained variable y, we should not use them for estimating a regression of y on x. If the data are grouped by the explanatory variable x, we can use the weighted-least-squares method to estimate the regression equation. If we have two or more explanatory variables and the data are classified by only one of these variables, we will get misleading results if we use these data to estimate the regression equation. There is no problem if we have a complete cross classification by *all* the explanatory variables simultaneously. If this is not available and we have data classified by each variable separately, we can use Houthakker's method if the frequencies for the cross classification are given. If these are not available and all we have are data from the separate one-way groupings as in Table 12-3, the Haitovsky method described above should be used. A method that is simpler to compute and that worked well in this example, though its merits have to be investigated, is to use weighted least squares on the entire set of data obtained by all the classifications.

Returning now to the data considered by Lau and Yotoupolos[1] and de-

[1] These data have been further analyzed in P. A. Yotoupolos and L. J. Lau, A Test for Relative Economic Efficiency: Some Further Results, *The American Economic Review*, March, 1973.

scribed in Chap. 6, Table 6-5, the main problem is that the data are classified by only one of the explanatory variables (land input). In addition there is the problem of heteroscedasticity that Lau and Yotopoulos ignored. The detailed data have been analyzed by Bardhan,[1] but since comparable equations are not presented for the grouped and ungrouped data, we cannot tell the extent of the biases. However, the fact that Lau and Yotoupolos find capital elasticity negative and Bardhan found positive elasticities for his measures (though different) of capital inputs (irrigation, fertilizer, etc.) suggests that the former result is perhaps due to the use of grouped data.

12-5 AUTOCORRELATED ERRORS

The third assumption we mentioned at the beginning is that the residuals u_i are mutually independent. This assumption will not always be valid, particularly in time-series data. In time-series data the successive residuals tend to be highly correlated, and this correlation is known as serial correlation or autocorrelation (these terms are used to denote the fact that it is the correlation of the series, not with some other series but with past values of the same series). The explanation often given for the existence of serial correlation in the residuals is that the residuals comprise a number of omitted variables which are themselves serially correlated. There is, however, one problem with this interpretation. It is that we should also be saying that these autocorrelated omitted variables, whatever they are, are independent of the explanatory variables included in the equation, or else we run into the problem that the residuals are correlated with the explanatory variables. We will return to this problem later. For the present we will assume that the residuals are independent of the explanatory variables; i.e., the autocorrelated omitted variables in the residuals that are causing the serial correlation in the residuals are independent of the included explanatory variables. Also, the problem of correlated residuals is often thought to be a problem only in time-series data. But if the correlation is due to omitted variables, it can also occur in cross-section data. The residuals tend to be correlated with those of the neighboring units.

In the case of time-series data we often find that the residuals are serially correlated. What we do about the correlation in the u_t series depends on what our hypothesis is about u_t. The usual assumptions about u_t are that they form

1. An *autoregressive process* (AR)
2. A *moving-average process* (MA)
3. A *mixed autoregressive moving-average process* (ARMA)

In the following discussion we will denote by e_t a series that is serially

[1] P. K. Bardhan, Size, Productivity, and Returns to Scale: An Analysis of Farm-Level Data in Indian Agriculture, *Journal of Political Economy*, November–December, 1973.

uncorrelated and has zero mean and common variance σ_e^2; i.e., $E(e_t) = 0$ and $V(e_t) = \sigma_e^2$ for all t and $\text{cov}(e_t, e_s) = 0$ for all $t \neq s$.

If $u_t = \theta_1 u_{t-1} + e_t$, then u_t is said to follow an autoregressive process of the first order and is denoted by AR(1). If $u_t = \theta_1 u_{t-1} + \theta_2 u_{t-2} + e_t$, then u_t is said to follow an autoregressive process of the second order and is denoted by AR(2). In general, an AR(k) process is $u_t = \theta_1 u_{t-1} + \theta_2 u_{t-2} + \cdots + \theta_k u_{t-k} + e_t$.

If $u_t = e_t + \alpha_1 e_{t-1}$, then u_t is said to be a moving-average process of order 1 and is denoted by MA(1). In general, a moving-average process of order r, denoted by MA(r), is $u_t = e_t + \alpha_1 e_{t-1} + \cdots + \alpha_r e_{t-r}$.

A process of the kind $u_t = \theta_1 u_{t-1} + \theta_2 u_{t-2} + e_t + \alpha_1 e_{t-1}$ is a mixed autoregressive and moving-average process and is denoted by ARMA(2,1). In general, an ARMA(k,r) process is

$$u_t = \theta_1 u_{t-1} + \cdots + \theta_k u_{t-k} + e_t + \alpha_1 e_{t-1} + \cdots + \alpha_r e_{t-r}$$

It is customary to impose some restrictions on the parameters of these processes so that their variances do not explode. For example, in the AR(1) process we assume $|\theta_1| < 1$ and in the MA(1) process we assume $\alpha_1^2 < \infty$. Similar restrictions have to be imposed for higher-order processes; e.g., for the kth-order autoregressive process we impose the condition that the roots of the equation $x^k - \theta_1 x^{k-1} - \cdots - \theta_k = 0$ all lie in the unit circle and for the rth-order moving-average process we impose the condition $\sum_{i=1}^{r} \alpha_i^2 < \infty$.

Since $E(e_t) = 0$, we can easily check that $E(u_t) = 0$. Hence $\text{var}(u_t) = E(u_t^2)$ and $\text{cov}(u_t u_s) = E(u_t u_s)$. We will assume that $E(u_t^2)$ and $E(u_t u_{t+s})$ are independent of t; i.e., variance u_t is the same for all t and covariance between u_t and u_{t+s} is a function only of the distance s between the two time periods and not of the starting period t. This assumption is known as the *stationarity* assumption. $E(u_t u_{t-s})$ is called the lagged covariance with lag s. By the stationarity assumption $E(u_t u_{t-s}) = E(u_t u_{t+s})$. From the lagged covariances we can compute the lagged correlation ρ_s defined as $E(u_t u_{t-s}) / \sqrt{E(u_t^2) E(u_{t-s}^2)}$. Denote the variance of u_t by σ^2. By the stationarity assumption $E(u_{t-s}^2)$ is also equal to σ^2. Hence $\rho_s = E(u_t u_{t-s}) / \sigma^2$. Clearly $\rho_s = \rho_{-s}$ and $\rho_0 = 1$. A graph of ρ_s against s is called the *correlogram* of the series u_t. We will illustrate how to derive the correlograms for some simple series, though this discussion is not necessary for the methods we describe later.

For the AR(1) process $u_t = \theta_1 u_{t-1} + e_t$ we note that u_t depends on e_t and u_{t-1}, u_{t-1} depends on e_{t-1} and u_{t-2}, etc. Thus u_t depends on $e_t, e_{t-1}, e_{t-2}, \ldots$, etc. Hence $E(u_{t-1} e_t) = 0$, because e_t are serially independent and u_{t-1} involves $e_{t-1}, e_{t-2}, \ldots$, etc., but not e_t. Also

$$\begin{aligned}
\sigma^2 = E(u_t^2) &= E(\theta_1 u_{t-1} + e_t)^2 \\
&= \theta_1^2 E(u_{t-1}^2) + E(e_t^2) + 2\theta_1 E(u_{t-1} e_t) \\
&= \theta_1^2 \sigma^2 + \sigma_e^2 + 0
\end{aligned}$$

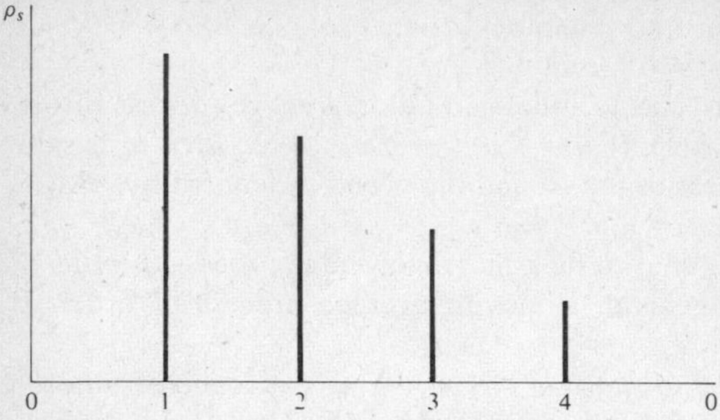

Figure 12-1 Correlogram for an autoregressive process of the first order.

Hence $\sigma^2 = \sigma_e^2/(1-\theta_1^2)$. Also $E(u_t u_{t-s}) = \theta_1 E(u_{t-1}u_{t-s}) + E(e_t u_{t-s})$. Hence $\sigma^2\rho_s = \theta_1\sigma^2\rho_{s-1} + 0$ or $\rho_s = \theta_1\rho_{s-1}$. Since $\rho_0 = 1$, we have $\rho_1 = \theta_1$, and by successive substitution we get $\rho_2 = \theta_1^2$, $\rho_3 = \theta_1^3$, etc. The correlogram for this process is shown in Fig. 12-1.

Consider the AR(2) process:

$$u_t = \theta_1 u_{t-1} + \theta_2 u_{t-2} + e_t$$

Multiplying throughout by u_{t-s} and taking expectations, we get, since $E(u_{t-s}e_t) = 0$,

$$E(u_t u_{t-s}) = \theta_1 E(u_{t-1}u_{t-s}) + \theta_2 E(u_{t-2}u_{t-s})$$

or

$$\sigma^2\rho_s = \theta_1\sigma^2\rho_{s-1} + \theta_2\sigma^2\rho_{s-2}$$

or

$$\rho_s = \theta_1\rho_{s-1} + \theta_2\rho_{s-2} \tag{12-12}$$

Put $s = 1$. Then we get $\rho_1 = \theta_1\rho_0 + \theta_2\rho_{-1}$.

But $\rho_0 = 1$ and $\rho_1 = \rho_{-1}$. Hence we get $\rho_1 = \theta_1/(1-\theta_2)$. We can easily find the other serial correlations by successive substitution into (12-12). The procedure for more general processes is similar. What we do is first derive a recurrence relation of the form (12-12). To find σ^2 in terms of σ_e^2, note that

$$\sigma^2 = E(u_t^2) = E(\theta_1 u_{t-1} + \theta_2 u_{t-2} + e_t)^2$$
$$= \theta_1^2\sigma^2 + \theta_2^2\sigma^2 + 2\theta_1\theta_2\rho_1\sigma^2 + \sigma_e^2$$

The other terms have zero expectation. Since $\rho_1 = \theta_1/(1-\theta_2)$, we can find σ^2 in terms of θ_1, θ_2, and σ_e^2. The procedure for higher-order processes is similar.

For the moving-average processes the algebra is different. What we have to do is note that $E(e_t e_s) = 0$ for all $t \neq s$ and gather the relevant terms in the products we consider. For example, for the MA(2) process,

$$u_t = e_t + \alpha_1 e_{t-1} + \alpha_2 e_{t-2}$$

we have

$$\sigma^2 = E(u_t^2) = \sigma_e^2(1 + \alpha_1^2 + \alpha_2^2)$$

$$E(u_t u_{t-1}) = E(e_t + \alpha_1 e_{t-1} + \alpha_2 e_{t-2})(e_{t-1} + \alpha_1 e_{t-2} + \alpha_2 e_{t-3})$$
$$= \sigma_e^2(\alpha_1 + \alpha_2\alpha_1)$$

Hence $$\rho_1 = \frac{\alpha_1 + \alpha_2\alpha_1}{1 + \alpha_1^2 + \alpha_2^2}$$

$$E(u_t u_{t-2}) = E(e_t + \alpha_1 e_{t-1} + \alpha_2 e_{t-2})(e_{t-2} + \alpha_1 e_{t-3} + \alpha_2 e_{t-4})$$
$$= \alpha_2\sigma_e^2$$

Hence $$\rho_2 = \frac{\alpha_2}{1 + \alpha_1^2 + \alpha_2^2}$$

It is easy to see that $E(u_t u_{t-3}), E(u_t u_{t-4}), \ldots$, etc., are all zero, because they involve nonoverlapping e's. Hence $\rho_3, \rho_4, \ldots$, etc., are all zero. In general, for an MA(r), process, all serial correlations of order $> r$ are zero—unlike the case of the AR process where they progressively decay but are not exactly equal to zero.

The purpose in deriving all these serial correlations is that if we want to apply GLS methods we need them all because the covariance matrix of the residuals is

$$\Lambda = \sigma^2 \begin{bmatrix} 1 & \rho_1 & \rho_2 & \cdots & \rho_{T-1} \\ \rho_1 & 1 & \rho_1 & \cdots & \rho_{T-2} \\ & \cdots & & & \vdots \\ \rho_{T-1} & \rho_{T-2} & \rho_{T-3} & \cdots & 1 \end{bmatrix}$$

Here we will not be concerned with the GLS solutions in general models. Since most of the discussion in the literature concerns the case when u_t follows the AR(1) process, we will first discuss this case.

12-6 ESTIMATION PROCEDURES WHEN RESIDUALS ARE AR(1)

Consider the model

$$y_t = \alpha + \beta x_t + u_t \tag{12-13}$$

$$u_t = \rho u_{t-1} + e_t \tag{12-14}$$

Then, by lagging (12-13) by one time period and multiplying by ρ, we get

$$\rho y_{t-1} = \alpha\rho + \beta\rho x_{t-1} + \rho u_{t-1} \tag{12-15}$$

Subtracting (12-15) from (12-13) and using (12-14), we get

$$y_t - \rho y_{t-1} = \alpha(1-\rho) + \beta(x_t - \rho x_{t-1}) + e_t \tag{12-16}$$

Since e_t are serially independent with a constant variance σ_e^2, we can estimate the parameters in this equation by an OLS procedure. Equation (12-16) is often known as a *quasi-first-difference* transformation of Eq. (12-13). What we do is transform the variables y_t and x_t to

$$\begin{aligned} y_t^* &= y_t - \rho y_{t-1} \\ x_t^* &= x_t - \rho x_{t-1} \qquad t = 2,3,\ldots,T \end{aligned} \tag{12-17}$$

and run a regression of y^* on x^*, with or without a constant term depending on whether the original equation has a constant term or not. In this method we use only $(T-1)$ observations because we lose one observation in the operation of taking differences. The procedure is not exactly the same as the GLS procedure in this model. The GLS procedure amounts to using

$$\begin{aligned} y_1^* &= \sqrt{1-\rho^2}\; y_1 \\ x_1^* &= \sqrt{1-\rho^2}\; x_1 \end{aligned} \tag{12-18}$$

and y_t^* and x_t^* for $t = 2,3,\ldots,T$ as defined in (12-17). Here we estimate the regression equation using the T observations on y_t^* and x_t^*. This procedure is known as the Prais-Winsten procedure.

In actual practice ρ is not known. So what is done is that we get a preliminary estimate of ρ and use it in the above procedures. There are two procedures that have been commonly used to find preliminary estimates of ρ. The first is known as the Cochrane-Orcutt[1] procedure and the second is known as the Durbin[2] procedure. The procedures differ only in the way $\hat{\rho}$, the estimate of ρ, is obtained. Once this is obtained, we transform the variables to y^* and x^* as defined in (12-17) and estimate a regression of y^* on x^*. The only thing to note is that the slope coefficient in this equation is β but the intercept is $\alpha(1-\rho)$. Thus, after estimating the regression of y^* on x^*, we have to adjust the constant term appropriately to get estimates of the parameters of the original equation (12-13).

In the Cochrane-Orcutt procedure, we estimate Eq. (12-16) by OLS, get the estimated residuals $\hat{u}_t$, and estimate ρ by $\hat{\rho} = \sum \hat{u}_t \hat{u}_{t-1} / \sum \hat{u}_t^2$. In the Durbin procedure, we estimate a regression equation of y_t on y_{t-1}, x_t, and x_{t-1} and take the coefficient of y_{t-1} as the estimate of ρ. The idea behind this procedure is that Eq. (12-16) can be written as

$$y_t = \alpha(1-\rho) + \rho y_{t-1} + \beta x_t - \beta\rho x_{t-1} + e_t$$

If there are many explanatory variables in the equation, Durbin's method involves a regression in too many variables (twice the number of explanatory variables plus y_{t-1}), and hence it is better to use the Cochrane-Orcutt procedure.

[1] D. Cochrane and G. H. Orcutt, Application of Least Squares Regressions to Relationships Containing Autocorrelated Error Terms, *Journal of the American Statistical Association*, 1949, pp. 32–61.

[2] J. Durbin, Estimation of Parameters in Time Series Regression Models, *Journal of the Royal Statistical Society*, B Series, 1960, pp. 139–153.

In actual practice, particularly if the number of observations is not large, it is better to use all the T observations as in the Prais-Winsten method, i.e., use y_1^* and x_1^* too, where y_1^* and x_1^* are as defined in (12-18). No extra computational effort is involved in this.

The procedures described till now are called *two-step procedures*. The first step involves getting an estimate of ρ. The second step involves getting estimates of the regression parameters. The procedures can be iterated. With the Cochran-Orcutt procedure, after we estimate a regression of y_t^* on x_t^*, we can recompute the residuals, get a new estimate of ρ, retransform the variables, and recompute the estimates. We can proceed with this iterative procedure till successive values of ρ are approximately the same.

In contrast to this, there are some *search procedures*, one of which is the one suggested by Hildreth and Lu.[1] The procedure they suggest is the following: Calculate y_t^* and x_t^* in (12-16) for different values of ρ at intervals of .1 in the range $-1 \leqslant \rho \leqslant 1$. Estimate the regression of y_t^* on x_t^* and calculate the residual sum of squares RSS in each case. Choose that value of ρ for which RSS is minimum. Again repeat this procedure for smaller intervals of ρ around this value. For instance, if the value of ρ for which RSS is minimum is -0.4, then repeat this search procedure for values of ρ at intervals of .01 in the range $-0.5 < \rho < -0.3$.

This procedure is not the same as the maximum-likelihood procedure for this model. Assuming the residuals to be normally distributed, we can write the log-likelihood function as (derivation is omitted)

$$\log L = \text{const.} - \frac{T}{2} \log \sigma_e^2 + \frac{1}{2} \log (1 - \rho^2) - \frac{Q}{2\sigma_e^2}$$

where $Q = \sum[y_t - \rho y_{t-1} - \alpha(1-\rho) - \beta(x_t - \rho x_{t-1})]^2$. Thus minimizing Q is not the same as maximizing $\log L$. There is the extra term $\frac{1}{2}\log(1-\rho^2)$. We can use the search procedure described above to get the ML estimates. The only difference is that after we compute the residual sum of squares RSS (ρ) for each ρ, we choose that value of ρ for which $(T/2) \log \text{RSS}(\rho) - \frac{1}{2}\log(1-\rho^2)$ is minimum.

If the number of observations is large, the latter term will be small compared with the former and hence the ML procedure and the search procedure described earlier will be the same.

We have described here four procedures for estimating the parameters in a regression model with residuals which are first-order autoregressive. These are the Cochrane-Orcutt procedure, the Durbin procedure, the Hildreth-Lu procedure, and the ML procedure. We will illustrate these with an example.

Consider the data in Table 10-4. The values of ρ obtained by the above four procedures for the 10 firms are given in Table 12-5. It can be easily seen that the values of ρ are widely different. In particular, the estimates produced by the

[1] Clifford Hildreth and John Y. Lu, "Demand Relations with Autocorrelated Disturbances," Michigan State University AES Technical Bulletin 276, November, 1960.

Durbin procedure are very different from those produced by the Hildreth and Lu or the ML procedure. In fact, in one case, the estimate of ρ is > 1. It has been found (in some experimental investigations) that the Hildreth-Lu (or the ML) procedure often performs better than the Durbin procedure in estimating the true autocorrelation coefficient.

After we estimate ρ, we transform the data to $(Y_t - \hat{\rho}Y_{t-1})$, $(x_t - \hat{\rho}x_{t-1})$, etc., and reestimate the regression equation. However, it should be noted that since the transformed equation is

$$Y_t - \hat{\rho}Y_{t-1} = \alpha(1 - \hat{\rho}) + \beta(x_t - \hat{\rho}x_{t-1}) + e_t$$

we have to adjust the constant term, though the slope coefficients do not need any adjustment. The estimated constant term from the transformed data should be divided by $(1 - \hat{\rho})$.

In Table 12-6 we present estimates of the regression parameters from the transformed equation. Since the Hildreth-Lu and the ML method produce very close results, we have presented only the latter. Also, since the estimates of ρ obtained by the Durbin method were widely different from those obtained by the ML method, this is the other method chosen for the comparison. The constant term reported is the adjusted one, with the adjustment described earlier. For the sake of brevity the standard errors are not reported. In any case, the standard errors obtained directly from the second step of the Durbin (or Cochrane-Orcutt) procedure or each step of the search procedure for the ML (or Hildreth-Lu) method are not the right ones to report because they do not take into account the fact that ρ has been estimated. One should note that if one is reporting the standard errors without taking into account the fact that ρ is estimated, these standard errors are lower than the correct standard errors. The results in Table 12-6 in conjunction with those in Table 12-5 show that in some cases even substantial differences in $\hat{\rho}$ produced only slight changes in the estimated regression coefficients.

Table 12-5 Estimates of first-order autocorrelation coefficient by different methods

	Method			
Firm	Cochrane-Orcutt	Durbin	Hildreth-Lu	ML
GM	.458	.816	.67	.64
U.S. Steel	.481	.874	.74	.69
GE	.461	1.061	.50	.47
Chrysler	−.020	−.346	−.05	−.04
Atlantic Richfield	−.236	−.737	−.22	−.21
IBM	.114	.624	.18	.17
Union Oil	.098	.125	.12	.11
Westinghouse	.241	.297	.30	.28
Goodyear	.246	.706	.39	.36
Diamond Match	.402	.385	.65	.57
Macro	.323	.349	.27	.26

Table 12-6 Comparison of regression estimates

Firm	Procedure	Coefficient of Constant	F_{-1}	C_{-1}
GM	Durbin	– 88.66	.09	.46
	ML	– 79.83	.09	.44
U.S. Steel	Durbin	– 151.50	.19	–.15
	ML	22.09	.20	.18
G.E.	Durbin	– 166.14	.02	–.39
	ML	– 16.98	.03	.14
Chrysler	Durbin	– 14.81	.09	.32
	ML	– 12.54	.09	.32
Atlantic Richfield	Durbin	26.88	.14	.004
	ML	27.62	.14	.001
IBM	Durbin	– 5.05	.07	.30
	ML	– 7.88	.11	.15
Union Oil	Durbin	– 7.39	.09	.13
	ML	– 7.47	.09	.13
Westinghouse	Durbin	.13	.05	.07
	ML	–.06	.05	.08
Goodyear	Durbin	22.59	.08	–.02
	ML	– 1.80	.07	.06
Diamond Match	Durbin	.48	.006	.37
	ML	1.02	.004	.30
Macro	Durbin	– 432.42	.10	.27
	ML	– 443.35	.11	.27
	Cochrane-Orcutt	–435.60	.11	.27

The above example illustrates how to use all these procedures. We will now discuss the following questions:

1. What do we gain by using all these procedures?
2. When should we use these procedures?

First, to the question of what do we gain, we have to know the consequences of using the OLS method in this model. As with heteroscedasticity, the result of autocorrelation in the residuals is that the OLS estimators are unbiased, but they are less efficient than the GLS estimates that take account of the autocorrelation. Also, the variances of the estimators are themselves biased. Thus the things we gain are higher efficiency and correct estimated variances. As to what the magnitude of the loss in efficiency and the magnitude of the bias in the estimated variances are if we use the OLS method, we can answer this question only by making special assumptions about the behavior of the residuals and by assuming the sample size to be large; i.e., our results are only asymptotic. It is hoped that similar results also hold good in samples of the size we often encounter.

To illustrate the problem, consider the simple regression model

$$y_\tau = \beta x_\tau + u_\tau$$

Let $V(u_\tau) = \sigma^2$ and $\text{cov}(u_\tau, u_{\tau-j}) = \rho_j\sigma^2$. If u_τ are first-order autoregressive, i.e., $u_\tau = \rho u_{\tau-1} + e_\tau$, then $\rho_j = \rho^j$. We will assume that the x's also follow a stochastic process which is independent of u_τ. We will also assume that the sample moments converge to some finite values. This excludes the cases of x series with a trend. Let $V(x_\tau) = \sigma_x^2$ and $\text{cov}(x_\tau, x_{\tau-j}) = r_j\sigma_x^2$. Under these assumptions, if $\hat{\beta}$ is the ordinary-least-squares estimator of β, then it has been shown[1] that the asymptotic variance of $\hat{\beta}$ is given by

$$V(\hat{\beta}) = \frac{\sigma^2}{T\sigma_x^2}\left(1 + 2\sum_{i=1}^{\infty} r_i\rho_i\right)$$

If both u_τ and x_t are first-order autoregressive so that $r_i = r^i$ and $\rho_i = \rho^i$, we have

$$V(\hat{\beta}) = \frac{\sigma^2}{T\sigma_x^2}\left(1 + \frac{2r\rho}{1 - r\rho}\right)$$

$$= \frac{\sigma^2}{T\sigma_x^2}\,\frac{1 + r\rho}{1 - r\rho}$$

On the other hand, if we ignore ρ, we would assume that this variance is $\sigma^2/T\sigma_x^2$. This will underestimate the true variance if r and ρ are of the same sign and overestimate the true variance if r and ρ are of opposite sign. If $r = \rho = .8$, the underestimation is of the order of close to 77 percent.

One further error is also involved. This is that we use $\hat{u}'\hat{u}/(T-1)$ as an estimate of σ^2. If $\rho = 0$, this is an unbiased estimator of σ^2. However, if ρ is not equal to zero, we have approximately[2] (under the assumption we are making)

$$E(\hat{u}'\hat{u}) = \sigma^2\left(T - \frac{1 + r\rho}{1 - r\rho}\right)$$

Again, if $\rho = r = .8$ and $T = 20$, we have

$$E\left(\frac{\hat{u}'\hat{u}}{T-1}\right) = \frac{15.45}{19}\sigma^2 \approx .81\sigma^2$$

Thus there is a further underestimation of 19 percent. Both these effects together result in an underestimation of the standard errors of more than 80 percent.

By contrast, the asymptotic variance of the maximum-likelihood estimator $\tilde{\beta}$ when both x and u are first-order autoregressive is [3]

$$V(\tilde{\beta}) = \frac{\sigma^2}{T\sigma_x^2}\,\frac{1 - \rho^2}{1 + \rho^2 - 2r\rho}$$

[1] H. Wold, "On Least Squares Regression with Autocorrelated Variables and Residuals," *Bulletin of the International Statistical Institute*, 1950, part 2.

[2] See J. Johnston, "Econometric Methods," 2d ed., pp. 247–249, McGraw-Hill Book Company, New York, 1972.

[3] See E. Manlinvaud, "Statistical Methods of Econometrics," 2d ed., p. 526, Rand McNally Company, Chicago, 1972.

Thus the efficiency of the OLS estimator is

$$\frac{V(\tilde{\beta})}{V(\hat{\beta})} = \frac{1 - r\rho}{1 + r\rho} \frac{1 - \rho^2}{1 + \rho^2 - 2r\rho}$$

One can compute this for different values of r and ρ. For $r = \rho = .8$ this efficiency is 0.21.

Thus the consequences of autocorrelated errors are:

1. The least-squares estimators are unbiased but are not efficient. Sometimes they are considerably less efficient than the procedures that take account of the autocorrelation.
2. The sampling variances are biased and sometimes likely to be seriously understated. Thus R^2 as well as t and F statistics tend to be exaggerated.

The solution to these problems is to use the maximum-likelihood procedure or some other procedure mentioned earlier that takes account of the autocorrelation. However, there are three important points to note:

1. If ρ is known, it is true that one can get estimators better than OLS that take account of autocorrelation. However, in practice ρ is not known and has to be estimated. In small samples it is not necessarily true that one gains (in terms of mean-square error for $\hat{\beta}$) by estimating ρ. This problem has been investigated by Rao and Griliches,[1] who suggest the rule of thumb (for samples of size 20) that one can use the methods that take account of autocorrelation if $|\hat{\rho}| \geqslant .3$, where $\hat{\rho}$ is the estimated first-order serial correlation from an OLS regression.[2] In samples of larger sizes it would be worthwhile using these methods for $\hat{\rho}$ smaller than .3.
2. All the above discussion assumes that the true residuals are first-order autoregressive. If they have a more complicated structure (e.g., second-order autoregressive), it might be thought that it would still be better to proceed on the assumption that the residuals are first-order autoregressive rather than ignore the problem completely and use the OLS method. Engle[3] shows that this is not necessarily true; i.e., sometimes one can be worse off making the assumption of first-order autocorrelation than ignoring the problem completely.
3. In regressions with quarterly (or monthly) data, one might find that the residuals exhibit fourth- (or twelfth-) order autocorrelation because of not making adequate allowance for seasonal effects. In such cases if one looks for

[1] P. Rao and Z. Griliches, Some Small Sample Properties of Several Two-Stage Regression Methods in the Context of Autocorrelated Errors, *Journal of the American Statistical Association*, March, 1969.

[2] Of course, it is not sufficient to argue in favor of OLS on the basis of mean-square errors of the estimators alone. What is also relevant is how seriously the sampling variances are biased.

[3] Robert F. Engle, Specification of the Disturbance for Efficient Estimation, *Econometrica*, 1973.

only first-order autocorrelation, one might not find any. This does not mean that autocorrelation is not a problem.[1]

All our discussion has been for the simple regression case. For the multiple-regression case similar results hold good.[2]

12-7 TESTS FOR SERIAL CORRELATION

There is a vast amount of literature on tests for serial correlation. The most commonly used test is the Durbin-Watson test. It is defined as

$$d = \frac{\sum_{\tau=2}^{N} (\hat{u}_\tau - \hat{u}_{\tau-1})^2}{\sum_{\tau=1}^{N} \hat{u}_\tau^2}$$

where $\hat{u}_\tau$ is the estimated residual from the least-square regression. In matrix notation d can be written as

$$d = \frac{\hat{\mathbf{u}}'\mathbf{A}\hat{\mathbf{u}}}{\hat{\mathbf{u}}'\hat{\mathbf{u}}} = \frac{\mathbf{u}'\mathbf{MAMu}}{\mathbf{u}'\mathbf{Mu}}$$

where

$$\mathbf{M} = \mathbf{I} - \mathbf{X}(\mathbf{X}'\mathbf{X})^{-1}\mathbf{X}'$$

$$\mathbf{u} = \text{true disturbance}$$

$$\mathbf{A} = \begin{bmatrix} 1 & -1 & 0 & 0 & 0 & & & 0 \\ -1 & 2 & -1 & 0 & 0 & & & 0 \\ 0 & -1 & 2 & -1 & 0 & & & 0 \\ & & & & & & & \\ 0 & 0 & & & & -1 & 2 & -1 \\ 0 & 0 & & & & 0 & -1 & 1 \end{bmatrix}$$

The sampling distribution of d involves X, and hence Durbin and Watson[3] derived upper (d_u) limits and lower (d_L) limits for the significance levels of d. The tables are to test the hypothesis of zero autocorrelation against the hypothesis of first-order autocorrelation.

If $d < d_L$, we reject the hypothesis of no autocorrelation.
If $d > d_u$, we do not reject the null hypothesis.
If $d_L < d < d_u$, the test is inconclusive.

[1] See K. F. Wallis, Testing for Fourth Order Autocorrelation in Quarterly Regression Equations, *Econometrica*, July, 1972.

[2] See G. S. Watson, Serial Correlation in Regression Analysis, I, *Biometrika*, 1955, pp. 327–341, for a discussion of the consequences for using the wrong covariance matrix of residuals in multiple-regression equations.

[3] J. Durbin and G. S. Watson, Testing for Serial Correlation in Least Squares Regression, *Biometrika*, 1950, pp. 409–428; 1951, pp. 159–178.

If $d > 2$, we wish to test the hypothesis $\rho = 0$ against $\rho < 0$. For this purpose we consider $4 - d$ and refer to the Durbin-Watson tables as if we are testing against positive autocorrelation.

The Durbin-Watson (DW) statistic d is approximately equal to $2(1 - \rho)$, so that it ranges from 0 to 4. It is in the range 0 to 2 for $\rho > 0$ and 2 to 4 for $\rho < 0$. Actually, its mean is given approximately by $E(d) = 2 + [2(r - 1)/(n - r)]$, where r is the number of regression parameters and n is the sample size. Thus even for zero serial correlation the statistic is biased upward from 2. If $r = 5$ and $n = 15$, the bias is as large as 0.8.

Most of the refinements suggested in the literature are designed to tackle the problem of the inconclusive region in the DW test. The suggestions that have been made are:

1. Theil-Nagar.[1] They use the assumption that economic time series are slowly changing to derive an approximation which is very close to the upper bound of the Durbin-Watson test.
2. Hannan-Terrell.[2] They show that the upper bound of the DW statistic is a good approximation to its distribution when the regressors are slowly changing. They argue that economic time series are slowly changing and hence one can use d_u as the correct significance point.
3. Henshaw.[3] He derives the first four moments of d and then fits a beta distribution. He obtains the critical values from the "Tables of the Incomplete Beta Distribution." The Henshaw approximation has been found to give very accurate results, but it is computationally burdensome and hence is not used much in economic work.
4. Durbin-Watson's $a + bd_u$ approximation. In their recent paper,[4] Durbin and Watson suggest approximating the distribution of d by that of $a + bd_u$. They suggest determining a and b by equating the mean and variance for the two statistics so that

$$E(d) = a + b\,E(d_u)$$
$$V(d) = b^2 V(d_u)$$

This gives

$$a = E(d) - \sqrt{\frac{V(d)}{V(d_u)}}\;E(d_u)$$

[1] H. Theil and A. L. Nagar, Testing the Independence of Regression Disturbances, *Journal of the American Statistical Association*, 1961, pp. 793–806.

[2] E. J. Hannan and R. D. Terrell, Testing for Serial Correlation After Least Squares Regression, *Econometrica*, 1968, pp. 133–150.

[3] R. C. Henshaw, Testing Single Equation Least Squares Regression Models for Autocorrelated Disturbances, *Econometrica*, 1966, pp. 646–660.

[4] J. Durbin and G. S. Watson, Testing for Serial Correlation in Least Square Regression, III, *Biometrika*, 1971, pp. 1–19.

and
$$b = \sqrt{\frac{V(d)}{V(d_u)}}$$

We reject the hypothesis of no serial correlation if

$$d < a + bd_u^0$$

or equivalently

$$d < E(d) + \gamma_0 \sqrt{V(d)}$$

where $\gamma_0 = [d_u^0 - E(d_u)]/\sqrt{V(d_u)}$ and d_u^0 is the critical value for the upper bound tabulated for the DW statistic. This test is also complicated but not as much as that of Henshaw. We have to compute $E(d)$ and $V(d)$ for each problem separately. In matrix notation they are given by

$$E(d) = \frac{\text{trace}\,(\mathbf{MA})}{n-r}$$

$$V(d) = \frac{2\,\text{trace}\,(\mathbf{MA})^2 - (n-r)[E(d)]^2}{(n-r)(n-r+2)}$$

Durbin and Watson argue that this approximation works very well, whereas the Hannan-Terrell and Theil-Nagar approximations can sometimes do very poorly. They do not recommend the latter two methods in empirical work.

5. Blattberg.[1] He suggests using $[d - E(d)]/\sqrt{V(d)}$ as a $N(0,1)$ variate. One major drawback with the DW test is (apart from the inconclusive region) that the tables are available only for selected significance levels (5, 2.5, and 1 percent). As Lindley[2] points out, for large samples lower significance levels are required and for small samples higher significance levels may be required. If we use the normal approximation, we can readily use any significance levels that we want. Blattberg finds that his normal approximation performs very well and does considerably better than the Hannan-Terrell (d_u) and the Theil-Nagar approximations, which do not use the information on the explanatory variables X.

All these refinements to the DW test are designed to produce the correct significance levels for the test. However, there is the more important question of the power of the DW test. Chipman[3] argues that in deriving their test statistic from a result by Anderson,[4] Durbin and Watson made some simplifying

[1] R. C. Blattberg, "Testing for Serial Correlation in Least Squares Regression Using a Normal Approximation to the Distribution of the Durbin-Watson Statistic," University of Chicago, August, 1972.

[2] D. V. Lindley, A Statistical Paradox, *Biometrika*, 1957, pp. 187–192.

[3] John S. Chipman, "The Problem of Testing for Serial Correlation in Regression Analysis: The Story of a Dilemma," University of Minnesota, June 1965.

[4] T. W. Anderson, On the Theory of Testing Serial Correlation, *Skandinavisk Aktuarietidskrift*, 1968, pp. 88–116.

assumptions but under these assumptions the ordinary-least-squares (OLS) estimators are expected to have high efficiency and thus there is no reason to reject the OLS method. On the other hand, in those circumstances when the use of OLS results in a considerable loss of efficiency, the DW test is expected to have low power. Thus the DW test is a good test in precisely those situations when it is not needed and it is not a very powerful test in precisely those situations when it is badly needed.

There is some evidence on the power of the DW test. Koerts and Abrahamse[1] made some calculations in connection with a comparison of the DW test and Theil's BLUS procedure. Blattberg[2] also does some calculations with seven different data sets— three artificially generated and four from real-life data. The powers for $\rho = .9$ were .84, .94, .93, .85, .59, .68, and .85. The fifth data set for which the DW test has such low power is the data set considered by Henshaw. Part of the reason could be the small sample size and the large number of explanatory variables ($n = 17$, $r = 5$).

In addition to the Durbin-Watson test, some other tests are commonly used. One such test is the one based on the von Neumann ratio,[3] which is the ratio of mean-square successive difference to the variance. It is given by

$$\frac{\delta^2}{s^2} = \frac{\sum_{\tau=2}^{n} (x_\tau - x_{\tau-1})^2/(n-1)}{\sum_{\tau=1}^{n} (x_\tau - \bar{x})/n}$$

If x_τ are independently distributed, then for large n, δ^2/s^2 can be taken as normally distributed with mean and variance given by

$$E\left(\frac{\delta^2}{s^2}\right) = \frac{2n}{n-1}$$

$$V\left(\frac{\delta^2}{s^2}\right) = \frac{4n^2(n-2)}{(n+1)(n-1)^3}$$

For finite samples one can use the tables prepared by Hart.[4] However, the basic assumption in the von Neumann ratio is that x_τ are independently distributed. The least-squares residuals $\hat{u}_\tau$ are not independently distributed even if the true residuals u_τ are. Thus it is inappropriate to use the von Neumann ratio in regression models, though this fact is not often recognized. The von Neumann

[1] J. Koerts and A. P. J. Abrahamse, On the Power of the BLUS Procedure, *Journal of the American Statistical Association*, 1968, pp. 1227–1236.

[2] R. C. Blattberg, "Evaluation of the Power of the Durbin-Watson Statistic for Non-first Order Serial Correlation Alternatives," University of Chicago, June, 1972.

[3] J. von Neumann, Distribution of the Ratio of the Mean Square Successive Difference to the Variance, *Annals of Mathematical Statistics*, 1941, pp. 367–395.

[4] B. I. Hart, Tabulation of the Probabilities of the Ratio of the Mean Square Difference to the Variance and Significance Levels for the Ratio of the Mean Square Difference to the Variance, *Annals of Mathematical Statistics*, 1962, pp. 207–214.

ratio and the DW statistic are, of course, intimately related. Specifically $d = (\delta^2/s^2)[(n-1)/n]$. Thus there is no point in reporting both the statistics, as is sometimes done in some empirical work.

Noting that the least-squares residuals are not independent, Theil[1] suggests constructing new residuals [he calls them BLUS (best linear unbiased scalar) residuals] which are independent and then suggests using the von Neumann ratio based on these transformed residuals. Since the least-squares residuals $\hat{u}_\tau$ are subject to r linear restrictions (where r is the number of regression parameters estimated) we have $(n-r)$ BLUS residuals. However, there is some arbitrariness in the way these $(n-r)$ residuals can be constructed from the n values of $\hat{u}_\tau$. Theil suggests some guidelines for solving this problem.

Durbin has extended the work on tests for serial correlation in several directions.

1. In a paper published in 1957, he showed that the DW test, with suitable modifications, can be used in simultaneous-equation problems.[2]
2. The DW test is derived under the assumption that the regressors are fixed. Hence it is not applicable in cases where some of the regressors are lagged dependent variables. To tackle this problem, Durbin suggests a new test (asymptotic) called the h test.[3] We will discuss this in the chapter on distributed-lag models.
3. To solve the problem of inconclusiveness of the DW test, Durbin suggests an alternative exact test.[4] However, since the approximations suggested also solve this problem, we will not consider it in detail here. Abrahamse and Louter[5] find that this test is less powerful than the BLUS procedure which was found earlier by Abrahamse and Koerts to be less powerful than the Durbin-Watson test. They also suggest a modification of the BLUS test that is uniquely defined and thus does not have the same arbitrariness as the BLUS test. They find that this modified test, which has higher power than the BLUS test, is almost as powerful as the Durbin-Watson test.
4. Finally, the DW test is applicable only if the alternative hypothesis is that of first-order autocorrelation. In practice the alternative hypothesis we have in mind is vague. In such cases Durbin suggests using the cumulated periodogram.[6] The method is as follows: Let the sample observations be y_1,

[1] Theil, "Principles of Econometrics," Chap. 5, John Wiley & Sons, Inc., New York, 1971.

[2] J. Durbin, Testing for Serial Correlation in Systems of Simultaneous Regression Equations, *Biometrika*, December 1957.

[3] J. Durbin, Testing for Serial Correlation in Least-Squares Regression When Some of the Regressors Are Lagged Dependent Variables, *Econometrica*, May, 1970.

[4] J. Durbin, An Alternative to the Bounds Test for Testing for Serial Correlation in Least Squares Regression, *Econometrica*, May, 1970.

[5] A. P. J. Abrahamse and A. S. Louter, On a New Test for Autocorrelation in Least Squares Regression, *Biometrika*, 1971, pp. 53–60.

[6] J. Durbin, Testing for Serial Correlation in Regression Analysis Based on the Periodogram of Least Squares Residuals, *Biometrika*, 1969, pp. 1–15.

$y_2, \ldots, y_T$. Define

$$a_j = \sqrt{\frac{2}{T}} \sum_{t=1}^{T} y_t \cos \frac{2\pi jt}{T}$$

$$b_j = \sqrt{\frac{2}{T}} \sum_{t=1}^{T} y_t \sin \frac{2\pi jt}{T}$$

$$\rho_j = a_j^2 + b_j^2 \qquad j = 1, 2, \ldots, m$$

where m is the largest integer in $T/2$. The graph of ρ_j against j is called the *periodogram* of y_t. The periodogram has a wildly fluctuating appearance, and hence Durbin suggests looking at the *cumulated periodogram* s_j, defined as

$$s_j = \sum_{r=1}^{j} \rho_r \Big/ \sum_{r=1}^{m} \rho_r \qquad j = 1, 2, \ldots, m$$

Durbin shows that $E(s_j) = j/m$ and considers the maximum positive distance of s_j from the mean and the maximum negative distance from the mean. Define

$$C^+ = \max_j \left(s_j - \frac{j}{m} \right)$$

$$C^- = \max_j \left(\frac{j}{m} - s_j \right)$$

$$C = \max\,(C^+, C^-)$$

Roughly speaking, large values of C^+ indicate positive serial correlations and large values of C^- indicate negative serial correlation. The statistic C is used to test both-sided alternatives. To test the significance of C^+, C^-, or C, we refer to the tables of the Kolmogorov-Smirnov statistic.[1] Another test based on the cumulated periodogram is to compute

$$\bar{s} = \frac{1}{m-1} \sum_{j=1}^{m-1} s_j$$

Again roughly speaking, large values of $\bar{s}$ indicate positive serial correlation and small values of $\bar{s}$ indicate negative serial correlation. Durbin argues that this test statistic has several advantages. First its exact significance points are tabulated by Stephens in *Biometrika*, 1966. Second it converges rapidly to normality with mean $\frac{1}{2}(m-1)$ and variance $1/12(m-1)$, so that the standard normal tables can be used even for moderate-sized samples.

These tests based on cumulated periodogram are not difficult to compute or use. Fast computer routines exist to compute the periodogram. However, there is

[1] These tables can be found in D. B. Owen, "Handbook of Statistical Tables," Addison-Wesley Publishing Company, Inc., Reading, Mass., 1962. Actually, Durbin suggests some slight modifications of C^+, C^-, and C, but we need not go into the details here.

one important point to note: With the alternative of first-order autocorrelation, we know what to do if the test rejects the null hypothesis. When the alternative is very general, as with this test, it is not clear exactly what one is supposed to do if the null hypothesis of no serial correlation is rejected. In this case we have to use generalized least-squares techniques based on very general assumptions about the residuals. These methods involve frequency-domain techniques which we cannot go into here.

Unlike the case considered by Durbin, if the alternative specifies the autocorrelation of a particular order (though not necessarily of the first order), we can use the extensions of the DW test given by Wallis (1972).[1] Wallis considers the specification[2]

$$u_\tau = \rho_4 u_{\tau-4} + e_\tau$$

and argues that this is a more plausible assumption than that of first-order autoregressive residuals in the case of regression models with quarterly data because serial correlation is most likely to be caused by omitted seasonal variables. The test statistic he considers is analogous to the DW statistic. It is defined as

$$d_4 = \sum_{\tau=5}^{n} (\hat{u}_\tau - \hat{u}_{\tau-4}) / \sum_{\tau=1}^{n} \hat{u}_\tau^2$$

Wallis provides tables like the DW tables (d_L and d_u at the 5 percent level of significance) to test the significance of d_4.

In Chap. 7 we discussed the desirability of using some simple nonparametric tests based on signs of the residuals. In a paper by Griliches et al.,[3] it was found that the Durbin-Watson test did not show any significant serial correlation but a χ^2 test based on a 2×2 contingency table of positive and negative signs at time t and time $(t-1)$ showed a significant correlation among residuals. The discrepancy was due to a single aberrant observation. Habibagahi and Pratschke[4] argue that this simple χ^2 test used by Griliches et al. is not very powerful but that a sign-change test (which is a runs test) suggested by Geary is better. They compare the Geary test with the Durbin-Watson test and find it only a little less powerful than the latter. However, what Griliches et al. suggest is to use the nonparametric tests in conjunction with the Durbin-Watson test, not as a substitute.

The literature on tests for serial correlation is voluminous (and growing), and one wonders whether the testing aspect has not been overdone. Often one finds the DW statistic reported (because the computer program prints it out along with R^2's, t ratios, etc.), but even if there is significant serial correlation

[1] See Wallis, *op.cit.*

[2] As Wallis points out, this should be distinguished from a general fourth-order autoregressive process

$$u_\tau = \sigma_1 u_{\tau-1} + \sigma_2 u_{\tau-2} + \sigma_3 u_{\tau-3} + \sigma_4 u_{\tau-4} + e_\tau$$

for which the test derived is not applicable.

[3] Griliches et al., *op. cit.*, *Econometrica*, July, 1962.

[4] H. Habibagahi and J. L. Pratschke, A Comparison of the Power of the von Neumann Ratio, Durbin-Watson and Geary Tests, *The Review of Economics and Statistics*, May, 1972, pp. 179–185.

nothing is done about it. The test for serial correlation is only a prelude to something further, and greater emphasis should be not on testing per se but on when one should proceed and estimate the regression parameters by generalized-least-squares or maximum-likelihood methods.[1]

12-8 CAUSES FOR SERIAL CORRELATION

It is often asserted that the source of serial correlation in the disturbances is that some variables that should have been included in the equation are omitted and that these omitted variables are themselves autocorrelated.[2] However, if this is ths argument for serial correlation, and it is an appealing one, then one should be careful in suggesting the methods we have discussed till now.

Suppose the true regression is

$$y_t = \beta_0 + \beta_1 x_t + \beta_2 x_t^2 + u_t \tag{12-19}$$

and instead we estimate

$$y_t = \beta_0 + \beta_1 x_t + V_t \tag{12-20}$$

Then since $V_t = \beta_2 x_t^2 + u_t$, if x_t is autocorrelated, this will produce autocorrelation in V_t. However, in Eq. (12-20) V_t is no longer independent of the included variable x_t. Thus, not only are the OLS estimators of β_0 and β_1 from (12-20) inefficient, they are inconsistent as well.

As yet another example, suppose the true relation is

$$y_t = \beta_1 x_t + \beta_2 z_t + u_t \tag{12-21}$$

and we estimate

$$y_t = \beta_1 x_t + w_t \tag{12-22}$$

Suppose again that z_t is autocorrelated. Then the residuals w_t will be autocorrelated as well. However, if z_t and x_t are independent, the methods we have discussed earlier are applicable. Thus to justify the models of autocorrelation we have discussed, we have to argue that the autocorrelated omitted variables that are producing the autocorrelation in the residuals are uncorrelated with the included explanatory variables. Further, if there are any time trends in these omitted variables, they will produce not only autocorrelated errors but also heteroscedastic errors—the error variance itself exhibiting a corresponding trend. Models of this sort can be analyzed more fruitfully with the "adaptive regression model" discussed later in the chapter on time-varying parameter models. In any case, when serial correlation in the residuals is due to omitted variables that are themselves autocorrelated, the question of whether or not the usual procedures of "efficient" estimation often suggested in textbooks are better than ordinary least squares is a point that needs more careful investigation.

[1] See Rao and Griliches, *op. cit.*, for one of the few discussions on this point, though in a limited context.

[2] See J. Johnston, "Econometric Methods," 2d ed., p. 244, McGraw-Hill Book Company, New York, 1972, as an example.

CHAPTER

THIRTEEN

ERRORS IN VARIABLES AND NONNORMAL ERRORS

13-1 ERRORS IN VARIABLES

So far we have assumed that the variables in our regression equation are all measured without error. This assumption is rarely justified. Most economic data contain observational errors. Further, the variables we actually measure are imperfect measurements of what we really want to measure. Here we will discuss the methods that have been suggested to analyze such problems. We will first discuss the classical errors-in-variables models where the errors are assumed to be random. The errors occurring in economic data are systematic rather than random. But we will discuss this extension later.

13-2 THE CLASSICAL MODELS

Suppose that the true model is

$$y = \beta x + e \tag{13-1}$$

Instead of y and x, we measure $Y = y + v$ and $X = x + u$, where u and v are measurement errors. x and y are called the systematic components. We will assume that the errors have zero means and variances σ_u^2 and σ_v^2, respectively, and that they are both mutually uncorrelated and uncorrelated with the systematic parts. That is, $E(u) = E(v) = 0, \text{var}(u) = \sigma_u^2, \text{var}(v) = \sigma_v^2, \text{cov}(u,v) = \text{cov}(u,x) = \text{cov}(y,v) = \text{cov}(x,v) = \text{cov}(u,y) = 0$.

Equation (13-1) can be written in terms of the observed variables as

$$Y - v = \beta(X - u) + e$$

or

$$Y = \beta X + w \tag{13-2}$$

where $w = e + v - \beta u$. The reason we cannot apply the OLS method to Eq. (13-2) is that $\text{cov}(w,X) = 0$. In fact,

$$\text{cov}(w,X) = \text{cov}(-\beta u, x + u) = -\beta\sigma_u^2$$

Thus one of the basic assumptions of least squares is violated. If only y is measured with error and x is measured without error, there is no problem because $\text{cov}(w,X) = 0$ in this case. Thus, given the specification (13-1) of the true relationship, it is errors in x that cause a problem.

If we estimate β by OLS applied to (13-2) we have

$$b_{YX} = \frac{\Sigma XY}{\Sigma X^2} = \frac{\Sigma(x+u)(y+v)}{\Sigma(x+u)^2}$$

$$\text{plim } b_{YX} = \frac{\text{cov}(xy)}{\text{var}(x) + \text{var}(u)} = \frac{\sigma_{xy}}{\sigma_x^2 + \sigma_u^2}$$

since all cross products vanish. Since $\beta = \sigma_{xy}/\sigma_x^2$, we have

$$\text{plim } b_{YX} = \frac{\beta}{1 + \sigma_u^2/\sigma_x^2} \tag{13-3}$$

Thus b_{YX} will underestimate β. The degree of underestimation depends on σ_u^2/σ_x^2.

If we run a reverse regression, i.e., regress X on Y, we have

$$b_{XY} = \frac{\Sigma XY}{\Sigma Y^2} = \frac{\Sigma(x+u)(y+v)}{\Sigma(y+v)^2}$$

Hence $$\text{plim } b_{XY} = \frac{\sigma_{xy}}{\sigma_y^2 + \sigma_v^2}$$

But from (13-1)

$$\sigma_y^2 = \beta^2\sigma_x^2 + \sigma_e^2 \qquad \text{and} \qquad \sigma_{xy} = \beta\sigma_x^2$$

Hence $$\text{plim } \frac{1}{b_{XY}} = \frac{\beta^2\sigma_x^2 + \sigma_e^2 + \sigma_v^2}{\beta\sigma_x^2} = \beta\left(1 + \frac{\sigma_e^2 + \sigma_v^2}{\beta^2\sigma_x^2}\right)$$

Thus $1/b_{XY}$ overestimates β, and we have

$$\text{plim } b_{YX} \leqslant \beta \leqslant \frac{1}{\text{plim } b_{XY}}$$

We can use the two regression coefficients b_{YX} and b_{XY} to get bounds on β (at least in large samples).

We have derived these results for a single explanatory variable. One question is: If we have more than one explanatory variable, do these results carry over? First, if there is only one explanatory variable measured with error and the others are measured without error, the previous results carry through. The direction of bias on the coefficient of the variable measured with error is unambiguously downward. As for the coefficients of the other variables measured without error, *the direction of bias can be either way*, but it can be calculated. All that is required is knowledge of the variance-covariance matrix of the observations.[1] However, if all the explanatory variables are measured with error, the expressions get very complicated. Theil[2] derives the following approximate formulas for the case of two variables:

$$\hat{\beta}_1 - \beta_1 \approx -\frac{1}{1-\rho^2}(\theta_1\beta_1 - \rho\theta_2\beta_2)$$

$$\hat{\beta}_2 - \beta_2 \approx -\frac{1}{1-\rho^2}(\theta_2\beta_2 - \rho\theta_1\beta_1)$$

where $\hat{\beta}_1$ and $\hat{\beta}_2$ are the OLS estimates of β_1 and β_2 from a regression of the measured variable Y on the measured variables X_1 and X_2, ρ is the correlation coefficient between the true values x_1 and x_2, and θ_1, θ_2 are the ratios of the error variances to the respective variances of the true values. If $\rho = 0$, we get the previous results for the case of simple regression. If $\rho \neq 0$, the magnitude of the bias depends on the signs of β_1, ρ, and β_2. If $\beta_1 > 0$ and ρ and β_2 are of opposite signs, the magnitude of underestimation is even larger than in the simple-regression case. In any case we can readily see that both underestimation and overestimation are possible now.

13-3 FUNCTIONAL RELATIONSHIP AND STRUCTURAL RELATIONSHIP

As we discussed earlier in the case of linear regression (Chap. 7, Sec. 7-8), we can distinguish between two types of models: least-squares regression model and bivariate regression model. The corresponding classifications in the case of errors-in-variables models are known as "functional relationship" and "structural relationship," respectively.

In a functional relationship we assume that there is a true relation (with no error in the equation)

$$y = \alpha + \beta x$$

If we observe y and x, any two points will determine the straight line. However, we observe only

$$Y_i = y_i + v_i = \alpha + \beta x_i + v_i \qquad i = 1,2,\ldots,n$$

[1] For detailed proofs, see Maurice D. Levi, Errors in the Variables Bias in the Presence of Correctly Measured Variables, *Econometrica*, September 1973, pp. 985–986.

[2] H. Theil, "Economic Forecasts and Policy," 2d rev. ed., pp. 328–329, North-Holland Publishing Company, Amsterdam, 1961.

and $$X_i = x_i + u_i$$

Thus we have $Y_i = \alpha + \beta X_i + (v_i - \beta u_i)$.

Since the x_i are constants, the unknowns to be estimated in this model are $\alpha,\beta,\sigma_u^2,\sigma_v^2$, and the x_i. The maximum-likelihood estimation of this model was first discussed by Lindley.[1] Without any loss of generality, we can assume $\alpha = 0$. If we assume that u_i and v_i are normally distributed, we have

$$\log L = \text{const.} - \frac{n}{2}\log \sigma_u^2\sigma_v^2 - \frac{1}{2}\frac{\Sigma(X_i - x_i)^2}{\sigma_u^2} - \frac{1}{2}\frac{\Sigma(Y_i - \beta x_i)^2}{\sigma_v^2}$$

and the ML estimates are obtained by maximizing this with respect to $\beta,\sigma_u^2,\sigma_v^2$, and x_i. The equations are, respectively,

$$\Sigma(Y_i - \beta x_i)x_i = 0$$

$$\Sigma(X_i - x_i)^2 = n\sigma_u^2$$

$$\Sigma(Y_i - \beta x_i)^2 = n\sigma_v^2$$

and $$\sigma_v^2(X_i - x_i) + \beta\sigma_u^2(Y_i - \beta x_i) = 0 \qquad i = 1,2,\ldots,n$$

Lindley shows that these equations lead to the solution

$$\hat{\beta}^2 = \frac{\hat{\sigma}_v^2}{\hat{\sigma}_u^2}$$

Thus the ML estimator for the slope coefficient β is equal to plus or minus the square root of ratio of the estimators of the error variances. The result is often interpreted to mean that the ML method breaks down in this case. The problem here is that with every extra observation on (Y_i,X_i) we have one extra parameter x_i to estimate. The parameters x_i have been rightly called "incidental parameters" by Neyman and Scott.[2] This sort of problem arises in other cases too where the number of parameters to be estimated increases with the sample size.

The problem can be solved if the ratio of the error variances is known a priori. Let $\lambda = \sigma_v^2/\sigma_u^2$, where λ is known. Then the log likelihood is given by

$$\log L = -\frac{n}{2}\log \lambda\sigma_u^4 - \frac{1}{2}\frac{\Sigma(X_i - x_i)^2}{\sigma_u^2} - \frac{1}{2}\frac{\Sigma(Y_i - Bx_i)^2}{\lambda\sigma_u^2}$$

[1] D. V. Lindley, Regression Lines and the Linear Functional Relationship, *Supplement to the Journal of the Royal Statistical Society*, 1947, pp. 218–244.

[2] J. Neyman and E. L. Scott, On Certain Methods of Estimating the Linear Structural Relationship, *Annals of Mathematical Statistics*, 1951, pp. 352–361.

This we maximize with respect to β, σ_u^2, and x_i. Writing down the normal equations and simplifying, we finally get

$$\hat{\beta} = \frac{\Sigma Y_i^2 - \lambda \Sigma X_i^2 \pm \sqrt{\left[(\Sigma Y_i^2 - \lambda \Sigma X_i^2)^2 + 4\lambda(\Sigma X_i Y_i)^2\right]}}{2\Sigma X_i Y_i}$$

It has been shown that the likelihood is maximized by taking the optional sign as positive in the above expression. This ensures that $\hat{\beta}$ always has the same sign as $\Sigma X_i Y_i$. Usually, it is unlikely that we know λ, and if we do it is the case that we know both σ_u^2 and σ_v^2. This case has been analyzed by Barnett.[1]

Thus the parameters in the functional relationship are estimable if we know the error variances or their ratio. The same is true of the structural relationship. In this case x_i's are random variables with mean m and variance σ_x^2. Then X and Y are normally distributed. The five parameters of this distribution are

$$\begin{aligned} E(X) &= m \\ E(Y) &= \alpha + \beta m \\ \operatorname{var}(X) &= \sigma_x^2 + \sigma_u^2 \\ \operatorname{var}(Y) &= \beta^2\sigma_x^2 + \sigma_v^2 \\ \operatorname{cov}(XY) &= \beta\sigma_x^2 \end{aligned} \tag{13-4}$$

The ML estimates of these parameters are the sample means, variances, and covariance. But in Eqs. (13-4) we have five equations and six unknowns, and thus we cannot solve the equations. The parameters are said to be nonidentifiable. If we are given σ_u^2, σ_v^2, or $\lambda = \sigma_u^2/\sigma_v^2$, we can solve the equations to get the remaining parameters. Another alternative is knowledge of α.

It should be noted that the nonidentifiability in this case is due to the assumption of normality in the distribution. It has been shown that if x_i are nonnormal, the parameters α and β are identifiable.[2] (We can then use higher-order moments of the distribution.) In many statistical problems we are better off assuming normality. In this case it is the reverse—we are worse off assuming normality.

13-4 INSTRUMENTAL-VARIABLE METHODS

Without some extra prior information, it is clear that ML procedures cannot be used in the errors-in-variables models. Hence some "grouping" methods have been suggested in the literature. All these methods can be regarded as "instrumental-variable" methods. Instrumental variables were first developed by

[1] V. D. Barnett, A Note on Linear Functional Relationships When Both Residual Variances Are Known, *Biometrika*, 1967, pp. 670–672.

[2] See the relevant references in A. Madansky, The Fitting of Straight Lines When Both Variables Are Subject to Error, *Journal of the American Statistical Association*, 1959, pp. 173–205.

Reiersøl.[1] Loosely stated, an instrumental variable is a variable uncorrelated with the error term but correlated with the other explanatory variables. The regression equation we have to estimate is

$$Y_i = \beta X_i + (v_i - \beta u_i)$$

The reason we cannot use OLS is that $(v_i - \beta u_i)$ is correlated with X_i. If Z_i is a variable uncorrelated with the residual $(v_i - \beta u_i)$ but correlated with X, the instrumental-variable estimator of β is $\beta^* = \sum Y_i Z_i / \sum X_i Z_i$. Hence

$$\begin{aligned}\operatorname{plim} \beta^* &= \operatorname{plim} \frac{\Sigma(\beta X_i + v_i - \beta u_i)Z_i}{\Sigma X_i Z_i} = \beta + \operatorname{plim} \frac{(1/n)\Sigma(v_i - \beta u_i)Z_i}{(1/n)\Sigma X_i Z_i} \\ &= \beta\end{aligned}$$

since Z_i is uncorrelated with $(v_i - \beta u_i)$, provided $\operatorname{plim}(1/n)\sum X_i Z_i = \operatorname{cov}(XZ) \neq 0$.

Three main grouping methods are suggested in the literature, by Wald, Bartlett, and Durbin.[2] In Wald's method we rank the X's and form those above the median X into one group and those below the median into another group. If the means in the two groups are, respectively, $\bar{Y}_1$, $\bar{X}_1$ and $\bar{Y}_2$, $\bar{X}_2$, we estimate the slope β by

$$\beta^* = (\bar{Y}_2 - \bar{Y}_1)/(\bar{X}_2 - \bar{X}_1)$$

This amounts to using the instrumental variable

$$\begin{aligned} Z_i &= 1 \qquad \text{if } X_i > \text{median} \\ &= -1 \qquad \text{if } X_i < \text{median} \end{aligned}$$

and using the estimator $\beta^* = \sum Y_i Z_i / \sum X_i Z_i$. Bartlett suggested ranking X's, forming three groups, and discarding the $n/3$ observations in the middle group. His estimator of β is

$$\beta^* = \frac{\bar{Y}_3 - \bar{Y}_1}{\bar{X}_3 - \bar{X}_1}$$

This amounts to using the instrumental variable

$$\begin{aligned} Z_i &= +1 \qquad \text{for the top } n/3 \text{ observations} \\ &= -1 \qquad \text{for the bottom } n/3 \text{ observations} \end{aligned}$$

Durbin suggests using the ranks of X_i as the instrumental variables. Thus

$$\beta^* = \frac{\Sigma i Y_i}{\Sigma i X_i}$$

[1] O. Reiersøl, Confluence Analysis by Means of Instrumental Sets of Variables, *Arkiv foer Mathematik*, 1945. The instrumental-variable method was discussed in Chap. 9 (Secs. 9-4 and 9-6) and Chap. 11 (Sec. 11-3).

[2] A. Wald, The Fitting of Straight Lines if Both Variables Are Subject to Errors, *Annals of Mathematical Statistics*, 1940, pp. 284–300; M. S. Bartlett, Fitting of Straight Lines When Both Variables Are Subject to Error, *Biometrics*, 1949, pp. 207–212; J. Durbin, Errors in Variables, *Review of International Statistical Institute*, 1954, pp. 23–32.

where the X_i are ranked in ascending order and the Y_i are the values of Y corresponding to the X_i. If the errors are large, the ranks will be correlated with the errors and then Durbin's procedure will give a poor instrumental variable. In this case Durbin suggests arranging the X values according to magnitude, forming them into groups, and taking the instrument $Z_i = i$ for all X's in the ith group.

With all these instrumental-variable estimators, there is a reduction in the bias but an increase in variance as compared with OLS estimators. Hence suggestions have been made to use a weighted linear combination of ordinary least squares and instrumental-variable estimators.[1]

With time-series data, if the errors u_i are serially uncorrelated but x_i are serially correlated, one can use lagged values of X_i as instrumental variables. This suggestion was made as early as 1941 by Reiersøl.[2]

As an illustration, consider the model

$$Y_t = \beta x_t + e_t$$

$$X_t = x_t + u_t$$

$$x_t = \rho x_{t-1} + v_t$$

(There is no error of observation in Y_t.) Then

$$\text{var}(X_t) = \sigma_{xx} + \sigma_{uu}$$

$$\text{var}(Y_t) = \beta^2\sigma_{xx} + \sigma_{ee}$$

$$\text{cov}(X_t, Y_t) = \beta\sigma_{xx}$$

$$\text{cov}(X_t, X_{t-1}) = \rho\sigma_{xx}$$

$$\text{cov}(Y_t, Y_{t-1}) = \beta^2\rho\sigma_{xx}$$

$$\text{cov}(Y_t, X_{t-1}) = \text{cov}(X_t, Y_{t-1}) = \beta\rho\sigma_{xx}$$

Thus we can estimate β by

$$\hat{\beta}_1 = \frac{\text{cov}(Y_t, X_{t-1})}{\text{cov}(X_t, X_{t-1})} \qquad \text{or} \qquad \hat{\beta}_2 = \frac{\text{cov}(Y_t, Y_{t-1})}{\text{cov}(X_t, Y_{t-1})}$$

The former amounts to using X_{t-1} as the instrumental variable, and the latter amounts to using Y_{t-1} as the instrumental variable.[3]

This method of using lagged values of variables as instruments (which is something like a "bootstrap" method) can, in theory, be used where the variables are unobserved (instead of being observed with error). As an illustra-

[1] M. S. Feldstein, Errors in Variables: A Consistent Estimator with Smaller Mean Square Error in Finite Samples, *Journal of the American Statistical Association*, December, 1974.

[2] O. Reiersøl, Confluence Analysis by Means of Lag Moments and Other Methods of Confluence Analysis, *Econometrica*, 1941, pp. 1–24.

[3] In actual practice, however, both X_{t-1} and Y_{t-1} are likely to be very poor instruments.

tion, consider the model

$$y_t = \beta x_t + v_t$$
$$x_{t+1} = \alpha x_t + w_t \qquad \text{with } |\alpha| < 1 \tag{13-5}$$

where the residuals v_t and w_t are mutually uncorrelated and also uncorrelated with x_t. Suppose that x_t is not observed. Which of the parameters β, α, σ_x^2, σ_v^2, and σ_w^2 are estimable?

Note that Eqs. (13-5) can be written in terms of the observables as

$$y_{t+1} - v_{t+1} = \beta x_{t+1} = \beta\alpha x_t + \beta w_t$$
$$= \alpha(y_t - v_t) + \beta w_t$$

Thus
$$y_{t+1} = \alpha y_t + u_t \tag{13-6}$$

where $u_t = v_{t+1} + \beta w_t - \alpha v_t$. We note that since u_t involves v_t and v_{t+1}, u_t is correlated with y_t and y_{t+1}. But it is uncorrelated with y_{t-1}. Thus we can use y_{t-1} as an instrumental variable and take $\hat{\alpha} = \sum y_{t+1}y_{t-1}/\sum y_t y_{t-1}$, and we will have plim $\hat{\alpha} = \alpha$.

We can next use the estimated residuals $\hat{u}_{t+1} = y_{t+1} - \hat{\alpha}y_t$ to get estimates of the residual variances. Since

$$\text{var}(u_{t+1}) = \text{var}(v_{t+1} + \beta w_t - \alpha v_t)$$
$$= \sigma_v^2(1 + \alpha^2) + \beta^2\sigma_w^2$$

and
$$\text{cov}(u_{t+1}, u_t) = -\alpha\sigma_v^2$$

we can first use $\text{cov}(\hat{u}_{t+1}, \hat{u}_t)$ to estimate σ_v^2 and then get an estimate of $\beta^2\sigma_w^2$ from $\text{var}(\hat{u}_t)$. Also since $\text{var}(x) = \sigma_w^2/(1 - \alpha^2)$, we can estimate $\beta^2\sigma_x^2$. Thus, in the model given by Eqs. (13-5), we can get consistent estimates for α, σ_v^2, $\beta^2\sigma_w^2$, and $\beta^2\sigma_x^2$. We cannot, however, get an estimate of β.

Another solution suggested by Griliches[1] to the errors-in-variables problem when only one explanatory variable is measured with error is the following: Suppose the model is

$$Y_t = \alpha_1 x_{1t} + \alpha_2 X_{2t} + u_t$$

and instead of X_{2t} we observe $x_{2t} = X_{2t} + v_t$, where the measurement error v_t is uncorrelated with y_t. In terms of observable variables the equation is

$$Y_t = \alpha_1 x_{1t} + \alpha_2 x_{2t} + (u_t - \alpha_2 v_t)$$

Since $\text{cov}(x_{2t}, u_t - \alpha_2 v_t) \neq 0$, the ordinary-least-squares estimates of α_1 and α_2 will not be consistent. However, if data are available at a disaggregated level, we can proceed as follows: Regress y on x_1 alone for each of the subgroups. If b^* is the estimated regression coefficient,

$$E(b^*) = \alpha_1 + \alpha_2 z$$

[1] Z. Griliches, Notes on the Role of Education in Production Functions and Growth Accounting, in W. Lee Hansen (ed.), "Education, Income and Human Capital," National Bureau of Economic Research, New York, 1970.

where z is the regression coefficient of the omitted variable x_2 on the included variable x_1. This can be done for each of the subaggregates. Assuming that variations in b_j^* (where j refers to the subaggregates) arise from variations in the relationship between x_2 and x_1 (i.e., variations in z_j) among the subaggregates, it is possible to get unbiased estimates of α_1 and α_2 by regressing b_j^* on z_j. This method is not fully efficient, since the error variances in the regression

$$E(b_j^*) = \alpha_1 + \alpha_2 z_j$$

are inversely proportional to $(\sum x_1^2)_j$. However, we can use weighted least squares to take account of this heteroscedasticity. Let w_j be the square root of $(\sum x_1^2)$ for the jth group. Then we estimate α_1 and α_2 by regressing $(w_j b_j^*)$ on w_j and $w_j z_j$ (with no constant term).

13-5 OTHER METHODS: REPEATED OBSERVATIONS AND MORE EQUATIONS

We have till now discussed two methods for the estimation of errors-in-variables models:

1. Prior knowledge of some parameters—usually error variances
2. Instrumental variables

We will now discuss two other methods:

3. Repeated observations
4. More equations

The case of replicated observations has been discussed in the statistical literature (see Tukey[1]), but it is not clear how relevant it is in economic applications. Suppose the true relationship is $y_i = \beta x_i + e_i$.

What these papers discuss is a model in which we have, say, N replications for each (y_i, x_i). That is, we observe

$$X_{ij} = x_i + u_{ij} \qquad \text{and} \qquad Y_{ij} = y_i + v_{ij} \qquad j = 1,2,\ldots,N \tag{13-7}$$

Then Tukey constructs consistent estimators for β from the between-group and within-group variances and covariances.[2] These are

$$\hat{\beta}_1 = \frac{B_{xy}}{B_{xx} - W_{xx}} \qquad \text{and} \qquad \hat{\beta}_2 = \frac{B_{yy} - W_{yy}}{B_{xy}}$$

[1] J. W. Tukey, Components in Regression, *Biometrics*, 1951, pp. 33–70. A good exposition of the methods is in Madansky, *op. cit.*

[2] Definitions of these terms are in Sec. 14-2.

Since the assumptions given by (13-7) are not very relevant in economics, we will not pursue this procedure here. A more relevant model in econometric applications is the model

$$Y_{ij} = \beta x_{ij} + e_{ij}$$
$$X_{ij} = x_{ij} + u_{ij}$$

X and Y observed.

The case of multiple equations can be illustrated as follows: Suppose

$$y_1 = \beta_1 x + e_1$$
$$y_2 = \beta_2 x + e_2$$

x is not observed. Instead we observe $X = x + u$. Suppose e_1, e_2, and u are mutually uncorrelated and also uncorrelated with x. Also let $\text{var}(e_1) = \sigma_1^2$, $\text{var}(e_2) = \sigma_2^2$, $\text{var}(u) = \sigma_u^2$, and $\text{var}(x) = \sigma_x^2$. Then we have

$$\text{var}(y_1) = \beta_1^2\sigma_x^2 + \sigma_1^2$$
$$\text{var}(y_2) = \beta_2^2\sigma_x^2 + \sigma_2^2$$
$$\text{cov}(y_1 y_2) = \beta_1\beta_2\sigma_x^2$$
$$\text{cov}(y_1, X) = \beta_1\sigma_x^2$$
$$\text{cov}(y_2, X) = \beta_2\sigma_x^2$$
$$\text{var}(X) = \sigma_x^2 + \sigma_u^2$$

These six equations can be solved to get estimates of β_1, β_2, σ_x^2, σ_u^2, σ_1^2, and σ_2^2. Specifically we have

$$\hat{\beta}_1 = \frac{\text{cov}(y_1, y_2)}{\text{cov}(X, y_2)} \quad \text{and} \quad \hat{\beta}_2 = \frac{\text{cov}(y_2, y_1)}{\text{cov}(X, y_1)}$$

In effect this is like using y_2 as an instrumental variable in the equation $y_1 = \beta_1 X + w_1$ and y_1 as an instrumental variable in the equation $y_2 = \beta_2 X + w_2$. Further elaboration of this approach of solving the errors-in-variables (and unobservable variables) problem by increasing the number of equations can be found in Goldberger.[1]

As an illustration, suppose

y_1 = expenditures on automobiles

y_2 = expenditures on other durables

x = permanent income

X = measured income

[1] A. S. Goldberger, Structural Equation Methods in the Social Sciences, *Econometrica*, 1972, pp. 979–1002.

If we are given only y_1 and X(or y_2 and X), we are in the single-equation errors-in-variables problem and we cannot get consistent estimators for β_1 (or β_2). But if we are given y_1,y_2, and X, we can get consistent estimators for both β_1 and β_2.

13-6 CORRELATED ERRORS

Till now we have assumed that the errors of observation are mutually uncorrelated and also uncorrelated with the systematic parts. If we drop these assumptions, things will get more complicated. For example, consider the model $y = \beta x + e$.

The observed values are $X = x + u$ and $Y = y + v$, where u and v are the measurement errors. Let σ_{xy} denote the covariance between x and y, with a similar notation for all the other covariances. If the least-squares estimate of β from a regression of Y on X is $\hat{\beta}$, then

$$\begin{aligned}
\text{plim } \hat{\beta} &= \frac{\text{cov}(YX)}{\text{var}(X)} = \frac{\text{cov}(x+u)(y+v)}{\text{var}(x+u)} \\
&= \frac{\sigma_{xy} + \sigma_{xv} + \sigma_{yu} + \sigma_{uv}}{\sigma_{xx} + 2\sigma_{xu} + \sigma_{uu}} \\
&= \frac{\beta\sigma_{xx} + \sigma_{xv} + \sigma_{yu} + \sigma_{uv}}{\sigma_{xx} + 2\sigma_{xu} + \sigma_{uu}}
\end{aligned}$$

Since $\sigma_{yu} = \beta\sigma_{xu}$ and $\sigma_{xv} = \text{cov}[(y - e)/\beta, v] = \sigma_{yv}/\beta$, we have

$$\text{plim } \hat{\beta} = \frac{\beta(\sigma_{xx} + \sigma_{xu}) + \sigma_{yv}/\beta + \sigma_{uv}}{\sigma_{xx} + 2\sigma_{xu} + \sigma_{uu}}$$

Now even if there is no error in x, i.e., $u = 0$, we find that plim $\hat{\beta} \neq \beta$ since $\sigma_{yv} \neq 0$. Thus it is not just errors in x that create a problem as in the earlier case.

One can calculate the nature of the bias in $\hat{\beta}$ making different assumptions about the different covariances. We need not pursue this further here. What is important to note is that one can get either underestimation or overestimation of β. With economic data where such correlations are more the rule than an exception, it is important not to believe that the slope coefficients are always underestimated in the presence of errors in observations, as is suggested by the classical analysis of errors-in-variables models.

We have all along omitted the intercept term. If there is an intercept term α, i.e., our true relationship is $y = \alpha + \beta x + e$, and instead we estimate $Y = \alpha + \beta X + w$, then the least-squares estimator $\hat{\beta}$ underestimates β and consequently the least-squares estimator $\hat{\alpha}$ will overestimate α. If, however, the errors do not have a zero mean, i.e., $X = x + u$ and $E(u) \neq 0$, then these conclusions need not hold.

With economic data the assumptions of zero means for the errors and of zero covariances between the errors and the systematic parts, and between errors themselves, may not be valid assumptions to make. To illustrate the nature of biases arising from errors in measurement in economic contexts, Haitovsky[1] used some data compiled by Cole. The data refer to provisional and revised figures for GNP and its components for the period 1947–1961. The provisional figures are considered the observations with errors, and the revised figures are assumed to be the correct measurements. Haitovsky finds that negative covariance between the measurement error and the systematic parts was a dominating feature. The reason for this, Haitovsky argues, is that predictions of economic time series tend to underestimate changes and since the provisional figures have a strong component of prediction in them, the variances of the revised figures tend to exceed the variances of the provisional figures, resulting in a negative $\text{cov}(x,u)$. Haitovsky also found that the least-squares slope coefficients were always overestimated rather than underestimated with the provisional figures. Further, since the mean of the errors was not zero, underestimated intercept values did not necessarily coincide with overestimated slope coefficients.

13-7 PREDICTION

Cole[2] and Denton and Kuiper[3] studied the effects of data errors on forecasting accuracy. These studies treat preliminary data as observations with error and revised data as the true values of the variables. Cole found that the use of preliminary data rather than revised data resulted in a doubling of the forecast error. The direct effect of using predicted values of the independent variables in the estimated equation was larger than the indirect effect on parameter estimates. She used the consumption function estimated by Zellner[4] and Griliches et al.[5] and found that methods of estimation produced more drastic changes in the estimates of the parameters than data errors. Denton and Kuiper found the opposite—that the choice of data had a stronger effect on the estimates of the parameters in their small econometric model than that resulting from the choice of estimation procedure (direct least squares vs. two-stage least squares).

These studies, however, do not give much guidance as to how to improve forecasting accuracy in the presence of errors in variables. If the classical

[1] Y. Haitovsky, On Errors of Measurement in Regression Analysis in Economics, *Review of International Statistical Institute*, 1972, pp. 23–35.

[2] Rosanne Cole, Data Errors and Forecasting Accuracy, in J. Mincer (ed.), "Economic Forecasts and Expectations—Analyses of Forecasting Behaviour and Performance," National Bureau of Economic Research, New York, 1969.

[3] Frank T. Denton and John Kuiper, The Effects of Measurement Errors on Parameter Estimates and Forecasts: A Case Study Based on the Canadian Preliminary National Accounts, *Review of Economics and Statistics*, May 1965.

[4] A. Zellner, The Short-Run Consumption Function, *Econometrica*, October, 1957.

[5] Griliches et al., *Econometrica*, July, 1962.

assumptions hold good, Johnston[1] shows that for some types of problems the OLS method can still be a useful technique even though the parameter estimates are biased. Suppose Y is measured consumption, X measured income, and x true income. Suppose

$$Y_t = \alpha + \beta x_{t-1} + e_t \qquad \text{and} \qquad X_t = x_t + u_t$$

Let $\hat{\beta}$ be the least-squares estimator for β from a regression of Y_t on X_{t-1} and let

$$\hat{Y}_{t+1} = \overline{Y} + \hat{\beta}(X_t - \overline{X})$$

Then Johnston shows that $\text{plim}(\hat{Y}_{t+1}) = E(Y_{t+1} \mid X_t)$ and thus the least-squares method can be used to get a consistent prediction of Y_{t+1}.

13-8 ERRORS IN VARIABLES AND OMITTED VARIABLES

Often we try to guard against the omitted-variable bias (see Chap. 9, Sec. 9-5) by including some proxies for the omitted variables. This procedure does not necessarily give better estimates than the one that ignores the proxies. A simple example is the one considered by Finis Welch[2] in connection with the estimation of the effects of schooling on income. Welch points out that often it has been argued that simple regressions of years of schooling on income overestimate the effect of schooling and people have tried to get proxies for ability and other such control variables so as to guard against the biases from omitted variables. If the variables are measured with error, this game of searching for control variables is not without pitfalls.

Consider the true regression equation

$$y = \beta_1 \bar{s} + \beta_2 \bar{a} + u$$

where y = income

$\bar{s}$ = marketable skills acquired in school scaled to the years of school completed

$\bar{a}$ = true initial (preschool) ability

Instead of $\bar{s}$ and $\bar{a}$, we observe s and a, where

$$s = \bar{s} + v_1$$

$$a = \bar{a} + v_2$$

where u, v_1, v_2 are mutually independent as well as independent of $\bar{s}$ and $\bar{a}$. Let b_{ys} be the regression coefficient from a simple regression of y on s and $b_{ys \cdot a}$ the regression coefficient of s in a multiple regression of y on s and a. Then, after

[1] J. Johnston, "Econometric Methods," 2d ed., pp. 290–291, McGraw-Hill Book Company, New York, 1972.

[2] Finis Welch, Human Capital Theory: Education, Discrimination and Life Cycles, *American Economic Review*, May, 1975, p. 67.

some algebraic simplifications, we can show that

$$\text{plim } b_{ys} = (\beta_1 + \beta_2 k) r^2_{s\bar{s}}$$

and

$$\text{plim } b_{ys\cdot a} = \beta_1 r^2_{s\bar{s}\cdot a} + \beta_2 k r^2_{s\bar{s}}(1 - r^2_{a\bar{a}\cdot s})$$

where k = OLS regression coefficient from the auxiliary regression of $\bar{a}$ on $\bar{s}$

$r_{s\bar{s}}$ = simple correlation between s and $\bar{s}$

$r_{s\bar{s}\cdot a}$ and $r_{a\bar{a}\cdot s}$ = partial correlation coefficients

We assume $\beta_1, \beta_2, k > 0$.

There are three points to note from these results:

1. b_{ys} is not necessarily an overestimate of β_1. There is an upward bias $\beta_2 k r^2_{s\bar{s}}$ and a downward bias $\beta_1(1 - r^2_{s\bar{s}})$.
2. The case with $b_{ys\cdot a}$ is similar. There is an upward bias $\beta_2 k r^2_{s\bar{s}}(1 - r^2_{a\bar{a}\cdot s})$ and a downward bias $\beta_1(1 - r^2_{s\bar{s}\cdot a})$.
3. Since $r^2_{s\bar{s}\cdot a} < r^2_{s\bar{s}}$ in this case, we have, unambiguously, plim $b_{ys\cdot a} <$ plim b_{ys}. But this does not necessarily mean that the (asymptotic) bias in $b_{ys\cdot a}$ is less than that in b_{ys}.

A similar argument is made by Griliches,[1] who shows that the more variables which are related to the systematic components of schooling we put into the equation, the more we try to "protect" ourselves against various possible biases due to omitted variables, the worse we make the errors-of-measurement problem.

13-9 NONNORMAL ERRORS

The least-squares estimators have the property that they are minimum-variance linear unbiased estimators and this property does not depend on the normality assumption. However, the assumption of normality of residuals plays a crucial role in the tests of significance we apply and other inferential procedures we use for the parameters we estimate. As with the other assumptions in our model, we have to ask the questions:

1. How to detect nonnormality?
2. What are the consequences?
3. What are the solutions?

As far as tests for normality are concerned, several tests are available, of which we might mention the following which are commonly used:

[1] Z. Griliches, "Estimating the Returns to Schooling: Some Econometric Problems," Presidential Address, 3d World Congress of the Econometric Society, Toronto, Aug., 22, 1975, Section "On Over Doing It: A Digression."

1. Tests based on $\sqrt{\beta_1}$ and β_2 where

$$\beta_1 = \mu_3^2/\mu_2^3 \qquad \text{and} \qquad \beta_2 = \mu_4/\mu_2^2$$

μ_2, μ_3, μ_4 are the second, third, and fourth moments about the mean, respectively. For the normal distribution $\beta_1 = 0$ and $\beta_2 = 3$. The former measures skewness and the latter kurtosis (or peakedness).

2. The Kolmogorov-Smirnov test.[1] Let $y_1 \leqslant y_2 \leqslant y_3 \leqslant \cdots \leqslant y_n$ denote the ordered observations from a sample of size n, $\bar{y}$ the sample mean, and $F_n(\cdot)$ the empirical distribution function. The Kolmogorov-Smirnov test uses the statistic

$$KS = \max_i \left| \frac{i}{n} - F(y_i) \right|$$

where $F(\cdot)$ is the hypothesized normal cumulative distribution function. Tables for testing the significance of KS are available, among other places, in D. B. Owen.[2]

3. The Shapiro-Wilk statistic.[3] This is defined as

$$W = \left[\sum_{i=1}^{m} a_{n-i+1}(y_{n-i+1} - y_i) \right]^2 \Big/ \sum_{i=1}^{n} (y_i - \bar{y})^2$$

where m = greatest integer in $n/2$

a_{n-i+1} = coefficient tabulated in the paper by Shapiro and Wilk (pp. 603–604)

Shapiro, Wilk, and Chen[4] did an empirical sampling study of the sensitivities of the above test statistics and five others for 45 alternative distributions and 5 sample sizes. They conclude that the W statistic provides a generally superior measure of nonnormality. Distance tests like KS are typically poor. A combination of $\sqrt{\beta_1}$ and β_2 usually provides a good judgment, but even their combined performance is dominated by W.

These tests all assume independent distributions for the random variables. However, in regression analysis we use the estimated residuals $\hat{u}_t$ rather than the true residuals u_t. Huang and Bolch[5] compare by means of a Monte Carlo study the powers of the W test, KS test, and some other tests when the alternative distributions are exponential, log-normal, and uniform. They used the true disturbances, the OLS residuals, and Theil's BLUS residuals. They found that

[1] This test is described, among other places, in M. G. Kendall and A. Stuart, "The Advanced Theory of Statistics," vol. II, pp. 452–457, Charles Griffin & Company, Ltd., London, 1961.

[2] "Handbook of Statistical Tables," Addison-Wesley Publishing Company, Inc., Reading, Mass., 1962.

[3] S. S. Shapiro and M. B. Wilk, An Analysis of Variance Test for Normality (Complete Samples), *Biometrika*, December, 1965, pp. 591–611.

[4] S. S. Shapiro, M. B. Wilk, and H. J. Chen, A Comparative Study of Various Tests for Normality, *Journal of the American Statistical Association*, December, 1968, pp. 1343–1372.

[5] C. J. Huang and B. W. Bolch, On the Testing of Regression Disturbances for Normality, *Journal of the American Statistical Association*, June, 1974, pp. 330–335.

the Shapiro-Wilk test was generally superior to the others and that the power was highest with the true residuals (which are unknown in practice) and lowest with the BLUS residuals. Thus they suggest using OLS residuals and the Shapiro-Wilk test in testing for nonnormality.[1]

Turning next to the question "What are the consequences?" we need to know what happens to the significance levels and the powers of the tests we apply on the assumption of normality if the assumption is not satisfied. Box and Watson[2] studied the "robustness" of tests for regression coefficients when the errors are nonnormal. They argue that if the empirical distribution of the explanatory variable x is approximately normal, the usual tests have the assumed significance levels. In the case of simple regression they suggest using the usual t and F tests but with degrees of freedom $k(T-2)$ instead of $(T-2)$, where

$$\frac{1}{k} = 1 + \frac{(\beta_2^u - 3)(\beta_2^x - 3)}{2T}$$

where β_2^u and β_2^x are the values of the β_2 coefficient (measuring kurtosis) defined earlier for the residuals u and the explanatory variable x, respectively. Note that for the log-normal distribution β_2 is very high and the degrees-of-freedom correction will indeed be very large.

Some nonparametric tests are suggested in the statistical literature, but these are cumbersome to use and are also applicable in only very simple models. Hence we will not discuss them here.

Finally, we come to the question of what to do if indeed we find the residuals to be nonnormal. If we have a specific distribution in mind—gamma, log-normal, etc.—we should carry out the analysis under these assumptions. The assumption of log-normal residuals is possibly quite justified in econometric work.[3] Unfortunately the nature of the errors affecting economic relations has not been investigated to any great extent. Hence one has to proceed with some plausible assumptions like gamma, χ^2, log-normal, and the Pareto distributions. Bradu and Mundlak,[4] and Teekens and Koerts[5] describe analysis when the residuals are log-normally distributed but enter the regression equation in a multiplicative fashion. The Pareto distribution is given by

$$f(u) = k(u - u_0)^{-\alpha - 1}$$

[1] Ramsay also found it better to use the OLS residuals than the BLUS residuals for the Shapiro-Wilk test. See J. B. Ramsay, Classical Model Selection through Specification Error Tests, p. 36 in P. Zarembka (ed.), "Frontiers in Econometrics," Academic Press, Inc., New York, 1974.

[2] G. E. P. Box and G. S. Watson, Robustness to Non-Normality of Regression Tests, *Biometrika*, June, 1962.

[3] J. Aitchison and J. A. C. Brown, "The Lognormal Distribution," Cambridge University Press, Cambridge, 1966.

[4] D. Bradu and Y. Mundlak, Estimation in Lognormal Linear Models, *Journal of the American Statistical Association*, March, 1970.

[5] R. Teekens and J. Koerts, Some Statistical Implications of the Log Transformation of Multiplicative Models, *Econometrica*, September, 1972.

where k, u_0, and α are constants. Mandelbrot[1] has argued that the Pareto distribution with $\alpha < 2$ is a reasonable distribution for many speculative prices. This distribution does not have a finite variance. Empirical researchers in the field of security prices have found estimates of α in the range 1.7 to 1.95.

Indeed if we assume that the variance of the residuals does not exist, the least-squares estimators do not have even the minimum-variance linear unbiasedness property. Though distributions with an infinite variance are an idealization, it cannot be ruled out that in most econometric applications the frequency of extreme outcomes is underestimated by the normal distribution. The empirical distributions of many economic variables certainly show "thick" tails.

The solutions to the problem of thick tails and extreme outcomes (outliers) fall in two categories:

1. Devise new techniques.
2. Transform the data so as to achieve normality.

13-10 ALTERNATIVES TO LEAST SQUARES

Many new techniques are being developed under the title of "robust regression." Tukey calls those who develop and use them "robusticators." We will only describe some for illustration.[2]

Let the regression equation be

$$y_i = \sum_{j=1}^{P} x_{ij}\beta_j + u_i$$

The least-squares estimates are obtained by minimizing

$$\sum_i \left(y_i - \sum_{j=1}^{P} x_{ij}\beta_j \right)^2 \tag{13-8}$$

These give the normal equations

$$\sum_i \left(y_i - \sum_k x_{ik}\beta_k \right) x_{ij} = 0 \tag{13-9}$$

Instead of minimizing (13-8), Huber suggests minimizing

$$\sum_i f\left(y_i - \sum_k x_{ik}\beta_k \right) \tag{13-10}$$

where $f(z) = \frac{1}{2} z^2$ for $|z| < c$
$\qquad = c|z| - \frac{1}{2} c^2$ for $|z| \geq c$

[1] B. Mandelbrot, New Methods in Statistical Economics, *Journal of Political Economy*, October 1963. Also, The Variation of Certain Speculative Prices, *Journal of Business*, October, 1963.

[2] P. J. Huber, Robust Regression: Asymptotics, Conjectures and Monte Carlo, *Annals of Statistics*, 1973, pp. 799–821. See also P. J. Huber, Robust Statistics: A Review, *Annals of Mathematical Statistics*, 1972, pp. 1041–1067.

and c is a preassigned constant. For OLS, $c = \infty$. The normal equations that Huber suggests solving are

$$\sum_i \phi\left(\frac{y_i - \sum_k x_{ik}\beta_k}{\sigma}\right) x_{ij} = 0 \tag{13-11}$$

where $\phi(z) = \max[-c, \min(c,z)]$. If $c = \infty$, $\phi(z) = z$, and we have the OLS estimator. We estimate the residual variance as

$$\frac{1}{n-p} \sum_i \phi\left(\frac{y_i - \sum_k x_{ik}\beta_k}{\sigma}\right)^2$$

To solve the nonlinear equations (13-11) iteratively, we need some starting values of the β's and σ. Despite their inadequacy, Huber says we have to start with the least-squares estimates. He finds his methods both computationally feasible and yielding good results in the case of nonnormal errors. Huber also has some suggestions for the standard errors of the estimators and describes the necessary computational procedures. We need not go into those details here.

Anscombe[1] has a similar suggestion. He suggests minimizing

$$\sum_{i=1}^{n} w_i\left(y_i - \sum_j x_{ij}\beta_j\right)^2 \tag{13-12}$$

where the w_i are defined as

$$\begin{aligned} w_i &= 1 && \text{if } |\hat{u}_i| \leqslant k_1 \\ w_i &= \frac{k_1}{\hat{u}_i} && \text{if } k_1 < |\hat{u}_i| \leqslant k_2 \\ w_i &= 0 && \text{if } |\hat{u}_i| \geqslant k_2 \end{aligned}$$

k_1, k_2 may be chosen a priori or as multiples of the error variance estimated from an application of OLS to the less extreme observations. k_1 may be chosen as twice the standard deviation and k_2 as four times the standard deviation. The w_i have to be iteratively estimated. Though the method makes intuitive sense, it is not easy to derive the sampling properties of the resulting estimators, nor can the procedure be derived as a maximum-likelihood procedure for any reasonable error distribution.

Another alternative that has been suggested is to minimize the sum of absolute errors rather than the sum of squared errors as in OLS. This will minimize the effect of large errors or outlying observations. Usually the common practice is to estimate the regression equation by OLS, look at the residuals, discard those observations for which the residuals are "large," and reestimate

[1] F. J. Anscombe, Topics in the Investigation of Linear Relations Fitted by the Method of Least Squares (with Discussion), *Journal of the Royal Statistical Society*, B Series, 1967, pp. 1–52.

the equations.[1] The problem with this procedure is that the conventional tests of significance are not applicable anymore. The method of minimizing the sum of absolute errors is probably less "ad hoc" than this procedure.

The estimator derived by minimizing the sum of absolute errors (MSAE) is also referred to as LAR (least absolute residual), LAE (least absolute error), and MAD (minimum absolute deviation). We will refer to it as LAR. Also, one often defines an L_P estimator as one which minimizes $(\sum |u_i|^P)^{1/P}$, and according to this definition the LAR estimator is an L_1 estimator and the OLS estimator is an L_2 estimator.

Consider the regression equation

$$y_i = \sum_j x_{ij}\beta_j + u_i$$

The LAR estimators of β_j are obtained by minimizing

$$\sum_i |y_i - \sum_j x_{ij}\beta_j|$$

The suggestion to use the LAR estimator goes as far back as Edgeworth (1888), but it was not popular because of the computational difficulties. It was Charnes et al.[2] who showed that the LAR estimator can be obtained as the solution to a linear-programming problem involving the auxiliary variables v_i and w_i. They show that the solution is to minimize, with respect to β_j, v_i, and w_i,

$$\sum_i (v_i + w_i)$$

subject to

$$v_i - w_i = y_i - \sum_j x_{ij}\beta_j$$

$$v_i \geqslant 0$$

$$w_i \geqslant 0$$

Though computationally cumbersome, the method is feasible. Meyer and Glauber[3] compare the forecasting performance of investment functions fitted by OLS and LAR and find that with very few exceptions the forecasts obtained from the latter equation were better. Fair[4] did a similar study for a simultaneous-equation model and found similar results. Fair computed the LAR

[1] For a defense and illustrations of this type of procedure, see F. M. Fisher, "A Priori Information and Time Series Analysis," North-Holland Publishing Company, Amsterdam, 1966. Robusticators too suggest some such procedures, which Tukey calls "trimming" and "peeling." However, they do this trimming in an iterative fashion rather than in a once-for-all way.

[2] A. Charnes, W. W. Cooper, and R. O. Ferguson, Optimal Estimation of Executive Compensation by Linear Programming, *Management Science*, 1955, pp. 138–151. See also H. Wagner, Linear Programming Techniques for Regression Analysis, *Journal of the American Statistical Association*, 1959, pp. 206–212, and W. D. Fisher, A Note on Curve Fitting with Minimum Deviations by Linear Programming, *Journal of the American Statistical Association*, June, 1961.

[3] J. R. Meyer and R. R. Glauber, "Investment Decisions, Economic Forecasting and Public Policy," Harvard Business School, Boston, 1964.

[4] R. C. Fair, "A Comparison of FIML and Robust Estimates of a Nonlinear Econometric Model," National Bureau of Economic Research Working Paper no. 15, October, 1973.

estimates by an iterative weighted-least-squares method as suggested by Tukey instead of the linear-programming method. The procedure suggested by Tukey is as follows: The LAR estimator minimizes

$$Q = \sum_{i=1}^{n} |u_i|$$

Now Q can be written as

$$\sum_i \frac{u_i^2}{|u_i|} = \sum_i w_i u_i^2$$

where $w_i = 1/|u_i|$. In OLS we minimize $\sum_i u_i^2$, and thus the problem of minimizing Q is a weighted-least-squares problem. Initial estimates of the residuals are obtained, say, by OLS. The reciprocals of the absolute values of these residuals are used as the weights w_i. Then new estimates of the regression parameters are obtained by minimizing $\sum_i w_i u_i^2$. These enable us to get new residuals, and the procedure is repeated. Fair performed four iterations but found that the estimates did not change much after the second or third iteration. In cases where the estimated residual at any iteration was zero (or close to zero), making it impossible to use it as a weight at the next iteration, it was set at $\epsilon = .00001$. Fair calls this method WLS-I.

In a second variant of weighted least squares, Fair used OLS for small residuals and LAR for large residuals; i.e., the weights w_i are taken as $1/|u_i|$ if $|u_i| \geqslant k$ but they are $1/k$ if $|u_i| < k$. The value of k was chosen as $\hat{m}/.6745$, where $\hat{m}$ is the median of the absolute values of the residuals. The WLS-I estimates were used as starting points, and the program was allowed to run four iterations. k was reestimated at each iteration. Fair calls this estimator WLS-II.

In the third variant Fair used the weights

$$w_i = \left[1 - \left(\frac{z_i}{k_1}\right)^2\right]^2 \qquad \text{if } |z_i| < k_1$$

$$= 0 \qquad \text{otherwise}$$

where $z_i = u_i/k_2$. k_1 was chosen as 6 and k_2 was $\hat{m}/.6745$. The value of k_2 was changed from iteration to iteration. This estimator was proposed by Tukey, and Fair calls it WLS-III. Fair found that WLS-I gave the best predictions in his example.

Though computing the LAR estimators is not a major problem, there is no well-developed theory about the sampling distributions of these estimators. The conditions under which they are unbiased and consistent are known,[1] but what is desired are standard errors (for confidence intervals and tests of significance), and these are not known. Since no closed form exists for these estimators, it is not possible to derive the sampling distributions. There are some sampling experiments, but these do not lead to any useful guidelines on what standard

[1] For a survey of the results, see Lester D. Taylor, Estimation by Minimizing the Sum of Absolute Errors, in P. Zarembka (ed.), "Frontiers in Econometrics," *op. cit.*

errors to report. Blattberg and Sargent[1] show that if the residuals u_i follow the second law of Laplace (two-tailed exponential distribution) with density function

$$f(u) = \frac{1}{2\lambda} \exp\left(-\frac{|u|}{\lambda}\right)$$

where $\mathrm{var}(u) = 2\lambda^2$, then the log of the likelihood function is

$$\log L = T \log\left(\frac{1}{2\lambda}\right) - \frac{1}{\lambda} \sum_{i=1}^{T} |u_i|$$

Thus maximizing the likelihood function amounts to minimizing $\sum_i |u_i|$, and the LAR estimator is the ML estimator. The two-tailed exponential is: compared with the normal, both more peaked and denser in the extreme tails.

Zeckhauser and Thompson[2] consider the case where the residuals follow the distribution (considered by Box and Tiao[3])

$$f(u) = k(\sigma,\theta) \exp\left(-\left|\frac{u}{\sigma}\right|^{\theta}\right) \tag{13-13}$$

where $$k(\sigma,\theta) = \left[2\sigma\Gamma\left(1 + \frac{1}{\theta}\right)\right]^{-1} \qquad \sigma > 0,\ \theta > 0$$

θ measures the degree of peakedness of the distribution. If $\theta = 2$, we have the normal distribution. If $\theta = 1$, we have the double exponential distribution. For the distribution given by (13-13) the maximum-likelihood estimates of the regression parameters are obtained by minimizing $S = \sum_{i=1}^{n} |u_i|^{\theta}$; i.e., the estimators are L_θ estimators. If the regression equation is

$$y_i = \alpha + \beta x_i + u_i$$

then we minimize

$$S = \sum_i |y_i - \alpha - \beta x|^{\theta}$$

Zeckhauser and Thompson suggest estimating α, β, θ simultaneously by the ML method. The likelihood function is

$$L = k^n(\sigma,\theta) \exp(-S/\sigma^{\theta})$$

The procedure is: For given θ, minimize S. Then the estimate of σ is given by $(\theta S/n)^{1/\theta}$

Substituting these values in L, we find the maximum value for this value of θ, say $L(\theta)$. We do this for selected values of θ and choose the value for which $L(\theta)$ is maximum. This is the ML estimate of θ, and the corresponding estimates of α, β, and σ are the ML estimates of those parameters. For the four empirical

[1] R. Blattberg and T. Sargent, Regression with Non-Gaussian Stable Disturbances: Some Sampling Results, *Econometrica*, May, 1971, pp. 501–510.

[2] Richard Zeckhauser and Mark Thompson, Linear Regression with Non-normal Error Terms, *Review of Economics and Statistics*, 1970, pp. 280–286.

[3] G. E. P. Box and G. C. Tiao, A Further Look at Robustness via Bayes' Theorem, *Biometrika*, 1962, pp. 419–432.

examples that Zeckhauser and Thompson considered, they found the ML estimates of θ in the range .45 to .675. Given the shape of the error distribution (13-13) for values of $\theta < 1$, the estimates they obtained can be considered implausibly low.[1] Many statisticians have voiced their opinions about the distribution (13-13) that it is an implausible distribution for $\theta = 1$ and possibly even 1.5.

Anscombe[2] rejects (13-13) and suggests what he thinks is a more plausible error distribution:

$$f(u) = k(m,\sigma)\left(1 + \frac{c_m u^2}{\sigma^2}\right)^{-m}$$

where $\quad c_m = \dfrac{4m^2}{(2m-1)^3} \quad$ and $\quad k(m,\sigma) = \dfrac{1}{\sqrt{2\pi}\,\sigma}\,\dfrac{\sqrt{2c_m}\,\gamma(m)}{\gamma\left(m - \frac{1}{2}\right)}$

As $m \to \infty$, this distribution tends to the normal distribution. The maximization of the likelihood function for this distribution, says Anscombe, is almost like minimizing (13-12) because observations with small residuals are given nearly equal weight, those with larger residuals less, and if $\hat{u}_i$ is large, the weight falls off as $1/\hat{u}_i^2$. Thus extreme deviant observations are almost ignored.

The advantage in deriving any estimator as a maximum-likelihood estimator is that we hope to use the general theory (even if applicable only to large samples) of the properties of ML estimators and the associated tests of significance. These are not available for the ad hoc procedures. On the other hand, as Tukey remarked in his discussion of Anscombe's paper, "Arguments as to what we would do if we 'know' that the residuals have a particular non-normal distribution can only be utopian—even more so than arguments based on 'knowing' the variances." However, it is always interesting to know for what type of error distribution the estimator we are considering is a ML estimator.

Though the LAR estimator can be derived as a maximum-likelihood estimator for the two-tailed exponential distribution, it is often justified by many econometricians as the appropriate one to use for what are known as symmetric stable Paretian distributions. These are distributions popularized by Mandelbrot, and their characteristic function is given by

$$\phi(t) = \exp(-|\sigma t|^{\alpha})$$

If $\alpha = 2$, we have the normal distribution, and if $\alpha = 1$, we have the Cauchy distribution. For $\alpha < 2$, the variance does not exist.[3]

[1] In their comments on Zeckhauser and Thompson's paper, Sims and Mandelbrot observed that heteroscedasticity in the residuals could have given a mistaken impression of nonnormality in the examples that Zeckhauser and Thompson considered. See comments by Sims and Mandelbrot in *Review of Economics and Statistics*.

[2] See Anscombe, *op. cit.*

[3] The important characteristic of these distributions is that the sum of independent symmetric stable variates with parameter α is also distributed as a symmetric stable variate with the same parameter α.

For the symmetric stable Paretian distributions an alternative to the LAR estimator is the estimator proposed by Wise.[1] He suggested generalizing the concept of best linear unbiased estimation to include the case where the residuals are stable Paretian. For simplicity let $y_i = \beta x_i + u_i$ be the regression model. Suppose that we take $\hat{\beta} = \sum_{i=1}^{n} a_i y_i$ as an estimator for β. If it is unbiased, we have

$$E(\Sigma a_i y_i) = (\Sigma a_i x_i)\,\beta = \beta$$

Hence $\sum a_i x_i = 1$. Because of the additive property of the stable distributions, $\hat{\beta} - \beta = \sum a_i u_i$ has a stable Paretian distribution with dispersion parameter $\sigma^\alpha \sum_{i=1}^{n} |a_i|^\alpha$. Since σ is a constant, minimizing the dispersion amounts to minimizing $\sum |a_i|^\alpha$ subject to the condition $\sum a_i x_i = 1$. Blattberg and Sargent show that this leads to the result

$$\hat{\beta} = \frac{\sum_i |x_i|^{1/(\alpha-1)} y_j \operatorname{sign} x_i}{\sum_i |x_i|^{\alpha/(\alpha-1)}}$$

For $\alpha = 2$, this gives

$$\hat{\beta} = \frac{\Sigma x_i y_i}{\Sigma x_i^2}$$

which is the OLS estimator. Kadiyala[2] shows that the estimator that John Wise suggested is a minimum mean absolute error estimator among the class of all linear unbiased estimators; i.e., if we consider the class of linear unbiased estimators, the estimator suggested by Wise minimizes $E(|\hat{\beta} - \beta|)$. He also shows that if we have more than one regressor we do not get closed-form expressions for $\hat{\beta}$, but we can compute the estimates on an electronic computer.

13-11 DATA TRANSFORMATIONS

Another alternative to the new methods suggested earlier is to transform the data so that the assumption of normality holds good. If we have reason to believe that the distribution is skew, it may be possible to symmetrize the distribution, usually by raising y to a power (or taking logs). On the other hand, if the distribution of the residuals is symmetric but different from normal, it is usually not possible to bring the distribution closer to normality by making a simple transformation of the y's. In this case the previously suggested alternatives to least squares should be used. Thus the solutions we discuss here are specifically to be used if we believe that the error distributions are skew.

[1] John Wise, "Linear Estimators for Linear Regression Systems Having Infinite Residual Variances," manuscript, 1966.

[2] K. R. Kadiyala, Regression with Non-Gaussian Stable Disturbances: Some Sampling Results, *Econometrica*, July, 1972.

Tukey,[1] who first gave a detailed discussion of transformations, suggested that transformations of data will help in making the model more nearly linear, the errors more homoscedastic and normal. A transformation is good if it achieves all these objectives simultaneously. On the other hand, it might achieve one of these objectives at the expense of the others; e.g., if the model was linear to start with, transformations to produce normality in the errors might make the model nonlinear. Tukey considers a wide family of transformations $(x + c)^\lambda$, but he assumes c and λ are known. Box and Tidwell[2] describe the procedure of estimating c and λ for the explanatory variables in the regression equation. The basic idea is to expand the function $(x + c)^\lambda$ in a Taylor series around initial guesses of the parameters. For simplicity assume $c = 0$ and consider the regression equation

$$y = \beta_1 x_1^{\lambda 1} + \beta_2 x_2^{\lambda 2} + u$$

The function $f(\lambda) = x^\lambda$ can be expanded to two terms in the Taylor series as

$$\begin{aligned} f(\lambda) &= f(\lambda_0) + (\lambda - \lambda_0) f'(\lambda_0) \\ &= x^{\lambda 0} + (\lambda - \lambda_0) x^{\lambda 0} \log x \end{aligned}$$

Thus, if λ_{10} and λ_{20} are the initial guesses of λ_1 and λ_2, respectively, we estimate a regression of y on $x_1^{\lambda 10}$, $x_2^{\lambda 20}$, $x_1^{\lambda 10} \log x_1$, and $x_2^{\lambda 20} \log x_2$. Let the estimated coefficients be b_1, b_2, a_1, and a_2, respectively. Then b_1, b_2 are estimates of β_1 and β_2 and $\lambda_{10} + a_1/b_1$ and $\lambda_{20} + a_2/b_2$ are, respectively, the new estimates of λ_1 and λ_2. These new estimates of λ_1 and λ_2 are used to repeat the process. Box and Tidwell give some examples that indicate that this iterative process converges rapidly. The (asymptotic) standard errors of b_1 and b_2 are the standard errors obtained for the final iteration. The standard errors of λ_1 and λ_2 are those of (a_1/b_1) and (a_2/b_2), and these can be obtained using Fieller's method described in Chap. 7, Sec. 7-9.

Box and Cox[3] consider transformations of the dependent variables (and also of the independent variables). Their transformation is defined as

$$\begin{aligned} y^{(\lambda)} &= \frac{y^\lambda - 1}{\lambda} \qquad && \lambda \neq 0 \\ &= \log y && \lambda = 0 \end{aligned}$$

The advantage with this transformation as compared with the simple power transformation y^λ is that it is continuous at $\lambda = 0$, since

$$Lt_{\lambda \to 0} \frac{y^\lambda - 1}{\lambda} = \log y$$

[1] J. W. Tukey, On the Comparative Anatomy of Transformations, *Annals of Mathematical Statistics*, 1957, pp. 602–632.

[2] G. E. P. Box and P. W. Tidwell, Transformation of the Independent Variables, *Technometrics*, 1962, pp. 531–550. See also M. E. Turner, R. J. Monroe, and H. L. Lucas, Generalized Asymptotic Regression and Non-linear Path Analysis, *Biometrics*, 1961, pp. 120–143.

[3] G. E. P. Box and D. R. Cox, An Analysis of Transformations (with Discussion), *Journal of the Royal Statistical Society*, Series B, 1962, pp. 211–243.

Box and Cox consider the regression model[1]

$$y_i^{(\lambda)} = \beta x_i + u_i$$

where $u_i \sim IN(0,\sigma^2)$. Then the joint density of the observations $y_1, y_2, \ldots, y_n$ is

$$\left(\frac{1}{2\pi\sigma^2}\right)^{n/2} \exp\left[-\frac{1}{2\sigma^2}\sum_i \left(y_i^{(\lambda)} - \beta x_i\right)^2\right] J$$

where J is the Jacobian of the transformation from the variables $y_i^{(\lambda)}$ to y_i. Thus

$$J = \prod_{i=1}^{n} \left| \frac{dy_i^{(\lambda)}}{dy_i} \right| = \prod_{i=1}^{n} y_i^{\lambda - 1}$$

The log-likelihood function therefore is

$$\log L = \text{const.} - n \log \sigma - \frac{1}{2\sigma^2} \sum_i \left[y_i^{(\lambda)} - \beta x_i \right]^2 + (\lambda - 1) \sum_i \log y_i \qquad \text{(13-14)}$$

If we divide each y_i by the geometric mean of the y's, then for the redefined variables we will have $\sum_i \log y_i = 0$. Thus the last term in (13-14) vanishes and the maximum values of $\log L$ will be, apart from a constant, equal to $-(n/2) \log \hat{\sigma}^2(\lambda)$ where $\hat{\sigma}^2(\lambda)$ is the residual sum of squares from a regression of $y_i^{(\lambda)}$ on x_i. Thus the procedure would be

1. Divide each y by the geometric mean of the y's.
2. For each value of λ regress $y_i^{(\lambda)}$ on x_i and compute the residual sum of squares $\hat{\sigma}^2(\lambda)$.
3. Choose that value of λ for which $\hat{\sigma}^2(\lambda)$ is minimum. This value, say $\hat{\lambda}$, is the ML estimate of λ.

The standard errors of the regression coefficients for any given value of λ can be obtained from the usual regression programs. These will, of course, be conditional standard errors—conditional on the assumed values of λ. The standard error or confidence interval for $\hat{\lambda}$ can be obtained by an inversion of the likelihood-ratio test statistic. This is done as follows.

Suppose we are testing the hypothesis $\lambda = \lambda_0$. The LR test statistic is

$$\theta = \frac{\max L(\lambda_0, \beta, \sigma^2)}{\max L(\lambda, \beta, \sigma^2)} = \left[\frac{\hat{\sigma}^2(\hat{\lambda})}{\hat{\sigma}^2(\lambda_0)}\right]^{n/2}$$

and $-2 \log \theta \sim \chi^2$ degrees of freedom 1. Thus if we want a 95 percent confidence interval for λ, we have to consider all values of λ_0 for which $-2 \log \theta$ is

[1] For ease of exposition, we are considering a single explanatory variable. The procedure is the same for multiple regressions.

less than 3.84, since $\Pr(-2 \log \theta < 3.84) = 0.95$ from the χ^2 tables with 1 degree of freedom. Thus we consider all values of λ for which

$$n \log \hat{\sigma}(\lambda) - n \log \hat{\sigma}(\hat{\lambda}) < 3.84$$

Since we will be evaluating $\hat{\sigma}^2(\lambda)$ for different values of λ in finding the ML estimate $\hat{\lambda}$, we can easily find the range of λ for which this condition is satisfied. This will give us the 95 percent confidence interval for λ.

The same procedure can be used to transform the explanatory variables. We define

$$x^{(\lambda)} = \frac{x^\lambda - 1}{\lambda} \qquad \text{for } \lambda \neq 0$$
$$= \log x \qquad \text{for } x = 0$$

In principle we can estimate different values of λ for the dependent variable y and the explanatory variables x. The search procedure cannot be used efficiently if there are more than 2 or 3 λ's. In such cases one can use the search procedure for estimating the value of λ for y and the Box-Tidwell procedure for estimating the values of λ for the explanatory variables x. In any case the computations will get cumbersome.

As a special case we can consider the problem where the value of λ is the same for y and all the explanatory variables. Also if we confine ourselves to the more practically interesting cases of $\lambda = 1$ and $\lambda = 0$, we end up with the two functional forms

$$y = \beta_0 + \beta_1 x_1 + \beta_2 x_2 + \cdots + \beta_k x_k + u$$

and $$\log y = \alpha_0 + \alpha_1 \log x_1 + \alpha_2 \log x_2 + \cdots + \alpha_k \log x_k + u$$

One cannot choose between these two models on the basis of R^2's alone because the R^2's are not comparable. The Box-Cox procedure amounts to the following: Divide each y_i by the geometric mean of the y's. Then estimate the two equations and choose the one with the smaller residual variance.

13-12 FRONTIER PRODUCTION FUNCTIONS: AN EXAMPLE OF NONNORMAL ERRORS

An obvious example of nonnormal errors is the case of "frontier" production functions. Let $Q^*(x,\theta)$ be the maximum output that can be produced technologically with inputs x. θ is a set of parameters in the production function. The actual output produced will be

$$Q = Q^*(x,\theta) - u$$

where u is a residual that is necessarily positive (since the firm cannot produce more than the technological maximum). Q^* is called the "frontier" production function, and our objective is to estimate the parameters θ of this frontier production function given observations on Q and x. Obviously we cannot assume the residuals u to be normally distributed. But we can assume them to have any of the following distributions:

1. The *half-normal* distribution

$$f(u) = \frac{2}{\sqrt{2\pi}\,\sigma} \exp\left(-\frac{u^2}{2\sigma^2}\right) \qquad u \geqslant 0 \tag{13-15}$$

2. The *exponential* distribution

$$f(u) = \frac{1}{\beta} \exp\left(-\frac{u}{\beta}\right) \qquad u \geqslant 0$$

3. The *log-normal* distribution where log u is assumed to be normal with mean μ and variance σ^2.

Given any of these assumptions and given data on Q and x, one can write the appropriate likelihood function and estimate the parameters θ by ML methods. Since the algebra of writing the first and second derivatives is tedious (though straightforward), it is omitted here.

The half-normal distribution (13-15) has the following mean and variance:

$$E(u) = \frac{\sqrt{2}}{\sqrt{\pi}}\,\sigma$$
$$V(u) = \frac{\pi - 2}{\pi}\,\sigma^2 \tag{13-16}$$

Sometimes the technological "frontier" production function itself can be assumed to be stochastic, i.e.,

$$Q^*(x,\theta) = f(x,\theta) + v$$

The random error v is due to variations in weather or some exogenous changes in the production process itself. In this case we are perhaps justified in assuming that v takes on positive as well as negative values. We can thus assume that v is normally distributed. Combining all these elements, we can write

$$Q = f(x,\theta) + v - u \tag{13-17}$$

where v can assume both positive and negative values and u can assume positive values only. A reasonable assumption is to assume v to be normally distributed as $N(0,\alpha^2)$ and u to have the half-normal distribution (13-15). To write the likelihood function, we need the density of the composite residual $v - u$ in (13-17). To do this, we define $\epsilon = v - u$. We write the joint density of v and u and transform this to a joint density in ϵ and u and integrate u (from 0 to ∞). After simplification, we get

$$f(\epsilon) = \frac{\sqrt{2}}{\sigma\sqrt{\pi}}\left[1 - F\left(\frac{\epsilon\lambda}{\delta}\right)\right] \exp\left(-\frac{\epsilon^2}{2\delta^2}\right) \qquad -\infty < \epsilon < \infty \tag{13-18}$$

where $\delta^2 = \sigma^2 + \alpha^2$ and $\lambda = \sigma/\alpha$ and $F(\cdot)$ is the cumulative distribution function of the standard normal.

$$F(t) = \frac{1}{\sqrt{2\pi}} \int_{-\infty}^{t} \exp\left(-\frac{z^2}{2}\right) dz$$

The density function (13-18) involves cumulative normals, and hence the computation of the ML estimates has to be done by the same procedures as those used for probit and logit models discussed in Sec. 9-7. The ML estimation of the parameters of this model is discussed in Aigner,[1] who reports some disappointing results with this method in Monte Carlo experiments. Schmidt and Lovell[2] applied this model to some actual data and found that in all cases σ^2 was very small compared with α^2; i.e., the error component u was negligible compared with the error v. This suggests that the usual specification of normal errors is not unreasonable.

In any case the above example illustrates a model where nonnormal errors have been assumed and the models estimated on that assumption.

[1] D. J. Aigner, "An Alternative Error Specification for the Estimation of Production Frontiers," S.S.R.I., University of Wisconsin Report 7524, October, 1975.

[2] P. Schmidt and C. A. Knox Lovell, "Formulation and Estimation of Stochastic Frontier Production Function Models," University of North Carolina, mimeo, January, 1976.

CHAPTER

FOURTEEN

COVARIANCE ANALYSIS AND POOLING CROSS-SECTION AND TIME-SERIES DATA

14-1 ANALYSIS OF VARIANCE AND COVARIANCE

Suppose we have a set of variables $x_1, x_2, \ldots, x_k$. We can compute the variances and covariances of these variables. In analysis of variance and covariance we try to decompose these variances and covariances into various components due to different identifiable sources. In Chap. 8 we saw how the variance of a variable y can be analyzed into two components: that due to regression and that due to the residual factors. What we study now is a more general analysis.

As an illustration consider the data in Table 14-1 for 30 individuals. Y is income in thousands of dollars and X is years of schooling. The data are not real-world data. They are just hypothetical and are used here for illustrative purposes to highlight the relevant computational aspects. From the observed data we can compute the variances and covariances. What we want to do is analyze these into their sources of variation, which in this case are race and sex. The residual is due to all other causes (presumably unknown).

One way of analyzing these data is to estimate a dummy-variable regression equation of the form

$$Y = \mu + \alpha D_1 + \gamma D_2 + \delta D_3 + u \tag{14-1}$$

where $D_1 = 1$ for whites, 0 for blacks

$D_2 = 1$ for males, 0 for females

$D_3 = 1$ for white males and black females, 0 for others

The equation we get is

$$\underset{(11.4)}{Y = 9.0} + \underset{(3.8)}{3.0D_1} + \underset{(2.03)}{1.6D_2} + \underset{(.51)}{0.4D_3} \qquad R^2 = .474 \tag{14-2}$$

(Figures in parentheses are t ratios.)

Table 14-1 Education and Income

White males		White females		Black males		Black females	
Y	X	Y	X	Y	X	Y	X
12.7	8	12.7	10	10.1	8	9.0	8
14.0	12	13.3	11	9.6	8	8.5	8
18.3	16	10.8	8	10.1	10	9.0	7
13.0	11	11.1	7	10.3	10	11.1	9
13.5	11	12.1	11	9.8	8		
11.2	8	12.0	13	14.1	10		
14.3	10			10.2	9		
13.7	10						
12.4	7						
9.8	7						
14.3	12						
15.7	15						
19.1	16						

How do we take the effect of years of schooling X on income Y? We can estimate an equation of the form

$$Y = \mu + \alpha D_1 + \gamma D_2 + \delta D_3 + \beta X + u \tag{14-3}$$

where D_1, D_2, and D_3 are defined as before. The variable X is usually known in analysis-of-variance literature as a *concomitant* variable. The estimated equation is

$$\underset{(4.16)}{Y = 3.568} + \underset{(3.39)}{1.642D_1} + \underset{(2.01)}{.921D_2} + \underset{(.89)}{.4D_3} + \underset{(7.44)}{.679X} \qquad R^2 = .836$$

In these equations only D_1 is significant at the 5 percent level. If the slope coefficient is not the same between the different groups, what we should be testing is whether both the slope and intercept terms differ between the groups. The necessary tests can be performed by estimating the equation

$$Y = \mu + \alpha D_1 + \gamma D_2 + \rho D_3 + \beta X + \beta_1(D_1X) + \beta_2(D_2X) + \beta_3(D_3X) + u \tag{14-4}$$

An F test for $\alpha = 0$, $\beta_1 = 0$ is a test for race effects; an F test for $\gamma = 0$, $\beta_2 = 0$ is a test for sex effects; and an F test for $\rho = 0$, $\beta_3 = 0$ is a test for the interaction effect.

We can apply corresponding tests for the data in Table 14-1. An overall test for equality of the regression is

$$F = \frac{(56.80 - 26.71)/6}{26.71/22} = 4.13$$

The 5 percent value of F for degrees of freedom 6,22 is 2.55. Thus the differences are significant at the 5 percent level. The question is: How do we know what these differences are due to race, sex, or interaction? This question can be answered if we can estimate an equation like (14-4) and apply the necessary F tests. This is left as an exercise for the reader.

Analyses like this have often been performed in econometric work. We usually have data on income, years of schooling, hours worked, wage rates, occupational status, etc., by race and sex. The relevant equations have often been estimated by the use of dummy variables for race and sex but no interaction dummy, or if the investigator felt that the slope coefficients were different, separate regressions would be estimated for the different groups. The above analysis illustrates how these differences between groups can be decomposed into three different components: race, sex, and interaction. The interaction effects are rarely estimated in these econometric studies, though the literature on analysis of variance and covariance has extensive discussion of this.

14-2 POOLING CROSS-SECTION AND TIME-SERIES DATA

One major application of analysis of variance and covariance is in the problem of pooling cross-section and time-series data—to decide on questions like whether or not to pool and to estimate the pooled regressions with different degrees of pooling.

To start with, let us consider the case of a single explanatory variable and suppose we have data on y and x for a number of firms over time. Let us postulate a separate regression for each firm

$$y_{it} = \alpha_i + \beta_i x_{it} + u_{it} \qquad \begin{aligned} i &= 1,2,\ldots,N \\ t &= 1,2,\ldots,T_i \end{aligned} \tag{14-5}$$

There are N firms and T_i observations on the ith firm. Let $\bar{x}_i$, $\bar{y}_i$ be the means of x and y, respectively, for the ith firm. Define

$$W_{xxi} = \sum_t (x_{it} - \bar{x}_i)^2$$

$$W_{xyi} = \sum_t (x_{it} - \bar{x}_i)(y_{it} - \bar{y}_i)$$

$$W_{yyi} = \sum_t (y_{it} - \bar{y}_i)^2$$

The symbol W and the subscript i are used to denote that these are all within the ith group. Then

$$\hat{\beta}_i = \frac{W_{xyi}}{W_{xxi}} \qquad \text{and} \qquad \hat{\alpha}_i = \bar{y}_i - \hat{\beta}_i \bar{x}_i$$

The residual sum of squares is $\text{RSS}_i = W_{yyi} - W_{xyi}^2/W_{xxi}$, which has $(T_i - 2)$ degrees of freedom. To test the hypothesis

$$H_1: \quad \begin{aligned} \alpha_1 &= \alpha_2 = \cdots = \alpha_N \\ \beta_1 &= \beta_2 = \cdots = \beta_N \end{aligned}$$

we have to estimate a common regression equation

$$y_{it} = \alpha + \beta x_{it} + u_{it}$$

Let $\bar{x}$, $\bar{y}$ be the means of x and y, respectively, based on *all* the observations. Again define

$$T_{xx} = \sum_i \sum_t (x_{it} - \bar{x})^2$$

$$T_{xy} = \sum_i \sum_t (x_{it} - \bar{x})(y_{it} - \bar{y})$$

$$T_{yy} = \sum_i \sum_t (y_{it} - \bar{y})^2$$

Then $\hat{\beta} = T_{xy}/T_{xx}$ and $\hat{\alpha} = \bar{y} - \hat{\beta}\bar{x}$. The residual sum of squares is RSS $= T_{yy} - T_{xy}^2/T_{xx}$ degrees of freedom $(\sum_i T_i) - 2$. To test the hypothesis of homogeneity of the regressions, we use an F test. In effect what we are doing is estimating the regression equations (14-5) subject to the $(2N - 2)$ linear restrictions implied by H_1, which says $\alpha_1 = \alpha_N$, $\alpha_2 = \alpha_N$, ..., $\alpha_{N-1} = \alpha_N$ and $\beta_1 = \beta_N$, $\beta_2 = \beta_N$, ..., $B_{N-1} = \beta_N$. Hence we use the F test described in Chap. 10.

$$S_1 = \text{unrestricted residual sum of squares}$$

$$= \sum_i \text{RSS}_i \qquad \text{df} = \sum_i (T_i - 2) = \left(\sum_i T_i\right) - 2N$$

$$S_2 = \text{restricted residual sum of squares}$$

$$= \text{RSS} \qquad \text{df} \left(\sum_i T_i\right) - 2$$

The F ratio is

$$F = \frac{(S_2 - S_1)/(2N - 2)}{S_1/\left(\sum_i T_i - 2N\right)}$$

If this F ratio is significant, since there are significant differences in the coefficients, we do not pool the data. If the F ratio is not significant, we pool the data and estimate a single equation.

Instead of testing the hypothesis that the slope coefficients as well as the intercepts are equal for all firms, we might be interested in testing the hypothesis that only the slope coefficients are equal. The hypothesis is H_2: $\beta_1 = \beta_2 = \cdots = \beta_N$. Now we have to estimate a regression equation with a constant β but different α's. The regression model is

$$y_{it} = \alpha_i + \beta x_{it} + u_{it}$$

Minimizing $Q = \sum_{it}(y_{it} - \alpha_i - \beta x_{it})^2$ with respect to α_i and β, we find that the estimates $\tilde{\alpha}_i$ and $\tilde{\beta}$ of these parameters are obtained from the equations

$$\frac{\partial Q}{\partial \alpha_i} = 0 \rightarrow \sum_t \left(y_{it} - \tilde{\alpha}_i - \tilde{\beta} x_{it}\right) = 0 \qquad \text{or} \qquad \tilde{\alpha}_i = \bar{y}_i - \tilde{\beta}\bar{x}_i$$

$$\frac{\partial Q}{\partial \beta} = 0 \rightarrow \sum_{it} x_{it}\left(y_{it} - \tilde{\alpha}_i - \tilde{\beta} x_{it}\right) = 0$$

Substituting the value of $\tilde{\alpha}_i$, we get

$$\sum_{it} x_{it}\left[y_{it} - \bar{y}_i - \tilde{\beta}(x_{it} - \bar{x}_i)\right] = 0$$

or

$$\tilde{\beta} = \frac{W_{xy}}{W_{xx}}$$

where

$$W_{xy} = \sum_{it} x_{it}(y_{it} - \bar{y}_i) = \sum_i W_{xyi}$$

$$W_{xx} = \sum_{it} x_{it}(x_{it} - \bar{x}_i) = \sum_i W_{xxi}$$

The residual sum of squares can be simplified to

$$S_3 = W_{yy} - \frac{W_{xy}^2}{W_{xx}} \qquad \text{df} \left(\sum T_i\right) - (N+1)$$

since we are estimating $(N+1)$ parameters ($N\alpha_i$ and a single β). To test the hypothesis H_2, we again use the F test. The restricted residual sum of squares is now S_3. The F test is given by

$$F = \frac{(S_3 - S_1)/(N-1)}{S_1/\left(\sum T_i - 2N\right)}$$

One can also consider the hypothesis of a common intercept and different slopes, though this model is not often used in practice. The hypothesis is now H_3: $\alpha_1 = \alpha_2 = \cdots = \alpha_N$. What we have to do now is minimize $\sum_{it} (y_{it} - \alpha - \beta_i x_{it})^2$ with respect to the common α and the N different β_i. The expressions we get are not as neat as before. The best way to compute the restricted residual sum of squares in this case is to pool the data and run the dummy-variable regression:

$$\begin{bmatrix} y_1 \\ y_2 \\ \vdots \\ y_N \end{bmatrix} = \alpha \begin{bmatrix} 1 \\ 1 \\ \vdots \\ 1 \end{bmatrix} + \beta_1 \begin{bmatrix} x_1 \\ 0 \\ 0 \\ \vdots \\ 0 \end{bmatrix} + \beta_2 \begin{bmatrix} 0 \\ x_2 \\ 0 \\ \vdots \\ 0 \end{bmatrix} + \cdots + \beta_N \begin{bmatrix} 0 \\ 0 \\ 0 \\ \vdots \\ x_N \end{bmatrix} + \begin{bmatrix} u_1 \\ u_2 \\ \vdots \\ u_N \end{bmatrix}$$

We pool all the data and regress the entire set of y observations on N dummies with a constant term. The dummy variables are

$$\begin{aligned} D_{1t} &= x_{1t} && \text{for the observations of the first group} \\ &= 0 && \text{for others} \\ D_{2t} &= x_{2t} && \text{for the observations of the second group} \\ &= 0 && \text{for others, etc.} \end{aligned}$$

Then the coefficients of the dummies are the estimates of the β's. The coefficient of the constant term is the estimate of α. If S_4 is the residual sum of squares from this equation, then the F test to test H_3 is

$$F = \frac{(S_4 - S_1)/(N-1)}{S_1/\left(\sum T_i - 2N\right)}$$

One can also apply some *conditional* tests. For instance, if we want to test the hypothesis

$$H_4\colon \alpha_1 = \alpha_2 = \cdots = \alpha_N \qquad \textit{given} \qquad \beta_1 = \beta_2 = \cdots = \beta_N$$

then the unrestricted residual sum of squares is S_3 with degrees of freedom $\sum_i T_i - (N+1)$ and the restricted residual sum of squares is S_2 with degrees of freedom $\sum_i T_i - 2$. Hence the F test is given by

$$F = \frac{(S_2 - S_3)/(N-1)}{S_3/\left[\sum T_i - (N+1)\right]}$$

Similarly, if we want to test the hypothesis

$$H_5\colon \beta_1 = \beta_2 = \cdots = \beta_N \qquad \textit{given} \qquad \alpha_1 = \alpha_2 = \cdots = \alpha_N$$

then the unrestricted residual sum of squares is S_4 with degrees of freedom $\sum_i T_i - (N+1)$ and the restricted residual sum of squares is S_2 with degrees of freedom $\sum_i T_i - 2$. The F test is given by

$$F = \frac{(S_2 - S_4)/(N-1)}{S_4/\left[\sum T_i - (N+1)\right]}$$

In many practical applications when pooling is done, the equations are estimated with a common intercept and slope or with different intercepts but a common slope. Thus the tests needed are those for hypotheses H_1, H_2, and H_4, but not the others. From the computational point of view we need the means and covariances within each group: $\bar{x}_i$, $\bar{y}_i$, W_{xxi}, W_{xyi}, W_{yyi}, and the corresponding values for the totals: $\bar{x}$, $\bar{y}$, T_{xx}, T_{xy}, T_{yy}.

If we estimate separate regressions, we get

$$\hat{\beta}_i = \frac{W_{xyi}}{W_{xxi}} \qquad \text{and} \qquad \hat{\alpha}_i = \bar{y}_i - \hat{\beta}_i \bar{x}_i$$

If we estimate a regression with a common slope and intercept, we get

$$\hat{\beta} = \frac{T_{xy}}{T_{xx}} \qquad \text{and} \qquad \hat{\alpha}_i = \bar{y} - \hat{\beta}\bar{x}$$

If we estimate a regression with a common slope but different intercepts, we get

$$\tilde{\beta} = \frac{W_{xy}}{W_{xx}} \qquad \text{and} \qquad \tilde{\alpha}_i = \bar{y}_i - \tilde{\beta}\bar{x}_i$$

The last one is known commonly as the dummy-variable regression. In production-function studies where y is output and x is input, α_i may be assumed to be a measure of the managerial input that is specific to the ith firm. In this case, if one wants to obtain estimates of the production-function coefficients free of the management bias, one can use the dummy-variable regression.[1]

The least-squares-with-dummy-variables (LSDV) method is a commonly used method of pooling. As mentioned earlier, this method assumes that the slope coefficient is the same for all cross-section units and only the intercepts are different. If enough observations are available, it is better to test whether the slope coefficients are indeed equal, using the test described above, before any pooling is done. Another problem is that sometimes we have to treat the "intercepts" as random variables rather than fixed parameters and they are also correlated with the explanatory variable x. For instance, in studies in farm management, if the α_i are supposed to capture the effects of an unobserved managerial input, it is reasonable to assume that this is highly correlated with the other inputs used, and thus farms with higher levels of $\bar{x}_i$ are also farms with higher levels of managerial input and hence α_i. In such cases it is best to reformulate the problem with another explicit equation for α_i or use the first-difference method. In the latter case, we estimate the model

$$y_{it} - y_{i,t-1} = \beta_i(x_{it} - x_{i,t-1}) + w_{it} \tag{14-6}$$

where the $w_{it} = u_{it} - u_{i,t-1}$ are a set of moving-average errors. (We are assuming that T_i, the number of observations on the ith firm, is the same for all i.) In actual practice, since the residuals u_{it} are likely to be highly positively correlated, it may not be unreasonable to estimate Eq. (14-6) by ordinary least squares. In most studies of pooling cross-section and time-series data it is best to estimate a first-difference equation like (14-6) along with the other equations. The first-difference method is a drastic remedy for the effects of all time-invariant omitted variables.

14-3 VARIANCE-COMPONENTS MODELS

Another type of model that is becoming increasingly popular is the "variance-components" model. Balestra and Nerlove[2] used this in their study of the demand for natural gas, and they found the LSDV method unsatisfactory. In the variance-components model the intercept terms α_i are treated as random variables rather than fixed and α_i are independent of the residuals u_{it}, and also mutually independent. We will also assume that the residuals u_{it} have zero mean

[1] See Y. Mundlak, Empirical Production Functions Free of Management Bias, *Journal of Farm Economics*, 1961, pp. 44–56.

[2] P. Balestra and M. Nerlove, Pooling Cross-Section and Time-Series Data in the Estimation of a Dynamic Model: The Demand for Natural Gas, *Econometrica*, July, 1966, pp. 585–612.

and common variance σ_u^2 and that they are both serially independent and independent across cross-section units. These assumptions can be written as

$$E(\alpha_i) = 0 \qquad E(u_{it}) = 0$$

$$\begin{aligned}
\text{cov}(\alpha_i, \alpha_j) &= \sigma_\alpha^2 && \text{for } i = j \\
&= 0 && \text{otherwise} \\
\text{cov}(u_{it}, u_{js}) &= \sigma_u^2 && \text{if } i = j, t = s \\
&= 0 && \text{otherwise} \\
\text{cov}(\alpha_i, u_{jt}) &= 0 && \text{for all } i,j,t
\end{aligned}$$

For the sake of simplicity in exposition, we use only one explanatory variable. Also, we consider what is known as a "balanced model"; i.e., the number of observations on each cross-section unit is the same, viz., T. If the model is "unbalanced," the variance-components method gets messier. In most econometric applications this is not a restrictive assumption. Thus the model is

$$y_{it} = \beta x_{it} + \alpha_i + u_{it} \qquad \begin{aligned} i &= 1,2, \ldots, N \\ t &= 1,2, \ldots, T \end{aligned}$$

Since α_i are also random, the residuals are now $v_{it} = \alpha_i + u_{it}$ and the presence of α_i produces a correlation among residuals of the same cross-section unit though the residuals from the different cross-section units are independent. We have

$$\begin{aligned}
\text{cov}(v_{it}, v_{is}) &= \sigma_u^2 + \sigma_\alpha^2 && \text{for } t = s \\
&= \sigma_u^2 && \text{for } t \neq s
\end{aligned}$$

$\text{cov}(v_{it}, v_{js}) = 0$ for all t, s if $i \neq j$. Since the residuals are correlated, we have to use generalized least squares (GLS) to get efficient estimates. However, in this model the GLS estimator for β can be written in a simple instructive form[1]

$$\hat{\beta}_{\text{GLS}} = \frac{W_{xy} + \theta B_{xy}}{W_{xx} + \theta B_{xx}} \qquad \text{where} \qquad \theta = \frac{\sigma_u^2}{\sigma_u^2 + T\sigma_\alpha^2} \tag{14-7}$$

W refers to within groups and B refers to between groups.

$$\begin{aligned}
B_{xx} &= T_{xx} - W_{xx} \\
B_{xy} &= T_{xy} - W_{xy} \\
B_{yy} &= T_{yy} - W_{yy}
\end{aligned}$$

T_{xx}, T_{xy}, T_{yy} are the total sums of squares and sums of products and W_{xx}, W_{xy}, W_{yy} are the within-group sums of squares and sums of products defined earlier. Also, as derived earlier,

$$\hat{\beta}_{\text{OLS}} = \frac{T_{xy}}{T_{xx}} = \frac{W_{xy} + B_{xy}}{W_{xx} + B_{xx}}$$

[1] See G. S. Maddala, The Use of Variance Components Models in Pooling Cross-Section and Time-Series Data, *Econometrica*, March, 1971, pp. 341–358.

and
$$\hat{\beta}_{\text{LSDV}} = \frac{W_{xy}}{W_{xx}}$$

Thus the ordinary-least-squares estimator and the least-squares-with-dummy-variable estimator are special cases of the generalized-least-squares estimator given by (14-7), corresponding to $\theta = 1$ and $\theta = 0$. The arguments in favor of this model are that the LSDV method often results in a loss of a large number of degrees of freedom and also eliminates a large portion of the total variation if B_{xx}, B_{xy}, and B_{yy} are large relative to W_{xx}, W_{xy}, and W_{yy}, respectively. Also, α_i are the total effect of several factors that are specific to the cross-section units, and thus α_i, which represent "specific ignorance," can be treated as random variables by much the same argument as the u_{it}, which can be regarded as representing "general ignorance."

There are two things to note about the GLS estimator in (14-7). First, if T is large or σ_α^2 is large relative to σ_u^2, θ will be very close to zero and the GLS estimator is very close to the LSDV estimator. Second, in actual practice θ is not known and must be estimated based on preliminary estimates of σ_u^2 and σ_α^2. Several methods are suggested in the literature.[1] One of these is the procedure suggested by Nerlove.[2] In this procedure we first estimate the equation by the LSDV method. The variance of the $\hat{\alpha}_i$ is taken to be an estimate of σ_α^2, and the estimate of the residual variance from this equation is taken as an estimate of σ_u^2. From these two estimates we get an estimate of θ and obtain the GLS estimate as given in Eq. (14-7). The estimates of σ_α^2 and σ_u^2 from this method are biased and are not consistent, but Nerlove found in his Monte Carlo study that the GLS estimator so obtained outperforms (in terms of mean-square error) the estimators from the other methods. Nerlove's two-step procedure has been widely used in several empirical studies besides the study by Balestra and Nerlove. However, unlike the case with the Balestra-Nerlove study, most of these subsequent studies found the GLS estimates obtained from the variance-components model very close to the LSDV estimates.[3] This result is not surprising, because in these studies $T\hat{\sigma}_\alpha^2$ is large compared with $\hat{\sigma}_u^2$. Further, most of these studies estimate a dynamic model with a lagged dependent variable. The coefficient of this variable was found to be close to 1 when the equation was estimated by the OLS method (thus implying long lags in adjustment), but this coefficient was smaller when the LSDV or variance-components (VC) method was used. For instance, in the Houthakker et al. study on demand for gasoline based on time-series data for 1960 to 1971 for 49 states, the results of estimation from different methods were the following (standard errors in parentheses, all variables in log form):

[1] See G. S. Maddala and T. D. Mount, A Comparative Study of Alternative Estimators for Variance Components Models, *Journal of the American Statistical Association*, June, 1973, pp. 324–328.

[2] M. Nerlove, Further Evidence on the Estimation of Dynamic Economic Relations from a Time Series of Cross Sections, *Econometrica*, March, 1971, pp. 359–382.

[3] See, for example, H. S. Houthakker, P. K. Verleger, Jr., and D. P. Sheehan, Dynamic Demand Analysis for Gasoline and Residential Electricity Demand, *American Journal of Agricultural Economics*, May 1974, pp. 412–418. This has also been the experience in several energy-demand studies done at the Oak Ridge National Laboratory by W. S. Chern, G. S. Gill, and T. J. Tyrrell.

		Coefficient of	
Method	Price	Income	Lagged consumption
OLS	−.023	.0031	.9894
	(.012)	(.0039)	(.0037)
LSDV	−.081	.341	.6595
	(.013)	(.018)	(.0171)
VC	−.075	.303	.6957
	(.013)	(.017)	(.0164)

Note that there is very little difference between the estimates obtained by the LSDV and VC methods. Also, the price and income elasticities are much higher when these methods are used than when the OLS method is used.

The extension of the above procedures to the cases of several explanatory variables is straightforward. W_{xx} and B_{xx} will now be matrices of sums of squares and sums of products for the several explanatory variables, and W_{xy} and B_{xy} will be vectors. Equation (14-7) will now read as

$$\hat{\beta}_{\text{GLS}} = (W_{xx} + \theta B_{xx})^{-1}(W_{xy} + \theta B_{xy})$$

Also, it is easy to extend these models to the case where in addition to the cross-section dummies we have time dummies and both sets of dummies are treated as random.[1]

When models with the intercepts α_i are treated as constants, it is customary to perform tests for equality of the slope coefficients. However, in the variance-components framework this is rarely done, and it is customary to assume a common slope coefficient β. Tests for equality of the slope coefficients β_i can be performed even in the variance-components framework. These are tests of linear restrictions when GLS procedures are used. Since the parameter θ is estimated, these tests are valid only if the samples are sufficiently large. In the case of a single explanatory variable where the model is

$$y_{it} = \beta_i x_{it} + \alpha_i + u_{it} \qquad \begin{aligned} i &= 1,2, \ldots, N \\ t &= 1,2, \ldots, T \end{aligned} \tag{14-8}$$

the test for the equality of the slope coefficients β_i is performed as follows: Compute

$$R_1^2 = W_{yy} + \theta B_{yy} - \frac{(W_{xy} + \theta B_{xy})^2}{W_{xx} + \theta B_{xx}}$$

$$R_0^2 = \sum_i \left[W_{yyi} + \theta T \bar{y}_i^2 - \frac{(W_{xyi} + \theta T \bar{x}_i \bar{y}_i)^2}{W_{xxi} + \theta T \bar{x}_i^2} \right]$$

R_1^2 = restricted residual sum of squares, degrees of freedom $NT - 1$

R_0^2 = unrestricted residual sum of squares, degrees of freedom $NT - N$

[1] See Maddala, *op. cit.* Also T. D. Wallace and A. Hussain, The Use of Error Component Models in Combining Cross-Section and Time Series Data, *Econometrica*, January, 1969, pp. 55–72.

Hence we use

$$F = \frac{(R_1^2 - R_0^2)/(N-1)}{R_0^2/(NT-N)}$$

as an F ratio with degrees of freedom $N-1$, $NT-N$. The extension to the case of several explanatory variables is straightforward.

In the variance-components model only the α_i are treated as random. There is another class of models where the β_i are also treated as random.[1]

Many believe that this is a generalization of the variance-components model because even the slope coefficients β_i are treated as random. However, this is not so, and there is a lot of conceptual difference between the two models. In the variance-component model our main interest is in the slope coefficients β_i, and when we treat α_i as random, this is because we are considering them, as argued earlier, as a combination of several factors we are ignorant about. We treat them as we treat the residuals u_{it} except that they constitute the time-invariant component in the residual. If we alternatively treat the residuals as, say, first-order autoregressive,

$$u_{it} = \rho_i u_{i,t-1} + e_{it}$$

then the correlation between two residuals u_{it} and u_{is} damps down as the distance $t-s$ increases. In the variance-components model this correlation is a constant.

When it comes to assuming β_i as random, we are in an entirely different ballpark. Here we assume that β_i are random, drawn from a distribution with mean $\bar{\beta}$ and variance σ_β^2, and we are interested in making inferences only about this mean and variance. Clearly there are situations where this sort of inference is valid. For instance, suppose we draw a random sample of firms and gather data on y and x. And we are interested in making inferences about the β coefficients not for just this group of firms but for the entire population of firms of which the firms drawn are a random sample. Then the random-coefficient regression model makes sense. What we are concerned with in this problem is the population of β's. It is clear that many of the cross-section time-series data we have do not fall in this category.

There may be cases where we know from economic reasoning that β_i vary in response to some policy variables, say z_i, and suppose we make this equation a stochastic equation because we have no exact specification of how the β_i vary in response to these policy variables. Then the specification is $\beta_i = \gamma z_i + v_i$, so that the model now becomes

$$\begin{aligned} y_{it} &= \alpha_i + (\gamma z_i + v_i)x_{it} + u_{it} \\ &= \alpha_i + \gamma z_i x_{it} + w_{it} \end{aligned}$$

where $w_{it} = u_{it} + v_i x_{it}$. Now the residuals w_{it} have a covariance structure as in

[1] See, for example, P. A. V. B. Swamy, Efficient Inference in a Random Coefficient Regression Model, *Econometrica*, May, 1970, pp. 311–323.

the random-coefficient regression models. But this model makes more economic sense than the one that says that β_i are random and that we are interested in the population of β's. In this problem we are interested in the coefficient γ. Models of this type where all parameters vary are discussed in Chap. 17.

One can also introduce problems of heteroscedasticity and autocorrelation among residuals in the variance-components models, but the computations get very burdensome. If these problems are considered important, it is better to stay within the framework of the LSDV method where these problems can be tackled more easily. Further, if there is any systematic relationship between α_i and the level of x's (as would often be the case in many econometric applications), it is not reasonable to assume that the α_i are random, and thus the variance-components model would not be appropriate.

14-4 THE SEEMINGLY UNRELATED REGRESSION MODEL[1]

The variance-components model results in a certain type of correlation among the residuals. The residuals for each cross-section unit are correlated over time (and this correlation is constant), but the residuals for different cross-section units are uncorrelated. This type of correlation would arise if each cross-section unit has a specific time-invariant variable omitted from the equation (like managerial input). In the seemingly unrelated regression model introduced by Zellner, the residuals are uncorrelated over time but correlated across cross-section units. That is,

$$\begin{aligned} \operatorname{cov}(u_{it}, u_{js}) &= \sigma_{ij} \qquad \text{if } t = s \\ &= 0 \qquad \text{if } t \neq s \end{aligned}$$

This type of correlation would arise if there are some omitted variables that are common to all equations. Both these models can, in principle, be extended to include the other type of correlation. Also, in both the models it is possible to apply tests for equality of the slope coefficients before any pooling is done. For the seemingly unrelated regression model we first estimate each equation separately by ordinary least squares. We then obtain the estimated residuals $\hat{u}_{it}$. From these estimated residuals we compute the estimates of the covariances σ_{ij}. $\hat{\sigma}_{ij} = [1/(T-k)]\sum \hat{u}_{it}\hat{u}_{jt}$, where k is the number of regression parameters estimated. After we estimate σ_{ij}, we reestimate all the N cross-sectional equations jointly, using generalized least squares. This joint estimation can be carried out both for separate β_i and for a common β, and one can test the hypothesis that the β_i are equal. (The details are given in Zellner's paper.)

If we have a large number of cross-section units and the time series is short, this method is not feasible. Also, the method is appropriate only if the residuals are generated by a true multivariate distribution. When the correlations are due

[1] A. Zellner, An Efficient Method of Estimating Seemingly Unrelated Regressions and Tests for Aggregation Bias, *Journal of the American Statistical Association*, June, 1962, pp. 348–368.

to common omitted variables, it is not clear whether Zellner's GLS method is superior to the OLS.[1]

In all problems of pooling, it is first important to estimate each equation individually by OLS and check whether there is any systematic behavior in the slope and intercept coefficients. If there is a systematic pattern in the intercepts, the variance-components model is inappropriate. In addition, we should also study whether there is a systematic pattern in the residuals. This will reveal whether the residuals are autocorrelated and/or correlated across cross-section units and what model is appropriate.

14-5 SIMULTANEOUS-EQUATION MODELS

Turning next to simultaneous-equation models estimated from a time series of cross sections, suppose the model is

$$y_{1it} = \alpha_{1i} + \beta_{12}y_{2it} + \gamma_{11}x_{1it} + \gamma_{12}x_{2it} + u_{1it} \tag{14-9}$$

$$y_{2it} = \alpha_{21} + \beta_{21}y_{1it} + \gamma_{23}x_{3it} + \gamma_{24}x_{4it} + u_{2it} \tag{14-10}$$

Such examples arise in, say, models of sales (y_1) and advertising (y_2). The estimation of models where α_{1i} and α_{2i} are constants is straightforward and need not be discussed here. There are, however, several alternatives available when we consider the variance-components models. One of these is the following. Suppose

$$\alpha_{1i} \sim IN(0,\sigma_{\alpha 1}^2)$$

$$\alpha_{2i} \sim IN(0,\sigma_{\alpha 2}^2)$$

To implement the 2SLS procedure, we note first of all that it is only necessary to get consistent estimates of the reduced-form parameters. It is not necessary to get efficient estimates. Thus the reduced-form equations for y_{1it} and y_{2it} can be estimated by ordinary least squares. We next substitute $\hat{y}_{2it}$ in Eq. (14-9) and $\hat{y}_{1it}$ in Eq. (14-10) and estimate both equations by using the variance-components method.

14-6 SOME ALTERNATIVES TO POOLING

As mentioned earlier, one often tests the hypothesis that the slope coefficients are equal, and if this hypothesis is not rejected, the LSDV method is used. Also, as mentioned earlier, it is possible to apply such tests for homogeneity for the variance-components models. In fact one should apply such tests before estimating a model with constant slopes. This procedure of pooling after some prelim-

[1] See P. Rao, Specification Bias in Seemingly Unrelated Regressions, in W. Sellekaerts (ed.), "Essays in Honor of Tinbergen," vol. 2, pp. 101–113, International Arts and Sciences Press, New York, 1974.

inary tests of significance raises problems about inference from the pooled model, and also there is the question of what significance level to use when deciding whether or not to pool.[1]

An alternative that has recently been suggested by Lindley is to estimate each equation in (14-8) separately and adjust the coefficients toward a common mean. This procedure has been applied with some success in studies of college-admissions tests.[2] The idea is to bear all the available information for the estimation of each regression parameter while at the same time allowing for potential differences that may exist between the different regressions.

In essence we compute $\hat{\beta}_i$ and $\hat{\alpha}_i$ as

$$\hat{\beta}_i = \frac{W_{xyi}}{W_{xxi}} \qquad \hat{\alpha}_i = \bar{y}_i - \hat{\beta}_i \bar{x}_i$$

Let $\hat{\beta} = (1/N)\sum_i \hat{\beta}_i$ be the mean of the estimated β's. Then the suggested estimate of β_i is

$$\beta_i^* = \frac{W_1 \hat{\beta}_i + W_2 \hat{\beta}}{W_1 + W_2}$$

where $W_1 = \dfrac{1}{\text{estimated variance of } \hat{\beta}_i} = \dfrac{W_{xxi}}{\hat{\sigma}_i^2}$

$$W_2 = \frac{N}{N-1} \frac{1}{\hat{\tau}_\beta}$$

$$\hat{\tau}_\beta = \frac{1}{N-1} \sum_i \left(\hat{\beta}_i - \hat{\beta} \right)^2 - \frac{1}{N} \sum \left(\frac{\hat{\sigma}_i^2}{W_{xxi}} \right)$$

This expression is analogous to the one encountered in between-group sum of squares in variance-components models. Apparently, this method has provided good results in some studies of educational data, and it needs to be explored in econometric problems of pooling cross-section and time-series data. The method is a compromise between estimating each equation separately and pooling and estimating a single equation.

[1] It is not possible to decide this question without getting into details of losses from different actions. But a rough rule of thumb is to use a significance level of 25 to 30 percent rather than the customary 5 percent in the preliminary test. See G. S. Maddala, The Likelihood Approach to Pooling Cross-Section and Time-Series Data, *Econometrica*, November, 1971, pp. 939–953.

[2] See M. R. Novick, P. H. Jackson, D. T. Thayer, and N. S. Cole, Estimating Multiple Regressions in *m* Groups: A Cross Validation Study, *British Journal of Mathematical and Statistical Psychology*, 1972, pp. 33–50, and references therein.

CHAPTER

FIFTEEN

TREND, SEASONAL VARIATION, AND FORECASTING

Most time series exhibit some regular patterns of movement, and it is common practice to decompose them into the following components:

1. Trend T (this is also known as the trend-cycle component)
2. Seasonal variation S
3. Irregular (or random) variation I

The two usual assumptions are that the observed series X is the product or sum of these different components. The multiplicative model says

$$X = (T) \times (S) \times (I)$$

This is the approach the Bureau of Labor Statistics uses. The additive model says

$$X = T + S + I$$

This is often the approach the mathematical statisticians use. The former approach amounts to assuming additivity in the log form.

15-1 TREND

The trend is the long-term movement in the series. This component is sometimes called *cyclical trend* or *trend cycle*. Different economic time series exhibit different trends. Some grow or decline linearly, and for these a linear function of time t is an appropriate one to use to describe the trend. Some curvilinear trends

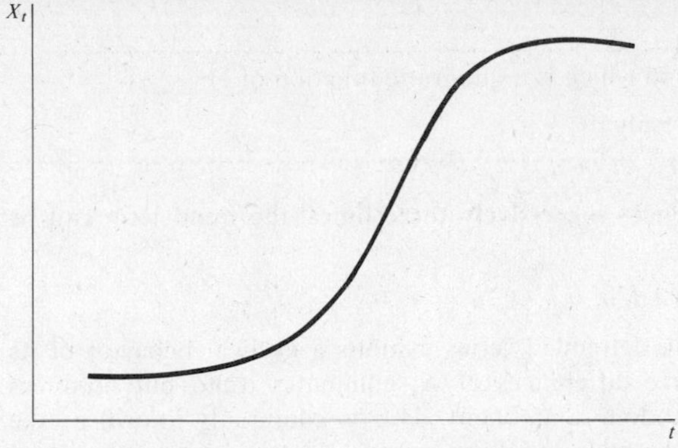

Figure 15-1 A logistic trend.

can be captured by fitting a polynomial in t to the series. Sometimes the trend is estimated by a moving-polynomial method. Some other series like growth of TV industry or growth of any new product first show a rapid growth and then a gradual tapering off. This is often described by a logistic curve which is given by

$$X_t = \frac{C}{1 + e^{-(\alpha + \beta t)}}$$

The curve is as shown in Fig. 15-1. C is the ceiling and β the proportionality factor in the growth rate. The growth rate at any time is given by

$$\frac{dX_t}{dt} = \beta \frac{X_t(C - X_t)}{C}$$

i.e., the rate of growth at any time t is proportional to the size already achieved and the amount by which the size falls short of the maximum (distance from the ceiling).

An economic time series from which the trend has been removed is called a *detrended series*.

15-2 METHODS OF TREND ELIMINATION

Polynomial Methods

Suppose

$$X_t = a + bt + ct^2$$

then $\delta X_t = X_t - X_{t-1} = a + bt + ct^2 - \left[a + b(t-1) + c(t-1)^2\right]$

$$= (b - c) + 2ct$$

$$\delta^2 X_t = \delta(\delta X_t) = 2c$$

$$\delta^3 X_t = 0$$

Thus, if

$$\begin{aligned} X_t &= (\text{a trend which is a quadratic function of } t) \\ &\quad + \text{a residual} \\ &= a + bt + ct^2 + u_t \end{aligned}$$

then by taking first differences successively three times, the trend term can be eliminated. However, since

$$\delta^3 X_t = 0 + \delta^3 u_t = u_t - 3u_{t-1} + 3u_{t-2} - u_{t-3}$$

the resulting residual in the detrended series exhibits a cyclical behavior of its own. Thus taking successive differences of X_t eliminates trend but produces serial correlation in the random component. This is commonly known as the Slutsky-Yule effect. If, on the other hand, we remove the trend by a polynomial regression, i.e., by regressing X_t on t and t^2 with a constant term in this case, this produces a different sort of correlation in the residuals which now satisfy the three linear restrictions

$$\sum \hat{u}_t = 0$$

$$\sum t\hat{u}_t = 0$$

$$\sum t^2\hat{u}_t = 0$$

Thus some induced correlation in the resulting residuals is unavoidable, but we will see later that regression methods have some advantages over the other methods.

Sometimes it is not possible to capture the trend-cycle component by the same polynomial over the entire range; e.g., consider a series as in Fig. 15-2. In this case we can use a piecewise polynomial. It is best to fit separate quadratic trends to the ranges (t_0,t_1), (t_1,t_2), (t_2,t_3), etc. We then have

$$\begin{aligned} X_t &= a_1 + b_1 t + c_1 t^2 + u_{1t} \qquad \text{for the range } t_0 \leqslant t \leqslant t_1 \\ &= a_2 + b_2 t + c_2 t^2 + u_{2t} \qquad \text{for the range } t_1 \leqslant t \leqslant t_2 \\ &= a_3 + b_3 t + c_3 t^2 + u_{3t} \qquad \text{for the range } t_2 \leqslant t \leqslant t_3 \end{aligned} \qquad (15\text{-}1)$$

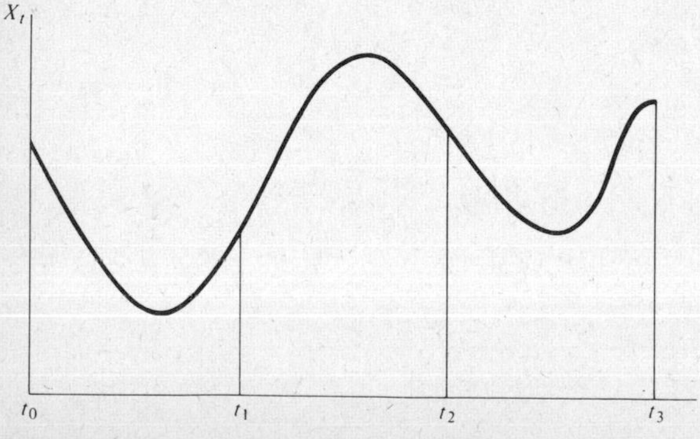

Figure 15-2 A piecewise polynomial trend.

Also note that the values of the polynomials have to be equal at the joining points, i.e.,

$$a_1 + b_1t_1 + c_1t_1^2 = a_2 + b_2t_1 + c_2t_1^2$$

and

$$a_2 + b_2t_2 + c_2t_2^2 = a_3 + b_3t_2 + c_3t_2^2 \tag{15-2}$$

Thus the parameters in the three equations (15-1) have to be estimated subject to the two constraints given by (15-2). The piecewise polynomial method gives greater flexibility than the simple polynomial method. The purpose in fitting moving polynomials is also the same—to give a more flexible representation for the trend component. The moving-polynomial method works as follows: Suppose we have 40 observations and we decide to fit a quadratic trend to each 20 observations. Then we estimate a polynomial for the first 20 observations, another one for observations 2 to 21, another one for observations 3 to 22, etc. Thus, for the second observation we have estimates of trend values from 2 equations (1 to 20 and 2 to 21), for the third observation we have estimates from 3 equations (1 to 20, 2 to 21, 3 to 22), etc. We can take the average of all the available estimates as the estimate of the trend value for that observation. A practically used variant of the moving-polynomial method is the centered-moving-average method; e.g., with monthly data, you take the average

$$\frac{1}{25}\sum_{j=-12}^{+12} X_{t+j} \left(\text{or } \frac{1}{24}\sum_{j=-11}^{12} X_{t+j} \right)$$

as an estimate for the trend value for X_t.

Logistic Trends

Logistic trends are not so commonly used, but they can represent a large number of growth curves. There are several methods of fitting the logistic, but the easiest one is to note that

$$\frac{1}{X_t}\frac{dX_t}{dt} = \beta - \frac{\beta}{C}X_t$$

In practice we can use δX_t for dX_t/dt.

Thus we regress $\delta X_t/X_t$ on X_t. The intercept term gives an estimate of β, and the slope gives an estimate of $-\beta/C$. Also since

$$\log\left(\frac{C}{X_t} - 1\right) = -(\alpha + \beta t)$$

the parameter α can be estimated as the mean value of $[-\hat{\beta}t - \log(\hat{C}/X_t - 1)]$. However, this parameter is usually not of great interest. The parameters that are of interest are the ceiling C and the proportionate rate of growth β. Griliches[1]

[1] See Zvi Griliches, Hybrid Corn: An Exploration in the Economics of Technological Change, *Econometrica*, October, 1957, pp. 501–522. For alternative methods of estimating the logistic, see F. R. Oliver, Methods of Estimating the Logistic Growth Function, *Applied Statistics*, 1964, pp. 57–66.

estimated the values of β and C for a number of corn-growing regions in the United States and tried to explain the differences in these parameters in terms of some economic variables.

15-3 SEASONAL VARIATION

The term seasonal variation refers to systematic though not necessarily regular intrayear movements in economic time series. Seasonal movements are assumed to be caused by exogenous forces, are deemed uncontrollable, and hence are removed before further analysis. "The relative predictability of the seasonal component (albeit imperfect) is part of the economists' desire to remove it before analyzing the remainder, for not only is it due to basic forces of a fundamental nature which it would be folly to try to modify by fiscal means but the rhythm is a recognizable one, to which we are accustomed and whose removal we do not desire."[1]

Given the definition and objective of seasonal adjustment, we will now turn to the following two problems:

1. Deseasonalizing a given quarterly, monthly, or weekly series
2. Estimation of economic relationships from both seasonally adjusted and unadjusted data

Deseasonalizing a Given Series

Broadly speaking, there are two methods of seasonal adjustment: the official method and the least-squares method. The usual method used by official agencies is called the ratio to moving average method. In brief it consists of taking a central moving average of the original series, dividing the original series by the moving average to get a preliminary estimate of the seasonal component, and then adjusting these estimates so that the sum of the seasonally adjusted series for the calendar year is equal to the sum of the original series.

In contrast, the least-squares methods estimate the seasonal component by running a regression of the original series on some seasonal variables. Usually, these seasonal variables are taken to be dummies; e.g., with quarterly data we run a regression of X_t on three dummies

$$
\begin{aligned}
D_1 &= 1 \quad \text{if the observation is for the first quarter} \\
&= 0 \quad \text{otherwise} \\
D_2 &= 1 \quad \text{if the observation is for the second quarter} \\
&= 0 \quad \text{otherwise} \\
D_3 &= 1 \quad \text{if the observation is for the third quarter} \\
&= 0 \quad \text{otherwise}
\end{aligned}
$$

[1] E. J. Hannan, The Estimation of a Changing Seasonal Pattern, *Journal of the American Statistical Association*, December, 1964, p. 1073.

We then take the residuals from this equation as the seasonally adjusted series.

There are two problems with this method. First, the sum of the residuals from a regression equation is zero and thus the sum of the seasonally adjusted series is equal to zero. What we want is to have the sum of the seasonally adjusted series equal the sum of the original series. This we can accomplish by adding the mean $\bar{X}$ to each observation in the seasonally adjusted series obtained from the regression equation.

The second problem is that the estimates of the regression coefficients corresponding to the seasonal dummies are merely $\bar{X}_1$, $\bar{X}_2$, $\bar{X}_3$, and $\bar{X}_4$, the means of the first, second third, and fourth quarters, respectively, and this does not sound very plausible. This problem does not arise if we estimate moving seasonals and also include some trend terms in the equation.[1]

In his discussion of seasonal adjustment, Lovell[2] talks of some logical implications of certain simple consistency requirements that seasonal-adjustment procedures should satisfy. If X_t is the unadjusted series and X_t^a is the adjusted series, the properties that Lovell defines are

1. Sum preserving: $(X_t + Y_t)^a = X_t^a + Y_t^a$
   As an illustration let X_t be employment and Y_t be unemployment so that $X_t + Y_t =$ total labor force. Then seasonally adjusted labor force should be equal to the sum of seasonally adjusted employment and seasonally adjusted unemployment.
2. Product preserving: $(X_t Y_t)^a = (X_t^a)(Y_t^a)$
   As an illustration suppose X_t is real quantity and Y_t is the price index so that $X_t Y_t$ is the nominal quantity. What the product-preserving property says is that the seasonally adjusted nominal quantity should be equal to the product of the seasonally adjusted real quantity and seasonally adjusted price index. If the adjustment is product preserving, it does not matter whether we seasonally adjust any deflated series or deflate the seasonally adjusted nominal series by a seasonally adjusted price index.
   Lovell proves that if an adjustment procedure is both sum preserving and product preserving, it is trivial because it implies $X_t^a = X_t$ or $X_t^a = 0$. Thus we cannot insist on both these properties simultaneously.
3. Orthogonality: This property says that we should havs $\sum_t (X_t - X_t^a)X_t^a = 0$. If this condition is not met, it implies that seasonal-correction terms are correlated with the adjustment series, which means that some seasonality remains in the data.
4. Idempotency: This property says that $(X_t^a)^a = X_t^a$ for all t. If this condition is not met, subjecting the series X_t once more to seasonal adjustment will produce a different series. This implies that the procedure is deficient.

[1] See D. J. Cowden, Moving Seasonal Indexes, *Journal of the American Statistical Association*, 1942, pp. 523–524. Cowden proposes that for each season the corresponding seasonal component be represented by a polynomial.

[2] Michael C. Lovell, Seasonal Adjustment of Economic Time Series and Multiple Regression Analysis, *Journal of the American Statistical Association*, December, 1963, pp. 993–1010.

5. Symmetry: This property says

$$\frac{\partial X_t^a}{\partial X_s} = \frac{\partial X_s^a}{\partial X_t}$$

for all t and S. This requirement states that whether we change observation X_t or any other observation, the seasonally adjusted series should be affected in a symmetric fashion.

Lovell then proves that any sum-preserving procedure that possesses two of the properties orthogonality, idempotency, and symmetry also satisfies the third property. He also argues that the official adjustment procedures do not satisfy the above-mentioned elementary properties but that least-squares methods do. He therefore advocates least-squares procedures.

15-4 REGRESSION ANALYSIS WITH SEASONAL DATA

In regression analysis with seasonal data where seasonal variation is removed by the inclusion of dummy variables, one need not regress each of the dependent and independent variables on the dummy variables and then run the regression with the deseasonalized data. One can as well run the regression equation with the unadjusted values with the dummy variables included as additional explanatory variables. This result was first noted by Frisch and Waugh in connection with regression analysis with detrended series and is known as the Frisch-Waugh theorem. In general let X_1 and X_2 be two sets of explanatory variables. Let $\hat{y}$ be the residual from a regression of y on X_2 and $\hat{X}_1$ the residual from a regression of X_1 on X_2. Let b be the regression coefficient of $\hat{y}$ on $\hat{X}_1$. If X_2 are the seasonal variables, clearly b is the set of regression coefficients obtained by running a regression with seasonally adjusted data. If X_2 are trend variables, b is the set of regression coefficients obtained by running a regression with detrended series, and so on. What the Frisch-Waugh theorem says is that b is the same as the estimate of β in the regression equation[1]

$$y = X_1\beta + X_2\gamma + u$$

Another theoretically attractive property of the least-squares methods is that one has a clear idea of the degrees of freedom involved because one knows how many parameters are being estimated in the process of trend elimination and seasonal adjustment. With the official methods the precise number of degrees of freedom lost (in the ratio to moving average method) may be intractable, but because it is not precisely known one should not ignore it. Lovell suggests that the degrees of freedom is $d = 3m - 1$, where m is the number of seasons. Thus it is 35 for monthly data and 11 for quarterly data. Since usually this problem is ignored in regression analysis with seasonally adjusted data, the overstatement in the degrees of freedom results in overstatement of the significance of regression coefficients.

[1] This proposition is proved in Appendix B in the section Prior Adjustment.

In estimating the seasonal component of a time series, the usual procedure is to specify, estimate, and eliminate the trend—including any cycles of more than one year—before proceeding to the estimation of seasonal variation. Jorgenson[1] suggests estimating by least-squares methods both trend and seasonal variation simultaneously. The procedure is to use a polynomial for the trend component and the seasonal dummies for the seasonal component.[2] One problem with this procedure is that it may not be possible to approximate the trend component by any simple polynomial, and thus the resulting seasonal adjustment could be poorer than that given by the usual ratio to moving average method. But this drawback can be eliminated by using the piecewise-polynomial method outlined earlier.

The procedure of using seasonal dummies in the regression equation implicitly assumes that only the intercept term varies seasonally but the slope coefficient does not. If we have a lot of data, we can fit a separate regression equation for each season (month or quarter) and check whether the intercepts or slopes or both vary seasonally. Thus we can test any hypothesis that we want about the pattern of seasonal variation. The use of seasonally unadjusted data permits testing of some hypotheses about seasonal variation in parameters.[3] The seasonally adjusted data, made available by the official agencies and often used in regression analyses, does not permit testing any hypotheses about seasonal variation in parameters. In fact the problems with the use of seasonally adjusted data may be more serious than this in dynamic models. Even if the true relationship between y_t and x_t is static of the type $y_t = \beta x_t + u_t$, we will get a dynamic model due to seasonal adjustment; i.e., y_t^a will depend on x_t^a, x_{t-1}^a, x_{t-2}^a, etc. Also, even if the relationship between y_t and x_t is dynamic, the estimated relationship will be distorted because of the process of seasonal adjustment. Wallis[4] shows that if the true relationship is

$$y_t = \sum_{j=0}^{\infty} \beta_j x_{t-j} + u_t$$

so that x_t affects y_t with only a lag, but we try to estimate the relationship between y_t and x_t from the seasonally adjusted data (given by the official agencies), we will find y_t depending not only on past x's but also on future x's;

[1] D. W. Jorgenson, Minimum Variance, Linear, Unbiased Seasonal Adjustment of Economic Time Series, *Journal of the American Statistical Association*, September, 1964, pp. 681–724.

[2] Lovell points out that Jorgenson's procedure is sum-preserving and idempotent but is neither orthogonal nor symmetric. See Michael C. Lovell, Alternative Axiomatizations of Seasonal Adjustment, *Journal of the American Statistical Association*, September, 1966, pp. 800–802.

[3] See G. W. Ladd, Regression Analyses of Seasonal Data, *Journal of the American Statistical Association*, June, 1974, pp. 402–420, for illustrations of such tests. See also J. J. Thomas and K. F. Wallis, Seasonal Variation in Regression Analysis, *Journal of the Royal Statistical Society*, Series A, 1971, pp. 57–72.

[4] K. F. Wallis, Seasonal Adjustment and Relations between Variables, *Journal of the American Statistical Association*, March, 1974, pp. 18–31. See also C. A. Sims, Seasonality in Regression, *Journal of the American Statistical Association*, September, 1974, pp. 618–626.

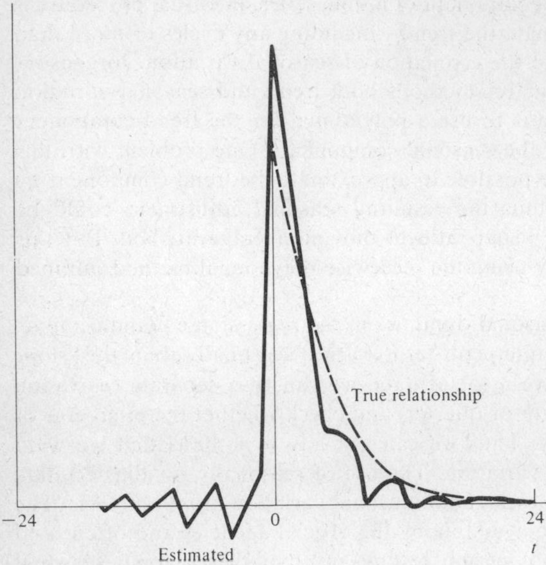

Figure 15-3 Bias due to the estimation of a distributed-lag model from seasonally adjusted data.

i.e., we will get an impression of y_t affecting x_t with a lag. The true pattern of β's and the pattern of β's estimated from seasonally adjusted data are shown in Fig. 15-3.

15-5 FORECASTING

A *forecast* or a *prediction* is generally defined as a statement concerning future events. Here we are confined to only quantitative economic predictions. Forecasting is one of the most common uses of econometric methods. Businessmen make forecasts of sales for their company and for the industry. Macro economists make forecasts of GNP, employment, etc.

Broadly speaking, there are two methods of forecasting:

1. Naive methods
2. Regression methods

In regression methods we can distinguish between two kinds:

1. Pure autoregression (or more generally Box-Jenkins methods)
2. Regression on related variables (or more generally econometric methods)

Suppose a company has to forecast sales for period t and suppose our time period is a quarter. Since quarterly sales have a seasonal effect, one naive way of forecasting is to say that sales in this quarter will be the same as the sales in the corresponding quarter last year adjusted for the most recent trend; i.e.,

$$S_t^* = S_{t-4} \frac{S_{t-1}}{S_{t-5}}$$

where S_t^* = forecast value of S_t

S_{t-4} = sales in the corresponding quarter last year

S_{t-1}/S_{t-5} = adjustment factor for the latest trend

In regression methods, we first estimate the relationship between the forecast variable and some other explanatory variables over the period for which we have data. Then we predict for future time periods the forecast variable, given the other variables from the regression equation. For example, suppose a firm wants to predict sales and it thinks that its sales depend on its advertising outlays (A) and on general economic activity, which we will measure by disposable income (Y). So $S = \alpha + \beta Y + \gamma A$. It can estimate α, β, γ from past data on S, Y, and A. Then the forecast for sales in period t will be $S_t^* = \hat{\alpha} + \hat{\beta} Y_t + \hat{\gamma} A_t$. There are several problems with this procedure: (1) The relationship may not be stable over the period of estimation and period of forecast. (2) The explanatory variables Y_t and A_t themselves have to be forecast. A_t is a variable over which the firm may have control, but Y_t is not.

In autoregressive methods, instead of regressing the forecast variable on other variables, we regress on the past values of the forecast variable itself; e.g., we estimate a regression equation of the sort $S_t = \alpha_0 + \alpha_1 S_{t-1} + \alpha_2 S_{t-2}$ and after estimating α_0, α_1, and α_2 from past data, estimate sales in period T as $S_T^* = \hat{\alpha}_0 + \hat{\alpha}_1 S_{T-1} + \hat{\alpha}_2 S_{T-2}$. Here the problem of forecasting the explanatory variables does not arise unless one is forecasting for several periods in the future. But the problem of stability of the relationship over the estimation period and period of forecast is still there.

Exercise For the consumption data given in Table 7-1 use the following methods for forecasting:

1. Naive method

$$C_t^* - C_{t-1} \frac{C_{t-1}}{C_{t-2}}$$

2. Regression method

$$C_t = \alpha + \beta Y_t$$

3. Autoregressive method

$$C_t = \alpha' + \beta' C_{t-1}$$

Use the period 1919–1959 for estimation and use the estimated regressions to predict C_t for 1960–1970. Which of the three methods gives the most accurate forecasts? (For measuring accuracy, use the measures discussed below.)

15-6 MEASURING THE ACCURACY OF FORECASTS

Let A_t be the actual value of a variable in period t and P_t the predicted or forecast value for the same period. The actual relative change is $a_t = (A_t - A_{t-1})/A_{t-1}$, and the predicted relative change is $p_t = (P_t - A_{t-1})/A_{t-1}$.

The following measures are commonly used to measure the accuracy of forecasts.

1 Mean-square error. The first measure is the mean-square error

$$\text{MSE} = \frac{1}{n} \sum_{t=1}^{n} (p_t - a_t)^2 = \frac{1}{n} \sum_{t=1}^{n} \left(\frac{P_t - A_t}{A_{t-1}} \right)^2$$

This can be written as

$$\text{MSE} = (\bar{p} - \bar{a})^2 + S_{p-a}^2$$

where S_{p-a}^2 is the variance of the prediction errors.

The first term, called the *bias component*, indicates the extent to which the magnitude of the MSE is the consequence of a tendency to estimate too high or too low a level of the forecast variable. Theil (1966) has pointed out that a further decomposition of the MSE is possible. If we let r denote the correlation between a and p, we have the identities

$$S_{p-a}^2 = S_p^2 + S_a^2 - 2rS_pS_a$$

$$= (S_p - S_a)^2 + 2(1 - r)S_pS_a$$

Also

$$S_{p-a}^2 = (S_p - rS_a)^2 + (1 - r^2)S_a^2$$

Theil calls $(S_p - S_a)^2$ the variance component, $2(1 - r)S_pS_a$ the covariance component, $(S_p - rS_a)^2$ the regression component, and $(1 - r^2)S_a^2$ the disturbance component of the MSE.

Thus we can decompose the MSE into either one of the two sets of components: (1) bias, variance, and covariance, or (2) bias, regression, and disturbance. Each of these decompositions gives us some information. The variance component suggests that the magnitude of the MSE may be influenced by the extent to which the variance of predictions is larger or smaller than the variance of the actual values. However, there is no a priori reason to insist that the variances should be equal. The decomposition into bias, regression, and disturbance components is perhaps more illuminating. The disturbance component is the variance of the residuals obtained by regressing the actual relative changes on the predicted changes. The other two components measure what can be called "systematic" errors.

Corresponding to these two decompositions of MSE, Theil defines two sets of statistics

$$U^M = \frac{(\bar{p} - \bar{a})^2}{\text{MSE}} = \text{bias proportion}$$

$$U^S = \frac{(S_p - S_a)^2}{\text{MSE}} = \text{variance proportion}$$

$$U^C = \frac{2(1 - r)S_pS_a}{\text{MSE}} = \text{covariance proportion}$$

and $$U^M = \frac{(\bar{p} - \bar{a})^2}{\text{MSE}} = \text{bias proportion}$$

$$U^R = \frac{(S_p - rS_a)^2}{\text{MSE}} = \text{regression proportion}$$

$$U^D = \frac{(1 - r^2)S_a^2}{\text{MSE}} = \text{disturbance proportion}$$

Note that $U^M + U^S + U^C = U^M + U^R + U^D = 1$.

Consider first U^M. If it is large, it means that the average predicted change deviates substantially from the average actual change. This is clearly a serious error, because we should expect that forecasters must be able to reduce such errors in the course of time. Of the other decompositions, the decomposition U^R, U^D is more meaningful than the decomposition U^S, U^C. If we consider the regression of actual on predicted values, i.e.,

$$A_t = \alpha + \beta P_t$$

then U^M will be zero if $\hat{\alpha} = 0$ and U^R will be zero if $\hat{\beta} = 1$. If we plot the predicted values against the actual values, the spread of values around the line of perfect forecasts $A_t = P_t$ yields information on possible inadequacies of the forecasts, and the decomposition U^M, U^R, and U^D yields information on this.

It is common practice to report the decomposition of mean-square error into the components U^M, U^S, and U^C. However, as Granger and Newbold[1] argue, it is hard to give any meaningful interpretation to U^S and U^C. They consider the case where the actual series is generated by the process

$$A_t = \alpha A_{t-1} + \epsilon_t \qquad 0 \leqslant \alpha \leqslant 1$$

where ϵ_t is a zero mean independently distributed disturbance term. Consider the predictor $P_t = \alpha A_{t-1}$. Then in the limit in large samples

$$U^M = 0 \qquad U^S = \frac{1 - \alpha}{1 + \alpha} \qquad \text{and} \qquad U^C = \frac{2\alpha}{1 + \alpha}$$

If one varies α from 0 to 1, U^S and U^C can take on any values subject to the restrictions $0 \leqslant U^S$, $U^C \leqslant 1$, and $U^S + U^C = 1$. Thus interpretation of these quantities is impossible. On the other hand, both U^M and U^R tend to zero for the optimal predictor.

2 Regression and correlation measures. A second measure of accuracy of forecasts is the coefficient of correlation between predicted and actual changes. The disadvantage with this is that it does not penalize the forecaster for systematic linear bias. Thus a forecaster who always underestimates actual changes by 50% receives a perfect score. A related suggestion is that of Mincer and Zarnowitz,[2]

[1] C. W. J. Granger and P. Newbold, Some Comments on the Evaluation of Economic Forecasts, *Applied Economics*, 1973, pp. 35–47.

[2] J. Mincer and V. Zarnowitz, The Evaluation of Economic Forecasts, in "Economic Forecasts and Expectations," J. Mincer (ed.), National Bureau of Economic Research, New York, 1969.

who suggest regressing actual values on predicted values, i.e., running the regression

$$A_t = \alpha + \beta P_t$$

According to them the predictor P_t is called "efficient" if $\alpha = 0$ and $\beta = 1$ (or in practice if the sample estimates of α and β do not differ significantly from 0 and 1, respectively). Granger and Newbold argue that the Mincer-Zarnowitz definition "hardly constitutes a definition of 'efficiency' according to any acceptable interpretation of the word." They argue that any measure that looks at only the relationship between the predictor and predicted series and not the magnitude and behavior of the prediction errors will give a misleading impression about the accuracy of forecasts.[1]

3 Theil's U statistics. Theil first defined a statistic measuring the accuracy of forecasts by[2]

$$U = \frac{\sqrt{\text{MSE}}}{\sqrt{\sum A_t^2/n} + \sqrt{\sum P_t^2/n}} \tag{15-3}$$

This statistic lies between zero and 1. It is equal to zero if P_t is a perfect forecast for A_t, and it is equal to 1 if $P_t = -bA_t$ ($b > 0$). Furthermore, unlike the r^2 criterion, it penalizes systematic linear bias. However, it does not provide a good ranking of forecasts. Granger and Newbold give the following example as an illustration: Let

$$A_t = \alpha A_{t-1} + \epsilon_t \qquad 0 \leqslant \alpha \leqslant 1$$

and consider the predictor

$$P_t = \beta A_{t-1} \qquad 0 \leqslant \beta \leqslant 1$$

Then they show that in large samples U^2 tends to $1 - [2\beta(1+\alpha)]/(1+\beta)^2]$, which is minimized for $\beta = 1$ rather than the optimal value of $\beta = \alpha$. This sort of problem arises with any measure of forecasting accuracy that is not a simple function of mean-square error.

Because of these problems with the U statistic defined in (15-3), Theil suggested in his later book[3] the use of

$$U_1 = \sqrt{\frac{\text{MSE}}{\sum A_t^2/n}} \tag{15-4}$$

[1] Dhrymes et al. suggest that "cross-spectral analysis can be used to investigate the relationship between predicted and actual values." See Dhrymes et al., Criteria for Evaluation of Economic Models, *Annals of Economic and Social Measurement*, 1972, pp. 291–324. Granger and Newbold argue that rather than consider the properties of the predictor and actual series, as is commonly done, one should consider the distributional and time-series properties of the forecast-error series.

[2] H. Theil, "Economic Forecasts and Policy," North-Holland Publishing Company, Amsterdam, 1961.

[3] H. Theil, "Applied Economic Forecasting," Rand McNally & Company, 1966.

This measure is again zero in the case of perfect forecasts and does not suffer from the defects of the other statistic. U_1^2 in the limit tends to $(1-\alpha)^2 + (\beta - \alpha)^2$ in the above example considered by Granger and Newbold and thus is minimum for the optimal value $\beta = \alpha$.

In summary, of the two statistics U and U_1 defined in (15-3) and (15-4), the statistic U is not a useful measure and U_1 should be preferred, as was also suggested by Theil. Further, of the two decompositions of mean-square error into bias, variance, and covariance proportions, and bias, regression, and residual proportions, though the former is often reported, it is not a useful decomposition, and the latter decomposition should be used.

4 Other measures. Some other measures that have been suggested are the average absolute error

$$AAE = \frac{1}{n} \sum |A_t - P_t|$$

and errors in the turning points of the cycle. Ferber[1] compared the accuracy of naive forecasts given by the formula

$$P_t = A_{t-4} \frac{A_{t-1}}{A_{t-5}}$$

with the actual forecasts based on the carload shipments ex ante data collected by the American Railway Association. He used the average absolute error AAE to judge the accuracy of the forecasts. He found that for the prewar period 1929–1941 the naive forecasts were more accurate than observed anticipations for the total nonfarm aggregate and for each of the five component industries he considered. For the period 1946–1950 the same was true for the nonfarm aggregate, but the actual forecasts were slightly better than naive forecasts in three industries, iron and steel, flour, and cement. Ferber therefore concluded that firms are not too accurate in their forecasting, though he said that the railroad shippers' survey is perhaps not a reasonable measure of actual anticipations.

Hirsch and Lovell[2] studied the accuracy of anticipations data provided by the Manufacturers' Inventory and Sales Expectations Survey of the Office of Business Economics, U.S. Department of Commerce. They used turning-point errors, Theil's U statistics, mean-square errors, and the various decompositions of MSE described earlier, to measure forecast accuracy. They found that the actual forecasts were more accurate than those implied by naive models. The only naive model they tried that did better than the actual forecasts was one that exploited knowledge of the seasonal pattern for the entire sample period. Obviously, this information is not available at the time the forecasts are made. Thus these recent data show that firms do better in forecasting than using naive models.

[1] Robert Ferber, "The Railroad Shippers' Forecasts," Bureau of Economic Research, University of Illinois, Urbana, 1953.

[2] Albert A. Hirsch and Michael C. Lovell, "Sales Anticipations and Inventory Behavior," John Wiley and Sons, Inc., New York, 1969.

15-7 FORECASTING FROM PAST OBSERVED VALUES

We have till now discussed measures of forecasting accuracy. We will now briefly discuss some models of expectation formation based on past observed values. Ferber suggested the following law to describe expectation formation:

$$P_t = \alpha + A_{t-4}\left(\beta + \gamma \frac{A_{t-1} - A_{t-5}}{A_{t-5}}\right) \tag{15-5}$$

$$P_t = \alpha + \beta A_{t-4} + \gamma\left(A_{t-4} \frac{A_{t-1} - A_{t-5}}{A_{t-5}}\right) \tag{15-6}$$

where P_t = anticipated carloadings in period t

A_t = actual carloadings in period t

If $\alpha = \gamma = 0$ and $\beta = 1$, we assume no change from the corresponding quarter last year. The naive formula discussed earlier amounts to $\alpha = 0$, $\beta = \gamma = 1$. When Ferber estimated Eq. (15-5) for aggregate over all commodities except farm products for the period 1929–1941, he obtained the coefficients $\alpha = .09$, $\beta = .986$, $\gamma = .43$, and $R^2 = .972$. This equation describes the way expectations were formed.

One major point in Eq. (15-5) is the regressivity of expectations. This is a tendency to predict a return toward a situation of the corresponding quarter of the previous year, rather than extrapolate the recent trend. Equation (15-5) can be written as

$$P_t = \alpha + \beta A_{t-1} \frac{A_{t-4}}{A_{t-5}} - (\beta - \gamma)(A_{t-1} - A_{t-5}) \frac{A_{t-4}}{A_{t-5}} \tag{15-7}$$

The ratio A_{t-4}/A_{t-5} is a crude form of allowing for seasonal movements. $(\beta - \gamma)$ is the "reversal coefficient." Ferber's aggregate railroad shippers' data yielded $\beta = .986$ and $\gamma = .43$, thus showing that expectations were indeed regressive. Hirsch and Lovell found that the expectations data they considered also showed regressivity. They found that the actual data also had a strong regressive component, and this explains why the anticipations data are regressive.

Another formula for expectation formation is the adaptive-expectations formula used by Cagan[1] and Nerlove.[2] It is given by

$$P_t - P_{t-1} = \lambda(A_{t-1} - P_{t-1}) \qquad 0 < \lambda < 1 \tag{15-8}$$

This says that expectations are revised (upward or downward) based on the most recent error. Suppose you predicted P_{t-1} to be 100 but A_{t-1} was 120. So your error was 20. Your prediction for period t, i.e., P_t, will be > 100 but less than 120.

[1] Phillip D. Cagan, The Monetary Dynamics of Hyperinflations, in M. Friedman (ed.), "Studies in the Quantity Theory of Money," University of Chicago Press, Chicago, 1956, pp. 25–117.

[2] Marc Nerlove, "The Dynamics of Supply: Estimation of Farmers' Response to Price," The Johns Hopkins Press, Baltimore, 1958.

Hirsch and Lovell extended the adaptive-expectations model to include seasonal factors, and they estimated the equation

$$\frac{P_t - A_{t-1}}{A_{t-1}} = \alpha_0 + \lambda \frac{P_{t-1} - A_{t-1}}{A_{t-1}} + \alpha S_1 + \alpha_2 S_2 + \alpha_3 S_3 \qquad (15\text{-}9)$$

where the dummy variable $S_i = 1$ in quarter i
$= 0$ otherwise

They compared the adaptive-expectations model with Ferber's and found that for short-period forecasts Ferber's model did better than the adaptive-expectations model. For longer-period forecasts they found the reverse, however. For two-period-ahead forecasts, for example, Ferber's model would be

$$P_t = \alpha + \beta A_{t-4} + \gamma A_{t-4} \frac{A_{t-2} - A_{t-4}}{A_{t-6}}$$

and the adaptive model would be obtained by changing all the lags $(t-1)$ to $(t-2)$ in Eq. (15-9).

15-8 BOX-JENKINS METHODS[1]

The above methods of extrapolative, adaptive, and regressive forecasting are simple methods based on past values. More general methods are known as Box-Jenkins methods. Let B be a backward-shift operator[2] defined as

$$Bx_t = x_{t-1}$$

or more generally $B^j x_t = x_{t-j}$. We discussed earlier autoregressive moving-average (ARMA) models of the sort

$$x_t - \phi_1 x_{t-1} - \phi_2 x_{t-2} - \cdots - \phi_p x_{t-p} = e_t - \theta_1 e_{t-1} - \cdots - \theta_q e_{t-q}$$

In the notation of the backward-shift operator B this can be written as

$$\phi_p(B) x_t = \theta_q(B) e_t$$

where $\phi_p(B)$ is a pth-degree polynomial in B defined as

$$\phi_p(B) = 1 - \phi_1 B - \phi_2 B^2 - \cdots - \phi_p B^p$$

and similarly

$$\theta_q(B) = 1 - \theta_1 B - \theta_2 B^2 - \cdots - \theta_q B^q$$

This is an ARMA (p,q) model. It can be used to model stationary time series. Since most time series also contain a trend and are thus nonstationary, we first

[1] G. E. P. Box and G. M. Jenkins, "Time Series Analysis: Forecasting and Control," Holden-Day, Inc., Publisher, San Francisco, 1970. The discussion in this section is very brief and is merely intended to give the reader a brief overview of what the method involves. Interested readers should refer to the book by Box and Jenkins.

[2] In the next chapter the operator L is used for the same purpose.

eliminate the trend by successive first differences. Let $\delta x_t = (1 - B)x_t = x_t - x_{t-1}$. If we take first differences of x_t d times, we can represent this by $\delta^d x_t$. The model that Box and Jenkins suggest is an ARMA representation for $\delta^d x_t$, i.e.,

$$\phi_p(B)\delta^d x_t = \theta_q(B)e_t$$

This is an ARIMA (p,d,q) model (autoregressive integrated moving-average model).

Sometimes there are strong seasonal elements in the data. To eliminate these, we have to use higher-order differences instead of first differences. Define

$$\delta_s x_t = (1 - B^s)x_t = x_t - x_{t-s}$$

e.g., for monthly data we might use $\delta_{12}x_t$ and for quarterly data we might use $\delta_4 x_t$. Thus we can use the ARIMA model

$$\phi_p(B)\delta^d\delta_s x_t = \theta_q(B)e_t$$

The operator $\delta^d\delta_s$ will eliminate both the trend and the seasonal.

In actual practice the degrees (p,d,q) have to be determined before any estimation. This can be done by studying the autocorrelation function using some judgment and some trial and error. Box and Jenkins suggest three steps: identification, estimation, and diagnostic checking.

Identification is the procedure for obtaining an approximate idea of the structure of the model, i.e., the degree of (p,d,q). This term should not be confused with "identification" in econometric literature, which was discussed earlier in the context of simultaneous-equation models.

The next step is estimation. Regarding estimation, autoregressive parameters can be easily estimated by least-squares methods. But moving-average parameters cause difficulties. One procedure that Box and Jenkins suggest is to use a grid-search procedure. To illustrate, suppose the model is

$$x_t - \phi_1 x_{t-1} - \phi_2 x_{t-2} = e_t - \theta_1 e_{t-1} - \theta_2 e_{t-2}$$

This can be written as

$$(1 - \phi_1 B - \phi_2 B^2)x_t = e_t - \theta_1 e_{t-1} - \theta_2 e_{t-2}$$

or
$$x_t = \frac{1}{1 - \phi_1 B - \phi_2 B^2}(e_t - \theta_1 e_{t-1} - \theta_2 e_{t-2})$$

Define
$$v_t = \frac{1}{1 - \phi_1 B - \delta_2 B^2}e_t$$

or
$$v_t - \phi_1 v_{t-1}\phi_2 v_{t-2} = e_t \tag{15-10}$$

Then we have
$$x_t = v_t - \theta_1 v_{t-1} - \theta_2 v_{t-2}$$

or
$$v_t = x_t + \theta_1 v_{t-1} + \theta_2 v_{t-2} \tag{15-11}$$

The grid-search procedure is as follows.

Within the stability region for (θ_1,θ_2) we choose a plausible value $(\hat{\theta}_1,\hat{\theta}_2)$. Starting with $\hat{v}_0 = 0$ and $\hat{v}_1 = 0$, we generate successive estimated values of $\hat{v}_t$ using (15-11), e.g.,

$$\hat{v}_2 = x_2$$

$$\hat{v}_3 = x_3 + \hat{\theta}_1\hat{v}_2$$

$$\hat{v}_4 = x_4 + \hat{\theta}_1\hat{v}_3 + \hat{\theta}_2\hat{v}_2 \qquad \text{etc.}$$

Then, using the $\hat{v}_t$, we estimate ϕ_1 and ϕ_2 by using ordinary least squares on Eq. (15-10), i.e., by regressing $\hat{v}_t$ on $\hat{v}_{t-1}$ and $\hat{v}_{t-2}$. We then compute the residual sum of squares

$$\sum \hat{e}_t^2 = \sum \left(\hat{v}_t - \hat{\phi}_1\hat{v}_{t-1} - \hat{\phi}_2\hat{v}_{t-2}\right)^2$$

Since we are interested in minimizing the residual sum of squares, we choose those values of $\hat{\theta}_1$ and $\hat{\theta}_2$ for which the residual sum of squares $\sum \hat{e}_t^2$ is minimum. If the number of parameters in the moving-average part of the ARMA model is high, this procedure is not very efficient. In practice, however, one does not need more than a couple of parameters to have an adequate representation and the grid-search procedure is operational.

Finally, after estimating the model, one has to use some diagnostic checking. This consists of computing the residuals $\hat{e}_t$ and seeing whether they exhibit any systematic pattern. If they do, we should change the specification of the model and estimate it again. If the residuals are random, we can use the model for forecasting purposes.

As an illustrative example, consider the problem of forecasting hog marketings considered by Leuthold et al.[1] The data consist of 257 daily observations in 1964. The autocorrelation functions for the original data, first differences, and fifth differences are shown in Figs. 15-4, 15-5, and 15-6, respectively. Figure 15-4 shows that the data have a strong 5-day weekly effect (because of the peaks at lags 5, 10, 15). Figure 15-6 again shows a strong weekly effect. Since the peaks are not damping progressively, it suggests the presence of a weekly first-order component. Also, within each week there is a certain amount of damping, thus suggesting a first- or second-order autoregressive component within weeks. Thus Fig. 15-5 suggests the model $(1 - \psi B^5)\phi_p(B)x_t = (1 - \epsilon B^5)\theta_q(B)e_t$. Figure 15-6, which has a deep trough at lag 5, confirms the existence of a weekly moving-average component $(1 - \epsilon B^5)$. The oscillatory nature apart from this deep trough suggests a second-order autoregressive component within weeks. The oscillations are quite small after lag 8, and this suggests a second-order moving-average component interacting with the autoregressive component.

Thus Leuthold et al. argue that Figs. 15-5 and 15-6 suggest the model

$$(1 - \psi B^5)(1 - \phi_1 B - \phi_2 B^2)x_t = (1 - \epsilon B^5)(1 - \theta_1 B - \theta_2 B^2)e_t$$

[1] R. M. Leuthold, A. M. A. MacCormick, A. Smitz, and D. G. Watts, Forecasting Daily Hog Prices and Quantities: A Study of Alternative Forecasting Techniques, *Journal of the American Statistical Association*, March, 1970, pp. 90–107.

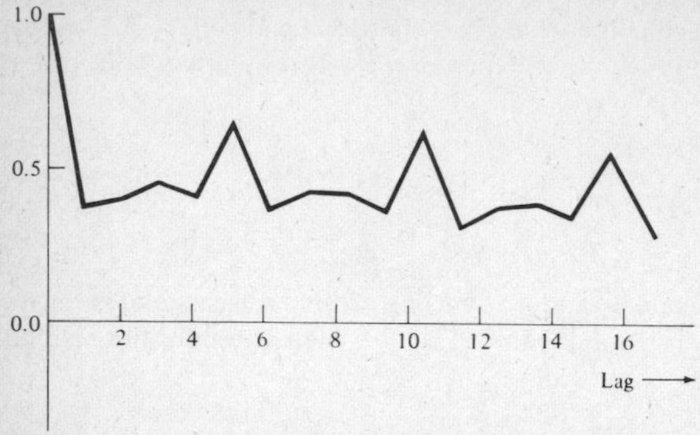

Figure 15-4 Autocorrelation function of levels.

They estimate this model by a grid-search procedure on ϵ, θ_1, and θ_2. The estimated parameters were

$$\psi = 0.90 \quad \phi_1 = 1.44 \qquad \theta_1 = 1.52$$
$$\epsilon = 0.70 \quad \phi_2 = -0.47 \quad \theta_2 = -0.66$$

and the model is

$$(1 - .90B^5)(1 - 1.44B + 0.47B^2)x_t = (1 - 0.70B^5)(1 - 1.52B - .66B^2)e_t$$

For forecasting purposes we multiply out and gather coefficients for like powers of B, and we get

$$x_t = 1.44x_{t-1} - 0.47x_{t-2} + 0.90x_{t-5} - (0.90 \times 1.44)x_{t-6}$$
$$+ (0.90 \times 0.47)x_{t-7} + e_t - 1.52e_{t-1} + 0.66e_{t-2}$$
$$- 0.70e_{t-5} + (0.70 \times 1.52)e_{t-6} - (0.70 \times 0.66)e_{t-7}$$

At the time of forecasting x_t we have all the lagged x's and the lagged errors e, but we do not have e_t. Since e_t are zero mean independently distributed

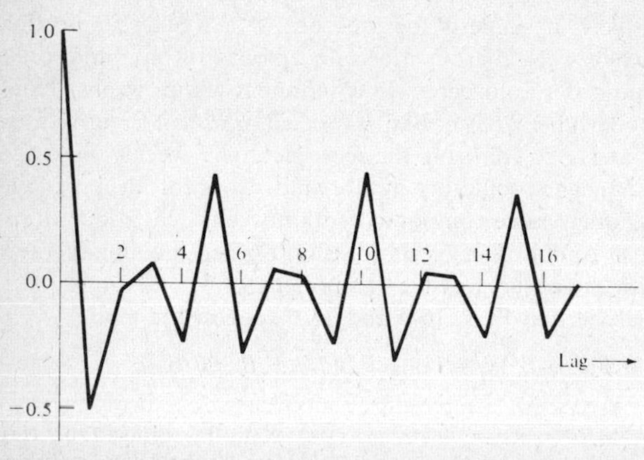

Figure 15-5 Autocorrelation function of first differences.

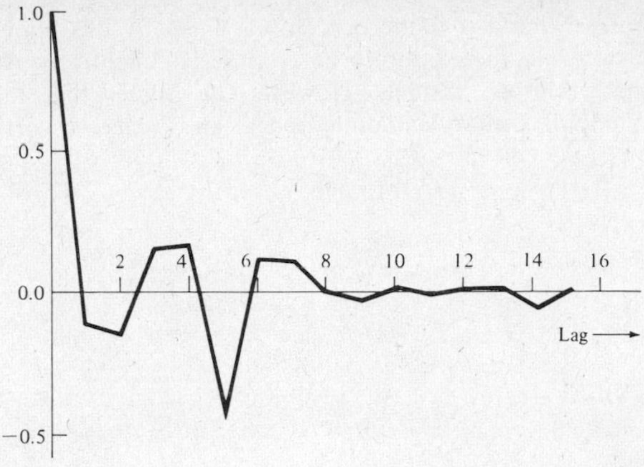

Figure 15-6 Autocorrelation function of fifth differences.

variables, we substitute $e_t = 0$ in the above equation. Leuthold et al. show that the forecasting performance of this equation is almost as good as that of an econometric model using both dummy variables and economic explanatory variables (price variables).

Nerlove[1] suggests a different procedure of identification from that of the Box-Jenkins procedure. His procedure depends on the assumption that the observed time series x_t is the sum of three unobserved components—a trend-cycle component, a seasonal component, and a residual. He suggests that the trend-cycle component be approximated by

$$\frac{1 + \beta_1 B + \beta_2 B^2}{(1 - \alpha_1 B)(1 - \alpha_2 B)} e_{1t}$$

where B is the backward-shift operator defined earlier and e_{1t} are independently and identically distributed random variables with zero mean and variance σ_1^2; i.e., $e_{1t} \sim IID(0,\sigma_1^2)$.

Similarly, the seasonal component (assuming monthly data) can be represented by

$$\frac{1 + \beta_3 B + \beta_4 B^2}{1 - \alpha_3 B^{12}} e_{2t}$$

where $e_{2t} \sim IID(0,\sigma_2^2)$. These considerations lead to the model

$$x_t = \frac{1 + \beta_1 B + \beta_2 B^2}{(1 - \alpha_1 B)(1 - \alpha_2 B)} e_{1t} + \frac{1 + \beta_3 B + \beta_4 B^2}{1 - \alpha_3 B^{12}} e_{2t} + e_{3t}$$

[1] Marc Nerlove, Analysis of Economic Time-Series by Box-Jenkins and Related Techniques, *Report* 7156, Center for Mathematical Studies in Business and Economics, University of Chicago, December, 1971.

where $e_{3t} \sim IID(0, \sigma_3^2)$. Nerlove found that the predictions given by this unobserved-components model were, in the examples he considered, slightly worse than those given by simple ARIMA models. However, he argues that the unobserved-components model has more economic appeal and hence is worth trying in other cases.[1]

[1] "Beginning with blotting paper may not be the best way to make a palatable pudding but gunpowder and sealing wax will surely make a considerable difference! Of course, the proof of the pudding is in the eating, and it is possible that a sensible ARIMA model may prove the better bargain in the end." *Op. cit.*

CHAPTER

SIXTEEN

DISTRIBUTED-LAG MODELS

16-1 FINITE LAG DISTRIBUTIONS

Often the effect of a variable x on another variable y is not contemporaneous but is spread out (or distributed) over a period of time. For instance, if y_t denotes consumption expenditures and x_t income, both in period t, a change in x_t will affect not just current consumer expenditures y_t but also future expenditures y_{t+1}, y_{t+2}, etc. This implies that the current value of y_t depends not just on x_t but also on some past values of x_t. If the effects last k periods, we write this as

$$y_t = \beta_0 x_t + \beta_1 x_{t-1} + \cdots + \beta_k x_{t-k} + u_t \tag{16-1}$$

This is known as a distributed-lag regression model. The problems with the direct least-squares estimation of (16-1) are: First we lose k degrees of freedom because Eq. (16-1) can be estimated from only $(n - k)$ observations, and if k is large, this results in a considerable decrease in the number of effective observations used. Second, often there is high multicollinearity among the x's, and this results in imprecise estimates for the β's. There have therefore been many suggestions in the literature to put some "structure" on the β's in (16-1). These are:

1. The arithmetic lag. This assumes that the lag coefficients β_i decline arithmetically as shown in Fig. 16-1. This was proposed by Irving Fisher[1] long ago. We have

$$\begin{aligned} \beta_i &= (k + 1 - i)\,\beta \qquad && 0 \leqslant i \leqslant k \\ &= 0 && \text{for } i > k \end{aligned} \tag{16-2}$$

[1] Irving Fisher, Note on a Short-Cut Method for Calculating Distributed Lags, *International Statistical Institute Bulletin*, 1937, pp. 323–327.

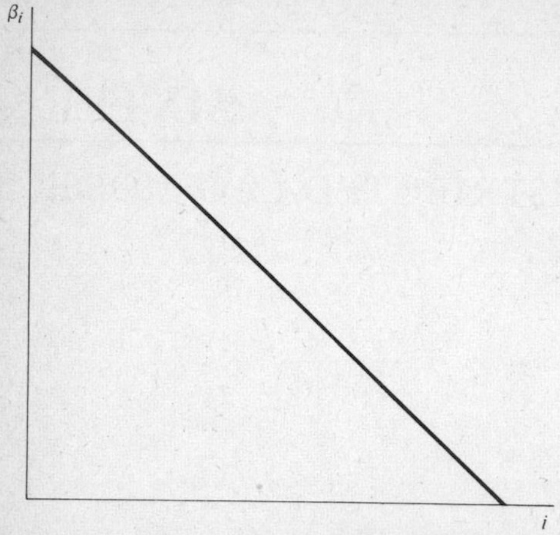

Figure 16-1 A linear distributed lag.

Substituting this in (16-1), we get

$$y_t = \left[\sum_{i=0}^{k} (k + 1 - i)x_{t-i} \right] \beta + u_t$$

$$= z_t \beta + u_t$$

Thus we regress y_t on the "constructed" variable z_t to get an estimate of β, and using Eq. (16-2), we get estimates of the β_i.

2. The inverted V lag. This was suggested and used by DeLeeuw.[1] It is shown in Fig. 16-2. For simplicity suppose k is even, and $\beta_0 = 0$ and $\beta_k = 0$. Then

$$\beta_i = i\beta \qquad \text{for } 0 \leqslant i \leqslant \frac{k}{2}$$

$$= (k - i)\beta \qquad \text{for } \frac{k}{2} \leqslant i \leqslant k \tag{16-3}$$

Again substituting these values in (16-1), we get

$$y_t = \beta z_t + u_t \qquad \text{where} \qquad z_t = \sum_{i=0}^{k/2} ix_{t-i} + \sum_{(k/2)+1}^{k} (k - i)x_{t-i}$$

and we estimate β by regressing y_t on the constructed variable z_t and using Eq. (16-3) we get estimates of β_i.

3. The Almon polynomial lag.[2] This is a generalization of the linear lag considered by Irving Fisher. We assume that the β_i follow a polynomial in i,

[1] Frank DeLeeuw, The Demand for Capital Goods by Manufacturers: A Study of Quarterly Time Series, *Econometrica*, 1962.

[2] S. Almon, The Distributed Lag between Capital Appropriations and Net Expenditures, *Econometrica*, January, 1965, pp. 178–196.

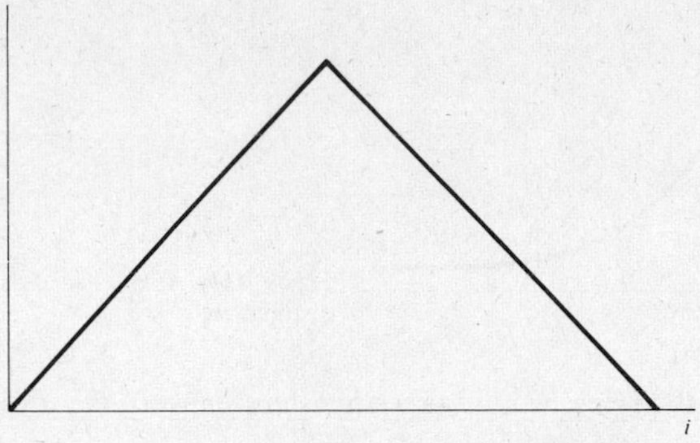

Figure 16-2 An inverted *V*-shaped distributed lag.

as shown in Fig. 16-3. For illustration we will assume a quadratic polynomial so that

$$\beta_i = \alpha_0 + \alpha_1 i + \alpha_2 i^2 \tag{16-4}$$

Substituting this in (16-1), we get

$$\begin{aligned} y_t &= \sum_{i=0}^{k} (\alpha_0 + \alpha_1 i + \alpha_2 i^2) x_{t-i} + u_t \\ &= \alpha_0 z_{0t} + \alpha_1 z_{1t} + \alpha_2 z_{2t} + u_t \end{aligned} \tag{16-5}$$

where $\quad z_{0t} = \sum_{i=0}^{k} x_{t-i}, z_{1t} = \sum_{i=0}^{k} i x_{t-i}, \text{ and } z_{2t} = \sum_{i=0}^{k} i^2 x_{t-i}$

Thus we regress y_t on the constructed variables z_{0t}, z_{1t}, and z_{2t}. After we get the estimates of the α's, we use Eq. (16-4) to get estimates of the β_i.

Following the suggestion of Almon, often some "endpoint constraints" are used. For instance, if we use the constraints that $\beta_{-1} = 0$ and $\beta_{k+1} = 0$ in

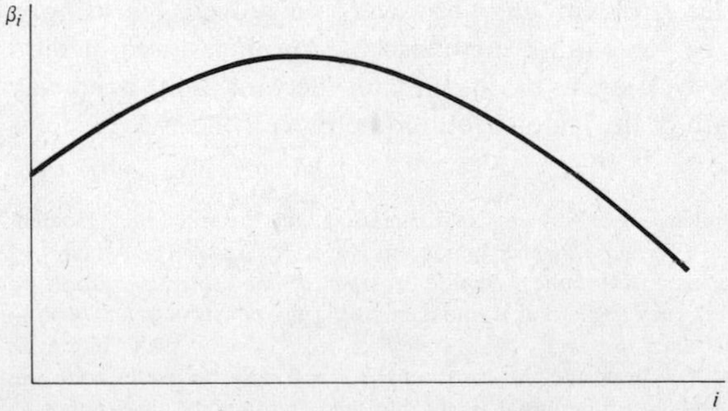

Figure 16-3 A polynomial distributed lag.

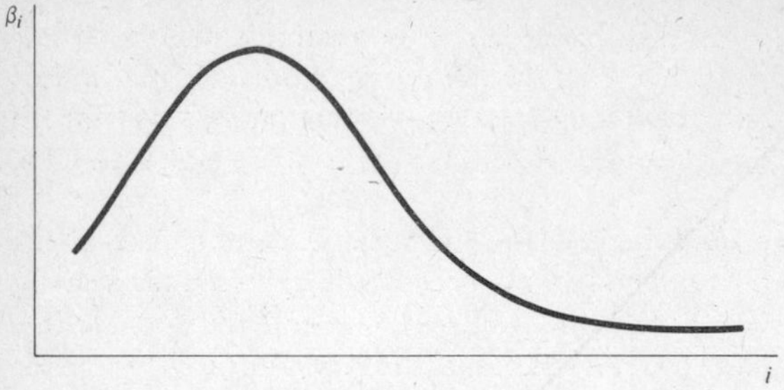

Figure 16-4 A long-tailed lag distribution.

Eq. (16-1), we have the following two linear relationships between the α's in (16-4):

$$\alpha_0 - \alpha_1 + \alpha_2 = 0 \qquad \text{and} \qquad \alpha_0 + \alpha_1(k+1) + \alpha_2(k+1)^2 = 0 \tag{16-6}$$

These give the conditions

$$\alpha_0 = -\alpha_2(k+1) \qquad \text{and} \qquad \alpha_1 = -\alpha_2 k \tag{16-7}$$

Thus we can simplify (16-5) to

$$y_t = z_t\alpha_2 + u_t$$

where $z_t = \sum(i^2 - ki - k - 1)x_{t-i}$.

We get an estimate of α_2 by regressing y_t on z_t, and we can get estimates of α_0 and α_1 from (16-7). Using (16-4), we then get estimates of the β_i.

The imposition of endpoint constraints has been criticized on the grounds that these are often responsible for the "plausible" shapes for the lag distribution fitted by the Almon method and the consequent popularity of the method.[1] Instead of imposing the endpoint constraints a priori, one can actually test them because once Eq. (16-5) is estimated, tests of hypotheses like (16-6) are standard tests of linear hypotheses. These tests will also give some indication of the adequacy of the length of the specified lag and the degree of the polynomial fitted.

There are some other problems with the Almon lag specification. First, it is difficult to capture any long-tailed distribution as in Fig. 16-4 by means of a single polynomial. This problem can, however, be solved by using a piecewise polynomial or by some other methods of using the Almon method in conjunction with the Koyck lag, as discussed later. Second, there is no way of knowing what the length of the lag distribution is. Even if the true model is

[1] See P. J. Dhrymes, "Distributed Lags: Problems of Estimation and Formulation," Holden-Day, Inc., Publisher, San Francisco, 1971. Also Peter Schmidt and Roger N. Waud, The Almon Lag Technique and the Monetary versus Fiscal Policy Debate, *Journal of the American Statistical Association*, March, 1973, pp. 11–19. They argue that if one is imposing the constraints $\beta_{-1} = \beta_{k+1} = 0$, one should also impose constraints $\beta_{-2} = \beta_{-3} = \cdots = \beta_{k+2} = \beta_{k+3} = \cdots = 0$. However, this is stretching the argument too far. Imposing the constraint $\beta_{-1} = 0$ may be overly strong in dictating the shape of the lag distribution in the initial stages, but the condition $\beta_{k+1} = 0$ is not an unreasonable one if one believes in a decaying lag distribution.

$y_t = \beta x_t + u_t$ so that there is no distributed lag, if we assume a distributed-lag model as in (16-1), no matter what k is, the Almon method will "distribute" the β over this range and thus give the impression of there being a distributed lag when there is none.[1] The presence or absence of a lag is not a testable proposition.

Once the length of the lag k in Eq. (16-1) is specified, the choice of the degree of the polynomial is a simple one because it reduces to tests of successive α's in an equation like (16-5). The tests for endpoint constraints like (16-6) can also be applied like any standard tests for linear hypotheses. The most difficult problem in the use of the Almon-lag method is the choice of the length of the lag k. Some investigators have suggested trying different values of k and choosing the optimal value on the basis of $\bar{R}^2$ or minimum-standard-error criteria.

16-2 INFINITE LAG DISTRIBUTIONS

A model like (16-1) is called a finite lag distribution because the lag terminates at point k. As discussed earlier, one basic problem with a finite lag distribution is that we do not know how to specify k. It might be thought that by specifying a sufficiently large k we would not be committing any serious error, but this is indeed not a desirable thing to do. First, we lose a large number of degrees of freedom. Second, as was seen in the case of the Almon-lag method, by considering a longer lag distribution we merely spread out the total effect, particularly if endpoint constraints are imposed. There is no way of inferring that the true length of the lag is shorter than the one considered. One way of tackling this problem is to use an infinite lag distribution that decays after a while. Since it is more convenient to write these lag distributions in terms of lag operators L, we will first define them. We will write Lx_t for x_{t-1}, L^2x_t for x_{t-2}, etc. In this notation Eq. (16-1) is

$$y_t = \sum_{i=0}^{k} \beta_i L^i x_t + u_t$$

When we use the infinite lag distribution, we will write (16-1) as

$$y_t = \sum_{i=0}^{\infty} \beta_i x_{t-i} + u_t \tag{16-8}$$

Obviously we cannot estimate the parameters in this equation with any finite data series without imposing some conditions on the β_i. The usual procedure is to write (16-8) as

$$y_t = \beta \sum_{i=0}^{\infty} w_i x_{t-i} + u_t \tag{16-9}$$

and define w_i as the probabilities given by some probability distribution. Since

[1] See Schmidt and Waud, *ibid*.

w_i are probabilities, we have $\sum w_i = 1$. β is the sum of the lag coefficients and is interpreted as the "long-run" effect of x_t on y_t. Since w_i are probabilities, this formulation enables us to use some standard algebraic manipulations from probability theory. Corresponding to the mean and variance of the probability distribution, we can talk of the mean and variance of the lag distribution. The following are some of the lag distributions suggested in the literature.

1 Geometric or Koyck lag. This model was suggested by Koyck.[1] It assumes that the w_i in (16-9) are generated by a geometric distribution

$$w_i = (1 - \lambda)\lambda^i \qquad 0 < \lambda < 1 \tag{16-10}$$

Clearly $\sum w_i = (1 - \lambda)\sum \lambda^i = 1$.

Also, the higher the value of λ, the slower the decay in the lag distribution. The mean of this probability distribution is $\lambda/(1 - \lambda)$ and the variance is $\lambda/(1 - \lambda)^2$. Thus the higher the value of λ, the higher the mean lag and the variance of the lag distribution. Substituting (16-10) in (16-9), we get

$$y_t = \beta(1 - \lambda) \sum \lambda^i x_{t-i} + u_t \tag{16-11}$$

In terms of the lag operator L we can write this as

$$\begin{aligned} y_t &= \beta(1 - \lambda) \sum \lambda^i L^i x_t + u_t \\ &= \frac{\beta(1 - \lambda)}{1 - \lambda L} x_t + u_t \end{aligned} \tag{16-12}$$

The earliest method of estimating (16-11) was the following: Multiply (16-12) throughout by $(1 - \lambda L)$ to get

$$(1 - \lambda L) y_t = \beta(1 - \lambda)x_t + (1 - \lambda L)u_t$$

or

$$y_t - \lambda y_{t-1} = \beta(1 - \lambda)x_t + u_t - \lambda u_{t-1}$$

or

$$y_t = \lambda y_{t-1} + \beta(1 - \lambda)x_t + v_t \tag{16-13}$$

where v_t is the residual $u_t - \lambda u_{t-1}$. If we can assume that the residuals v_t are serially independent, we can estimate Eq. (16-13) by ordinary least squares. The coefficient of y_{t-1} will give an estimate of λ and the coefficient of x_t an estimate of $\beta(1 - \lambda)$. The estimate of β will be obtained as a ratio of two regression coefficients, and thus its distribution is somewhat complicated.[2] Of course, if u_t are serially independent to start with, v_t will be serially correlated. The latter are serially independent only if u_t follow a first-order autoregressive process with the same parameter λ; i.e., $u_t = \lambda u_{t-1} + \epsilon_t$, where ϵ_t are serially independent.

[1] L. M. Koyck, "Distributed Lags and Investment Analysis," North-Holland Publishing Company, Amsterdam, 1954. An extensive and thorough discussion of the Koyck model can be found in M. Nerlove, "Distributed Lags and Demand Analysis," U.S. Department of Agriculture Handbook 141, Washington, D.C., 1958.

[2] One can, however, obtain confidence intervals for β using Fieller's method in Chap. 7, Sec. 7-9.

It has indeed been observed that a direct ordinary-least-squares estimation of (16-13) often yielded a high value of λ, thus giving an impression of slowly decaying or long lags. As will be seen later, this can be explained by the serial correlation in the residuals. The first suggestion that was made was to use an instrumental-variable estimation method[1] to estimate Eq. (16-13). The instrumental variables used are x_t and x_{t-1}. The estimates of λ and $\beta(1-\lambda)$ are obtained as solutions of the two equations

$$\sum x_t[y_t - \lambda y_{t-1} - \beta(1-\lambda)x_t] = 0$$

$$\sum x_{t-1}[y_t - \lambda y_{t-1} - \beta(1-\lambda)x_t] = 0$$

Often, since x_t and x_{t-1} are highly correlated, there is not much independent information in x_{t-1}, and the instrumental-variable estimators, though consistent, are very inefficient.

It is customary to call (16-12) the distributed-lag form and (16-13) the autoregressive form of the distributed-lag model. Initially it was thought that estimating the distributed-lag model in its autoregressive form was easier because one could apply ordinary least squares. However, the use of ordinary least squares is valid only if the residuals in the original equation follow a special first-order autoregression. One can, however, make some assumptions about the residuals v_t in (16-13), say, that they are first-order autoregressive $v_t = \rho v_{t-1} + e_t$, and then estimate the equation by either a nonlinear-least-squares program or by searching over the autoregressive parameter ρ.

The direct estimation of the distributed-lag model, as suggested by Klein,[2] is as follows: Write (16-12) as

$$y_t = \beta(1-\lambda)\sum_{i=0}^{t-1} \lambda^i x_{t-i} + \beta(1-\lambda)\sum_{i=t}^{\infty} \lambda^i x_{t-i} + u_t \tag{16-14}$$

The first term in (16-14) can be computed from the actual observations for any given value of λ. The second term cannot be computed because x_0, x_{-1}, x_{-2}, etc., are not observed. But writing $i - t = j$ (or $i = t + j$), it can be seen to be equal to

$$\lambda^t\beta(1-\lambda)\sum_{j=0}^{\infty} \lambda^j x_{-j} = \lambda^t \eta_0$$

where
$$\eta_0 = E(y_0) = \beta(1-\lambda)\sum_{i=0}^{\infty} \lambda^i x_{-i}$$

Thus (16-14) can be written as

$$y_t = \beta z_{1t} + \eta_0 z_{2t} + u_t \tag{16-15}$$

[1] See N. Liviatan, Consistent Estimation of Distributed Lags, *International Economic Review*, 1963, pp. 44–52.

[2] L. R. Klein, The Estimation of Distributed Lags, *Econometrica*, October, 1958, pp. 553–565.

where
$$z_{1t} = (1-\lambda)\sum_{i=0}^{t-1}\lambda^i x_{t-i}$$
$$z_{2t} = \lambda^t \tag{16-16}$$

η_0 is a parameter corresponding to the truncation remainder, and since $\eta_0 = E(y_0)$ it can be called an "initial-value parameter." The procedure for the estimation of λ and β is as follows: For each value of λ we construct the variables z_{1t} and z_{2t} in (16-16), regress y_t on z_{1t} and z_{2t}, and look at the residual sum of squares. We choose that value of λ for which this is a minimum. This is the maximum-likelihood estimate of λ, and the corresponding values of β and η_0 are the ML estimates of those parameters. It can be shown that the estimators for β and λ are consistent but that for η_0 is not. This is because for large values of t, z_{2t} is almost zero. Thus as we increase the sample size we do not get any more information on η_0. In fact for large samples we can ignore η_0 and regress y_t on just z_{1t}.

Even though the ML estimator of η_0 is not consistent, and in large samples η_0 can be ignored, it has been found in practice that even for sample sizes as large as 60, it is desirable not to ignore η_0, because this might often produce drastically different estimates for the parameters β and λ. Maddala and Rao[1] present evidence of this in connection with the Solow distributed-lag model.

Instead of estimating η_0, one can drop an observation and write

$$y_t = \beta z_t + \lambda^{t-1}\eta_1 + u_t$$

where
$$\eta_1 = E(y_1) \qquad \text{and} \qquad z_t = (1-\lambda)\sum_{i=0}^{t-2}\lambda^i x_{t-i}$$

and then use y_1 as a proxy for η_1, i.e., regress $(y_t - \lambda^{t-1}y_1)$ on z_t to get an estimate of β for each λ. The procedure of searching over λ can be repeated as before. This suggestion was made by Pesaran.[2] Schmidt[3] did a Monte Carlo study and compared the mean-square errors of the estimates of λ and β to see whether it is worthwhile to take account of the initial-value parameters as suggested by Maddala and Rao. He finds that even in samples as large as 100, it is worthwhile including the truncation remainders and that of the two procedures of estimating η_0 and using y_1 as a proxy for η_1 as suggested by Pesaran, there is not much difference.

If one assumes that the residuals in (16-15) are, say, first-order autoregressive, i.e., $u_t = \rho u_{t-1} + e_t$, then one can use the search procedure on both λ and ρ,

[1] G. S. Maddala and A. S. Rao, Maximum Likelihood Estimation of Solow's and Jorgenson's Distributed Lag Models, *The Review of Economics and Statistics*, February, 1971, pp. 80–88.

[2] M. H. Pesaran, The Small Sample Problem of Truncation Remainders in the Estimation of Distributed Lag Models with Autocorrelated Errors, *International Economic Review*, February, 1973, pp. 120–131.

[3] Peter Schmidt, The Small Sample Effects of Various Treatments of Truncation Remainders in the Estimation of Distributed Lag Models, *The Review of Economics and Statistics*, 1976.

as done by Dhrymes.[1] Thus the estimation of the distributed-lag model in the distributed-lag form is not very difficult. Also, there is something to be said in favor of estimating the model in its distributed-lag form (16-12) rather than the autoregressive form (16-13). In the autoregressive form, because of the presence of lagged dependent variables among the explanatory variables, if the error term is misspecified, we get inconsistent estimates of the parameters. In the distributed-lag form even if there is any such misspecification, the estimators are still consistent. They will be only inefficient.

One disadvantage with the Koyck model is that not all lag distributions are continuously declining. However, as Koyck himself suggested, if we believe that there is an initial buildup before the decline (as in Fig. 16-4), then we can leave the first few coefficients free and start the geometric decline, i.e., estimate a model of the sort

$$y_t = \beta_0 x_t + \beta_1 x_{t-1} + \frac{\beta(1-\lambda)}{1-\lambda L} x_{t-2} + u_t \tag{16-17}$$

In actual practice this might prove to be sufficient to capture lag patterns actually observed, and also be less restrictive and problematical than the Solow and Jorgenson lag distributions considered later. Another alternative is to combine the Koyck lag with a low-degree polynomial lag. Hall and Sutch[2] suggested that the initial part of the lag distribution be represented by a polynomial and the latter part by a Koyck distribution. Thus they graft a Koyck tail to an Almon lag. This is merely an extension of the idea in (16-17), that if there are many terms before the Koyck distribution, we are again faced with the problem of not being able to estimate the β_i efficiently and we want to reduce the number of parameters using the Almon method.

An alternative method of combining the Almon lag with the Koyck lag is to say that (for illustration we are again assuming a quadratic polynomial)

$$\beta_i = (\alpha_0 + \alpha_1 i + \alpha_2 i^2)\lambda^i \tag{16-18}$$

Here, in the initial stages of the lag distribution the polynomial portion will dominate and in the latter stages the Koyck portion will dominate.[3] Again, as with any infinite lag distribution, we have to consider what to do with the terms for which no observations are available. Write

$$y_t = \sum_{i=0}^{t-1} (\alpha_0 + \alpha_1 i + \alpha_2 i^2)\lambda^i x_{t-i} + \sum_{i=t}^{\infty} (\alpha_0 + \alpha_1 i + \alpha_2 i^2)\lambda^i x_{t-i} + u_t \tag{16-19}$$

The first expression in (16-19) can be written as

$$\alpha_0 z_{0t} + \alpha_1 z_{1t} + \alpha_2 z_{2t}$$

[1] P. J. Dhrymes, Efficient Estimation of Distributed Lags with Autocorrelated Errors, *International Economic Review*, 1969, pp. 47–67.

[2] R. E. Hall and R. C. Sutch, A Flexible Infinite Distributed Lag, presented at 1967 Econometric Society Meetings, abstracted in *Econometrica*, 1968 (Supplementary Issue, pp. 91–92).

[3] See Peter Schmidt, A Modification of the Almon Distributed Lag, *Journal of the American Statistical Association*, September, 1974, pp. 679–681.

where
$$z_{0t} = \sum_{0}^{t-1} \lambda^i x_{t-i}$$
$$z_{1t} = \sum_{0}^{t-1} i\lambda^i x_{t-i}$$
and
$$z_{2t} = \sum_{0}^{t-1} i^2\lambda^i x_{t-i}$$

As for the second term in (16-19), writing $j = i - t$, we can write it as
$$\lambda^t \sum_{j=0}^{\infty} \left[\alpha_0 + \alpha_1(t + j) + \alpha_2(t + j)^2\right]\lambda^j x_{-j} = (\lambda^t)\eta_0 + (t\lambda^t)\eta_1 + (t^2\lambda^t)\eta_2$$

where $\eta_0 = \sum_{j=0}^{\infty} (\alpha_0 + \alpha_1 j + \alpha_2 j^2)\lambda^j x_{-j}$
$$\eta_1 = \sum_{j=0}^{\infty} (\alpha_1 + 2\alpha_2 j)\lambda^j x_{-j}$$
$$\eta_2 = \sum_{j=0}^{\infty} \alpha_2 \lambda^j x_{-j}$$

We can treat η_0, η_1, η_2 as "initial-value parameters," though only η_0 has an interpretation, viz., $\eta_0 = E(y_0)$. We cannot get consistent estimates for these parameters, and they are asymptotically unimportant. However, we can, in practice, include them and estimate the regression equation
$$y_t = \alpha_0 z_{0t} + \alpha_1 z_{1t} + \alpha_2 z_{2t} + (\lambda^t)\eta_0 + (t\lambda^t)\eta_1 + (t^2\lambda^t)\eta_2 + u_t$$
Schmidt applied this method to the Almon data and got reasonably good results.

2 The Pascal lag distribution. Solow[1] suggested that the w_i in (16-9) be represented by the Pascal distribution
$$w_i = \text{coefficient of } L^i \text{ in } \frac{(1 - \lambda)^r}{(1 - \lambda L)^r}$$
$$= (1 - \lambda)^r \binom{r+i-1}{i} \lambda^i$$
The distributed-lag model is then
$$y_t = \frac{\beta(1 - \lambda)^r}{(1 - \lambda L)^r} x_t + u_t \qquad (16\text{-}20)$$
For $r = 2$,
$$w_i = (1 - \lambda)^2(i + 1)\lambda^i$$

[1] R. M. Solow, On a Family of Lag Distributions, *Econometrica*, April, 1960, pp. 393–406.

For $r = 3$,
$$w_i = (1 - \lambda)^3 \frac{(i+1)(i+2)}{2} \lambda^i$$

These expressions are similar to (16-18) except that the polynomial part has known coefficients. Thus the Pascal model can be considered as a special case of the model (16-18).

The autoregressive form of the model is

$$(1 - \lambda L)^r y_t = \beta(1 - \lambda)^r x_t + v_t \tag{16-21}$$

where $v_t = (1 - \lambda L)^r u_t$. Again, as with the Koyck model, if one assumes the residuals v_t to be serially independent (which implies that the residuals u_t follow a very special process), then one can estimate (16-21) by ordinary least squares. However, one has to take the nonlinearities into account. For example, with $r = 2$, Eq. (16-21) gives

$$y_t = 2\lambda y_{t-1} - \lambda^2 y_{t-2} + \beta(1 - \lambda)^2 x_t + v_t$$

Thus one cannot just regress y_t on y_{t-1}, y_{t-2}, and x_t. The simplest procedure in this case would be to search on λ, i.e., for each λ regress $y_t^* = y_t - 2\lambda y_{t-1} + \lambda^2 y_{t-2}$ on x_t and choose that value of λ for which the residual sum of squares is minimum. This gives the ML estimate of λ and the corresponding estimate of β gives the ML estimate of β. It is possible to use the same search procedure to estimate the distributed-lag version (16-20). For illustrative purposes let us consider the case $r = 3$ so that

$$y_t = \beta \frac{(1 - \lambda)^3}{(1 - \lambda L)^3} x_t + u_t$$

Define

$$z_t^* = \frac{(1 - \lambda)^3}{(1 - \lambda L)^3} x_t$$

Then

$$(1 - \lambda L)^3 z_t^* = (1 - \lambda)^3 x_t$$

or

$$z_t^* - 3\lambda z_{t-1}^* + 3\lambda^2 z_{t-2}^* - \lambda^3 z_{t-3}^* = (1 - \lambda)^3 x_t$$

or

$$z_t^* = 3\lambda z_{t-1}^* - 3\lambda^2 z_{t-2}^* + \lambda^3 z_{t-3}^* + (1 - \lambda)^3 x_t \tag{16-22}$$

For any given λ, we can generate (16-22) in a recursive fashion starting from $t = 1$. However, to start the successive generation of z_t^*, we need some initial values. Denote z_0^* by η_0, z_{-1}^* by η_{-1}, and z_{-2}^* by η_{-2}, and treat them as unknown parameters. Then, using (16-22), we can generate the z_t^* series. Regressing y_t on z_t^*, we get an estimate of β. As before, we do this for different values of λ and pick that value of λ for which the residual sum of squares is minimum. This will give the ML estimate of λ, and the corresponding estimate of β is the ML estimate of β. As before, the estimators of the initial-value parameters η_0, η_{-1}, and η_{-2} will not be consistent. But often it is desirable to estimate them as done by Maddala and Rao.[1]

One can find the ML estimates of λ and β by the above method for any given r. The problem is choosing the degree r. Maddala and Rao suggest choosing that value of r for which $\bar{R}^2$ is highest. In reporting the standard errors of the estimated parameters, the point that r itself is estimated is often ignored. Schmidt[2] points out that one should take account of this fact in reporting the estimated standard errors. This problem, however, is not peculiar to the Solow model. It arises in the Almon model and in the Jorgenson model considered later, where the degrees of the polynomials themselves have to be estimated.

One major problem with the Pascal lag distribution is that if there is a sharp peak at the beginning of the lag distribution, it is impossible to pick it up with this model. In this respect a model of the sort (16-17) or the Jorgenson model considered later would be useful.

3 Jorgenson's rational lag distribution.[3] Jorgenson suggested approximating the lag distribution by the ratio of two polynomials $A(L)/B(L)$ in the lag operator L. The distributed-lag model is now

$$y_t = \frac{A(L)}{B(L)} x_t + u_t \tag{16-23}$$

For simplicity let $A(L) = \alpha_0 + \alpha_1 L + \alpha_2 L^2$ and $B(L) = 1 - \beta_1 L - \beta_2 L^2$. The autoregressive form of (16-23) is then

$$(1 - \beta_1 L - \beta_2 L^2) y_t = (\alpha_0 + \alpha_1 L + \alpha_2 L^2) x_t + v_t$$

or

$$y_t = \beta_1 y_{t-1} + \beta_2 y_{t-2} + \alpha_0 x_t + \alpha_1 x_{t-1} + \alpha_2 x_{t-2} + v_t \tag{16-24}$$

where $v_t = (1 - \beta_1 L - \beta_2 L^2) u_t$. In his empirical work Jorgenson estimated (16-24) by ordinary least squares, ignoring the fact that if the residuals in (16-23) are independent, the residuals in (16-24) are serially correlated. As with the Koyck model, the ordinary-least-squares estimation of the autoregressive form is valid only if the residuals in the original distributed-lag model follow a special autoregressive process.

The procedures described earlier for the estimation of the Koyck and Solow models can also be used for the direct estimation of the distributed-lag model (16-23). Maddala and Rao[4] suggest the following procedure:

[1] See Maddala and Rao, *op. cit.*

[2] Peter Schmidt, On the Difference between Conditional and Unconditional Asymptotic Distributions of Estimates in Distributed Lag Models with Integer-Valued Parameters, *Econometrica*, January, 1973, pp. 165–170.

[3] D. W. Jorgenson, Rational Distributed Lag Functions, *Econometrica*, January, 1966, pp. 135–149.

[4] Maddala and Rao, *op. cit.*

Define

$$x_t^* = \frac{1}{B(L)} x_t$$

Since $B(L)x_t^* = x_t$, we have

$$x_t^* = \beta_1 x_{t-1}^* + \beta_2 x_{t-2}^* + x_t \qquad (16\text{-}25)$$

This equation can be used recursively to generate x_t^* given x_t. But x_0^* and x_{-1}^* are not known. Suppose we treat them as unknown parameters, say, θ_1 and θ_2, respectively. Then we have

$$\begin{aligned} x_1^* &= x_1 + \beta_1\theta_1 + \beta_2\theta_2 \\ x_2^* &= x_2 + \beta_1 x_1^* + \beta_2\theta_1 \\ x_t^* &= x_t + \beta_1 x_{t-1}^* + \beta_2 x_{t-2}^* \qquad \text{for } t \geqslant 3 \end{aligned}$$

These simplify into

$$x_t^* = z_{1t} + \theta_1 z_{2t} + \theta_2 z_{3t}$$

$$\begin{aligned} \text{where } z_{1t} &= x_1 && \text{for } t = 1 \\ &= x_2 + \beta_1 x_1 && \text{for } t = 2 \\ &= x_t + \beta_1 z_{1,t-1} + \beta_2 z_{1,t-2} && \text{for } t \geqslant 3 \\ z_{2t} &= \beta_1 && \text{for } t = 1 \\ &= \beta_1^2 + \beta_2 && \text{for } t = 2 \\ &= \beta_1 z_{2,t-1} + \beta_2 z_{2,t-2} && \text{for } t \geqslant 3 \\ z_{3t} &= \beta_2 && \text{for } t = 1 \\ &= \beta_1\beta_2 && \text{for } t = 2 \\ &= \beta_1 z_{3,t-1} + \beta_2 z_{3,t-2} && \text{for } t \geqslant 3 \end{aligned}$$

If we assume the residuals u_t in (16-23) to be $IN(0,\sigma^2)$, the ML estimates of the parameters will be obtained by minimizing

$$\Sigma\left[y_t - (\alpha_0 + \alpha_1 L + \alpha_2 L^2)(z_{1t} + \theta_1 z_{2t} + {}_3z_{3t})\right]^2$$

If we assume θ_1 and θ_2 to be zero,[1] this is a simple problem. We first generate z_{1t} for given values of β_1 and β_2, then regress y_t on z_{1t}, $z_{1,t-1}$, and $z_{1,t-2}$ to get

[1] Dhrymes et al. suggest assuming θ_1 and θ_2 to be zero. See P. J. Dhrymes, L. R. Klein, and K. Stiglitz, Estimation of Distributed Lags, *International Economic Review*, June, 1970, pp. 235–250. Maddala and Rao found that even if the estimators of θ_1 and θ_2 are not consistent, and even if asymptotically these parameters can be ignored, the estimates of the other parameters of interest were very sensitive to whether θ_1 and θ_2 were estimated or assumed to be zero.

estimates of α_0, α_1, and α_2. We repeat this for different values of β_1 and β_2, look at the residual sum of squares in each case, and choose those values for which the residual sum of squares is minimum. The corresponding estimates of α_0, α_1, and α_2 are the ML estimates of those parameters. If we do not assume θ_1 and θ_2 to be zero, we have to use a nonlinear estimation procedure, or get some preliminary estimates of these parameters, or as done by Pesaran with the Koyck model, we can omit the first two observations, start the iterative process (16-25) from the third observation, and use y_1 and y_2 as proxies for $A(L)x_1^*$ and $A(L)x_2^*$.

4 Gamma distributed lag. Tsurumi[1] suggests using the gamma distribution for the distributed-lag weights. Essentially this amounts to taking

$$\beta_i = \beta i^{s-1} e^{-i} \tag{16-26}$$

This has the problem that for $s \neq 1$ we have $\beta_0 = 0$. This difficulty can be remedied by replacing i^{s-1} by $(i+1)^{s-1}$. Also we can generalize (16-26) by writing it as

$$\beta_i = \beta(i+1)^{s-1} e^{-\lambda i} \tag{16-27}$$

Schmidt[2] suggests that since the ML estimates will be computed by searching over s, it is convenient to replace $(s-1)$ with $\alpha/(1-\alpha)$, where $0 \leqslant \alpha \leqslant 1$ so as to facilitate the search procedure. Also he replaces $e^{-\lambda i}$ by λ^i, as is usually done with discrete data. These modifications yield

$$\beta_i = \beta(i+1)^{\alpha/(1-\alpha)} \lambda^i \qquad 0 \leqslant \alpha \leqslant 1, 0 \leqslant \lambda < 1 \tag{16-28}$$

The peak for this lag distribution occurs later the larger the value of α or the larger the value of λ.

As with any of the infinite lag distributions we have to consider what to do with the infinite sum. We can write the distributed lag as

$$y_t = \sum_{i=0}^{t-1} \beta_i x_{t-i} + \sum_{i=t}^{\infty} \beta_i x_{t-i} + u_t$$

With the Koyck, Solow, and Jorgenson models we can express the second term in terms of some "initial-value parameters." This is not exactly possible with the gamma lag, though one can approximate it.

All these lag models, Almon, Koyck, Solow, Jorgenson, gamma, etc., depend on imposing some strong restrictions on the parameters, and there is little economic theory to guide us in the choice of which sort of restrictions to impose on the data. It has been found that incorrect restrictions result in biased

[1] H. Tsurumi, A Note on Gamma Distributed Lags, *International Economic Review*, June, 1971, pp. 317–324. The gamma lag was suggested earlier by Theil and Stern. See H. Theil and R. M. Stern, A Simple Unimodal Lag Distribution, *Metroeconomica*, vol. 12, pp. 111–119, 1960.

[2] Peter Schmidt, An Argument for the Usefulness of the Gamma Distributed Lag Model, *International Economic Review*, February, 1974, pp. 246–250.

estimation of key parameters. It is likely that these models have been popular for too long (because of the computational ease and the nice-looking lag shapes they give). It is also likely that the above discussion summarizing these methods is also too long. In later sections we will discuss some weak parametric specifications and "form-free" lags.

Finally, for the estimation of distributed-lag models in the autoregressive form, particularly the Koyck model in (16-13), other methods have been suggested in the literature. Liviatan[1] suggested estimating Eq. (16-13) by the instrumental-variable method using x_{t-1} as an instrumental variable for y_{t-1}. Though these estimates are consistent, they have been shown by Hannan[2] to be inefficient compared with the ML estimates. In some sampling experiments Sargent,[3] too, found the performance of the instrumental-variable estimators very poor. Klein[4] suggested writing (16-13) as

$$y_t - u_t = \beta(1-\lambda)x_t + \lambda(y_{t-1} - u_{t-1})$$

and using a weighted regression method similar to that suggested in errors-in-variables literature. Amemiya and Fuller[5] show this method to be less efficient than the ML method. Oi[6] derives some bracketing rules for the estimates obtained by the weighted-regression method. In addition to these methods there is the three-pass least-squares method suggested by Taylor and Wilson,[7] which was popular for a while but was later discarded because it does not, in general, yield consistent estimates and other methods that yield consistent estimates have been found to be superior.[8]

All these methods are now rather outdated. First, the autoregressive form of the distributed-lag model was suggested because it was thought that one could use ordinary-least-squares methods. Soon it was discovered that these estimates were not, in general, consistent, and then some methods producing consistent estimates were suggested. Next it was discovered that these methods did not produce efficient estimates, and then some efficient procedures were suggested. Some of these efficient procedures are what are known as two-step procedures. But the important thing is that the ML procedures are not very difficult to

[1] N. Liviatan, Consistent Estimation of Distributed Lags, *International Economic Review*, 1963, pp. 44–52.

[2] E. J. Hannan, The Estimation of Relationships Involving Distributed Lags, *Econometrica*, 1965, pp. 206–224.

[3] T. J. Sargent, Some Evidence on the Small Sample Properties of Distributed Lag Estimators in the Presence of Autocorrelated Disturbances, *Review of Economics and Statistics*, 1968, pp. 87–95.

[4] L. R. Klein, The Estimation of Distributed Lags, *Econometrica*, 1958, pp. 553–565.

[5] T. Amemiya and W. A. Fuller, A Comparative Study of Alternative Estimators in a Distributed Lag Model, *Econometrica*, 1967, pp. 509–529.

[6] W. Oi, A Bracketing Rule for the Estimation of Simple Distributed Lag Models, *Review of Economics and Statistics*, November, 1969, pp. 445–452.

[7] L. D. Taylor and T. A. Wilson, Three-Pass Least Squares: A Method for Estimating Models with a Lagged Dependent Variable, *Review of Economics and Statistics*, 1964, pp. 329–346.

[8] See K. F. Wallis, Lagged Dependent Variables and Serially Correlated Errors: A Reappraisal of Three-Pass Least Squares, *Review of Economics and Statistics*, 1967, pp. 555–567.

implement for either the distributed-lag form or the autoregressive form of the distributed-lag models. Of course, if there are several explanatory variables, the estimation in the distributed-lag form can get very complicated. In any case, the several procedures suggested are designed to reduce the computational burden, which in former days was a desirable motive but is not so any more.

16-3 AN ILLUSTRATIVE EXAMPLE

As an illustration of the several procedures discussed above, we will consider Almon's data on capital expenditures (y) and appropriations (x).[1] These data are reported in Table 16-1 for the years 1953–1967 on a quarterly basis. There are thus 60 observations. The data are from the National Industrial Conference Board. Table 16-2 lists the estimates obtained by the several procedures. The rational distributed lag is the one suggested by Jorgenson. m is the degree of the numerator polynomial and n the degree of the denominator polynomial. The results are from the paper by Maddala and Rao (*op. cit.*). The Solow and rational distributed-lag models were estimated with the initial conditions terms included.

Table 16-1

N	*Y*	*X*	*N*	*Y*	*X*	*N*	*Y*	*X*
1	2072	1660	21	2697	1511	41	2601	2629
2	2077	1926	22	2338	1631	42	2648	3133
3	2078	2181	23	2140	1990	43	2840	3449
4	2043	1897	24	2012	1993	44	2937	3764
5	2062	1695	25	2071	2520	45	3136	3983
6	2067	1705	26	2192	2804	46	3299	4381
7	1964	1731	27	2240	2919	47	3514	4786
8	1981	2151	28	2421	3024	48	3815	4094
9	1914	2556	29	2639	2725	49	4093	4870
10	1991	3152	30	2733	2321	50	4262	5344
11	2129	3763	31	2721	2131	51	4531	5433
12	2309	3903	32	2640	2552	52	4825	5911
13	2614	3912	33	2513	2234	53	5160	6109
14	2896	3571	34	2448	2282	54	5319	6542
15	3058	3199	35	2429	2533	55	5574	5785
16	3309	3262	36	2516	2517	56	5749	5707
17	3446	3476	37	2534	2772	57	5715	5412
18	3466	2993	38	2494	2380	58	5637	5465
19	3435	2262	39	2596	2568	59	5383	5550
20	3183	2011	40	2572	2944	60	5467	5465

[1] These data are used very often (in fact too often) in illustrations of new methods of estimation for distributed-lag models. Hence they are reproduced here.

Table 16-2

Lag	Koyck	Solow $r = 2$	Solow $r = 3$	Solow $r = 4$	Solow $r = 5$	Almon	Rational $m = 0$ $n = 2$	Rational $m = 1$ $n = 2$	Rational $m = 2$ $n = 2$
0	.180	.109	.085	.073	.060	.068	.099	.077	.021
1	.148	.146	.143	.140	.129	.122	.144	.142	.187
2	.121	.147	.160	.169	.167	.156	.155	.161	.177
3	.099	.131	.150	.162	.167	.168	.146	.154	.155
4	.081	.110	.126	.136	.144	.157	.126	.133	.127
5	.067	.088	.099	.104	.112	.127	.102	.107	.100
6	.055	.069	.074	.075	.080	.084	.079	.081	.075
7	.045	.053	.053	.052	.054	.038	.058	.058	.055
8	.037	.040	.037	.034	.035	0	.040	.040	.039
9	.030	.030	.025	.022	.022	0	.026	.025	.026
10	.025	.022	.017	.014	.013	0	.015	.015	.017
11	.020	.016	.011	.008	.008	0	.009	.007	.010
12	.017	.012	.007	.005	.004	0	.004	.003	.006
13	.014	.008	.005	.003	.003	0	0	0	.003
14	.011	.006	.003	.002	.001	0	0	0	.001
Sum	.949	.986	.995	.995	.998	.920	.986	.986	.992
Mean lag	4.5	4.0	3.8	3.7	3.8		3.4	3.5	3.7

16-4 SERIAL-CORRELATION PROBLEMS

When the distributed-lag model is estimated in the distributed-lag form, so that no lagged dependent variables occur on the right-hand side, there is not much danger in using the Durbin-Watson test statistic to test for serial correlation.[1] Further, ignoring the serial correlation merely results in inefficient estimates but not inconsistent estimates of the parameters. Serial-correlation problems are especially serious in distributed-lag models estimated in the autoregressive form. In these models the DW test statistic is not applicable, and ignoring the serial-correlation problems results in inconsistent estimates of the parameters.

Griliches[2] and Malinvaud[3] discuss the serial-correlation biases in the estimates of the parameters of distributed-lag models estimated by ordinary least squares. Suppose the model is

$$y_t = \alpha y_{t-1} + \beta x_t + u_t \qquad u_t = \rho u_{t-1} + e_t \qquad e_t \text{ are } IID(0, \sigma_e^2)$$

[1] The DW tables are, strictly speaking, not valid because we have a nonlinear problem here. But the bias in the DW statistic is not serious as in the case of distributed-lag models in the autoregressive form.

[2] Z. Griliches, A Note on Serial Correlation Bias in Estimates of Distributed Lags, *Econometrica*, January, 1961, pp. 65–73.

[3] E. Malinvaud, "Statistical Methods of Econometrics," 2d rev. ed., pp. 554–560, North-Holland Publishing Company, Amsterdam, 1970.

and
$$x_t = \theta x_{t-1} + v_t \qquad v_t \text{ are } IID(0,\sigma_v^2)$$
$$|\alpha|,|\rho|,|\theta| < 1$$

We have, for simplicity, assumed both u_t and x_t to be first-order autoregressive. In this case we can obtain expressions that are easy to interpret. If $\hat{\alpha}$ and $\hat{\beta}$ are the ordinary-least-squares estimates of α and β, then

$$\text{plim } \hat{\alpha} = \alpha + \frac{\rho\sigma_x^2\sigma_u^2}{(1-\alpha\rho)D}$$

$$\text{plim } \hat{\beta} = \beta - \frac{\beta\theta\rho\sigma_x^2\sigma_u^2}{(1-\alpha\theta)(1-\alpha\rho)D}$$

where $D = \text{var}(y_{-1})\ \text{var}(x) - \text{cov}^2(y_{-1},x) > 0$. Thus, if ρ is positive, $\hat{\alpha}$ overestimates α. Thus with positively autocorrelated residuals we get an impression of very long lags. It can also be shown that if $\hat{\rho}$ is the estimated first-order serial correlation computed from $\hat{u}_t$, the estimated residuals from the ordinary-least-squares regression, then

$$\text{plim } \hat{\rho} = \rho - A$$

where A is the asymptotic bias in $\hat{\alpha}$, the least-squares estimator of α.[1] Thus the estimated $\hat{\rho}$ is biased toward zero and we are more likely to accept the null hypothesis that $\rho = 0$ even when $\rho \neq 0$. Note that the danger here is in accepting the null hypothesis. If the DW test rejects it, we can use the test.

Since the DW test is not applicable in these models, Durbin suggests an alternative test[2] that can be used with the least-squares residuals. He suggests using

$$h = \hat{\rho}\sqrt{\frac{T}{1 - T\hat{V}(\hat{\alpha})}}$$

as a standard normal deviate to test the hypothesis $\rho = 0$. Here $\hat{\rho}$ is the estimated first-order serial correlation computed from OLS residuals, $\hat{V}(\hat{\alpha})$ is the estimated variance of the OLS estimate $\hat{\alpha}$, and T is the sample size. If $T\hat{V}(\hat{\alpha}) > 1$, the test is not applicable, but Durbin gives an alternative procedure in this case.

Often there are problems of errors of measurement in the x variable in addition to serial correlation in residuals. Grether and Maddala[3] discuss this

[1] This result is derived in Malinvaud, *op. cit.*, for the case with no exogenous variables. It is derived for the case of an included first-order x in G. S. Maddala and A. S. Rao, Tests for Serial Correlation in Regression Models with Lagged Dependent Variables and Serially Correlated Errors, *Econometrica*, July, 1973, p. 773.

[2] J. Durbin, Testing for Serial Correlation in Least Squares Regression When Some of the Regressors Are Lagged Dependent Variables, *Econometrica*, 1970, pp. 410–421. This modified test by Durbin is for the case when there is only one lagged dependent variable. There is no similar modification if there are more lagged dependent variables.

[3] D. M. Grether and G. S. Maddala, Errors in Variables and Serially Correlated Disturbances in Distributed Lag Models, *Econometrica*, March, 1973, pp. 255–262.

problem, give generalization of the expressions for serial-correlation bias derived earlier by Griliches and Malinvaud, and argue that though the two biases, due to errors in variables and serial correlation in residuals, can theoretically run in opposite directions, in the cases of practical interest, the two biases run in the same direction. In models with serially correlated residuals, the solution to the serial-correlation-bias problem is to estimate the complete model by nonlinear-regression procedures. When errors in variables are also present, these procedures are not necessarily better than ordinary least squares. One can, however, get consistent estimates for all the parameters by using lagged values of the independent variable (measured with error) as instrumental variables.[1] But in actual practice, with the type of economic time series we often get, this method cannot be expected to give any good results.

16-5 SEASONALITY IN DISTRIBUTED-LAG MODELS

Often distributed-lag models are estimated with seasonally adjusted data. The seasonal-adjustment procedures often introduce distortions in the patterns of estimated responses. As was argued earlier (in the discussion on seasonal adjustment[2]), even if the true relationship between y_t and x_t is contemporaneous of the type $y_t = \beta x_t + u_t$, we will discover a distributed-lag relation between the adjusted series; i.e., y_t^a will depend on x_t^a, x_{t-1}^a, x_{t-2}^a, . . . , etc. Also, even if the true relationship between y_t and x_t is a one-sided lag, i.e.,

$$y_t = \sum_{j=0}^{\infty} \beta_j x_{t-j} + u_t$$

we will find the estimated relationship to be one of a two-sided lag; i.e., y_t depends on not only past x's but also on future x's, and consequently we get an impression that y_t affects x_t with a lag. Because of these problems it is often better to estimate the distributed-lag models with seasonally unadjusted data rather than seasonally adjusted data. However, the question arises as to what to do if the dependent variable has a pronounced seasonal pattern which cannot be attributed to the seasonal behavior of the independent variable. One alternative to using seasonally adjusted data is to use seasonal dummies. Another is to make the distributed-lag coefficients themselves functions of the seasonal dummies. Pesando[3] illustrates the latter method with reference to a study of the distributed lag between the commitment and disbursement of life insurance company mortgage investment funds. The acquisition of residential mortgages by life insurance companies exhibits a distinct seasonal pattern, peaking in the fourth quarter and dropping sharply in the first quarter the following year. This reflects

[1] See *ibid.*, p. 261, footnote 7, where this suggestion is made.

[2] See the references to the papers by Wallis and Sims cited there (Chap. 15, Sec. 15-4).

[3] James E. Pesando, Seasonal Variability in Distributed Lag Models, *Journal of the American Statistical Association*, June, 1972, pp. 311–312.

in part the pronounced seasonal pattern in residential construction, but Pesando found that residential mortgage commitments made in the winter months for new construction have a longer takedown lag than the corresponding commitments made in the spring and summer. Thus a fixed-weight distributed-lag model is inappropriate for this problem.

Pesando estimates the distributed-lag model

$$y_t = \sum_{i=0}^{n} w(i)x_{t-i}$$

where $w(i) = c_i + S_{1i}D_{1,t-i} + S_{2i}D_{2,t-i} + S_{3i}D_{3,t-i}$; D_1, D_2, and D_3 are seasonal dummy variables; y_t are mortgage disbursements; and x_t are new mortgage commitments. He estimates this relationship by constraining c_i, S_{1i}, S_{2i}, and S_{3i} to lie along low-order polynomials, thus employing four sets of "Almon" variables. However, the coefficients of seasonal dummies S_{1i}, S_{2i}, and S_{3i} are constrained to sum to zero, thus permitting the quarter in which the commitment is made to determine the shape of the lag pattern but not the sum of the weights.

16-6 AGGREGATION OVER TIME IN DISTRIBUTED-LAG MODELS

One question that has often been asked is: What happens to the estimated distributed-lag relationships when the reaction interval of the economic units is smaller than the interval at which we have observations? This is the problem often discussed under the title of aggregation over time. That time aggregation could lead to systematic biases in estimating distributed-lag models can be easily seen from a study by Bryan.[1] In his paper, Bryan reports results analyzing microdata on bank holdings of excess reserves. When he estimated his equations with the microdata, he found that banks take about 3.2 weeks to close 95 percent of the gap between excess reserves and actual plus anticipated change in excess reserves. Using data aggregated over banks, the period required rose to 5.2 weeks. When Bryan aggregated the data over banks and over time (from a weekly to a monthly basis), the corresponding figure was 28.7 months. Bryan argued that if the time period for adjustment is a matter of weeks, estimating a stock-adjustment model using monthly or quarterly data amounts to a serious specification error.

From the existing literature it seems well established that time aggregation can produce seriously biased estimates of rates of adjustment. Generally, the theoretical analysis of time aggregation has dealt with two kinds of questions.

[1] W. R. Bryan, Bank Adjustments to Monetary Policy: Alternative Estimates of the Lag, *American Economic Review*, September, 1967, pp. 855–864.

The first is the question asked by Engle and Liu,[1] and Moriguchi,[2] which is the following: If the true distributed-lag model is of the Koyck type with, say, quarterly time units, what can be said about the probability limits of estimates obtained from fitting the Koyck model to annual data? In particular, how does the estimated mean lag compare with the true mean lag? The answer to this question has been that no general conclusions can be derived about the direction of the biases even if we make some assumptions about the behavior of the x_t series.

A more fruitful question, in this context, for which we can get some answers if we make some assumptions about the behavior of the x_t series, is the following: If the true model is the Koyck model at the quarterly level, and we have annual data, what is the model we should be estimating at the annual level that will enable us to get consistent estimates of the parameters of the original model?

What can be done about time aggregation depends on whether we are considering the distributed-lag model in the distributed-lag form or the autoregressive form and whether the data we have arise from (1) skip sampling—when the data available are (y_m, x_m), (y_{2m}, x_{2m}), (y_{3m}, x_{3m}), . . . , etc., or (2) time aggregates

$$X_t = x_t + x_{t-1} + \cdots + x_{t-m+1}$$
$$Y_t = y_t + y_{t-1} + \cdots + y_{t-m+1}$$

These two situations correspond to cases where the data are on stocks or flows, respectively.[3]

In case (1) we wish to estimate the parameters from a skip sample on x and y. Since time-aggregated data are generally available only for nonoverlapping time intervals, in case (2) we need estimates from a skip sample on X and Y. Thus in both cases the problems are essentially the same. The only differences seem to be in the kinds of assumptions that can reasonably be made about the nature of the disturbances.

In any case what can be done in actual practice depends on what assumptions we make about the behavior of the x_t series. Suppose we assume that the x_t series is first-order autoregressive, i.e.,

$$x_t = \theta x_{t-1} + e_t$$

Suppose we have a skip sample on x_t and y_t with every alternative observation missing; i.e., we observe only x_{2t} and y_{2t}, and suppose the true model is the

[1] R. F. Engle and T. C. Liu, Effects of Aggregation Over Time on Dynamic Characteristics of an Econometric Model, in B. G. Hickman (ed.), "Econometric Models of Cyclical Behavior," vol. II, Studies in Income and Wealth, no. 36, National Bureau of Economic Research, Columbia University Press, New York, 1972.

[2] C. Moriguchi, Aggregation Over Time in Macroeconomic Relations, *International Economic Review*, October, 1970, pp. 427–440.

[3] Obviously, other combinations are possible, e.g., one stock variable and one flow variable. See Moriguchi, *op. cit.*

Koyck model

$$y_t = \frac{\beta x_t}{1 - \lambda L} + u_t$$

then it can be shown that we should be estimating the model

$$y_{2t} = \beta_0 x_{2t} + \frac{\beta_1}{1 - \lambda^2 L^2} x_{2t-2} + w_{2t}$$

i.e., estimating a geometrically declining lag distribution leaving the first coefficient free. In addition to correctly estimating λ, the rate at which the coefficients decay, the total response is likely to be well estimated. We get the total response as $[\beta(1 + 2\lambda\theta + \theta^2)]/[(1 - \lambda^2)(1 + \theta^2)]$, whereas the true sum is $\beta/(1 - \lambda)$. For $\theta = 0$, the total is underestimated by a factor of $(1 + \lambda)$. It can be checked that for reasonable values of θ (say, .7 or .8) the bias in the estimated total response is negligible.

If the distributed-lag model is specified in its autoregressive form so that

$$y_t = \alpha y_{t-1} + \beta x_t + u_t$$

and we have the skip sample (x_{2t}, y_{2t}), then we can write

$$\begin{aligned} y_t &= \alpha^2 y_{t-2} + \beta x_t + \alpha\beta x_{t-1} + u_t + \alpha u_{t-1} \\ &= \alpha^2 y_{t-2} + \beta x_t + \frac{\alpha\beta\theta}{1 + \theta^2}(x_t + x_{t-2}) + w_t \end{aligned} \tag{16-29}$$

where $$w_t = u_t + \alpha u_{t-1} + \alpha\beta\left[x_{t-1} - \frac{\theta}{1 + \theta^2}(x_t + x_{t-2})\right]$$

It can be shown that

$$\frac{1}{T}\sum x_t w_t \to 0 \quad \text{and} \quad \frac{1}{T}\sum x_{t-2} w_t \to 0 \quad \text{as } T \to \infty$$

It can also be shown that $(1/T)\Sigma y_{t-2} w_t \to 0$ as $T \to \infty$ if the u_t are serially independent. In this case Eq. (16-29) can be estimated by OLS to get consistent estimates of all the parameters. If the u_t are serially correlated, we need an instrumental variable for y_{t-2}. We can use x_{t-4} as an instrumental variable and get consistent estimates of all the parameters.

The above examples show that if, instead of asking what we can say about the estimates of the parameters when we estimate the same model with time-aggregated data (as Engle and Liu did), we ask the question: "What is the appropriate model to estimate with time-aggregated data?" Then we can get more definitive and practically useful answers.[1]

[1] Some other discussion on time aggregation that makes this argument can be found in the papers by Telser, Zellner, and Sims. See L. G. Telser, Discrete Samples and Moving Terms in Stochastic Processes, *Journal of the American Statistical Association*, June, 1967, pp. 484–499. A. Zellner, On the Analysis of First Order Autoregressive Models with Incomplete Data, *International Economic Review*, January, 1966, pp. 72–76. C. Sims, Discrete Approximations to Continuous Time Distributed Lags in Econometrics, *Econometrica*, May, 1971, pp. 545–564.

16-7 COMPUTATION OF MEAN LAGS

It has become customary for investigators estimating distributed-lag models to report "mean lags." The mean lag is defined as follows:[1] Suppose that the weights of the lag distribution are

$$w_i = (1 - \lambda)\lambda^i$$

Then, taking $|z| \leqslant 1$, the generating function of this sequence is

$$W(z) = (1 - \lambda)(1 + \lambda z + \lambda^2 z^2 + \lambda^3 z^3 + \cdots)$$
$$= \frac{1 - \lambda}{1 - \lambda z}$$

The mean of the nonnegative variable distributed with this probability distribution is $\sum_{i=0}^{\infty} i w_i = W'(1)$, where $W'(1)$ is the derivative of $W(z)$ at $z = 1$. In this case $W'(z) = [\lambda(1 - \lambda)]/(1 - \lambda z)^2$ so that $W'(1) = \lambda/(1 - \lambda)$. One major defect of looking at the mean lags in this fashion becomes apparent when we consider the following problem: Suppose that we have a skip sample in which we observe only x_{mt} and y_{mt} (m is an integer > 1). The lag coefficients will decline at the rate λ^m, and if we succeed in estimating the lag coefficients correctly, since the implied lag-generating function is $(1 - \lambda^m)/(1 - \lambda^m z)$, we will be estimating the mean lag as $m\lambda^m/(1 - \lambda^m)$. For example, if the original data are quarterly, the mean lag is $\lambda/(1 - \lambda)$ quarters. With annual data it is $4\lambda^4/(1 - \lambda^4)$ quarters. Thus, even if one succeeds in correctly estimating the shape of the lag distribution, the calculated mean lag will depend upon the time unit chosen. Since we have captured the lag distribution exactly, it seems reasonable to expect that the mean lag calculated from the skip sample will be the same as that calculated from the complete sample. This suggests that when one is computing mean lags from models with different time units, one should not compute mean lags in the usual fashion.

An alternative procedure is to compute the mean lag from the continuous-time version of the distributed-lag model. Consider a continuous-time distributed-lag model

$$y(t) = \int_0^{\infty} b(s)x(t - s) + u(t)$$

where $b(\ )$ is nonnegative and integrates to one. The mean lag can easily be calculated from the Fourier transform of the lag distribution:[2]

$$F(\omega) = \int_0^{\infty} b(s)e^{-i\omega s}\,ds$$

In this case the mean lag is given by

$$\mu = iF'(0)$$

[1] See Zvi Griliches, Distributed Lags: A Survey, *Econometrica*, January, 1967, pp. 16–49.

[2] Those unfamiliar with Fourier transforms can read any book on spectral analysis. However, to understand the argument being made here, this is not necessary.

The continuous-time lag distribution corresponding to the Koyck model is $\beta e^{t \ln \lambda}$, for which

$$F(\omega) = \frac{-\ln \lambda}{-\ln \lambda + i\omega}$$

and the mean lag is $1/(-\ln \lambda)$. Note that if, because of skip sampling, the time units are multiplied by m, but estimated lag distribution has the correct shape, the calculated mean lag will be $m/(-\ln \lambda^m) = -[1/(\ln \lambda)]$. Thus, when analyzing the effects of time aggregation or skip sampling on the estimates of mean lags, we suggest that the mean lags be computed so that the observed discrepancies depend upon the statistical biases introduced but not upon the time interval used. This is not to suggest that differences in the time unit are unimportant. In fact, $(m\lambda^m)/(1-\lambda^m)$ can be quite different from $\lambda/(1-\lambda)$ even for moderate size m; e.g., $\lambda = .7$ and $m = 3$ gives 1.58 and 2.33, respectively. The point is that it seems reasonable to separate this effect from the statistical biases.

16-8 WEAK PARAMETRIC SPECIFICATIONS IN DISTRIBUTED LAGS

Till now we have discussed methods where the successive coefficients β_i in the lag distribution have been assumed to follow some functional forms which depend on fewer parameters. The Almon, Koyck, Solow, and Jorgenson methods all fall in this category. These methods might be called "strong parametric specifications." It has been often argued that these specifications really impose strong constraints on the lag distribution, and there is often no prior information to justify that. No one knows how far the results obtained are a consequence of these constraints.[1] Some functional forms like the Almon lag are very popular because if one imposes the endpoint constraints, one gets a very "plausible" lag pattern that is often very appealing. But this method, as argued earlier, can really produce severe distortions in the true lag distribution. In recent times there has been a shift to the estimation of distributed-lag models through unconstrained least squares with possibly some weak structure imposed on the coefficients.[2] In this category we will discuss the methods suggested by Hannan.

[1] Take, for instance, the data in Table 9-2. Ordinary-least-squares estimations of distributed-lag models with 1 to 8 lags all give the sum of the coefficients about .929 to .935 with a standard error of .002 to .004. But when a Koyck lag is imposed and the model is estimated by the maximum-likelihood method, the sum of the coefficients is found to be greater than 1.

[2] See C. Sims, Distributed Lags, in M. D. Intrilligator and D. A. Kendrick (eds.), "Frontiers of Quantitative Economics," North-Holland Publishing Company, Amsterdam, 1974. Sims argues for the estimation of long unconstrained lags and says that they give sensible results. Griliches, in his comment on the paper, says that he is surprised that estimation of such long unconstrained lags leads to "sensible" results. He argues that he often thought that this would give "garbage" but that possibly we see more in the "garbage" than we used to. This is because some prior information is used in an informal way. But if one formally incorporates this prior information, the results would roughly be the same.

Two methods for distributed-lag estimation suggested by Hannan are often used. One is called the Hannan "efficient" method (HE) and the other the Hannan "inefficient" method (HI). Though the methods are discussed in frequency domain using spectral analysis, it is not necessary to be familiar with these techniques to understand what these methods are about and where their merit and usefulness lie. The HE method is useful for any regression model—with distributed lags or not—but the HI method is specifically for distributed-lag models. The HI method is computationally much simpler than the HE method, and Hannan feels that for most economic time series it would produce efficient estimates.[1]

The HE method is essentially a generalized-least-squares estimation of a regression model

$$\mathbf{y} = \mathbf{X}\boldsymbol{\beta} + \mathbf{u}$$

where the error $\mathbf{u}$ is assumed to follow a general stationary stochastic process. In the usual time-series-regression models we assume $\mathbf{u}$ to be a serially independent series or sometimes a first-order autoregressive series. The advantage with the frequency-domain methods like the HE method is that we do not have to make such a restrictive assumption. The estimator for β is

$$\hat{\boldsymbol{\beta}} = (\mathbf{X}'\boldsymbol{\Omega}^{-1}\mathbf{X})^{-1}\mathbf{X}'\boldsymbol{\Omega}^{-1}\mathbf{y}$$

where $\boldsymbol{\Omega}$ is the covariance matrix of a very general stationary process. The other advantage is computational—that computational tricks are available for the inversion of the covariance matrix $\boldsymbol{\Omega}$, which is of a large order ($T \times T$). Thus, the two advantages are generality in the assumptions about u and computational ease in the inversion of $\boldsymbol{\Omega}$.

The HI method, on the other hand, is specifically designed for the estimation of distributed-lag models. The main advantage of the HI method that Hannan claims is that it can be used when the exact length of the lag distribution is not known and also one can add coefficients without having to recompute the estimates all over again. Further, the variance of each coefficient is the same and an estimate of this variance can be obtained once for all before any of the lag coefficients are estimated. A simple explanation of the method without using any frequency-domain methods is as follows: Let

$$y_t = \sum_{i=0}^{p} \beta_i x_{t-i} + u_t$$

where the length of the lag p is not known. Suppose we can transform the x's into a mutually uncorrelated series, i.e., there exists a transformation T such that

[1] These methods were both suggested in E. J. Hannan, Regression for Time Series, in M. Rosenblatt (ed.), "Proceedings of a Symposium in Time Series Analysis," John Wiley & Sons, Inc., New York, 1963. The Hannan "inefficient" method was later elaborated in E. J. Hannan, The Estimation of a Lagged Regression Relation, *Biometrika*, 1967, pp. 409–418.

$Tx_t = x_t^*$ is serially independent. Let $y_t^* = Ty_t$ and $u_t^* = Tu_t$. Then the given distributed lag can be transformed to

$$y_t^* = \Sigma\beta_i x_{t-i}^* + u_t^*$$

Since the x_t^* are serially independent, we can compute the β_i successively and stop at a point where they are zero. If the serial-correlation structure of x_t and u_t is similar (which is quite likely with most economic data, because u_t are omitted variables whose behavior is similar to that of x_t), then the transformation that orthogonalizes the x_t series will also orthogonalize the u_t series, and then the HI method is also efficient. If the u_t^* series is not serially independent, the HI method is of course inefficient. It is customary to say that the HI method is efficient if the signal-to-noise ratio is constant at all frequencies. What this means is that the structure of the x_t series and u_t series is similar, and the procedure that orthogonalizes one also orthogonalizes the other. In essence the basic problem is finding the transformation T. One can perhaps use Nerlove's "universal formula" for economic time series. This is to take $x_t^* = (1 - .75L)^2 x_t$. In any case those reporting HI estimates should start reporting what transformation was used so that the readers can appraise the results more thoroughly.

The HI and the HE methods are now standard tools for distributed-lag estimation. See, for example, the applications by Cargill and Meyer, Sargent, and Sims.[1] However, none of these studies report the ordinary-least-squares estimates for the sake of comparison. If one is arguing for unconstrained estimation of the distributed-lag models, it would help to see what the OLS estimates also look like and what differences are being produced by the use of the HI and HE methods.

Table 16-3 HI estimates

Lag	1 year	2 years	3 years	4 years	5 years	10 years	20 years
0	.711*	.543*	.451*	.398*	.359*	.229*	.179*
1	.025	−.002	−.004	−.012	−.027	−.047	−.034
2	−.088	−.039	−.061	−.033	−.012	−.020	−.037
3	.039	−.034	−.044	−.069	−.074	−.010	−.004
4	.073	.093	.115*	.107*	.097*	.017	.027
5	−.038	.024	−.032	−.029	−.036	−.017	−.013
6	.051	.045	.092	.063	.046	.007	.011
7	−.048	−.056	−.087	−.054	−.031	−.003	−.012
8	.022	−.002	.039	.037	.028	.021	.019
9	−.001	−.010	−.016	−.012	−.001	.007	−.011
R^2	.735	.522	.396	.328	.277	.122	.080

[1] Thomas F. Cargill and Robert A. Meyer, A Spectral Approach to Estimating the Distributed Lag Relationship between Long- and Short-Term Interest Rates, *International Economic Review*, 1972, pp. 223–238. Thomas J. Sargent, Rational Expectations and the Term Structure of Interest Rates, *Journal of Money, Credit, and Banking*, 1972. C. A. Sims, Are There Exogenous Variables in Short-Run Production Relations? *Annals of Economic and Social Measurement*, 1972, pp. 17–36.

Table 16-4 HE estimates

Lag	1 year	2 years	3 years	4 years	5 years	10 years	20 years
0	.773*	.636*	.555*	.510*	.467*	.289*	.196*
1	.061	.060	.040	.016	−.007	−.009	.002
2	−.045	.015	−.018	.011	.029	−.021	−.045
3	.020	−.076	−.077	−.102*	−.098*	−.040	−.022
4	.039	.040	.068	.045	.030	−.022	.003
5	−.053	.020	−.030	−.010	−.007	.007	−.012
6	.043	.038	.097*	.059	.033	.006	.025
7	−.006	.006	−.055	−.020	.004	.021	−.006
8	.044	.018	.064	.055	.040	.028	.032
9	.023	−.040	−.038	−.035	−.021	−.003	−.016
R^2	.703	.522	.467	.423	.385	.278	.235

Cargill and Meyer estimate the relationship between long and short rates of interest over a wide maturity range. The long rate R_t is represented by 1-, 2-, 3-, 4-, 5-, 10-, and 20-year government bond rates and the short-rate S_t by rates on 3-month bills. The data are monthly (April 1951 to December 1968). Tables 16-3 and 16-4 present the HI and HE estimates. (Asterisk denotes the coefficient is significant at the 5 percent level.) As can be easily seen from these tables, there is a discernible pattern in the results. First the R^2 falls as the maturity rises. Second often only the first coefficient is significant, and the magnitude of this coefficient also falls as the maturity rises. Cargill and Meyer argue that there is no evidence of a long lag between R_t and S_t, as was found by some who used the Almon procedure.

There are some puzzling things in the results, however. Cargill and Meyer exhibit the signal-to-noise ratios for $R_t = 1$ year and $R_t = 5$ years, and this ratio is not constant. However, the HE estimates are close to the HI estimates. But more importantly, the first coefficient for the HE method is always higher than the corresponding coefficient for the HI method. Further, in a case like this where unconstrained distributed-lag estimation gave "sensible" results, we would like to see what the OLS estimates look like and how they compare with the HI estimates. If these two are different, one also needs an explanation of why they are different. Unfortunately, Cargill and Meyer do not report the OLS estimates.[1] Finally, in this example it is possible that we are able to get more information from the unconstrained estimates because we have a large number of observations (over 200).

[1] In a subsequent Monte Carlo study, Cargill and Meyer compare the OLS, HI, and Almon methods. They conclude that the OLS is better than the HI method, which in turn is better than the Almon method. It is not clear whether the HI method should be abandoned in favor of OLS, because the main merit of the HI method is that the length of the lag need not be specified, whereas for the others it has to be specified. What their results perhaps suggest is that it would be useful to use the HI method to determine the length of the lag distribution and then use OLS once this is determined. See T. Cargill and R. A. Meyer, Some Time and Frequency Domain Distributed Lag Estimators: A Comparative Monte Carlo Study, *Econometrica*, November, 1974, pp. 1031–1044.

What all this suggests is that even those using the Koyck, Solow, Jorgenson, and Almon types of models would do well first to report the estimates of unconstrained distributed-lag models by the OLS and HI methods. Those reporting results of the HI and HE methods should also report the results of OLS. This will throw light on some peculiarities of the data and will also reveal what information can be obtained without imposing any constraints. For instance, the OLS results reported in Table 10-2 show a systematic negative coefficient for the fourth lag, thus suggesting that seasonality may be a serious problem and that without correcting for it, one should not do any constrained estimation. It also suggests that there is strong evidence in the data about the long-run marginal propensity to consume. In a later section (Sec. 16-10) we will see how much information there is in the "garbage" of the ordinary least-squares estimates.

16-9 SHILLER'S METHOD[1] AND RIDGE ESTIMATORS

Consider the distributed-lag model

$$y_t = \sum_{i=0}^{p} \beta_i x_{t-i} + u_t \tag{16-30}$$

where u_t are $IN(0,\sigma_u^2)$; $t = 1,2, \ldots, n$.

In the Almon method we assume that the β_i in (16-30) lie on a low-degree polynomial. For the sake of illustration, we will assume that it is a quadratic.

$$\beta_i = \alpha_0 + \alpha_1 i + \alpha_2 i^2 \tag{16-31}$$

Then Eq. (16-30) can be written as

$$\begin{aligned} y_t &= \sum_{i=0}^{p} (\alpha_0 + \alpha_1 i + \alpha_2 i^2) x_{t-i} + u_t \\ &= a_0 z_{0t} + \alpha_1 z_{1t} + \alpha_2 z_{2t} + u_t \end{aligned}$$

where

$$z_{jt} = \sum_{i=0}^{p} i^j x_{t-i} \tag{16-32}$$

Equation (16-31) can be written as

$$\boldsymbol{\beta} = \mathbf{H}\boldsymbol{\alpha} \tag{16-33}$$

where

$$\mathbf{H} = \begin{bmatrix} 1 & 0 & 0 \\ 1 & 1 & 1 \\ 1 & 2 & 4 \\ \cdot & \cdot & \cdot \\ 1 & p & p^2 \end{bmatrix}$$

[1] Shiller, Robert J., A Distributed Lag Estimator Derived from Smoothness Priors, *Econometrica*, July, 1973, pp. 775–788.

Define

$$\mathbf{M} = \mathbf{I} - \mathbf{H}(\mathbf{H}'\mathbf{H})^{-1}\mathbf{H}' \tag{16-34}$$

Then Eq. (16-33) implies the set of restrictions

$$\mathbf{M}\boldsymbol{\beta} = \mathbf{0} \tag{16-35}$$

Thus, to get Almon's estimator, we minimize $(\mathbf{y} - \mathbf{X}\boldsymbol{\beta})'(\mathbf{y} - \mathbf{X}\boldsymbol{\beta})$ subject to (16-35). The resulting estimator is[1]

$$\hat{\boldsymbol{\beta}}_A = \hat{\boldsymbol{\beta}} - (\mathbf{X}'\mathbf{X})^{-1}\mathbf{M}'\left[\mathbf{M}(\mathbf{X}'\mathbf{X})^{-1}\mathbf{M}'\right]^{-1}\mathbf{M}\hat{\boldsymbol{\beta}} \tag{16-36}$$

where $\hat{\boldsymbol{\beta}}_A$ is the Almon estimator of $\boldsymbol{\beta}$ and $\hat{\boldsymbol{\beta}}$ is the ordinary-least-squares estimator of $\boldsymbol{\beta}$.

The basic argument in Shiller's method is that we often specify a restriction such as (16-31) not because we believe in it but because we believe the lag distribution to be smooth.

One can add an error term to (16-31) and write

$$\beta_i = \alpha_0 + \alpha_1 i + \alpha_2 i^2 + v_i \tag{16-37}$$

where v_i are $IN(0, \sigma_v^2)$. This will result in the model

$$y_t = \alpha_0 z_{0t} + \alpha_1 z_{1t} + \alpha_2 z_{2t} + w_t$$

where z_{jt} are as defined in (16-32) and

$$w_t = u_t + \sum_{i=0}^{p} v_i x_{t-i}$$

This results in a complicated covariance matrix for the residuals. The residuals are heteroscedastic and autocorrelated.

Instead of making Eq. (16-31) stochastic, Shiller notes that assumption (16-31) implies that

$$\Delta^3 \beta_i = 0 \tag{16-38}$$

where $\Delta\beta_i = \beta_i - \beta_{i-1}$. Shiller makes Eq. (16-38) stochastic by adding an error term to it, i.e.,

$$\Delta^3 \beta_i = w_i \qquad \text{where } w_i \text{ are } IN\left(0, \sigma_w^2\right) \tag{16-39}$$

This can be written as

$$\mathbf{R}\boldsymbol{\beta} = \mathbf{w} \tag{16-40}$$

$$\text{where} \quad \mathbf{R} = \begin{bmatrix} 1 & -3 & +3 & -1 & 0 & 0 & \cdot & \cdot & 0 \\ 0 & 1 & -3 & +3 & -1 & 0 & \cdot & \cdot & 0 \\ \cdot & \cdot & \cdot & \cdot & \cdot & \cdot & \cdot & \cdot & \cdot \\ \cdot & \cdot & \cdot & \cdot & \cdot & \cdot & \cdot & \cdot & \cdot \\ 0 & 0 & 0 & 0 & 0 & 1 & -3 & +3 & -1 \end{bmatrix}$$

$\mathbf{R}$ is a $(p-1) \times (p+1)$ matrix. Using the Theil-Goldberger mixed-estimation

[1] See Appendix B, section on tests of linear restrictions, Eq. (B-10).

method,[1] we get the estimator of β as

$$\hat{\beta}_s = (\mathbf{X}'\mathbf{X} + k\mathbf{R}'\mathbf{R})^{-1}\mathbf{X}'\mathbf{y} \tag{16-41}$$

where $k = \sigma_u^2/\sigma_w^2$ is assumed known. If we follow the nonstochastic version of Shiller's method, we minimize $(\mathbf{y} - \mathbf{X}\boldsymbol{\beta})'(\mathbf{y} - \mathbf{X}\boldsymbol{\beta})$ subject to $\mathbf{R}\boldsymbol{\beta} = \mathbf{0}$, and the estimator of $\boldsymbol{\beta}$ we obtain is

$$\hat{\boldsymbol{\beta}}_A = \hat{\boldsymbol{\beta}} - (\mathbf{X}'\mathbf{X})^{-1}\mathbf{R}'\left[\mathbf{R}(\mathbf{X}'\mathbf{X})^{-1}\mathbf{R}'\right]^{-1}\mathbf{R}\hat{\boldsymbol{\beta}} \tag{16-42}$$

where $\hat{\boldsymbol{\beta}}$ is the OLS estimator of $\boldsymbol{\beta}$. This expression can be shown to be equivalent to the expression in (16-36). However, when we introduce the stochastic term, it makes a difference whether we make (16-31) or (16-38) stochastic.

Ridge Estimators

Hoerl and Kennard[2] present a set of biased least-squares estimators which they call "ridge estimators." Their suggestion is to use, instead of the least-squares estimator

$$\hat{\boldsymbol{\beta}} = (\mathbf{X}'\mathbf{X})^{-1}\mathbf{X}'\mathbf{y}$$

the modified estimator

$$\hat{\boldsymbol{\beta}}_R = (\mathbf{X}'\mathbf{X} + k\mathbf{I})^{-1}\mathbf{X}'\mathbf{y} \tag{16-43}$$

They suggest an iterative procedure to decide on a suitable k. Instead of (16-43) we can consider a more general form

$$\hat{\boldsymbol{\beta}}_R = (\mathbf{X}'\mathbf{X} + k\mathbf{Q})^{-1}\mathbf{X}'\mathbf{y} \tag{16-44}$$

where $\mathbf{Q}$ is a positive semidefinite matrix, and written this way it can be seen that Shiller's estimator (16-41) is also a ridge estimator.

One can give a Bayesian interpretation to all these estimators, and in fact this way of looking at the estimators is more revealing.[3] Consider the ridge estimator (16-43). If the prior distribution of $\boldsymbol{\beta}$ is $N(\mathbf{0},\tau^2\mathbf{I})$, the mean of the posterior distribution of $\boldsymbol{\beta}$ is given by (16-43) with $k = \sigma^2/\tau^2$. Instead, if we assume the prior distribution of $\boldsymbol{\beta}$ to be $N(\delta,\tau^2\boldsymbol{\Delta})$, the posterior distribution of $\boldsymbol{\beta}$ is also normal with mean

$$(\mathbf{X}'\mathbf{X} + k\boldsymbol{\Delta}^{-1})^{-1}(\mathbf{X}'\mathbf{y} + k\boldsymbol{\Delta}^{-1}\boldsymbol{\delta}) \tag{16-45}$$

and variance $\sigma^2(\mathbf{X}'\mathbf{X} + k\boldsymbol{\Delta}^{-1})^{-1}$. If $\boldsymbol{\Delta} = \mathbf{I}$, the posterior mean is

$$(\mathbf{X}'\mathbf{X} + k\mathbf{I})^{-1}(\mathbf{X}'\mathbf{y} + k\boldsymbol{\delta}) \tag{16-46}$$

The important point to note is that the commonly used ridge estimator given by (16-43) implies a prior distribution for $\boldsymbol{\beta}$ with mean zero. This may not be a

[1] See Appendix B, section on extraneous estimates and mixed estimation.

[2] A. E. Hoerl and R. W. Kennard, Ridge Regression: Biased Estimation for Non-orthogonal Problems, *Technometrics*, 1970, pp. 55–67.

[3] For an introduction to Bayesian inference, see Chap. 18.

plausible assumption to make in many applications, and if so, Eq. (16-45) or (16-46) should be used. These modifications can be made very easily.

The Bayesian approach to the stochastic version of the Almon lag given by (16-37) can easily be seen to yield the ridge estimator as the posterior mean. Equation (16-37) can be written as

$$\boldsymbol{\beta} = \mathbf{H}\boldsymbol{\alpha} + \mathbf{v}$$

where **H** is defined in (16-33).

Following Lindley and Smith,[1] we can say that

$$\mathbf{y} \sim N(\mathbf{X}\boldsymbol{\beta}, \mathbf{I}\sigma_u^2)$$

and
$$\boldsymbol{\beta} \sim N(\mathbf{H}\boldsymbol{\alpha}, \mathbf{I}\sigma_v^2) \tag{16-47}$$

This still leaves us with the specification of the priors for $\boldsymbol{\alpha}$. We can assume a diffuse prior for $\boldsymbol{\alpha}$. Lindley and Smith prove the following theorem: If

$$\mathbf{y} \sim N(\mathbf{A}_1\boldsymbol{\theta}_1, \mathbf{C}_1)$$
$$\boldsymbol{\theta}_1 \sim N(\mathbf{A}_2\boldsymbol{\theta}_2, \mathbf{C}_2)$$

and we assume a diffuse prior for $\boldsymbol{\theta}_2$, then the posterior distribution of $\boldsymbol{\theta}_1$ is $N(\mathbf{D}_0\mathbf{d}_0, \mathbf{D}_0)$, where

$$\mathbf{D}_0^{-1} = \mathbf{A}_1'\mathbf{C}_1^{-1}\mathbf{A}_1 + \mathbf{C}_2^{-1} - \mathbf{C}_2^{-1}\mathbf{A}_2(\mathbf{A}_2'\mathbf{C}_2^{-1}\mathbf{A}_2)^{-1}\mathbf{A}_2'\mathbf{C}_2^{-1}$$

and
$$\mathbf{d}_0 = \mathbf{A}_1'\mathbf{C}_1^{-1}\mathbf{y}$$

In our case the posterior mean of $\boldsymbol{\beta}$ is (after simplification)

$$\boldsymbol{\beta}^* = ((\mathbf{X}'\mathbf{X}) + k\mathbf{M})^{-1}\mathbf{X}'\mathbf{y} \tag{16-48}$$

where **M** is as defined in (16-34) and $k = \sigma_u^2/\sigma_v^2$. Thus we see that the mean of the posterior distribution for the Bayesian version of the stochastic Almon-lag specification is a ridge estimator of $\boldsymbol{\beta}$. As $\sigma_v^2 \to 0$, this should give the usual Almon estimator defined in (16-36). This can be checked as follows:

$$\begin{aligned}\boldsymbol{\beta}^* &= (\mathbf{X}'\mathbf{X} + k\mathbf{M})^{-1}\mathbf{X}'\mathbf{y} \\ &= (\mathbf{X}'\mathbf{X} + k\mathbf{M}^2)^{-1}\mathbf{X}'\mathbf{y} \qquad \text{since } \mathbf{M} \text{ is idempotent}\end{aligned}$$

Now $(\mathbf{X}'\mathbf{X} + k\mathbf{M}^2)^{-1}$ can be written as[2]

$$(\mathbf{X}'\mathbf{X})^{-1} - (\mathbf{X}'\mathbf{X})^{-1}\mathbf{M}\left[\mathbf{M}'(\mathbf{X}'\mathbf{X})^{-1}\mathbf{M} + \frac{1}{k}\mathbf{I}\right]^{-1}\mathbf{M}'(\mathbf{X}'\mathbf{X})^{-1}$$

As $\sigma_v^2 \to 0$, $1/k \to 0$, and thus $\boldsymbol{\beta}^*$ = the expression in (16-36). Henceforth we will call the estimator (16-48) the Bayesian Almon estimator.[3] The fact that $k = \sigma_u^2/\sigma_v^2$ suggests an iterative procedure for estimating k. We first estimate σ_u^2 from the least-squares residuals and σ_v^2 from the estimated least-square $\boldsymbol{\beta}$'s.

[1] D. V. Lindley and A. F. M. Smith, Bayes Estimates for the Linear Model (with Discussion), *Journal of the Royal Statistical Society*, B Series, 1972, pp. 1–41.

[2] In Eq. (A-18) of Appendix A, put $\mathbf{D} = k\mathbf{I}$, $\mathbf{B} = \mathbf{M}$, and $\mathbf{A} = \mathbf{X}'\mathbf{X}$. Then the result follows.

[3] Throughout our discussion of the Bayesian Almon estimator, we assumed σ_u^2 and σ_v^2 known. When these are not known, one has to assume priors for them. Since the analysis is similar to that given in Lindley and Smith, we will not repeat it here.

Instead of making the assumption (16-47), Lindley and Smith assume

$$\boldsymbol{\beta} \sim N(\mu\mathbf{1}, \sigma_v^2 \mathbf{I})$$

where $\mathbf{1}$ is the unit vector and we have a vague prior for μ. This is just a special case of the Almon lag (with zero-degree polynomial). Thus the posterior mean they get is the same as in (16-48) except that instead of $\mathbf{H}$ we have the unit vector $\mathbf{1}$ and hence $\mathbf{M} = \mathbf{I}_{p+1} - (1/p+1)\ \mathbf{J}_{p+1}$ when $\mathbf{J}$ is a matrix with all elements unity.

In all these methods there is the problem of how to determine k. Shiller gives a rule of thumb for determining k in his method. Since $k = \sigma_u^2/\sigma_w^2$, he suggests taking σ_u^2 as the estimate of the residual variance from the OLS regression and σ_w^2 as $64S^2/p^2$, where S is the sum of the lag coefficients (obtained from the OLS regression). Though this rule of thumb seems to have worked well for the examples that Shiller used in his paper, experiments with the Almon data gave very high values of k (which imply very low values of σ_w^2 or very tight priors). Thus one should be cautious in using Shiller's rule of thumb. There is also the further problem with choosing a constant value for σ_w^2. With changes in the units of measurement of y (and of x so that S remains constant), the value of σ_u^2 changes. Thus k is not invariant to changes in units of measurement of the variables.

Lindley and Smith suggest an iterative procedure of estimating k which essentially consists of starting with the OLS estimates of the β_i and taking the variance of the estimates as an estimate of σ_v^2. That is, $\hat{\sigma}_v^2 = (1/p)\sum_{i=0}^{p}(\hat{\beta}_i - \bar{\beta})^2$, where $\bar{\beta}$ is the mean of the $\hat{\beta}_i$. After the new estimates are computed, the estimate of σ_v^2 is revised based on the new estimates. The procedure is repeated until some satisfactory level of convergence is attained. One can also use this iterative procedure for Shiller's method.

For illustrative purposes, we will present the results obtained by using these procedures on the Almon data. In all cases the lag distribution was arbitrarily terminated at x_{t-8}. For the Bayes-Almon method we used a polynomial of degrees zero, one, and two. The iterative procedure in each case was terminated when the sum of the absolute values of the changes in the coefficients was less than .001.

First, there are some procedures that were found unsatisfactory to start with. The straight ridge estimator of Hoerl and Kennard really smoothed the lag distribution even for as low values of k as .01. The estimated coefficients were all almost equal (each close to .11). Thus the total response was equally distributed.[1] This suggests that the Hoerl and Kennard type of ridge estimator is not appropriate for the estimation of distributed-lag models.

Second, Shiller's rule of thumb suggested a value of $k = 729.3$ for the Almon data. Such tight priors produce exactly the same estimates as those obtained by

[1] We noticed this even in the estimation of other distributed-lag models as well. Using the procedure for the choice of k suggested in their paper, we always arrived at a lag distribution where the coefficients were all almost equal.

the Almon method. This suggests that if one is using Shiller's method, it is better to use some iterative procedure (like the Lindley-Smith procedure) rather than use a fixed value of k.

Table 16-5 presents the results of the Bayes-Almon procedure with polynomials of degree 0, 1, 2. The iterative procedure converged after 8, 6, and 5 iterations, respectively. Actually, this is an example where the OLS estimates are not too erratic. The zero-degree polynomial is, as discussed earlier, the Lindley-Smith estimator. As can be seen, this method also smooths the lag distribution and distributes the weights almost equally, though not as much as the Hoerl-Kennard method.

In summary, the ridge estimators discussed here can be regarded as weak parametric specifications for the distributed-lag models and are designed to overcome the multicollinearity problem and at the same time not impose very strong assumptions. However, the Hoerl and Kennard method and the Lindley-Smith method are not too promising for distributed-lag estimation. It is the Shiller method and the Bayes-Almon method that need more investigation. At present, there is not much empirical evidence on these methods. There is, however, the problem that all these procedures are, like the Almon procedure, applicable only to finite lag distributions and the length of the lag needs to be specified.

The Almon procedure depends on the specification of the restriction $\boldsymbol{\beta} = \mathbf{H}\boldsymbol{\alpha}$, where $\mathbf{H}$ is a matrix of the form (16-33). It can, however, be improved by changing $\mathbf{H}$ to correspond to, say, a piecewise linear function or a piecewise polynomial. These changes still lead to the linear restrictions on β. All these linear parametrizations are convenient and computationally easy, but unless we keep the number of columns in $\mathbf{H}$ small, we cannot prevent erratic shapes for the lag distribution.

Shiller argues[1] that his "smoothness prior" prevents getting such erratic

Table 16-5 Estimates for Almon Data

Lag	OLS	Zero-degree	First-degree	Second-degree
0	.07272	.11441	.12116	.09142
1	.08121	.11648	.12857	.12446
2	.23184	.11845	.14052	.15607
3	.18436	.11698	.13647	.15540
4	.13406	.11314	.12201	.13508
5	.01382	.10820	.10191	.10678
6	.13647	.10517	.09336	.09980
7	.06380	.10220	.07708	.07331
8	.06870	.10086	.06515	.04225
Sum	.98698	.99589	.98623	.98457

[1] R. J. Shiller, "Alternative Prior Representations of Smoothness for Distributed Lag Estimation," National Bureau of Economic Research Working Paper 89, June, 1975.

shapes and that the formulation (16-37) need not. The difference between the two stochastic versions (16-37) and (16-39), according to Shiller, is that the prior (16-37) would assert that the coefficients cannot deviate far from some polynomial and is indifferent as to how irregular are the deviations of the coefficients from the polynomial. The smoothness prior (16-39), on the other hand, asserts (if σ_w^2 is small) that the β_i can deviate dramatically from any polynomial if it does so gradually, i.e., in a "smooth" manner. For instance, if we have $\Delta\beta_i = w_i$, the prior allows any shape which does not allow adjacent coefficients to be much different. If $\Delta^2\beta_i = w_i$, the prior allows any shape in which the slopes do not change quickly; i.e., it does not allow "jagged" shapes.

Shiller also modifies his smoothness prior by changing Eq. (16-40) to $\mathbf{R} \log \boldsymbol{\beta} = \mathbf{w}$. This is an appropriate formulation if we believe that the coefficients are all positive. Now the priors are about proportionate changes rather than absolute changes. The advantage of this formulation is that the priors "tighten" up in regions in which the coefficients are small, as in the tail of the lag distribution. From the computational point of view, Shiller uses a quadratic approximation to $(\log \boldsymbol{\beta})'\mathbf{R}'\mathbf{R}(\log \boldsymbol{\beta})$ around an initial guess of $\boldsymbol{\beta}$ and then uses an iterative procedure. The computations are not complicated if one assumes a particular value of k. They will get messier if one also has to iterate on k.

16-10 FORM-FREE LAGS

In the previous sections we discussed some weak parametric specifications. Strictly speaking, even the assumption of smoothness does not have a universal theoretical basis. It can be justified only in some cases. Sims argues that if a random economic time series Y_t is projected on current and lagged values of another time series x_t, there is no reason to expect a "smooth" distributed lag even if the time series themselves are smooth. In view of this, it would be interesting to ask what features of the lag distribution we can capture without imposing any constraints on the lag distribution. Suppose we are interested only in some moments of the lag distribution. More specifically, suppose we are interested in the sum of the lag coefficients (the long-run response), the mean lag, and the variance of the lag distribution.[1] Then we can consider the following nonsingular transformation of the β's:

$$\mu_j = \sum_{s=0}^{k} s^j \beta_j \qquad j = 0, 1, 2, \ldots, k$$

The μ_j are the $k+1$ ordered moments of the nonnormalized lag distribution. Thus the model in (16-1) can be transformed to a linear model in the lag moments. Further, if the x_t follow a first-order autoregressive process and if σ_{jj} is the variance of μ_j, then Wallace shows that in large samples

$$\sigma_{00} < \sigma_{11} < \cdots < \sigma_{kk}$$

[1] The following discussion is based on a paper by T. D. Wallace, "Form Free Distributed Lags," Duke University, summer, 1975.

i.e., if the problem in getting precise estimates of the β's is that x_t are autoregressive, then the transformation to μ's orders the precision in the data so that the long-run effect is estimated most precisely, the mean of the (nonnormalized) lag distribution next most precisely, etc.

Wallace applies this method to the consumption data in Table 10-1 for which we presented earlier in Table 10-2 some OLS estimates of the distributed-lag models with k from 0 to 8. Wallace computes the results for $k = 18, 19, 20, 21$, and 22. He also allows for a first-order serial correlation in the residuals. For $k = 19$, he gets the following results (figures in parentheses are standard errors):

$$\hat{\mu}_0 = .9609\ (.0091)$$

$$\hat{\mu}_1 = 6.23\ (.901)$$

$$\hat{\mu}_2 = 115.099\ (16.549)$$

$$\hat{\mu}_3 = 1973.82\ (293.8)$$

$$\hat{\rho} = .3 \qquad R^2 = .9992 \qquad \text{DW} = 1.9694$$

From these results, Wallace concludes that

1. A 90 percent confidence interval for the long-run marginal propensity to consume is $\Pr(.945 < \mu_0 < .977) = .90$.
2. A point estimate for the mean of the normalized lag distribution is $\hat{M}_1 = \hat{\mu}_1/\hat{\mu}_0 = 6.5$ quarters, with an approximate 90 percent confidence interval[1] $\Pr(4.9 < M_1 < 8.1) = .90$.
3. A point estimate of the variance about the mean of the normalized lag distribution is $\hat{M}_2 = \hat{\mu}_2/\hat{\mu}_0 - \hat{M}_1^2 = 77.8$ with an approximate confidence interval $\Pr(67.0 < M_2 < 88.6) = .90$.
4. The estimated skewness coefficient is $\hat{M}_3 = \hat{\mu}_3/\hat{\mu}_0 - 3M_1M_2 - M_1^3 = 267.6$. The approximate standard error is 653.9.

Hence Wallace concludes that we can get an estimate of the long-run marginal propensity to consume with quite good precision, an estimate of the mean lag with fair precision, an estimate of the variance of the lag distribution with less precision, and not much of a notion about the skewness.

[1] The approximate confidence interval is constructed from the asymptotic normal distribution. See Goldberger, "Econometric Theory," p. 125, John Wiley & Sons, Inc., New York, 1964.

CHAPTER

SEVENTEEN

VARYING-PARAMETER MODELS

One of the assumptions we have made till now is that the parameters are constant over all the observations. It has often been suggested that this may not be a valid assumption to make. In cross-section studies there can be heterogeneity in the parameters across different cross-section units. In time-series studies there can be variation over time in the parameters.

Several models to tackle such problems are suggested in the literature. To illustrate the principles we will consider the case of only one explanatory variable. Generalization to multiple regression is often straightforward. Where this is not so, we will illustrate the principles with reference to the case of several explanatory variables.

17-1 CASE 1: EXPLANATORY VARIABLES FOR CHANGES IN THE PARAMETERS ARE KNOWN

This is the simplest and most easily interpretable case. Let

$$y_t = \beta_t x_t + u_t \qquad t = 1,2, \ldots, n \tag{17-1}$$

be the regression equation.

If there is some variable z_t that can explain the movements in β_t, we can write

$$\beta_t = \alpha + \delta z_t \tag{17-2}$$

Substituting this in Eq. (17-1), we get

$$y_t = \alpha x_t + \delta z_t x_t + u_t \tag{17-3}$$

The hypothesis that β_t in (17-1) are constant is equivalent to the hypothesis that δ in (17-3) is zero. Thus we can easily test the hypothesis of constancy of β_t. In actual practice if z_t is a policy variable and if a relation like (17-1) is obtained by the maximization behavior of firms or individuals, then z_t should not enter Eq.

(17-1) additively. It should be entering as a determining variable for the parameters as in Eq. (17-2).

If Eq. (17-2) is made stochastic, i.e.,

$$\beta_t = \alpha + \delta z_t + v_t \tag{17-4}$$

then substituting (17-4) in (17-1), we get

$$y_t = \alpha x_t + \delta x_t z_t + w_t \tag{17-5}$$

where $\qquad w_t = u_t + v_t x_t$

If we assume

$$\begin{aligned} \operatorname{cov}(u_t, v_s) &= 0 \qquad \text{for all } t \text{ and } s \\ \operatorname{var}(u_t) &= \sigma_u^2 \qquad \text{for all } t \\ \operatorname{var}(v_t) &= \sigma_v^2 \qquad \text{for all } t \end{aligned}$$

and $\qquad \operatorname{cov}(u_t, u_s) = \operatorname{cov}(v_t, v_s) = 0 \qquad \text{for all } t \neq s$

then $\qquad \operatorname{var}(w_t) = \sigma_u^2 + x_t^2 \sigma_v^2$

and $\qquad \operatorname{cov}(w_t, w_s) = 0 \qquad \text{for } t \neq s$

Thus Eq. (17-5) is a usual regression model with heteroscedastic residuals, the variances being proportional to $(1 + \lambda x_t^2)$, where $\lambda = \sigma_v^2/\sigma_u^2$.

The maximum-likelihood estimates for this model can be easily obtained as follows: The log likelihood is given by (under the assumption that u_t and v_t are normally distributed)

$$\log L = \text{const.} - \frac{n}{2} \log \sigma_u^2 - \frac{1}{2} \sum_{t=1}^{n} \log(1 + \lambda x_t^2) - \frac{1}{2\sigma_u^2} \sum_{t=1}^{n} \frac{(y_t - \alpha x_t - \delta x_t z_t)^2}{1 + \lambda x_t^2}$$

The estimation would proceed as follows:

For given λ we estimate the regression equation

$$\frac{y_t}{r_t} = \alpha \frac{x_t}{r_t} + \delta \frac{x_t z_t}{r_t}$$

where $r_t = \sqrt{1 + \lambda x_t^2}$ and compute the residual sum of squares $\hat{\sigma}_u^2(\lambda)$. Let

$$F(\lambda) = -\frac{n}{2} \log \hat{\sigma}_u^2(\lambda) - \frac{1}{2} \sum_{t=1}^{n} \log(1 + \lambda x_t^2)$$

Then the value of λ for which $F(\lambda)$ is maximum is the ML estimate of λ, and the corresponding estimates of α and δ are the ML estimates of α and δ.

Generalization of the above models to the case of several explanatory variables is straightforward. In the case where equations like (17-2) are non-stochastic, we have no problems. All we end up with is models like (17-3) with just more variables. In the case where these equations are stochastic as in (17-4), the residual w_t has a complicated structure. $\operatorname{var}(w_t)$ is now $\sigma_u^2 + \mathbf{x}_t' \boldsymbol{\Sigma}_v x_t$, where

$\boldsymbol{\Sigma}_v$ is the covariance matrix of the residuals in the different equations like (17-4) and x_t is the vector of explanatory variables. One can simplify this by assuming $\boldsymbol{\Sigma}_v$ to be diagonal so that

$$\boldsymbol{\Sigma}_v = \begin{bmatrix} \sigma_1^2 & & & \\ & \sigma_2^2 & & 0 \\ & 0 & \ddots & \\ & & & \sigma_k^2 \end{bmatrix}$$

where k is the number of explanatory variables. In this case

$$\text{var}(w_t) = \sigma_u^2(1 + \lambda_1 x_{1t}^2 + \lambda_2 x_{2t}^2 + \cdots + \lambda_k x_{kt}^2)$$

where $$\lambda_i = \frac{\sigma_i^2}{\sigma_u^2} \qquad i = 1,2, \ldots, k$$

We can no longer use the search procedure outlined earlier, but we can still compute the maximum-likelihood estimates by an iterative procedure (at least in principle). Hildreth and Houck considered this model with no error term in Eq. (17-1). Thus $\text{var}(w_t) = \sigma_1^2 x_{1t}^2 + \sigma_2^2 x_{2t}^2 + \cdots + \sigma_k^2 x_{kt}^2$.

17-2 CASE 2: HILDRETH AND HOUCK MODEL[1]

The model considered by Hildreth and Houck is

$$y_t = \sum_{j=1}^{k} \beta_{jt} x_{jt} \qquad t = 1,2, \ldots, n$$

$$\beta_{jt} = \beta_j + v_{jt}$$

where $\text{var}(v_{jt}) = \sigma_j^2$. These two equations together can be written as

$$y_t = \sum_{j=1}^{k} \beta_j x_{jt} + w_t \tag{17-6}$$

where $$w_t = \sum_j x_{jt} v_{jt} \tag{17-7}$$

We can write this in matrix notation as

$$\mathbf{y} = \mathbf{X}\boldsymbol{\beta} + \mathbf{w}$$

where $\mathbf{y}$, $\mathbf{X}$, $\boldsymbol{\beta}$, and $\mathbf{w}$ are suitably defined. If we assume the v_{jt} to be mutually independent and independent over time, we have

$$\text{var}(w_t) = \sum_j x_{jt}^2 \sigma_j^2 \tag{17-8}$$

[1] Clifford Hildreth and James Houck, Some Estimators for a Linear Model with Random Coefficients, *Journal of the American Statistical Association*, 1968, pp. 584–595.

The parameters that are of interest in this model are σ_j^2 and β_j. Hildreth and Houck suggest the following method for estimating σ_j^2.

We first estimate Eq. (17-6) by ordinary least squares. Let $\mathbf{r}$ be the vector of estimated residuals. Then $\mathbf{r} = \mathbf{Mw}$ where $\mathbf{M} = \mathbf{I} - \mathbf{X}(\mathbf{X}'\mathbf{X})^{-1}\mathbf{X}'$. Thus $r_t = m_{t1}w_1 + m_{t2}w_2 + \cdots + m_{tn}w_n$, where $(m_{t1}, m_{t2}, \ldots, m_{tn})$ is the tth row of $\mathbf{M}$. Since $E(w_j) = 0$ for all j, we have $E(r_t) = 0$.

$$\operatorname{var}(r_t) = E(r_t^2) = \sum_{j=1}^{n} m_{tj}^2 \operatorname{var}(w_j)$$

$$= \sum_{j=1}^{n} m_{tj}^2 \sum_{i=1}^{k} x_{ij}^2 \sigma_i^2$$

This relationship can be compactly written as

$$E(\dot{\mathbf{r}}) = \dot{\mathbf{M}}\dot{\mathbf{X}}\dot{\boldsymbol{\sigma}} \tag{17-9}$$

where $\dot{\mathbf{r}}$ = vector with elements r_t^2

$\dot{\mathbf{M}}$ = matrix M with each element in M replaced by its square

$\dot{\mathbf{X}}$ = matrix X with each element in X replaced by its square

$\dot{\boldsymbol{\sigma}}$ = vector with elements σ_j^2

We can write Eq. (17-9) as

$$\dot{\mathbf{r}} = \dot{\mathbf{M}}\dot{\mathbf{X}}\dot{\boldsymbol{\sigma}} + \boldsymbol{\epsilon} = \mathbf{Z}\dot{\boldsymbol{\sigma}} + \boldsymbol{\epsilon} \qquad \text{(say)} \tag{17-10}$$

Hildreth and Houck suggest estimating $\dot{\boldsymbol{\sigma}}$ from the multiple regression equation (17-10). This estimator is $(\mathbf{Z}'\mathbf{Z})^{-1}\mathbf{Z}'\dot{\mathbf{r}}$. They show that this estimator is consistent.

There are two problems with this method. First it does not guarantee positive estimates for the σ_j^2. For this Hildreth and Houck suggest estimating Eq. (17-10) subject to the constraints $\dot{\boldsymbol{\sigma}} > 0$. This is a computationally burdensome procedure. The other problem is that the estimator does not take into account the covariances between the ϵ's in Eq. (17-10). However, this problem can be solved. One can obtain an estimate of the covariance matrix of the ϵ's and use generalized least squares. Froehlich[1] found that this GLS estimator was better (in the mean-square-error sense) than the estimator obtained from applying OLS to (17-10) and that this in turn was better than the ML estimator. Froehlich had only three regressors, and thus if one uses the search method to compute the ML estimates, this merely involves searching over two parameters $\lambda_1 = \sigma_1^2/\sigma_3^2$ and $\lambda_2 = \sigma_2^2/\sigma_3^2$. It is indeed surprising that Froehlich got such poor estimates by using the ML method. Further, Froehlich (following Hildreth and Houck) concentrates on the estimates for σ_j^2 and does not discuss estimation of the parameters β_j. Also for purposes of prediction, say for period T, we have to estimate the actual regression coefficients β_{jT} for that time period.[2] Froehlich did not consider this problem in his Monte Carlo study.

[1] B. R. Froehlich, Some Estimators for a Random Coefficient Regression Model, *Journal of the American Statistical Association*, June 1973, pp. 329–335.

[2] W. E. Griffiths, Estimating Actual Response Coefficients in the Hildreth-Houck Random Coefficient Model, *Journal of the American Statistical Association*, September 1972, pp. 633–635.

17-3 CASE 3: SWITCHING REGRESSION MODEL

This is the model considered by Quandt[1] and later studied by Goldfeld and Quandt, Hinkley, McGee and Carlton, among others.

Suppose we have n observations on y and x. The switching regression model says that

$$y_t = \alpha_1 + \beta_1 x_t + u_{1t} \qquad \text{for } 1 \leqslant t \leqslant n_0 \tag{17-11}$$

$$y_t = \alpha_2 + \beta_2 x_t + u_{2t} \qquad \text{for } n_0 < t < n \tag{17-12}$$

i.e., the relationship between y and x has switched at the point $t = n_0$ from relationship (17-11) to relationship (17-12). If n_0 is known, there is really no problem. One estimates a separate regression equation for each of the "regimes." In actual practice n_0 needs to be estimated. If we assume the error variances to be equal for both the regimes, all that we have to do is estimate (17-11) and (17-12) for different values of n_0 (i.e., different partitions of the entire sample), look at the sum of the two residual sums of squares, and choose that value of n_0 for which this sum is minimum.

If the error variances are unequal, one has to maximize the log-likelihood function (assuming the residuals u_{1t} and u_{2t} to be independently and normally distributed).

$$\begin{aligned}\log L = \text{const.} - n_0 \log \sigma_1 & \\ - (n - n_0)\log \sigma_2 - \frac{1}{2\sigma_1^2} \sum_{1}^{n_0} (y_i - \alpha_1 - \beta_1 x_i)^2 & \\ - \frac{1}{2\sigma_2^2} \sum_{n_0+1}^{n} (y_i - \alpha_2 - \beta_2 x_i)^2 &\end{aligned}$$

with respect to α_1, β_1, α_2, β_2, σ_1, and σ_2 for different values of n_0. There are, however, some problems with this procedure. If $n_0 \leqslant 2$ or $\geqslant n - 2$, $\log L$ tends to ∞.

Goldfeld and Quandt discuss further modifications of this switching regression model to cases where there is continuous switching back and forth. They also consider deterministic and stochastic switching models. In the deterministic models there are some other variables $z_1, z_2, \ldots, z_k$, such that we are in regime 1 if $\lambda = \pi_1 z_1 + \pi_2 z_2 + \cdots + \pi_k z_k < c$ and in regime 2 if $\lambda > c$. The π's have to be estimated, and c is a given constant. In the stochastic switching model there is a probability λ that each observation belongs to regime 1 and a probability $(1 - \lambda)$ that it belongs to regime 2. All this can be generalized to cases of more than one regime.

[1] R. E. Quandt, The Estimation of the Parameters of a Linear Regression System Obeying Two Separate Regimes, *Journal of the American Statistical Association*, 1958, pp. 873–880.

Hinkley,[1] McGee and Carlton,[2] and Gallant and Fuller[3] consider the cases where there are no discontinuities in the regression function. For the two-regime case considered in Eqs. (17-11) and (17-12), if the two regression lines meet at the point $t = n_0$, this implies a constraint on the parameters. $\alpha_1 + \beta_1 x^* = \alpha_2 + \beta_2 x^*$, where x^* is the value of x at the point $t = n_0$.

If the regression parameters do change in response to any changes in the policy variables, it is questionable that they change in an abrupt fashion as hypothesized in the simplest form of the switching regression model. Any switch from one regime to the other is likely to be smooth. In this respect one modification considered by Goldfeld and Quandt[4] is promising. This is to combine Eqs. (17-11) and (17-12) as

$$y_i = (\alpha_1 + \beta_1 x_i)D_i + (a_2 + \beta_2 x_i)(1 - D_i) + D_i u_{1i} + (1 - D_i)u_{2i}$$

where D_i will be a function of the policy variables and other exogenous variables. D_i could be assumed to follow a smooth curve as in Fig. 17-1. It can be taken to be the cumulative probability corresponding to a normal, Cauchy, or any other convenient density.

Goldfeld and Quandt suggest estimating this model under the assumption that the residuals u_{1i} and u_{2i} have a common variance σ^2. This is because the model they consider is a mixture of two normal distributions, and if we assume

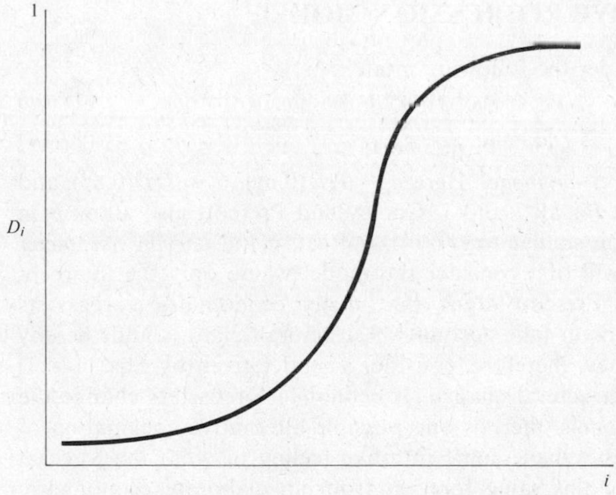

Figure 17.1 Cumulative response to a policy.

[1] D. V. Hinkley, Inference in Two-Phase Regression, *Journal of the American Statistical Association*, 1971, pp. 736–743.

[2] V. E. McGee and W. T. Carlton, Piecewise Regression, *Journal of the American Statistical Association*, 1970, pp. 1109–1124.

[3] A. R. Gallant and W. A. Fuller, Fitting Segmented Polynomials Whose Joint Points Have to Be Estimated, *Journal of the American Statistical Association*, 1973, pp. 144–147.

[4] See the references in S. M. Goldfeld and R. E. Quandt, The Estimation of Structural Shifts by Switching Regressions, *Annals of Economic and Social Measurement*, October, 1973, pp. 475–485.

different variances σ_1^2 and σ_2^2 for the residuals in (17-11) and (17-12), the likelihood function for such a mixture distribution[1] tends to ∞ as $\sigma_1 \to 0$ and $\sigma_2 \to 0$.

An alternative to the Goldfeld and Quandt procedure that is different from the switching regression model, and that does not involve problems of mixture distributions, is obtained by considering a continuously varying parameter regression model (17-1) and changing the specification (17-2) from the linear function to a cumulative density function based on the normal or any other convenient distribution. For instance, if we consider this cumulative density to be described by the logistic curve, we can write

$$\beta_t = \bar{\beta} + \frac{c}{1 + e^{\alpha - \delta z_t}}$$

Assuming that $\delta < 0$, we get as $z_t \to -\infty$, $\beta_t \to \bar{\beta} + c$. As $z_t \to \infty$, $\beta_t \to \bar{\beta}$. Substituting this expression for β_t in (17-1), we get, instead of the simple linear equation (17-3), the more complicated equation

$$y_t = \bar{\beta} x_t + \frac{c x_t}{1 + e^{\alpha - \delta z_t}} + u_t$$

The parameters of this equation can be estimated by nonlinear least-squares methods.

17-4 CASE 4: ADAPTIVE REGRESSION MODEL[2]

Cooley and Prescott consider the following model:

$$y_t = \alpha_t + \beta x_t + u_t \tag{17-13}$$

$$\alpha_t = \alpha_{t-1} + v_{t-1} \tag{17-14}$$

and call it an *adaptive regression model*. Here $u_t \sim IID(0, \sigma_u^2)$, $v_t \sim IID(0, \sigma_v^2)$, and u_t and v_s are independent for all t and s. Cooley and Prescott also allow β in (17-13) to vary in a fashion similar to (17-14) and call it the *varying-parameter regression model*, but we will first consider the model where only the intercept term varies. Cooley and Prescott argue that many econometric forecasters change their constant terms to take account of structural changes and thereby obtain better forecasts. They, therefore, consider a model given by Eqs. (17-13) and (17-14) as depicting structural change. If economic forecasters change the constant terms in their models, there is one possible alternative explanation of why they do it. Perhaps they have some intuitive feeling of what the forecast should be, and generating this same forecast from an elaborate econometric model lends an aura of respectability (and also salability) to the forecast. The simplest way of doing this is to change the constant term. The term "adaptive regression" originates from the fact that the residual in (17-13) is the sum of a

[1] See N. E. Day, Estimating the Components of a Mixture of Normal Distributions, *Biometrika*, 1969, pp. 463–474.

[2] T. Cooley and E. C. Prescott, An Adaptive Regression Model, *International Economic Review*, June 1973. See also their paper, Varying Parameter Regression: A Theory and Some Applications, *Annals of Economic and Social Measurement*, October 1973, pp. 463–473, and the references in it.

random walk and an independent error. For such structures[1] adaptive forecasting is appropriate. One can also give an alternative justification for the adaptive regression model that is entirely different from that given by Cooley and Prescott. This is in terms of omitted variables. Suppose we have a regression equation

$$y_t = \alpha + \beta x_t + \delta z_t + u_t \tag{17-15}$$

and z_t is unobservable and hence omitted. Equation (17-15) is the same as (17-13) with $\alpha_t = \alpha + \delta z_t$. If z_t is first-order autoregressive with a high autoregression coefficient, (17-14) is a reasonably approximate representation of α_t. With this interpretation, what Eq. (17-14) is supposed to capture is not "structural change" but the effect of omitted variables. Looking at Eq. (17-15), it is clear that the omitted variables can as well be combined with the residual u_t. In this case we end up with a regression model in which the residuals are both heteroscedastic and autocorrelated. In fact this is also what Eqs. (17-13) and (17-14) imply. To write these equations in the form of the usual regression model, we have to choose one of the α's as the basis of reference. Cooley and Prescott choose α_{n+1} because this facilitates prediction for the first postsample period. Let $\alpha_{n+1} = \alpha$. Then

$$\begin{aligned}
\alpha_n &= \alpha_{n+1} - v_n = \alpha - v_n \\
\alpha_{n-1} &= \alpha_{r} - v_{n-1} = \alpha - v_n - v_{n-1} \qquad \text{etc.} \\
&\cdots\cdots\cdots \\
\alpha_2 &= \alpha - v_n - v_{n-1} - \cdots - v_2 \\
\alpha_1 &= \alpha - v_n - v_{n-1} - \cdots - v_1
\end{aligned}$$

Hence Eq. (17-13) can be written as

$$\begin{aligned}
y_1 &= \alpha + \beta x_1 + u_1 - v_1 - v_2 - \cdots - v_n \\
y_2 &= \alpha + \beta x_2 + u_2 - v_2 - v_3 - \cdots - v_n \\
&\cdots\cdots\cdots \\
y_n &= \alpha + \beta x_n + u_n - v_n
\end{aligned}$$

This implies a regression equation $y_t = \alpha + \beta x_t + w_t$, where the residuals w_t have a covariance matrix (assuming u_t and v_t are independently and identically distributed with variances σ_u^2 and σ_v^2, respectively)

$$\sigma_u^2 \begin{bmatrix}
1 + n\lambda & (n-1)\lambda & \cdots & 3\lambda & 2\lambda & \lambda \\
(n-1)\lambda & 1 + (n-1)\lambda & \cdots & 3\lambda & 2\lambda & \lambda \\
 & & & & & \\
3\lambda & 3\lambda & & 1 + 3\lambda & 2\lambda & \lambda \\
2\lambda & 2\lambda & & 2\lambda & 1 + 2\lambda & \lambda \\
\lambda & \lambda & & \lambda & \lambda & 1 + \lambda
\end{bmatrix} \tag{17-16}$$

where $\lambda = \sigma_v^2/\sigma_u^2$. Since the covariance matrix is known up to a multiplicative constant if λ is known, the ML estimates can be computed by searching over λ.

[1] See J. F. Muth, Optimal Properties of Exponentially Weighted Forecasts, *Journal of the American Statistical Association*, June 1960, pp. 299–306.

Cooley and Prescott discuss a transformation that reduces the computational burden of inverting the matrix (17-16) at each value of λ that we search on.

The extension of this model to the case where the slope parameters also vary is the model that Cooley and Prescott call the varying-parameter regression model. We can no longer rationalize this type of model in terms of omitted variables. Perhaps one important rationalization is computational tractability and that it picks up structural "drifts" rather than "shifts." The model they consider is

$$y_t = \boldsymbol{\beta}_t'\mathbf{x}_t$$

$$\boldsymbol{\beta}_t = \boldsymbol{\beta}_t^p + \mathbf{u}_t$$

$$\boldsymbol{\beta}_t^p = \boldsymbol{\beta}_{t-1}^p + \mathbf{v}_t \tag{17-17}$$

The superscript p denotes the permanent component of the parameter. They assume the following covariance matrices for u_t and v_t.

$$\text{cov}(u_t) = (1-\theta)\sigma^2\boldsymbol{\Sigma}_u$$

$$\text{cov}(v_t) = \theta\sigma^2\boldsymbol{\Sigma}_v \qquad 0 < \theta < 1$$

where $\boldsymbol{\Sigma}_u$ and $\boldsymbol{\Sigma}_v$ are assumed *known*. Since they are assumed known, we can for simplicity, and without any loss of generality, assume them to be identity matrices. Thus our problem is to estimate σ^2, θ, and β_t^p. Again, one cannot estimate the β_t^p for all t. Cooley and Prescott suggest taking β_{n+1}^p as the reference value, since this is the value needed for prediction for the first postsample period. The method of estimation is similar to the one discussed for the adaptive regression model.

It has been found that for most economic time series adaptive forecasting is better than forecasting from autoregressive models. Cooley and Prescott also argue that their model has given good results in practice. What their model in effect implies is an ordinary regression model with residuals showing both heteroscedasticity and autocorrelation. Regression models where both these problems are handled simultaneously have not been estimated, and it might be reasonable to assume that both these problems are present if we have omitted variables (which we often do in econometric work). This might also explain why the Cooley and Prescott model "works." It would be interesting to consider a usual regression model with the residuals exhibiting both heteroscedasticity and autocorrelation and compare its performance with that of the Cooley and Prescott model. The Monte Carlo study by Cooley and Prescott,[1] though interesting, does not consider all the relevant alternatives. However, other alternative formulations could be computationally more cumbersome. Since the adaptive regression model can also be considered as a model that accounts for the omitted variables, it is important to compare it with models where we use

[1] T. Cooley and E. C. Prescott, Tests of an Adaptive Regression Model, *Review of Economics and Statistics*, May 1973, pp. 248–256. Their basic argument is that econometricians have extensively used structures with autocorrelated errors, not because they believe in them but because they are easy to handle and that the alternative they suggest is easy to handle and gives better forecasts.

proxies for the omitted variables. With time-series data one commonly used proxy is time—either a linear or polynomial trend term.

17-5 CASE 5: STOCHASTICALLY CONVERGENT PARAMETER MODELS

One problem with the adaptive regression model (and also the varying-parameter model considered by Cooley and Prescott) is that the parameters vary over time but do not converge to any fixed values. (Actually this may not be a problem if there are structured "drifts.") Rosenberg[1] considers a model similar to that of Cooley and Prescott. Instead of making the β_t a random walk, he considers a stochastically convergent parameter structure. The model that Rosenberg considers is

$$y_t = \boldsymbol{\beta}_t' \mathbf{x}_t + u_t \tag{17-18}$$

where

$$\boldsymbol{\beta}_t = (1-\lambda)\bar{\boldsymbol{\beta}} + \lambda \boldsymbol{\beta}_{t-1} + \mathbf{v}_t \tag{17-19}$$

The paper by Rosenberg is rather lengthy, but the essence of the estimation procedure is as follows: For illustrative purposes let us consider the model where only the constant term is changing, i.e., the adaptive regression model of Cooley and Prescott:

$$y_t = \alpha_t + \beta x_t + u_t$$

But now we specify

$$\alpha_t = (1-\lambda)\bar{\alpha} + \lambda \alpha_{t-1} + v_t$$

In terms of the lag operator L we can write this as

$$(1-\lambda L)\alpha_t = (1-\lambda)\bar{\alpha} + v_t \qquad \text{or} \qquad \alpha_t = \frac{(1-\lambda)\bar{\alpha} + v_t}{1-\lambda L}$$

Hence we have

$$y_t = \frac{(1-\lambda)\bar{\alpha}}{1-\lambda L} + \beta x_t + \frac{v_t}{1-\lambda L} + u_t \tag{17-20}$$

or

$$y_t = \bar{\alpha} + \beta x_t + \left(u_t + \frac{v_t}{1-\lambda L}\right) \tag{17-21}$$

We can estimate this equation by generalized least squares or maximum-likelihood procedures after deriving the covariance matrix of the residual $u_t + [v_t/(1-\lambda L)]$. Or else we can write (17-20) as

$$(1-\lambda L)y_t = (1-\lambda)\bar{\alpha} + (1-\lambda L)\beta x_t + v_t + (1-\lambda L)u_t$$

or

$$y_t = (1-\lambda)\bar{\alpha} + \lambda y_{t-1} + \beta x_t - \beta\lambda x_{t-1} + w_t \tag{17-22}$$

where $w_t = u_t - \lambda u_{t-1} + v_t$.

[1] B. Rosenberg, The Analysis of a Cross-Section of Time Series by Stochastically Convergent Parameter Regression, *Annals of Economic and Social Measurement*, October 1973, pp. 399–450.

Again we can estimate (17-22) by generalized least squares or maximum-likelihood procedures after deriving the covariance matrix of w_t. The covariance matrices of the residuals in Eqs. (17-21) and (17-22) are not any more complicated than those in the adaptive regression model.

For the model given by Eqs. (17-18) and (17-19) the procedure is similar. Now the residuals in the equations like (17-21) and (17-22) involve also the variables x_t. We can write down the expressions formally, but in practice we will have computational difficulties.

17-6 CASE 6: KALMAN-FILTER MODELS[1]

In these models we assume $\boldsymbol{\beta}_t = \mathbf{T}\boldsymbol{\beta}_{t-1} + \mathbf{v}_t$, where $\mathbf{T}$ is a known matrix. Since $\mathbf{T}$ is known, as in the case of the adaptive regression model, we can express all the $\boldsymbol{\beta}_t$ in terms of one of the $\boldsymbol{\beta}$'s, say $\boldsymbol{\beta}_0$.

Then

$$\begin{aligned}\boldsymbol{\beta}_t &= \mathbf{T}\boldsymbol{\beta}_{t-1} + \mathbf{v}_t \\ &= \mathbf{T}(\mathbf{T}\boldsymbol{\beta}_{t-2} + \mathbf{v}_{t-1}) + \mathbf{v}_t \qquad \text{etc.} \\ &= \mathbf{T}^t\boldsymbol{\beta}_0 + \sum_{j=1}^{t} \mathbf{T}^{t-j}\mathbf{v}_j\end{aligned}$$

Thus the regression model reduces to

$$y_t = (\mathbf{T}^t\boldsymbol{\beta}_0)'\mathbf{x}_t + \sum_{j=1}^{t} (\mathbf{T}^{t-j}\mathbf{v}_j)'\mathbf{x}_t + \mathbf{u}_t$$

We can now formally write the covariance matrix of the residuals and the likelihood function. Since $\mathbf{T}$ is a known matrix, the computational burden in obtaining the ML estimates is not any greater than that in the Cooley-Prescott varying-parameter regression model. We will not go into the details here.[2]

17-7 CASE 7: PURE-RANDOM-COEFFICIENT MODELS

All the above models have some systematic variation in the parameters. The pure-random-coefficient models assume that the $\boldsymbol{\beta}_t$ are distributed with mean $\bar{\boldsymbol{\beta}}$

[1] These models are popular in engineering literature. The earliest work is by Kalman and Bucy in 1961. A good survey can be found in textbooks like A. P. Sage and J. L. Melsa, "Estimation Theory with Applications to Communications Control," McGraw-Hill Book Company, New York, 1971. They were introduced into econometrics by Rosenberg. A good exposition for econometricians is in the paper by J. Phillip Cooper referred to below.

[2] For a good and concise discussion of this model, see J. Phillip Cooper, Time Varying Regression Coefficients: A Mixed Estimation Approach and Operational Limitations of the General Markov Structure, *Annals of Economic and Social Measurement*, October 1973, pp. 525–530.

and covariance matrix Λ. Rao[1] first discussed this model, and Swamy[2] extended it to the problem of pooling cross-section and time-series data. The model considered by Swamy is the following: We have N cross-section units with T observations on each. For illustrative purposes we will consider the case of only one explanatory variable. We have

$$y_{ij} = \beta_i x_{ij} + u_{ij} \qquad i = 1,2, \ldots, N \qquad j = 1,2, \ldots, T \tag{17-23}$$

The u_{ij} are all independent with mean 0 and $\mathrm{var}(u_{ij}) = \sigma_i^2$. The β_i are independent with mean β and variance δ^2. We can write $\beta_i = \beta + v_i$, where $E(v_i) = 0$ and $\mathrm{var}(v_i) = \delta^2$. The v_i are independent of the u_{ij}.

Under these assumptions we can write the regression model (17-23) as

$$y_{ij} = \beta x_{ij} + w_{ij} \tag{17-24}$$

where

$$w_{ij} = u_{ij} + v_i x_{ij} \tag{17-25}$$

Hence

$$\mathrm{var}(w_{ij}) = \sigma_i^2 + \delta^2 x_{ij}^2$$

$$\mathrm{cov}(w_{ij}, w_{ik}) = \mathrm{cov}(u_{ij} + v_i x_{ij})(u_{ik} + v_i x_{ik}) = \delta^2 x_{ij} x_{ik}$$

$$\mathrm{cov}(w_{ij}, w_{i'k}) = 0$$

for $i \neq i'$ for all j and k because v_i are independent and u_{ij} are independent. Thus the covariance matrix of the w_{ij} is

$$\mathbf{V} = \begin{bmatrix} \sigma_1^2\mathbf{I} + \delta^2\mathbf{x}_1\mathbf{x}_1' & 0 & 0 \\ 0 & \sigma_2^2\mathbf{I} + \delta^2\mathbf{x}_2\mathbf{x}_2' & 0 \\ & & \ddots \\ 0 & 0 & \sigma_N^2\mathbf{I} + \delta^2\mathbf{x}_N\mathbf{x}_N' \end{bmatrix} \tag{17-26}$$

where $\mathbf{x}_i$ is the vector of observations $(x_{i1}, x_{i2}, \ldots, x_{iT})$ on the ith cross-section unit.

The parameters to estimate are β, δ^2, and $\sigma_i^2 (i = 1,2, \ldots, N)$. If we estimate (17-24) by ordinary least squares, the estimator of β will be consistent but not efficient because $\mathrm{var}(w_{ij})$ is not constant. To get an efficient estimator we have to use generalized least squares. The generalized-least-squares estimator of β is

$$\hat{\boldsymbol{\beta}} = \left[\sum_{i=1}^{N} \mathbf{x}_i'(\sigma_i^2\mathbf{I} + \delta^2\mathbf{x}_i\mathbf{x}_i')^{-1}\mathbf{x}_i \right]^{-1} \left[\sum \mathbf{x}_i'(\sigma_i^2\mathbf{I} + \delta^2\mathbf{x}_i\mathbf{x}_i')\mathbf{y}_i \right] \tag{17-27}$$

[1] C. R. Rao, The Theory of Least Squares When the Parameters Are Stochastic, *Biometrika*, 1965, pp. 447–458.

[2] P. A. V. B. Swamy, Efficient Inference in a Random Coefficient Regression Model, *Econometrica*, 1970, pp. 311–323.

Now

$$\left(\sigma_i^2\mathbf{I} + \delta^2\mathbf{x}_i\mathbf{x}_i'\right)^{-1} = \frac{1}{\sigma_i^2}\mathbf{I} - \frac{\delta^2}{\sigma_i^2\left(\sigma_i^2 + \delta^2\mathbf{x}_i'\mathbf{x}_i\right)}\mathbf{x}_i\mathbf{x}_i'$$

Substituting this and simplifying, we get

$$\hat{\beta} = \sum_{i=1}^{N} w_i\hat{\beta}_i \qquad \text{(17-28)}$$

where $\hat{\beta}_i = (\mathbf{x}_i'\mathbf{y}_i)/(\mathbf{x}_i'\mathbf{x}_i)$ is the estimator of β_i from Eqs. (17-23) corresponding to the ith cross-section unit and

$$w_i = \frac{1/\left[\delta^2 + \sigma_i^2/(\mathbf{x}_i'\mathbf{x}_i)\right]}{\sum_{j=1}^{N}\left\{1/\left[\delta^2 + \sigma_j^2/(\mathbf{x}_j'\mathbf{x}_j)\right]\right\}} \qquad \text{(17-29)}$$

Note that $\sigma_i^2/(\mathbf{x}_i'\mathbf{x}_i)$ is var$(\hat{\beta}_i)$. Hence if $\delta^2 = 0$, what Eqs. (17-28) and (17-29) say is that $\hat{\beta}$ is a weighted average of $\hat{\beta}_i$, the weights being inversely proportional to the variances. If δ^2 is very large compared with $\sigma_i^2/(\mathbf{x}_i'\mathbf{x}_i)$, the weights (17-29) are almost equal, and $\hat{\beta}$ is then close to a simple unweighted average of $\hat{\beta}_i$. The same would be the case if $\sigma_i^2/(\mathbf{x}_i'\mathbf{x}_i)$ are almost equal.

Suppose $\sigma_i^2/(\mathbf{x}_i'\mathbf{x}_i)$ are all equal. Then the estimator $\hat{\beta}$ in (17-28) would be the same no matter what δ^2 is. Thus the estimator obtained with the random-coefficient model would be the same as the estimator obtained from a model where the coefficients are nonrandom (i.e., $\delta^2 = 0$). However, the variance of $\hat{\beta}$ would be different. It is given by

$$\frac{1}{\sum_{j=1}^{N}\left[1/\delta^2 + \sigma_j^2/(\mathbf{x}_j'\mathbf{x}_j)\right]} \qquad \text{(17-30)}$$

which, for different values of δ^2, assumes different values.

In actual practice the GLS estimator (17-28) cannot be computed because the parameters δ^2 and σ_i^2 in (17-29) are not known. We can proceed by using some preliminary consistent estimators for these parameters. To obtain these, we estimate Eqs. (17-23) separately for each cross section. We get $\hat{\beta}_i$ and the vector of residuals $\hat{u}_i$. Then we can use

$$\hat{\sigma}_i^2 = \frac{1}{T}\hat{\mathbf{u}}_i'\hat{\mathbf{u}}_i$$

and

$$\hat{\delta}^2 = \frac{1}{N}\sum\hat{\beta}_i^2 - \left(\frac{1}{N}\sum\hat{\beta}_i\right)^2 \qquad \text{(17-31)}$$

Swamy suggests using unbiased estimators, which in the case under consideration are

$$\bar{\sigma}_i^2 = \frac{1}{T-1}\hat{\mathbf{u}}_i'\hat{\mathbf{u}}_i$$

and $$\bar{\delta}^2 = \frac{1}{N-1}\left[\Sigma\hat{\beta}_i^2 - \frac{1}{N}\left(\Sigma\hat{\beta}_i\right)^2\right] - \frac{1}{N}\Sigma\left(\frac{\bar{\sigma}_i^2}{\mathbf{x}_i'\mathbf{x}_i}\right)$$

One major problem with this procedure is that the estimator for δ^2 can assume negative values. Further, there is no reason to insist on using unbiased estimators for the parameters in the weight functions to be used in generalized least squares. Thus the estimators in (17-31) should prove adequate in actual practice.

17-8 WHY AND WHEN TO USE VARYING-PARAMETER MODELS

It is always tempting to argue that the parameters in our models cannot, in general, be expected to be constant and hence we have to consider a varying-parameter model in almost all circumstances. However, this type of argument can be made about every assumption we make, and if we are given voluminous data we can afford the luxury of very general models. If we have limited data, as we often do, there is a limit to the generality we can postulate. Further, even if we have a large data set, the more general the models, the "woollier" the questions we ask, and if we ask "woolly" questions all we can expect to get are "woolly" answers.

Anyway, in some situations it becomes necessary to resort to varying-parameter models. Consider the case where the econometric relationships we estimate are derived from some maximizatiom (or minimization) problem which involves some policy variables. Often these policy variables are assumed to enter the econometric models in an additive fashion and the effects of changes in policies are analyzed on this assumption. However, if economic agents are indeed maximizing, they would be taking these policy variables into account in their decisions and thus the variables would be entering the model not in an additive fashion but as determinants of the parameters in the model. Thus we necessarily end up with a varying-parameter model, and any econometric evaluation of the effects of economic policies would have to be done within the framework of such models.[1]

There are also some problems in which our main interest is in the means and variances of what look like parameters in a linear regression model. As an illustrative example, suppose we have a court that deals with civil and criminal

[1] See R. E. Lucas, Jr., Econometric Policy Evaluation: A Critique, *Journal of Monetary Economics*, 1976 Special Supplement on Phillips Curve, pp. 19–46. Though this is the main point in Lucas' paper, he seems to suggest the adaptive regression model as a solution to this problem. Cooley and Prescott, too, quote Lucas' paper to justify their procedure. However, the adaptive regression model is not necessarily the best solution to this problem. In fact, the model of the type given by Eqs. (17-1), (17-2), and (17-3) seems to be the more logical one to consider. In all these models, when we go to simultaneous equations, problems get more complicated. For a discussion of these problems, see H. H. Kelejian, Random Parameters in a Simultaneous Equation Framework: Identification and Estimation, *Econometrica*, May 1974, pp. 517–527.

cases. We are given data on the total time spent in deciding all cases, and the *number* of civil and criminal cases.

We want to estimate the means and variances of the time spent on each of the two types of cases. The model, therefore, is

$$y = \beta_1 x_1 + \beta_2 x_2 \tag{17-32}$$

where y = total time spent
x_1 = number of civil cases
x_2 = number of criminal cases
β_1 = average time spent on each civil case
β_2 = average time spent on each criminal case

If the times spent on civil cases have a mean $\bar{\beta}_1$ and variance σ_1^2, then $E(\beta_1) = \bar{\beta}_1$ and $\text{var}(\beta_1) = \sigma_1^2/x_1$. Similarly, if the times spent on criminal cases have a mean $\bar{\beta}_2$ and variance σ_2^2, then $E(\beta_2) = \bar{\beta}_2$ and $\text{var}(\beta_2) = \sigma_2^2/x_2$.

Suppose we are given n observations on y, x_1, and x_2 and we are asked to estimate $\bar{\beta}_1$, $\bar{\beta}_2$, σ_1^2, and σ_2^2, we can proceed as follows: We can write $\beta_1 = \bar{\beta}_1 + u_1$, where $E(u_1) = 0$, $V(u_1) = \sigma_1^2/x_1$, and $\beta_2 = \bar{\beta}_2 + u_2$, where $E(u_2) = 0$, $V(u_2) = \sigma_2^2/x_2$. Equation (17-32) can be written as

$$y = \bar{\beta}_1 x_1 + \bar{\beta}_2 x_2 + w \tag{17-33}$$

where $w = u_1 x_1 + u_2 x_2$. Hence

$$E(w) = 0 \qquad \text{and} \qquad v(w) = x_1\sigma_1^2 + x_2\sigma_2^2 = \sigma_1^2(x_1 + x_2\lambda)$$

where $\lambda = \sigma_2^2/\sigma_1^2$. The estimation now is similar to that of Eq. (17-5) described earlier and need not be repeated here.

We have here an example of a regression model (17-32), and our main interest is in the means and variances of the regression parameters β_1 and β_2, which are random.

CHAPTER

EIGHTEEN

BAYESIAN METHODS IN ECONOMETRICS

In Chap. 5, we discussed the basic elements of Bayesian inference. We also said that the main discussion in this book will be in terms of classical methods. This is not because these methods are superior to Bayesian methods (in fact the questions one asks and the answers one gets are different in the two cases), but because most of the econometric literature is in the classical tradition and because, in order to understand the basic problems discussed in this book, we need not go into any ideological controversies. The main aim in this book has been to keep algebraic detail to a minimum, and Bayesian methods often entail more algebra than classical methods. In this chapter we will give an outline of some Bayesian procedures useful in econometric work. More details can be found in the book by Zellner,[1] and the references cited in the footnotes in this chapter.

The basic formula that is used throughout is formula (5-1), which says: Posterior distribution varies with prior distribution times likelihood function, or algebraically:

$$f(\theta \mid y) \propto h(\theta)L(y \mid \theta)$$

If many parameters are involved, one has to take the joint posterior distribution of all these parameters and integrate out all but the one of interest to get the marginal distribution[2] of this parameter. Then inferences about this parameter can be made from this marginal distribution. Needless to say, we have to confine our attention to functional forms that will facilitate these

[1] A. Zellner, "An Introduction to Bayesian Inference in Econometrics," John Wiley & Sons, Inc., New York, 1971.

[2] See Sec. 3-4 for a definition of "marginal distribution."

integrations. However, this may not be as restrictive in practice as it sounds at first. Also, if the final posterior distribution involves two or three parameters, the extra one or two parameters can be integrated out using numerical-integration methods.[1]

18-1 SOME PROBABILITY DISTRIBUTIONS

In our analysis, we will be using some probability distributions and integrals. It will facilitate our further discussion if they are listed here. Some of these have been discussed in Chap. 3. Throughout we will use the notation $\binom{N}{r}$ for $(N!/r!(n-r)!)$, where $N! = 1 \cdot 2 \cdot 3 \cdot \ldots \cdot (N-1)(N)$.

1. *Binomial distribution:* The probability density function of the binomial distribution is

$$f(x) = \binom{n}{x} p^x (1-p)^{n-x} \qquad x = 0, 1, 2, \ldots, n$$
$$0 \leqslant p \leqslant 1$$

If n independent trials, each with probability of success p, are made, the probability of x successes is given by the binomial distribution. The mean of this distribution is np and the variance $np(1-p)$.

2. *The negative binomial distribution*: If independent trials, each with probability of success p, are performed until the rth failure occurs, the number of observed successes follows the negative binomial distribution. The probability density function is

$$f(x) = \binom{r+x-1}{x} (1-p)^r p^x \qquad x = 0, 1, 2, \ldots$$

where $0 \leqslant p < 1$ and $r \geqslant 0$. This distribution has mean $rp/(1-p)$ and variance $rp/(1-p)^2$. We shall denote the negative binomial by $NB(p,r)$.

3. *The geometric distribution:* This is a special case of the negative binomial for $r = 1$.

4. *The Pascal distribution:* The Pascal distribution is related to the negative binomial. It is the distribution of the total number of trials required to produce r successes. The probability density function of this distribution is

$$f(x) = \binom{x-1}{r-1} p^r (1-p)^{x-r} \qquad x \geqslant r$$
$$0 \leqslant p < 1$$
$$x, r = 1, 2, \ldots$$

Let us denote the Pascal distribution by $\text{Pa}(p,r)$. The relationship between the Pascal distribution and the negative binomial is the following: If $x \sim \text{Pa}(p,$

[1] These use the univariate or bivariate Simpson's rule. The procedures are easy and can be found in Zellner's book.

r), then $(x - r) \sim NB(1 - p, r)$. We shall henceforth use the symbol $\sim$ to denote "is distributed as." The mean of the Pascal distribution is r/p and the variance $[r(1 - p)]/p^2$. The Pascal distribution is also related to the beta distribution discussed later by the following relation: If $x \sim \mathrm{Pa}(p, r)$, then $p \sim B_1(r, x - r + 1)$.

5. *The Poisson distribution:* This has the probability density function

$$p(x) = e^{-\lambda} \frac{\lambda^x}{x!} \qquad x = 0, 1, 2, \ldots$$
$$\lambda > 0$$

Its mean and variance are both equal to λ. It has the additive property. If X_1 and X_2 are independent Poisson variates with parameters λ_1 and λ_2, respectively, $X_1 + X_2$ also has a Poisson distribution with parameter $\lambda_1 + \lambda_2$.

6. *The uniform or rectangular distribution:* The probability density function is given by

$$f(x)\, dx = \frac{1}{\beta - \alpha}\, dx \qquad \alpha \leqslant x \leqslant \beta$$

The mean of the distribution is $(\alpha + \beta)/2$ and the variance $(\beta - \alpha)^2/12$.

7. *The normal distribution:* Its probability density function is given by

$$f(x)\, dx = \frac{1}{\sigma\sqrt{2\pi}} \qquad \exp\left[-\frac{1}{2\sigma^2}(x - \mu)^2 \right] dx \qquad \sigma > 0, -\infty < x < \infty$$

The mean is μ and variance σ^2. We shall denote the normal distribution by $N(\mu, \sigma^2)$.

8. *The gamma distribution:* The probability density function is

$$f(x)\, dx = \frac{1}{\gamma(n)}\, e^{-x} x^{n-1}\, dx \qquad 0 \leqslant x \leqslant \infty$$

where $\gamma(n)$ represents the gamma function

$$\gamma(n) = \int_0^\infty e^{-x} x^{n-1}\, dx$$

Integrating this by parts, we see that $\gamma(n) = (n - 1)\gamma(n - 1)$, and hence if n is an integer $\gamma(n) = (n - 1)!$

If αx has the gamma distribution with parameter n, then

$$f(x)\, dx = \frac{1}{\gamma(n)}\, e^{-\alpha x} (\alpha x)^{n-1}\, d(\alpha x)$$
$$= \frac{\alpha^n}{\gamma(n)}\, e^{-\alpha x} x^{n-1}\, dx$$

We shall denote this by $G(\alpha, n)$. It can be verified that

$$E(x^r) = \frac{n(n+1) \ldots (n + r - 1)}{\alpha^r}$$

from which we get the mean $= n/\alpha$ and variance $= n/\alpha^2$. If $\alpha = 1$, the mean and variance are both equal to n.

The gamma variate also satisfies the additive property. If $x_1 \sim G(\alpha,n_1)$ and $x_2 \sim G(\alpha,n_2)$ and x_1 amd x_2 are independent, then $x_1 + x_2 \sim G(\alpha,n_1 + n_2)$.

Raiffa and Schlaifer[1] call this the gamma-1 distribution and define a gamma-2 distribution which can be obtained from this by making the transformation

$$\alpha = \beta n \qquad \text{and} \qquad n = \frac{m}{2}$$

We will call this $G_2(\beta,m)$.

The motivation behind this is that the gamma-2 distribution is a flexible prior distribution for the precision parameter $(1/\sigma^2)$ in the Bayesian analysis of a normal process. Of course, instead of defining the prior for $1/\sigma^2$ we could have defined a prior for a transformation of this parameter and used the standard gamma function $G(\alpha,n)$. It is merely a matter of convenience in notation.

9. *The beta distribution:* The beta distribution of the *first kind* has the probability density function

$$f(x)\,dx = \frac{1}{B(m,n)} x^{m-1}(1-x)^{n-1}\,dx \qquad 0 \leqslant x \leqslant 1$$

where $B(m,n)$ is the beta function defined by

$$B(m,n) = \int_0^1 x^{m-1}(1-x)^{n-1}\,dx$$

The beta function satisfies the relation

$$B(m,n) = \frac{\gamma(m)\gamma(n)}{\gamma(m+n)}$$

The mean of this distribution is $m/(m+n)$ and the variance $[mn/(m+n)^2][1/(m+n+1)]$. The beta distribution with $m = 1$, $n = 1$ is the uniform distribution in the range (0,1).

The beta distribution of the *second kind* is given by

$$f(x)\,dx = \frac{1}{B(m,n)} \frac{x^{m-1}}{(1+x)^{m+n}}\,dx \qquad 0 \leqslant x \leqslant \infty$$

The mean of this distribution is $m/(n-1)$ and variance is $[m(m+n-1)]/[(n-1)^2(n-2)]$. If X has a beta distribution with parameters m and n, we shall denote it as $B_1(m,n)$ if it is of the first kind and $B_2(m,n)$ if it is of the second kind. The relationship between beta and gamma distributions is the following: If X_1 and X_2 are independent gamma variates with distributions $X_1 \sim G(\alpha,n_1)$ and $X_2 \sim G(\alpha,n_2)$, then

$$\frac{X_1}{X_1 + X_2} \sim B_1(n_1,n_2)$$

[1] H. Raiffa and R. Schlaifer, "Applied Statistical Decision Theory," Harvard Business School, Boston, 1961.

and this is independent of $X_1 + X_2$, which has the gamma distribution $G(\alpha, n_1 + n_2)$. Also

$$\frac{X_1}{X_2} \sim B_2(n_1, n_2)$$

though this is *not* independent of $X_1 + X_2$. Also, in general, if $X_1, X_2, \ldots, X_R$ are independent gamma variates

$$G(\alpha, N_1), G(\alpha, N_2), \ldots, G(\alpha, N_R)$$

respectively, then

$$\frac{X_1}{X_1 + X_2}, \frac{X_1 + X_2}{X_1 + X_2 + X_3}, \ldots, \frac{X_1 + X_2 + \cdots + X_{R-1}}{X_1 + X_2 + \cdots + X_R}$$

are independent beta variates of the first kind

$$B_1(N_1, N_2), B_1(N_1 + N_2, N_3), \ldots, B_1(N_1 + N_2 + \cdots + N_{R-1}, N_R)$$

respectively, and they are all distributed independently of $X_1 + X_2 + \cdots + X_R$, which has a gamma distribution $G(\alpha, N_1 + N_2 + \ldots + N_R)$.

10. *The χ^2 distribution*: If $X \sim N(0, \sigma^2)$, then $X^2 \sim G(\frac{1}{2}\sigma^2, \frac{1}{2})$. Also, by the additive property of the gamma distribution, if $X_1, X_2, \ldots, X_n$ are independent normal with mean 0 and variance σ^2, i.e., $X_i \sim IN(0, \sigma^2)$, then

$$\sum_{i=1}^{n} X_i^2 \sim G\left(\frac{1}{2\sigma^2}, \frac{n}{2}\right) \qquad \text{or} \qquad \frac{\sum_{i=1}^{n} X_i^2}{\sigma^2} \sim G\left(\frac{1}{2}, \frac{n}{2}\right)$$

The distribution of $(1/\sigma^2)\sum X_i^2$ is known as the χ^2 distribution degrees of freedom (df)n. Thus, if $u \sim \chi^2(n)$, then $u \sim G(\frac{1}{2}, \frac{n}{2})$. By the results stated earlier for the gamma distribution, we have $E(u) = n$ and $V(u) = 2n$. That is, the expected value of a χ^2 variate = its degrees of freedom and the variance = 2(df). The explicit probability density function for a χ^2 variate x with n degrees of freedom is

$$f(x)\,dx = \frac{1}{2^{n/2}\gamma(n/2)} e^{-x/2} x^{n/2-1}\,dx \qquad 0 \leqslant x \leqslant \infty$$

11. *The F distribution:* The F distribution is the distribution of the ratio of two independent χ^2 variates divided by their respective degrees of freedom. Let X_1 and X_2 be two independent χ^2 variates with degrees of freedom N_1 and N_2, respectively:

$$F = \frac{X_1/N_1}{X_2/N_2} \qquad \text{or} \qquad \frac{N_1 F}{N_2} = \frac{X_1}{X_2}$$

But $X_1 \sim G(\frac{1}{2}, N_1/2)$ and $X_2 \sim G(\frac{1}{2}, N_2/2)$. Hence the ratio has a beta distribution of the second kind $B_2(N_1/2, N_2/2)$. Hence the probability density function of the F distribution is given by

$$f(F)\,dF = \frac{1}{B(N_1/2, N_2/2)} \frac{(N_1F/N_2)^{(N_1/2)-1}}{(N_1F/N_2 + 1)^{(N_1+N_2)/2}}\, d\,\frac{(N_1F)}{N_2}$$

$$= \frac{N_1^{N_1/2} N_2^{N_2/2}}{B(N_1/2, N_2/2)} \frac{F^{(N_1/2)-1}}{(N_1F + N_2)^{(N_1+N_2)/2}}\, dF \qquad 0 \leqslant F < \infty$$

We can deduce the mean of the F distribution from the mean of the beta distribution of the second kind. The mean of the F distribution is $N_1N_2/N_1(N_2 - 2)$ for $N_2 > 2$.

12. *The t distribution:* It is the distribution of $\sqrt{F}$ with $N_1 = 1$. Denote N_2 by n for convenience. Substituting in the previous expression for the F distribution (noting that $F = t^2$), we get the probability density function of the t distribution with n degrees of freedom as

$$f(t)\,dt = \frac{1}{\sqrt{n}\, B(1/2, n/2)} \frac{1}{(1 + t^2/n)^{(n+1)/2}}\, dt \qquad -\infty < t < \infty \qquad (18\text{-}1)$$

When $n = 1$, this reduces to the Cauchy distribution defined below.

13. *The Cauchy distribution:* It has the probability density function

$$f(x)\,dx = \frac{\beta}{\pi} \frac{1}{\beta^2 + (x - \alpha)^2}\, dx \qquad \beta > 0 \qquad -\infty < x < \infty$$

The mean and variance of this distribution do not exist. Yet it is symmetric about its median, and the distance between its first and third quartiles is 2β. If $X_1, X_2, \ldots, X_n$ are independent random variables, all having the Cauchy distribution with parameters (α, β), their average $(1/n) \sum X_i$ has also the same distribution.

14. *The log-normal distribution:* x is said to have the log-normal distribution if $y = \log_e x$ has a normal distribution $N(\mu, \sigma^2)$. We have $x = e^y$. Hence $E(x) = e^{\mu + 1/2\sigma^2}$ and $E(x^2) = e^{2\mu + 2\sigma^2}$. We shall denote the log-normal distribution by $LN(\mu, \sigma^2)$.

15. *The beta-binomial distribution:* This is, in fact, a discrete distribution, but it is derived from a continuous distribution. Suppose $Y \sim B_1(\alpha, \beta)$ and let the conditional distribution of X given $Y = y$ be binomial with parameters y and n. The marginal distribution of X is the beta binomial. Its probability density function is given by

$$f(x) = \binom{n}{x} \frac{B(x + \alpha, n + \beta - x)}{B(\alpha, \beta)} \qquad x = 0, 1, 2, \ldots, n$$

This distribution can be derived by writing down the joint distribution of X and Y and integrating out Y.

$$P(X, Y) = P(X \mid Y)P(Y) = \left[\binom{n}{x} y^x (1 - y)^{n-x}\right]\left[\frac{1}{B(\alpha, \beta)}\, y^{\alpha-1}(1 - y)^{\beta-1} dy\right]$$

Integrating out Y, we get the required result. Also, noting that $E(x) = E_y E(x \mid y)$ and $V(x) = V_y[E(x \mid y)] + E_y[V(x \mid y)]$, we can verify that $E(x) = n\alpha/(\alpha + \beta)$ and $V(x) = [n\alpha\beta(n + \alpha + \beta)]/[(\alpha + \beta)^2(\alpha + \beta + 1)]$.

The beta binomial is an illustration of some compound distributions that are common in Bayesian work. Suppose that a salesman is trying to sell a product to n customers. The probability of any of them accepting is p. Then the probability distribution of the number of acceptances X is a binomial distribution with parameters p and n. Suppose his prior distribution for p is a beta distribution $B_1(\alpha,\beta)$. Then the marginal distribution of X is a beta binomial.

16. *The inverted gamma distribution:* Its probability density function is given by

$$f(x)\,dx = \frac{e^{-y/x}(y/x)^{r+1}}{\gamma(r)}\frac{1}{y}\,dx \qquad x \geqslant 0 \qquad r,y > 0 \tag{18-2}$$

We shall denote this by $iG(y,r)$. The relationship between the inverted gamma distribution and the gamma distribution is

$$\text{If } x \sim iG(y,r) \qquad \text{then} \qquad y \sim G\left(\frac{1}{x},r\right) \qquad \text{and} \qquad \frac{1}{x} \sim G(y,r)$$

The mean and variance of the inverted gamma distribution are $y/(r-1)$, and $y^2/[(r-1)^2(r-2)]$, respectively. Actually, Raiffa and Schlaifer call this the inverted gamma-1 distribution and define an inverted gamma-2 distribution by making the transformation

$$y = rs^2$$

$$x = \sigma^2$$

and

$$r = \frac{\nu}{2}$$

Since $dx = 2\sigma\,d\sigma$, we now get after some simplifications

$$f(\sigma)\,d\sigma \propto \sigma^{-\nu}e^{-(1/2)\nu s^2/\sigma^2}\,d\sigma \tag{18-3}$$

We will denote this by $iG_2(s,\nu)$. Their idea in doing this is that it gives a flexible prior for σ in the Bayesian analysis of the normal distribution. This inverted gamma-2 distribution is related to the gamma distributions discussed earlier by the following relationships:

$$\text{If } \sigma \sim iG_2(s,\nu) \qquad \text{then} \qquad \frac{1}{\sigma^2} \sim G_2(s^2,\nu) \qquad \text{and} \qquad \frac{1}{2}\nu s^2 \sim G\left(\frac{1}{\sigma^2},\frac{\nu}{2}\right)$$

17. *The inverted beta distribution:* Its probability density function is given by

$$f(x)\,dx = \frac{1}{\beta(\alpha,\beta)}\frac{b^\alpha(x-b)^{\beta-1}}{x^{\alpha+\beta}}\,dx \qquad 0 \leqslant b \leqslant x < \infty \qquad \alpha,\beta > 0$$

Since this is related to the beta distribution of the first kind, we shall denote it by $iB_1(b,\alpha,\beta)$. The relationship between the inverted beta distribution and the standard beta distribution is

$$\text{If } x \sim iB_1(b,\alpha,\beta) \qquad \text{then} \qquad \frac{b}{x} \sim B_1(\alpha,\beta)$$

We can define an inverted beta distribution of the second kind in an analogous fashion. The mean and variance of the inverted beta distribution of the first kind are, respectively,

$$\frac{b(\alpha+\beta-1)}{\alpha-1} \quad \text{and} \quad \frac{b^2(\alpha+\beta-1)\beta}{(\alpha-1)^2(\alpha-2)}$$

18-2 BAYESIAN ANALYSIS OF THE SIMPLE REGRESSION MODEL

We will discuss the Bayesian analysis of the simple regression model with what are known as "conjugate" priors. A conjugate prior is a prior that when combined with the likelihood function yields a posterior distribution that has the same functional form as the prior. The advantage of this prior is that as we get new sample information we can combine it with the posterior distribution obtained from the previous stage in an easy way.

Consider $y_i = \beta x_i + u_i$ where $u_i \sim IN(0,\sigma^2)$. The likelihood function based on n observations is

$$L(\beta,\sigma) \propto \sigma^{-n} \exp\left[-\frac{1}{2\sigma^2}\sum(y_i-\beta x_i)^2\right]$$

Let the OLS estimator of β be $\hat{\beta} = \sum x_i y_i / \sum x_i^2$. Its variance is $\sigma^2/\sum x_i^2$. We can write $\sum(y_i-\beta x_i)^2 = \sum(y_i-\hat{\beta}x_i)^2 + (\beta-\hat{\beta})^2\sum x_i^2$. Define

$$\hat{\sigma}^2 = \frac{1}{n-1}\sum(y_i-\hat{\beta}x_i)^2$$

We can write the likelihood function as

$$L(\beta,\sigma) \propto \sigma^{-n} \exp\left\{-\frac{1}{2\sigma^2}\left[(n-1)\hat{\sigma}^2 + (\beta-\hat{\beta})^2\sum x_i^2\right]\right\} \tag{18-4}$$

Consider the following cases.

Case 1: σ known. Now we can write

$$L(\beta) \propto \exp\left[-\frac{1}{2\sigma^2}(\beta-\hat{\beta})^2\left(\sum x_i^2\right)\right]$$

This form suggests that the normal distribution is an appropriate prior distribution. Suppose the prior is

$$P(\beta) \propto \exp\left[-\frac{m}{2\sigma^2}(\beta-\beta_0)^2\right] \qquad m > 0$$

The prior mean is β_0 and the prior variance σ^2/m. Then the posterior density is

$$P(\beta \mid y) \propto \exp\left\{-\frac{1}{2\sigma^2}\left[(\beta-\hat{\beta})^2\left(\sum x_i^2\right) + (\beta-\beta_0)^2 m\right]\right\}$$

This is again a normal distribution. To find its mean and variance, we simplify the expression in the brackets. We can write it as $\beta^2(\sum x_i^2 + m) - 2\beta(\hat{\beta}\sum x_i^2 + \beta_0 m) + \hat{\beta}^2\sum x_i^2 + \beta_0^2 m = (\sum x_i^2 + m)(\beta - \beta^*)^2 +$ some terms independent of β where

$$\beta^* = \frac{\hat{\beta}\sum x_i^2 + \beta_0 m}{\sum x_i^2 + m} \tag{18-5}$$

Thus the posterior distribution is

$$P(\beta \mid y) \propto \exp\left[-\frac{\sum x_i^2 + m}{2\sigma^2}(\beta - \beta^*)^2\right]$$

We shall henceforth call the reciprocal of the variance "precision." In this case the prior precision is m/σ^2 and the sample precision (the precision of $\hat{\beta}$) is $\sum x_i^2/\sigma^2$. The precision of the posterior distribution of $\beta = (m + \sum x_i^2)/\sigma^2 =$ the sum of the prior precision and sample precision.

Also the posterior mean β^* is a weighted average of the OLS estimator $\hat{\beta}$ and the prior mean β_0 with weights inversely proportional to their variances (or directly proportional to their respective precision).

Case 2: σ unknown. In this case we consider a prior similar in form to the likelihood function (18-4). The prior is

$$P(\beta,\sigma) \propto \sigma^{-k}\exp\left\{-\frac{1}{2\sigma^2}\left[M + m(\beta - \beta_0)^2\right]\right\} \tag{18-6}$$

For given σ, this distribution gives a normal distribution with mean β_0 and variance σ^2/m. For given β, the distribution of σ is a gamma distribution [actually it is the inverted gamma-2 distribution given in (18-3) with $\nu = k$ and $M = \nu s^2$]. Its variance decreases as k increases. The prior (18-6) is called a gamma-normal prior. The four parameters to be chosen are β_0, k, M, and m. β_0 is the mean of β, and the mean of σ is $M/k - 1$.

We choose β_0 and M/k based on our notions about the means of β and σ. We choose large values of m and k if we have more precise notions about β and σ.

The posterior distribution now is

$$P(\beta,\sigma \mid y) \propto \sigma^{-(n+k)}\exp\left\{-\frac{1}{2\sigma^2}\left[(n-1)\hat{\sigma}^2 + M + m(\beta - \beta_0)^2 + \left(\sum x_i^2\right)(\beta - \hat{\beta})^2\right]\right\} \tag{18-7}$$

To get the marginal distribution of σ, we have to integrate (18-7) with respect to β. It can be easily seen that the marginal posterior distribution of σ is an inverted gamma-2 density. To get the marginal distribution of β, we have to integrate (18-7) with respect to σ. To do this, we make use of the following integral:

$$\int \frac{1}{\sigma^{n+1}}\exp\left(-\frac{Q}{2\sigma^2}\right)d\sigma = \text{const.}\,\frac{1}{Q^{n/2}} \tag{18-8}$$

This integral can be derived by noting that the integral with respect to σ of the inverted gamma-2 density given in (18-3) is 1.

Using the formula (18-8) to integrate σ from (18-7), we get

$$P(\beta) \propto \left[(n-1)\hat{\sigma}^2 + M + m(\beta-\beta_0)^2 + \sum x_i^2(\beta-\hat{\beta})^2\right]^{-(n+k-1)/2} \tag{18-9}$$

The distribution of β is now the t distribution given in (18-1) with $n+k-2$ degrees of freedom.

The marginal distribution of β implied by the gamma-normal prior (18-6) is a t distribution. To see this integrate (18-6) with respect to σ using (18-8), we get

$$P(\beta) \propto \frac{1}{\left[M + m(\beta-\beta_0)^2\right]^{(k-1)/2}} \propto \frac{1}{\left[1 + (m/M)(\beta-\beta_0)^2\right]^{(k-1)/2}} \tag{18-10}$$

Comparing this with the t distribution (18-1), we find that

$$\left[\frac{m(k-2)}{M}\right]^{1/2}(\beta-\beta_0)$$

has a t distribution with degrees of freedom $k-2$. We can similarly simplify the expression in (18-9). The expression in the brackets can be written as

$$F + G(\beta-\beta^*)^2 \tag{18-11}$$

where β^* is as defined by (18-5), $F = (n-1)\hat{\sigma}^2 + M + m\beta_0^2 + (\sum x_i^2)\hat{\beta}^2 - (m + \sum x_i^2)\beta^{*2}$, and $G = m + \sum x_i^2$. Thus

$$\left[\frac{(n+k-2)G}{F}\right]^{1/2}(\beta-\beta^*)$$

has a t distribution degrees of freedom $n+k-2$. This distribution can be used to construct Bayesian confidence intervals for β in much the same way that we construct the confidence intervals in the classical procedures.

18-3 THE CASE OF DIFFUSE PRIORS

When we know nothing a priori about the parameters of the model, we let the variances of the prior distributions of β and σ increase without limit. In the normal gamma prior (18-6) we let M and $m \to 0$ and put $k = 1$. The prior distribution now is

$$p(\beta,\sigma) \propto \frac{1}{\sigma} \tag{18-12}$$

Now it can be readily verified that

$$\beta^* = \hat{\beta}$$

and we find that in (18-11), $F = (n-1)\hat{\sigma}^2$ and $G = \sum x_i^2$. Also since $k = 1$, we now get the result that

$$\frac{(\beta-\hat{\beta})(\sum x_i^2)^{1/2}}{\hat{\sigma}}$$

has a t distribution degrees of freedom $n-1$. This is precisely the result we have using classical statistical inference. Thus the Bayesian interval and the classical confidence interval are precisely the same, though their interpretations are of course different. Often the results obtained by Bayesian methods with the use of diffuse priors coincide with the results obtained by the classical procedures.

The prior (18-12) is referred to as a diffuse prior, but it is also (and more appropriately) called an *improper prior* because it does not integrate to 1. It is also called a Jeffreys prior after H. Jeffreys[1] and is extensively used by Zellner and also Lindley.[2] A criticism of these improper priors, particularly in problems involving many parameters, can be found in two papers by Charles Stein.[3]

18-4 BAYESIAN ANALYSIS OF THE MULTIPLE REGRESSION MODEL

The Bayesian analysis of the multiple regression model proceeds along similar lines. First we need the density of the multivariate normal distribution. This is discussed at length in Appendix B. The density of the p-dimensional vector random variable $\boldsymbol{\beta}$ with mean $\boldsymbol{\beta}_0$ and covariance matrix $\mathbf{V}$ is

$$P(\boldsymbol{\beta})\,d\boldsymbol{\beta} = \frac{1}{|\mathbf{V}|^{1/2}(2\pi)^{p/2}} \exp\left[-\frac{1}{2}(\boldsymbol{\beta}-\boldsymbol{\beta}_0)'\mathbf{V}^{-1}(\boldsymbol{\beta}-\boldsymbol{\beta}_0)\right] d\boldsymbol{\beta} \tag{18-13}$$

Since the integral of this with respect to $\boldsymbol{\beta}$ is 1, we have the following integral that we will use repeatedly in our further discussion.

$$\int \exp\left[-\frac{1}{2}(\boldsymbol{\beta}-\boldsymbol{\beta}_0)'\mathbf{V}^{-1}(\boldsymbol{\beta}-\boldsymbol{\beta}_0)\right] d\boldsymbol{\beta} = |\mathbf{V}|^{1/2}(2\pi)^{p/2} \tag{18-14}$$

Consider the multiple regression model

$$\mathbf{y} = \mathbf{X}\boldsymbol{\beta} + \mathbf{u} \qquad E(\mathbf{uu}') = \mathbf{I}\sigma^2$$

$\mathbf{y}$ is an $n \times 1$ vector, $\mathbf{X}$ is an $n \times p$ matrix, and $\boldsymbol{\beta}$ is a $p \times 1$ vector. $\mathbf{u}$ is an $n \times 1$ vector of residuals. The likelihood function is

$$L(\boldsymbol{\beta},\sigma) \propto \sigma^{-n} \exp\left[-\frac{1}{2\sigma^2}(\mathbf{y}-\mathbf{X}\boldsymbol{\beta})'(\mathbf{y}-\mathbf{X}\boldsymbol{\beta})\right] \tag{18-15}$$

Let $\hat{\boldsymbol{\beta}}$ be the OLS estimator of $\boldsymbol{\beta}$ so that $\hat{\boldsymbol{\beta}} = (\mathbf{X}'\mathbf{X})^{-1}\mathbf{X}'\mathbf{y}$. Then we can write $(\mathbf{y}-\mathbf{X}\boldsymbol{\beta})'(\mathbf{y}-\mathbf{X}\boldsymbol{\beta}) = R + (\boldsymbol{\beta}-\hat{\boldsymbol{\beta}})'\mathbf{X}'\mathbf{X}(\boldsymbol{\beta}-\hat{\boldsymbol{\beta}})$, where R is the residual sum of

[1] H. Jeffreys, "Theory of Probability," 3d ed., Clarendon Press, Oxford, 1961.

[2] D. V. Lindley, "Introduction to Probability amd Statistics from a Bayesian Point of View," part 2, Inference, Cambridge University Press, New York, 1965.

[3] C. Stein, Confidence Sets for the Mean of the Multivariate Normal Distribution (with Discussion), *Journal of the Royal Statistical Society*, ser. B, 1962, pp. 265–296; C. Stein, Approximation of Improper Prior Measures by Prior Probability Measures, in Neyman and LeCam (eds.), "Bernoulli, Bayes, Laplace Volume," pp. 217–240, Springer-Verlag OHG, Berlin, 1965. See also the paper by Mervyn Stone and the subsequent comments in *Journal of the American Statistical Association*, March 1976, pp. 114–125, for a discussion of the deficiencies of uniform priors.

squares $(\mathbf{y} - \mathbf{X}\hat{\boldsymbol{\beta}})'(\mathbf{y} - \mathbf{X}\hat{\boldsymbol{\beta}})$. Hence the likelihood function (18-15) can be written as

$$L(\boldsymbol{\beta},\sigma) \propto \sigma^{-n}\exp\left\{-\frac{1}{2\sigma^2}\left[R + (\boldsymbol{\beta} - \hat{\boldsymbol{\beta}})'\mathbf{X}'\mathbf{X}(\boldsymbol{\beta} - \hat{\boldsymbol{\beta}})\right]\right\} \tag{18-16}$$

As a prior for $\boldsymbol{\beta}$ and σ, we choose

$$P(\boldsymbol{\beta},\sigma) \propto \sigma^{-m}\exp\left\{-\frac{1}{2\sigma^2}\left[M + (\boldsymbol{\beta} - \boldsymbol{\beta}_0)'\mathbf{Q}(\boldsymbol{\beta} - \boldsymbol{\beta}_0)\right]\right\} \tag{18-17}$$

where $M > 0$, $m > 0$, and $\mathbf{Q}$ is a positive definite matrix. This is called a gamma-normal prior and is the conjugate prior for this problem. For given σ, the vector $\boldsymbol{\beta}$ has a p-variate normal distribution with mean $\boldsymbol{\beta}_0$ and covariance matrix $\mathbf{Q}^{-1}\sigma^2$. For given value of $\boldsymbol{\beta}$ the distribution of σ is the inverted gamma-2 distribution. Integrating (18-17) with respect to $\boldsymbol{\beta}$, we see that the marginal distribution of σ is

$$P(\sigma) \propto \sigma^{-(m-p)}\exp\left(-\frac{M}{2\sigma^2}\right) \tag{18-18}$$

This is also an inverted gamma-2 distribution. Integrating (18-17) with respect to σ (using 18-8), we see that the marginal distribution of $\boldsymbol{\beta}$ is

$$P(\boldsymbol{\beta}) \propto \left[M + (\boldsymbol{\beta} - \boldsymbol{\beta}_0)'\mathbf{Q}(\boldsymbol{\beta} - \boldsymbol{\beta}_0)\right]^{-(m-1)/2} \tag{18-19}$$

This is called a *multivariate t distribution.* Raiffa and Schlaifer[1] write the multivariate t distribution in the form

$$P(\boldsymbol{\beta}) \propto \left[\nu + (\boldsymbol{\beta} - \boldsymbol{\beta}_0)'\mathbf{H}(\boldsymbol{\beta} - \boldsymbol{\beta}_0)\right]^{-(\nu+p)/2} \tag{18-20}$$

and show that the first two moments are

$$E(\boldsymbol{\beta}) = \boldsymbol{\beta}_0 \qquad \text{if } \nu > 1$$

and

$$V(\boldsymbol{\beta}) = \frac{\nu}{\nu - 2}\mathbf{H}^{-1} \qquad \text{if } \nu > 2$$

In our case $\nu + p = m - 1$ or $\nu = m - p - 1$ and $\mathbf{H} = [(m - p - 1)/M]\mathbf{Q}$. Hence if $m > p + 2$, $E(\boldsymbol{\beta}) = \boldsymbol{\beta}_0$, and if $m > p + 3$

$$V(\boldsymbol{\beta}) = \frac{M}{m - p - 3}\mathbf{Q}^{-1}$$

The marginal distribution of any component β_j of $\boldsymbol{\beta}$ is a t distribution

$$P(\beta_j) \propto \left[(m - p - 1) + \frac{(\beta_j - \beta_{j0})^2}{\sigma_j^2}\right]^{-(m-p)/2} \tag{18-21}$$

where σ_j^2 is the jth diagonal element of $[M/(m - p - 1)]\mathbf{Q}^{-1}$. Hence $(\beta_j - \beta_{j0})/\sigma_j$ has a t distribution degrees of freedom $(m - p - 1)$.

[1] See Raiffa and Schlaifer, *op. cit.*, pp. 256–258.

In general, suppose we partition $\boldsymbol{\beta}$ into two components $\boldsymbol{\beta}_1$ and $\boldsymbol{\beta}_2$ of dimensions p_1 and p_2 $(p_1 + p_2 = p)$, respectively, $\boldsymbol{\beta}_0$ into corresponding components $\boldsymbol{\beta}_{10}$ and $\boldsymbol{\beta}_{20}$, and $\mathbf{H}$ in (18-20) conformably into

$$\begin{bmatrix} \mathbf{H}_{11} & \mathbf{H}_{12} \\ \mathbf{H}_{21} & \mathbf{H}_{22} \end{bmatrix}$$

Then we can write[1] $(\boldsymbol{\beta} - \boldsymbol{\beta}_0)'\mathbf{H}(\boldsymbol{\beta} - \boldsymbol{\beta}_0)$ as $Q_1 + Q_{2\cdot 1}$, where

$$Q_1 = (\boldsymbol{\beta}_1 - \boldsymbol{\beta}_{10})'(\mathbf{H}_{11} - \mathbf{H}_{12}\mathbf{H}_{22}^{-1}\mathbf{H}_{21})(\boldsymbol{\beta}_1 - \boldsymbol{\beta}_{10})$$
$$Q_{2\cdot 1} = (\boldsymbol{\beta}_2 - \boldsymbol{\beta}_{20}^*)'\mathbf{H}_{22}(\boldsymbol{\beta}_2 - \boldsymbol{\beta}_{20}^*)$$

where $\boldsymbol{\beta}^*_{20} = \boldsymbol{\beta}_{20} - \mathbf{H}_{22}^{-1}\mathbf{H}_{21}(\boldsymbol{\beta}_1 - \boldsymbol{\beta}_{10})$. The marginal distribution of $\boldsymbol{\beta}_1$ is

$$P(\boldsymbol{\beta}_1) \propto (\nu + Q_1)^{-(p_1+\nu)/2}$$

and the conditional distribution of $\boldsymbol{\beta}_2$ given $\boldsymbol{\beta}_1$ is

$$p(\boldsymbol{\beta}_2 \mid \boldsymbol{\beta}_1) \propto (\nu + Q_1)^{-(p_2/2)}\left(1 + \frac{Q_{2\cdot 1}}{\nu + Q_1}\right)^{-(p+\nu)/2}$$

Thus both the marginal and conditional distributions are multivariate t distributions. Finally, we can also establish that the quantity

$$\frac{m(m-p-1)}{M}(\boldsymbol{\beta} - \boldsymbol{\beta}_0)\mathbf{Q}(\boldsymbol{\beta} - \boldsymbol{\beta}_0)$$

has an F-distribution degrees of freedom p and $m - p - 1$.

We will be using all these results in the Bayesian inference of the multiple regression model. Combining the likelihood function (18-16) with the prior (18-17), we get the posterior distribution

$$P(\boldsymbol{\beta},\sigma \mid \mathbf{y}) \propto \sigma^{-(n+m)}\exp\left\{-\frac{1}{2\sigma^2}\left[R + M + (\boldsymbol{\beta} - \boldsymbol{\beta}_0)'\mathbf{Q}(\boldsymbol{\beta} - \boldsymbol{\beta}_0) + (\boldsymbol{\beta} - \hat{\boldsymbol{\beta}})'\mathbf{X}'\mathbf{X}(\boldsymbol{\beta} - \hat{\boldsymbol{\beta}})\right]\right\} \tag{18-22}$$

The expression in the brackets of (18-22) can be written as

$$Z + (\boldsymbol{\beta} - \boldsymbol{\beta}^*)'(\mathbf{Q} + \mathbf{X}'\mathbf{X})(\boldsymbol{\beta} - \boldsymbol{\beta}^*) \tag{18-23}$$

where

$$\boldsymbol{\beta}^* = (\mathbf{Q} + \mathbf{X}'\mathbf{X})^{-1}(\mathbf{Q}\boldsymbol{\beta}_0 + \mathbf{X}'\mathbf{X}\hat{\boldsymbol{\beta}}) \tag{18-24}$$

and

$$Z = R + M + \boldsymbol{\beta}_0'\mathbf{Q}\boldsymbol{\beta}_0 + \hat{\boldsymbol{\beta}}'(\mathbf{X}'\mathbf{X})\hat{\boldsymbol{\beta}} - \boldsymbol{\beta}^{*\prime}(\mathbf{Q} + \mathbf{X}'\mathbf{X})\boldsymbol{\beta}^* \tag{18-25}$$

[1] This decomposition and simplification is similar to the one done in the derivation of marginal and conditional densities from the multivariate normal distribution (see Appendix B). Those interested in further details can refer to Zellner's book, pp. 387–388.

The expression (18-24) shows that $\boldsymbol{\beta}^*$ is a matrix weighted average of the prior mean $\boldsymbol{\beta}_0$ and the OLS estimator $\hat{\boldsymbol{\beta}}$ with weights proportional to the inverses of the covariance matrices. The formula (18-24) is similar to (18-5) considered earlier. Integrating (18-22) with respect to σ, we get the posterior distribution of $\boldsymbol{\beta}$ as

$$P(\boldsymbol{\beta}) \propto \left[Z + (\boldsymbol{\beta} - \boldsymbol{\beta}^*)'(\mathbf{Q} + \mathbf{X}'\mathbf{X})(\boldsymbol{\beta} - \boldsymbol{\beta}^*)\right]^{-(n+m-1)/2} \tag{18-26}$$

This is a multivariate t density. By the results stated earlier

$$\frac{(n+m)(n+m-p-1)}{Z}(\boldsymbol{\beta} - \boldsymbol{\beta}^*)'(\mathbf{Q} + \mathbf{X}'\mathbf{X})(\boldsymbol{\beta} - \boldsymbol{\beta}^*)$$

has an F-distribution degrees of freedom p and $n+m-p-1$, and if β_j is the jth element of $\boldsymbol{\beta}$, β_j^* the jth element of $\boldsymbol{\beta}^*$, and σ_j^2 the jth diagonal element of

$$\frac{Z}{n+m-p-1}(\mathbf{Q} + \mathbf{X}'\mathbf{X})^{-1}$$

then $(\beta_j - \beta_j^*)/\sigma_j$ has a t-distribution degrees of freedom $(n+m-p-1)$. These results can be used to construct Bayesian confidence intervals and confidence regions for the β's.

Again, it might be instructive to see what the results look like when we know nothing about the parameters $\boldsymbol{\beta}$ and σ. Using the diffuse prior (18-12), we get the posterior distribution as

$$P(\boldsymbol{\beta},\sigma) \propto \sigma^{-(n+1)}\exp\left\{-\frac{1}{2\sigma^2}\left[R + (\boldsymbol{\beta} - \hat{\boldsymbol{\beta}})'\mathbf{X}'\mathbf{X}(\boldsymbol{\beta} - \hat{\boldsymbol{\beta}})\right]\right\} \tag{18-27}$$

Integrating (18-27) with respect to σ, we get the marginal posterior distribution of $\boldsymbol{\beta}$ as

$$P(\boldsymbol{\beta}) \propto \left[R + (\boldsymbol{\beta} - \hat{\boldsymbol{\beta}})'\mathbf{X}'\mathbf{X}(\boldsymbol{\beta} - \hat{\boldsymbol{\beta}})\right]^{-n/2} \tag{18-28}$$

If β_j is the jth element of $\boldsymbol{\beta}$, $\hat{\beta}_j$ the jth element of $\hat{\boldsymbol{\beta}}$, and σ_j^2 the jth diagonal element of $[R/(n-p)](\mathbf{X}'\mathbf{X})^{-1}$, then $(\beta_j - \hat{\beta}_j)/\sigma_j$ has the t-distribution degrees of freedom $n-p$. Note that this result is the same as the one obtained by the use of classical methods. Note that since R is the residual sum of squares $R/(n-p) = \hat{\sigma}^2$ is the usual unbiased estimator for σ^2.

To make inferences about σ, we integrate the posterior distribution (18-27) with respect to $\boldsymbol{\beta}$. As noted earlier, this is an inverted gamma-2 density.

18-5 BAYESIAN ANALYSIS OF THE REGRESSION MODEL WITH AUTOCORRELATED ERRORS

Sometimes the posterior distributions obtained are not analytically tractable but can be graphed and their mean and variance computed by numerical-integration methods. As an illustration, consider the following model:[1]

$$y_t = \beta x_t + u_t \qquad e_t \sim IN(0,\sigma^2)$$
$$u_t = \rho u_{t-1} + e_t \qquad t = 1,2, \ldots, T$$

Combining the two equations, we can write

$$y_t = \rho y_{t-1} + \beta x_t - \beta\rho x_{t-1} + e_t \qquad t = 1,2, \ldots, T$$

Since this is a dynamic model, we have to make some assumptions about the initial value of y_0. We can either assume it known or assume that it has a distribution with an unknown mean. In the latter case we can integrate it out. The likelihood function in either case is

$$L(\beta,\rho,\sigma \mid y_0 y_1 \cdots y_T) \propto \sigma^{-T} \exp\left[-\frac{1}{2\sigma^2}\sum_{t=1}^{T}(y_t - \rho y_{t-1} - \beta x_t + \beta\rho x_{t-1})^2\right]$$

The diffuse prior we assume for the parameters is

$$P(\beta) \propto \text{const.}$$
$$P(\rho) \propto \text{const.}$$
$$P(\sigma) \propto \frac{1}{\sigma}$$

Combining the priors with the likelihood function, we get the posterior distribution of β, ρ, σ as $(1/\sigma)L(\beta,\rho,\sigma)$. Integrating this with respect to σ using formula (18-8), we get the joint posterior distribution of β and ρ as

$$P(\beta,\rho \mid y) \propto \left\{\sum\left[y_t - \rho y_{t-1} - \beta(x_t - \rho x_{t-1})\right]^2\right\}^{T/2}$$

The normalizing constant cannot be evaluated analytically, but it can be evaluated numerically given any data set. The marginal distributions of β and ρ are obtained by integrating out the other parameter. They are

$$P(\beta \mid y) \propto \left(\sum \bar{y}_{t-1}^2\right)^{-1/2}\left[\sum \bar{y}_t^2 - \frac{\sum(\bar{y}_t \bar{y}_{t-1})^2}{\sum \bar{y}_{t-1}^2}\right]^{-(T-1)/2}$$

where $\bar{y}_t = y_t - \beta x_t$, and

$$P(\rho \mid y) \propto \left(\sum x_t^{*2}\right)^{-1/2}\left[\sum y_t^{*2} - \frac{(\sum x_t^* y_t^*)^2}{\sum x_t^{*2}}\right]^{-(T-1)/2}$$

where $x_t^* = x_t - \rho x_{t-1}$ and $y_t^* = y_t - \rho y_{t-1}$.

Zellner and Tiao analyze these posterior distributions by numerical-integration methods. In this analysis the parameter ρ is not restricted to the

[1] This analysis is based on A. Zellner and G. C. Tiao, Bayesian Analysis of the Regression Model with Autocorrelated Errors, *Journal of the American Statistical Association*, September 1964, pp. 763–778. Further details can be found in the paper.

range $-1 \leqslant \rho \leqslant 1$ (in fact we have assumed a uniform prior over an unlimited range for ρ). The posterior means of β and ρ are not the same as the maximum-likelihood estimates of β and ρ (respectively) in this model, though if the sample is large enough, the posterior mean will be close to the maximum-likelihood estimate. With diffuse priors, the posterior mean is like a mean-likelihood estimate, and if the likelihood functions are almost symmetric (as in large samples), the mean and the mode will be close to each other. Though the Bayesian estimators (mean of the posterior distribution) with diffuse priors are of interest for those interested in Bayesian inference, an investigation of their sampling properties often showed that they have lower mean square errors than the maximum-likelihood and other estimators usually used in classical methods.[1] Thus they might also be of interest to nonbayesians.

The above example illustrates the case where the posterior density does not have a neat analytic form but can be evaluated and analyzed by numerical-integration methods. This sort of procedure is applicable[2] to other models like distributed-lag models. However, since computer time builds up in a geometric fashion, one cannot conveniently analyze posterior distributions involving more than two or three parameters by numerical-integration methods.

18-6 BAYESIAN INFERENCE IN SYSTEMS OF EQUATIONS

Till now we have discussed the Bayesian analysis of the multiple regression model with conjugate priors and diffuse priors and noted that with diffuse priors there is a close similarity between the results obtained from the Bayesian analysis and those from the classical analysis. Several other problems like pooling information from different samples can be analyzed in a similar way, and since the algebra is very much the same as we have encountered till now, we will not go into these problems here. We will see that when we come to systems of equations and to simultaneous-equation models, the results based on the so-called diffuse priors will again be asymptotically the same as those obtained from classical procedures, though in small samples the results are somewhat different.

Let us first consider a set of p regression equations (like the reduced-form equations in a simultaneous-equation model)

$$\mathbf{y}_i = \mathbf{X}\boldsymbol{\beta}_i + \mathbf{u}_i \qquad i = 1, 2, \ldots, p \tag{18-29}$$

We will assume that the residuals from the different equations are mutually correlated and have a covariance matrix $\boldsymbol{\Sigma}$. The "diffuse" or "noninformative" prior often used in this case is the Geisser-Cornfield prior.[3]

$$p(\boldsymbol{\Sigma}) \propto |\boldsymbol{\Sigma}|^{-(p+1)/2} \tag{18-30}$$

[1] See Zellner's book, pp. 276–286, for some evidence from Monte Carlo experiments.

[2] See, for example, A. Zellner and M. S. Geisel, Analysis of Distributed Lag Models with Applications to Consumption Function Estimation, *Econometrica*, 1970, pp. 865–888.

[3] S. Geisser and J. Cornfield, Posterior Distributions for Multivariate Normal Parameters, *Journal of the Royal Statistical Society*, ser. B, 1963.

In the case $p = 1$, this reduces to the prior considered earlier $p(\sigma) \propto (1/\sigma)$.

Before we proceed with an analysis of the multiple-equation models, we need some more distributions like the Wishart distribution, the inverted Wishart distribution, and the generalized multivariate t distribution. The Wishart distribution is a multivariate generalization of the gamma distribution. Just as the sample variance obtained from a sample of observations from the univariate normal distribution has a gamma-type distribution, the sample covariance matrix $\mathbf{S}$ obtained from a sample of n observations from a multivariate normal distribution with mean zero and covariance matrix $\mathbf{\Sigma}$ has the Wishart distribution defined below. Here we will not derive the distribution but will merely state its functional form, because that is all we need.[1]

If $\mathbf{S}$ is an $m \times m$ symmetric positive definite matrix, then the $[n(m+1)]/2$ distinct elements of $\mathbf{S}$ are said to have a *Wishart distribution* if the probability density is

$$f(\mathbf{S}) \propto \mathbf{S}^{(n-m-1)/2}|\mathbf{\Sigma}|^{n/2}\exp\left(-\frac{1}{2}\operatorname{tr}\mathbf{\Sigma}^{-1}\mathbf{S}\right) \tag{18-31}$$

where tr denotes "trace" (see Appendix A for a definition), $\mathbf{\Sigma}$ is an $m \times m$ symmetric positive definite matrix, and $n \geqslant m$. We will write this as $\mathbf{S} \sim W(\mathbf{\Sigma}, n, m)$.

Just as we found the inverted gamma distribution more useful in Bayesian applications, we will also find the *inverted Wishart distribution* very useful. The symmetric positive definite $(m \times m)$ matrix $\mathbf{G}$ has an inverted Wishart distribution if

$$f(\mathbf{G}) \propto |\mathbf{V}|^{n/2}|\mathbf{G}|^{-(n+m+1)/2}\exp\left(-\frac{1}{2}\operatorname{tr}\mathbf{G}^{-1}\mathbf{V}\right) \tag{18-32}$$

where $\mathbf{V}$ is a symmetric $m \times m$ positive definite matrix and $n \geqslant m$. We will write $\mathbf{G} \sim IW(\mathbf{V}, n, m)$. The relationship of this distribution to the Wishart distribution is the following: If

$$\mathbf{G} \sim IW(\mathbf{V}, n, m) \qquad \text{then} \qquad \mathbf{G}^{-1} \sim W(\mathbf{V}^{-1}, n, m)$$

Since the integral of (18-32) with respect to $\mathbf{G}$ is 1 (it being a probability density), we have the following integration formula which we will often find useful in our further discussion:

$$\int |\mathbf{G}|^{-(n+m+1)/2}\exp(-1/2\operatorname{tr}\mathbf{G}^{-1}\mathbf{V})\,d\mathbf{G} \propto |\mathbf{V}|^{-n/2} \tag{18-33}$$

Another distribution that we will be needing is the *generalized multivariate t distribution*. This is also known as the matricvariate t distribution.[2] It is defined as follows:

[1] Details of derivation can be found in any textbook of multivariate analysis. See T. W. Anderson, "An Introduction to Multivariate Statistical Analysis," John Wiley & Sons, Inc., New York, 1958; or C. R. Rao, "Linear Statistical Inference and Applications," John Wiley & Sons, Inc., New York, 1965.

[2] See J. M. Dickey, Matricvariate Generalizations of the Multivariate t-Distribution and the Inverted Multivariate t-Distribution, *Annals of Mathematical Statistics*, 1967, pp. 511–518.

If **T** is a $p \times q$ random matrix, the elements of **T** have a matricvariate t distribution if

$$f(\mathbf{T}) \propto |\mathbf{Q}|^{(n-p)/2}|\mathbf{P}|^{q/2}|\mathbf{Q} + \mathbf{T}'\mathbf{P}\mathbf{T}|^{-n/2} \tag{18-34}$$

where $n > p + q - 1$ and **P** and **Q** are symmetric positive definite matrices of orders $p \times p$ and $q \times q$, respectively.

With these preliminaries, we can now discuss our models. Equations (18-29) can be written as

$$\mathbf{Y} = \mathbf{X}\mathbf{B} + \mathbf{U} \tag{18-35}$$

where $\mathbf{Y} = (\mathbf{y}_1, \mathbf{y}_2, \ldots, \mathbf{y}_p)$ is an $n \times p$ matrix of observation on the dependent variables, **X** is an $n \times k$ matrix of observations on k independent variables, $\mathbf{B} = (\boldsymbol{\beta}_1, \boldsymbol{\beta}_2, \ldots, \boldsymbol{\beta}_p)$ is a $k \times p$ matrix of regression parameters, and $\mathbf{U} = (\mathbf{u}_1, \mathbf{u}_2, \mathbf{u}_3, \ldots, \mathbf{u}_p)$ is an $n \times p$ matrix of disturbances. We assume that the rows of **U** are independently distributed each with a p-dimensional normal distribution with mean **0** and covariance matrix $\boldsymbol{\Sigma}$. Under these assumptions, the likelihood function is

$$L(\mathbf{B}, \boldsymbol{\Sigma} \mid \mathbf{Y}) \propto |\boldsymbol{\Sigma}|^{-n/2} \exp\left[-\frac{1}{2}\operatorname{tr}(\mathbf{Y} - \mathbf{X}\mathbf{B})'(\mathbf{Y} - \mathbf{X}\mathbf{B})\boldsymbol{\Sigma}^{-1}\right] \tag{18-36}$$

Note that we can write

$$(\mathbf{Y} - \mathbf{X}\mathbf{B})'(\mathbf{Y} - \mathbf{X}\mathbf{B}) = \mathbf{S} + (\mathbf{B} - \hat{\mathbf{B}})'\mathbf{X}'\mathbf{X}(\mathbf{B} - \hat{\mathbf{B}})$$

where $\hat{\mathbf{B}} = (\mathbf{X}'\mathbf{X})^{-1}\mathbf{X}'\mathbf{Y}$ is the matrix of least-squares estimators and $\mathbf{S} = (\mathbf{Y} - \mathbf{X}\hat{\mathbf{B}})'(\mathbf{Y} - \mathbf{X}\hat{\mathbf{B}})$ is the matrix of sums of squares and sums of products of least-squares residuals. We can now write the likelihood functions as

$$L(\mathbf{B}, \boldsymbol{\Sigma} \mid \mathbf{Y}) \propto |\boldsymbol{\Sigma}|^{-n/2} \exp\left[-\frac{1}{2}\operatorname{tr}\mathbf{S}\boldsymbol{\Sigma}^{-1} - 1/2\operatorname{tr}(\mathbf{B} - \hat{\mathbf{B}})'\mathbf{X}'\mathbf{X}(\mathbf{B} - \hat{\mathbf{B}})\boldsymbol{\Sigma}^{-1}\right] \tag{18-37}$$

Combining the likelihood function with the prior (18-30) we get the posterior distribution as

$$P(\mathbf{B}, \boldsymbol{\Sigma} \mid \mathbf{Y}) \propto |\boldsymbol{\Sigma}|^{-(n+p+1)/2} \exp\left\{-\frac{1}{2}\operatorname{tr}\left[\mathbf{S} + (\mathbf{B} - \hat{\mathbf{B}})'\mathbf{X}'\mathbf{X}(\mathbf{B} - \hat{\mathbf{B}})\right]\boldsymbol{\Sigma}^{-1}\right\} \tag{18-38}$$

Integrating this with respect to $\boldsymbol{\Sigma}$ using formula (18-33), we get the marginal density of **B** as

$$P(\mathbf{B} \mid \mathbf{Y}) \propto |\mathbf{S} + (\mathbf{B} - \hat{\mathbf{B}})'\mathbf{X}'\mathbf{X}(\mathbf{B} - \hat{\mathbf{B}})|^{-n/2} \tag{18-39}$$

This is a generalized multivariate t distribution of the form (18-34). We will not analyze this distribution any further here. The derivation of the marginal distributions of any subsets of **B** is a matter of algebraic manipulations. The marginal distribution of any particular element of **B** is a univariate t distribution which is the same as the one derived in the classical framework. Also, if we consider

$$V = \frac{|\mathbf{S}|}{|\mathbf{S} + (\mathbf{B} - \hat{\mathbf{B}})'\mathbf{X}'\mathbf{X}(\mathbf{B} - \hat{\mathbf{B}})|}$$

then Geisser[1] shows that the posterior distribution of V where $\mathbf{B}$ is random and the other quantities are fixed is the same as the sampling distribution of V where $\mathbf{B}$ is fixed and $\mathbf{S}$ and $\hat{\mathbf{B}}$ are considered random variables. Thus there is a close similarity between the Bayesian analysis (with diffuse priors) of the multivariate regression model and the classical analysis.

The above analysis has been with the diffuse prior (18-30). It would be interesting to ask what the appropriate conjugate prior for this problem is. Rothenberg[2] argues that if we treat $\boldsymbol{\Sigma}$ as known, the function (18-37) describes a normal density for $\mathbf{B}$. Thus a natural conjugate is a normal density for $\mathbf{B}$. But Eq. (18-37) is not a *general* normal density. It implies severe restriction on the variances. In particular, a density proportional to (18-37) implies

$$\operatorname{var}(\beta_{ij}) = \sigma_{ii} m_{jj} \tag{18-40}$$

where σ_{ii} is a diagonal element of $\boldsymbol{\Sigma}$ and m_{jj} a diagonal element of $(\mathbf{X}'\mathbf{X})^{-1}$. Equation (18-40) implies that

$$\frac{\operatorname{var} \beta_{ri}}{\operatorname{var} \beta_{si}} = \frac{\operatorname{var} \beta_{rj}}{\operatorname{var} \beta_{sj}}$$

i.e., variances of all parameters in the rth equation must be proportional to the variances of the corresponding parameters in the sth equation. Since there is no reason why our prior beliefs about the β_{ij} should be related in this way, Rothenberg concludes that the conjugate family is too restrictive for this model. If $\boldsymbol{\Sigma}$ is known, one can have an arbitrary normal density on $\mathbf{B}$. But if $\boldsymbol{\Sigma}$ is not known, an arbitrary normal density on $\mathbf{B}$ does not combine with the likelihood function to form a tractable posterior density. The joint conjugate density on $\mathbf{B}$ and $\boldsymbol{\Sigma}$ derived from (18-37) by replacing the data matrices with arbitrary matrices of constants may be interpreted as a normal density on $\mathbf{B}$ conditional on $\boldsymbol{\Sigma}^{-1}$ and a Wishart density on $\boldsymbol{\Sigma}^{-1}$. This is the density that yields tractable posteriors, but as pointed out above, the variances of $\mathbf{B}$ are restricted.[3] Rothenberg argues that a similar result applies if we consider the structural equations in a simultaneous-equation system. Again the prior distribution implied by the natural conjugate theory has unsatisfactory constraints on the choice of prior variances. He concludes that when *systems* of interrelated equations are analyzed, the conjugate family is not rich enough to incorporate the prior beliefs that economists typically possess.

[1] S. Geisser, Bayesian Estimation in Multivariate Analysis, *Annals of Mathematical Statistics*, 1965, pp. 150–159.

[2] T. J. Rothenberg, "A Bayesian Analysis of Simultaneous Equations Systems," Econometric Institute, Report 6315, Rotterdam, 1963. This paper in a revised form appears as Chap. 6 in The Bayesian Approach to Econometrics, in T. J. Rothenberg, "Efficient Estimation with A-Priori Information," Cowles Foundation Monograph 23, Yale University Press, New Haven, Conn., 1973.

[3] An analysis of the conjugate normal Wishart distribution can be found in A. Ando and G. M. Kaufman, Bayesian Analysis of the Independent Multinormal Process—Neither Mean nor Precision Known, *Journal of the American Statistical Association*, 1965, pp. 347–358. It is also discussed in M. H. DeGroot, "Optimal Statistical Decisions," McGraw-Hill Book Company, New York, 1970.

18-7 BAYESIAN ANALYSIS OF SIMULTANEOUS-EQUATION MODELS[1]

Consider a simultaneous-equation model

$$\begin{aligned} Y_{1t} &= \beta Y_{2t} + U_{1t} \\ Y_{2t} &= U_{2t} \qquad t = 1,2, \ldots, n \end{aligned} \tag{18-41}$$

Let the n observation Y_{1t} and Y_{2t} be denoted by the vectors $\mathbf{Y}_1$ and $\mathbf{Y}_2$. Suppose the covariance matrix of (U_1, U_2) is

$$\mathbf{\Sigma} = \begin{bmatrix} \sigma_{11} & \sigma_{12} \\ \sigma_{12} & \sigma_{22} \end{bmatrix}$$

Let

$$\mathbf{\Sigma}^{-1} = \begin{bmatrix} \sigma^{11} & \sigma^{12} \\ \sigma^{12} & \sigma^{22} \end{bmatrix}$$

Then the likelihood function, given $\mathbf{\Sigma}$, is

$$L(\beta) \propto \exp\left\{ -\tfrac{1}{2}\left[\sigma^{11}(\mathbf{Y}_1 - \beta\mathbf{Y}_2)'(\mathbf{Y}_1 - \beta\mathbf{Y}_2) + 2\sigma^{12}(\mathbf{Y}_1 - \beta\mathbf{Y}_2)'\mathbf{Y}_2 + \sigma^{22}\mathbf{Y}_2'\mathbf{Y}_2\right]\right\} \tag{18-42}$$

If we assume a diffuse prior for β, the posterior density of β is proportional to $L(\beta)$. The expression in the brackets of (18-42) can be written as

$$\begin{aligned} &\sigma^{11}\mathbf{Y}_1'\mathbf{Y}_1 + 2\sigma^{12}\mathbf{Y}_1'\mathbf{Y}_2 + \sigma^{22}\mathbf{Y}_2'\mathbf{Y}_2 + \beta^2(\sigma^{11}\mathbf{Y}_2'\mathbf{Y}_2) - 2\beta(\sigma^{12}\mathbf{Y}_2'\mathbf{Y}_2 + \sigma^{11}\mathbf{Y}_1'\mathbf{Y}_2) \\ &\quad = \sigma^{11}(\mathbf{Y}_2'\mathbf{Y}_2)(\beta - \beta^*)^2 \end{aligned}$$

plus some terms that do not involve β, where we define β^* as

$$\beta^* = \frac{\sigma^{12}\mathbf{Y}_2'\mathbf{Y}_2 + \sigma^{11}\mathbf{Y}_1'\mathbf{Y}_2}{\sigma^{11}\mathbf{Y}_2'\mathbf{Y}_2} \tag{18-43}$$

If we define $\hat{\beta}$ as the OLS estimator of β so that

$$\hat{\beta} = \frac{\mathbf{Y}_1'\mathbf{Y}_2}{\mathbf{Y}_2'\mathbf{Y}_2}$$

since

$$\frac{\sigma^{12}}{\sigma^{11}} = -\frac{\sigma_{12}}{\sigma_{22}}$$

we have

$$\beta^* = \hat{\beta} - \frac{\sigma_{12}}{\sigma_{22}}$$

[1] The following discussion is based on T. J. Rothenberg, Analysis of Simultaneous Equations Models, in S. E. Fienberg and A. Zellner (eds.), "Studies in Bayesian Econometrics and Statistics in Honor of L. J. Savage," North-Holland Publishing Company, Amsterdam, 1975.

We thus find that β has a normal distribution with mean β^* and variance

$$\frac{1}{\sigma^{11}\mathbf{Y}_2'\mathbf{Y}_2} = \frac{1}{\mathbf{Y}_2'\mathbf{Y}_2}\left(\sigma_{11} - \frac{\sigma_{12}^2}{\sigma_{22}}\right)$$

Thus, conditional on $\boldsymbol{\Sigma}$, we have $E(\beta) = \hat{\beta} - \sigma_{12}/\sigma_{22}$ and $V(\beta) = (\mathbf{Y}_2'\mathbf{Y}_2\sigma^{11})^{-1}$. If $\sigma_{12} = 0$, the mean of the posterior distribution is just the OLS estimator, and the variance of the posterior distribution is the same as the variance of the sampling distribution of $\hat{\beta}$.

If $\boldsymbol{\Sigma}$ is not known but we have some prior notions about $\boldsymbol{\Sigma}$ which can be represented by an inverted Wishart distribution

$$P(\boldsymbol{\Sigma}) \propto |\mathbf{S}|^{p/2}|\boldsymbol{\Sigma}|^{-(p-3)/2}\exp(-1/2 \operatorname{tr} \mathbf{S}\boldsymbol{\Sigma}^{-1}) \tag{18-44}$$

where $\mathbf{S}$ is a 2×2 positive definite matrix proportional to the mean of $\boldsymbol{\Sigma}$ and p is a positive integer, then the posterior distribution of β can be shown to be a t distribution with mean $E(\beta) = \hat{\beta} - S_{12}/S_{22}$; that is, to get the mean of the posterior distribution of β, we subtract from the OLS estimator the ratio of our prior expectations about σ_{12} and σ_{22}.

In the model considered in Eqs. (18-41) it is well known that the parameter β is not identified unless we put some restrictions like $\sigma_{12} = 0$ or have some prior information on $\boldsymbol{\Sigma}$. What the above analysis suggests is that we need not put any such exact restriction or possess any exact knowledge about the elements of $\boldsymbol{\Sigma}$. It is sufficient to have some prior notions about the covariance matrix [as in (18-44)]. This was the point made by Dreze[1] (in an unpublished paper in 1962), who suggested that instead of imposing deterministic or exact restrictions in simultaneous-equations model, it is more reasonable to impose stochastic prior restrictions.

Consider next the model

$$\begin{aligned} Y_{1t} &= \beta Y_{2t} + U_{1t} \\ Y_{2t} &= \alpha_1 X_{1t} + \alpha_2 X_{2t} + \cdots + \alpha_k X_{kt} + U_{2t} \end{aligned} \tag{18-45}$$

where Y_1 and Y_2 are the endogenous variables and the X's are the exogenous variables. Assume that U_1 and U_2 have the covariance matrix $\boldsymbol{\Sigma}$ defined earlier, and let the elements of $\boldsymbol{\Sigma}^{-1}$ be denoted by superscripts as before. If we have n observations, we can write Eqs. (18-45) in matrix notation as

$$\mathbf{Y}_1 = \beta\mathbf{Y}_2 + \mathbf{U}_1 \qquad \mathbf{Y}_2 = \mathbf{X}\boldsymbol{\alpha} + \mathbf{U}_2$$

The likelihood function, given $\boldsymbol{\Sigma}$, is $L(\beta,\boldsymbol{\alpha}) \propto \exp\{-\frac{1}{2}[\sigma^{11}(\mathbf{Y}_1 - \beta\mathbf{Y}_2)'(\mathbf{Y}_1 - \beta\mathbf{Y}_2) + 2\sigma^{12}(\mathbf{Y}_1 - \beta\mathbf{Y}_2)'(\mathbf{Y}_2 - \mathbf{X}\boldsymbol{\alpha}) + \sigma^{22}(\mathbf{Y}_2 - \mathbf{X}\boldsymbol{\alpha})'(\mathbf{Y}_2 - \mathbf{X}\boldsymbol{\alpha})]\}$. First complete the quadratic in $\boldsymbol{\alpha}$ and integrate out $\boldsymbol{\alpha}$. The terms involving $\boldsymbol{\alpha}$ are

$$\sigma^{22}\boldsymbol{\alpha}'\mathbf{X}'\mathbf{X}\boldsymbol{\alpha} - 2\sigma^{22}\boldsymbol{\alpha}'\mathbf{X}'\mathbf{Y}_2 - 2\sigma^{12}\boldsymbol{\alpha}'\mathbf{X}'(\mathbf{Y}_1 - \beta\mathbf{Y}_2)$$

[1] J. Dreze, "The Bayesian Approach to Simultaneous Equation Estimation," O.N.R. Research Memorandum 67, Northwestern University, 1962.

This can be written as $(\boldsymbol{\alpha} - \boldsymbol{\alpha}^*)'(\sigma^{22}\mathbf{X}'\mathbf{X})(\boldsymbol{\alpha} - \boldsymbol{\alpha}^*) - (\boldsymbol{\alpha}^{*\prime}\sigma^{22}\mathbf{X}'\mathbf{X}\boldsymbol{\alpha}^*)$ where $\boldsymbol{\alpha}^* = (\mathbf{X}'\mathbf{X})^{-1}\mathbf{X}'\mathbf{Y}_2 + (\sigma^{12}/\sigma^{22})(\mathbf{X}'\mathbf{X})^{-1}\mathbf{X}'(\mathbf{Y}_1 - \beta\mathbf{Y}_2)$. Thus, integrating out $\boldsymbol{\alpha}$, we are left with the following terms involving β:

$$\sigma^{11}(\mathbf{Y}_1 - \beta\mathbf{Y}_2)'(\mathbf{Y}_1 - \beta\mathbf{Y}_2) + 2\sigma^{12}(\mathbf{Y}_1 - \beta\mathbf{Y}_2)'\mathbf{Y}_2 - \left[(\sigma^{12})^2/\sigma^{22}\right]$$

$$\times(\mathbf{Y}_1 - \beta\mathbf{Y}_2)'\mathbf{X}(\mathbf{X}'\mathbf{X})^{-1}\mathbf{X}'(\mathbf{Y}_1 - \beta\mathbf{Y}_2) - 2\sigma^{12}(\mathbf{Y}_1 - \beta\mathbf{Y}_2)'\mathbf{X}(\mathbf{X}'\mathbf{X})^{-1}\mathbf{X}'\mathbf{Y}_2$$

We can write this in the form $(1/\sigma^{*2})(\beta - \beta^*)^2$ + some terms not involving β. After considerable simplification, it can be verified that

$$E(\beta) = \beta^* = \frac{1}{1 - \rho^2 R^2}\left[\hat{\beta} - \rho^2 R^2 \tilde{\beta} - (1 - R^2)\frac{\sigma_{12}}{\sigma_{22}}\right] \qquad (18\text{-}46)$$

and

$$V(\beta) = \sigma^{*2} = \frac{\sigma_{11}(1 - \rho^2)}{Y_2'Y_2(1 - \rho^2 R^2)} \qquad (18\text{-}47)$$

where $\hat{\beta}$ is the OLS estimate of β, $\rho^2 = \sigma_{12}^2/(\sigma_{11}\sigma_{22})$, $R^2 = \mathbf{Y}_2'\mathbf{X}(\mathbf{X}'\mathbf{X})^{-1}\mathbf{X}'\mathbf{Y}_2/\mathbf{Y}_2'\mathbf{Y}_2$, and $\tilde{\beta} = \mathbf{Y}_2'\mathbf{X}(\mathbf{X}'\mathbf{X})^{-1}\mathbf{X}'\mathbf{Y}_1/\mathbf{Y}_2'\mathbf{X}(\mathbf{X}'\mathbf{X})^{-1}\mathbf{X}'\mathbf{Y}_2$ is the 2SLS estimate of β.

ρ^2 is the square of the correlation coefficient between the residuals U_{1t} and U_{2t}, and R^2 is the square of the multiple correlation coefficient from the reduced form for Y_2.

Again, if $\sigma_{12} = 0$, $\beta^* = \hat{\beta}$; i.e., the mean of the posterior distribution of β is the OLS estimate of β and the variance is the same as the variance of the sampling distribution of β.

We will now consider the Bayesian analog of 2SLS and LIML methods for a single structural equation. We can write the equation as [see Eq. (C-14) in Appendix C]

$$\begin{aligned} \mathbf{y} &= \mathbf{Y}_1\beta + \mathbf{X}_1\gamma + \mathbf{U} \\ &= \mathbf{Z}_1\boldsymbol{\delta} + \mathbf{U} \end{aligned} \qquad (18\text{-}48)$$

where $\mathbf{y}$ is a $T \times 1$ vector of observations on the "dependent" endogenous variable, $\mathbf{Y}_1$ is a $T \times (G_1 - 1)$ matrix of observations on the other included endogenous variables, $\mathbf{X}_1$ is a $T \times K_1$ matrix of observations on the included exogenous variables, $\boldsymbol{\delta} = [{}^{\beta}_{\gamma}]$ is a $(G_1 - 1 + K_1) \times 1$ vector of parameters to be estimated, $\mathbf{U}$ is a $T \times 1$ vector of disturbances, and $\mathbf{Z}_1 = (\mathbf{Y}_1\mathbf{X}_1)$.

Let $\mathbf{X}$ be the $T \times K$ matrix of observations on all the exogenous variables in the system. Also suppose we can write the reduced form corresponding to the endogenous variables $\mathbf{Y}_1$ as $\mathbf{Y}_1 = \mathbf{X}\pi' + \mathbf{V}$. Let the covariance matrix of the errors $(\mathbf{U},\mathbf{V})$ be

$$\boldsymbol{\Sigma} = \begin{bmatrix} \sigma_{11} & \omega' \\ \omega & \Omega \end{bmatrix}$$

Then Rothenberg shows that one gets as a straightforward generalization of formulas (18-46) and (18-47) that the mean and the covariance matrix of the posterior distribution of $\boldsymbol{\delta}$ in (18-48) are given by

$$E(\boldsymbol{\delta}) = (\mathbf{I} - \rho^2\mathbf{R}^2)^{-1}\left[\hat{\boldsymbol{\delta}} - \rho^2\mathbf{R}^2\tilde{\boldsymbol{\delta}} - (\mathbf{I} - \mathbf{R}^2)\boldsymbol{\Phi}\right] \tag{18-49}$$

and

$$\text{cov}(\boldsymbol{\delta}) = \sigma_{11}(1 - \rho^2)(\mathbf{I} - \rho^2\mathbf{R}^2)^{-1}(\mathbf{Z}_1'\mathbf{Z}_1)^{-1} \tag{18-50}$$

where $\hat{\boldsymbol{\delta}} = (\mathbf{Z}_1'\mathbf{Z}_1)^{-1}\,\mathbf{Z}_1'\mathbf{y}$ is the OLS estimate of $\boldsymbol{\delta}$.

$$\tilde{\boldsymbol{\delta}} = \left[\mathbf{Z}_1'\mathbf{X}(\mathbf{X}'\mathbf{X})^{-1}\mathbf{X}'\mathbf{Z}_1\right]^{-1}\mathbf{Z}_1'\mathbf{X}(\mathbf{X}'\mathbf{X})^{-1}\mathbf{X}'\mathbf{y}$$

is the 2SLS estimate of $\boldsymbol{\delta}$, $\mathbf{R}^2 = (\mathbf{Z}_1'\mathbf{Z}_1)^{-1}\mathbf{Z}_1'\mathbf{X}(\mathbf{X}'\mathbf{X})^{-1}\,\mathbf{X}'\mathbf{Z}_1$ is the matrix generalization of the reduced-form squared multiple correlation coefficient considered earlier, $\mathbf{I}$ is an identity matrix of the same order as $\mathbf{R}^2$, $\boldsymbol{\Phi} = \boldsymbol{\Omega}^{-1}\boldsymbol{\omega}$ = vector of regression coefficients from a regression of $\mathbf{U}$ on $\mathbf{V}$ (corresponding to σ_{12}/σ_{22} earlier), and $\rho^2 = \boldsymbol{\omega}'\boldsymbol{\Omega}^{-1}\boldsymbol{\omega}/\sigma_{11}$ = squared multiple correlation coefficient between $\mathbf{U}$ and $\mathbf{V}$.

Equations (18-49) and (18-50) are generalizations in matrix form of Eqs. (18-46) and (18-47), respectively.

The preceding analysis is with a diffuse prior for $\boldsymbol{\delta}$ and $\boldsymbol{\Sigma}$ known. If $\boldsymbol{\Sigma}$ is not known, we use either a "noninformative" prior for $\boldsymbol{\Sigma}$ of the form (18-30) or an inverted Wishart distribution of the form (18-32). When we use a diffuse prior for $\boldsymbol{\delta}$ and a noninformative prior for $\boldsymbol{\Sigma}$,

$$P(\boldsymbol{\Sigma}) \propto |\boldsymbol{\Sigma}|^{-(m-2)/2}$$

the posterior density of $\boldsymbol{\delta}$ can be shown to be proportional to (the algebra is tedious, and the details can be found in Dreze)[1]

$$\left[(\mathbf{y} - \mathbf{Z}_1\boldsymbol{\delta})'\mathbf{M}(\mathbf{y} - \mathbf{Z}_1\boldsymbol{\delta})\right]^{(T^*-K)/2}\left[(\mathbf{y} - \mathbf{Z}_1\boldsymbol{\delta})'(\mathbf{y} - \mathbf{Z}_1\boldsymbol{\delta})\right]^{-T^*/2} \tag{18-51}$$

where $\mathbf{M} = \mathbf{I} - \mathbf{X}(\mathbf{X}'\mathbf{X})^{-1}\mathbf{X}'$ and $T^* = T + m$. If T^* is very large, the posterior density is normal with mean given by the 2SLS estimate. However, if K is large compared with T^*, the posterior mean can depart significantly from the 2SLS estimate. Dreze shows that (18-51) is a proper density if $G_1 + K_1 - 1 \leqslant K$, i.e., the order condition for identification is satisfied, and that the rth moment of $\boldsymbol{\delta}$ exists if $r \leqslant$ the degree of overidentification $K - (G_1 + K_1 - 1)$.

One major problem with the above analysis is that (18-51) would be a proper density if the order condition is satisfied even if the rank condition is not. Thus one is likely to get neat posterior distributions with "noninformative" priors even for underidentified models.[2] Of course, a similar problem exists with even the 2SLS method if one computes the 2SLS estimates without checking whether the rank condition is satisfied (which is quite often done).

[1] J. Dreze, "Bayesian Limited Information Analysis of the Simultaneous Equations Model," CORE Discussion Paper 7111, 1971.

[2] See G. S. Maddala, Weak Priors and Sharp Posteriors in Simultaneous Equations Models, *Econometrica*, 1976.

If we use an informative prior for $\boldsymbol{\Sigma}$ like the inverted Wishart distribution with density proportional to

$$|\boldsymbol{\Sigma}|^{-(m-2)/2}\exp(-\tfrac{1}{2}\operatorname{tr}\mathbf{S}\boldsymbol{\Sigma}^{-1})$$

then Rothenberg shows that the posterior density of $\boldsymbol{\delta}$ is proportional to (the algebra is tedious)

$$|\mathbf{A}+\mathbf{S}|^{-(T^*+K+1)/2}\left[S_{11}+(\mathbf{y}-\mathbf{Z}_1\boldsymbol{\delta})'\mathbf{M}(\mathbf{y}-\mathbf{Z}_1\boldsymbol{\delta})\right]^{(T^*-K)/2} \times\left[S_{11}+(\mathbf{y}-\mathbf{Z}_1\boldsymbol{\delta})'(\mathbf{y}-\mathbf{Z}_1\boldsymbol{\delta})\right]^{-T^*/2}$$

where $T^* = T + m$, S_{11} is the upper left-hand element of $\mathbf{S}$, and $\mathbf{A}$ is the $G_1 \times G_1$ matrix.

$$\mathbf{A} = \begin{bmatrix} (\mathbf{y}-\mathbf{Z}_1\boldsymbol{\delta})'\mathbf{M}(\mathbf{y}-\mathbf{Z}_1\boldsymbol{\delta}) & (\mathbf{y}-\mathbf{Z}_1\boldsymbol{\delta})'\mathbf{M}\mathbf{Y}_1 \\ \mathbf{Y}_1'\mathbf{M}(\mathbf{y}-\mathbf{Z}_1\boldsymbol{\delta}) & \mathbf{Y}_1'\mathbf{M}\mathbf{Y}_1 \end{bmatrix}$$

18-8 OTHER MODELS AND CONCLUDING REMARKS

It is clear from the preceding discussion that there is a close similarity between the Bayesian results and the classical results if we use "noninformative" priors (and this is not surprising). However, the interpretation of the results is different, and also in the Bayesian framework one can incorporate prior information more easily. There is a large amount of literature on the "construction" of priors (see Savage[1] for an excellent survey). However, this literature refers mostly to subjective or intuitive priors. The priors commonly used in econometric work are "data-based" priors. Some of them are based on the same data being analyzed (and thus are not, strictly speaking, priors). For instance, in the analysis of the multiple regression models with Jeffreys priors, the prior distribution is taken as proportional to $|X'X|^{1/2}$, where X is the matrix of observations on the explanatory variables. This is a common case of a prior that is based on the data being analyzed. But often the priors are based on earlier empirical studies of a "similar" problem. In this case one has to be careful in specifying the covariances if the priors for different parameters are selected from different "similar" problems.

Suppose we have a regression model with two explanatory variables and because of the multicollinearity problem we cannot estimate the two parameters with any precision. Obviously, a prior will help, and a prior which has a diagonal covariance matrix will help more than a prior with a covariance matrix close to singularity, which would be the case if our prior is based on a "similar" study where multicollinearity was severe. Suppose we take two "similar" studies

[1] L. J. Savage, Elicitation of Personal Probabilities and Expectations, *Journal of the American Statistical Association*, 1971, pp. 783–801.

and pick the prior for one parameter from one study and the prior for the other parameter from another study and argue that since these studies were independently done our priors are independent (or the covariance matrix of the prior distribution is diagonal). This will "solve" our multicollinearity problem, but this argument is not a valid one to make. Simply because we are constructing priors for different parameters from different "independent" sources, it does not follow that we can assume the prior covariances to be zero.

Not all Bayesian inference depends on the analysis of the mean and variance of the posterior distribution. Often the posterior distribution may not have any moments, and if we use a quadratic loss function (so that the posterior mean is the optimal estimator), we may not be able to find an optimal estimator. In this case, if we change the loss function *suitably*, we will have a solution to the estimation problem. This is what Zellner[1] does in his MELO (minimum expected loss) approach. Zellner applies the method to different classes of single-equation and simultaneous-equation models, and studies the properties of the resulting estimators (existence of their moments, etc.).

To illustrate the procedure, suppose the regression model is

$$Y_i = \beta X_i + U_i$$

where $U_i \sim IN(0,\sigma^2)$. We are interested in an estimator $\hat{\theta}$ of $\theta = 1/\beta$. If the loss function is $L(\hat{\theta},\theta) = (\hat{\theta} - \theta)^2$, we take the posterior mean of θ as an estimator and it may not exist. We can, however, get the posterior distribution of β very easily so that its first two moments exist. Then if we use the loss function

$$L(\hat{\theta},\theta) = \left(\frac{\hat{\theta} - \theta}{\theta}\right)^2 = (1 - \beta\hat{\theta})^2$$

we have the expected loss as

$$E(L) = 1 - 2\hat{\theta}E(\beta) + \hat{\theta}^2 E(\beta^2)$$

which is minimum for

$$\hat{\theta} = \frac{E(\beta)}{E(\beta^2)} = \frac{\bar{\beta}}{\bar{\beta}^2 + \operatorname{var}(\beta)} = \frac{1}{\bar{\beta}}\,\frac{1}{1 + \operatorname{var}(\beta)/\bar{\beta}^2}$$

where $\bar{\beta}$ is the mean of the posterior distribution of β. Thus $\hat{\theta}$ is equal to the reciprocal of the posterior mean multiplied by a factor which lies between 0 and 1. In this problem if we use diffuse priors, $\bar{\beta}$ will also be the ML estimate of β, and the ML estimate of θ will merely be $1/\bar{\beta}$. The moments of the MLE do not exist, but the moments of $\hat{\theta}$ exist.

Note that the particular loss function for which we can *easily* derive the MELO estimator will be different for different problems, and thus the loss functions chosen in this approach are problem-specific.

[1] A. Zellner, "Estimation of Functions of Population Means and Regression Coefficients Including Structural Coefficients: A Minimum Expected Loss (MELO) Approach," paper presented at the Third World Congress, Toronto, August 1975.

Another area in which considerable work has been done is the problem of model selection (see Gaver and Geisel[1] for an excellent survey). The general approach is to start with some priors for models, and priors for the parameters in each model, and then derive the posterior probabilities for the models. Though the mechanics of the approach involve merely a straightforward use of Bayes' theorem, some fundamental issues are involved in the procedure.

We will be discussing some of these issues here. The discussion is not a criticism of the posterior-odds approach as such, which is a very useful approach to model selection, but a warning about the consequences of a mechanical application of the method. Some other comments on this approach can be found in Leamer.[2]

Consider two models with the same dependent variable but one model containing some extra explanatory variables. More simply,

$$\left\{\begin{array}{ll} M_1 : y = \beta_1 x_1 + \beta_2 x_2 + u_1 & u_1 \sim IN(0,\sigma_1^2) \\ M_2 : y = \beta_1 x_1 + u_2 & u_2 \sim IN(0,\sigma_2^2) \end{array}\right\}$$

In the $\bar{R}^2$ criterion, we ask whether the additional reduction in the unexplained variance due to the inclusion of x_2 compensates for the additional loss in degrees of freedom. In the Bayesian analysis, one starts with some prior probabilities $P(M_1)$ and $P(M_2)$ for the two models and computes the posterior odds as

$$\frac{P(M_1 \mid \text{data})}{P(M_2 \mid \text{data})} = \frac{P(M_1)}{P(M_2)} \frac{\int L_1 P_1(\beta_1,\beta_2)\, d\beta_1\, d\beta_2}{\int L_2 P_2(\beta_1)\, d\beta_1\, d\beta_2}$$

where L_1 and L_2 are the respective likelihoods and P_1 and P_2 are the respective prior distributions for the parameters in models 1 and 2. Also, in the Bayesian framework we do not select one of the models as "true" or "best" and eliminate the others. For purposes of prediction, the predictive distributions from all the models are combined with weights equal to the posterior probabilities of the models. Also the marginal distributions of the common parameters are derived from a combination of all the models.

Since the posterior odds are weighted averages of the likelihoods, care should be exercised in the computations if one uses diffuse priors—because it is not clear what the weighted averages mean when the weights sum to infinity. If the number of parameters is the same in both the models (say k), the posterior odds with diffuse priors can be regarded as the limit of expressions of the sort

$$\frac{(1/N^k)\int_0^N L_1\, d\alpha_1}{(1/N^k)\int_0^N L_2\, d\alpha_2} \qquad \text{as } N \to \infty$$

[1] K. M. Gaver and M. S. Geisel, Discriminating among Alternative Models: Bayesian and Non-Bayesian Methods, in P. Zarembka (ed.), "Frontiers in Econometrics," Academic Press Inc., New York, 1974.

[2] E. E. Leamer, "On Probabilities of Linear Hypotheses," Harvard University (Mimeo), 1972.

and one could give a meaningful interpretation to the posterior odds. If, however, the number of parameters is different and we use diffuse priors, the model with the larger number of parameters will have zero posterior probability, because the integrated likelihood for this model has a divisor which is a higher power of N. Thus one cannot hope to discriminate among such models unless one has some proper prior for at least the extra parameters.

In connection with the problem of discriminating between models M_1 and M_2, the minimum prior information we need to feed in is a prior on β_2. Also if we are formulating priors for the residual variances, it seems reasonable to formulate the priors to take account of the fact that the residual variance for the larger model is expected to be less than that for the smaller model. The posterior odds for the two models will then depend on:

1. The reduction in the unexplained variance.
2. How much reduction in the residual variance there is relative to what we expected—what we expected shows up in the priors we formulate for σ_1^2 and σ_2^2.
3. How informative we are about β_2.
4. How our prior information about β_2 conflicts with the sample information.

The degrees-of-freedom question does not enter the analysis, and it is also clear that the $\bar{R}^2$ criterion and the posterior-odds analysis can give quite different answers.

The posterior-odds analysis takes into account both the reduction in unexplained variance and the problem of "plausibility" of the estimated coefficients. The two factors that classical statisticians have been worried about and that do not enter the analysis are the problem of degrees of freedom and the problem of stability of the coefficients. One can, however, argue that the former factor enters the analysis implicitly, because as you increase the number of coefficients to be estimated, you are under increasing pressure to specify for more and more coefficients. It makes sense that so long as you have prior information on the extra coefficients, you need not worry about increasing the size of the model, that this should be of concern only when you have weak prior information. As for the problem of stability of coefficients over time, though this factor does show up to some extent in the posterior odds computed, it is conceivable that a model that exhibits greater instability could be the one that has higher posterior odds. For the Bayesian what is of consequence is the final result at the end of the period of analysis and not what happened in between. Thus the problem of stability of coefficients over time that worries many empirical practitioners in econometrics and that forms a criterion for choosing between models has no place in the Bayesian setup—at least not explicitly.

One thing that a straightforward Bayesian posterior-odds computation will not show is whether both the models considered are inadequate. If the performance of the models considered is unsatisfactory in terms of either the explained variance or the plausibility of the estimated coefficients, we might not want to take the posterior odds too seriously. In this case a first step would be a report of the maximum-likelihood (ML) estimates with an analysis of the residuals to uncover any omitted factors that might have escaped our attention in the initial formulation of the models.

In discriminating between models M_1 and M_2, one simplifying factor was that the dependent variable was the same for both the models. Once this assumption is dropped and/or nonlinearities are introduced, the $\bar{R}^2$ criterion can no longer be even applied. As for the posterior-odds analysis, superficially there is no problem. For instance, if one were discriminating between the following two models:

$$\left\{\begin{array}{ll} M_3 : y = \beta_3 x + u_3 & u_3 \sim IN(0,\sigma_3^2) \\ M_4 : \log y = \beta_4 \log x + u_4 & u_4 \sim IN(0,\sigma_4^2) \end{array}\right\}$$

all one has to do is start with some prior probabilities for the two models and compute posterior odds. But this raises as many questions as it answers. The first question is: Are the likelihoods comparable? One has to answer this when one puts prior probabilities on the models. Usually, this is assumed away. Further, in the above case prior notions about β_3 and β_4 cannot be independent. Another question that needs to be answered is whether it makes sense to put priors on models independently of the priors on the parameters in the models.

Usually, in econometric work, when we consider prior probabilities on models, we do not really believe that any of the models is a description of the "true" state. What we have in mind is some notion about how satisfactory the models are in terms of explanatory power, predictive ability, etc. For instance, consider the two models (this is what Geisel[1] analyzed in the Friedman-Meiselman and Ando-Modigliani controversy):

$$\left\{\begin{array}{ll} M_5 : y = \beta x + u & u \sim IN(0,\sigma_u^2) \\ M_6 : y = \gamma z + v & v \sim IN(0,\sigma_v^2) \end{array}\right\}$$

What is meant by saying that we give equal prior odds for the two models? One possible interpretation, and not an unreasonable one, is that we expect x and z to explain the same amount of variations in y. If this is so, σ_u^2 and σ_v^2 should have the same prior distributions.[2] Further, since our prior notions were about residual variances, after we observe the sample what we should be looking at is $P(\sigma_u^2 > \sigma_v^2 \mid \text{data})$, which can be easily obtained from the well-defined posterior distributions of σ_u^2 and σ_v^2.

In any case, the first step taken in the computation of posterior odds, viz., putting prior probabilities on models, is a very big step. Unless there is some

[1] M. S. Geisel, Bayesian Comparisons of Simple Macroeconomic Models, *Journal of Money, Credit and Banking*, August 1973, pp. 751–772.

[2] Perhaps what Friedman had in mind in the controversy was also that one relationship is more stable over time than the other. As to how this can be articulated in prior odds and posterior odds is not clear.

operational meaning that can be given to these prior probabilities, it does not make much sense to talk of prior odds on models, and when such meaning is given to the concept of prior odds, it might impose some restrictions on the prior distributions of the parameters in the models. The probabilities assigned to the models and the prior probabilities assigned to the parameters need not be independent.

In some of the instances where the posterior odds computed have been used in further analysis, there are alternative possible solutions to the problem considered. For instance, Geisel considers the two models

$$C_t = \alpha_1 + \beta_1 M_t + u_{1t}$$

$$C_t = \alpha_2 + \beta_2 A_t + u_{2t}$$

where C is consumption expenditures, M is the stock of money, and A is autonomous expenditures. He derives the posterior odds for the two models—which in this case are the ratio of the residual variances raised to the power $n/2$—and then combines the predictive densities for C based on each of the two models by weighting them with the posterior probabilities. If the objective is to obtain a predictive distribution of C, based on both M and A, it is not clear why one should obtain it from the separate models and weight them by the posterior probabilities, rather than obtaining the predictive density from the extended model $C_t = \alpha_3 + \beta_3 M + \gamma_3 A + W$. Given the fact that both M and A influence C, and that the extended model also takes into account the correlation between M and A, it seems logical in this case to use the latter procedure for this purpose. Of course, one would not want to push this argument in every case. It all depends on whether the extended model makes economic sense.

APPENDIX

A

MATRIX ALGEBRA

A *matrix* is a rectangular array of elements, e.g.,

$$\begin{bmatrix} 2 & 3 & 7 & 1 \\ 1 & 2 & 3 & -4 \\ -7 & 0 & 2 & 1 \end{bmatrix}$$

We will denote this by **A** and say that it is of order 3 × 4. The first number is the number of rows and the second number is the number of columns. A matrix of order $1 \times n$ is called a *row vector*, and a matrix of order $m \times 1$ is called a *column vector*, e.g., $\mathbf{b} = (2,\ 3,\ 7,\ 1)$ is a row vector.

$$c = \begin{bmatrix} 2 \\ 1 \\ -7 \end{bmatrix}$$

is a column vector. To economize on space, we shall write $\mathbf{c} = [2,\ 1,\ -7]$

A *transpose* of a matrix **A**, denoted by **A**′, is the same matrix with rows and columns interchanged. In the above example

$$\mathbf{A}' = \begin{bmatrix} 2 & 1 & -7 \\ 3 & 2 & 0 \\ 7 & 3 & 2 \\ 1 & -4 & 1 \end{bmatrix}$$

Henceforth, we will follow the convention of writing all column vectors without a prime and writing row vectors with a prime; e.g., if

$$\mathbf{b} = \begin{bmatrix} 2 \\ 3 \\ 7 \\ 1 \end{bmatrix}$$

is a column vector, then $\mathbf{b}' = [2,\ 3,\ 7,\ 1]$ is a row vector.

Matrix addition (or subtraction) is done by adding (or subtracting) the corresponding elements and is defined only if the matrices are of the same order. For example, if

$$\mathbf{A} = \begin{bmatrix} 2 & 3 & 1 \\ 0 & 1 & 7 \end{bmatrix} \quad \text{and} \quad \mathbf{B} = \begin{bmatrix} 1 & 0 & 3 \\ 0 & 1 & 2 \end{bmatrix}$$

then $$\mathbf{A} + \mathbf{B} = \begin{bmatrix} 3 & 3 & 4 \\ 0 & 2 & 9 \end{bmatrix} \quad \text{and} \quad \mathbf{A} - \mathbf{B} = \begin{bmatrix} 1 & 3 & -2 \\ 0 & 0 & 5 \end{bmatrix}$$

Obviously, $\mathbf{A} + \mathbf{B}'$ is not defined because $\mathbf{A}$ is 2×3 and $\mathbf{B}'$ is 3×2. Also note that $\mathbf{A} + \mathbf{B} = \mathbf{B} + \mathbf{A}$. (The same is not true of multiplication, as will be seen later.) Multiplying a matrix by a number (scalar) is defined as multiplying each element of the matrix by this scalar, e.g., if

$$\mathbf{A} = \begin{bmatrix} 2 & 3 & 1 \\ 0 & 1 & 7 \end{bmatrix}$$

then $$3\mathbf{A} = \begin{bmatrix} 6 & 9 & 3 \\ 0 & 3 & 21 \end{bmatrix}$$

Two matrices $\mathbf{A}$ and $\mathbf{B}$ are said to be equal if they are of the same order and they have all corresponding elements equal. In this case $\mathbf{A} - \mathbf{B} = \mathbf{0}$ (a matrix with all elements equal to 0).

Scalar product of vectors: If $\mathbf{b}$ and $\mathbf{c}$ are two vectors of the same order, $\mathbf{b}' = [b_1 b_2 \cdots b_n]$ and $\mathbf{c}' = [c_1 c_2 \cdots c_n]$; then $\mathbf{b}'\mathbf{c} = b_1c_1 + b_2c_2 + \cdots + b_nc_n$. For example, if $\mathbf{b}' = [2, -1, 2]$ and $\mathbf{c}' = [0, 3, 3]$, $\mathbf{b}'\mathbf{c} = (0 \times 2) + (-1 \times 3) + (2 \times 3) = 3$. The scalar product is not defined if the vectors are not of the same order.

Matrix multiplication: Let $\mathbf{B}$ be an $m \times n$ matrix and $\mathbf{C}$ an $n \times k$ matrix. We can write $\mathbf{B}$ as a set of m row vectors each of order n, and we can write $\mathbf{C}$ as a set of k column vectors each of order n, i.e.,

$$\mathbf{B} = \begin{bmatrix} \mathbf{b}'_1 \\ \mathbf{b}'_2 \\ \mathbf{b}'_m \end{bmatrix} \quad \text{and} \quad \mathbf{C} = [\mathbf{c}_1 \mathbf{c}_2 \cdots \mathbf{c}_k]$$

where $\mathbf{b}'_1 \mathbf{b}'_2 \ldots$ etc., are $1 \times n$ row vectors and $\mathbf{c}_1 \mathbf{c}_2 \ldots$ etc., are $n \times 1$ column vectors. Then $\mathbf{BC}$ is defined as

$$\mathbf{BC} = \begin{bmatrix} \mathbf{b}'_1\mathbf{c}_1 & \mathbf{b}'_1\mathbf{c}_2 & \mathbf{b}'_1\mathbf{c}_k \\ \mathbf{b}'_2\mathbf{c}_1 & \mathbf{b}'_2\mathbf{c}_2 & \mathbf{b}'_2\mathbf{c}_k \\ \vdots & \vdots & \vdots \\ \mathbf{b}'_m\mathbf{c}_1 & \mathbf{b}'_m\mathbf{c}_2 & \mathbf{b}'_m\mathbf{c}_k \end{bmatrix} \tag{A-1}$$

$\mathbf{BC}$ is of order $m \times k$. Matrix multiplication is thus done by row and column; i.e., we take scalar products of row vectors in the first matrix $\mathbf{B}$ with column vectors of the second matrix $\mathbf{C}$. The matrix product $\mathbf{BC}$ is defined only if the number of columns in **B** equals the number of rows in **C**. Also **BC** has as many rows as **B** and as many columns as **C**. For example, consider

$$\mathbf{B} = \begin{bmatrix} 2 & 1 & 3 \\ 0 & 1 & 2 \end{bmatrix} \quad \text{and} \quad \mathbf{C} = \begin{bmatrix} 7 & 5 \\ 8 & 6 \end{bmatrix}$$

Since **B** is 2 × 3 and **C** is 2 × 2, **BC** is not defined. But **B′C** is defined. We have

$$\mathbf{B}'\mathbf{C} = \begin{bmatrix} 2 & 0 \\ 1 & 1 \\ 3 & 2 \end{bmatrix} \cdot \begin{bmatrix} 7 & 5 \\ 8 & 6 \end{bmatrix} = \begin{bmatrix} 2\times 7 + 0\times 8 & 2\times 5 + 0\times 6 \\ 1\times 7 + 1\times 8 & 1\times 5 + 1\times 6 \\ 3\times 7 + 2\times 8 & 3\times 5 + 2\times 6 \end{bmatrix}$$

$$= \begin{bmatrix} 14 & 10 \\ 15 & 11 \\ 37 & 27 \end{bmatrix}$$

Note that **BC** is not defined but **CB** is defined. Here

$$\mathbf{CB} = \begin{bmatrix} 7 & 5 \\ 8 & 6 \end{bmatrix} \begin{bmatrix} 2 & 1 & 3 \\ 0 & 1 & 2 \end{bmatrix} = \begin{bmatrix} 14 & 12 & 31 \\ 16 & 14 & 36 \end{bmatrix}$$

Also, given two matrices **B** and **C**, one or both of the products **BC** and **CB** may be undefined, and even if both **BC** and **CB** are defined, they may not be of the same order. For example, if **B** is 2 × 3 and **C** is 3 × 2, then **BC** is defined and of order 2 × 2 and **CB** is defined but of order 3 × 3. Further, even if **BC** and **CB** are of the same order, they may not be equal, e.g., if

$$\mathbf{B} = \begin{bmatrix} 2 & 0 \\ 1 & 1 \end{bmatrix} \quad \text{and} \quad \mathbf{C} = \begin{bmatrix} 3 & 6 \\ 1 & 3 \end{bmatrix}$$

then $$\mathbf{BC} = \begin{bmatrix} 6 & 12 \\ 4 & 9 \end{bmatrix} \quad \text{and} \quad \mathbf{CB} = \begin{bmatrix} 12 & 6 \\ 5 & 3 \end{bmatrix}$$

Thus **BC** ≠ **CB**, even though they are of the same order.

Reversal law for transpose of a product: If **B** and **C** are matrices such that **BC** is defined, then $(\mathbf{BC})' = \mathbf{C}'\mathbf{B}'$. This can be easily verified and hence will not be proved here.

A *unit* or *identity matrix* $\mathbf{I}_n$ is defined as an $n \times n$ matrix with 1 in the diagonal and zeros elsewhere, e.g.,

$$\mathbf{I}_3 = \begin{bmatrix} 1 & 0 & 0 \\ 0 & 1 & 0 \\ 0 & 0 & 1 \end{bmatrix}$$

The identity matrix plays the same role in matrix multiplication as the number 1 in scalar multiplication—except that the order of $\mathbf{I}_n$ must be defined properly; e.g., if **B** is a 4 × 5 matrix, $\mathbf{I}_4\mathbf{B} = \mathbf{B}$ and $\mathbf{B}\mathbf{I}_5 = \mathbf{B}$.

Determinant: The determinant of an $n \times n$ square matrix, to be denoted by $|\mathbf{A}|$, is an algebraic function of the n^2 elements which is defined as $|\mathbf{A}| = \sum(\pm)$ $a_{1i_1}a_{2i_2} \cdots a_{ni_n}$ where the summation is over all $n!$ permutations of the numbers $(1, 2, \ldots, n)$ and the sign of any element is positive if it is an even permutation and negative if it is an odd permutation. A permutation is said to be even (or odd) if we need an even (or odd) number of interchanges in the elements to arrive at that permutation; e.g., with numbers (1,2,3) we say that (1,3,2) is an odd permutation and (2,3,1) is an even permutation. The former requires only one interchange and the latter two. If we have a 3×3 matrix, there are $3! = 6$ permutations of the numbers (1,2,3). These are, with the appropriate signs: $+(1,2,3), -(1,3,2), -(2,1,3), +(2,3,1), -(3,2,1), +(3,1,2)$.

$$\mathbf{A} = \begin{bmatrix} a_{11} & a_{12} & a_{13} \\ a_{21} & a_{22} & a_{23} \\ a_{31} & a_{32} & a_{33} \end{bmatrix}$$

Hence $|\mathbf{A}|$ is the sum of six terms. The first subscript is always (1,2,3), and the second subscript is one of the six permutations above, i.e.,

$$|\mathbf{A}| = a_{11}a_{22}a_{33} - a_{11}a_{23}a_{32} - a_{12}a_{21}a_{33} + a_{12}a_{23}a_{31} - a_{13}a_{22}a_{31} + a_{13}a_{21}a_{32}$$

We can write this in terms of the elements of the first row, i.e.,

$$|\mathbf{A}| = a_{11}(a_{22}a_{33} - a_{23}a_{32}) + a_{12}(-a_{21}a_{33} + a_{23}a_{31}) + a_{13}(a_{21}a_{32} - a_{22}a_{31})$$

The terms in the brackets are called the *cofactors* of the respective elements. Thus, if we denote the cofactor of a_{11} by A_{11}, of a_{12} by A_{12}, and of a_{13} by A_{13}, then $|\mathbf{A}| = a_{11}A_{11} + a_{12}A_{12} + a_{13}A_{13}$.

We can as well write the expansion of $|\mathbf{A}|$ in terms of the elements of the second or third row and its cofactors, or the elements in any column and their cofactors. The cofactor is nothing but the determinant of a submatrix obtained by deleting that row and column, with an appropriate sign. If we want the cofactor of an element a_{ij} in a matrix A, we delete the ith row and jth column in A, compute the determinant, and multiply by $(-1)^{i+j}$.

Given the definition of the determinant, we can easily see that the following properties hold:

1. If $\mathbf{A}^*$ is a matrix with two columns or rows of $\mathbf{A}$ interchanged, then $|\mathbf{A}^*| = -|\mathbf{A}|$. This is because all odd permutations become even and even permutations become odd—with one extra interchange.
2. From property 1 it follows that if two columns (or rows) of a matrix $\mathbf{A}$ are identical, then $|\mathbf{A}| = 0$, because by interchanging these columns (or rows) the value is unaltered. Thus $|\mathbf{A}| = |\mathbf{A}^*| = -|\mathbf{A}|$. Hence $|\mathbf{A}| = 0$.
3. Expansion of the determinant in terms of "alien" cofactors is equal to zero. By alien cofactors we mean cofactors of another row (or column). For example, suppose we consider the first and second rows. $|\mathbf{A}| = a_{11}A_{11} + a_{12}A_{12} + \cdots + a_{1n}A_{1n}$. This is called *expansion by own cofactors*. Suppose instead we consider the sum $a_{11}A_{21} + a_{12}A_{22} + \cdots + a_{1n}A_{2n}$, where A_{21}, $A_{22}, \ldots, A_{2n}$ are the cofactors of the elements in the second row. This is called an expansion by "alien" cofactors. This is a correct expansion for $|\mathbf{A}|$ if the first and second rows of $\mathbf{A}$ are identical. But in this case by the result 2 above we have $|\mathbf{A}| = 0$. Hence

$$a_{11}A_{21} + a_{12}A_{22} + \cdots + a_{1n}A_{2n} = 0$$

4. The value of a determinant is unaltered by adding to any of its rows (or columns) any multiples of other rows (or columns.) For example, suppose we add c times the second row to the first row. We have

$$\begin{vmatrix} a_{11}+ca_{21} & a_{12}+ca_{22} & \cdots & a_{1n}+ca_{2n} \\ a_{21} & a_{22} & \cdots & a_{2n} \\ a_{n1} & a_{n2} & \cdots & a_{nn} \end{vmatrix}$$

$$\begin{aligned} \text{This determinant} &= (a_{11}+ca_{21})A_{11} + (a_{12}+ca_{22})A_{12} + \cdots + (a_{1n}+ca_{2n})A_{1n} \\ &= (a_{11}A_{11} + a_{12}A_{12} + \cdots + a_{1n}A_{2n}) + c(a_{21}A_{11} \\ &\quad + a_{22}A_{12} + \cdots + a_{2n}A_{1n}) \end{aligned}$$

The first bracket is $|\mathbf{A}|$ and the second bracket is equal to zero because it is an expansion by alien cofactors.

5. It follows from property 4 that if a row (or column) of a matrix $\mathbf{A}$ can be expressed as a linear combination of the other rows (or columns), the determinant of $\mathbf{A}$ is zero. For example, consider

$$\mathbf{A} = \begin{bmatrix} 3 & -1 & 1 \\ 4 & 2 & 8 \\ 10 & 3 & 16 \end{bmatrix}$$

Here the third column of $\mathbf{A}$ = (first column) + 2(second column). In such cases we say that the columns are *linearly dependent*. The determinant of a matrix $\mathbf{A}$ is nonzero if and only if there are no linear dependencies between the columns (or rows) of $\mathbf{A}$.

Inverse of a matrix: The inverse of a matrix $\mathbf{A}$ defined as $\mathbf{A}^{-1}$ is a matrix such that $\mathbf{A}^{-1}\mathbf{A} = \mathbf{A}\mathbf{A}^{-1} = \mathbf{I}$. This is analogous to the result in ordinary scalar multiplication $yy^{-1} = 1$. To get the inverse of a matrix $\mathbf{A}$, we first replace each element of $\mathbf{A}$ by its cofactor, transpose the matrix, and then divide each element by $|\mathbf{A}|$. That is,

$$\mathbf{A}^{-1} = \frac{1}{|\mathbf{A}|}\begin{bmatrix} A_{11} & A_{21} & \cdots & A_{n1} \\ A_{12} & A_{22} & \cdots & A_{n2} \\ \vdots & \vdots & & \vdots \\ A_{1n} & A_{2n} & \cdots & A_{nn} \end{bmatrix} \tag{A-2}$$

Multiplying $\mathbf{A}^{-1}$ by $\mathbf{A}$, we get (noting that expansion of a determinant by alien cofactors is zero)

$$\mathbf{A}^{-1}\mathbf{A} = \frac{1}{|\mathbf{A}|}\begin{bmatrix} A_{11} & A_{21} & \cdots & A_{n1} \\ A_{12} & A_{22} & \cdots & A_{n2} \\ \vdots & \vdots & & \vdots \\ A_{1n} & A_{2n} & \cdots & A_{nn} \end{bmatrix}\begin{bmatrix} a_{11} & a_{12} & \cdots & a_{1n} \\ a_{21} & a_{22} & \cdots & a_{2n} \\ \vdots & \vdots & & \vdots \\ a_{n1} & a_{n2} & \cdots & a_{nn} \end{bmatrix}$$

$$= \frac{1}{|\mathbf{A}|}\begin{bmatrix} |\mathbf{A}| & 0 & \cdots & 0 \\ 0 & |\mathbf{A}| & \cdots & 0 \\ \vdots & \vdots & & \vdots \\ 0 & 0 & \cdots & |\mathbf{A}| \end{bmatrix} = \mathbf{I}$$

If $|\mathbf{A}| = 0$, the matrix $\mathbf{A}$ is said to be *singular*. Its inverse does not exist.

Inverses follow a reversal law like transposes. If $\mathbf{B}$ and $\mathbf{C}$ both have an inverse and $\mathbf{BC}$ is defined, then $(\mathbf{BC})^{-1} = \mathbf{C}^{-1}\mathbf{B}^{-1}$.

Finally, since $\mathbf{BC}$ and $\mathbf{CB}$ are not in general equal, when we talk of multiplication of matrices, we have to specify whether we are premultiplying or postmultiplying. For example, $\mathbf{BC}$ is referred to as $\mathbf{C}$ premultiplied by $\mathbf{B}$ or $\mathbf{B}$ postmultiplied by $\mathbf{C}$. For an inverse both pre- and postmultiplication by the original matrix should give an identity matrix. (In generalized inverses we talk of left-inverse and right-inverse because these are not necessarily the same.)

Linear independence: If $\mathbf{x}_1, \mathbf{x}_2, \ldots, \mathbf{x}_k$ are k vectors of order n, that is,

$$\mathbf{x}_j = \begin{bmatrix} x_{j1} \\ x_{j2} \\ x_{jn} \end{bmatrix} \qquad j = 1,2, \ldots, k$$

the vector $\mathbf{x} = \sum_{j=1}^{k} a_j \mathbf{x}_j$ is called a linear combination of the vectors. The ith element of $\mathbf{x}$ is $\sum_j a_j x_{ji}$. A set of vectors $\mathbf{x}_1, \mathbf{x}_2, \ldots, \mathbf{x}_k$ is said to be linearly independent if none can be expressed as a linear combination of the rest. For example, $[1,-1,0]$, $[2,3,1]$, and $[4,1,1]$ are not linearly independent because the third vector = 2 (first vector) + (second vector). There cannot be more than n linearly independent vectors of order n.

Orthogonal matrices: Two vectors $\mathbf{x}_1$ and $\mathbf{x}_2$ are said to be orthogonal if $\mathbf{x}_1'\mathbf{x}_2 = 0$. Let $\mathbf{X}$ be an $n \times n$ matrix with columns $\mathbf{x}_1, \mathbf{x}_2, \ldots, \mathbf{x}_n$. If the vectors are orthogonal and also of unit length so that

$$\begin{aligned} \mathbf{x}_i'\mathbf{x}_j &= 0 \qquad \text{if } i \neq j \\ &= 1 \qquad \text{if } i = j \end{aligned}$$

then the matrix $\mathbf{X}$ is said to be an orthogonal matrix. Note that

$$\mathbf{X}'\mathbf{X} = \begin{bmatrix} \mathbf{x}_1' \\ \mathbf{x}_2' \\ \mathbf{x}_n' \end{bmatrix} \begin{bmatrix} \mathbf{x}_1 \; \mathbf{x}_2 \cdots \mathbf{x}_n \end{bmatrix} = \begin{bmatrix} 1 & 0 & \cdots & 0 \\ 0 & 1 & \cdots & 0 \\ 0 & 0 & \cdots & 1 \end{bmatrix}$$

$$= \mathbf{I} \text{ the identity matrix}$$

Postmultiplying both sides of this relationship by $\mathbf{X}^{-1}$, we get $\mathbf{X}' = \mathbf{X}^{-1}$. Also, premultiplying both sides by $\mathbf{X}$, we get $\mathbf{XX}' = \mathbf{I}$. Thus for an orthogonal matrix the transpose and the inverse are the same and the rows as well as columns are orthogonal. Also $|\mathbf{X}'\mathbf{X}| = 1$. Hence $|\mathbf{X}| = \pm 1$.

Rank of matrices: If we are given an $m \times n$ matrix

$$\mathbf{A} = \begin{bmatrix} a_{11} & a_{12} & \cdots & a_{1n} \\ a_{21} & a_{22} & \cdots & a_{2n} \\ \vdots & \vdots & \vdots & \\ a_{m1} & a_{m2} & \cdots & a_{mn} \end{bmatrix}$$

then we can consider this as a set of n (column) vectors of order m or a set of m (row) vectors of order n. The row rank of the matrix is the number of linearly independent row vectors and the column rank of the matrix is the number of linearly independent column vectors. For the matrix $\mathbf{A}$, row rank is $\leqslant m$ and column rank $\leqslant n$.

1. It can be shown that the number of linearly independent row vectors equals the number of linearly independent column vectors, i.e., row rank = column rank.
2. Also if **A** and **B** are two matrices such that their product **AB** is defined, then rank(**AB**) $\ngtr$ rank **A** or rank **B**. The proof is as follows: the product **AB** can be obtained by suitable linear combinations of the rows of **B**. This does not increase the number of linearity independent rows of **B**. Hence rank (**AB**) is not greater than rank **B**. Also $(\mathbf{AB})' = \mathbf{B}'\mathbf{A}'$. Repeating the above argument, we get rank (**AB** $\ngtr$ rank **A**′, i.e., rank **AB** $\ngtr$ rank **A**.
3. If **B** is a matrix of the form $m \times n$ and **A** of the form $n \times n$ with rank n, then rank **B** = rank **BA**. This can be proved as follows: Let rank **B** = s and rank **BA** = r. Then $r \ngtr s$. Since $\mathbf{B} = (\mathbf{BA})(\mathbf{A}^{-1})$, we have $s \ngtr r$. Hence $r = s$. This result shows that rank is unaltered by postmultiplication by a nonsingular matrix. Similarly we can show that rank is unaltered by premultiplication by a nonsingular matrix.

Solution of systems of equations: Consider m equations in n unknowns $x_1, x_2, \ldots, x_n$.

$$a_{11}x_1 + a_{12}x_2 + \cdots + a_{1n}x_n = 0$$
$$a_{21}x_1 + a_{22}x_2 + \cdots + a_{2n}x_n = 0$$
$$a_{m1}x_1 + a_{m2}x_2 + \cdots + a_{mn}x_n = 0$$

These can be written as $\mathbf{Ax} = 0$, where **x** is the column vector

$$\begin{bmatrix} x_1 \\ x_2 \\ \vdots \\ x_n \end{bmatrix} \quad \text{and} \quad \mathbf{A} = \begin{bmatrix} a_{11} & a_{12} & \cdots & a_{1n} \\ a_{21} & a_{22} & \cdots & a_{2n} \\ \vdots & \vdots & & \vdots \\ a_{m1} & a_{m2} & \cdots & a_{mn} \end{bmatrix}$$

The equations imply that the vector **x** is orthogonal to the row vectors of **A**. Since **x** is a vector of order n and there can be at most n linearly independent vectors of order n, a necessary and sufficient condition for the existence of a nonnull solution to this set of equations is that rank $\mathbf{A} < n$. If rank $\mathbf{A} = r$, there will be $(n - r)$ linearly independent vectors that are solutions to this set of equations, and any linear combination of these $(n - r)$ vectors is also a solution.

The above set of equations is called a set of homogeneous equations. Replacing the zeros on the right-hand side of the above equations by b_1, $b_2, \ldots, b_m$, we get a system of nonhomogeneous equations. This set of equations in essence means

$$x_1 \begin{bmatrix} a_{11} \\ a_{21} \\ \vdots \\ a_{m1} \end{bmatrix} + x_2 \begin{bmatrix} a_{12} \\ a_{22} \\ \vdots \\ a_{m2} \end{bmatrix} + \cdots + x_n \begin{bmatrix} a_{1n} \\ a_{2n} \\ \vdots \\ a_{mn} \end{bmatrix} = \begin{bmatrix} b_1 \\ b_2 \\ \vdots \\ b_m \end{bmatrix}$$

i.e., the vector **b** is a linear combination of the columns of **A**. Hence the necessary and sufficient condition for the existence of a solution to this set of equations is rank $(\mathbf{A}) = \text{rank}\ [\mathbf{A}\ \mathbf{b}]$.

As an exercise, find the value of c for which the following equations admit a solution:

$$\begin{aligned} 2x_1 - x_2 + 5x_3 &= 4 \\ 4x_1 \qquad + 6x_3 &= 1 \\ -2x_2 + 4x_3 &= 7 + c \end{aligned}$$

As another exercise, find the basic solutions for the set of equations:

$$\begin{aligned} 3x_1 + 4x_2 + \ \ x_3 - 7x_n &= 0 \\ 2x_1 - \ \ x_2 + \ 6x_3 - \ \ x_n &= 0 \\ 7x_1 + 2x_2 + 13x_3 - 9x_n &= 0 \end{aligned}$$

Trace of a matrix: The trace of a matrix is defined to be the sum of its diagonal elements. The following are some results regarding traces:

$$\begin{aligned} \text{Tr}\ \mathbf{A} &= \text{Tr}\ \mathbf{A}' \\ \text{Tr}\ (\mathbf{A} + \mathbf{B}) &= \text{Tr}\ \mathbf{A} + \text{Tr}\ \mathbf{B} \\ \text{Tr}\ (\mathbf{AB}) &= \text{Tr}\ (\mathbf{BA}) \qquad \text{provided both } \mathbf{BA} \text{ and } \mathbf{AB} \text{ are defined} \\ \text{Tr}\ (c\mathbf{A}) &= c\ \text{Tr}\ (\mathbf{A}) \qquad \text{where } c \text{ is a scalar} \end{aligned} \tag{A-3}$$

The third result is one that will often be used subsequently.

Linear and quadratic forms: If $\mathbf{a}$,$\mathbf{x}$,$\mathbf{y}$ are vectors of order n and $\mathbf{A}$ is a matrix of order $n \times n$, then $\mathbf{a}'\mathbf{x} = a_1x_1 + a_2x_2 + \cdots + a_nx_n = \sum_i a_ix_i$ is said to be a linear form.

$$\begin{aligned} \mathbf{x}'\mathbf{A}\mathbf{x} &= a_{11}x_1^2 + a_{12}x_1x_2 + \cdots + a_{1n}x_1x_n \\ &\quad + a_{21}x_2x_1 + a_{22}x_2^2 + \cdots + a_{2n}x_2x_n \\ &\quad + a_{n1}x_nx_1 + a_{n2}x_nx_2 + \cdots + a_{nn}x_n^2 \\ &= \sum_i \sum_j a_{ij}x_ix_j \end{aligned}$$

is said to be a quadratic form and $\mathbf{x}'\mathbf{A}\mathbf{y} = \sum_i \sum_j a_{ij}x_iy_j$

is said to be a bilinear form. Consider the set of nonnull vectors $\mathbf{x}$ (i.e., vectors which have at least one element nonzero). Then

A is said to be positive definite if $\mathbf{x}'\mathbf{A}\mathbf{x} > 0$ for all $\mathbf{x}$
A is said to be positive semidefinite if $\mathbf{x}'\mathbf{A}\mathbf{x} \geqslant 0$ for all $\mathbf{x}$
A is said to be negative definite if $\mathbf{x}'\mathbf{A}\mathbf{x} < 0$ for all $\mathbf{x}$
A is said to be negative semidefinite if $\mathbf{x}'\mathbf{A}\mathbf{x} \leqslant 0$ for all $\mathbf{x}$

Vector and matrix differentiation: Let us denote by $\partial F/\partial \mathbf{x}$ the vector of partial derivatives

$$\begin{bmatrix} \dfrac{\partial F}{\partial x_1} \\ \dfrac{\partial F}{\partial x_n} \end{bmatrix}$$

and let us denote by $\partial F/\partial \mathbf{A}$ the $m \times n$ matrix of partial derivatives

$$\left[\frac{\partial F}{\partial a_{ij}}\right] \qquad \begin{matrix} i = 1,2,\ldots,m \\ j = 1,2,\ldots,n \end{matrix}$$

Then

$$\frac{\partial}{\partial \mathbf{x}}(\mathbf{a}'\mathbf{x}) = \begin{bmatrix} a_1 \\ a_2 \\ \vdots \\ a_n \end{bmatrix} = \mathbf{a} \tag{A-4}$$

$$\frac{\partial}{\partial \mathbf{x}}(\mathbf{x}'\mathbf{A}\mathbf{x}) = \mathbf{A}\mathbf{x} + \mathbf{A}'\mathbf{x} = 2\mathbf{A}\mathbf{x} \text{ if } \mathbf{A} \text{ is symmetric} \tag{A-5}$$

$$\frac{\partial}{\partial \mathbf{x}}(\mathbf{x}'\mathbf{A}\mathbf{y}) = \mathbf{A}\mathbf{y} \tag{A-6}$$

$$\frac{\partial}{\partial \mathbf{A}}\mathbf{x}'\mathbf{A}\mathbf{x} = \begin{bmatrix} x_1^2 & x_1x_2 & x_1x_n \\ x_1x_2 & x_2^2 & x_2x_n \\ \vdots & \vdots & \vdots \\ x_1x_n & x_2x_n & x_n^2 \end{bmatrix} = \mathbf{x}\mathbf{x}' \tag{A-7}$$

Suppose $\mathbf{A}$ is an $m \times n$ matrix and $\mathbf{B}$ an $n \times m$ matrix. Consider trace $\mathbf{AB}$. The ith diagonal element of $\mathbf{AB}$ is obtained as the scalar product of the ith row of $\mathbf{A}$ and ith column of $\mathbf{B}$, which is

$$\sum_j a_{ij} b_{ji}$$

Hence $$\operatorname{Tr} \mathbf{AB} = \sum_i \sum_j a_{ij} b_{ji}$$

Hence $(\partial/\partial\mathbf{A})(\operatorname{Tr} \mathbf{AB}) = \mathbf{B}'$. In particular $(\partial/\partial\mathbf{A})(\operatorname{Tr} \mathbf{A}) = \mathbf{I}$. We will be encountering cases where $\mathbf{A}$ and $\mathbf{B}$ are symmetric matrices. In this case

$$\frac{\partial}{\partial \mathbf{A}}(\operatorname{Tr} \mathbf{AB}) = \mathbf{B} \tag{A-8}$$

For instance, we can write $\mathbf{x}'\mathbf{A}\mathbf{x} = \operatorname{Tr} \mathbf{x}'\mathbf{A}\mathbf{x}$ (since $\mathbf{x}'\mathbf{A}\mathbf{x}$ is a scalar) $= \operatorname{Tr} \mathbf{A}\mathbf{x}\mathbf{x}'$. Hence

$$\frac{\partial}{\partial \mathbf{A}}(\mathbf{x}'\mathbf{A}\mathbf{x}) = \frac{\partial}{\partial \mathbf{A}} \operatorname{Tr} \mathbf{A}\mathbf{x}\mathbf{x}' = \mathbf{x}\mathbf{x}'$$

as obtained earlier. Sometimes we need derivatives of determinants. Expanding the determinant $|\mathbf{A}|$ in terms of the elements of the ith row and the corresponding cofactors, we get

$$|\mathbf{A}| = a_{i1}A_{i1} + a_{i2}A_{i2} + \cdots + a_{in}A_{in}$$

where A_{ij} is the cofactor of a_{ij}. Hence

$$\frac{\partial |\mathbf{A}|}{\partial a_{ij}} = A_{ij} \tag{A-9}$$

or
$$\frac{\partial |\mathbf{A}|}{\partial \mathbf{A}} = \left[A_{ij} \right] = |\mathbf{A}|(\mathbf{A}')^{-1} \tag{A-10}$$

because $(\mathbf{A}')^{-1}$ is defined to be $1/|\mathbf{A}|$ times the matrix of cofactors A_{ij}. Also
$$\frac{\partial \log |\mathbf{A}|}{\partial \mathbf{A}} = \frac{1}{|\mathbf{A}|} \frac{\partial |\mathbf{A}|}{\partial \mathbf{A}} = (\mathbf{A}')^{-1} \tag{A-11}$$

In some problems we need the derivatives of inverses. We have the formula (the product rule in differentiation)
$$\frac{\partial (\mathbf{AB})}{\partial x} = \mathbf{A} \frac{\partial \mathbf{B}}{\partial x} + \mathbf{B} \frac{\partial \mathbf{A}}{\partial x}$$

Putting $\mathbf{B} = \mathbf{A}^{-1}$, since
$$\frac{\partial (\mathbf{AB})}{\partial x} = \frac{\partial \mathbf{I}}{\partial x} = 0$$

we get
$$\frac{\partial \mathbf{A}^{-1}}{\partial x} = -\mathbf{A}^{-1} \frac{\partial \mathbf{A}}{\partial x} \mathbf{A}^{-1} \tag{A-12}$$

If x is a_{ij}, then $\partial \mathbf{A}/\partial x$ has 1 in the ith row, jth column and zeros elsewhere. Hence when we premultiply by $\mathbf{A}^{-1}$ we pick up the elements of the jth column of $\mathbf{A}^{-1}$ and when we postmultiply by $\mathbf{A}^{-1}$ we pick up the elements in the ith row of $\mathbf{A}^{-1}$. Hence
$$\text{The } (h,k)\text{th element of } \frac{\partial \mathbf{A}^{-1}}{\partial a_{ij}} = -a^{hi}a^{jk} \tag{A-13}$$

(This formula is easy to remember because h,i,j,k are in alphabetical order.)

Characteristic roots and vectors: We will be considering only symmetric matrices $\mathbf{A}$ because that is what we will encounter in our applications. We maximize the quadratic form $\mathbf{x}'\mathbf{A}\mathbf{x}$ subject to the condition $\mathbf{x}'\mathbf{x} = 1$. Introducing the lagrangian multiplier λ, we maximize $\mathbf{x}'\mathbf{A}\mathbf{x} - \lambda(\mathbf{x}'\mathbf{x} - 1)$. Differentiating with respect to $\mathbf{x}$ and equating the derivatives to zero, we get
$$2\mathbf{A}\mathbf{x} - \lambda \cdot 2\mathbf{x} = 0 \qquad \text{or} \qquad (\mathbf{A} - \lambda\mathbf{I})\mathbf{x} = 0$$

In order that this set of equations can have a nonnull solution, the rank of $(\mathbf{A} - \lambda\mathbf{I})$ should be $< n$. Hence $|\mathbf{A} - \lambda\mathbf{I}| = 0$. The roots of this determinantal equation are called the characteristic roots of $\mathbf{A}$, and the corresponding solution vectors $\mathbf{x}$ are called the characteristic vectors. The determinantal equation $|\mathbf{A} - \lambda\mathbf{I}| = 0$ is an nth-degree equation in λ and has n roots. For instance, if $\mathbf{A}$ is a 3×3 matrix, we have to solve the equation
$$\begin{vmatrix} a_{11} - \lambda & a_{12} & a_{13} \\ a_{21} & a_{22} - \lambda & a_{23} \\ a_{31} & a_{32} & a_{33} - \lambda \end{vmatrix} = 0$$

which is a cubic in λ and has three roots. Let $\lambda_1, \lambda_2, \ldots, \lambda_n$ be the n characteristic roots and $\mathbf{x}_1, \mathbf{x}_2, \ldots, \mathbf{x}_n$ be the corresponding characteristic vectors. We can show that the characteristic vectors corresponding to two distinct characteristic roots are orthogonal. For instance, if λ_1 and λ_2 are two distinct roots, we have

$$\mathbf{A}\mathbf{x}_1 = \lambda_1\mathbf{x}_1 \quad \text{and hence} \quad \mathbf{x}_2'\mathbf{A}\mathbf{x}_1 = \lambda_1\mathbf{x}_2'\mathbf{x}_1$$

$$\mathbf{A}\mathbf{x}_2 = \lambda_2\mathbf{x}_2 \quad \text{and hence} \quad \mathbf{x}_1'\mathbf{A}\mathbf{x}_2 = \lambda_2\mathbf{x}_1'\mathbf{x}_2$$

By subtraction we get $0 = (\lambda_1 - \lambda_2)(\mathbf{x}_1'\mathbf{x}_2)$.

Since $\lambda_1 \neq \lambda_2$, we have $\mathbf{x}_1'\mathbf{x}_2 = 0$ or $\mathbf{x}_1$ and $\mathbf{x}_2$ are orthogonal. Let $\mathbf{X}$ be the matrix whose columns are the vectors $\mathbf{x}_1, \mathbf{x}_2, \ldots, \mathbf{x}_n$. That is, $\mathbf{X} = [\mathbf{x}_1\mathbf{x}_2 \ldots \mathbf{x}_n]$. Then if $\lambda_1, \lambda_2, \ldots, \lambda_n$ are distinct roots, the columns of $\mathbf{X}$ are orthogonal and since $\mathbf{x}_i'\mathbf{x}_i = 1$ for all i, $\mathbf{X}$ is an orthogonal matrix. We can write the system of equations $\mathbf{A}\mathbf{x}_j = \lambda_j\mathbf{x}_j$ where $j = 1, 2, \ldots, n$ together as

$$\mathbf{A}[\mathbf{x}_1\mathbf{x}_2 \ldots \mathbf{x}_n] = [\lambda_1\mathbf{x}_1 \quad \lambda_2\mathbf{x}_2 \quad \lambda_n\mathbf{x}_n]$$

or

$$\mathbf{AX} = \mathbf{XD}$$

where $\mathbf{D}$ is the diagonal matrix

$$\begin{bmatrix} \lambda_1 & & & \\ & \lambda_2 & & \\ & & \ddots & \\ & & & \lambda_n \end{bmatrix}$$

with all nondiagonal terms zero. Premultiplying both sides by $\mathbf{X}^{-1}$, we get $\mathbf{X}^{-1}\mathbf{AX} = \mathbf{D}$ or $\mathbf{X}'\mathbf{AX} = \mathbf{D}$, since $\mathbf{X}$ is an orthogonal matrix and its inverse is its transpose. Though we derived this result for the case of distinct roots λ_j, it can be shown to be true even for repeated roots; i.e., given a symmetric matrix, $\mathbf{A}$, there exists an orthogonal matrix $\mathbf{X}$ (whose columns are the characteristic vectors of $\mathbf{A}$) such that $\mathbf{X}'\mathbf{AX} = \mathbf{D}$ where $\mathbf{D}$ is a diagonal matrix whose elements are the characteristic roots of $\mathbf{A}$. Also, since $|\mathbf{X}'\mathbf{AX}| = |\mathbf{D}| = \lambda_1\lambda_2 \cdots \lambda_n$ and since $|\mathbf{X}'| = |\mathbf{X}| = \pm 1$, we have $|\mathbf{A}| = \lambda_1\lambda_2 \cdots \lambda_n$. Thus the determinant of any matrix is equal to the product of its characteristic roots. Further

$$\text{Tr } \mathbf{D} = \lambda_1 + \lambda_2 + \cdots + \lambda_n$$

and

$$\begin{aligned} \text{Tr } \mathbf{X}'\mathbf{AX} &= \text{Tr } \mathbf{AXX}' \\ &= \text{Tr } \mathbf{A} \qquad \text{since } \mathbf{XX}' = \mathbf{I} \end{aligned}$$

Thus the trace of a matrix is equal to the sum of its characteristic roots. Further, since the rank of a matrix is unaltered by pre- or postmultiplication by nonsingular matrices, rank $\mathbf{A}$ = rank $\mathbf{X}'\mathbf{AX}$ = rank $\mathbf{D}$. Thus the rank of a matrix is equal to the number of its nonzero characteristic roots. Since $\mathbf{AX} = \mathbf{XD}$, postmultiplying by $\mathbf{X}^{-1}$, we get

$$\begin{aligned} \mathbf{A} &= \mathbf{XDX}' \\ &= \lambda_1\mathbf{x}_1\mathbf{x}_1' + \lambda_2\mathbf{x}_2\mathbf{x}_2' + \cdots + \lambda_n\mathbf{x}_n\mathbf{x}_n' \end{aligned}$$

(Note that $\mathbf{x}_j\mathbf{x}_j'$ is an $n \times n$ matrix of rank 1.) Also

$$\begin{aligned} \mathbf{A}^2 &= (\mathbf{XDX}')(\mathbf{XDX}') = \mathbf{XD}^2\mathbf{X}' \qquad \text{since } \mathbf{X}'\mathbf{X} = \mathbf{I} \\ &= \lambda_1^2\mathbf{x}_1\mathbf{x}_1' + \lambda_2^2\mathbf{x}_2\mathbf{x}_2' + \cdots + \lambda_n^2\mathbf{x}_n\mathbf{x}_n' \end{aligned}$$

Thus if we consider the rth power of $\mathbf{A}$, the characteristic roots of $\mathbf{A}^r$ are the rth powers of the characteristic roots of $\mathbf{A}$, but the characteristic vectors are the same as those of $\mathbf{A}$.

If $\mathbf{A}$ is positive definite, all its characteristic roots are positive. Consider the equation $\mathbf{A}\mathbf{x}_j = \lambda\mathbf{x}_j$. We have $\mathbf{x}_j'\mathbf{A}\mathbf{x}_j$ is greater than 0 for all nonnull $\mathbf{x}_j$. Hence $\lambda_j > 0$ for all $j = 1,2, \ldots, n$. By a similar argument we can show that if $\mathbf{A}$ is positive semidefinite, all the characteristic roots are $\geqslant 0$. If $\mathbf{A}$ is negative definite, all the roots are < 0, and if $\mathbf{A}$ is negative semidefinite, all the roots are $\leqslant 0$. Another important result which we will have occasion to use is the following: If $\mathbf{B}$ is positive definite and $\mathbf{A} - \mathbf{B}$ is positive semidefinite, then

1. $|\mathbf{A} - \lambda\mathbf{B}| = 0$ has all roots $\lambda \geqslant 1$
2. $|\mathbf{A}| \geqslant |\mathbf{B}|$ (A-14)
3. $\mathbf{B}^{-1} - \mathbf{A}^{-1}$ is positive semidefinite

Result (1) follows from the fact that $\mathbf{B}^{-1}(\mathbf{A} - \mathbf{B})$ is positive semidefinite and hence its roots are all $\geqslant 0$. This means that the roots of $|\mathbf{B}^{-1}(\mathbf{A} - \mathbf{B}) - \mu\mathbf{I}| = 0$ or $|\mathbf{A} - \mathbf{B} - \mu\mathbf{B}| = 0$ or $|\mathbf{A} - (1 + \mu)\mathbf{B}| = 0$ are all greater than 0. Hence substituting $\lambda = 1 + \mu$, we get the result.

Result (2) follows from the fact that $|\mathbf{B}^{-1}\mathbf{A}| =$ product of the roots of $|\mathbf{A} - \lambda\mathbf{B}| = 0$. Hence $|\mathbf{B}^{-1}\mathbf{A}| \geqslant 1$ or $|\mathbf{A}|/|\mathbf{B}| \geqslant 1$.

Result (3) can be proved by noting that the roots of $|\mathbf{B}^{-1} - \lambda\mathbf{A}^{-1}| = 0$, which are the same as the roots of $|\mathbf{A} - \lambda\mathbf{B}| = 0$, are all greater than 1. The detailed proof is omitted here.

There is alternative terminology in the literature for characteristic roots and vectors. They are also termed latent roots and vectors or eigenvalues and vectors, respectively.

Idempotent matrices: In econometric applications we often encounter symmetric matrices $\mathbf{A}$ with the property that $\mathbf{A} = \mathbf{A}^2$. Such a matrix is said to be idempotent. Since the characteristic roots of $\mathbf{A}^r$ are the same as those of $\mathbf{A}$ in this case, every characteristic root of $\mathbf{A}$ is either 0 or 1. Hence $|\mathbf{A}| = 0$ or 1. Also

$$\begin{aligned} \operatorname{Tr} \mathbf{A} &= \text{number of nonzero characteristic roots of } \mathbf{A} \\ &= \text{rank } \mathbf{A} \end{aligned}$$

Some formulas for inverses: We will present the inverses for some special matrices that occur in econometrics. Let $\mathbf{e}$ be an $n \times 1$ vector with all elements equal to 1. Then $\mathbf{e}'\mathbf{e} = n$ and $\mathbf{J} = \mathbf{e}\mathbf{e}'$ is an $n \times n$ matrix with all elements equal to n. We encounter covariance matrices of the form $\mathbf{I} + \lambda\mathbf{e}\mathbf{e}'$. The inverse of this matrix is of the form $\mathbf{I} + \mu\mathbf{e}\mathbf{e}'$. Since $(\mathbf{I} + \lambda\mathbf{e}\mathbf{e}')(\mathbf{I} + \mu\mathbf{e}\mathbf{e}') = \mathbf{I}$, we have $\lambda\mathbf{e}\mathbf{e}' + \mu\mathbf{e}\mathbf{e}' + n\lambda\mu\mathbf{e}\mathbf{e}' = 0$ or $\lambda + \mu + n\lambda\mu = 0$. Hence

$$\mu = -\frac{\lambda}{1 + n\lambda}$$

Then
$$(\mathbf{I} + \lambda\mathbf{e}\mathbf{e}')^{-1} = \mathbf{I} - \left(\frac{\lambda}{1 + n\lambda}\right)\mathbf{e}\mathbf{e}' \tag{A-15}$$

Suppose we have two $n \times 1$ vectors $\mathbf{x}$ and $\mathbf{y}$ so that $\mathbf{x}\mathbf{y}'$ is an $n \times n$ matrix. The inverse of $[\mathbf{I} + \mathbf{x}\mathbf{y}']$ will be of the form $[\mathbf{I} + \lambda\mathbf{x}\mathbf{y}']$. Since $[\mathbf{I} + \mathbf{x}\mathbf{y}'][\mathbf{I} + \lambda\mathbf{x}\mathbf{y}'] = \mathbf{I}$, we have $\mathbf{xy}' + \lambda\mathbf{xy}' + (\lambda\mathbf{y}'\mathbf{x})\mathbf{xy}' = 0$ or

$$\lambda = -\left(\frac{1}{1 + \mathbf{y}'\mathbf{x}}\right)$$

Thus
$$[\mathbf{I} + \mathbf{xy}']^{-1} = \mathbf{I} - \left(\frac{1}{1 + \mathbf{y}'\mathbf{x}}\right)\mathbf{xy}'$$

or more generally,

$$[\mathbf{A} + \mathbf{xy}']^{-1} = \mathbf{A}^{-1} - \left(\frac{1}{1 + \mathbf{y}'\mathbf{A}^{-1}\mathbf{x}}\right)\mathbf{A}^{-1}\mathbf{xy}'\mathbf{A}^{-1} \tag{A-16}$$

This follows from the fact that

$$\begin{aligned}[\mathbf{A} + \mathbf{xy}']^{-1} &= [\mathbf{A}(\mathbf{I} + \mathbf{A}^{-1}\mathbf{xy}')]^{-1} \\ &= (\mathbf{I} + \mathbf{A}^{-1}\mathbf{xy}')^{-1}\mathbf{A}^{-1} \\ &= \left[\mathbf{I} - \frac{1}{1 + \mathbf{y}'\mathbf{A}^{-1}\mathbf{x}}\mathbf{A}^{-1}\mathbf{xy}'\right]\mathbf{A}^{-1}\end{aligned}$$

(substituting $\mathbf{A}^{-1}\mathbf{x}$ for $\mathbf{x}$ in the previous result). Let $\mathbf{X}$ and $\mathbf{Y}$ be two $m \times n$ matrices, $\mathbf{I}_m$ an identity matrix of order m, and $\mathbf{I}_n$ an identity matrix of order n. Then

$$[\mathbf{I}_m + \mathbf{XY}']^{-1} = \mathbf{I}_m - \mathbf{X}(\mathbf{I}_n + \mathbf{Y}'\mathbf{X})^{-1}\mathbf{Y}' \tag{A-17}$$

The result can be easily verified by pre- or postmultiplying the right-hand side by $\mathbf{I}_m + \mathbf{XY}'$ and noting that the result is $\mathbf{I}_m$.

More generally, let $\mathbf{A}$ and $\mathbf{D}$ be nonsingular matrices of orders m and n, respectively, and $\mathbf{B}$ an $m \times n$ matrix. Then

$$[\mathbf{A} + \mathbf{BDB}']^{-1} = \mathbf{A}^{-1} - \mathbf{A}^{-1}\mathbf{B}\,(\mathbf{B}'\mathbf{A}^{-1}\mathbf{B} + \mathbf{D}^{-1})^{-1}\mathbf{B}'\mathbf{A}^{-1} \tag{A-18}$$

This formula can easily be derived from the previous result by writing $\mathbf{A} + \mathbf{BDB}'$ as $\mathbf{A}(\mathbf{I} + \mathbf{A}^{-1}\mathbf{BDB}')$ and putting $\mathbf{A}^{-1}\mathbf{B} = \mathbf{X}$ and $\mathbf{DB}' = \mathbf{Y}'$. We will be using this formula in a discussion of regression models subject to linear restrictions.

Another result we will be using is that of inversion of partitioned matrices. Since most of the matrices we consider are symmetric (they are covariance matrices), we will consider the partitioned inversion of a symmetric matrix. The formula is

$$\begin{bmatrix}\mathbf{A} & \mathbf{B} \\ \mathbf{B}' & \mathbf{D}\end{bmatrix} = \begin{bmatrix}\mathbf{A}^{-1} + \mathbf{FEF}' & -\mathbf{FE} \\ -\mathbf{EF}' & \mathbf{E}\end{bmatrix} \tag{A-19}$$

where $\mathbf{E} = [\mathbf{D} - \mathbf{B}'\mathbf{A}^{-1}\mathbf{B}]^{-1}$ and $\mathbf{F} = \mathbf{A}^{-1}\mathbf{B}$. The formula can be readily verified by pre- or postmultiplying the right-hand side by

$$\begin{bmatrix}\mathbf{A} & \mathbf{B} \\ \mathbf{B}' & \mathbf{D}\end{bmatrix}$$

and noting that we get an identity matrix after simplification. Also consider the product

$$\begin{bmatrix}\mathbf{A} & \mathbf{B} \\ \mathbf{B}' & \mathbf{D}\end{bmatrix}\begin{bmatrix}\mathbf{I} & -\mathbf{A}^{-1}\mathbf{B} \\ \mathbf{0} & \mathbf{I}\end{bmatrix} = \begin{bmatrix}\mathbf{A} & \mathbf{0} \\ \mathbf{B}' & \mathbf{D} - \mathbf{B}'\mathbf{A}^{-1}\mathbf{B}\end{bmatrix}$$

Taking determinants, we get

$$\begin{vmatrix} \mathbf{A} & \mathbf{B} \\ \mathbf{B}' & \mathbf{D} \end{vmatrix} = |\mathbf{A}||\mathbf{D} - \mathbf{B}'\mathbf{A}^{-1}\mathbf{B}| \tag{A-20}$$

Generalized inverses: Consider a set of equations $\mathbf{Ax} = \mathbf{b}$. If $\mathbf{A}$ is square and nonsingular, we have a unique solution to this set of equations, given by

$$\mathbf{x} = \mathbf{A}^{-1}\mathbf{b}$$

If $\mathbf{A}$ is a rectangular matrix, we can write the solution as $\mathbf{x} = \mathbf{A}^{-}\mathbf{b}$, where $\mathbf{A}^{-}$ is said to be a generalized inverse or, for short, g inverse. Rao[1] defines the g inverse as a matrix $\mathbf{A}^{-}$ such that

$$\mathbf{AA}^{-}\mathbf{A} = \mathbf{A}$$

The g inverse as defined by Rao is not unique. But Rao shows that for many theorems in least-squares theory the g inverse defined need not be unique. He argues that in particular applications some further conditions may be imposed.

In econometric work sometimes we need a unique inverse. Moore[2] and Penrose[3] define the generalized inverse, to be denoted by $\mathbf{A}^{+}$ to distinguish it from Rao's g inverse $\mathbf{A}^{-}$, to be a matrix such that

1. $\mathbf{AA}^{+}\mathbf{A} = \mathbf{A}$ (this is also Rao's condition)
2. $\mathbf{A}^{+}\mathbf{AA}^{+} = \mathbf{A}^{+}$
3. $(\mathbf{AA}^{+})' = \mathbf{AA}^{+}$ (A-21)
4. $(\mathbf{A}^{+}\mathbf{A})' = \mathbf{A}^{+}\mathbf{A}$

Such an inverse is unique. In most of our discussions we will be using the Moore-Penrose inverse. If $(\mathbf{A}'\mathbf{A})$ is nonsingular, it can be easily checked that

$$\mathbf{A}^{+} = (\mathbf{A}'\mathbf{A})^{-1}\mathbf{A}'$$

This will actually be the inverse we will be using in many cases.

Kronecker products: Let $\mathbf{A} = [a_{ij}]$ be an $m \times n$ matrix and $\mathbf{B}$ a $p \times q$ matrix. Then the $mp \times nq$ matrix obtained by multiplying each element of $\mathbf{A}$ by $\mathbf{B}$ is called the Kronecker product of $\mathbf{A}$ and $\mathbf{B}$.

$$\mathbf{A} \otimes \mathbf{B} = \begin{bmatrix} a_{11}\mathbf{B} & a_{12}\mathbf{B} & a_{1n}\mathbf{B} \\ a_{21}\mathbf{B} & a_{22}\mathbf{B} & a_{2n}\mathbf{B} \\ a_{m1}\mathbf{B} & a_{m2}\mathbf{B} & a_{mn}\mathbf{B} \end{bmatrix} \tag{A-22}$$

There are several properties of Kronecker products, but the one that we require in our work (which can be easily verified) is

$$[\mathbf{A} \otimes \mathbf{B}]^{-1} = \mathbf{A}^{-1} \otimes \mathbf{B}^{-1} \tag{A-23}$$

[1] C. R. Rao, "Linear Statistical Inference and Its Applications," 2d ed., John Wiley & Sons, Inc., New York, 1974.

[2] E. H. Moore, "General Analysis," American Philosophical Society, Philadelphia, 1935.

[3] R. Penrose, A Generalized Inverse for Matrices, *Proceedings of the Cambridge Philosophical Society*, 1955, pp. 406–413.

APPENDIX

B

THE LINEAR MODEL IN MATRIX NOTATION

The general linear model with full rank:

Let $y_1, y_2, \ldots, y_n$ be a set of random variables with means $E(y_i) = \mu_i$ $i = 1, 2, \ldots, n$ and covariances $\text{cov}(y_i, y_j) = \sigma_{ij}$ $i,j = 1, 2, \ldots, n$. We will denote these in matrix notation as

$$E(\mathbf{y}) = \boldsymbol{\mu} \qquad \text{and} \qquad V(\mathbf{y}) = E(\mathbf{y} - \boldsymbol{\mu})(\mathbf{y} - \boldsymbol{\mu})' = \boldsymbol{\Sigma}$$

where $\mathbf{y}$ = an $n \times 1$ vector with elements y_i
$\boldsymbol{\mu}$ = an $n \times 1$ vector with elements μ_i
$\boldsymbol{\Sigma}$ = an $n \times n$ matrix with the (i,j)th element σ_{ij}

We will first consider the case where $\boldsymbol{\mu} = \mathbf{X}\boldsymbol{\beta}$ and $\boldsymbol{\Sigma} = \sigma^2\mathbf{I}$. We can write our model as

$$\mathbf{y} = \mathbf{X}\boldsymbol{\beta} + \mathbf{u} \tag{B-1}$$

where $\mathbf{y}$ = an $n \times 1$ vector of observations on the explained variable
$\mathbf{X}$ = an $n \times k$ matrix of observations on k explanatory variables
$\mathbf{u}$ = an $n \times 1$ vector of residuals
$\boldsymbol{\beta}$ = a $k \times 1$ vector of parameters to be estimated

We assume that:

1. The residuals are independently and identically distributed with mean 0 and variance σ^2, that is,

$$E(\mathbf{u}) = 0, V(\mathbf{u}) = \mathbf{I}\sigma^2$$

2. The x's are nonstochastic and hence independent of the u's, that is,

$$E(\mathbf{X}'\mathbf{u}) = 0$$

3. The x's are linearly independent. Hence rank $(\mathbf{X}'\mathbf{X})$ = rank $\mathbf{X} = k$ and $(\mathbf{X}'\mathbf{X})^{-1}$ exists.

Under these assumptions the best (minimum variance) unbiased linear estimator $\hat{\boldsymbol{\beta}}$ of $\boldsymbol{\beta}$ is given by minimizing

$$Q = (\mathbf{y} - \mathbf{X}\boldsymbol{\beta})'(\mathbf{y} - \mathbf{X}\boldsymbol{\beta})$$
$$= \mathbf{y}'\mathbf{y} - 2\boldsymbol{\beta}'\mathbf{X}'\mathbf{y} + \boldsymbol{\beta}'\mathbf{X}'\mathbf{X}\boldsymbol{\beta}$$

$\partial Q/\partial\boldsymbol{\beta} = 0$ gives $-2\mathbf{X}'\mathbf{y} + 2\mathbf{X}'\mathbf{X}\boldsymbol{\beta} = \mathbf{0}$ or $(\mathbf{X}'\mathbf{X})\boldsymbol{\beta} = \mathbf{X}'\mathbf{y}$. These are called the "normal equations." Hence

$$\hat{\boldsymbol{\beta}} = (\mathbf{X}'\mathbf{X})^{-1}\mathbf{X}'\mathbf{y} \tag{B-2}$$

Since $(\mathbf{X}'\mathbf{X})^{-1}\mathbf{X}'$ is a matrix of constants, the elements of $\hat{\boldsymbol{\beta}}$ are linear functions of $\mathbf{y}$. Hence $\hat{\boldsymbol{\beta}}$ is called a linear estimator. Substituting (B-1) in (B-2), we get

$$\begin{aligned}\hat{\boldsymbol{\beta}} &= (\mathbf{X}'\mathbf{X})^{-1}\mathbf{X}'(\mathbf{X}\boldsymbol{\beta} + \mathbf{u}) \\ &= \boldsymbol{\beta} + (\mathbf{X}'\mathbf{X})^{-1}\mathbf{X}'\mathbf{u}\end{aligned} \tag{B-3}$$

$E(\hat{\boldsymbol{\beta}}) = \boldsymbol{\beta} + (\mathbf{X}'\mathbf{X})^{-1}\mathbf{X}'\mathbf{E}(\mathbf{u}) = \boldsymbol{\beta}$ since $\mathbf{E}(\mathbf{u}) = \mathbf{0}$. Thus $\hat{\boldsymbol{\beta}}$ is unbiased.

$$\begin{aligned}V(\hat{\boldsymbol{\beta}}) &= E(\hat{\boldsymbol{\beta}} - \boldsymbol{\beta})(\hat{\boldsymbol{\beta}} - \boldsymbol{\beta})' \\ &= (\mathbf{X}'\mathbf{X})^{-1}\mathbf{X}'\mathbf{E}(\mathbf{uu}')\mathbf{X}(\mathbf{X}'\mathbf{X})^{-1} \\ &= \sigma^2(\mathbf{X}'\mathbf{X})^{-1} \qquad \text{since} \qquad \mathbf{E}(\mathbf{uu}') = \mathbf{I}\sigma^2\end{aligned}$$

If $\boldsymbol{\beta}^*$ is any other linear estimator of $\boldsymbol{\beta}$ different from $\hat{\boldsymbol{\beta}}$, we will show that $V(\boldsymbol{\beta}^*) \geqslant V(\hat{\boldsymbol{\beta}})$. The inequality is to be interpreted as saying that $V(\boldsymbol{\beta}^*) - V(\hat{\boldsymbol{\beta}})$ is a positive semidefinite matrix. In particular, the diagonal elements of $V(\beta^*) - V(\hat{\beta})$ are all $\geqslant 0$; that is, $V(\beta_i^*) \geqslant V(\hat{\beta}_i)$ for $i = 1, 2, \ldots, k$.

Any arbitrary linear estimator β^* can be written as

$$\begin{aligned}\boldsymbol{\beta}^* &= \left[(\mathbf{X}'\mathbf{X})^{-1}\mathbf{X}' + \mathbf{C}\right]\mathbf{y} \\ &= \hat{\boldsymbol{\beta}} + \mathbf{Cy} \\ &= \boldsymbol{\beta} + \mathbf{CX}\boldsymbol{\beta} + \left[(\mathbf{X}'\mathbf{X})^{-1}\mathbf{X}' + \mathbf{C}\right]\mathbf{u}\end{aligned}$$

If $\boldsymbol{\beta}^*$ is unbiased, $E(\boldsymbol{\beta}^*) = \boldsymbol{\beta}$, and since this relation is true for all possible values of $\boldsymbol{\beta}$, we have $\mathbf{CX} = \mathbf{0}$.

$$\begin{aligned}V(\boldsymbol{\beta}^*) &= E(\boldsymbol{\beta}^* - \boldsymbol{\beta})(\boldsymbol{\beta}^* - \boldsymbol{\beta})' \\ &= \left[(\mathbf{X}'\mathbf{X})^{-1}\mathbf{X}' + \mathbf{C}\right]E(\mathbf{uu}')\left[(\mathbf{X}'\mathbf{X})^{-1}\mathbf{X}' + \mathbf{C}\right]' \\ &= \sigma^2\left[(\mathbf{X}'\mathbf{X})^{-1} + \mathbf{CC}'\right]\end{aligned}$$

The other terms vanish because of the condition $\mathbf{CX} = \mathbf{0}$. Thus $V(\boldsymbol{\beta}^*) - V(\hat{\boldsymbol{\beta}}) = \sigma^2\mathbf{CC}'$, which is a positive semidefinite matrix. This proves that $\hat{\boldsymbol{\beta}}$ is the best linear unbiased estimator (denoted BLUE) of $\boldsymbol{\beta}$. The minimum value of $(\mathbf{y} - \mathbf{X}\boldsymbol{\beta})'(\mathbf{y} - \mathbf{X}\boldsymbol{\beta})$ is therefore $(\mathbf{y} - \mathbf{X}\hat{\boldsymbol{\beta}})'(\mathbf{y} - \mathbf{X}\hat{\boldsymbol{\beta}})$. This is usually called the residual sum of squares. It is equal to $\mathbf{y}'\mathbf{y} + \hat{\boldsymbol{\beta}}'(\mathbf{X}'\mathbf{X})\hat{\boldsymbol{\beta}} - 2\hat{\boldsymbol{\beta}}'\mathbf{X}'\mathbf{y}$. But $\hat{\boldsymbol{\beta}}'\mathbf{X}'\mathbf{y} = \hat{\boldsymbol{\beta}}'\mathbf{X}'\mathbf{X}\hat{\boldsymbol{\beta}}$.

Hence

$$\text{Residual sum of squares } \mathbf{y'y} - \hat{\boldsymbol\beta}'\mathbf{X'X}\hat{\boldsymbol\beta} = \mathbf{y'y} - \hat{\boldsymbol\beta}'\mathbf{X'y} \tag{B-4}$$

We can now relax the basic assumptions. First, suppose $E(\mathbf{uu'})$ is an arbitrary positive definite matrix $\boldsymbol\Sigma$, instead of $\sigma^2\mathbf{I}$. Then the model (B-1) can be transformed to the model

$$\mathbf{y}^* = \mathbf{X}^*\boldsymbol\beta + \mathbf{u}^*$$

where $\mathbf{y}^* = \boldsymbol\Sigma^{-1/2}\mathbf{y}$

$\mathbf{X}^* = \boldsymbol\Sigma^{-1/2}\mathbf{X}$

$\mathbf{u}^* = \boldsymbol\Sigma^{-1/2}\mathbf{u}$

Then $E(\mathbf{u}^*\mathbf{u}^{*\prime}) = \boldsymbol\Sigma^{-1/2}E(\mathbf{uu'})\boldsymbol\Sigma^{-1/2} = \mathbf{I}$. By the previous result, the BLUE of $\boldsymbol\beta$ is given by

$$\hat{\boldsymbol\beta}_{\text{GLS}} = (\mathbf{X}^{*\prime}\mathbf{X}^*)^{-1}\mathbf{X}^{*\prime}\mathbf{y} = (\mathbf{X'}\boldsymbol\Sigma^{-1}\mathbf{X})^{-1}\mathbf{X'}\boldsymbol\Sigma^{-1}\mathbf{y} \tag{B-5}$$

We use the subscript GLS to denote "generalized least squares." The variance of this estimator is given by

$$V(\hat{\boldsymbol\beta}_{\text{GLS}}) = \sigma^2(\mathbf{X}^{*\prime}\mathbf{X}^*)^{-1} = \sigma^2(\mathbf{X'}\boldsymbol\Sigma^{-1}\mathbf{X})^{-1} \tag{B-6}$$

In this case the ordinary-least-squares estimator

$$\begin{aligned}\hat{\boldsymbol\beta}_{\text{OLS}} &= (\mathbf{X'X})^{-1}\mathbf{X'y}\\ &= \boldsymbol\beta + (\mathbf{X'X})^{-1}\mathbf{X'u}\end{aligned}$$

is still unbiased, since $E(\mathbf{u}) = \mathbf{0}$. But its variance is given by

$$\begin{aligned}V(\hat{\boldsymbol\beta}_{\text{OLS}}) &= (\mathbf{X'X})^{-1}\mathbf{X'}E(\mathbf{uu'})\mathbf{X}(\mathbf{X'X})^{-1}\\ &= (\mathbf{X'X})^{-1}\mathbf{X'}\boldsymbol\Sigma\mathbf{X}(\mathbf{X'X})^{-1}\end{aligned}$$

The GLS estimator is more efficient than the OLS estimator in the sense that $V(\hat{\boldsymbol\beta}_{\text{OLS}}) - V(\hat{\boldsymbol\beta}_{\text{GLS}})$ is a positive semidefinite matrix. However, there are cases where $\boldsymbol\Sigma$ is not of the form $\mathbf{I}\sigma^2$, but still the OLS estimator is the same as the GLS estimator. Let $\mathbf{Z}$ be a matrix such that $\mathbf{X'Z} = 0$. Then a necessary and sufficient condition that the OLS and the GLS methods are equivalent is that $\boldsymbol\Sigma$ is of the form

$$\boldsymbol\Sigma = \mathbf{XCX'} + \mathbf{ZDZ'} + \mathbf{I}\sigma^2$$

where $\mathbf{C}$ and $\mathbf{D}$ are arbitrary (nonnegative definite) matrices.[1] A special case of this is the following model:

$$\begin{aligned} y_i &= \alpha + \delta x_i + u_i \qquad && i = 1,2, \ldots, n\\ \text{var}(u_i) &= 1 &&\\ \text{cov}(u_i,u_j) &= \rho && \text{for } i \neq j (\rho > 0)\end{aligned}$$

[1] C. R. Rao, Least Squares Theory Using an Estimated Dispersion Matrix and Its Application to the Measurement of Signals, *Proceedings of the Fifth Berkeley Symposium*, vol. I, pp. 355–372.

In matrix form we can write this as

$$\mathbf{y} = \mathbf{X}\boldsymbol{\beta} + \mathbf{u}$$

where
$$\mathbf{X} = \begin{bmatrix} 1 & x_1 \\ 1 & x_2 \\ \vdots & \vdots \\ 1 & x_n \end{bmatrix} \qquad \boldsymbol{\beta} = \begin{bmatrix} \alpha \\ \delta \end{bmatrix}$$

and
$$E(\mathbf{uu}') = \boldsymbol{\Sigma} = \begin{bmatrix} 1 & \rho & \cdots & \rho \\ \rho & 1 & \cdots & \rho \\ \rho & \rho & \cdots & 1 \end{bmatrix}$$
$$= (1 - \rho)\mathbf{I} + \rho\mathbf{ee}'$$

where $\mathbf{e}$ is an $n \times 1$ vector with all elements unity (first column of $\mathbf{X}$).

Thus $\boldsymbol{\Sigma} = \mathbf{XCX}' + \sigma^2\mathbf{I}$, where $\sigma^2 = (1 - \rho)$ and

$$\mathbf{C} = \begin{bmatrix} \rho & 0 \\ 0 & 0 \end{bmatrix}$$

Hence the OLS and GLS estimators are equivalent in this model. The next assumption we relax is that the x's are nonstochastic. If the x's are random variables, we replace the assumption $E(\mathbf{X}'\mathbf{u}) = \mathbf{0}$ by the assumption $\text{plim}(\mathbf{X}'\mathbf{u}/n) = 0$. Also, we will assume that $\text{plim}(\mathbf{X}'\mathbf{X}/n) = \mathbf{M}$, a finite positive definite matrix. In this case instead of proving $E(\hat{\boldsymbol{\beta}}) = \boldsymbol{\beta}$, we prove that $\text{plim}(\hat{\boldsymbol{\beta}}) = \boldsymbol{\beta}$; that is, instead of proving unbiasedness we prove the consistency. We have

$$\hat{\boldsymbol{\beta}} = \boldsymbol{\beta} + \left(\frac{\mathbf{X}'\mathbf{X}}{n}\right)^{-1} \frac{\mathbf{X}'\mathbf{u}}{n}$$

Taking probability limits and using the assumptions we have made, we get the result $\text{plim } \hat{\boldsymbol{\beta}} = \boldsymbol{\beta}$.

The final assumption we made is that the x's are linearly independent. If we relax this assumption, $(\mathbf{X}'\mathbf{X})^{-1}$ will not exist. Thus there is no unique solution to the normal equations

$$(\mathbf{X}'\mathbf{X})\,\hat{\beta} = \mathbf{X}'\mathbf{y}$$

However, consider two different solutions $\hat{\boldsymbol{\beta}}_1$ and $\hat{\boldsymbol{\beta}}_2$. We have

$$(\mathbf{X}'\mathbf{X})\,\hat{\boldsymbol{\beta}}_1 = \mathbf{X}'\mathbf{y}$$

and
$$(\mathbf{X}'\mathbf{X})\,\hat{\boldsymbol{\beta}}_2 = \mathbf{X}'\mathbf{y}$$

Premultiply the first equation by $\hat{\boldsymbol{\beta}}_2'$ and the second equation by $\hat{\boldsymbol{\beta}}_1$ and subtract. Since $\hat{\boldsymbol{\beta}}_2'\mathbf{X}'\mathbf{X}\hat{\boldsymbol{\beta}}_1 = \hat{\boldsymbol{\beta}}_1'\mathbf{X}'\mathbf{X}\hat{\boldsymbol{\beta}}_2$ (the transpose of a scalar is the same), we get $\hat{\boldsymbol{\beta}}_1'\mathbf{X}'\mathbf{y} = \hat{\boldsymbol{\beta}}_2'\mathbf{X}'\mathbf{y}$. Thus from (B-4) we see that the residual sum of squares will be the same, whichever solution of the normal equations we take. In the case where

$(\mathbf{X}'\mathbf{X})$ is a singular matrix, we cannot get a unique estimate for $\boldsymbol{\beta}$ but there will be some linear functions of $\boldsymbol{\beta}$ that will have unique estimates. Let $\mathbf{a}$ be a vector which is a linear combination of the columns of $\mathbf{X}'\mathbf{X}$. Thus $\mathbf{a} = (\mathbf{X}'\mathbf{X})\boldsymbol{\lambda}$. Then all linear functions of the form $\mathbf{a}'\boldsymbol{\beta}$ are uniquely estimable. To see this, consider

$$\mathbf{a}'\hat{\boldsymbol{\beta}} = \boldsymbol{\lambda}'\mathbf{X}'\mathbf{X}\hat{\boldsymbol{\beta}} = \boldsymbol{\lambda}'\mathbf{X}'\mathbf{y}$$

Thus $\mathbf{a}'\hat{\boldsymbol{\beta}}$ is a unique linear function of $\mathbf{y}$. Also $E(\boldsymbol{\lambda}'\mathbf{X}'\mathbf{y}) = \boldsymbol{\lambda}'\mathbf{X}'\mathbf{X}\boldsymbol{\beta} = \mathbf{a}'\boldsymbol{\beta}$. Thus $\mathbf{a}'\hat{\boldsymbol{\beta}}$ is a unique unbiased linear estimator for $\mathbf{a}'\boldsymbol{\beta}$. It can also be proved (along the lines of the earlier proofs) that it is the best (minimum variance) linear unbiased estimator. If $(\mathbf{X}'\mathbf{X})$ is of full rank, every $k \times 1$ vector $\mathbf{a}$ can be expressed as a linear combination of the columns of $\mathbf{X}'\mathbf{X}$. Thus all linear parametric functions $\mathbf{a}'\boldsymbol{\beta}$ are estimable.

In addition to the earlier assumptions, there is also one additional assumption that is often made, and this is that the residuals have a normal distribution. This assumption is not necessary to obtain the best linear unbiased estimator $\hat{\boldsymbol{\beta}}$ in Eq. (B-2). It is needed only for deriving some tests of significance. Also, if we assume normality, we can show that $\hat{\boldsymbol{\beta}}$ is the best unbiased estimator (i.e., it has the minimum variance property among all unbiased estimators, linear or nonlinear).

We can also prove, without adding the assumption of normality, that

$$\hat{\sigma}^2 = \frac{1}{n-k}(\mathbf{y} - \mathbf{X}\hat{\boldsymbol{\beta}})'(\mathbf{y} - \mathbf{X}\hat{\boldsymbol{\beta}})$$

is an unbiased estimator for σ^2. To show this, note that

$$\mathbf{y} - \mathbf{X}\hat{\boldsymbol{\beta}} = \mathbf{X}(\boldsymbol{\beta} - \hat{\boldsymbol{\beta}}) + \mathbf{u} = \mathbf{N}\mathbf{u}$$

where $\mathbf{N} = \mathbf{I}_n - \mathbf{X}(\mathbf{X}'\mathbf{X})^{-1}\mathbf{X}'$, $\mathbf{I}_n$ is an identity matrix of order n, and hence its trace $= n$. Also

$$\begin{aligned} \text{tr}\,\mathbf{X}(\mathbf{X}'\mathbf{X})^{-1}\mathbf{X}' &= \text{tr}(\mathbf{X}'\mathbf{X})^{-1}\mathbf{X}'\mathbf{X} \qquad (\text{tr}\,\mathbf{AB} = \text{tr}\,\mathbf{BA}) \\ &= \text{tr}\,\mathbf{I}_k \qquad \text{since } \mathbf{X}'\mathbf{X} \text{ is order } k \times k \\ &= k \end{aligned}$$

Hence $\text{tr}\,\mathbf{N} = n - k$. It can also be easily verified that $\mathbf{N}^2 = \mathbf{N}$, and thus $\mathbf{N}$ is an idempotent matrix.

$$\begin{aligned} E(\mathbf{y} - \mathbf{X}\hat{\boldsymbol{\beta}})'(\mathbf{y} - \mathbf{X}\hat{\boldsymbol{\beta}}) &= E\mathbf{u}'\mathbf{N}'\mathbf{N}\mathbf{u} \\ &= E\mathbf{u}'\mathbf{N}\mathbf{u} \qquad \text{since } \mathbf{N} \text{ is idempotent} \\ &= E(\text{tr}\,\mathbf{N}\mathbf{u}\mathbf{u}') \\ &= \text{tr}\,\mathbf{N}E(\mathbf{u}\mathbf{u}') = \sigma^2\,\text{tr}\,\mathbf{N} = (n-k)\sigma^2 \end{aligned}$$

Hence we have $E(\hat{\sigma}^2) = \sigma^2$.

The multivariate normal distribution: To derive the sampling distributions of the estimators and tests of significance in the general linear model (B-1), we need to assume that the residuals follow a normal distribution. Here we will derive the distributions of quadratic forms in normally distributed variables which will be needed in our derivations.

Let $Z_1, Z_2, \ldots, Z_n$ be n independent normally distributed random variables with mean 0 and variance 1. Consider k linearly independent functions

$$y_i = C_{i1}Z_1 + C_{i2}Z_2 + \cdots + C_{in}Z_n \qquad i = 1,2, \ldots, k$$

or $\mathbf{y} = \mathbf{CZ}$, where $\mathbf{C}$ is a $k \times n$ matrix of rank k. We want the joint distribution of the y_i. Define another $(n-k)$ linear function:

$$x_j = d_{j1}Z_1 + d_{j2}Z_2 + \cdots + d_{jn}Z_n \qquad j = k+1, \ldots, n$$

or $\mathbf{x} = \mathbf{DZ}$ where $\mathbf{D}$ is an $(n-k) \times n$ matrix of rank $(n-k)$ such that $\mathbf{CD}' = \mathbf{0}$. Then

$$\mathbf{B} = \begin{bmatrix} \mathbf{C} \\ \mathbf{D} \end{bmatrix}$$

is a nonsingular $n \times n$ matrix. Also

$$\mathbf{BB}' = \begin{bmatrix} \mathbf{CC}' & \mathbf{CD}' \\ \mathbf{DC}' & \mathbf{DD}' \end{bmatrix} = \begin{bmatrix} \mathbf{CC}' & \mathbf{0} \\ \mathbf{0} & \mathbf{DD}' \end{bmatrix}$$

Hence

$$(\mathbf{BB}')^{-1} = \begin{bmatrix} (\mathbf{CC}')^{-1} & \mathbf{0} \\ \mathbf{0} & (\mathbf{DD}')^{-1} \end{bmatrix}$$

Now

$$\begin{bmatrix} \mathbf{y} \\ \mathbf{x} \end{bmatrix} = \mathbf{BZ} \qquad \text{or} \qquad \mathbf{Z} = \mathbf{B}^{-1}\begin{bmatrix} \mathbf{y} \\ \mathbf{x} \end{bmatrix}$$

The Jacobian of the transformation is

$$\left| \frac{\partial \mathbf{Z}}{\partial (\mathbf{y},\mathbf{x})} \right| = |\mathbf{B}^{-1}|$$

Since the joint distribution of Z_i is

$$P(\mathbf{Z})\, d\mathbf{Z} = \frac{1}{(2\pi)^{n/2}} e^{-(1/2)\mathbf{Z}'\mathbf{Z}}\, d\mathbf{Z}$$

we have

$$P(\mathbf{y},\mathbf{x})\, d\mathbf{y}\, d\mathbf{x} = \frac{1}{|\mathbf{B}|(2\pi)^{n/2}} e^{-(1/2)Q}\, d\mathbf{y}\, d\mathbf{x}$$

where

$$Q = \mathbf{Z}'\mathbf{Z} = [\mathbf{y}'\mathbf{x}'](\mathbf{BB}')^{-1}\begin{bmatrix} \mathbf{y} \\ \mathbf{x} \end{bmatrix}$$

$$= \mathbf{y}'(\mathbf{CC}')^{-1}\mathbf{y} + \mathbf{x}'(\mathbf{DD}')^{-1}\mathbf{x}$$

Also $|\mathbf{B}| = |\mathbf{BB}'|^{1/2} = |\mathbf{CC}'|^{1/2} \cdot |\mathbf{DD}'|^{1/2}$. Hence

$$P(\mathbf{y},\mathbf{x})\, d\mathbf{y}\, d\mathbf{x} = \left[\frac{1}{|\mathbf{CC}'|^{1/2}} \frac{1}{(2\pi)^{k/2}} e^{-(1/2)\mathbf{y}'(\mathbf{CC}')^{-1}\mathbf{y}}\, d\mathbf{y} \right]$$

$$\cdot \left[\frac{1}{|\mathbf{DD}'|^{1/2}} \frac{1}{(2\pi)^{(n-k)/2}} e^{-(1/2)\mathbf{x}'(\mathbf{DD}')^{-1}\mathbf{x}}\, d\mathbf{x} \right]$$

Denote $\mathbf{CC}'$ by $\mathbf{V}$. Then it is easy to see that the covariance matrix of $\mathbf{y}$ is

$$\begin{aligned} E(\mathbf{yy}') &= E(\mathbf{CZZ'C}') \\ &= \mathbf{CC}' = \mathbf{V} \end{aligned}$$

The distribution of $\mathbf{y}$ is therefore

$$P(\mathbf{y})\ d\mathbf{y} = \frac{1}{|\mathbf{V}|^{1/2}(2\pi)^{k/2}} e^{-(1/2)\mathbf{y}'\mathbf{V}^{-1}\mathbf{y}}\ d\mathbf{y}$$

where $\mathbf{V}$ is the covariance matrix of $\mathbf{y}$. This is the probability density of the k-variate normal distribution. We write this as $\mathbf{y} \sim N_k(\mathbf{0},\mathbf{V})$. If the mean is $\boldsymbol{\mu}$ instead of $\mathbf{0}$, we write $\mathbf{y} \sim \mathrm{N}_k(\boldsymbol{\mu},\mathbf{V})$.

Marginal and conditional distributions: Let $\mathbf{y} \sim N_k(\mathbf{0},\mathbf{V})$. Partition $\mathbf{y}$ into

$$\begin{bmatrix} \mathbf{y}_1 \\ \mathbf{y}_2 \end{bmatrix}$$

of k_1 and k_2 variates, respectively ($k_1 + k_2 = k$). Partition $\mathbf{V}$ conformably as

$$\begin{bmatrix} \mathbf{V}_{11} & \mathbf{V}_{12} \\ \mathbf{V}_{21} & \mathbf{V}_{22} \end{bmatrix}$$

We will show that the marginal distribution of $\mathbf{y}_1$ is $N_{k_1}(\mathbf{0},\mathbf{V}_{11})$ and the conditional distribution of $\mathbf{y}_2$ given $\mathbf{y}_1$ is $N_{k_2}(\mathbf{V}_{21}\mathbf{V}_{11}^{-1}\mathbf{y}_1, \mathbf{V}_{22} - \mathbf{V}_{21}\mathbf{V}_{11}^{-1}\mathbf{V}_{12})$. Note that [see Appendix A, Eq. (A-20)]

$$|\mathbf{V}| = |\mathbf{V}_{11}| \cdot |\mathbf{V}_{22} - \mathbf{V}_{21}\mathbf{V}_{11}^{-1}\mathbf{V}_{12}|$$

and

$$\mathbf{V}^{-1} = \begin{bmatrix} \mathbf{V}_{11}^{-1} & \mathbf{0} \\ \mathbf{0} & \mathbf{0} \end{bmatrix} + \begin{bmatrix} -\mathbf{V}_{11}^{-1}\mathbf{V}_{12} \\ \mathbf{I}_{k_2} \end{bmatrix} \left[\mathbf{V}_{22} - \mathbf{V}_{21}\mathbf{V}_{11}^{-1}\mathbf{V}_{12}\right]^{-1} \left[-\mathbf{V}_{21}\mathbf{V}_{11}^{-1}, \mathbf{I}_{k_2}\right]$$

Hence

$$\begin{aligned} \mathbf{y}'\mathbf{V}^{-1}\mathbf{y} &= \begin{bmatrix} \mathbf{y}_1 \\ \mathbf{y}_2 \end{bmatrix}' \mathbf{V}^{-1}[\mathbf{y}_1\mathbf{y}_2] \\ &= \mathbf{y}_1'\mathbf{V}_{11}^{-1}\mathbf{y}_1 + (\mathbf{y}_2 - \mathbf{V}_{21}\mathbf{V}_{11}^{-1}\mathbf{y}_1)'\left[\mathbf{V}_{22} - \mathbf{V}_{21}\mathbf{V}_{11}^{-1}\mathbf{V}_{12}\right]^{-1}(\mathbf{y}_2 - \mathbf{V}_{21}\mathbf{V}_{11}^{-1}\mathbf{y}_1) \\ &= Q_1 + Q_2 \qquad \text{(say)} \end{aligned}$$

Thus, we can divide $|\mathbf{V}|$ and the exponent in the expression for $P(\mathbf{y})\,d\mathbf{y}$ into two parts, one involving $\mathbf{y}_1$ and $\mathbf{V}_{11}$ only.

$$\begin{aligned} P(\mathbf{y}_1,\mathbf{y}_2) = &\left[\frac{1}{|\mathbf{V}_{11}|^{1/2}(2\pi)^{k_1/2}} e^{-(1/2)Q_1}\ d\mathbf{y}_1\right] \\ &\cdot \left[\frac{1}{|\mathbf{V}_{22} - \mathbf{V}_{21}\mathbf{V}_{11}^{-1}\mathbf{V}_{12}|^{1/2}(2\pi)^{k_2/2}} e^{(1/2)Q_2}\ d\mathbf{y}_2\right] = P(\mathbf{y}_1) \cdot P(\mathbf{y}_2 \mid \mathbf{y}_1) \end{aligned}$$

This shows that the marginal distribution of $\mathbf{y}_1$ is $N_{k_1}(\mathbf{0},\mathbf{V}_{11})$ and the conditional distribution of $\mathbf{y}_2$ given $\mathbf{y}_1$ is $N_{k_2}(\mathbf{V}_{21}\mathbf{V}_{11}^{-1}\mathbf{y}_1, \mathbf{V}_{22}-\mathbf{V}_{21}\mathbf{V}_{11}^{-1}\mathbf{V}_{12})$.

Distributions of quadratic forms: We need some preliminary definitions and results. If $x_1, x_2, \ldots, x_n$ are $IN(0,1)$ or $\mathbf{x} \sim N_n(\mathbf{0},\mathbf{I})$, the distribution of $Z = \sum_{i=1}^{n} x_i^2 = \mathbf{x}'\mathbf{x}$ is said to be the chi-square-distribution degrees of freedom n. We will write this as $Z \sim \chi^2(n)$. If x is a random variable, $\phi(t) = E(e^{itx})$ is said to be the characteristic function of x. ($i = \sqrt{-1}$ and t is a real number.) There are two important theorems in characteristic functions:

1. *Uniqueness Theorem:* There exists a one-to-one correspondence between characteristic functions and probability distribution functions. This result enables us to determine the distribution function from the characteristic function.
2. *Independence Theorem:* If x_1 and x_2 are two random variables with characteristic functions $\phi_1(t)$ and $\phi_2(t)$, respectively, and $\phi(t)$ is the characteristic function of $x_1 + x_2$, then x_1 and x_2 are independent if and only if $\phi(t) = \phi_1(t) \cdot \phi_2(t)$.

Using these definitions and results, we will now state the results on quadratic forms:

1. Let $\mathbf{y} \sim N_k(\mathbf{0},\mathbf{V})$. Then $\mathbf{y}'\mathbf{V}^{-1}\mathbf{y} \sim \chi^2(k)$.
   Proof: Let $\mathbf{Z} = \mathbf{V}^{-1/2}\mathbf{y}$. Then $\mathbf{Z} \sim N_k(\mathbf{0},\mathbf{I})$. Hence $\mathbf{Z}'\mathbf{Z} \sim \chi^2(k)$, that is, $\mathbf{y}'\mathbf{V}^{-1}\mathbf{y} \sim \chi^2(k)$.
2. Let $\mathbf{y} \sim N_k(\mathbf{0},\mathbf{I})$ and $\mathbf{A}$ be a $k \times k$ matrix of rank $r(< k)$. Then $\mathbf{y}'\mathbf{A}\mathbf{y} \sim \chi^2(r)$ if and only if $\mathbf{A}$ is idempotent.
   Proof: There exists an orthogonal matrix $\mathbf{C}$ such that $\mathbf{C}'\mathbf{A}\mathbf{C}$ is a diagonal matrix with the characteristic roots of $\mathbf{A}$ along the diagonal. Consider the transformation $\mathbf{Z} = \mathbf{C}'\mathbf{y}$ or $\mathbf{y} = \mathbf{C}\mathbf{Z}$. Hence $\mathbf{y}'\mathbf{A}\mathbf{y} = \mathbf{Z}'\mathbf{C}'\mathbf{A}\mathbf{C}\mathbf{Z} = \sum \lambda_i Z_i^2$. Since the transformation is orthogonal, if $\mathbf{y} \sim N(\mathbf{0},\mathbf{I})$, then $\mathbf{Z} \sim N(\mathbf{0},\mathbf{I})$. Thus $\mathbf{y}'\mathbf{A}\mathbf{y} \sim \chi^2(k)$ if and only if r of the λ_i are equal to 1 and the rest zero, i.e., if and only if $\mathbf{A}$ is an idempotent matrix of rank r.
3. If $\mathbf{y} \sim N_k(\mathbf{0},\mathbf{V})$, $\mathbf{y}'\mathbf{A}\mathbf{y} \sim \chi^2(k)$ iff $\mathbf{AVA} = \mathbf{A}$.
   Proof: Put $\mathbf{Z} = \mathbf{V}^{-1/2}\mathbf{y}$. Then $\mathbf{Z} \sim N_k(\mathbf{0},\mathbf{I})$ and $\mathbf{y}'\mathbf{A}\mathbf{y} = \mathbf{Z}'\mathbf{V}^{1/2}\mathbf{A}\mathbf{V}^{1/2}\mathbf{Z}$. Hence the necessary and sufficient condition required is that $\mathbf{V}^{1/2}\mathbf{A}\mathbf{V}^{1/2}$ be idempotent or $\mathbf{AVA} = \mathbf{A}$.
4. If $\mathbf{y} \sim N_k(\mathbf{0},\mathbf{I})$, the characteristic function of $\mathbf{y}'\mathbf{A}\mathbf{y}$ is $|\mathbf{I} - 2it\mathbf{A}|^{-1/2}$.
   Proof: Suppose that $\mathbf{x} \sim N_k(\mathbf{0},\mathbf{V})$. Then since the integral of a probability density is 1, we have

$$\frac{1}{|\mathbf{V}|^{1/2}} \int \frac{1}{(2\pi)^{k/2}} e^{-(1/2)\mathbf{x}'\mathbf{V}^{-1}\mathbf{x}} \, d\mathbf{x} = 1$$

or

$$\int \frac{1}{(2\pi)^{k/2}} e^{-(1/2)\mathbf{x}'\mathbf{V}^{-1}\mathbf{x}} \, d\mathbf{x} = \frac{1}{|\mathbf{V}^{-1}|^{1/2}}$$

We will use this integral in our derivation. Since $\mathbf{y} \sim N_k(\mathbf{0},\mathbf{I})$, the characteristic function of $\mathbf{y}'\mathbf{A}\mathbf{y}$ is

$$E(e^{it\mathbf{y}'\mathbf{A}\mathbf{y}}) = \frac{1}{(2\pi)^{k/2}} \int e^{-(1/2)\mathbf{y}'\mathbf{y} + it\mathbf{y}'\mathbf{A}\mathbf{y}}\, d\mathbf{y}$$

$$= \frac{1}{(2\pi)^{k/2}} \int e^{-(1/2)\mathbf{y}'(\mathbf{I} - 2it\mathbf{A})\mathbf{y}}\, d\mathbf{y}$$

$$= \frac{1}{|\mathbf{I} - 2it\mathbf{A}|^{1/2}} \quad \text{from the integral derived above}$$

5. If $\mathbf{y} \sim N_k(\mathbf{0},\mathbf{I})$, $\mathbf{y}'\mathbf{A}_1\mathbf{y}$ and $\mathbf{y}'\mathbf{A}_2\mathbf{y}$ are independently distributed iff $\mathbf{A}_1\mathbf{A}_2 = \mathbf{0}$.
Proof: The characteristic functions of $\mathbf{y}'\mathbf{A}_1\mathbf{y}, \mathbf{y}'\mathbf{A}_2\mathbf{y}$, and $\mathbf{y}'(\mathbf{A}_1 + \mathbf{A}_2)\mathbf{y}$ are, respectively, $|\mathbf{I} - 2it\mathbf{A}_1|^{-1/2}$, $|\mathbf{I} - 2it\mathbf{A}_2|^{-1/2}$, and $|\mathbf{I} - it(\mathbf{A}_1 + \mathbf{A}_2)|^{-1/2}$.
By the independence theorem, $\mathbf{y}'\mathbf{A}_1\mathbf{y}$ and $\mathbf{y}'\mathbf{A}_2\mathbf{y}$ are independently distributed iff

$$|\mathbf{I} - 2it(\mathbf{A}_1 + \mathbf{A}_2)|^{-1/2} = |\mathbf{I} - 2it\mathbf{A}_1|^{-1/2} \cdot |\mathbf{I} - 2it\mathbf{A}_2|^{-1/2}$$

that is, iff $\mathbf{A}_1\mathbf{A}_2 = \mathbf{0}$.
6. If $\mathbf{y} \sim N_k(\mathbf{0},\mathbf{I})$ and $\mathbf{A}_1$ and $\mathbf{A}_2$ are $k \times k$ matrices of ranks r_1 and r_2, respectively, then $\mathbf{y}'\mathbf{A}_1\mathbf{y}$ and $\mathbf{y}'\mathbf{A}_2\mathbf{y}$ are independent χ^2 variates iff $\mathbf{A}_1\mathbf{A}_2 = \mathbf{0}$ and $\mathbf{A}_1$ and $\mathbf{A}_2$ are both idempotent.
Proof: Result follows from results 2 and 5.
7. If $\mathbf{y} \sim N_k(\mathbf{0},\mathbf{V})$, the necessary sufficient conditions for the above result to hold good are

$$\mathbf{A}_1\mathbf{V}\mathbf{A}_1 = \mathbf{A}_1 \qquad \mathbf{A}_2\mathbf{V}\mathbf{A}_2 = \mathbf{A}_2 \qquad \text{and} \qquad \mathbf{A}_1\mathbf{V}\mathbf{A}_2 = \mathbf{0}$$

Proof: Result follows from the transformation $\mathbf{Z} = \mathbf{V}^{-1/2}\mathbf{y}$ and result 6.
8. Suppose $\mathbf{y} \sim N_k(\boldsymbol{\mu},\mathbf{I})$. Then $(\mathbf{y} - \boldsymbol{\mu}) \sim N_k(\mathbf{0},\mathbf{I})$, and we know that $(\mathbf{y} - \boldsymbol{\mu})' \cdot (\mathbf{y} - \boldsymbol{\mu})$ has a χ^2-distribution degrees of freedom k. This is often called the central χ^2 distribution. The distribution of $\mathbf{y}'\mathbf{y}$ is said to be noncentral χ^2 with noncentrality parameter $\boldsymbol{\mu}'\boldsymbol{\mu}$. We have the following result as an extension of result 2: $(\mathbf{y} - \boldsymbol{\mu})'\mathbf{A}(\mathbf{y} - \boldsymbol{\mu}) \sim \chi^2(r)$ iff $\mathbf{A}$ is of rank r and idempotent. Also, if $\mathbf{A}$ is idempotent, $\mathbf{y}'\mathbf{A}\mathbf{y}$ has a noncentral χ^2-distribution degrees of freedom r and noncentrality parameter $\boldsymbol{\mu}'\mathbf{A}\boldsymbol{\mu}$.

Tests of significance in the linear model: With these preliminaries we return to the linear model (B-1). We make the additional assumption that the residuals are normally distributed. Hence $\mathbf{u} \sim N_n(\mathbf{0},\mathbf{I}\sigma^2)$. We have, from (B-3), $\mathbf{X}(\hat{\boldsymbol{\beta}} - \boldsymbol{\beta}) = \mathbf{X}(\mathbf{X}'\mathbf{X})^{-1}\mathbf{X}'\mathbf{u} = \mathbf{M}\mathbf{u}$ and $\mathbf{y} - \mathbf{X}\hat{\boldsymbol{\beta}} = \mathbf{X}\boldsymbol{\beta} + \mathbf{u} - \mathbf{X}\hat{\boldsymbol{\beta}} = [\mathbf{I} - \mathbf{X}(\mathbf{X}'\mathbf{X})^{-1}\mathbf{X}']\mathbf{u} = \mathbf{N}\mathbf{u}$ where

$$\mathbf{M} = \mathbf{X}(\mathbf{X}'\mathbf{X})^{-1}\mathbf{X}' \qquad \text{and} \qquad \mathbf{N} = \mathbf{I} - \mathbf{M} \tag{B-7}$$

It can be easily verified that $\mathbf{M}^2 = \mathbf{M}$ and $\mathbf{N}^2 = \mathbf{N}$, that is, **M** and **N** are idempotent. Also $\mathbf{MN} = \mathbf{0}$.

$$\text{Rank } \mathbf{M} = \text{tr } \mathbf{M} = \text{tr } \mathbf{X}(\mathbf{X}'\mathbf{X})^{-1}\mathbf{X}' = \text{tr}(\mathbf{X}'\mathbf{X})^{-1}\mathbf{X}'\mathbf{X}$$
$$= \text{tr } \mathbf{I}_k = k$$
$$\text{Rank } \mathbf{N} = n - k$$

Hence $(1/\sigma^2)\ \mathbf{u}'\mathbf{M}\mathbf{u}$ and $(1/\sigma^2)\ \mathbf{u}'\mathbf{N}\mathbf{u}$ have independent χ^2 distributions with degrees of freedom k and $n-k$, respectively. But $(\hat{\boldsymbol{\beta}} - \boldsymbol{\beta})'\mathbf{X}'\mathbf{X}(\hat{\boldsymbol{\beta}} - \boldsymbol{\beta}) = \mathbf{u}'\mathbf{M}^2\mathbf{u} = \mathbf{u}'\mathbf{M}\mathbf{u}$ and $(\mathbf{y} - \mathbf{X}\hat{\boldsymbol{\beta}})'(\mathbf{y} - \mathbf{X}\hat{\boldsymbol{\beta}}) = \mathbf{u}'\mathbf{N}^2\mathbf{u} = \mathbf{u}'\mathbf{N}\mathbf{u}$. Hence

$$\frac{(\hat{\boldsymbol{\beta}} - \boldsymbol{\beta})'\mathbf{X}'\mathbf{X}(\hat{\boldsymbol{\beta}} - \boldsymbol{\beta})/k}{(\mathbf{y} - \mathbf{X}\hat{\boldsymbol{\beta}})'(\mathbf{y} - \mathbf{X}\hat{\boldsymbol{\beta}})/(n-k)}$$

has an F-distribution degrees of freedom k and $n-k$. This result can be used to construct confidence regions for $\boldsymbol{\beta}$ and also to apply any tests of significance. To test the hypothesis $\boldsymbol{\beta} = \boldsymbol{\beta}_0$, we substitute the value $\boldsymbol{\beta}_0$ for $\boldsymbol{\beta}$ in the above test statistic and use it as an F variate. Whether or not the hypothesis is true, the denominator, which depends on $\hat{\boldsymbol{\beta}}$ only, always has a χ^2-distribution degrees of freedom $n-k$. The numerator has a χ^2 distribution only if the null hypothesis is true. When it is false, it has a noncentral χ^2 distribution, and this can be used to find the power of this test.

Tests of linear restrictions: Consider the estimation of $\boldsymbol{\beta}$ in (B-1) subject to $r(<k)$ linearly independent restrictions $\mathbf{R}\boldsymbol{\beta} = \mathbf{d}$, where $\mathbf{R}$ is an $r \times k$ matrix of rank r and $\mathbf{d}$ is an $r \times 1$ vector. To get the constrained least-squares estimator, we minimize $(\mathbf{y} - \mathbf{X}\boldsymbol{\beta})'(\mathbf{y} - \mathbf{X}\boldsymbol{\beta})$ subject to $\mathbf{R}\boldsymbol{\beta} = \mathbf{d}$. Hence we minimize

$$Q = (\mathbf{y} - \mathbf{X}\boldsymbol{\beta})'(\mathbf{y} - \mathbf{X}\boldsymbol{\beta}) - 2\boldsymbol{\lambda}'(\mathbf{R}\boldsymbol{\beta} - \mathbf{d})$$
$$= \mathbf{y}'\mathbf{y} - 2\boldsymbol{\beta}'\mathbf{X}'\mathbf{y} + \boldsymbol{\beta}'\mathbf{X}'\mathbf{X}\boldsymbol{\beta} + 2\boldsymbol{\lambda}'(\mathbf{R}\boldsymbol{\beta} - \mathbf{d})$$

where $\boldsymbol{\lambda}$ is the vector of lagrangian multipliers.

$$\frac{\partial Q}{\partial \boldsymbol{\beta}} = \mathbf{0} \quad \text{gives} \quad -2\mathbf{X}'\mathbf{y} + 2\mathbf{X}'\mathbf{X}\boldsymbol{\beta} + 2\mathbf{R}'\boldsymbol{\lambda} = \mathbf{0} \tag{B-8}$$

$$\frac{\partial Q}{\partial \boldsymbol{\lambda}} = \mathbf{0} \quad \text{gives} \quad \mathbf{R}\boldsymbol{\beta} - \mathbf{d} = \mathbf{0} \tag{B-9}$$

We have to eliminate $\boldsymbol{\lambda}$ from Eq. (B-8). Premultiply (B-8) by $\mathbf{R}(\mathbf{X}'\mathbf{X})^{-1}$. We get

$$\left[\mathbf{R}(\mathbf{X}'\mathbf{X})^{-1}\mathbf{R}'\right]\boldsymbol{\lambda} = \mathbf{R}(\mathbf{X}'\mathbf{X})^{-1}\mathbf{X}'\mathbf{y} - \mathbf{R}\boldsymbol{\beta}$$
$$= \mathbf{R}\hat{\boldsymbol{\beta}} - \mathbf{d}$$

where $\hat{\boldsymbol{\beta}} = (\mathbf{X}'\mathbf{X})^{-1}\mathbf{X}'\mathbf{y}$ is the unconstrained least-squares estimator. Since $\mathbf{R}$ is of rank r, $\mathbf{R}(\mathbf{X}'\mathbf{X})^{-1}\mathbf{R}'$ is an $r \times r$ matrix of rank r, and its inverse exists. Hence

$$\boldsymbol{\lambda} = \left[\mathbf{R}(\mathbf{X}'\mathbf{X})^{-1}\mathbf{R}'\right]^{-1}\left[\mathbf{R}\hat{\boldsymbol{\beta}} - \mathbf{d}\right]$$

Substituting this in (B-8) and premultiplying throughout by $(\mathbf{X}'\mathbf{X})^{-1}$, we get the constrained least-squares estimator $\boldsymbol{\beta}^*$ as

$$\begin{aligned}\boldsymbol{\beta}^* &= \hat{\boldsymbol{\beta}} - (\mathbf{X}'\mathbf{X})^{-1}\mathbf{R}'\boldsymbol{\lambda} \\ &= \hat{\boldsymbol{\beta}} - (\mathbf{X}'\mathbf{X})^{-1}\mathbf{R}'\left[\mathbf{R}(\mathbf{X}'\mathbf{X})^{-1}\mathbf{R}'\right]^{-1}(\mathbf{R}\hat{\boldsymbol{\beta}} - \mathbf{d}) \qquad \text{(B-10)}\end{aligned}$$

Let us define the unrestricted residual sum of squares as URSS $= (\mathbf{y} - \mathbf{X}\hat{\boldsymbol{\beta}})'(\mathbf{y} - \mathbf{X}\hat{\boldsymbol{\beta}})$ and the restricted residual sum of squares as RRSS $= (\mathbf{y} - \mathbf{X}\boldsymbol{\beta}^*)'(\mathbf{y} - \mathbf{X}\boldsymbol{\beta}^*)$. We will show that, when the hypothesis $\mathbf{R}\boldsymbol{\beta} = \mathbf{d}$ is true, (RRSS − URSS) and URSS have independent χ^2 distributions and hence one can use

$$\frac{(\text{RRSS} - \text{URSS})/r}{\text{URSS}/(n-k)}$$

as an F variate with degrees of freedom r and $(n - k)$ to test this hypothesis. Consider

$$\begin{aligned}(\mathbf{y} - \mathbf{X}\boldsymbol{\beta}^*)'(\mathbf{y} - \mathbf{X}\boldsymbol{\beta}^*) &= (\mathbf{y} - \mathbf{X}\hat{\boldsymbol{\beta}} + \mathbf{X}\hat{\boldsymbol{\beta}} - \mathbf{X}\boldsymbol{\beta}^*)'(\mathbf{y} - \mathbf{X}\hat{\boldsymbol{\beta}} + \mathbf{X}\hat{\boldsymbol{\beta}} - \mathbf{X}\boldsymbol{\beta}^*) \\ &= (\mathbf{y} - \mathbf{X}\hat{\boldsymbol{\beta}})'(\mathbf{y} - \mathbf{X}\hat{\boldsymbol{\beta}}) + (\hat{\boldsymbol{\beta}} - \boldsymbol{\beta}^*)'\mathbf{X}'\mathbf{X}(\hat{\boldsymbol{\beta}} - \boldsymbol{\beta}^*)\end{aligned}$$

The cross-product terms vanish by virtue of the fact that $\mathbf{X}'(\mathbf{y} - \mathbf{X}\hat{\boldsymbol{\beta}}) = \mathbf{0}$. Hence RRSS − URSS $= (\hat{\boldsymbol{\beta}} - \boldsymbol{\beta}^*)'\mathbf{X}'\mathbf{X}(\hat{\boldsymbol{\beta}} - \boldsymbol{\beta}^*)$. But from Eq. (B-10) we have

$$\mathbf{X}(\hat{\boldsymbol{\beta}} - \boldsymbol{\beta}^*) = \mathbf{X}(\mathbf{X}'\mathbf{X})^{-1}\mathbf{R}'\left[\mathbf{R}(\mathbf{X}'\mathbf{X})^{-1}\mathbf{R}'\right]^{-1}\mathbf{R}(\hat{\boldsymbol{\beta}} - \boldsymbol{\beta})$$

Since $\hat{\boldsymbol{\beta}} - \boldsymbol{\beta} = (\mathbf{X}'\mathbf{X})^{-1}\mathbf{X}'\mathbf{u}$, we have

$$\mathbf{X}(\hat{\boldsymbol{\beta}} - \boldsymbol{\beta}^*) = (\mathbf{BDB}')\mathbf{u}$$

where $\mathbf{B} = \mathbf{X}(\mathbf{X}'\mathbf{X})^{-1}\mathbf{R}'$ and $\mathbf{D} = [\mathbf{R}(\mathbf{X}'\mathbf{X})^{-1}\mathbf{R}']^{-1}$. But $\mathbf{B}'\mathbf{B} = \mathbf{D}^{-1}$. Hence $(\mathbf{BDB}')(\mathbf{BDB}') = (\mathbf{BDB}')$. Thus $\mathbf{BDB}'$ is idempotent. Also

$$\begin{aligned}\text{rank } \mathbf{BDB}' &= \text{tr } \mathbf{BDB}' \\ &= \text{tr } \mathbf{DB}'\mathbf{B} \\ &= \text{tr } \mathbf{DD}^{-1} = \text{tr } \mathbf{I}_r = r\end{aligned}$$

Hence $(1/\sigma^2)$ (RRSS − URSS) $= (1/\sigma^2)(\hat{\boldsymbol{\beta}} - \boldsymbol{\beta}^*)'\mathbf{X}'\mathbf{X}(\hat{\boldsymbol{\beta}} - \boldsymbol{\beta}^*)$ has a χ^2-distribution degrees of freedom r. Also we noted earlier that

$$\frac{1}{\sigma^2}\text{URSS} = \frac{1}{\sigma^2}(\mathbf{y} - \mathbf{X}\hat{\boldsymbol{\beta}})'(\mathbf{y} - \mathbf{X}\hat{\boldsymbol{\beta}}) = \frac{1}{\sigma^2}\mathbf{u}'\mathbf{N}\mathbf{u}$$

has a χ^2-distribution degrees of freedom $(n - k)$. Further it can be easily verified that $\mathbf{B}'\mathbf{N} = 0$ and thus $\mathbf{BDB}'\mathbf{N} = \mathbf{0}$. Hence the two χ^2's are independent. Thus we get the F test

$$F = \frac{(\text{RRSS} - \text{URSS})/r}{\text{URSS}/n - k} \sim F_{r,n-k}$$

Addition of observations: Suppose we estimate the linear model (B-1) with n_1 observations. Let RSS_1 be the residual sum of squares. Suppose we reestimate it with n_2 extra observations. The number of observations is now $n = n_1 + n_2$. Let RSS be the residual sum of squares. Then $(\text{RSS} - \text{RSS}_1)$ and RSS_1 have independent χ^2 distributions.

Before we prove this, we note the result that if **A** and **B** are symmetric idempotent matrices and $(\mathbf{A} - \mathbf{B})\mathbf{B} = \mathbf{0}$, then $\mathbf{A} - \mathbf{B}$ is idempotent.
Proof: Since $(\mathbf{A} - \mathbf{B})\mathbf{B} = \mathbf{0}$, we have $\mathbf{AB} = \mathbf{B}^2 = \mathbf{B}$ and $\mathbf{BA} = \mathbf{B}$. Hence $(\mathbf{A} - \mathbf{B})(\mathbf{A} - \mathbf{B}) = \mathbf{A}^2 + \mathbf{B}^2 - \mathbf{AB} - \mathbf{BA} = \mathbf{A} + \mathbf{B} - 2\mathbf{B} = \mathbf{A} - \mathbf{B}$, that is, $(\mathbf{A} - \mathbf{B})$ is idempotent.

Now let us write

$$\mathbf{y}_1 = \mathbf{X}_1\boldsymbol{\beta} + \mathbf{u}_1 \qquad \text{for the first } n_1 \text{ observations}$$
$$\mathbf{y}_2 = \mathbf{X}_2\boldsymbol{\beta} + \mathbf{u}_2 \qquad \text{for the second } n_2 \text{ observations}$$

Write

$$\mathbf{u} = \begin{bmatrix} \mathbf{u}_1 \\ \mathbf{u}_2 \end{bmatrix} \qquad \text{and} \qquad \mathbf{X} = \begin{bmatrix} \mathbf{X}_1 \\ \mathbf{X}_2 \end{bmatrix}$$

$$\text{RSS}_1 = \mathbf{u}_1'\mathbf{N}_1\mathbf{u}_1 \qquad \text{where} \qquad \mathbf{N}_1 = \mathbf{I}_{n_1} - \mathbf{X}_1(\mathbf{X}_1'\mathbf{X}_1)^{-1}\mathbf{X}_1'$$
$$\text{RSS} = \mathbf{u}'\mathbf{N}\mathbf{u} \qquad \text{where} \qquad \mathbf{N} = \mathbf{I}_n - \mathbf{X}(\mathbf{X}'\mathbf{X})^{-1}\mathbf{X}'$$

We can write

$$\mathbf{N}_1^* = \begin{bmatrix} \mathbf{N}_1 & \mathbf{0} \\ \mathbf{0} & \mathbf{0} \end{bmatrix}$$

so that $\text{RSS}_1 = \mathbf{u}'\mathbf{N}_1^*\mathbf{u}$. Also, we can write **N** as

$$\mathbf{N} = \begin{bmatrix} \mathbf{N}_{11} & \mathbf{N}_{12} \\ \mathbf{N}_{21} & \mathbf{N}_{22} \end{bmatrix}$$

where
$$\mathbf{N}_{11} = \mathbf{I}_{n_1} - \mathbf{X}_1(\mathbf{X}'\mathbf{X})^{-1}\mathbf{X}_1'$$
$$\mathbf{N}_{12} = -\mathbf{X}_1(\mathbf{X}'\mathbf{X})^{-1}\mathbf{X}_2'$$
$$\mathbf{N}_{21} = -\mathbf{X}_2(\mathbf{X}'\mathbf{X})^{-1}\mathbf{X}_1'$$
$$\mathbf{N}_{22} = \mathbf{I}_{n_2} - \mathbf{X}_2(\mathbf{X}'\mathbf{X})^{-1}\mathbf{X}_2'$$

We know that **N** and $\mathbf{N}_1^*$ are idempotent matrices of ranks $(n - k)$ and $(n_1 - k)$, respectively. All we want to prove is that $(\mathbf{N} - \mathbf{N}_1^*)\mathbf{N}_1^* = \mathbf{0}$. Then our result follows. Now

$$(\mathbf{N} - \mathbf{N}_1^*)\mathbf{N}_1^* = \begin{bmatrix} \mathbf{N}_{11} - \mathbf{N}_1 & \mathbf{N}_{12} \\ \mathbf{N}_{21} & \mathbf{N}_{22} \end{bmatrix}\begin{bmatrix} \mathbf{N}_1 & \mathbf{0} \\ \mathbf{0} & \mathbf{0} \end{bmatrix}$$
$$= \begin{bmatrix} (\mathbf{N}_{11} - \mathbf{N}_1)\mathbf{N}_1 & \mathbf{0} \\ \mathbf{N}_{21}\mathbf{N}_1 & \mathbf{0} \end{bmatrix}$$

Since $\mathbf{X}_1'\mathbf{N}_1 = \mathbf{0}$, we have $\mathbf{N}_{21}\mathbf{N}_1 = \mathbf{0}$. Also $\mathbf{N}_{11} - \mathbf{N}_1 = \mathbf{X}_1[(\mathbf{X}'\mathbf{X})^{-1} - (\mathbf{X}_1'\mathbf{X}_1)^{-1}]\mathbf{X}_1'$. Again since $\mathbf{X}_1'\mathbf{N}_1 = \mathbf{0}$, we have $(\mathbf{N}_{11} - \mathbf{N}_1)\mathbf{N}_1 = \mathbf{0}$. Thus $(\mathbf{N} - \mathbf{N}_1^*)\mathbf{N}_1^* = \mathbf{0}$. Hence $(\mathbf{N} - \mathbf{N}_1^*)$ is also idempotent.

$$\text{Rank}(\mathbf{N} - \mathbf{N}_1^*) = \text{tr}(\mathbf{N} - \mathbf{N}_1^*) = (n - k) - (n_1 - k) = n_2$$

Hence $(\text{RSS} - \text{RSS}_1) = \mathbf{u}'(\mathbf{N} - \mathbf{N}_1^*)\mathbf{u}$ and $\text{RSS}_1 = \mathbf{u}'\mathbf{N}_1^*\mathbf{u}$ have independent χ^2 distributions and

$$\frac{(\text{RSS} - \text{RSS}_1)/n_2}{\text{RSS}/(n_1 - k)}$$

has an F-distribution degrees of freedom $n_2, n_1 - k$.

Tests for stability: Often we estimate the same regression model for two different time periods and we are interested in knowing whether there has been a structural change. Suppose the model is $\mathbf{y}_1 = \mathbf{X}_1\boldsymbol{\beta}_1 + \mathbf{u}_1$ with n_1 observations for period 1 and $\mathbf{y}_2 = \mathbf{X}_2\boldsymbol{\beta}_2 + \mathbf{u}_2$ with n_2 observations for period 2.The absence of structural change implies $\beta_1 = \beta_2$. There are two ways of going about testing this hypothesis. One is to pool the data and write

$$\begin{bmatrix} \mathbf{y}_1 \\ \mathbf{y}_2 \end{bmatrix} = \begin{bmatrix} \mathbf{X}_1 & \mathbf{0} \\ \mathbf{0} & \mathbf{X}_2 \end{bmatrix} \begin{bmatrix} \boldsymbol{\beta}_1 \\ \boldsymbol{\beta}_2 \end{bmatrix} + \begin{bmatrix} \mathbf{u}_1 \\ \mathbf{u}_2 \end{bmatrix}$$

and estimate it with and without the restrictions $\boldsymbol{\beta}_1 = \boldsymbol{\beta}_2$. If there are k elements each in $\boldsymbol{\beta}_1$ and $\boldsymbol{\beta}_2$, the unrestricted residual sum of squares URSS has $n_1 + n_2 - 2k$ degrees of freedom. The restricted residual sum of squares RRSS has $n_1 + n_2 - k$ degrees of freedom. Hence we use the F test

$$\frac{(\text{RRSS} - \text{URSS})/k}{\text{URSS}/(n_1 + n_2 - 2k)} \sim F_{k, n_1 + n_2 - 2k} \tag{B-11}$$

The URSS can be computed by estimating each regression equation separately and taking the sum of the separate residual sums of squares. The RRSS can be computed by pooling the data and estimating a single regression equation. Clearly, the test cannot be applied if either n_1 or n_2 is less than k.

An alternative way of testing the hypothesis of no structural change is to see whether the later n_2 observations are generated by the same model as the first n_1 observations. In this case we compute RSS_1, the residual sum of squares for the first n_1 observations, and RSS, the residual sum of squares for the $n = n_1 + n_2$ observations, and use

$$\frac{(\text{RSS} - \text{RSS}_1)/n_2}{\text{RSS}_1/(n_1 - k)} \sim F_{n_2, n_1 - k} \tag{B-12}$$

This test is not as powerful as that given by the statistic (B-11). However, it can be applied even if $n_2 < k$. Thus Eq. (B-12) is useful when (B-11) cannot be applied.

Sets of regression equations: We saw that if we consider the regression of $\mathbf{y}$ on $\mathbf{X}$, the estimates of the regression parameters are

$$\hat{\boldsymbol{\beta}} = (\mathbf{X}'\mathbf{X})^{-1}\mathbf{X}'\mathbf{y}$$

and the residual sum of squares is $\mathbf{y}'\mathbf{y} - \mathbf{y}'\mathbf{X}(\mathbf{X}'\mathbf{X})^{-1}\mathbf{X}'\mathbf{y}$. Consider m variables $\mathbf{y}_1, \mathbf{y}_2, \ldots, \mathbf{y}_m$. Denote the observations by $\mathbf{Y}$, which is an $n \times m$ matrix. Let the matrix of regression parameters be $\mathbf{B}$, which is a $k \times m$ matrix. The ith column of $\mathbf{B}$ is the set of regression parameters of $\mathbf{y}_i$ on $\mathbf{X}$. Then $\hat{\mathbf{B}} = (\mathbf{X}'\mathbf{X})^{-1}\mathbf{X}'\mathbf{Y}$ and the matrix of residual sums of squares and sums of products is $\mathbf{Y'Y} - \mathbf{Y'X(X'X)^{-1}X'Y}$. We will be using these expressions in further work.

Specification errors: misspecified variables: Suppose that the true model is

$$\mathbf{y} = \mathbf{X}\boldsymbol{\beta} + \mathbf{u} \qquad \mathbf{X} \text{ is an } n \times k \text{ matrix} \tag{B-13}$$

Instead we estimate

$$\mathbf{y} = \mathbf{Z}\boldsymbol{\delta} + \mathbf{v} \qquad \mathbf{Z} \text{ is an } n \times r \text{ matrix} \tag{B-14}$$

r can be less than, equal to, or greater than k. The variables in $\mathbf{Z}$ may include some variables in $\mathbf{X}$. Then $\hat{\boldsymbol{\delta}} = (\mathbf{Z'Z})^{-1}\mathbf{Z'y}$

$$= (\mathbf{Z'Z})^{-1}\mathbf{Z'}(\mathbf{X}\boldsymbol{\beta} + \mathbf{u})$$

$$= \mathbf{P}\boldsymbol{\beta} + (\mathbf{Z'Z})^{-1}\mathbf{Z'u}$$

$$E(\hat{\boldsymbol{\delta}}) = \mathbf{P}\boldsymbol{\beta} \qquad \text{since} \qquad E(\mathbf{u}) = \mathbf{0} \tag{B-15}$$

$\mathbf{P} = (\mathbf{Z'Z})^{-1}\mathbf{Z'X}$ is the matrix of regression coefficients of the variables $\mathbf{X}$ in the true model on the variables $\mathbf{Z}$ in the misspecified model.

As an illustration, suppose the true equation is

$$y = \beta_1 x_1 + \beta_2 x_2 + u$$

Instead we estimate

$$y = \delta_1 x_1 + \delta_2 z + V$$

Then P is obtained by regressing each of x_1 and x_2 on x_1 and z. The regression of x_1 on x_1 and z gives coefficients 1 and 0. The regression of x_2 on x_1 and z gives coefficients (say) b_{21} and b_{2Z}. These regressions are known as "auxiliary regressions." Hence

$$E\begin{bmatrix} \hat{\delta}_1 \\ \hat{\delta}_2 \end{bmatrix} = \begin{bmatrix} 1 & b_{21} \\ 0 & b_{2Z} \end{bmatrix} \begin{bmatrix} \beta_1 \\ \beta_2 \end{bmatrix}$$

or $$E(\hat{\delta}_1) = \beta_1 + b_{21}\beta_2 \qquad \text{and} \qquad E(\hat{\delta}_2) = b_{2Z}\beta_2$$

Consider now the estimate of the residual variance from the misspecified equation (B-14). It is

$$\tilde{\sigma}^2 = \frac{1}{n-r}\mathbf{y'N_Zy} \qquad \text{where} \qquad \mathbf{N_Z} = \mathbf{I} - \mathbf{Z(Z'Z)^{-1}Z'}$$

Since $\mathbf{y} = \mathbf{X}\boldsymbol{\beta} + \mathbf{u}$ and $E(\mathbf{uu'}) = \mathbf{I}\sigma^2$, we have

$$\mathbf{y'N_Zy} = (\mathbf{X}\boldsymbol{\beta} + \mathbf{u})'\mathbf{N_Z}(\mathbf{X}\boldsymbol{\beta} + \mathbf{u})$$

$$= \boldsymbol{\beta}'\mathbf{X'N_ZX}\boldsymbol{\beta} + u'\mathbf{N_Zu} + 2\boldsymbol{\beta}'\mathbf{X'N_Zu}$$

Since $E(\mathbf{u}) = \mathbf{0}$, the last term has the expected value 0. Also

$$E(\mathbf{u'N_Zu}) = \text{tr } E(\mathbf{N_Zuu'}) = \sigma^2 \text{ tr } \mathbf{N_Z} = (n-r)\sigma^2$$

Hence $$E(\tilde{\sigma}^2) = \sigma^2 + \frac{1}{n-r}\boldsymbol{\beta}'\mathbf{X'N_ZX}\boldsymbol{\beta}$$

Since the second term in this expression is $\geqslant 0$, we have

$$E(\tilde{\sigma}^2) \geqslant \sigma^2$$

Thus the estimate of the residual variance from the misspecified equation is upward-biased. This is the basis of what is known as the "minimum s^2" or the "maximum $\bar{R}^2$" rule. The rule says that if we are considering some alternative regression models we should choose the one with the minimum estimated residual variance. The idea behind it is that "on the average" the misspecified model has a larger estimated residual variance than the "true model." Of course, the suggested rule is based on the assumption that one of the models being considered is the "true" model. It should be noted, however, that $E(\tilde{\sigma}^2) = \sigma^2$ even for misspecified models if $\mathbf{X}'\mathbf{N}_Z = 0$. This will be the case if $\mathbf{Z}$ consists of the variables $\mathbf{X}$ and any number of irrelevant variables. This does not make these models any better than models with a few omitted variables for which $E(\tilde{\sigma}^2) > \sigma^2$.

Prior adjustment: Sometimes we estimate the regression equation with data adjusted for trend and seasonal variables. If these prior adjustments are done by regressing each variable on some trend variables (say, a polynomial in t) and seasonal variables (some dummies), then the estimates of the regression coefficients from data with prior adjustment will be the same as the estimates of the regression coefficients from unadjusted data with the trend and seasonal variables included as extra explanatory variables.

To prove this, consider the regression model

$$\mathbf{y} = \mathbf{X}_1\boldsymbol{\beta} + \mathbf{X}_2\boldsymbol{\gamma} + \mathbf{u} \tag{B-16}$$

where $\mathbf{X}_2$ are the trend or seasonal variables. Let $\mathbf{M} = \mathbf{I} - \mathbf{X}_2(\mathbf{X}_2'\mathbf{X}_2)^{-1}\mathbf{X}_2'$. Then $\hat{\mathbf{y}} = \mathbf{My}$ and $\hat{\mathbf{X}}_1 = \mathbf{MX}_1$ are the adjusted variables. The regression coefficients estimated from the adjusted data are

$$\begin{aligned}\mathbf{b} &= \left(\hat{\mathbf{X}}_1'\hat{\mathbf{X}}_1\right)^{-1}\hat{\mathbf{X}}_1'\hat{\mathbf{y}} \\ &= (\mathbf{X}_1'\mathbf{MX}_1)^{-1}\mathbf{X}_1'\mathbf{My}\end{aligned}$$

On the other hand, the estimates from (B-16) are

$$\begin{bmatrix} \hat{\boldsymbol{\beta}} \\ \hat{\boldsymbol{\gamma}} \end{bmatrix} = \begin{bmatrix} \mathbf{X}_1'\mathbf{X}_1 & \mathbf{X}_1'\mathbf{X}_2 \\ \mathbf{X}_2'\mathbf{X}_1 & \mathbf{X}_2'\mathbf{X}_2 \end{bmatrix}^{-1} \begin{bmatrix} \mathbf{X}_1'\mathbf{y} \\ \mathbf{X}_2'\mathbf{y} \end{bmatrix}$$

These equations can be written as

$$\mathbf{X}_1'\mathbf{X}_1\hat{\boldsymbol{\beta}} + \mathbf{X}_1'\mathbf{X}_2\hat{\boldsymbol{\gamma}} = \mathbf{X}_1'\mathbf{y}$$

and

$$\mathbf{X}_2'\mathbf{X}_1\hat{\boldsymbol{\beta}} + \mathbf{X}_2'\mathbf{X}_2\hat{\boldsymbol{\gamma}} = \mathbf{X}_2'\mathbf{y}$$

From the second equation we have

$$\hat{\boldsymbol{\gamma}} = (\mathbf{X}_2'\mathbf{X}_2)^{-1}\left[\mathbf{X}_2'\mathbf{y} - \mathbf{X}_2'\mathbf{X}_1\hat{\boldsymbol{\beta}}\right]$$

Substituting this in the first equation, we get

$$\mathbf{X}_1'\mathbf{X}_1\hat{\boldsymbol{\beta}} + \mathbf{X}_1'\mathbf{X}_2(\mathbf{X}_2'\mathbf{X}_2)^{-1}\left[\mathbf{X}_2'\mathbf{y} - \mathbf{X}_2'\mathbf{X}_1\hat{\boldsymbol{\beta}}\right] = \mathbf{X}_1'\mathbf{y}$$

or

$$(\mathbf{X}_1'\mathbf{MX}_1)\,\hat{\boldsymbol{\beta}} = \mathbf{X}_1'\mathbf{My}$$

Thus $\hat{\boldsymbol{\beta}} = \mathbf{b}$.

Extraneous estimates; mixed estimation: Suppose we have a regression equation

$$\mathbf{y} = \mathbf{X}_1\boldsymbol{\beta}_1 + \mathbf{X}_2\boldsymbol{\beta}_2 + \mathbf{u} \tag{B-17}$$

Sometimes an extraneous estimate is available for some of the parameters. Call these $\boldsymbol{\beta}_2$. If $\hat{\boldsymbol{\beta}}_2$ is this estimate, one procedure is to substitute $\tilde{\boldsymbol{\beta}}_2$ for $\boldsymbol{\beta}_2$ and estimate $\boldsymbol{\beta}_1$ by regressing $(\mathbf{y} - \mathbf{X}_2\tilde{\boldsymbol{\beta}}_2)$ on $\mathbf{X}_1$. This was the procedure used in early demand studies where an estimate of the income elasticity was obtained from budget studies and the price elasticity was estimated from time-series data after substituting this estimate of the income elasticity in the demand equation. A better procedure is to combine the two pieces of information by using a GLS procedure. Write $\tilde{\boldsymbol{\beta}}_2 = \boldsymbol{\beta}_2 + \tilde{\mathbf{u}}$. Combine this with (B-17) and write

$$\begin{bmatrix} \mathbf{y} \\ \tilde{\boldsymbol{\beta}}_2 \end{bmatrix} = \begin{bmatrix} \mathbf{X}_1 & \mathbf{X}_2 \\ \mathbf{0} & \mathbf{I} \end{bmatrix} \begin{bmatrix} \boldsymbol{\beta}_1 \\ \boldsymbol{\beta}_2 \end{bmatrix} + \begin{bmatrix} \mathbf{u} \\ \tilde{\mathbf{u}} \end{bmatrix} \tag{B-18}$$

Suppose

$$E(\mathbf{uu}') = \mathbf{I}\sigma^2$$
$$E(\tilde{\mathbf{u}}\tilde{\mathbf{u}}') = \boldsymbol{\Omega}$$

and it is reasonable to assume that $E(\mathbf{u}\tilde{\mathbf{u}}') = \mathbf{0}$. Then the covariance matrix of the residuals in (B-18) is block diagonal

$$\boldsymbol{\Sigma} = \begin{bmatrix} \mathbf{I}\sigma^2 & \mathbf{0} \\ \mathbf{0} & \boldsymbol{\Omega} \end{bmatrix}$$

To use the GLS procedure we have to know $\boldsymbol{\Sigma}$. Since we do not know $\boldsymbol{\Sigma}$, we obtain a preliminary estimate. For $\boldsymbol{\Omega}$ we can use the estimated covariance matrix of the extraneous estimates. For $\mathbf{I}\sigma^2$ we can obtain an estimate of σ^2 from the OLS estimation of Eq. (B-17).

More generally, Theil and Goldberger consider extraneous information in the form

$$\mathbf{r} = \mathbf{R}\boldsymbol{\beta} + \mathbf{v} \qquad E(\mathbf{vv}') = \boldsymbol{\Omega}$$

Combining this with (B-17), which can be written as

$$\mathbf{y} = \mathbf{X}\boldsymbol{\beta} + \mathbf{u}$$

we get

$$\begin{bmatrix} \mathbf{y} \\ \mathbf{r} \end{bmatrix} = \begin{bmatrix} \mathbf{X} \\ \mathbf{R} \end{bmatrix} + \begin{bmatrix} \mathbf{u} \\ \mathbf{v} \end{bmatrix}$$

Suppose, more generally, that $E(\mathbf{uu}') = \mathbf{V}\sigma^2$. Then the covariance matrix of

$$\begin{bmatrix} \mathbf{u} \\ \mathbf{v} \end{bmatrix} \text{ is } \boldsymbol{\Sigma} = \begin{bmatrix} \mathbf{V}\sigma^2 & 0 \\ 0 & \boldsymbol{\Omega} \end{bmatrix}$$

Hence

$$\boldsymbol{\Sigma}^{-1} = \begin{bmatrix} \dfrac{1}{\sigma^2}\mathbf{V}^{-1} & 0 \\ 0 & \boldsymbol{\Omega}^{-1} \end{bmatrix}$$

and the GLS estimator, which Theil and Goldberger[1] call a mixed estimator, is

$$\hat{\boldsymbol{\beta}} = \left[\frac{1}{\sigma^2}\mathbf{X}'\mathbf{V}^{-1}\mathbf{X} + \mathbf{R}'\boldsymbol{\Omega}^{-1}\mathbf{R}\right]^{-1}\left[\frac{1}{\sigma^2}\mathbf{X}'\mathbf{V}^{-1}\mathbf{y} + \mathbf{R}'\boldsymbol{\Omega}^{-1}\mathbf{r}\right]$$

with covariance matrix $[(1/\sigma^2)\mathbf{X}'\mathbf{V}^{-1}\mathbf{X} + \mathbf{R}'\boldsymbol{\Omega}^{-1}\mathbf{R}]^{-1}$. Where parameters are not known, we substitute preliminary consistent estimates for them.

Unbiased prediction in the linear model: Suppose we estimate the model (B-1) on the basis of n observations. We are interested in predicting m future observations $\mathbf{y}^*$, given the matrix of future observations $\mathbf{X}^*$ on the explanatory variables. Let us write

$$\mathbf{y}^* = \mathbf{X}^*\boldsymbol{\beta} + \mathbf{u}^* \tag{B-19}$$

$\mathbf{y}^*$ is an $m \times 1$ vector, $\mathbf{X}^*$ an $m \times k$ matrix, $\boldsymbol{\beta}$ a $k \times 1$ vector, and $\mathbf{u}^*$ an $m \times 1$ vector.

Under the assumption that the observations in (B-19) are generated by the same model as (B-1), i.e.,

$$V\begin{bmatrix}\mathbf{u}\\ \mathbf{u}^*\end{bmatrix} = \begin{bmatrix}\mathbf{I}_n\sigma^2 & 0\\ 0 & \mathbf{I}_m\sigma^2\end{bmatrix}$$

we can show that the "best" unbiased predictor of $\mathbf{y}^*$ is given by

$$\hat{\mathbf{y}}^* = \mathbf{X}^*\hat{\boldsymbol{\beta}} \tag{B-20}$$

Note that

$$\hat{\mathbf{y}}^* - \mathbf{y}^* = \mathbf{X}^*(\hat{\boldsymbol{\beta}} - \boldsymbol{\beta}) - \mathbf{u}^* \tag{B-21}$$

Thus the prediction error consists of two parts—one arising from the error in Eq. (B-19) and the other arising from the sampling error in $\hat{\boldsymbol{\beta}}$. From Eq. (B-21) we have $E(\hat{\mathbf{y}}^* - \mathbf{y}^*) = 0$ or $E(\hat{\mathbf{y}}^*) = E(\mathbf{y}^*)$. Thus our prediction $\hat{\mathbf{y}}^*$ is unbiased in the sense that its expectation is equal to the expectation of $\mathbf{y}^*$. We do not assert that $E(\hat{\mathbf{y}}^*) = \mathbf{y}^*$.

The covariance matrix of the prediction error in (B-21) is

$$\sigma^2\left[\mathbf{X}^*(\mathbf{X}'\mathbf{X})^{-1}\mathbf{X}^{*\prime} + \mathbf{I}\right]$$

To prove that (B-20) gives the "best" unbiased prediction, we proceed the same way as we did in proving that $\hat{\boldsymbol{\beta}}$ is the best unbiased linear estimator. We write

$$\hat{\mathbf{y}}^* = \mathbf{X}^*(\mathbf{X}'\mathbf{X})^{-1}\mathbf{X}'\mathbf{y}$$

Any other predictor which is linear in $\mathbf{y}$ can be written as $\tilde{\mathbf{y}}^* = [\mathbf{X}^*(\mathbf{X}'\mathbf{X})^{-1}\mathbf{X}' + \mathbf{C}]\mathbf{y}$. If it is an unbiased predictor, we get $\mathbf{CX} = 0$. We next show that the covariance matrix of the prediction error $\tilde{\mathbf{y}}^* - \mathbf{y}^*$ is $\sigma^2[\mathbf{X}^*(\mathbf{X}'\mathbf{X})^{-1}\mathbf{X}^{*\prime} + \mathbf{I} + \mathbf{CC}']$. Hence the result follows.

[1] H. Theil and A. S. Goldberger, On Pure and Mixed Statistical Estimation in Economics, *International Economic Review*, 1961, pp. 65–78.

The above result says that for purposes of prediction all we need is $\hat{\boldsymbol{\beta}}$. However, if the residuals $\mathbf{u}$ and $\mathbf{u}^*$ are correlated, this is not so. We can use the estimated residuals $\hat{\mathbf{u}}$ to improve the prediction. This was noted by Goldberger.[1] Let

$$V\begin{bmatrix} \mathbf{u} \\ \mathbf{u}^* \end{bmatrix} = \begin{bmatrix} \mathbf{V}_{11} & \mathbf{V}_{12} \\ \mathbf{V}_{21} & \mathbf{V}_{22} \end{bmatrix}$$

Then the best unbiased prediction is

$$\hat{\mathbf{y}}^* = \mathbf{X}^*\hat{\boldsymbol{\beta}}_{\mathrm{GLS}} + \mathbf{V}_{21}\mathbf{V}_{11}^{-1}\hat{\mathbf{u}}$$

where $$\hat{\boldsymbol{\beta}}_{\mathrm{GLS}} = (\mathbf{X}'\mathbf{V}_{11}^{-1}\mathbf{X})^{-1}\mathbf{X}'\mathbf{V}_{11}^{-1}\mathbf{y}$$

and $$\hat{\mathbf{u}} = \hat{\mathbf{y}} - \mathbf{X}\hat{\boldsymbol{\beta}}_{\mathrm{GLS}}$$

The algebra is somewhat tedious and is omitted here.

Systems of equations: Suppose we have a set of m equations

$$\begin{aligned} \mathbf{y}_1 &= \mathbf{X}_1\boldsymbol{\beta}_1 + \mathbf{u}_1 \\ \mathbf{y}_2 &= \mathbf{X}_2\boldsymbol{\beta}_2 + \mathbf{u}_2 \\ &\cdots\cdots \\ \mathbf{y}_m &= \mathbf{X}_m\boldsymbol{\beta}_m + \mathbf{u}_m \end{aligned} \tag{B-22}$$

Each of the vectors $\mathbf{y}_1,\mathbf{y}_2, \ldots, \mathbf{y}_m$ and $\mathbf{u}_1,\mathbf{u}_2, \ldots, \mathbf{u}_m$ are $n \times 1$ vectors. The matrix $\mathbf{X}_j$ is of order $n \times k_j$ and the vector $\boldsymbol{\beta}$ is of order $k_j \times 1$. Zellner,[2] who calls it a "seemingly unrelated regression model," considers the joint estimation of the parameters $\boldsymbol{\beta}_1,\boldsymbol{\beta}_2, \ldots, \boldsymbol{\beta}_m$ by GLS under the assumption

$$E(\mathbf{u}_i\mathbf{u}_j') = \sigma_{ij}\mathbf{I} \qquad i,j = 1,2, \ldots, m \tag{B-23}$$

Suppose the n observations are observations over time and the m equations are for different cross-section units. The assumption (B-23) implies that the residuals are independent over time but are contemporaneously correlated across cross-section units. We can generalize the assumption and assume $E(\mathbf{u}_i\mathbf{u}_j') = \sigma_{ij}\mathbf{V}$ or more generally V_{ij}, but this adds considerable complexity which we need not get into here to illustrate the "system method."

We can write Eq. (B-22) in "stacked form"

$$\begin{bmatrix} \mathbf{y}_1 \\ \mathbf{y}_2 \\ \vdots \\ \mathbf{y}_m \end{bmatrix} = \begin{bmatrix} \mathbf{X}_1 & 0 & \cdots & 0 \\ 0 & \mathbf{X}_2 & \cdots & 0 \\ \cdots & \cdots & \cdots & \cdots \\ 0 & 0 & \cdots & \mathbf{X}_m \end{bmatrix} \begin{bmatrix} \boldsymbol{\beta}_1 \\ \boldsymbol{\beta}_2 \\ \vdots \\ \boldsymbol{\beta}_m \end{bmatrix} + \begin{bmatrix} \mathbf{u}_1 \\ \mathbf{u}_2 \\ \vdots \\ \mathbf{u}_m \end{bmatrix}$$

[1] A. S. Goldberger, Best Linear Unbiased Prediction in the Generalized Linear Regression Model, *Journal of the American Statistical Association*, 1962, pp. 369–375.

[2] A. Zellner, An Efficient Method of Estimating Seemingly Unrelated Regressions and Tests for Aggregation Bias, *Journal of the American Statistical Association*, 1962, pp. 348–368.

or $\mathbf{y} = \mathbf{X}\boldsymbol{\beta} + \mathbf{u}$. Then $E(\mathbf{uu}') = \sum \otimes \mathbf{I}_n$, the Kronecker-product matrix, where

$$\sum = [\sigma_{ij}] \qquad i,j = 1,2, \ldots, m$$

The inverse of the covariance matrix is $\sum^{-1} \otimes \mathbf{I}_n$. Hence the GLS estimator is

$$\hat{\boldsymbol{\beta}} = \left[\mathbf{X}'(\Sigma^{-1} \otimes \mathbf{I}_n)\mathbf{X}\right]^{-1}\left[\mathbf{X}'(\Sigma^{-1} \otimes \mathbf{I}_n)\mathbf{y}\right]$$

Let $\sum^{-1} = [\sigma^{ij}]$. Then

$$\begin{bmatrix} \hat{\boldsymbol{\beta}}_1 \\ \hat{\boldsymbol{\beta}}_2 \\ \hat{\boldsymbol{\beta}}_m \end{bmatrix} = \begin{bmatrix} \sigma^{11}\mathbf{X}_1'\mathbf{X}_1 & \sigma^{12}\mathbf{X}_1'\mathbf{X}_2 & \cdots & \sigma^{1m}\mathbf{X}_1'\mathbf{X}_m \\ \sigma^{21}\mathbf{X}_2'\mathbf{X}_1 & \sigma^{22}\mathbf{X}_2'\mathbf{X}_2 & \cdots & \sigma^{2m}\mathbf{X}_2'\mathbf{X}_m \\ \sigma^{m1}\mathbf{X}_m'\mathbf{X}_1 & \sigma^{m2}\mathbf{X}_m'\mathbf{X}_2 & \cdots & \sigma^{mm}\mathbf{X}_m'\mathbf{X}_m \end{bmatrix}^{-1} \begin{bmatrix} \sum_j \sigma^{1j}\mathbf{X}_1'\mathbf{y}_j \\ \sum_j \sigma^{2j}\mathbf{X}_2'\mathbf{y}_j \\ \sum_j \sigma^{mj}\mathbf{X}_m'\mathbf{y}_j \end{bmatrix} \tag{B-24}$$

(all summations running from $j = 1$ to m).

The covariance matrix of $\hat{\boldsymbol{\beta}}$ is $[\mathbf{X}'(\sum^{-1} \otimes \mathbf{I}_n)\mathbf{X}]^{-1}$ or $[\sigma^{ij}\mathbf{X}_i'\mathbf{X}_j]^{-1}$. In actual practice σ_{ij} are not known. What we do is estimate each of Eqs. (B-22) by OLS, get the estimated residuals $\hat{\mathbf{u}}_i$, and estimate σ_{ij} by

$$s_{ij} = \frac{1}{n}\hat{\mathbf{u}}_i'\hat{\mathbf{u}}_j$$

and then invert the matrix $\mathbf{S} = [s_{ij}]$. If the inverse is $\mathbf{S}^{-1} = [s^{ij}]$, we substitute s^{ij} for σ^{ij} in (B-24) and obtain the GLS estimates.

With all these GLS procedures based on a consistent estimate of the covariance matrix (the seemingly unrelated regression model here and the mixed regression model considered earlier), it can be shown that the estimators are consistent and that they are asymptotically as efficient as the GLS estimator based on the true covariance matrix. This property holds good so long as there is no correlation between the **X**'s and the **u**'s. If this condition is violated, the GLS estimates based on an estimated covariance matrix are not as efficient as those based on the true covariance matrix $\boldsymbol{\Sigma}$. In this case we can distinguish among three different estimators of $\boldsymbol{\beta}$:

$\hat{\boldsymbol{\beta}}_1$, the estimator of $\boldsymbol{\beta}$ obtained by GLS when $\boldsymbol{\Sigma}$ is known
$\hat{\boldsymbol{\beta}}_2$, the estimator of $\boldsymbol{\beta}$ when $\sum$ is not known but both $\sum$ and $\boldsymbol{\beta}$ are estimated jointly
$\hat{\boldsymbol{\beta}}_3$, the estimator of $\boldsymbol{\beta}$ obtained by GLS based on a preliminary consistent estimate of $\sum$

Then $V(\hat{\boldsymbol{\beta}}_1) \leqslant V(\hat{\boldsymbol{\beta}}_2) \leqslant V(\hat{\boldsymbol{\beta}}_3)$. In the case where X's and u's are uncorrelated, we have $V(\hat{\boldsymbol{\beta}}_1) = V(\hat{\boldsymbol{\beta}}_2) = V(\hat{\boldsymbol{\beta}}_3)$. All these variances are, of course, asymptotic.

In the special case $\sigma_{ij} = 0$ for $i \neq j$ it is easy to see that the GLS estimator in Eq. (B-24) reduces to the OLS estimator of each equation in (B-22) separately. The GLS estimator also reduces to the OLS estimator when all equations in

(B-22) contain the identical explanatory variables, that is, $\mathbf{X}_1 = \mathbf{X}_2 = \mathbf{X}_3 = \cdots = \mathbf{X}_m = \mathbf{Z}$ (say). In this case the first bracket on the right-hand side of (B-24) is $[\boldsymbol{\Sigma}^{-1} \otimes (\mathbf{Z}'\mathbf{Z})]^{-1} = \boldsymbol{\Sigma} \otimes (\mathbf{Z}'\mathbf{Z})^{-1}$. Denote $(\mathbf{Z}'\mathbf{Z})^{-1}$ by $\mathbf{D}$. Also note that

$$\sum_j \sigma_{ij}\sigma^{kj} = 1 \qquad \text{if } i = k$$
$$= 0 \qquad \text{otherwise}$$

Hence

$$\begin{bmatrix} \hat{\boldsymbol{\beta}}_1 \\ \hat{\boldsymbol{\beta}}_2 \\ \vdots \\ \hat{\boldsymbol{\beta}}_m \end{bmatrix} = \begin{bmatrix} \sigma_{11}\mathbf{D} & \sigma_{12}\mathbf{D} & \cdots & \sigma_{1m}\mathbf{D} \\ \sigma_{21}\mathbf{D} & \sigma_{22}\mathbf{D} & \cdots & \sigma_{2m}\mathbf{D} \\ \vdots & \vdots & & \vdots \\ \sigma_{m1}\mathbf{D} & \sigma_{m2}\mathbf{D} & \cdots & \sigma_{mm}\mathbf{D} \end{bmatrix} \begin{bmatrix} \sum_j \sigma^{1j}\mathbf{Z}'\mathbf{y}_j \\ \sum_j \sigma^{2j}\mathbf{Z}'\mathbf{y}_j \\ \vdots \\ \sum_j \sigma^{mj}\mathbf{Z}'\mathbf{y}_j \end{bmatrix} = \begin{bmatrix} \mathbf{DZ}'\mathbf{y}_1 \\ \mathbf{DZ}'\mathbf{y}_2 \\ \vdots \\ \mathbf{DZ}'\mathbf{y}_m \end{bmatrix}$$

But the OLS estimator of β_j is $\mathbf{DZ}'\mathbf{y}_j$. Thus the GLS method reduces to the OLS estimation of each equation in (B-22) separately.

Stepwise least squares:[1] Sometimes if we have a regression equation $y = \beta_1 x_1 + \beta_2 x_2 + u$, instead of estimating this equation by multiple regression methods, y is regressed on x_1 in the first step to get an estimate $\tilde{\beta}_1$ of β_1, the residuals $(y - \tilde{\beta}_1 x_1)$ are computed, and these residuals are then regressed on x_2 in the second step to get an estimate $\tilde{\beta}_2$ of β_2. This procedure is known as two-step least squares. Obviously, both $\tilde{\beta}_1$ and $\tilde{\beta}_2$ will be biased, but they have smaller variances than the OLS estimates. If $\hat{\beta}_1$ and $\hat{\beta}_2$ are the OLS estimates, we have

$$E(\hat{\beta}_1) = \beta_1$$
$$E(\hat{\beta}_2) = \beta_2$$
$$V(\hat{\beta}_1) = \frac{\sigma^2}{\sum x_1^2(1 - r_{12}^2)}$$

Here $\qquad \sigma^2 = V(u) \qquad$ and $\qquad r_{12}^2 = \dfrac{\left(\sum x_1 x_2\right)^2}{\left(\sum x_1^2\right)\left(\sum x_2^2\right)}$

$$V(\hat{\beta}_2) = \frac{\sigma^2}{\sum x_2^2(1 - r_{12}^2)}$$

and $\qquad \operatorname{cov}(\hat{\beta}_1, \hat{\beta}_2) = \dfrac{-\sigma^2 r_{12}}{(1 - r_{12}^2)\sqrt{\left(\sum x_1^2\right)\left(\sum x_2^2\right)}}$

[1] See A. S. Goldberger, Stepwise Least Squares: Residual Analysis and Specification Errors, *Journal of the American Statistical Association*, December 1961, pp. 998–1000.

On the other hand, for the two-step estimates $\tilde{\beta}_1$ and $\tilde{\beta}_2$ we have

$$\tilde{\beta}_1 = \beta_1 + \beta_2 \frac{\sum x_1 x_2}{\sum x_1^2} + \frac{\sum x_1 u}{\sum x_1^2}$$

$$\tilde{\beta}_2 = \beta_2(1 - r_{12}^2) + \frac{\sum x_2 u}{\sum x_2^2} - r_{12}^2 \frac{\sum x_1 u}{\sum x_1 x_2}$$

Hence

$$E(\tilde{\beta}_1) = \beta_1 + \beta_2 \frac{\sum x_1 x_2}{\sum x_1^2}$$

$$E(\tilde{\beta}_2) = \beta_2(1 - r_{12}^2)$$

$$V(\tilde{\beta}_1) = \frac{\sigma^2}{\sum x_1^2} \qquad \text{and hence} \qquad V(\tilde{\beta}_1) \leqslant V(\hat{\beta}_1)$$

$$V(\tilde{\beta}_2) = \frac{\sigma^2}{\sum x_2^2}(1 - r_{12}^2) \qquad \text{and hence} \qquad V(\tilde{\beta}_2) \leqslant V(\hat{\beta}_2)$$

and $\text{cov}(\tilde{\beta}_1, \tilde{\beta}_2) = 0$. Thus $\tilde{\beta}_1$ and $\tilde{\beta}_2$ have smaller variances than $\hat{\beta}_1$ and $\hat{\beta}_2$, respectively, unless $r_{12}^2 = 0$, in which case they have the same variances. The generalized variance of $\hat{\beta}_1$ and $\hat{\beta}_2$, which is the determinant of the covariance matrix, is

$$|V(\hat{\beta}_1, \hat{\beta}_2)| = \frac{\sigma^4}{\left(\sum x_1^2\right)\left(\sum x_2^2\right)(1 - r_{12}^2)}$$

and for $\tilde{\beta}_1$ and $\tilde{\beta}_2$ it is

$$|V(\tilde{\beta}_1, \tilde{\beta}_2)| = \frac{\sigma^4(1 - r_{12}^2)}{\left(\sum x_1^2\right)\left(\sum x_2^2\right)}$$

The mean square errors are

$$\text{MSE}(\tilde{\beta}_1) = \frac{\sigma^2 + \beta_2^2 r_{12}^2 \sum x_2^2}{\sum x_1^2}$$

$$\text{MSE}(\tilde{\beta}_2) = \frac{\sigma^2(1 - r_{12}^2)}{\sum x_2^2} + \beta_2^2 r_{12}^4$$

For $\hat{\beta}_1$ and $\hat{\beta}_2$, the mean square errors are the variances, since they are unbiased. Hence

$$\text{MSE}(\tilde{\beta}_1) \lesseqgtr \text{MSE}(\hat{\beta}_1) \qquad \text{according as} \qquad \frac{\beta_2^2}{V(\hat{\beta}_2)} \lesseqgtr 1$$

and

$$\text{MSE}(\tilde{\beta}_2) \lesseqgtr \text{MSE}(\hat{\beta}_2) \qquad \text{according as} \qquad \frac{\beta_2^2}{V(\hat{\beta}_2)} \lesseqgtr \frac{2 - r_{12}^2}{r_{12}^2}$$

Sometimes the two-step estimators are preferred to the OLS estimators because they have smaller mean square errors.[1] However, the condition depends on the "true" t ratio for β_2, viz., $\beta_2/\sqrt{V(\hat{\beta}_2)}$. In actual practice one has to use the estimated t value, viz., $\hat{\beta}_2/\text{SE}(\hat{\beta}_2)$.

[1] See T. D. Wallace, Efficiencies for Step-wise Regressions, *Journal of the American Statistical Association*, December 1964, pp. 1179–1182.

APPENDIX

C

SIMULTANEOUS-EQUATION MODELS

Identification: Consider a simultaneous-equation model consisting of G endogenous variables (denoted by $\mathbf{y}$) and K exogenous variables (denoted by $\mathbf{x}$). We write the model as

$$\mathbf{B}\mathbf{y}_t + \mathbf{\Gamma}\mathbf{x}_t = \mathbf{u}_t \qquad t = 1, 2, \ldots, T \tag{C-1}$$

where $\mathbf{y}_t =$ a $G \times 1$ vector of observations on the endogenous variables
$\mathbf{x}_t =$ a $K \times 1$ vector of observations on the exogenous variables
$\mathbf{u}_t =$ a $G \times 1$ vector of disturbances
$\mathbf{B} =$ a $G \times G$ matrix of coefficients of the endogenous variables
and $\mathbf{\Gamma} =$ a $G \times K$ matrix of coefficients of the exogenous variables

We assume that $\mathbf{B}$ is a nonsingular matrix. Hence we can solve (C-1) for $\mathbf{y}_t$ to get

$$\begin{aligned} \mathbf{y}_t &= -\mathbf{B}^{-1}\mathbf{\Gamma}x_t + \mathbf{B}^{-1}u_t \\ &= \mathbf{\Pi}\mathbf{x}_t + \mathbf{v}_t \end{aligned} \tag{C-2}$$

This is called the "reduced form." We have

$$\mathbf{B\Pi} = -\mathbf{\Gamma} \qquad \text{and} \qquad \mathbf{v}_t = \mathbf{B}^{-1}\mathbf{u}_t \tag{C-3}$$

Equations (C-1) are called "structural equations." About the residuals $\mathbf{u}_t$ we assume that $E(\mathbf{u}_t) = \mathbf{0}$ and $E(\mathbf{u}_t\mathbf{u}_t') = \mathbf{\Sigma}$, a nonsingular matrix. Thus the covariance matrix of the $\mathbf{u}_t$ is $\mathbf{\Sigma}$. It follows that $E(\mathbf{v}_t) = \mathbf{0}$ and the covariance matrix of the $\mathbf{v}_t$, to be denoted by $\mathbf{\Omega} = E(\mathbf{v}_t\mathbf{v}_t')$, is given by $\mathbf{\Omega} = \mathbf{B}^{-1}\mathbf{\Sigma}(\mathrm{B}^{-1})'$. We also assume that the residuals $\mathbf{u}_t$ are independent over time so that $p(\mathbf{u}_t\mathbf{u}_{t+s}) = p(\mathbf{u}_t) \cdot p(\mathbf{u}_{t+s})$ for all t and s. Regarding the exogenous variables, we assume that they are independent of the residuals. Hence

$$\text{plim}\left(\frac{1}{T}\sum_{t=1}^{T} x_{it}u_{jt}\right) = 0 \quad \text{for } i = 1, 2, \ldots, K$$

$$j = 1, 2, \ldots, G$$

Also we assume that $\text{plim}(1/T)\mathbf{X}'\mathbf{X}$ is a positive definite matrix, where

$$\mathbf{X} = \begin{bmatrix} \mathbf{x}_1' \\ \mathbf{x}_2' \\ \mathbf{x}_T' \end{bmatrix}$$

is the $T \times K$ matrix observations on the exogenous variables.

Since the $\mathbf{u}_t$ are independent over time, we can write their joint density as $\prod_{t=1}^{T} p(\mathbf{u}_t)$. Because the $\mathbf{u}_t$ are unobservable, we have to convert this into the density of the observables $\mathbf{y}_t$. We have

$$p(\mathbf{y}_t \mid \mathbf{x}_t) = p(\mathbf{u}_t) \cdot J$$

where J, the Jacobian of the transformation $|\partial \mathbf{u}_t / \partial \mathbf{y}_t| = |\mathbf{B}|$ by virtue of Eq. (C-1). Hence the joint density of the endogenous variables (given the exogenous variables) is

$$p(\mathbf{y}_1\mathbf{y}_2 \ldots \mathbf{y}_T \mid \mathbf{x}_1\mathbf{x}_2 \ldots \mathbf{x}_T) = |\mathbf{B}|^T \prod_{t=1}^{T} p(\mathbf{u}_t)$$

Considered as a function of the unknown parameters $\mathbf{B}$, $\mathbf{\Gamma}$, $\mathbf{\Sigma}$, this is the likelihood function. Thus

$$L(\mathbf{B},\mathbf{\Gamma},\mathbf{\Sigma}) = |\mathbf{B}|^T \prod_{t=1}^{T} p(\mathbf{u}_t)$$

Consider a transformation of Eq. (C-1)

$$(\mathbf{FB})\mathbf{y}_t + (\mathbf{F\Gamma})\mathbf{x}_t = \mathbf{Fu}_t$$

where $\mathbf{F}$ is a nonsingular matrix. Write this as

$$\mathbf{B}^*\mathbf{y}_t + \mathbf{\Gamma}^*\mathbf{x}_t = \mathbf{u}_t^* \tag{C-1a}$$

where $\mathbf{B}^* = \mathbf{FB}$, $\mathbf{\Gamma}^* = \mathbf{F\Gamma}$, and $\mathbf{u}_t^* = \mathbf{Fu}_t$.

$$p(\mathbf{u}_t^*) = p(\mathbf{u}_t)\frac{\partial \mathbf{u}_t}{\partial \mathbf{u}_t^*} = \mathbf{F}^{-1}p(\mathbf{u}_t)$$

The joint density of the endogenous variables (given the exogenous variables) is now

$$|\mathbf{FB}|^T|\mathbf{F}^{-1}|^T \prod_{t=1}^{T} p(\mathbf{u}_t) = |\mathbf{B}|^T \prod_{t=1}^{T} p(\mathbf{u}_t)$$

Since this is the likelihood function for the new set of parameters $\mathbf{B}^*$, $\mathbf{\Gamma}^*$, and $\mathbf{\Sigma}^*$, we have

$$L(\mathbf{B}^*,\mathbf{\Gamma}^*,\mathbf{\Sigma}^*) = L(\mathbf{B},\mathbf{\Gamma},\mathbf{\Sigma})$$

Thus $(\mathbf{B},\mathbf{\Gamma},\mathbf{\Sigma})$ and $(\mathbf{B}^*,\mathbf{\Gamma}^*,\mathbf{\Sigma}^*)$ are said to be indistinguishable structures, if there are no restrictions on $(\mathbf{B},\mathbf{\Gamma},\mathbf{\Sigma})$, because they both lead to the same likelihood function. This we express by saying that the parameters $(\mathbf{B},\mathbf{\Gamma},\mathbf{\Sigma})$ are not identified. On the other hand, if there are some restrictions on $(\mathbf{B},\mathbf{\Gamma},\mathbf{\Sigma})$, this and the transformed structure $(\mathbf{B}^*,\mathbf{\Gamma}^*,\mathbf{\Sigma}^*)$ will be indistinguishable only if the transformed structure also satisfies the same restrictions. If we cannot find any $\mathbf{F}$ such that the transformed structure also satisfies the same restrictions as those on $(\mathbf{B},\mathbf{\Gamma},\mathbf{\Sigma})$, we say that the structure $(\mathbf{B},\mathbf{\Gamma},\mathbf{\Sigma})$ is said to be identified.

One transformed structure that is of special interest is the one corresponding to $\mathbf{F} = \mathbf{B}^{-1}$. Then (C-1*a*) is the reduced form (C-2). The reduced-form equations can be estimated by OLS, since the residuals are independent of the regressors. One way of looking at the identification problem is to see whether we can get estimates of the structural parameters $(\mathbf{B},\mathbf{\Gamma},\mathbf{\Sigma})$ from the estimates of the reduced-form parameters $(\mathbf{\Pi},\Omega)$.

We will say that the structure $(\mathbf{B},\mathbf{\Gamma},\mathbf{\Sigma})$ is identified if each equation in the system (C-1) is identified. Hence we will discuss the identification of each equation separately. Also we will discuss the problem in terms of getting estimates of the structural parameters from the estimates of the reduced-form parameters and also in terms of being able to distinguish the parameters of each equation from the parameters of a linear combination of all equations. (Premultiplication by the matrix $\mathbf{F}$ amounts to considering linear combinations of the equations.)[1]

Without any loss of generality, consider the identification of the first equation in (C-1). Let $\boldsymbol{\beta}'$ be the first row of $\mathbf{B}$ and $\boldsymbol{\gamma}'$ the first row of $\mathbf{\Gamma}$. Partition these vectors, each into two components corresponding to the included and excluded variables in this equation.

$$\boldsymbol{\beta}' = [\,\boldsymbol{\beta}_1'\boldsymbol{\beta}_2'\,]$$

$$\boldsymbol{\gamma}' = [\,\boldsymbol{\gamma}_1'\boldsymbol{\gamma}_2'\,]$$

$\boldsymbol{\beta}_1'$ corresponds to G_1 included and $\boldsymbol{\beta}_2'$ corresponds to G_2 excluded endogenous variables ($G_1 + G_2 = G$). Similarly $\boldsymbol{\gamma}_1'$ corresponds to K_1 included and $\boldsymbol{\gamma}_2'$ corresponds to K_2 excluded exogenous variables.

We have $\boldsymbol{\beta}_2' = \boldsymbol{\gamma}_2' = \mathbf{0}$. Partition the $G \times K$ matrix $\mathbf{\Pi}$ conformably into

	K_1 columns	K_2 columns
G_1 rows	$\mathbf{\Pi}_{11}$	$\mathbf{\Pi}_{12}$
G_2 rows	$\mathbf{\Pi}_{21}$	$\mathbf{\Pi}_{22}$

[1] In our derivations we will be considering only linear systems with within-equation linear constraints on the parameters.

Then, since $\mathbf{B\Pi} = -\mathbf{\Gamma}$, we have, taking the first rows of $\mathbf{B}$ and $\mathbf{\Gamma}$,

$$[\beta_1' \quad \mathbf{0}]\begin{bmatrix} \mathbf{\Pi}_{11} & \mathbf{\Pi}_{12} \\ \mathbf{\Pi}_{21} & \mathbf{\Pi}_{22} \end{bmatrix} = -[\gamma_1' \quad \mathbf{0}]$$

Hence

$$\gamma_1' = -\beta_1'\mathbf{\Pi}_{11} \tag{C-4}$$

and

$$\beta_1'\mathbf{\Pi}_{12} = \mathbf{0} \tag{C-5}$$

Equation (C-5) is a set of K_2 homogeneous equations in G_1 unknowns. Hence it has a solution only if $K_2 \geqslant G_1 - 1$. This condition is known as the "order condition" of identification. It is only a necessary condition. The necessary and sufficient condition is

$$\text{Rank}(\mathbf{\Pi}_{12}) = G_1 - 1 \tag{C-6}$$

This is called the "rank condition" for identification. The order condition can alternatively be written as

$$G_2 + K_2 \geqslant G_2 + G_1 - 1 \qquad \text{or} \qquad G_2 + K_2 \geqslant G - 1$$

But $G_2 + K_2$ is the number of variables (endogenous and exogenous) excluded from the equation. Thus the number of excluded variables should be greater than or equal to the number of equations minus one.

If $G_2 + K_2 = G - 1$, the equation is said to be exactly identified.
If $G_2 + K_2 > G - 1$, the equation is said to be overidentified.

Investigating the rank of $\mathbf{\Pi}_{12}$ is difficult. An alternative rank condition is the following. Partition the matrices $\mathbf{B}$ and $\mathbf{\Gamma}$ also conformably to the partitioning of $\boldsymbol{\beta}$ and $\boldsymbol{\gamma}$.

$$\mathbf{B} = \begin{bmatrix} \beta_1' & \mathbf{0} \\ \mathbf{B}_1 & \mathbf{B}_2 \end{bmatrix} \qquad \text{and} \qquad \mathbf{\Gamma} = \begin{bmatrix} \gamma_1' & \mathbf{0} \\ \mathbf{\Gamma}_1 & \mathbf{\Gamma}_2 \end{bmatrix}$$

Then an alternative rank condition for identification, which is easier to check, is rank $\mathbf{D} = G - 1$, where

$$\mathbf{D} = \begin{bmatrix} \mathbf{0} & \mathbf{0} \\ \mathbf{\Gamma}_2 & \mathbf{B}_2 \end{bmatrix} \tag{C-7}$$

$\mathbf{D}$ is the matrix of coefficients corresponding to the missing endogenous and exogenous variables. It can be easily shown that conditions (C-6) and (C-7) are equivalent.

Note that $\mathbf{B\Pi} = -\mathbf{\Gamma}$ implies that $\beta_1'\mathbf{\Pi}_{12} = \mathbf{0}$ and $\mathbf{B}_1\mathbf{\Pi}_{12} + \mathbf{B}_2\mathbf{\Pi}_{22} = -\mathbf{\Gamma}_2$ and hence that $\mathbf{D} = \mathbf{BC}$, where

$$\mathbf{C} = \begin{bmatrix} -\mathbf{\Pi}_{12} & \mathbf{0} \\ -\mathbf{\Pi}_{22} & \mathbf{I}_{G_2} \end{bmatrix}$$

Since rank is unaltered by premultiplication by a nonsingular matrix,

$$\text{rank } \mathbf{D} = \text{rank } \mathbf{BC} = \text{rank } \mathbf{C}$$

Again, since rank is unaltered by postmultiplication by a nonsingular matrix, we have

$$\begin{aligned}\text{rank } \mathbf{C} &= \text{rank}\begin{bmatrix} -\mathbf{\Pi}_{12} & \mathbf{0} \\ -\mathbf{\Pi}_{22} & \mathbf{I}_{G_2} \end{bmatrix}\begin{bmatrix} \mathbf{I}_{K_2} & \mathbf{0} \\ \mathbf{\Pi}_{22} & \mathbf{I}_{G_2} \end{bmatrix} \\ &= \text{rank}\begin{bmatrix} -\mathbf{\Pi}_{12} & \mathbf{0} \\ \mathbf{0} & \mathbf{I}_{G_2} \end{bmatrix} \\ &= \text{rank}(\mathbf{\Pi}_{12}) + G_2\end{aligned}$$

Hence rank $\mathbf{D} = G - 1 \Leftrightarrow \text{rank}(\mathbf{\Pi}_{12}) = G_1 - 1$. Thus conditions (C-6) and (C-7) are equivalent. The two conditions are based on two different ways of looking at the identification problem. Condition (C-6) is based on the requirement that we should be able to go from the reduced-form parameters to the structural parameters. Condition (C-7), on the other hand, is based on the requirement that there should be no linear combination of the other $(G - 1)$ equations which when added to the first equation results in an equation that "looks like" it. If $\text{rank}[\mathbf{B}_2\mathbf{\Gamma}_2] < G - 1$, there will exist a nonnull vector $\mathbf{a}$ such that $\mathbf{a}'[\mathbf{B}_2\mathbf{\Gamma}_2] = [\mathbf{0} \quad \mathbf{0}]$ and hence we can find a linear combination of the other $G - 1$ equations, which, when added to the first equations, results in a similar equation. Thus it is not possible to identify the parameters of the first equation.

Till now we have considered "exclusion restrictions." We will now derive the condition corresponding to (C-7) for linear homogeneous restrictions.

Write Eq. (C-1) as

$$\mathbf{AZ}_t = \mathbf{u}_t \tag{C-8}$$

where $\mathbf{A} = [\mathbf{B} \; \mathbf{\Gamma}]$ and $\mathbf{Z}_t = \begin{bmatrix} \mathbf{y}_t \\ \mathbf{x}_t \end{bmatrix}$

Let $\boldsymbol{\alpha}_1'$ be the first row of $\mathbf{A}$ and let the restrictions on the first row of $\mathbf{A}$ be expressible as

$$\boldsymbol{\alpha}_1'\boldsymbol{\phi} = 0 \tag{C-9}$$

For example, if $\boldsymbol{\alpha}_1' = [\beta_{11}\beta_{12} \cdots \beta_{1G}\gamma_{11} \cdots \gamma_{1K}]$ and the restrictions are $\beta_{11} + \beta_{12} = 0$ and $\gamma_{11} - \gamma_{1K} = 0$, we have

$$\boldsymbol{\phi} = \begin{bmatrix} 1 & 1 \\ 1 & 0 \\ 0 & 0 \\ \vdots & \vdots \\ 0 & -1 \end{bmatrix}$$

Since α_1' can be written as $\mathbf{e}_1'\mathbf{A}$, where $\mathbf{e}_1'$ is a row vector with unity in the first element and zeros elsewhere, we can write (C-9) as

$$\mathbf{e}_1'\mathbf{A}\boldsymbol{\phi} = \mathbf{0} \tag{C-10}$$

Consider now a nonsingular $G \times G$ matrix $\mathbf{F}$ and the transformed system

$$\mathbf{FAz}_t = \mathbf{Fu}_t \tag{C-11}$$

The first row of the transformed (C-11) is given by $\mathbf{f}'_1\mathbf{A}$, where $\mathbf{f}'_1$ is the first row of $\mathbf{F}$. If this obeys the restrictions (C-9), we have

$$\mathbf{f}'_1\mathbf{A}\boldsymbol{\phi} = \mathbf{0} \tag{C-12}$$

If the first equation of the model (C-8) is to be identified, the coefficients of the transformed equations must be identical to the coefficients of the original equation (except for a scalar multiple). Thus $\mathbf{f}_1$ must be a scalar multiple of $\mathbf{e}_1$. The necessary and sufficient condition for this is

$$\text{rank}(\mathbf{A}\boldsymbol{\phi}) = G - 1 \tag{C-13}$$

[Note that if rank $(\mathbf{A}\boldsymbol{\phi}) < G - 1$, there will be a solution to Eq. (C-12), which will be different from a scalar multiple of $\mathbf{e}_1$.] It can be easily checked that in the case of the exclusion restrictions considered earlier, $\mathbf{A}\boldsymbol{\phi}$ equals the matrix $\mathbf{D}$ defined in (C-7).

Methods of estimation; two-stage least squares: Broadly speaking, we have to divide the methods into single-equation methods and system methods. In the former we estimate each equation separately, taking into account the restrictions on only that equation, and in the latter we estimate all equations together, taking into account all the restrictions in the system. Further, in each category we have least-squares methods and maximum-likelihood methods. The former methods depend on the normalization rule we adopt (though not in exactly identified equations) and the latter methods are independent of the normalization rules. Normalization rules specify the coefficient of a particular variable to be 1. A common normalization rule is to assume that the diagonal elements of the matrix B in (C-1) are all unity; i.e., the ith equation is normalized with respect to the variable y_i. In the least-squares methods the variable whose coefficient is 1 is usually termed the "dependent" endogenous variable, though strictly speaking this terminology is contrary to the spirit of simultaneous-equation models where all the endogenous variables are jointly dependent.

We will first consider the estimation of a single equation by least-squares methods. Let the particular equation be written as

$$\mathbf{y} = \mathbf{Y}_1\boldsymbol{\beta} + \mathbf{X}_1\boldsymbol{\gamma} + \mathbf{u} = \mathbf{Z}_1\boldsymbol{\delta} + \mathbf{u} \tag{C-14}$$

where $\mathbf{y}$ = the $T \times 1$ vector of observations on the "dependent" endogenous variable.

$\mathbf{Y}_1$ = a $T \times (G_1 - 1)$ matrix of observations on the other included endogenous variables
$\mathbf{X}_1$ = a $T \times K_1$ matrix of observations on the included exogenous variables
$\boldsymbol{\delta} = \binom{\boldsymbol{\beta}}{\boldsymbol{\gamma}}$ = a $(G_1 - 1 + K_1) \times 1$ vector of parameters to be estimated
$\mathbf{u}$ = a $T \times 1$ vector of disturbances
$\mathbf{Z}_1 = [\mathbf{Y}_1\mathbf{X}_1]$.

Also $E(\mathbf{uu}') = \sigma^2\mathbf{I}_T$. Let $\mathbf{X}$ be the $T \times K$ matrix of observations on all the exogenous variables and K_2 the number of excluded exogenous variables. We have $K = K_1 + K_2$ and $G = G_1 + G_2$. Equation (C-14) is identified (by the order condition) only if $G_2 + K_2 \geqslant G - 1$. We will assume that this condition is satisfied.

Since $\mathbf{Y}_1$ and $\mathbf{u}$ are correlated, the OLS estimators of the parameters in (C-14) will be inconsistent. To get consistent estimates, we use instrumental variables for $\mathbf{Y}_1$. Let us consider the instrumental variables $\hat{\mathbf{Y}}_1$ where $\hat{\mathbf{Y}}_1$ is the estimated value of $\mathbf{Y}_1$ from the reduced form. Then $\hat{\mathbf{Y}}_1 = \mathbf{X}(\mathbf{X}'\mathbf{X})^{-1}\mathbf{X}'\mathbf{Y}_1$. Also let $\hat{\mathbf{V}}_1$ be the matrix of estimated residuals from the reduced form so that $\mathbf{Y}_1 = \hat{\mathbf{Y}}_1 + \hat{\mathbf{V}}_1$. Then we have the relations

$$\mathbf{X}'\hat{\mathbf{Y}}_1 = \mathbf{X}'\mathbf{Y}_1 \qquad \mathbf{X}'\hat{\mathbf{V}}_1 = \mathbf{0} \qquad \text{and} \qquad \hat{\mathbf{Y}}_1'\hat{\mathbf{V}}_1 = \mathbf{0} \tag{C-15}$$

Note that

$$\text{plim}\left(\frac{1}{T}\hat{\mathbf{Y}}_1'\mathbf{u}\right) = \text{plim}\left(\frac{1}{T}\mathbf{Y}_1'\mathbf{X}\right)\cdot\text{plim}\left(\frac{1}{T}\mathbf{X}'\mathbf{X}\right)^{-1}\cdot\text{plim}\left(\frac{1}{T}\mathbf{X}'\mathbf{u}\right) = 0 \tag{C-16}$$

since the last term is zero and the other terms are finite.

Define $\hat{\mathbf{Z}}_1 = [\hat{\mathbf{Y}}_1\mathbf{X}_1]$. Then, using the relations in (C-15) we can easily check that

$$(\hat{\mathbf{Z}}_1'\hat{\mathbf{Z}}_1) = (\hat{\mathbf{Z}}_1'\mathbf{Z}_1) \tag{C-17}$$

The instrumental-variable (IV) estimator of $\boldsymbol{\delta}$ is

$$\begin{aligned}
\hat{\boldsymbol{\delta}}_{\text{IV}} &= (\hat{\mathbf{Z}}_1'\mathbf{Z}_1)^{-1}\hat{\mathbf{Z}}_1'\mathbf{y} \\
&= (\hat{\mathbf{Z}}_1'\mathbf{Z}_1)^{-1}\hat{\mathbf{Z}}_1'(\mathbf{Z}_1\boldsymbol{\delta} + \mathbf{u}) \\
&= \boldsymbol{\delta} + (\hat{\mathbf{Z}}_1'\mathbf{Z}_1)^{-1}\hat{\mathbf{Z}}_1'\mathbf{u}
\end{aligned}$$

$$\begin{aligned}
\text{plim}\ \hat{\boldsymbol{\delta}}_{\text{IV}} &= \boldsymbol{\delta} + \text{plim}\left(\frac{1}{T}\hat{\mathbf{Z}}_1'\mathbf{Z}_1\right)^{-1}\cdot\text{plim}\left(\frac{1}{T}\hat{\mathbf{Z}}_1'\mathbf{u}\right) \\
&= \boldsymbol{\delta} \qquad \text{since plim}\left(\frac{1}{T}\hat{\mathbf{Z}}_1'\mathbf{u}\right) = 0 \text{ by (C-16)}
\end{aligned}$$

and $\text{plim}\left(\frac{1}{T}\hat{\mathbf{Z}}_1'\mathbf{Z}_1\right)^{-1}$ is finite.

Thus, as is to be expected, the IV estimator is consistent. The asymptotic covariance matrix of $\hat{\boldsymbol{\delta}}_{\text{IV}}$ is given by

$$\begin{aligned}
A\cdot E\ T(\hat{\boldsymbol{\delta}}_{\text{IV}} - \boldsymbol{\delta})(\hat{\boldsymbol{\delta}}_{\text{IV}} - \boldsymbol{\delta})' &= \text{plim}\ T(\hat{\boldsymbol{\delta}}_{\text{IV}} - \boldsymbol{\delta})(\hat{\boldsymbol{\delta}}_{\text{IV}} - \boldsymbol{\delta})' \\
&= \text{plim}\left(\frac{1}{T}\hat{\mathbf{Z}}_1'\mathbf{Z}_1\right)^{-1}\text{plim}\left(\frac{1}{T}\hat{\mathbf{Z}}_1'\mathbf{u}\mathbf{u}'\hat{\mathbf{Z}}_1\right)\text{plim}\left(\frac{1}{T}\hat{\mathbf{Z}}_1'\hat{\mathbf{Z}}_1\right)^{-1} \\
&= \sigma^2\text{plim}\left(\frac{1}{T}\hat{\mathbf{Z}}_1'\hat{\mathbf{Z}}_1\right)^{-1}
\end{aligned} \tag{C-18}$$

since $E(\mathbf{u}\mathbf{u}') = \sigma^2\mathbf{I}_T$ and $\hat{\mathbf{Z}}_1'\hat{\mathbf{Z}}_1 = \hat{\mathbf{Z}}_1'\mathbf{Z}_1$. In practice we estimate σ^2 by

$$\hat{\sigma}^2 = \frac{(\mathbf{y} - \mathbf{y}_1\hat{\boldsymbol{\beta}} - \mathbf{X}_1\hat{\boldsymbol{\gamma}})'(\mathbf{y} - \mathbf{y}_1\hat{\boldsymbol{\beta}} - \mathbf{X}_1\hat{\boldsymbol{\gamma}})}{T - G_1 - K_1}$$

and $\text{plim}[(1/T)\hat{\mathbf{Z}}_1'\hat{\mathbf{Z}}_1]^{-1}$ by

$$\left(\frac{1}{T}\hat{\mathbf{Z}}_1'\hat{\mathbf{Z}}_1\right)^{-1} = T\begin{bmatrix} \mathbf{Y}_1'\mathbf{X}(\mathbf{X}'\mathbf{X})^{-1}\mathbf{X}'\mathbf{Y}_1 & \mathbf{Y}_1'\mathbf{X}_1 \\ \mathbf{X}_1'\mathbf{Y}_1 & \mathbf{X}_1'\mathbf{X}_1 \end{bmatrix}^{-1}$$

In the two-stage least-squares (2SLS) estimation method we use $\hat{\mathbf{Y}}_1$ as regressors rather than instrumental variables; i.e., we substitute $\hat{\mathbf{Y}}_1$ for $\mathbf{Y}_1$ on the right-hand side of (C-14) and estimate the equation by OLS. The equation is

$$\begin{aligned} \mathbf{y} &= \hat{\mathbf{Y}}_1\boldsymbol{\beta} + \hat{\mathbf{X}}_1\boldsymbol{\gamma} + (\mathbf{u} + \hat{\mathbf{V}}_1\boldsymbol{\beta}) \\ &= \hat{\mathbf{Z}}_1\boldsymbol{\delta} + (\mathbf{u} + \hat{\mathbf{V}}_1\boldsymbol{\beta}) \\ \hat{\boldsymbol{\delta}}_{2SLS} &= (\hat{\mathbf{Z}}_1'\hat{\mathbf{Z}}_1)^{-1}\hat{\mathbf{Z}}_1'\mathbf{y} \\ &= (\hat{\mathbf{Z}}_1'\hat{\mathbf{Z}}_1)^{-1}\hat{\mathbf{Z}}_1'[\mathbf{Z}_1\boldsymbol{\delta} + \mathbf{u} + \hat{\mathbf{V}}_1\boldsymbol{\beta}] \\ &= \boldsymbol{\delta} + (\hat{\mathbf{Z}}_1'\hat{\mathbf{Z}}_1)^{-1}\hat{\mathbf{Z}}_1'\mathbf{u} \qquad \text{since } \hat{\mathbf{Z}}_1'\hat{\mathbf{V}}_1 = \mathbf{0} \end{aligned} \tag{C-19}$$

That $\hat{\boldsymbol{\delta}}_{2SLS} = \hat{\boldsymbol{\delta}}_{IV}$ follows from (C-17). The asymptotic covariance matrix of the 2SLS estimator is given by (C-18). Since $\hat{\mathbf{Z}}_1 = [\hat{\mathbf{Y}}_1\mathbf{X}_1] = \mathbf{X}(\mathbf{X}'\mathbf{X})^{-1}\mathbf{X}'[\mathbf{Y}_1\mathbf{X}_1]$, we can write this covariance matrix also as $V_{2SLS} = \sigma_T^2\,\text{plim}[\mathbf{Z}_1'\mathbf{X}(\mathbf{X}'\mathbf{X})^{-1}\mathbf{X}'\mathbf{Z}_1]^{-1}$.

The above discussion shows that the 2SLS estimator can be interpreted as an instrumental-variable estimator where $\hat{\mathbf{Y}}_1$ are used as instruments. We can also show that if we consider the class of instrumental variables which are linear functions of the exogenous variables, then $\hat{\mathbf{Y}}_1$ are the best instruments (best in the sense that they result in the minimum asymptotic covariance matrix). To prove this, consider an arbitrary set of instrumental variables $\mathbf{W} = \mathbf{XD}$, where $\mathbf{W}$ is of the same dimension as $\mathbf{Z}_1$. The asymptotic covariance matrix of this instrumental-variable estimator is $\mathbf{V}_{IV} = \sigma^2 T\,\text{plim}[\mathbf{W}'\mathbf{Z}_1]^{-1}[\mathbf{W}'\mathbf{W}][\mathbf{Z}_1'\mathbf{W}]^{-1}$. We will show that $\mathbf{V}_{IV} \geqslant \mathbf{V}_{2SLS}$ or $\mathbf{V}_{IV}^{-1} \leqslant \mathbf{V}_{2SLS}^{-1}$. (We say $\mathbf{A} \geqslant \mathbf{B}$ if $\mathbf{A} - \mathbf{B}$ is positive semidefinite and $\mathbf{A} \leqslant \mathbf{B}$ if $\mathbf{A} - \mathbf{B}$ is negative semidefinite.) Now

$$\begin{aligned} \mathbf{V}_{IV}^{-1} &= \frac{1}{T\sigma^2}\,\text{plim}[\mathbf{Z}_1'\mathbf{W}][\mathbf{W}'\mathbf{W}]^{-1}[\mathbf{W}'\mathbf{Z}_1] \\ &= \frac{1}{T\sigma^2}\,\text{plim}[\mathbf{Z}_1'\mathbf{XD}(\mathbf{D}'\mathbf{X}'\mathbf{XD})^{-1}\mathbf{D}'\mathbf{X}'\mathbf{Z}_1] \end{aligned}$$

and

$$\mathbf{V}_{2SLS}^{-1} = \frac{1}{T\sigma^2}\,\text{plim}[\mathbf{Z}_1'\mathbf{X}(\mathbf{X}'\mathbf{X})^{-1}\mathbf{X}'\mathbf{Z}_1]$$

Thus it is sufficient to show that

$$\mathbf{XD}(\mathbf{D}'\mathbf{X}'\mathbf{XD})^{-1}\mathbf{D}'\mathbf{X}' \leqslant \mathbf{X}(\mathbf{X}'\mathbf{X})^{-1}\mathbf{X}' \tag{C-20}$$

We know that $\mathbf{I} - \mathbf{C}(\mathbf{C}'\mathbf{C})^{-1}\mathbf{C}'$ is a positive semidefinite matrix.[1] Hence for any arbitrary $\mathbf{A}$

$$\mathbf{A}'[\mathbf{C}(\mathbf{C}'\mathbf{C})^{-1}\mathbf{C}' - \mathbf{I}]\mathbf{A} \leqslant 0$$

[1] Note that $\mathbf{y}[\mathbf{I} - \mathbf{C}(\mathbf{C}'\mathbf{C})^{-1}\mathbf{C}']\mathbf{y}$ is the residual sum of squares in a regression equation $\mathbf{y} = \mathbf{C}\boldsymbol{\beta} + \mathbf{u}$ and hence is $\geqslant 0$.

Put

$$\mathbf{A} = \mathbf{Q}^{-1}(\mathbf{X}'\mathbf{Z}_1)$$
$$\mathbf{C} = \mathbf{Q}'\mathbf{D} \qquad \text{where } \mathbf{QQ}' = \mathbf{X}'\mathbf{X}$$

Then we get the result (C-20), and hence $\mathbf{V}_{2SLS} \leqslant \mathbf{V}_{IV}$. Thus we have proved the optimality property of the 2SLS estimator as an instrumental-variable estimator.

There are some alternative ways of deriving the 2SLS estimator. Premultiply (C-14) by $\mathbf{X}'$. We get

$$\mathbf{X}'\mathbf{y} = \mathbf{X}'\mathbf{Z}_1\boldsymbol{\delta} + \mathbf{X}'\mathbf{u} \tag{C-21}$$

The covariance matrix of the residuals of the transformed system (C-21) is $E(\mathbf{X}'\mathbf{uu}'\mathbf{X}) = \sigma^2(\mathbf{X}'\mathbf{X})$. The GLS estimator of $\boldsymbol{\delta}$ from (C-21) is

$$\hat{\boldsymbol{\delta}} = \left[\mathbf{Z}_1'\mathbf{X}(\mathbf{X}'\mathbf{X})^{-1}\mathbf{X}'\mathbf{Z}_1\right]^{-1}\left[\mathbf{Z}_1'\mathbf{X}(\mathbf{X}'\mathbf{X})^{-1}\mathbf{X}'\mathbf{y}\right]$$
$$= \left[\hat{\mathbf{Z}}_1'\hat{\mathbf{Z}}_1\right]^{-1}\hat{\mathbf{Z}}_1'\mathbf{y}$$

which is the 2SLS estimator. Thus the 2SLS estimator of $\boldsymbol{\delta}$ is the GLS estimator of $\boldsymbol{\delta}$ from the transformed system (C-21). Actually, we can make one more transformation of Eq. (C-21). We can find a square nonsingular matrix $\mathbf{P}$ such that $(\mathbf{X}'\mathbf{X})^{-1} = \mathbf{PP}'$. Now premultiply (C-21) throughout by $\mathbf{P}'$. We get

$$\mathbf{P}'\mathbf{X}'\mathbf{y} = \mathbf{P}'\mathbf{X}'\mathbf{Z}_1\boldsymbol{\delta} + \mathbf{P}'\mathbf{X}'\mathbf{u} \tag{C-22}$$

The covariance matrix of the residuals is now

$$E\left[\mathbf{P}'\mathbf{X}'\mathbf{uu}''\mathbf{XP}\right] = \sigma^2\mathbf{P}'\mathbf{X}'\mathbf{XP} = \sigma^2\mathbf{I}$$

The 2SLS estimator can now easily be shown to be the OLS estimator of $\boldsymbol{\delta}$ from Eq. (C-22).

k-class estimators: The 2SLS estimators can be written as

$$\hat{\boldsymbol{\delta}}_{2SLS} = \begin{bmatrix} \hat{\mathbf{Y}}_1'\hat{\mathbf{Y}}_1 & \hat{\mathbf{Y}}_1'\mathbf{X}_1 \\ \mathbf{X}_1'\hat{\mathbf{Y}}_1 & \mathbf{X}_1'\mathbf{X}_1 \end{bmatrix}^{-1} \begin{bmatrix} \hat{\mathbf{Y}}_1'\mathbf{y} \\ \mathbf{X}_1'\mathbf{y} \end{bmatrix} \tag{C-23}$$

Since $\mathbf{Y}_1 = \hat{\mathbf{Y}}_1 + \hat{\mathbf{V}}_1$, we have $\mathbf{Y}_1'\mathbf{Y}_1 = \hat{\mathbf{Y}}_1'\hat{\mathbf{Y}}_1' + \hat{\mathbf{V}}_1'\hat{\mathbf{V}}_1$ (the cross products vanish because $\hat{\mathbf{Y}}_1'\hat{\mathbf{V}}_1 = \mathbf{0}$). Hence

$$\hat{\mathbf{Y}}_1'\hat{\mathbf{Y}}_1 = \mathbf{Y}_1'\mathbf{Y}_1 - \hat{\mathbf{V}}_1'\hat{\mathbf{V}}_1$$

Also $\qquad \hat{\mathbf{Y}}_1'\mathbf{X}_1 = \mathbf{Y}_1'\mathbf{X}_1 \qquad \text{since} \qquad \hat{\mathbf{V}}_1'\mathbf{X}_1 = \mathbf{0}$

Thus (C-23) can be written as

$$\hat{\boldsymbol{\delta}}_{2SLS} = \begin{bmatrix} \mathbf{Y}_1'\mathbf{Y}_1 - \hat{\mathbf{V}}_1'\hat{\mathbf{V}}_1 & \mathbf{Y}_1'\mathbf{X}_1 \\ \mathbf{X}_1'\mathbf{Y}_1 & \mathbf{X}_1'\mathbf{X}_1 \end{bmatrix}^{-1} \begin{bmatrix} (\mathbf{Y}_1 - \hat{\mathbf{V}}_1)'\mathbf{y} \\ \mathbf{X}_1'\mathbf{y} \end{bmatrix} \tag{C-24}$$

Theil defined a family of estimators called k-class estimators which are a generalization of (C-24).

$$\hat{\boldsymbol{\delta}}_k = \begin{bmatrix} \mathbf{Y}_1'\mathbf{Y}_1 - k\hat{\mathbf{V}}_1'\hat{\mathbf{V}}_1 & \mathbf{Y}_1'\mathbf{X}_1 \\ \mathbf{X}_1'\mathbf{Y}_1 & \mathbf{X}_1'\mathbf{X}_1 \end{bmatrix}^{-1} \begin{bmatrix} (\mathbf{Y}_1 - k\hat{\mathbf{V}}_1)'\mathbf{y} \\ \mathbf{X}_1'\mathbf{y} \end{bmatrix} \tag{C-25}$$

For $k = 1$ we have 2SLS. For $k = 0$ we have OLS. Earlier we saw that the 2SLS estimator is the same as the IV estimator where, $\hat{\mathbf{Y}}_1 = \mathbf{Y}_1 - \hat{\mathbf{V}}_1$ is used as the set of instrumental variables. The k-class estimator is also a IV estimator with $\mathbf{Y}_1 - k\hat{\mathbf{V}}_1$ used as the instruments.

$$\begin{bmatrix} (\mathbf{Y}_1 - k\hat{\mathbf{V}}_1)'\mathbf{Y}_1 & (\mathbf{Y}_1 - k\hat{\mathbf{V}}_1)'\mathbf{X}_1 \\ \mathbf{X}_1'\mathbf{Y}_1 & \mathbf{X}_1'\mathbf{X}_1 \end{bmatrix}^{-1} \begin{bmatrix} (\mathbf{Y}_1 - k\hat{\mathbf{V}}_1)'\mathbf{y} \\ \mathbf{X}_1'\mathbf{y} \end{bmatrix} \tag{C-26}$$

To show the equivalence of Eqs. (C-25) and (C-26), all we have to show is $(\mathbf{Y}_1 - k\hat{\mathbf{V}}_1)'\mathbf{Y}_1 = \mathbf{Y}_1'\mathbf{Y}_1 - k\hat{\mathbf{V}}_1'\hat{\mathbf{V}}_1$ and $(\mathbf{Y}_1 - k\hat{\mathbf{V}}_1)'\mathbf{X}_1 = \mathbf{Y}_1'\mathbf{X}_1$. The second relation follows easily from the fact that $\hat{\mathbf{V}}_1'\mathbf{X}_1 = 0$. The first relation follows from the fact that $(\mathbf{Y}_1 - k\hat{\mathbf{V}}_1)'\mathbf{Y}_1 = \mathbf{Y}_1'\mathbf{Y}_1 - k\hat{\mathbf{V}}_1'(\hat{\mathbf{Y}}_1 + \hat{\mathbf{V}}_1) = \mathbf{Y}_1'\mathbf{Y}_1 - k\hat{\mathbf{V}}_1'\hat{\mathbf{V}}_1$ since $\hat{\mathbf{V}}_1'\hat{\mathbf{Y}}_1 = 0$. To prove the consistency of the k-class estimators, we note that if $\mathbf{W}$ is the set of instruments, the IV estimator is consistent if $\text{plim}(1/T)\mathbf{W}'\mathbf{W}$ exists and $\text{plim}(1/T)\mathbf{W}'\mathbf{u} = 0$. Hence the k-class estimators are consistent if (1) $\text{plim}(1/T)$ $(\mathbf{Y}_1 - k\hat{\mathbf{V}}_1)'(\mathbf{Y}_1 - k\hat{\mathbf{V}}_1)$ exists (a condition that can be easily verified) and (2) $\text{plim}(1/T)(\mathbf{Y}_1 - k\hat{\mathbf{V}}_1)'\mathbf{u} = \mathbf{0}$. Since $\mathbf{Y}_1 - k\hat{\mathbf{V}}_1 = \mathbf{Y}_1 - k(\mathbf{Y}_1 - \hat{\mathbf{Y}}_1) = (1-k)\mathbf{Y}_1 + k\hat{\mathbf{Y}}_1$, we have

$$\text{plim}\,\frac{1}{T}(\mathbf{Y}_1 - k\hat{\mathbf{V}}_1)'\mathbf{u} = \text{plim}(1-k)\cdot\text{plim}\,\frac{1}{T}\mathbf{Y}_1'\mathbf{u} + \text{plim}\,k\cdot\text{plim}\left(\frac{1}{T}\hat{\mathbf{Y}}_1'\mathbf{u}\right)$$

Since $\text{plim}(1/T)\hat{\mathbf{Y}}_1'\mathbf{u} = 0$ and $\text{plim}(1/T)\mathbf{Y}_1'\mathbf{u} \neq 0$, this is zero iff $\text{plim}(1-k) = 0$. Thus the k-class estimators are consistent iff $\text{plim}(1-k) = 0$. The asymptotic covariance matrix of the k-class estimator is

$$\sigma^2 T\,\text{plim}[\mathbf{W}'\mathbf{Z}_1]^{-1}[\mathbf{W}'\mathbf{W}][\mathbf{Z}_1'\mathbf{W}]^{-1}$$

where $\mathbf{W} - [\mathbf{Y}_1 - k\hat{\mathbf{V}}_1\mathbf{X}_1]$. The expression can be simplified for special cases. If $\text{plim}\sqrt{T}\,(k-1) = 0$, this covariance matrix is the same as that of the 2SLS estimator.

Limited-information maximum-likelihood method: Another member of the k-class is the limited-information maximum-likelihood (LIML) estimator. This estimator is also called the least-variance-ratio (LVR) estimator, and Goldberger calls it the least generalized residual variance (LGRV) estimator.

In the LIML method (due to Anderson and Rubin) we consider the likelihood function for Eq. (C-1) under the assumption of normality of the disturbances and maximize it subject to the restrictions on only the particular equation under consideration. Since the algebra is somewhat tedious, we will not present it here. Goldberger's LGRV method proceeds to do the same via the reduced form. What we do is consider the likelihood function for the reduced form and maximize it subject to the implied restrictions on the reduced form. In this case the method reduces to maximizing $|\mathbf{V}_*'\mathbf{V}_*|$, where $\mathbf{V}_*$ is the matrix of reduced-form residuals for the included endogenous variables, subject to the restrictions (C-5) on the reduced form. That is why it is called the least generalized residual variance method. Again, since the algebra is somewhat tedious, we will not present it here.[1]

[1] See A. S. Goldberger, "Econometric Theory," pp. 338–342, John Wiley & Sons, Inc., New York, 1964.

The LVR method is easier to derive. We write

$$\mathbf{Y}_* = [\mathbf{y}\ \mathbf{Y}_1] \qquad \text{and} \qquad \boldsymbol{\beta}_* = \begin{bmatrix} 1 \\ -\boldsymbol{\beta} \end{bmatrix}$$

Then Eq. (C-14) can be written as

$$\mathbf{y}_* = \mathbf{Y}_*\boldsymbol{\beta}_* = \mathbf{X}_1\boldsymbol{\gamma} + \mathbf{u} \tag{C-27}$$

For given $\boldsymbol{\beta}_*$ this can be treated as an ordinary regression equation. What (C-27) says is that only the variables $\mathbf{X}_1$ are important in determining $\mathbf{y}_*$. If this is so, the incremental reduction in the residual sum of squares by including the other exogenous variables $\mathbf{X}_2$ in (C-27) should be minimal. The residual sum of squares from (C-27) is

$$\mathbf{y}_*'\mathbf{N}_1\mathbf{y}_* \qquad \text{where } \mathbf{N}_1 = \mathbf{I} - \mathbf{X}_1(\mathbf{X}_1'\mathbf{X}_1)^{-1}\mathbf{X}_1'$$

$$= \boldsymbol{\beta}_*'\mathbf{W}_1\boldsymbol{\beta}_* \qquad \text{where } \mathbf{W}_1 = \mathbf{Y}_*'\mathbf{Y}_* - \mathbf{Y}_*'\mathbf{X}_1(\mathbf{X}_1'\mathbf{X}_1)^{-1}\mathbf{X}_1'\mathbf{Y}_*$$

If we include all the exogenous variables $\mathbf{X}$ in (C-27), the residual sum of squares would be

$$\mathbf{y}_*'\mathbf{N}\mathbf{y}_* \qquad \text{where } \mathbf{N} = \mathbf{I} - \mathbf{X}(\mathbf{X}'\mathbf{X})^{-1}\mathbf{X}'$$

$$= \boldsymbol{\beta}_*'\mathbf{W}\boldsymbol{\beta}_* \qquad \text{where } \mathbf{W} = \mathbf{Y}_*'\mathbf{Y}_* - \mathbf{Y}_*'\mathbf{X}(\mathbf{X}'\mathbf{X})^{-1}\mathbf{X}'\mathbf{Y}_*$$

The incremental reduction in the residual sum of squares by introducing $\mathbf{X}_2$ in Eq. (C-27) is $\boldsymbol{\beta}_*'\mathbf{W}_1\boldsymbol{\beta}_* - \boldsymbol{\beta}_*'\mathbf{W}\boldsymbol{\beta}_*$. What the LVR method suggests is minimizing

$$\frac{\boldsymbol{\beta}_*'\mathbf{W}_1\boldsymbol{\beta}_* - \boldsymbol{\beta}_*'\mathbf{W}\boldsymbol{\beta}_*}{\boldsymbol{\beta}_*'\mathbf{W}_1\boldsymbol{\beta}_*}$$

or, equivalently, minimizing

$$\lambda = \frac{\boldsymbol{\beta}_*'\mathbf{W}_1\boldsymbol{\beta}_*}{\boldsymbol{\beta}_*'\mathbf{W}\boldsymbol{\beta}_*} \tag{C-28}$$

$$\frac{\partial \lambda}{\partial \boldsymbol{\beta}_*} = 0 \text{ gives}$$

$$\frac{1}{(\boldsymbol{\beta}_*'\mathbf{W}\boldsymbol{\beta}_*)^2}\left[(\boldsymbol{\beta}_*'\mathbf{W}\boldsymbol{\beta}_*)2\mathbf{W}_1\boldsymbol{\beta}_* - (\boldsymbol{\beta}_*'\mathbf{W}_1\boldsymbol{\beta}_*)2\mathbf{W}\boldsymbol{\beta}_*\right] = 0$$

or

$$(\mathbf{W}_1 - \lambda\mathbf{W})\,\boldsymbol{\beta}_* = \mathbf{0}$$

Hence the minimum value of the variance ratio (C-28) is given by the minimum root of the determinantal equation

$$|\mathbf{W}_1 - \lambda\mathbf{W}| = 0 \tag{C-29}$$

Since $\mathbf{W}_1 - \mathbf{W} \geqslant 0$, all the roots of this equation are $\geqslant 1$. $\boldsymbol{\beta}_*$ is obtained as the solution of the equations

$$(\mathbf{W}_1 - \hat{\lambda}\mathbf{W})\,\boldsymbol{\beta}_* = \mathbf{0} \tag{C-30}$$

where $\hat{\lambda}$ is the minimum root of (C-29). Since Eq. (C-30) determines $\boldsymbol{\beta}_*$ only up to a multiplicative constant, we impose some restriction like $\beta_{*1} = 1$ to determine $\hat{\boldsymbol{\beta}}_*$ uniquely. After getting $\hat{\boldsymbol{\beta}}_*$, we can estimate γ from an OLS estimation of (C-27). We get

$$\hat{\gamma} = (\mathbf{X}_1'\mathbf{X}_1)^{-1}\mathbf{X}_1'\mathbf{Y}_*\hat{\boldsymbol{\beta}}_* \qquad \text{(C-31)}$$

Anderson and Rubin[1] show, under general conditions, that $T(\hat{\lambda} - 1)$ has asymptotically a χ^2 distribution with degrees of freedom equal to the degree of overidentification $K_2 - G_1 + 1$. Since the expected value of a χ^2 variate is equal to its degrees of freedom and the variance is equal to 2 (degrees of freedom), it follows that

$$A \cdot E\sqrt{T}(\hat{\lambda} - 1) = \frac{K_2 - G_1 + 1}{\sqrt{T}}$$

and asymptotic variance of $\sqrt{T}(\hat{\lambda} - 1)$ is $(K_2 - G_1 + 1)/T$. Hence

$$\text{plim}\sqrt{T}(\hat{\lambda} - 1) = 0 \qquad \text{(C-32)}$$

and a fortiori $\text{plim}(\hat{\lambda} - 1) = 0$. We will show below that the LIML estimator is a k-class estimator with $k = \hat{\lambda}$. Hence by the condition derived earlier for the consistency of the k-class estimator, viz., $\text{plim}(k - 1) = 0$, it follows that the LIML estimator is consistent. Also, since all k-class estimators that satisfy $\text{plim}[\sqrt{T}(k - 1)] = 0$ have the same asymptotic covariance matrix as the 2SLS estimator, it follows from condition (C-32) that the LIML estimator has the same asymptotic covariance matrix as the 2SLS estimator. However, the estimated standard errors will be different because the estimates of the residual variance σ^2 will be different, each being computed from the respective estimates of the structural coefficients. In fact, the residual sum of squares for the LIML method will always be $\geqslant$ the residual sum of squares for the 2SLS method, and hence the LIML standard errors will be $\geqslant$ those of the 2SLS.

To show that the LIML estimator is a k-class estimator, we simplify Eq. (C-25) for the k-class estimator and Eqs. (C-30) and (C-31) for the LIML estimator and show their equivalence. Equations (C-25) can be written as

$$\left(\mathbf{Y}_1'\mathbf{Y}_1 - k\hat{\mathbf{V}}_1'\hat{\mathbf{V}}_1\right)\hat{\boldsymbol{\beta}}_k + \mathbf{Y}_1'\mathbf{X}_1\hat{\gamma}_k = \left(\mathbf{Y}_1 - k\hat{\mathbf{V}}_1\right)'\mathbf{y}$$

and

$$\mathbf{X}_1'\mathbf{Y}_1\hat{\boldsymbol{\beta}}_k + \mathbf{X}_1'\mathbf{X}_1\hat{\gamma}_k = \mathbf{X}_1'\mathbf{y}$$

The second equation gives

$$\hat{\gamma}_k = (\mathbf{X}_1'\mathbf{X}_1)^{-1}\mathbf{X}_1'\left[\mathbf{y} - \mathbf{Y}_1\hat{\boldsymbol{\beta}}_k\right] \qquad \text{(C-33)}$$

and substituting this in the first equation, we get

$$\left(\mathbf{Y}_1'\mathbf{Y}_1 - k\hat{\mathbf{V}}_1'\hat{\mathbf{V}}_1\right)\hat{\boldsymbol{\beta}}_k + \mathbf{Y}_1'\mathbf{X}_1(\mathbf{X}_1'\mathbf{X}_1)^{-1}\mathbf{X}_1'\mathbf{Y}_1\hat{\boldsymbol{\beta}}_k = \left(\mathbf{Y}_1 - k\hat{\mathbf{V}}_1\right)'\mathbf{y} - \mathbf{Y}_1'\mathbf{X}_1(\mathbf{X}_1'\mathbf{X}_1)^{-1}\mathbf{X}_1'\mathbf{y}$$

[1] T. W. Anderson and H. Rubin, The Asymptotic Properties of Estimates of the Parameters of a Single Equation in a Complete System of Stochastic Equations, *Annals of Mathematical Statistics*, December 1950, pp. 570–582.

or
$$\left(\mathbf{Y}_1'\mathbf{N}_1\mathbf{Y}_1 - k\hat{\mathbf{V}}_1'\hat{\mathbf{V}}_1\right)\hat{\boldsymbol{\beta}}_k = \left(\mathbf{Y}_1'\mathbf{N}_1 - k\hat{\mathbf{V}}_1'\right)\mathbf{y}$$
where
$$\mathbf{N}_1 = \mathbf{I} - \mathbf{X}_1(\mathbf{X}_1'\mathbf{X}_1)^{-1}\mathbf{X}_1'$$
Since $\hat{\mathbf{V}}_1 = \mathbf{N}\mathbf{Y}_1$, where $\mathbf{N} = \mathbf{I} - \mathbf{X}(\mathbf{X}'\mathbf{X})^{-1}\mathbf{X}'$, we can write this as

$$(\mathbf{Y}_1'\mathbf{N}_1\mathbf{Y}_1 - k\mathbf{Y}_1'\mathbf{N}\mathbf{Y}_1)\hat{\boldsymbol{\beta}}_k = \mathbf{Y}_1'\mathbf{N}_1\mathbf{y} - k\mathbf{Y}_1'\mathbf{N}\mathbf{y} \tag{C-34}$$

Noting that $\mathbf{Y}_* = [\mathbf{y}\ \mathbf{Y}_1]$ and $\boldsymbol{\beta}_* = [{}^{\ 1}_{-\boldsymbol{\beta}}]$, we can easily see that (C-33) and (C-31) are equivalent and that (C-34) follows from (C-30) (since $\mathbf{W}_1 = \mathbf{Y}_*'\mathbf{N}_1\mathbf{Y}_*$ and $\mathbf{W} = \mathbf{Y}_*'\mathbf{N}\mathbf{Y}_*$).

We thus see that the OLS, 2SLS, and LIML estimators are all different members of the k class. In the case of LIML, it should be noted that k is not a constant but is a stochastic variable, since it is obtained by minimizing (C-28). Oi[1] shows that the estimates of the coefficients of the endogenous variables for the 2SLS lie between those of the OLS and LIML estimates. Fisher[2] studies the sensitivity of the different k-class estimators to specification errors and finds that none is uniformly superior to the others.

One simple relationship between the 2SLS and LIML estimators is the following. The LIML estimator is obtained by minimizing the variance ratio in (C-28) whereas the 2SLS estimator is obtained by minimizing the variance difference $\boldsymbol{\beta}_*'\mathbf{W}_1\boldsymbol{\beta}_* - \boldsymbol{\beta}_*'\mathbf{W}\boldsymbol{\beta}_*$ and the k-class estimator by minimizing the difference $\boldsymbol{\beta}_*'\mathbf{W}_1\boldsymbol{\beta}_* - k\boldsymbol{\beta}_*'\mathbf{W}\boldsymbol{\beta}_*$ (subject to some normalization rule). Since the ratio (C-28) is invariant to any normalization rule adopted, the LIML estimates are invariant to normalization. However, the k-class estimators which minimize a difference are not invariant to the normalization rule adopted. If the equation is exactly identified, the 2SLS estimator and the LIML estimator (using the same normalization as the one used for 2SLS) are identical. Thus the 2SLS estimates are also invariant to normalization rules if the equation is exactly identified.

Three-stage least-squares: In three-stage least-squares, we write all the equations in a "stacked" form and apply generalized-least-squares methods to the system as a whole as in Zellner's "seemingly unrelated regression" model (after a transformation). Suppose we normalize the first equation with respect to y_1, the second equation with respect to y_2, etc. We will write the ith equation as

$$\mathbf{y}_i = \mathbf{Y}_i\boldsymbol{\beta}_i + \mathbf{X}_i\boldsymbol{\gamma}_i + \mathbf{u}_i \qquad i = 1, 2, \ldots, G \tag{C-35}$$

Where $[\mathbf{y}_i\mathbf{Y}_i]$ is a $T \times G_i$ matrix of observations on the G_i endogenous variables occurring in the ith equation, $\mathbf{X}_i$ is a $T \times K_i$ matrix of observations on the K_i exogenous variables occurring in the ith equation, $\mathbf{u}_i$ is a $T \times 1$ vector of disturbances in the ith equation. The order condition for identification is $G - G_i + K - K_i \geqslant G - 1$. We will assume that this is satisfied (and that the rank

[1] W. Y. Oi, On the Relationship among Different Members of the k-class, *International Economic Review*, 1969, pp. 36–46.

[2] F. M. Fisher, The Relative Sensitivity to Specification Error of Different k-class Estimators, *Journal of the American Statistical Association*, 1966, pp. 345–356.

condition is also). Equation (C-35) corresponds to Eq. (C-14) considered earlier in 2SLS estimation of a single equation. We can write Eq. (C-35) as

$$\mathbf{y}_i = \mathbf{Z}_i \boldsymbol{\delta}_i + \mathbf{u}_i \qquad i = 1,2,\ldots,G \tag{C-36}$$

where

$$\mathbf{Z}_i = \left[\mathbf{Y}_i \mathbf{X}_i\right] \qquad \text{and} \qquad \boldsymbol{\delta}_i = \begin{bmatrix} \boldsymbol{\beta}_i \\ \boldsymbol{\gamma}_i \end{bmatrix}$$

Let $E(\mathbf{u}_i\mathbf{u}_j') = \sigma_{ij}\mathbf{I}$, i.e., the errors in the different equations are contemporaneously correlated but are independent over time. As was done in the case of a single equation [see Eq. (C-21)], we can write

$$\mathbf{X}'\mathbf{y}_i = \mathbf{X}'\mathbf{Z}_i \boldsymbol{\delta}_i + \mathbf{X}'\mathbf{u}_i \qquad i = 1,2,\ldots,G \tag{C-37}$$

The residuals now have a covariance matrix

$$E(\mathbf{X}'\mathbf{u}_i\mathbf{u}_j'\mathbf{X}) = \sigma_{ij}(\mathbf{X}'\mathbf{X})$$

As was noted earlier, the 2SLS estimates are the GLS estimates of the transformed equations, each estimated separately. The 3SLS estimates are the GLS estimates of Eqs. (C-37) using the "seemingly unrelated regression" method. We can write the equations in a "stacked" form as

$$\begin{bmatrix} \mathbf{X}'\mathbf{y}_1 \\ \mathbf{X}'\mathbf{y}_2 \\ \vdots \\ \mathbf{X}'\mathbf{y}_G \end{bmatrix} = \begin{bmatrix} \mathbf{X}'\mathbf{Z}_1 & 0 & \cdots & 0 \\ 0 & \mathbf{X}'\mathbf{Z}_2 & \cdots & 0 \\ 0 & 0 & \cdots & \mathbf{X}'\mathbf{Z}_G \end{bmatrix} \begin{bmatrix} \boldsymbol{\delta}_1 \\ \boldsymbol{\delta}_2 \\ \vdots \\ \boldsymbol{\delta}_G \end{bmatrix} + \begin{bmatrix} \mathbf{X}'\mathbf{u}_1 \\ \mathbf{X}'\mathbf{u}_2 \\ \vdots \\ \mathbf{X}'\mathbf{u}_G \end{bmatrix}$$

The errors have a covariance matrix $\boldsymbol{\Sigma} \otimes (\mathbf{X}'\mathbf{X})$ where $\boldsymbol{\Sigma} = [\sigma_{ij}]$.[1] Its inverse is $\boldsymbol{\Sigma}^{-1} \otimes (\mathbf{X}'\mathbf{X})^{-1}$ We now apply Zellner's seemingly unrelated regression method as in Eq. (B-23). However, since the inverse of the covariance matrix is now $\boldsymbol{\Sigma}^{-1} \otimes (\mathbf{X}'\mathbf{X})^{-1}$ instead of $\boldsymbol{\Sigma}^{-1} \otimes \mathbf{I}$ as considered there and also we have $\mathbf{X}'\mathbf{Z}_i$ instead of $\mathbf{X}_i$ and $\mathbf{X}'\mathbf{y}_i$ instead of $\mathbf{y}_i$ as considered there, we will get expressions like $\mathbf{Z}_i'\mathbf{X}(\mathbf{X}'\mathbf{X})^{-1}\mathbf{X}'\mathbf{Z}_i$ instead of $\mathbf{X}_i'\mathbf{X}_i$ and $\mathbf{Z}_i'\mathbf{X}(\mathbf{X}'\mathbf{X})^{-1}\mathbf{X}'\mathbf{y}_j$ instead of $\mathbf{X}_i'\mathbf{y}_j$ in Eq. (B-23). Thus the 3SLS estimator is given by

$$\begin{bmatrix} \hat{\boldsymbol{\delta}}_1 \\ \hat{\boldsymbol{\delta}}_2 \\ \vdots \\ \hat{\boldsymbol{\delta}}_G \end{bmatrix} = \begin{bmatrix} \sigma^{11}\mathbf{Z}_1'\mathbf{M}\mathbf{Z}_1 & \sigma^{12}\mathbf{Z}_1'\mathbf{M}\mathbf{Z}_2 & \cdots & \sigma^{1G}\mathbf{Z}_1'\mathbf{M}\mathbf{Z}_G \\ \sigma^{21}\mathbf{Z}_2'\mathbf{M}\mathbf{Z}_1 & \sigma^{22}\mathbf{Z}_2'\mathbf{M}\mathbf{Z}_2 & \cdots & \sigma^{2G}\mathbf{Z}_2'\mathbf{M}\mathbf{Z}_G \\ \vdots & \vdots & & \vdots \\ \sigma^{G1}\mathbf{Z}_G'\mathbf{M}\mathbf{Z}_1 & \sigma^{G2}\mathbf{Z}_G'\mathbf{M}\mathbf{Z}_2 & \cdots & \sigma^{GG}\mathbf{Z}_G'\mathbf{M}\mathbf{Z}_G \end{bmatrix}^{-1} \begin{bmatrix} \sum_j \sigma^{1j}\mathbf{Z}_1'\mathbf{M}\mathbf{y}_j \\ \sum_j \sigma^{2j}\mathbf{Z}_2'\mathbf{M}\mathbf{y}_j \\ \vdots \\ \sum_j \sigma^{Gj}\mathbf{Z}_G'\mathbf{M}\mathbf{y}_j \end{bmatrix} \tag{C-38}$$

[1] ⊗ denotes Kronecker products. See the last section of Appendix A.

all summations running from $j = 1$ to G and $\mathbf{M} = \mathbf{X}(\mathbf{X}'\mathbf{X})^{-1}\mathbf{X}'$, $[\sigma^{ij}] = \mathbf{\Sigma}^{-1}$. The covariance matrix of the 3SLS estimator is given by the inverse matrix on the right-hand side of (C-38), i.e., $[\sigma^{ij}\mathbf{Z}'\mathbf{M}\mathbf{Z}_j]^{-1}$. In actual practice σ^{ij} is not known. Hence what we do is estimate each equation in (C-35) by 2SLS, get the estimated residuals $\hat{\mathbf{u}}_i$, estimate σ_{ij} by $S_{ij} = (1/T)\hat{\mathbf{u}}_i'\hat{\mathbf{u}}_j$, invert this matrix, to be denoted as $[S^{ij}]$, and use S^{ij} for σ^{ij} in (C-38).

As was done in the case of 2SLS estimation, if $(\mathbf{X}'\mathbf{X})^{-1} = \mathbf{PP}'$, we can make a further transformation of Eq. (C-37) to

$$\mathbf{P}'\mathbf{X}'\mathbf{y}_i = \mathbf{P}'\mathbf{X}'\mathbf{Z}_i\,\boldsymbol{\delta}_i + \mathbf{P}'\mathbf{X}'\mathbf{u}_i$$

or

$$\mathbf{r}_i = \mathbf{R}_i\,\boldsymbol{\delta}_i + \mathbf{V}_i \qquad i = 1,2,\ldots,G \tag{C-39}$$

where $\mathbf{r}_i = \mathbf{P}'\mathbf{X}'\mathbf{y}_i$
$\mathbf{R}_i = \mathbf{P}'\mathbf{X}'\mathbf{Z}_i$
$\mathbf{V}_i = \mathbf{P}'\mathbf{X}'\mathbf{u}_i$

It can be easily verified that $E(\mathbf{V}_i\mathbf{V}_j') = E[\mathbf{P}'\mathbf{X}'\mathbf{u}_i\mathbf{u}_j'\mathbf{X}\mathbf{P}] = \sigma_{ij}\mathbf{I}$ since $\mathbf{P}'\mathbf{X}'\mathbf{X}\mathbf{P} = \mathbf{I}$. The 2SLS estimator can easily be shown to be the estimator obtained by using OLS to each equation in (C-39) separately and the 3SLS estimator as that obtained by using the GLS method to all equations in (C-39) together. Note that

$$\mathbf{R}_i'\mathbf{R}_j = (\mathbf{Z}_i'\mathbf{X}\mathbf{P}\mathbf{P}'\mathbf{X}'\mathbf{Z}_j) = \mathbf{Z}_i'\mathbf{X}(\mathbf{X}'\mathbf{X})^{-1}\mathbf{X}'\mathbf{Z}_j$$

If we write $\mathbf{R} = \text{diag.}[\mathbf{R}_1\mathbf{R}_2\ldots\mathbf{R}_G]$

$$\boldsymbol{\delta} = \begin{bmatrix}\boldsymbol{\delta}_1\\ \boldsymbol{\delta}_2\\ \vdots\\ \boldsymbol{\delta}_G\end{bmatrix} \qquad \mathbf{r} = \begin{bmatrix}\mathbf{r}_1\\ \mathbf{r}_2\\ \vdots\\ \mathbf{r}_G\end{bmatrix} \qquad \text{and} \qquad \mathbf{V} = \begin{bmatrix}\mathbf{V}_1\\ \mathbf{V}_2\\ \vdots\\ \mathbf{V}_G\end{bmatrix}$$

and if $\mathbf{\Omega}$ is the covariance matrix of $\mathbf{V}$, that is,

$$\mathbf{\Omega} = \mathbf{\Sigma} \otimes \mathbf{I}$$

then the 2SLS estimator of $\boldsymbol{\delta}$ is

$$\hat{\boldsymbol{\delta}}_{2\text{SLS}} = (\mathbf{R}'\mathbf{R})^{-1}\mathbf{R}'\mathbf{r} \tag{C-40}$$

and the 3SLS estimator of $\boldsymbol{\delta}$ is

$$\hat{\boldsymbol{\delta}}_{3\text{SLS}} = (\mathbf{R}'\mathbf{\Omega}^{-1}\mathbf{R})^{-1}\mathbf{R}'\mathbf{\Omega}^{-1}\mathbf{r} \tag{C-41}$$

If $\sigma_{ij} = 0$ for all $i \neq j$, then 3SLS and 2SLS estimators are identical. This follows from the fact that in the seemingly unrelated regression model the GLS and OLS estimators are identical in this case. If all equations are exactly identified (by the order condition), then again 3SLS and 2SLS estimators are identical because in this case $\mathbf{Z}_i$ is of order $T \times (G_i + K_i - 1)$ and since by the order condition

$$G - G_i + K - K_i = G - 1 \qquad \text{or} \qquad G_i + K_i - 1 = K$$

$\mathbf{X}'\mathbf{Z}_i$ is of order $K \times K$, and hence $\mathbf{R}_i$ is of order $K \times K$. Thus $\mathbf{R}$ is a square matrix. Hence

$$\begin{aligned}\hat{\delta}_{2SLS} &= (\mathbf{R}'\mathbf{R})^{-1}\mathbf{R}'\mathbf{r} \\ &= \mathbf{R}^{-1}(\mathbf{R}')^{-1}\mathbf{R}'\mathbf{r} \\ &= \mathbf{R}^{-1}\mathbf{r}\end{aligned}$$

and

$$\begin{aligned}\hat{\delta}_{3SLS} &= (\mathbf{R}'\Omega^{-1}\mathbf{R})^{-1}\mathbf{R}'\Omega^{-1}\mathbf{r} \\ &= \mathbf{R}^{-1}\Omega(\mathbf{R}')^{-1}\mathbf{R}'\Omega^{-1}\mathbf{r} \\ &= \mathbf{R}^{-1}\mathbf{r}\end{aligned}$$

Thus the 2SLS and 3SLS estimators are identical.[1]

If the system consists of a subset of G^* equations that are exactly identified and $G - G^*$ other equations that are overidentified, the 3SLS estimator of the latter set is the same as that obtained by the application of the 3SLS method to the entire system.[2] That is, for the 3SLS estimation of the $G - G^*$ overidentified equations, the G^* exactly identified equations can be ignored. On the other hand, for the 3SLS estimation of the G^* exactly identified equations, we have to consider the overidentified equations. In particular, consider a system of two equations, and suppose the first equation is exactly identified and the second equation is overidentified. Then the 2SLS and 3SLS estimators of the parameters of the second equation are identical, but for the first equation they are not.

We can give an instrumental-variable interpretation to the 3SLS method just as we did for 2SLS. In the 2SLS method we use $\hat{\mathbf{Z}}_i$ as instrumental variables for the ith equation, where $\hat{\mathbf{Z}}_i = \mathbf{M}\mathbf{Z}_i$. Define

$$\mathbf{Z} = \begin{bmatrix} \mathbf{Z}_1 & & & \bigcirc \\ & \mathbf{Z}_2 & & \\ & & \ddots & \\ \bigcirc & & & \mathbf{Z}_G \end{bmatrix} \qquad \hat{\mathbf{Z}} = \begin{bmatrix} \hat{\mathbf{Z}}_1 & & & \bigcirc \\ & \hat{\mathbf{Z}}_2 & & \\ & & \ddots & \\ \bigcirc & & & \hat{\mathbf{Z}}_G \end{bmatrix} \tag{C-42}$$

and

$$\hat{\mathbf{W}}' = \hat{\mathbf{Z}}'(\mathbf{S}^{-1} \otimes \mathbf{I}_T)$$

Also let

$$\mathbf{y} = \begin{bmatrix} \mathbf{y}_1 \\ \mathbf{y}_2 \\ \vdots \\ \mathbf{y}_G \end{bmatrix} \qquad \boldsymbol{\delta} = \begin{bmatrix} \delta_1 \\ \delta_2 \\ \vdots \\ \delta_G \end{bmatrix} \qquad \text{and} \qquad \mathbf{u} = \begin{bmatrix} \mathbf{u}_1 \\ \mathbf{u}_2 \\ \vdots \\ \mathbf{u}_G \end{bmatrix}$$

[1] The more concise notation for 3SLS, from Eq. (C-39) on, can be found in an unpublished working paper: G. R. Fisher, "A Generalization of Generalized Least Squares," University of Birmingham, 1964; and P. J. Dhrymes, "Econometrics," chap. 4, Harper & Row, Publishers, Incorporated, New York, 1970.

[2] This has been proved in A. Zellner and H. Theil, Three Stage Least Squares: Simultaneous Estimation of Simultaneous Equations, *Econometrica*, 1962, pp. 54–78.

then Eq. (C-36) can be written as

$$\mathbf{y} = \mathbf{Z}\boldsymbol{\delta} + \mathbf{u} \tag{C-43}$$

and the 3SLS estimator given in (C-38) can be verified to be

$$\hat{\boldsymbol{\delta}}_{3SLS} = (\hat{\mathbf{W}}'\mathbf{Z})^{-1}\hat{\mathbf{W}}'\mathbf{y} \tag{C-44}$$

Thus the instrumental variables are $\hat{\mathbf{W}}$ defined in (C-42), and the 3SLS method is a "weighted" instrumental-variable method.

Full-information maximum-likelihood (FIML): Like the 3SLS method, the FIML method is a "system method" in which we estimate the parameters of all equations simultaneously using all the information in the model. Historically, it was the first method proposed for the estimation of simultaneous equations, and the other methods have been suggested and have gained popularity because of the computational complexity of FIML. The 3SLS estimates, like the 2SLS estimates, are not in general invariant to normalization. But the FIML estimates, like the LIML estimates, are invariant to normalization.

We will write the entire set of equations as

$$\mathbf{YB} + \mathbf{X\Gamma} = \mathbf{U} \tag{C-45}$$

where $\mathbf{Y}$ = a $T \times G$ matrix of observations on the G endogenous variables
$\mathbf{X}$ = a $T \times K$ matrix of observations on the K exogenous variables
$\mathbf{U}$ = a $T \times G$ matrix of disturbances

We assume that $\mathbf{B}$ is nonsingular, that all equations satisfy the rank condition for identification, that all identities in the system have been substituted out, and that rank $\mathbf{X} = K$, i.e., there are no linear dependencies among the exogenous variables. We will also assume that

$$\text{plim}\left(\frac{1}{T}\mathbf{X}'\mathbf{U}\right) = \mathbf{0}$$

and that the residuals have a normal distribution with covariance matrix $\boldsymbol{\Sigma}$ and are serially independent, i.e., if $\mathbf{u}_t$ is the tth row of $\mathbf{U}$,

$$\mathbf{u}_t \sim N(0,\boldsymbol{\Sigma}) \qquad (\boldsymbol{\Sigma} \text{ is positive definite})$$

and $E(\mathbf{u}_t\mathbf{u}_s') = \mathbf{0}$ for $t \neq s$. We will, without any loss of generality, assume exclusion restrictions on the matrices $\mathbf{B}$ and $\boldsymbol{\Gamma}$. (There are no restrictions on $\boldsymbol{\Sigma}$.) Suppose that G_i endogenous variables and K_i exogenous variables are included in the ith equation. If we assume a normalization rule, the equations can be written as (C-35) or (C-36). The reduced form corresponding to (C-45) is

$$\mathbf{Y} = \mathbf{X\Pi} + \mathbf{V}$$

where $\boldsymbol{\Pi} = -\boldsymbol{\Gamma}\mathbf{B}^{-1}$ and $\mathbf{V} = \mathbf{UB}^{-1}$. The joint density of the $\mathbf{u}$'s is

$$\frac{1}{(2\pi)^{GT/2}}\frac{1}{|\boldsymbol{\Sigma}|^{T/2}}\exp\left[-\frac{1}{2}\sum_{i=1}^{T}\mathbf{u}_i\boldsymbol{\Sigma}^{-1}\mathbf{u}_i'\right]$$

For convenience in notation we note that

$$\sum_{i=1}^{T}\mathbf{u}_i\boldsymbol{\Sigma}^{-1}\mathbf{u}_i' = \text{tr }\mathbf{U}\boldsymbol{\Sigma}^{-1}\mathbf{U}' = \text{tr }\boldsymbol{\Sigma}^{-1}\mathbf{U}'\mathbf{U}$$

Transforming this to the density of the observed y's, we have the joint density of the endogenous variables given the exogenous variables as

$$\frac{|\mathbf{B}|^T}{(2\pi)^{GT/2}|\mathbf{\Sigma}|^{T/2}} \exp\left[-\frac{1}{2}\operatorname{tr}\mathbf{\Sigma}^{-1}(\mathbf{YB}+\mathbf{X\Gamma})'(\mathbf{YB}+\mathbf{X\Gamma})\right]$$

We have the term $|\mathbf{B}|^T$ because the Jacobian of the transformation from $\mathbf{u}_t$ to $\mathbf{y}_t$ is $|\mathbf{B}|$. Considered as a function of the parameters, this is the likelihood function. Denoting the log-likelihood by L, we have

$$L(\mathbf{B},\mathbf{\Gamma},\mathbf{\Sigma}) = \text{const.} + \frac{T}{2}\log|\mathbf{\Sigma}^{-1}| + T\log|\mathbf{B}| - \frac{1}{2}\left[\operatorname{tr}\mathbf{\Sigma}^{-1}(\mathbf{YB}+\mathbf{X\Gamma})'(\mathbf{YB}+\mathbf{X\Gamma})\right] \tag{C-46}$$

In the differentiation of (C-46), we will use the results

$$\frac{\partial \log|\mathbf{A}|}{\partial \mathbf{A}} = (\mathbf{A}')^{-1}$$

$$\frac{\partial}{\partial \mathbf{A}}\operatorname{tr}\mathbf{AC} = \mathbf{C}'$$

$$\frac{\partial}{\partial \mathbf{A}}\operatorname{tr}\mathbf{DACA}' = 2\mathbf{DAC}$$

(where $\mathbf{C}$ and $\mathbf{D}$ do not involve elements of $\mathbf{A}$). Using these results, we get

$$\frac{\partial L}{\partial \mathbf{B}} = 0 \Rightarrow T(\mathbf{B}')^{-1} - \mathbf{Y}'(\mathbf{YB}+\mathbf{X\Gamma})\mathbf{\Sigma}^{-1} = \mathbf{0} \tag{C-47}$$

$$\frac{\partial L}{\partial \mathbf{\Gamma}} = 0 \Rightarrow -\mathbf{X}'(\mathbf{YB}+\mathbf{X\Gamma})\mathbf{\Sigma}^{-1} = \mathbf{0} \tag{C-48}$$

$$\frac{\partial L}{\partial \mathbf{\Sigma}^{-1}} = 0 \Rightarrow T\mathbf{\Sigma} - (\mathbf{YB}+\mathbf{X\Gamma})'(\mathbf{YB}+\mathbf{X\Gamma}) = \mathbf{0} \tag{C-49}$$

The last equation gives

$$\hat{\mathbf{\Sigma}} = \frac{1}{T}(\mathbf{YB}+\mathbf{X\Gamma})'(\mathbf{YB}+\mathbf{X\Gamma}) \tag{C-50}$$

Since there are no restrictions on $\mathbf{\Sigma}$, it is customary to replace the estimate of $\mathbf{\Sigma}$ from (C-50) in (C-46) and get the concentrated likelihood function

$$L^*(\mathbf{B},\mathbf{\Gamma}) = \text{const.} - \frac{T}{2}\log|(\mathbf{YB}+\mathbf{X\Gamma})'(\mathbf{YB}+\mathbf{X\Gamma})| + T\log|\mathbf{B}|$$

Since $\log|\mathbf{B}| = \frac{1}{2}\log|\mathbf{B}'\mathbf{Y}'\mathbf{YB}| - \frac{1}{2}\log|\mathbf{Y}'\mathbf{Y}|$ and $|\mathbf{Y}'\mathbf{Y}|$ is a constant (being a function of observations only), we can write this as

$$L^*(\mathbf{B},\mathbf{\Gamma}) = \text{const.} + \frac{T}{2}\log|\mathbf{B}'\mathbf{Y}'\mathbf{YB}| - \frac{T}{2}\log|(\mathbf{YB}+\mathbf{X\Gamma})'(\mathbf{YB}+\mathbf{X\Gamma})| \tag{C-51}$$

Thus, to obtain the ML estimates of $\mathbf{B}$ and $\mathbf{\Gamma}$, we have to maximize

$$L^{**} = \log|\mathbf{B}'\mathbf{Y}'\mathbf{YB}| - \log|(\mathbf{YB}+\mathbf{X\Gamma})'(\mathbf{YB}+\mathbf{X\Gamma})| \tag{C-52}$$

We will use the result that

$$\frac{\partial \log|\mathbf{AMA}'|}{\partial \mathbf{A}} = 2(\mathbf{AMA}')^{-1}\mathbf{AM} \tag{C-53}$$

If we write, for the sake of convenience,

$$(\mathbf{B}'\mathbf{Y}'\mathbf{YB}) = \mathbf{Q} \qquad \text{and} \qquad (\mathbf{YB} + \mathbf{X\Gamma})'(\mathbf{YB} + \mathbf{X\Gamma}) = \mathbf{S}$$

then, using the result (C-53), we get

$$\frac{\partial L^{**}}{\partial \mathbf{B}} = 0 \Rightarrow \mathbf{Y}'\mathbf{YBQ}^{-1} - \mathbf{Y}'(\mathbf{YB} + \mathbf{X\Gamma})\mathbf{S}^{-1} = 0 \tag{C-54}$$

$$\frac{\partial L^{**}}{\partial \mathbf{\Gamma}} = 0 \Rightarrow -\mathbf{X}'(\mathbf{YB} + \mathbf{X\Gamma})\mathbf{S}^{-1} = 0 \tag{C-55}$$

We can write Eqs. (C-54) and (C-55) in a notation comparable with that of 3SLS. To do that, consider the system, after normalization, to be written in the form (C-35) or (C-36). Then

$$\mathbf{Q} = [q_{ij}] \qquad \text{where } q_{ij} = (\mathbf{y}_i - \mathbf{Y}_i\boldsymbol{\beta}_i)'(\mathbf{y}_j - \mathbf{Y}_j\boldsymbol{\beta}_j)$$

$$\mathbf{S} = [s_{ij}] \qquad \text{where } s_{ij} = (\mathbf{y}_i - \mathbf{Z}_i\boldsymbol{\delta}_i)'(\mathbf{y}_j - \mathbf{Z}_j\boldsymbol{\delta}_j)$$

What we have to maximize is $|\mathbf{Q}| - |\mathbf{S}|$. Note that $|\mathbf{Q}|$ involves β_i only and does not involve γ_i. If we write $\overline{\mathbf{Z}}_i = [\mathbf{Y}_i\mathbf{0}]$, then $\mathbf{Y}_i\boldsymbol{\beta}_i = \overline{\mathbf{Z}}_i\,\boldsymbol{\delta}_i$. After carrying out the necessary differentiation, we get[1]

$$\hat{\boldsymbol{\delta}} = \mathbf{P}^{-1}\mathbf{d} \tag{C-56}$$

where $\mathbf{P} = [p_{ij}]$.

$$p_{ij} = s^{ij}\mathbf{Z}_i'\mathbf{Z}_j - q^{ij}\overline{\mathbf{Z}}_i'\overline{\mathbf{Z}}_j$$

and the ith element of d is given by

$$d_i = \sum_{i=1}^{G} \left(s^{ij}\mathbf{Z}_i'\mathbf{y}_j - q^{ij}\overline{\mathbf{Z}}_i'\mathbf{y}_j\right)$$

The analogy between (C-56) and the 3SLS equations (C-38) is clear. In the case of 3SLS we have $\sigma^{ij}\mathbf{Z}_i'\mathbf{MZ}_j$ in place of p_{ij} and $\sum_j \sigma^{ij}\mathbf{Z}_j'\mathbf{My}_j$ in place of d_j. In Eq. (C-56) both s^{ij} and q^{ij} involve the unknown parameters β's and γ's. Chow suggests solving Eq. (C-56) in the same way as we do for 3SLS using a consistent estimator for $\mathbf{Q}$ and $\mathbf{S}$. For instance, in the case of 3SLS we use

$$s_{ij} = \frac{1}{T}(\mathbf{y}_i - \mathbf{Z}_i\tilde{\boldsymbol{\delta}}_i)'(\mathbf{y}_j - \mathbf{Z}_j\tilde{\boldsymbol{\delta}}_j) \tag{C-57}$$

where $\tilde{\boldsymbol{\delta}}_i$ is the 2SLS estimator of $\boldsymbol{\delta}_i$. Similarly, for the computations in (C-56) we use s_{ij} as in (C-57) and

$$q_{ij} = \frac{1}{T}(\mathbf{y}_i - \overline{\mathbf{Z}}_i\tilde{\boldsymbol{\delta}}_i)'(\mathbf{y}_j - \overline{\mathbf{Z}}_j\tilde{\boldsymbol{\delta}}_j) \tag{C-58}$$

[1] See G. C. Chow, Two Methods of Computing Full Information Maximum Likelihood Estimates in Simultaneous Stochastic Equations, *International Economic Review*, 1968, pp. 100–112.

The estimator of $\boldsymbol{\delta}$ so obtained is called a modified (linearized) maximum-likelihood estimator. If we define, as before,

$$\mathbf{Z} = \text{diag.}\left[\mathbf{Z}_1\mathbf{Z}_2 \cdots \mathbf{Z}_G\right]$$

and similarly define

$$\overline{\mathbf{Z}} = \text{diag.}\left[\overline{\mathbf{Z}}_1\overline{\mathbf{Z}}_2 \cdots \overline{\mathbf{Z}}_G\right]$$

then Eq. (C-56) can be written as[1]

$$\left[\mathbf{Z}'(\mathbf{S}^{-1} \otimes \mathbf{I}_T)\mathbf{Z} - \overline{\mathbf{Z}}'(\mathbf{Q}^{-1} \otimes \mathbf{I}_T)\overline{\mathbf{Z}}\right]\hat{\boldsymbol{\delta}} = \left[\mathbf{Z}'(\mathbf{S}^{-1} \otimes \mathbf{I}_T)\mathbf{y} - \overline{\mathbf{Z}}'(\mathbf{Q}^{-1} \otimes \mathbf{I}_T)\mathbf{y}\right] \tag{C-59}$$

One can also give an instrumental variable interpretation to the FIML estimator.[2] Note that (C-50) can be written as $T\mathbf{I} = (\mathbf{YB} + \mathbf{X\Gamma})'(\mathbf{YB} + \mathbf{X\Gamma})\boldsymbol{\Sigma}^{-1}$, and substituting this in (C-47), we get

$$(\mathbf{B}')^{-1}(\mathbf{YB} + \mathbf{X\Gamma})'(\mathbf{YB} + \mathbf{X\Gamma})\boldsymbol{\Sigma}^{-1} - \mathbf{Y}'(\mathbf{YB} + \mathbf{X\Gamma})\boldsymbol{\Sigma}^{-1} = \mathbf{0}$$

Hence $(\mathbf{B}')^{-1}\mathbf{\Gamma}'\mathbf{X}'(\mathbf{YB} + \mathbf{X\Gamma})\boldsymbol{\Sigma}^{-1} = \mathbf{0}$ or $\mathbf{\Pi}'\mathbf{X}'(\mathbf{YB} + \mathbf{X\Gamma})\boldsymbol{\Sigma}^{-1} = 0$ since $\mathbf{\Pi} = -\mathbf{\Gamma B}^{-1}$. This equation, together with Eq. (C-48), can be written as

$$\begin{bmatrix} \mathbf{X}' \\ \mathbf{\Pi}'\mathbf{X}' \end{bmatrix}(\mathbf{YB} + \mathbf{X\Gamma})\boldsymbol{\Sigma}^{-1} = 0 \tag{C-60}$$

Again, like Eqs. (C-54) and (C-55) earlier, Eq. (C-60) is not easily recognizable, but it becomes transparent if we consider the model in the form (C-36) after normalization. Note that $\mathbf{X\Pi}$ in (C-60) is the estimate of $\mathbf{Y}$ from the reduced form. Let $\tilde{\mathbf{Z}}_i = [\tilde{\mathbf{Y}}_i\mathbf{X}_i]$, where $\tilde{\mathbf{Y}}_i$ is the estimate of $\mathbf{Y}_i$ from the reduced form. (It is not $\hat{\mathbf{Y}}_i = \mathbf{X}(\mathbf{X}'\mathbf{X})^{-1}\mathbf{X}'\mathbf{Y}_i$. It is obtained as the appropriate submatrix of $\mathbf{B}^{-1}\mathbf{\Gamma X}$.) Also define

$$\tilde{\mathbf{Z}} = \text{diag.}\left[\tilde{\mathbf{Z}}_1\tilde{\mathbf{Z}}_2 \cdots \tilde{\mathbf{Z}}_G\right]$$

Then Eq. (C-60) amounts to

$$\hat{\boldsymbol{\delta}} = \left[\tilde{\mathbf{Z}}'(\boldsymbol{\Sigma}^{-1} \otimes \mathbf{I}_T)\mathbf{Z}\right]^{-1}\left[\tilde{\mathbf{Z}}'(\boldsymbol{\Sigma}^{-1} \otimes \mathbf{I}_T)\mathbf{y}\right] \quad \text{or} \quad \hat{\boldsymbol{\delta}} = (\tilde{\mathbf{W}}'\mathbf{Z})^{-1}\tilde{\mathbf{W}}'\mathbf{y} \tag{C-61}$$

where $\tilde{\mathbf{W}} = \tilde{\mathbf{Z}}'(\boldsymbol{\Sigma}^{-1} \otimes \mathbf{I}_T)$. Equation (C-61) now looks like an instrumental-variable estimator, and the analogy with Eq. (C-44), when we discussed the instrumental-variable interpretation of 3SLS, is clear. $\tilde{\mathbf{W}}$ is itself a function of the parameters $\boldsymbol{\delta}$. But one can think of an iterative procedure to solve Eq. (C-61). Let $\hat{\boldsymbol{\delta}}_k$ be the estimate of $\boldsymbol{\delta}$ at the kth iteration and $\tilde{\mathbf{W}}_k$ the value of $\tilde{\mathbf{W}}$ based on $\hat{\boldsymbol{\delta}}_k$. Then

$$\hat{\boldsymbol{\delta}}_{k+1} = (\tilde{\mathbf{W}}_k'\mathbf{Z})^{-1}\tilde{\mathbf{W}}_k'\mathbf{y} \tag{C-62}$$

[1] See P. J. Dhrymes, "Econometrics," p. 326, Harper & Row, Publishers, Incorporated, New York, 1970.

[2] The following discussion is based on J. Durbin, "Maximum Likelihood Estimation of the Parameters of a System of Simultaneous Regression Equations," 1963 mimeographed, presented at the Copenhagen Meetings of the Econometric Society; and J. A. Hausman, Full Information Instrumental Variable Estimation of Simultaneous Equation Models, *Econometrica*, 1975.

The iterative process, when converged, gives the FIML estimates. Though this particular way of computing the ML estimates is very inefficient, Hausman argues that this formula is instructive in studying the relationships between different instrumental-variable methods proposed in the literature.[1]

Relationship among different estimators:[2] The above discussion makes it clear that the currently available methods of estimation differ in the way the covariance matrix $\mathbf{\Sigma}$ and the reduced-form matrix $\mathbf{\Pi}$ are estimated for the construction of the instrumental variables $\mathbf{W}$. From the large-sample point of view all that is required is consistent estimators for $\mathbf{\Pi}$ and $\mathbf{\Sigma}$ and the asymptotic distribution is not affected. The 3SLS method uses the unrestricted reduced-form least-squares estimate of $\mathbf{\Pi}$ and an estimate of $\mathbf{\Sigma}$ obtained from the 2SLS residuals. The FIML method amounts to iterating on both $\mathbf{\Pi}$ and $\mathbf{\Sigma}$, the estimate of $\mathbf{\Pi}$ at each stage being obtained from the solved reduced form. The 3SLS method can be iterated using the revised estimator of $\mathbf{\Sigma}$ based on 3SLS residuals, but this does not produce the FIML estimator. On the other hand, iterating on *both* $\mathbf{\Pi}$ and $\mathbf{\Sigma}$ will produce FIML on convergence. This merely amounts to an iterative solution of Eq. (C-61).

In some situations the unrestricted reduced form is not estimable because of an insufficient number of observations in comparison with the number of exogenous variables. In such cases the 2SLS and 3SLS methods cannot be used. But some instrumental-variable methods can still be used. The FIVE (full-information instrumental-variable estimation method) suggested by Brundy and Jorgenson[3] amounts to obtaining preliminary consistent estimates $\hat{\mathbf{B}}$, $\hat{\mathbf{\Gamma}}$ of $\mathbf{B}$ and $\mathbf{\Gamma}$, respectively, by instrumental-variable methods and then constructing

$$\hat{\mathbf{\Pi}} = -\hat{\mathbf{\Gamma}}\hat{\mathbf{B}}^{-1} \qquad \text{and} \qquad \hat{\mathbf{\Sigma}} = \frac{1}{T}(\mathbf{Y}\hat{\mathbf{B}} + \mathbf{X}\hat{\mathbf{\Gamma}})'(\mathbf{Y}\hat{\mathbf{B}} + \mathbf{X}\hat{\mathbf{\Gamma}})$$

They then use the instrumental-variable method, as described earlier, based on these estimates. This method clearly amounts to a first iteration of the ML method.

Another method suggested in this same context is the iterative instrumental-variable method (IIV) discussed by Lyttkens.[4] In this method the instrumental variables are obtained from the solved reduced form at each stage. Thus the method iterates on $\mathbf{\Pi}$ but $\mathbf{\Sigma}$ is taken to be the identity matrix. Hence the IIV estimator is consistent but not as efficient as the FIML estimator. The LIVE (limited-information instrumental-variable estimation method) estimator sug-

[1] One problem with the iterative procedure in (C-62) is that $(\tilde{\mathbf{W}}_k'\mathbf{Z})$ may not be positive definite at each stage of the iteration. Hausman discusses some modifications of the procedure given by (C-62). One modification is to use $(\tilde{\mathbf{W}}_k'\tilde{\mathbf{Z}})$ if $\tilde{\mathbf{W}}_k'\mathbf{Z}$ is not positive definite. See Hausman, *op. cit.*

[2] For a unified treatment of all simultaneous equations estimators see D. F. Hendry, "The Structure of Simultaneous Equations Estimators," *Journal of Econometrics*, 1976, pp. 51–88.

[3] J. M. Brundy and D. W. Jorgenson, Efficient Estimation of Simultaneous Equations by Instrumental Variables, *Review of Economics and Statistics*, 1971, pp. 207–224.

[4] E. Lyttkens, The Iterative Instrumental Variable Method and the Full Information Maximum Likelihood Method for Estimating Interdependent Systems, *Journal of Multivariate Analysis*, 1974, pp. 283–307.

gested by Brundy and Jorgenson is the first iterate of the IIV estimator. It is the same as the FIVE estimator with $\mathbf{\Sigma}$ taken to be the identity matrix. In the LIVE method, as in the FIVE method, we first use some instrumental variables to get consistent estimates $\hat{\mathbf{B}}$, $\hat{\mathbf{\Gamma}}$ of $\mathbf{B}$, $\mathbf{\Gamma}$, respectively, and then get $\hat{\mathbf{\Pi}}$ from the solved reduced form, i.e., $\hat{\mathbf{\Pi}} = -\hat{\mathbf{\Gamma}}\hat{\mathbf{B}}^{-1}$. The estimates of the endogenous variables from the solved reduced form are used as instrumental variables. The LIVE and the IIV estimators as well as the 2SLS estimator have the same asymptotic distribution. However, the LIVE estimator will depend on what instrumental variables are used in the first stage, and thus we will get different answers depending on what variable we pick as instruments to get $\hat{\mathbf{B}}$ and $\hat{\mathbf{\Gamma}}$. Further, the LIVE estimator (and so also the IIV estimator) is not strictly speaking a limited-information estimator because the information on the structure of the entire $(\mathbf{B},\mathbf{\Gamma})$ matrix is used in its computation (because we use the solved reduced form in constructing the instruments). The merit of the LIVE and IIV estimator is that (in fact they have been suggested in exactly this context) they can be computed even when 2SLS estimates cannot be if the model is large and the unrestricted reduced form is not estimable.

In our discussion of 2SLS, we noted that if $\hat{\mathbf{Y}}$, the estimates of the endogenous variables, are obtained from the unrestricted reduced form, then $\hat{\mathbf{Y}}$ can be used as either regressors (2SLS) or as instrumental variables and the resultant estimators of the parameters are the same. This is no longer true if $\hat{\mathbf{Y}}$ are obtained from the restricted reduced form (as-solved reduced form). In fact we can talk of the RRF2SLS (restricted reduced-form two-stage least-squares) and RRFIV (restricted reduced-form instrumental-variable) estimators[1] and the two will be different. The difference between the two is that in RRF2SLS, $\hat{\mathbf{Y}}$'s are used as regressors and in RRFIV, $\hat{\mathbf{Y}}$'s are used as instrumental variables, and one can use both procedures in an iterative fashion. The RRFIV is the IIV estimator considered earlier. The RRF2SLS is the estimator that Wold suggests under the name fix-point method.[2] Though Wold suggested the fix-point method in the context of a respecified version of the simultaneous-equation system, which he called the GEID (generalized independent system), he intends his method also to be considered as an alternative to the other simultaneous-equation methods. But the fix-point (RRF2SLS) method has several drawbacks. Sometimes it does not converge and can give oscillatory solutions, and even if it converges it can converge to different points depending on the starting point.[3] Dhrymes and Pandit[4] consider the asymptotic distribution of the first iterate of

[1] G. S. Maddala, Simultaneous Estimation Methods for Large and Medium-Size Econometric Models, *Review of Economic Studies*, 1971, pp. 435–445.

[2] H. Wold, A Fix-Point Theorem with Econometric Background; Parts I and II, *Arkiv för Matematik*, 1965, pp. 209–240. An elaborate study of the method is contained in E. Mosbaek and H. Wold, "Interdependent Systems," North-Holland Publishing Company, Amsterdam, 1970.

[3] See Maddala, *op. cit.*

[4] P. J. Dhrymes and V. Pandit, The Asymptotic Distribution of the First Iterate of the Iterated Two Stage Least Squares Estimates, *Journal of the American Statistical Association*, 1971.

the RRF2SLS and find that it is not possible to rank it in relation to 2SLS. The estimators of some parameters can be more efficient than those of 2SLS, and the estimators of some other parameters can be less efficient than those of 2SLS. Thus, if the restricted reduced-form method is used, it is better to consider the instrumental-variable version than the 2SLS version.

Usefulness of Asymptotic Approximations

Most of the theoretical work on simultaneous equations has been concerned with obtaining asymptotic distributions of estimators, and it is common practice to report the confidence intervals and significance tests based on these asymptotic distributions. From the practical point of view we would like to know how good these significance tests are. It has been customary to study this problem through some Monte Carlo studies. However, such studies use up a lot of computer time, and different investigators often come to different conclusions based on the range of parameter variation they assume. It would be useful if these problems could be studied analytically. This important problem has been studied by Sargan and his associates in a series of papers. Sargan also gives some practical methods, based on asymptotic theory, to improve our significance tests and also suggests ways of evaluating the results of Monte Carlo studies. This work is, however, somewhat complicated to review here.[1]

[1] See J. D. Sargan, "Econometric Estimators and the Edgeworth Approximation," *Econometrica*, May 1976, pp. 421–448, and the references to other papers cited therein. This work builds on Sargan's earlier seminal work on instrumental variables and instrumental variable estimators.

APPENDIX

D

SOME EXERCISES

I. GENERAL QUESTIONS

1. Since the tax rate on capital gains is less than the tax rate on ordinary income, a premium for this advantage must be included in the price of growth stocks. It has been argued that universities should not be willing to pay this premium, since their income is tax-exempt. What can an econometrician do to help settle this question?

2. Empirical studies overstate the price elasticity of demand for whisky, since most of the observed price changes are due to tax changes that lead to increased purchases of whisky in nearby stores. How would you estimate the price elasticity of demand for whisky?

3. Suppose that, for each household in a cross section, you have data giving the household's income and its purchases (quantities) of each good. Suppose that some of these households have been compelled to purchase more of the first good than they would have purchased without compulsion, and that you know which households these are and how much extra they were compelled to purchase. How would you determine the effects of this compulsion on these households' purchases of other goods? Would your procedure change if you also knew the price of the first good? The prices of all goods?

4. A study was made in a certain firm of the relation between payroll in dollars (y) and number of hours worked (x). Both x and y were weekly totals. The usual least-squares straight line, taking y as the dependent variable, gave $y = 2468 + 1.1x$. This procedure was criticized on two grounds: (1) Since the intercept of the true relations is obviously zero, a regression showing a large positive intercept seems meaningless; (2) in the given circumstances, the conditional variance of y could not be expected to be independent of x.

(*a*) Are these criticisms valid? Discuss.

(*b*) Whether you accept or reject the objections, specify clearly and fully a model in which (1) the regression line in the population is straight and is restricted so as to pass through the origin, and (2) some reasonable assumption is made for the dependence of the variance of y on x. On the basis of this model, find the formula for the maximum-likelihood estimate of the slope of that line.

5. Suggest what you consider to be a good example of the use of mathematical economics to provide testable economic hypotheses. Explain the derivation of at least one such hypothesis and show how you would go about testing it.

6. What is "stepwise" multiple regression? What are the advantages and disadvantages of "stepwise" regression compared with "ordinary" regression?

7. In his study of the demand for aluminum ingot, F. M. Fisher estimates the following short-run demand equation for the U. S.:

$$\Delta \log Q_t = .0542 + \underset{(.124)}{.755}\,\Delta \log Y_t - \underset{(.426)}{.024}\,\Delta \log P_t \qquad R^2 = .747$$

where Q_t = quantity of aluminum ingot
Y_t = Federal Reserve index of durable output
P_t = money price of aluminum divided by BLS price index for metals

What would be the effect on the price coefficient of deflating the money price index of aluminum ingot by a general price index, e.g., wholesale price index? (During the sample period there was only one aluminum-ingot producer in the U. S.)

8. In a world with a fixed stock of financial assets and in which everyone had the same expectations, wealth, and utility function, there would be no markets for financial assets. If we were to relax these assumptions by allowing either differences in expectations or difference in utility functions, trading would occur in response to changes in expectations. How would you go about determining empirically the extent to which trading of financial assets is due to differences among individuals in (1) expectations and elasticities of expectations, and (2) the shape of the utility function?

9. If society is maximizing the value of lives saved by public expenditure on safety equipment, the value of lives saved through marginal expenditures on such things as air travel, highways, and public recreation are all equal. This need not imply that the number of lives saved by all such marginal expenditures are equal, since not all lives are of equal value to society. How would you determine whether society is maximizing the value of its safety expenditures?

10. An investigator tried to determine, among other things, the relationship between true property values and assessed values for tax purposes. For a sample of sales within a given time period, the investigator obtained data on the sales price and current assessed valuation. He then computed the regression of the *ratio* of assessed value to sales price on sales price and found a negative slope. Why might this procedure have given misleading results? How might the same basic data have been analyzed to avoid this difficulty? Under what circumstances, if any, could you defend the analysis actually made?

11. It is often said that underdeveloped countries face a low price elasticity of demand for their exports of primary products—food, fiber, and minerals. Discuss how you would test this hypothesis for a particular product, say coffee or tea. Construct an adequate but reasonably simple model, discuss whether time-series or cross-section data would be most appropriate for estimating the model, and explain fully the econometric problems that you might encounter and the available techniques for detecting and dealing with these problems.

12. Suppose the "true" demand relationship for a certain commodity is

$$Y_t^* = \delta + \beta P_t^* + u_t$$

where y_t^* is the "desired" quantity in period t (not observable) and P_t^* is the "expected" price in period t (also not observable).

Assume that two other relevant relationships are operative, viz., a "price-expectations" equation

$$P_t^* = \alpha P_{t-1} + (1-\alpha)P_{t-1}^* + V_t \qquad 0 < \alpha < 1$$

and a "quantity-adjustment" relationship

$$Y_t = \gamma Y_t^* + (1-\gamma)Y_{t-1} + W_t \qquad 0 < \gamma < 1$$

u_t, V_t, W_t are independent random variables with zero mean and unknown variances $\sigma_u^2, \sigma_V^2, \sigma_W^2$, respectively. Also u_t, V_t, W_t are independent of anything occurring prior to period t.

(*a*) Show how β can be estimated. What can you say about the properties of β? (State any additional assumptions required.)

(*b*) Can α and γ be estimated? If so, how? If not, why not? What can you say about the applicability of the above model in practical econometric investigations?

13. Let $y = X_1\beta_1 + X_2\beta_2 + e$. Instead of computing the least-squares estimates b_1 and b_2, we compute b_1^* from a regression of y on X_1 only, and b_2^* from a regression of the resulting residuals on X_2. Evaluate the biases in b_1^* and b_2^*. In the special case $y = \beta_1 x_1 + \beta_2 x_2 + e$, show that b_2^* is biased toward zero.

14. $Y_t = \beta x_t + u_t$, $u_t = \rho u_{t-1} + e_t$, e_t are $IN(0,\sigma^2)$ and $\rho < 1$. Discuss the different procedures for the estimation of β and ρ. How will your answer change if y_{t-1} is also included as an explanatory variable?

15. Discuss the choice of the form of econometric equations (e.g., linear in variables, linear in logarithms of variables, linear in unknown parameters) and the choice of variables to be included and variables to be excluded.

16. Suppose you have a priori convictions about the algebraic signs of certain parameters in an econometric equation. Discuss the issues involved in the choice between (1) estimating the parameters subject to the restrictions that the parameters in question have the signs that you believe to be correct, and (2) first estimating the parameters without restrictions and then revising the equation if any estimated parameters that differ significantly from zero fail to have the signs you believe to be correct.

17. You are interested in estimating the relationship of sugar consumption to income. You have the choice of working with data on individuals at a particular time, with group averages at a particular time, and with aggregate time-series data. Discuss the advantages and disadvantages of each body of data for your purposes. Also discuss how best you can use the three data sets together.

18. In a gambling experiment, subjects are offered several gambles, all relating to the same event, but differing in the odds offered. In each case the subject is asked whether he would like to bet for or against the event and how much. The answers tell the experimenter how much the subject is willing to risk on the given event at the given odds. The experimenter can calculate from the subject's answer the amount the subject hopes to win.

For example:

(*a*) If odds of 3 to 1 are offered and the subject offers to bet \$2 that the event will occur, he is risking \$2 and hopes to win \$6.

(*b*) If odds of 2 to 1 are offered and the subject offers to bet \$3 that the event will not occur, he risks \$3 and hopes to win \$1.50.

Let X_1 measure the outcome of a gamble if the event gambled on occurs, and X_2 measure the outcome if the event does not occur.

It follows from expected utility maximization that a curve, properly fitted to (X_1,X_2), should pass through the origin and that at the origin its slope should be $-p/(1-p)$, where p is the probability that the event in question will occur.

The difficulty here is that our observations consist of points (X_1,X_2) in which one measure or the other is the response of the subject and the remaining measure is derived from the response by simple multiplication. If one measure contains an error, so does the other. A regression of X_2 on X_1 will therefore suffer. How? What cures are commonly applied?

19. Suppose we are investigating two income concepts, one being disposable income, equal to

$$Y_D = A_1 + C$$

where C is consumption and A_1 is the autonomous-expenditure concept relevant to this income concept; and the other being disposable income plus undistributed corporate profits, equal to

$$Y = A_2 + C = A_1 + U + C$$

where U is undistributed corporate profits. To determine which income concept is more appropriate for estimating "the" Keynesian multiplier, one might take the simple correlation of Y_D with A_1 and that of Y with A_2 and find which gives the higher correlation.

An objection to this procedure might be that it involves "spurious" correlation. Does it? Why? If it does, give a preferable procedure. Suppose one wanted to estimate the relation between real consumption and real income. One approach is to deflate money income and money consumption by a common price index and correlate deflated consumption and deflated income. This also has been criticized for involving "spurious" correlation. Does it? Why? If so, give a preferable procedure.

20. Define plim, lim E, and A.E. and give examples of sequences of random variables for which:

(*a*) plim = lim E
(*b*) plim $\neq$ lim E
(*c*) plim = A.E.
(*d*) plim $\neq$ A. E.
(*e*) lim E = A.E.
(*f*) lim $E \neq$ A.E.

21.
$$X_t = a + bX_{t-1} + u_t \quad 0 < b < 1 \quad E(u_t) = E(v_t) = 0$$
$$Y_t = c + bY_{t-1} + v_t \quad V(u_t) = V(v_t) = \sigma^2 < \infty$$

X_t and Y_t are independent. Suppose we compute the regression of Y_t on X_t. Let the regression coefficient be $\hat{\beta}$. What is plim $\hat{\beta}$?

22. Suppose the true equation is

$$Y = \alpha_0 + \alpha_1 X + \alpha_2 X^2 + u$$

Suppose we estimate instead the equation

$$Y = \beta_0 + \beta_1 X + v$$

by OLS. Express $E(\hat{\beta}_1)$ in terms of α_0, α_1, and α_2.

23. Let $Y = X\beta + e$ be the "true" equation. The covariance matrix of e is $I\sigma^2$. Let $Y = Z\alpha + u$ be the "misspecified" equation. Show that the estimated residual variance computed from the "misspecified" equation will (on the average) be larger than σ^2.

24. Consider the set of demand functions for n commodities

$$X_{it} = a_i C_t + \sum_{j=1}^{n} b_{ij} P_{jt} + e_{it} \qquad \begin{array}{l} i = 1, 2, \ldots, n \\ t = 1, 2, \ldots, T \end{array}$$

where P_{jt} are prices and $C_t = \Sigma_i X_{it}$ is total consumption. But the coefficients are subject to certain a priori restrictions given by the consumption laws. These are:

(*a*) Additivity: $C_t = \Sigma_i X_{it}$ for all t.

(*b*) Homogeneity: If C_t and P_{jt} are all multiplied by the same number, the X_{it} are also multiplied by the same number.

(*c*) Symmetry conditions on the substitution matrix given by the Slutsky conditions. These conditions imply some restriction on the parameters. Derive these restrictions, and explain how you will carry out the estimation of the demand functions subject to these restrictions.

II. TRUE, FALSE, UNCERTAIN QUESTIONS

Examine whether the following statements are true (T), false, (F), or uncertain (U). Give a short explanation. If a statement is not true in general but is true under some conditions, state the conditions.

1. Deflating income and consumption by the same price index results in a higher estimate for the marginal propensity to consume.

2. Suppose you regress food expenditures on total consumption. Assuming that consumption and permanent income are highly correlated, this procedure gives us an unbiased estimate of the elasticity of demand for food with respect to permanent income.

3. The omission of a variable from a regression equation biases the estimates of the coefficients of the included variables toward one.

4. Multicollinearity among the independent variables in a regression equation implies that least-squares estimates of the coefficients are not best linear unbiased.

5. Errors in variables lead to estimates of the regression coefficients that are biased toward zero.

6. Consider three variables X_1, X_2, X_3. If r_{12} and r_{23} are significantly close to $+1$ or -1, then r_{13} will have the sign of the product $r_{12}r_{23}$.

7. If $r_{12} = 0$, no information as to the sign of r_{13} can be drawn from r_{23}, $+r_{13}^2$, and $r_{23}^2 < 1$ in this case.

8. Least-squares techniques when applied to economic time-series data usually yield biased estimates because many economic time series are autocorrelated.

9. The "standard error of an estimate" is a measure of the accuracy with which predictions can be made from the estimated regression equation.

10. Since inventory investment is such a small fraction of GNP, it can, for all practical purposes, be ignored in explanations of booms and recessions.

11. The correlation between two ratios which have the same denominator is always biased upward.

12. The method of instrumental variables gives unbiased estimates of the regression coefficients.

13. The omission of income variables in a demand function results in an underestimate of the price elasticity in absolute terms.

14. Several different forms of trend can be represented by the equation $Y = a + b \log t$.

15. If a variable X is uncorrelated with Z, the addition of Z to a regression in which X is used as an independent variable will not change either the coefficient of X or the standard error of the coefficient.

16. The residual from a regression of Y on X is uncorrelated with X but correlated with Y.

17. An estimation of the demand function for steel gave the price elasticity of demand for steel as $+.3$. This finding should be interpreted to mean that the price elasticity of supply is at least $+.3$.

18. Heteroscedasticity and serial correlation in the residuals u lead to biased estimates and biased standard errors in the estimated least-squares coefficients of the equation $Y = Xb + u$.

19. The Durbin-Watson test for serial correlation is not applicable if the residuals are heteroscedastic.

20. The Durbin-Watson test for serial correlation is not applicable in distributed-lag models.

21. An investigator estimated the demand function in the log-linear form $\log Q = \alpha + \beta \log \mathrm{P}$ and the linear form $Q = a + bP$, and chose the latter because the R^2's for the two formulations were, respectively, .85 and .90. This is not the correct procedure for choosing between the two formulations.

22. It is possible to obtain more efficient estimates than simple least-squares estimates of the reduced-form parameters by exploiting ths true correlations among the residuals of the various equations.

23. The matrix of variables in a four-equation, seven-variable simultaneous-equation system is

$$\begin{matrix} 1 & 0 & 1 & 1 & 1 & 0 & 0 \\ 1 & 1 & 1 & 0 & 0 & 1 & 1 \\ 0 & 0 & 1 & 0 & 1 & 0 & 0 \\ 1 & 0 & 1 & 1 & 0 & 1 & 0 \end{matrix}$$

The first equation is identified. (1 indicates presence, 0 absence.)

24. In a simultaneous-equation system, the more the number of exogenous variables, the better.

25. If multiple correlation coefficients of the reduced-form equations are nearly one, OLS estimates of the parameters of the structural equations will be nearly unbiased.

26. If one is interested in making predictions, estimates of the reduced-form equations of an economic model are all that are required.

27.

$$Y_{1t} = \beta_{12}Y_{2t} + r_{11}Z_{1t} + U_{1t}$$
$$Y_{2t} = \beta_{21}Y_{1t} \qquad + U_{2t}$$

The first equation is not identified.

28. Two-stage least-squares and three-stage least-squares estimates will be identical if and only if all equations are exactly identified.

29. If you iterate on three-stage least-squares you get full-information maximum-likelihood estimates, but there is no point in doing this because you do not gain anything.

30. Consistent estimators are asymptotically unbiased and conversely.

31.

$$Y_t = a + bX_t + U_t$$
$$U_t = \delta U_{t-1} + e_t \qquad 0 \leqslant \delta \leqslant 1$$

e_t are random variables independent of U_{t-1} and X_t. By taking first differences, it is possible to obtain more efficient least-squares estimates of b than by the OLS regression of Y_t on X_t.

32. In 31 above, if X_t satisfies a first-order autoregressive equation, OLS estimates of b will not be even consistent.

33. The Durbin-Watson test can be used to decide whether the residuals in a regression equation based on time-series data are serially independent.

34. It is sometimes preferable to use OLS instead of the instrumental-variable method even though the latter method gives consistent estimates and the former does not.

35. Consider the model $Y_t = \alpha Y_{t-1} + \beta X_t + U_t$, where the residuals U_t are autoregressive. In this case, even if the OLS estimation method gives inconsistent estimates of the parameters, we can use the equation for prediction purposes if the evolution of the exogenous variables during the prediction period follows the average evolution during the estimation period.

36. In the 2SLS method we should replace only the endogenous variables on the right-hand side of the equation by their estimated values from the reduced form. We should not replace the endogenous variable on the left-hand side by its estimated value from the reduced form.

37. Though 2SLS and LIML methods have been shown to be asymptotically the same, we should prefer the 2SLS method to the LIML method because the sum of squares of the residuals obtained from the 2SLS method is always less than or equal to the sum of squares of the residuals from the LIML method.

38. If one applies simple least squares to estimate the parameters of a regression equation with autocorrelated errors, one will obtain unbiased estimators, but one is likely to obtain a serious underestimate of their sampling variances.

39. If the residuals in a regression model are not independently distributed with a common variance σ^2, the OLS estimates are always less efficient than the GLS estimates for all finite sample sizes.

40. The statement in 39 is also true even asymptotically.

III. SIMULTANEOUS-EQUATION MODELS

1. T. C. Liu, in his quarterly econometric model (*Econometrica*, July 1963) reports results of both OLS and 2SLS estimates of his equations. In almost all equations the two estimates differ only at the third decimal place. Does this mean that there is no need to estimate this model by simultaneous-equation techniques?

2. Smith[1] has a four-equation model:

$$Y = C + I + U_1 \qquad I = b_0 + b_1Y_{-1} + b_2r_{-1} + U_3$$
$$C = a_0 + a_1Y + a_2T + U_2 \qquad M = h_0 + h_1Y + h_2r + U_4$$

[1] Paul Smith, Built-in-Flexibility of Income Tax, *Econometrica*, October 1963.

Y, C, I, M are endogenous variables; the rest predetermined. He says that everyone knows that OLS is inappropriate for estimating structural equations. Hence he estimates the equations by 2SLS. Comment on the normalization rules he has adopted. In his next model he makes T endogenous and adds the equation

$$T = t_0 + t_1 Y + U_5$$

How does your answer change now?

3. How do you decide which variables to treat as endogenous, which as exogenous, and which to use for normalization if you are using 2SLS?

4. Construct an example of an econometric model in which the order condition for identifiability is satisfied but the rank condition is not.

5. Discuss the identifiability of the parameters in the following system:

$$C = \alpha_0 + \alpha_1 W + \alpha_2 P + U_1$$

$$I = \beta_0 + \beta_1 P + \beta_2 k_{-1} + U_2$$

$$W = \gamma_0 + \gamma_1 Y_{-1} + U_3$$

where $C + I = Y$

$P + W = Y$

$I = k - k_{-1}$

C, I, W, P, Y, k are endogenous.

6. Give an example to show how a priori restrictions concerning the disturbance in a single equation or in a system of equations can be used to help "identify" the parameters of a particular equation.

7. Consider the model

(1) $$c = \alpha + \beta(y - t) + u$$

(2) $$i = \gamma + \delta y + v$$

(3) $$c + i + g = y$$

where c, y, and i are endogenous variables, t and g are exogenous variables, and u and v are two stochastic disturbances whose distribution is independent of g and t. Is equation (1) identified? Is equation (2) identified? Do not answer only yes or no, but explain how you reach your conclusions.

8. Consider the model

(1) $$x = \alpha p + \beta q + \gamma + u$$

(2) $$x = \delta p + \epsilon r + \mu + v$$

where x and p are endogenous variables, q and r are exogenous variables, and u and v are stochastic disturbances whose distribution is independent of q and r. Describe a method for getting estimates of α and δ. Compare the estimates you get in three situations I, II, and III, where the situations differ from each other only in the following way: In situation I the true value of ϵ is far from zero, in situation II the true value of ϵ is equal to zero, and in situation III the true value of ϵ is close to zero.

9. Consider the simultaneous-equation model consisting of the endogenous variables:

C = real consumption
I = real investment
N = employment
P = price level
R = interest rate
Y = real income
W = money wage rate

and exogenous variables:

$$G = \text{real government purchases}$$
$$T = \text{real tax receipts}$$
$$M = \text{nominal money stock}$$

$$\begin{array}{ll}
C = a_1 + b_1 Y - c_1 T + d_1 R + U_1 & \text{(consumption function)} \\
I = a_2 + b_2 Y + c_2 R + U_2 & \text{(investment function)} \\
Y = C + I + G & \text{(identity)} \\
M = a_3 + b_3 Y + c_3 R + d_3 P + U_3 & \text{(liquidity preference function)} \\
Y = a_4 + b_4 N + U_4 & \text{(production function)} \\
N = a_5 + b_5 W + c_5 P + U_5 & \text{(labor demand)} \\
N = a_6 + b_6 W + c_6 P + U_6 & \text{(labor supply)}
\end{array}$$

(*a*) Is the model complete?

(*b*) Which of these equations is underidentified, exactly identified, or overidentified?

(*c*) Suggest methods for estimating the investment function, labor-demand function, and labor-supply function.

10. It has been asserted that a correctly specified model of virtually any economic structure would be found to be underidentified and that identification is commonly achieved only by making a variety of invalid assumptions; for example, many variables assumed to be excluded from an equation do in fact have at least some influence on it, the true structure has many more equations than the assumed structure, and some variables assumed to be exogenous are in fact endogenous in the larger structure. Hence structural estimation is said to be logically impossible in most cases, and attempts to formulate and estimate "identified" models an exercise in futility; further, for purposes of prediction, the use of unrestricted estimates of the reduced form is said to be better than estimates based on incorrect "identifying" restrictions. The above argument was first presented by T. C. Liu in the late fifties, and yet econometricians continue to estimate structural parameters. What justifications of this practice can be advanced?

11. Suppose

$$q = \alpha p + u \qquad \text{and} \qquad q = \beta p + v$$

are two relations operating simultaneously, where q and p are observable variables, α and β are unknown constants, and u and v are nonobservable random variables with zero means, constant (unknown) variances (designated σ_u^2 and σ_v^2, respectively), and zero covariance.

(*a*) Show that, in the population of observations (q,p) generated by this system, the least-squares regression coefficient of q on p is equal to a weighted average of α and β, the weights being σ_v^2 and σ_u^2, respectively.

(*b*) If in addition it is known that $\sigma_v^2 = k\sigma_u^2$, where k is a known nonnegative constant, show how α and β might be estimated.

12. Suggest methods of estimating the following model:

$$Y_{1t} = \beta_{12} Y_{2t} + \gamma_{11} Y_{1,t-1} + \gamma_{12} Y_{2,t-1} + U_{1t}$$
$$Y_{1t} = \beta_{22} Y_{2t} + \gamma_{21} Z_{1t} + \gamma_{22} Z_{2t} + U_{2t}$$

where

$$U_{1t} = \delta_{11} U_{1,t-1} + \delta_{12} U_{2,t-1} + e_{1t}$$
$$U_{2t} = \delta_{21} U_{1,t-1} + \delta_{22} U_{2,t-1} + e_{2t}$$

e_{1t}, e_{2t} are serially independent. *Y*'s are endogenous and *Z*'s are exogenous variables.

13. Outline the salient features that distinguish each of the following estimation methods:

(*a*) Single-equation least-squares
(*b*) Indirect least-squares
(*c*) Limited-information maximum-likelihood
(*d*) Two-stage least-squares
(*e*) Three-stage least-squares

State the circumstances under which any of these are not distinct from the others.

14. Suppose that we estimate a given structural equation by 2SLS and LIML methods. Show that the sum of squares of the residuals obtained by 2SLS is not larger than the sum of squares of residuals obtained by the LIML method. Does this mean that 2SLS gives a better "fit"? Explain.

15. Basmann has shown that sometimes the variance of 2SLS estimators does not exist. However, the limiting distribution has a finite variance. Which limit should we prefer—the limits of the moments of a distribution or the moments of the limiting distribution? Why?

16. Consider the equation $Y_1 = \alpha X + \beta Y_2 + u$ where Y_1, Y_2 are endogenous and X is exogenous. Let α_1, β_1 be the 2SLS estimators of α, β, respectively, and let α_k, β_k be the k-class estimators. Show that $(\alpha_1 - \alpha_k)/(\beta_k - \beta_1) =$ the regression coefficient of Y_2 on X.

17. On p. 93 of their 1955 book, Klein and Goldberger summarized a comparison of their 1929–1950 and 1929–1952 limited-information models by saying: "The majority of differences in parameter estimates obtained by the revised and augmented sample are not large and can be accounted for by the presence of sampling errors." Karl Fox ("Intermediate Economic Statistics," p. 360, 1968) compares the least-squares and limited-information estimates for 1929–1952 and finds that these differences are still smaller. He concludes that Klein and Goldberger gained little of economic importance using the limited-information method. Examine the validity of this argument.

18. Comment in detail on the following procedure used to decide whether to use a simultaneous-equation model or a recursive model.

Karl Fox ("Intermediate Economic Statistics," 1968) considers the following model for pork:

Demand function: $$Q = a_1 + b_1 P + c_1 Y + u$$

Supply function: $$Q = a_2 + b_2 P + c_2 Z + v$$

Y is disposable income and Z is an estimate of production These two variables are considered exogenous. The equations are fitted for the period 1922–1941. The reduced-form equations are

$$P = -.0101 + \underset{(.1339)}{1.0813}Y - \underset{(.1159)}{.8320}Z \qquad R^2 = .893$$

$$Q = .0026 - \underset{(.0673)}{.0018}Y + \underset{(.0582)}{.6839}Z \qquad R^2 = .898$$

From these the structural estimates are:

Demand: $$Q = -.0063 - .8220P + .8870Y$$

Supply: $$Q = .0026 - 0017P + .6825Z$$

The OLS estimates of the demand function are as follows.
Using Q as the dependent variable:

$$Q = -.0049 - \underset{(.0594)}{.7205}P + \underset{(.0967)}{.7646}Y \qquad R^2 = .903$$

Using P as the dependent variable:

$$P = -.0070 - \underset{(.1032)}{1.2518}Q + \underset{(.0861)}{1.0754}Y \qquad R^2 = .956$$

When the structural demand function is normalized with respect to P, it is

$$P = -.0077 - 1.2165Q + 1.0791Y$$

Thus the coefficients of the least-squares regression using P as the dependent variable are almost identical with those of the structural equation. Also, the coefficient of P in the supply equation is close to zero (and has the wrong sign) and the coefficient of Y in the reduced-form equation for Q is not at all significant. These results lead us to conclude that the appropriate formulation of the model is the recursive model.

Demand function: $$P = \alpha_1 + \beta_1 Q + \delta_1 Y + u$$

$$Q = \alpha_2 + \delta_2 Z + v$$

and we can estimate each equation by OLS.

Fox next considers the model for beef (data 1922–1941). The demand function is $Q = a_1 + b_1 P + c_1 Y + d_1 W + u$, and the supply function is $Q = a_2 + b_2 P + c_2 Z + v$.

W is consumption of other meats assumed exogenous. The reduced-form estimates are

$$P = A_1 + \underset{(.1061)}{.8185}\,Y - \underset{(.1877)}{.8521}\,Z - \underset{(.1631)}{.4346}\,W \qquad R^2 = .87$$

$$Q = A_2 + \underset{(.0545)}{.0509}\,Y + \underset{(.0964)}{.8801}\,Z - \underset{(.0830)}{.0899}\,W \qquad R^2 = .87$$

$\hat{b}_1 = -1.0329$. For b_2 we have two estimates

$$\hat{b}_{2y} = \frac{.0509}{.8185} = .0622 \qquad \text{and} \qquad \hat{b}_{2w} = \frac{-.0899}{-.4346} = .2068$$

Now, neither of the numerators from which we compute $\hat{b}_2$ is significant. Therefore, Fox argues: "Starting from such unpromising materials it seems likely that any compromise estimate of b_2 which must be a weighted average of $\hat{b}_{2y}$ and $\hat{b}_{2w}$ will also be non-significant." Hence we can assume b_2 to be zero. This reduces the system to a recursive one, and we can estimate the demand function by OLS using P as the dependent variable.

APPENDIX

E

TABLES

Table E-1 Ordinates of the normal density function

$$\phi(x) = \frac{1}{\sqrt{2\pi}} e^{-x^2/2}$$

x	.00	.01	.02	.03	.04	.05	.06	.07	.08	.09
.0	.3989	.3989	.3989	.3988	.3986	.3984	.3982	.3980	.3977	.3973
.1	.3970	.3965	.3961	.3956	.3951	.3945	.3939	.3932	.3925	.3918
.2	.3910	.3902	.3894	.3885	.3876	.3867	.3857	.3847	.3836	.3825
.3	.3814	.3802	.3790	.3778	.3765	.3752	.3739	.3725	.3712	.3697
.4	.3683	.3668	.3653	.3637	.3621	.3605	.3589	.3572	.3555	.3538
.5	.3521	.3503	.3485	.3467	.3448	.3429	.3410	.3391	.3372	.3352
.6	.3332	.3312	.3292	.3271	.3251	.3230	.3209	.3187	.3166	.3144
.7	.3123	.3101	.3079	.3056	.3034	.3011	.2989	.2966	.2943	.2920
.8	.2897	.2874	.2850	.2827	.2803	.2780	.2756	.2732	.2709	.2685
.9	.2661	.2637	.2613	.2589	.2565	.2541	.2516	.2492	.2468	.2444
1.0	.2420	.2396	.2371	.2347	.2323	.2299	.2275	.2251	.2227	.2203
1.1	.2179	.2155	.2131	.2107	.2083	.2059	.2036	.2012	.1989	.1965
1.2	.1942	.1919	.1895	.1872	.1849	.1826	.1804	.1781	.1758	.1736
1.3	.1714	.1691	.1669	.1647	.1626	.1604	.1582	.1561	.1539	.1518
1.4	.1497	.1476	.1456	.1435	.1415	.1394	.1374	.1354	.1334	.1315
1.5	.1295	.1276	.1257	.1238	.1219	.1200	.1182	.1163	.1145	.1127
1.6	.1109	.1092	.1074	.1057	.1040	.1023	.1006	.0989	.0973	.0957
1.7	.0940	.0925	.0909	.0893	.0878	.0863	.0848	.0833	.0818	.0804
1.8	.0790	.0775	.0761	.0748	.0734	.0721	.0707	.0694	.0681	.0669
1.9	.0656	.0644	.0632	.0620	.0608	.0596	.0584	.0573	.0562	.0551
2.0	.0540	.0529	.0519	.0508	.0498	.0488	.0478	.0468	.0459	.0449
2.1	.0440	.0431	.0422	.0413	.0404	.0396	.0387	.0379	.0371	.0363
2.2	.0355	.0347	.0339	.0332	.0325	.0317	.0310	.0303	.0297	.0290
2.3	.0283	.0277	.0270	.0264	.0258	.0252	.0246	.0241	.0235	.0229
2.4	.0224	.0219	.0213	.0208	.0203	.0198	.0194	.0189	.0184	.0180
2.5	.0175	.0171	.0167	.0163	.0158	.0154	.0151	.0147	.0143	.0139
2.6	.0136	.0132	.0129	.0126	.0122	.0119	.0116	.0113	.0110	.0107
2.7	.0104	.0101	.0099	.0096	.0093	.0091	.0088	.0086	.0084	.0081
2.8	.0079	.0077	.0075	.0073	.0071	.0069	.0067	.0065	.0063	.0061
2.9	.0060	.0058	.0056	.0055	.0053	.0051	.0050	.0048	.0047	.0046
3.0	.0044	.0043	.0042	.0040	.0039	.0038	.0037	.0036	.0035	.0034
3.1	.0033	.0032	.0031	.0030	.0029	.0028	.0027	.0026	.0025	.0025
3.2	.0024	.0023	.0022	.0022	.0021	.0020	.0020	.0019	.0018	.0018
3.3	.0017	.0017	.0016	.0016	.0015	.0015	.0014	.0014	.0013	.0013
3.4	.0012	.0012	.0012	.0011	.0011	.0010	.0010	.0010	.0009	.0009
3.5	.0009	.0008	.0008	.0008	.0008	.0007	.0007	.0007	.0007	.0006
3.6	.0006	.0006	.0006	.0005	.0005	.0005	.0005	.0005	.0005	.0004
3.7	.0004	.0004	.0004	.0004	.0004	.0004	.0003	.0003	.0003	.0003
3.8	.0003	.0003	.0003	.0003	.0003	.0002	.0002	.0002	.0002	.0002
3.9	.0002	.0002	.0002	.0002	.0002	.0002	.0002	.0002	.0001	.0001

(Reprinted from Mood and Graybill, "Introduction to the Theory of Statistics," 3rd ed., McGraw-Hill Book Company, New York, 1973. By permission of the publishers.)

Table E-2 Cumulative normal distribution

$$\Phi(x)=\int_{-\infty}^{x} \frac{1}{\sqrt{2\pi}} e^{-t^2/2}\, dt$$

x	.00	.01	.02	.03	.04	.05	.06	.07	.08	.09
.0	.5000	.5040	.5080	.5120	.5160	.5199	.5239	.5279	.5319	.5359
.1	.5398	.5438	.5478	.5517	.5557	.5596	.5636	.5675	.5714	.5753
.2	.5793	.5832	.5871	.5910	.5948	.5987	.6026	.6064	.6103	.6141
.3	.6179	.6217	.6255	.6293	.6331	.6368	.6406	.6443	.6480	.6517
.4	.6554	.6591	.6628	.6664	.6700	.6736	.6772	.6808	.6844	.6879
.5	.6915	.6950	.6985	.7019	.7054	.7088	.7123	.7157	.7190	.7224
.6	.7257	.7291	.7324	.7357	.7389	.7422	.7454	.7486	.7517	.7549
.7	.7580	.7611	.7642	.7673	.7704	.7734	.7764	.7794	.7823	.7852
.8	.7881	.7910	.7939	.7967	.7995	.8023	.8051	.8078	.8106	.8133
.9	.8159	.8186	.8212	.8238	.8264	.8289	.8315	.8340	.8365	.8389
1.0	.8413	.8438	.8461	.8485	.8508	.8531	.8554	.8577	.8599	.8621
1.1	.8643	.8665	.8686	.8708	.8729	.8749	.8770	.8790	.8810	.8830
1.2	.8849	.8869	.8888	.8907	.8925	.8944	.8962	.8980	.8997	.9015
1.3	.9032	.9049	.9066	.9082	.9099	.9115	.9131	.9147	.9162	.9177
1.4	.9192	.9207	.9222	.9236	.9251	.9265	.9279	.9292	.9306	.9319
1.5	.9332	.9345	.9357	.9370	.9382	.9394	.9406	.9418	.9429	.9441
1.6	.9452	.9463	.9474	.9484	.9495	.9505	.9515	.9525	.9535	.9545
1.7	.9554	.9564	.9573	.9582	.9591	.9599	.9608	.9616	.9625	.9633
1.8	.9641	.9649	.9656	.9664	.9671	.9678	.9686	.9693	.9699	.9706
1.9	.9713	.9719	.9726	.9732	.9738	.9744	.9750	.9756	.9761	.9767
2.0	.9772	.9778	.9783	.9788	.9793	.9798	.9803	.9808	.9812	.9817
2.1	.9821	.9826	.9830	.9834	.9838	.9842	.9846	.9850	.9854	.9857
2.2	.9861	.9864	.9868	.9871	.9875	.9878	.9881	.9884	.9887	.9890
2.3	.9893	.9896	.9898	.9901	.9904	.9906	.9909	.9911	.9913	.9916
2.4	.9918	.9920	.9922	.9925	.9927	.9929	.9931	.9932	.9934	.9936
2.5	.9938	.9940	.9941	.9943	.9945	.9946	.9948	.9949	.9951	.9952
2.6	.9953	.9955	.9956	.9957	.9959	.9960	.9961	.9962	.9963	.9964
2.7	.9965	.9966	.9967	.9968	.9969	.9970	.9971	.9972	.9973	.9974
2.8	.9974	.9975	.9976	.9977	.9977	.9978	.9979	.9979	.9980	.9981
2.9	.9981	.9982	.9982	.9983	.9984	.9984	.9985	.9985	.9986	.9986
3.0	.9987	.9987	.9987	.9988	.9988	.9989	.9989	.9989	.9990	.9990
3.1	.9990	.9991	.9991	.9991	.9992	.9992	.9992	.9992	.9993	.9993
3.2	.9993	.9993	.9994	.9994	.9994	.9994	.9994	.9995	.9995	.9995
3.3	.9995	.9995	.9995	.9996	.9996	.9996	.9996	.9996	.9996	.9997
3.4	.9997	.9997	.9997	.9997	.9997	.9997	.9997	.9997	.9997	.9998

x	1.282	1.645	1.960	2.326	2.576	3.090	3.291	3.891	4.417
$\Phi(x)$	.90	.95	.975	.99	.995	.999	.9995	.99995	.999995
$2[1-\Phi(x)]$	.20	.10	.05	.02	.01	.002	.001	.0001	.00001

(Reprinted from Mood and Graybill, "Introduction to the Theory of Statistics," 3rd ed., McGraw-Hill Book Company, New York, 1973. By permission of the publishers.)

Table E-3 Cumulative chi-square distribution*

$$F(u) = \int_0^u \frac{x^{(n-2)/2} e^{-x/2}\, dx}{2^{n/2}\Gamma(n/2)}$$

n \ F	.005	.010	.025	.050	.100	.250	.500	.750	.900	.950	.975	.990	.995
1	$.0^4393$	$.0^3157$	$.0^3982$	$.0^2393$	.0158	.102	.455	1.32	2.71	3.84	5.02	6.63	7.88
2	.0100	.0201	.0506	.103	.211	.575	1.39	2.77	4.61	5.99	7.38	9.21	10.6
3	.0717	.115	.216	.352	.584	1.21	2.37	4.11	6.25	7.81	9.35	11.3	12.8
4	.207	.297	.484	.711	1.06	1.92	3.36	5.39	7.78	9.49	11.1	13.3	14.9
5	.412	.554	.831	1.15	1.61	2.67	4.35	6.63	9.24	11.1	12.8	15.1	16.7
6	.676	.872	1.24	1.64	2.20	3.45	5.35	7.84	10.6	12.6	14.4	16.8	18.5
7	.989	1.24	1.69	2.17	2.83	4.25	6.35	9.04	12.0	14.1	16.0	18.5	20.3
8	1.34	1.65	2.18	2.73	3.49	5.07	7.34	10.2	13.4	15.5	17.5	20.1	22.0
9	1.73	2.09	2.70	3.33	4.17	5.90	8.34	11.4	14.7	16.9	19.0	21.7	23.6
10	2.16	2.56	3.25	3.94	4.87	6.74	9.34	12.5	16.0	18.3	20.5	23.2	25.2
11	2.60	3.05	3.82	4.57	5.58	7.58	10.3	13.7	17.3	19.7	21.9	24.7	26.8
12	3.07	3.57	4.40	5.23	6.30	8.44	11.3	14.8	18.5	21.0	23.3	26.2	28.3
13	3.57	4.11	5.01	5.89	7.04	9.30	12.3	16.0	19.8	22.4	24.7	27.7	29.8
14	4.07	4.66	5.63	6.57	7.79	10.2	13.3	17.1	21.1	23.7	26.1	29.1	31.3
15	4.60	5.23	6.26	7.26	8.55	11.0	14.3	18.2	22.3	25.0	27.5	30.6	32.8
16	5.14	5.81	6.91	7.96	9.31	11.9	15.3	19.4	23.5	26.3	28.8	32.0	34.3
17	5.70	6.41	7.56	8.67	10.1	12.8	16.3	20.5	24.8	27.6	30.2	33.4	35.7
18	6.26	7.01	8.23	9.39	10.9	13.7	17.3	21.6	26.0	28.9	31.5	34.8	37.2
19	6.84	7.63	8.91	10.1	11.7	14.6	18.3	22.7	27.2	30.1	32.9	36.2	38.6
20	7.43	8.26	9.59	10.9	12.4	15.5	19.3	23.8	28.4	31.4	34.2	37.6	40.0
21	8.03	8.90	10.3	11.6	13.2	16.3	20.3	24.9	29.6	32.7	35.5	38.9	41.4
22	8.64	9.54	11.0	12.3	14.0	17.2	21.3	26.0	30.8	33.9	36.8	40.3	42.8
23	9.26	10.2	11.7	13.1	14.8	18.1	22.3	27.1	32.0	35.2	38.1	41.6	44.2
24	9.89	10.9	12.4	13.8	15.7	19.0	23.3	28.2	33.2	36.4	39.4	43.0	45.6
25	10.5	11.5	13.1	14.6	16.5	19.9	24.3	29.3	34.4	37.7	40.6	44.3	46.9
26	11.2	12.2	13.8	15.4	17.3	20.8	25.3	30.4	35.6	38.9	41.9	45.6	48.3
27	11.8	12.9	14.6	16.2	18.1	21.7	26.3	31.5	36.7	40.1	43.2	47.0	49.6
28	12.5	13.6	15.3	16.9	18.9	22.7	27.3	32.6	37.9	41.3	44.5	48.3	51.0
29	13.1	14.3	16.0	17.7	19.8	23.6	28.3	33.7	39.1	42.6	45.7	49.6	52.3
30	13.8	15.0	16.8	18.5	20.6	24.5	29.3	34.8	40.3	43.8	47.0	50.9	53.7

* This table is abridged from "Tables of percentage points of the incomplete beta function and of the chi-square distribution," *Biometrika*, Vol. 32 (1941). It is here published with the kind permission of its author, Catherine M. Thompson, and the editor of *Biometrika*.

Table E-4 Cumulative student's t distribution*

$$F(t) = \int_{-\infty}^{t} \frac{\Gamma\left(\frac{n+1}{2}\right)}{\Gamma(n/2)\sqrt{\pi n}\left(1+\frac{x^2}{n}\right)^{(n+1)/2}}\,dx$$

n \ F	.75	.90	.95	.975	.99	.995	.9995
1	1.000	3.078	6.314	12.706	31.821	63.657	636.619
2	.816	1.886	2.920	4.303	6.965	9.925	31.598
3	.765	1.638	2.353	3.182	4.541	5.841	12.941
4	.741	1.533	2.132	2.776	3.747	4.604	8.610
5	.727	1.476	2.015	2.571	3.365	4.032	6.859
6	.718	1.440	1.943	2.447	3.143	3.707	5.959
7	.711	1.415	1.895	2.365	2.998	3.499	5.405
8	.706	1.397	1.860	2.306	2.896	3.355	5.041
9	.703	1.383	1.833	2.262	2.821	3.250	4.781
10	.700	1.372	1.812	2.228	2.764	3.169	4.587
11	.697	1.363	1.796	2.201	2.718	3.106	4.437
12	.695	1.356	1.782	2.179	2.681	3.055	4.318
13	.694	1.350	1.771	2.160	2.650	3.012	4.221
14	.692	1.345	1.761	2.145	2.624	2.977	4.140
15	.691	1.341	1.753	2.131	2.602	2.947	4.073
16	.690	1.337	1.746	2.120	2.583	2.921	4.015
17	.689	1.333	1.740	2.110	2.567	2.898	3.965
18	.688	1.330	1.734	2.101	2.552	.2878	3.922
19	.688	1.328	1.729	2.093	2.539	2.861	3.883
20	.687	1.325	1.725	2.086	2.528	2.845	3.850
21	.686	1.323	1.721	2.080	2.518	2.831	3.819
22	.686	1.321	1.717	2.074	2.508	2.819	3.792
23	.685	1.319	1.714	2.069	2.500	2.807	3.767
24	.685	1.318	1.711	2.064	2.492	2.797	3.745
25	.684	1.316	1.708	2.060	2.485	2.787	3.725
26	.684	1.315	1.706	2.056	2.479	2.779	3.707
27	.684	1.314	1.703	2.052	2.473	2.771	3.690
28	.683	1.313	1.701	2.048	2.467	2.763	3.674
29	.683	1.311	1.699	2.045	2.462	2.756	3.659
30	.683	1.310	1.697	2.042	2.457	2.750	3.646
40	.681	1.303	1.684	2.021	2.423	2.704	3.551
60	.679	1.296	1.671	2.000	2.390	2.660	3.460
120	.677	1.289	1.658	1.980	2.358	2.617	3.373
∞	.674	1.282	1.645	1.960	2.326	2.576	3.291

* This table is abridged from the "Statistical Tables" of R. A. Fisher and Frank Yates published by Oliver & Boyd, Ltd., Edinburgh and London, 1938. It is here published with the kind permission of the authors and their publishers.

Table E-5[1] Durbin-Watson statistic (d). Significance points of d_L and d_U: 5%

n	$k' = 1$		$k' = 2$		$k' = 3$		$k' = 4$		$k' = 5$	
	d_L	d_U	d_L	d_U	d_L	d_U	d_L	d_U	d_L	d_U
15	1.08	1.36	0.95	1.54	0.82	1.75	0.69	1.97	0.56	2.21
16	1.10	1.37	0.98	1.54	0.86	1.73	0.74	1.93	0.62	2.15
17	1.13	1.38	1.02	1.54	0.90	1.71	0.78	1.90	0.67	2.10
18	1.16	1.39	1.05	1.53	0.93	1.69	0.82	1.87	0.71	2.06
19	1.18	1.40	1.08	1.53	0.97	1.68	0.86	1.85	0.75	2.02
20	1.20	1.41	1.10	1.54	1.00	1.68	0.90	1.83	0.79	1.99
21	1.22	1.42	1.13	1.54	1.03	1.67	0.93	1.81	0.83	1.96
22	1.24	1.43	1.15	1.54	1.05	1.66	0.96	1.80	0.86	1.94
23	1.26	1.44	1.17	1.54	1.08	1.66	0.99	1.79	0.90	1.92
24	1.27	1.45	1.19	1.55	1.10	1.66	1.01	1.78	0.93	1.90
25	1.29	1.45	1.21	1.55	1.12	1.66	1.04	1.77	0.95	1.89
26	1.30	1.46	1.22	1.55	1.14	1.65	1.06	1.76	0.98	1.88
27	1.32	1.47	1.24	1.56	1.16	1.65	1.08	1.76	1.01	1.86
28	1.33	1.48	1.26	1.56	1.18	1.65	1.10	1.75	1.03	1.85
29	1.34	1.48	1.27	1.56	1.20	1.65	1.12	1.74	1.05	1.84
30	1.35	1.49	1.28	1.57	1.21	1.65	1.14	1.74	1.07	1.83
31	1.36	1.50	1.30	1.57	1.23	1.65	1.16	1.74	1.09	1.83
32	1.37	1.50	1.31	1.57	1.24	1.65	1.18	1.73	1.11	1.82
33	1.38	1.51	1.32	1.58	1.26	1.65	1.19	1.73	1.13	1.81
34	1.39	1.51	1.33	1.58	1.27	1.65	1.21	1.73	1.15	1.81
35	1.40	1.52	1.34	1.58	1.28	1.65	1.22	1.73	1.16	1.80
36	1.41	1.52	1.35	1.59	1.29	1.65	1.24	1.73	1.18	1.80
37	1.42	1.53	1.36	1.59	1.31	1.66	1.25	1.72	1.19	1.80
38	1.43	1.54	1.37	1.59	1.32	1.66	1.26	1.72	1.21	1.79
39	1.43	1.54	1.38	1.60	1.33	1.66	1.27	1.72	1.22	1.79
40	1.44	1.54	1.39	1.60	1.34	1.66	1.29	1.72	1.23	1.79
45	1.48	1.57	1.43	1.62	1.38	1.67	1.34	1.72	1.29	1.78
50	1.50	1.59	1.46	1.63	1.42	1.67	1.38	1.72	1.34	1.77
55	1.53	1.60	1.49	1.64	1.45	1.68	1.41	1.72	1.38	1.77
60	1.55	1.62	1.51	1.65	1.48	1.69	1.44	1.73	1.41	1.77
65	1.57	1.63	1.54	1.66	1.50	1.70	1.47	1.73	1.44	1.77
70	1.58	1.64	1.55	1.67	1.52	1.70	1.49	1.74	1.46	1.77
75	1.60	1.65	1.57	1.68	1.54	1.71	1.51	1.74	1.49	1.77
80	1.61	1.66	1.59	1.69	1.56	1.72	1.53	1.74	1.51	1.77
85	1.62	1.67	1.60	1.70	1.57	1.72	1.55	1.75	1.52	1.77
90	1.63	1.68	1.61	1.70	1.59	1.73	1.57	1.75	1.54	1.78
95	1.64	1.69	1.62	1.71	1.60	1.73	1.58	1.75	1.56	1.78
100	1.65	1.69	1.63	1.72	1.61	1.74	1.59	1.76	1.57	1.78

n = number of observations.

k' = number of explanatory variables.

[1] This Table is reproduced from *Biometrika*, vol. 41, p. 173, 1951, with the permission of the Trustees.

Table E-6[1] Durbin-Watson statistic (d). Significance points of d_L and d_U: 1%

n	$k' = 1$		$k' = 2$		$k' = 3$		$k' = 4$		$k' = 5$	
	d_L	d_U	d_L	d_U	d_L	d_U	d_L	d_U	d_L	d_U
15	0.81	1.07	0.70	1.25	0.59	1.46	0.49	1.70	0.39	1.96
16	0.84	1.09	0.74	1.25	0.63	1.44	0.53	1.66	0.44	1.90
17	0.87	1.10	0.77	1.25	0.67	1.43	0.57	1.63	0.48	1.85
18	0.90	1.12	0.80	1.26	0.71	1.42	0.61	1.60	0.52	1.80
19	0.93	1.13	0.83	1.26	0.74	1.41	0.65	1.58	0.56	1.77
20	0.95	1.15	0.86	1.27	0.77	1.41	0.68	1.57	0.60	1.74
21	0.97	1.16	0.89	1.27	0.80	1.41	0.72	1.55	0.63	1.71
22	1.00	1.17	0.91	1.28	0.83	1.40	0.75	1.54	0.66	1.69
23	1.02	1.19	0.94	1.29	0.86	1.40	0.77	1.53	0.70	1.67
24	1.04	1.20	0.96	1.30	0.88	1.41	0.80	1.53	0.72	1.66
25	1.05	1.21	0.98	1.30	0.90	1.41	0.83	1.52	0.75	1.65
26	1.07	1.22	1.00	1.31	0.93	1.41	0.85	1.52	0.78	1.64
27	1.09	1.23	1.02	1.32	0.95	1.41	0.88	1.51	0.81	1.63
28	1.10	1.24	1.04	1.32	0.97	1.41	0.90	1.51	0.83	1.62
29	1.12	1.25	1.05	1.33	0.99	1.42	0.92	1.51	0.85	1.61
30	1.13	1.26	1.07	1.34	1.01	1.42	0.94	1.51	0.88	1.61
31	1.15	1.27	1.08	1.34	1.02	1.42	0.96	1.51	0.90	1.60
32	1.16	1.28	1.10	1.35	1.04	1.43	0.98	1.51	0.92	1.60
33	1.17	1.29	1.11	1.36	1.05	1.43	1.00	1.51	0.94	1.59
34	1.18	1.30	1.13	1.36	1.07	1.43	1.01	1.51	0.95	1.59
35	1.19	1.31	1.14	1.37	1.08	1.44	1.03	1.51	0.97	1.59
36	1.21	1.32	1.15	1.38	1.10	1.44	1.04	1.51	0.99	1.59
37	1.22	1.32	1.16	1.38	1.11	1.45	1.06	1.51	1.00	1.59
38	1.23	1.33	1.18	1.39	1.12	1.45	1.07	1.52	1.02	1.58
39	1.24	1.34	1.19	1.39	1.14	1.45	1.09	1.52	1.03	1.58
40	1.25	1.34	1.20	1.40	1.15	1.46	1.10	1.52	1.05	1.58
45	1.29	1.38	1.24	1.42	1.20	1.48	1.16	1.53	1.11	1.58
50	1.32	1.40	1.28	1.45	1.24	1.49	1.20	1.54	1.16	1.59
55	1.36	1.43	1.32	1.47	1.28	1.51	1.25	1.55	1.21	1.59
60	1.38	1.45	1.35	1.48	1.32	1.52	1.28	1.56	1.25	1.60
65	1.41	1.47	1.38	1.50	1.35	1.53	1.31	1.57	1.28	1.61
70	1.43	1.49	1.40	1.52	1.37	1.55	1.34	1.58	1.31	1.61
75	1.45	1.50	1.42	1.53	1.39	1.56	1.37	1.59	1.34	1.62
80	1.47	1.52	1.44	1.54	1.42	1.57	1.39	1.60	1.36	1.62
85	1.48	1.53	1.46	1.55	1.43	1.58	1.41	1.60	1.39	1.63
90	1.50	1.54	1.47	1.56	1.45	1.59	1.43	1.61	1.41	1.64
95	1.51	1.55	1.49	1.57	1.47	1.60	1.45	1.62	1.42	1.64
100	1.52	1.56	1.50	1.58	1.48	1.60	1.46	1.63	1.44	1.65

n = number of observations.
k' = number of explanatory variables.

[1] This Table is reproduced from *Biometrika*, vol. 41, p. 175, 1951, with the permission of the Trustees.

Table E-7 F distribution, upper 5% points ($F_{0.95}$).[1]

Degrees of freedom for numerator (columns); Degrees of freedom for denominator (rows)

	1	2	3	4	5	6	7	8	9	10	12	15	20	24	30	40	60	120	∞
1	161	200	216	225	230	234	237	239	241	242	244	246	248	249	250	251	252	253	254
2	18.5	19.0	19.2	19.2	19.3	19.3	19.4	19.4	19.4	19.4	19.4	19.4	19.4	19.5	19.5	19.5	19.5	19.5	19.5
3	10.1	9.55	9.28	9.12	9.01	8.94	8.89	8.85	8.81	8.79	8.74	8.70	8.66	8.64	8.62	8.59	8.57	8.55	8.53
4	7.71	6.94	6.59	6.39	6.26	6.16	6.09	6.04	6.00	5.96	5.91	5.86	5.80	5.77	5.75	5.72	5.69	5.66	5.63
5	6.61	5.79	5.41	5.19	5.05	4.95	4.88	4.82	4.77	4.74	4.68	4.62	4.56	4.53	4.50	4.46	4.43	4.40	4.37
6	5.99	5.14	4.76	4.53	4.39	4.28	4.21	4.15	4.10	4.06	4.00	3.94	3.87	3.84	3.81	3.77	3.74	3.70	3.67
7	5.59	4.74	4.35	4.12	3.97	3.87	3.79	3.73	3.68	3.64	3.57	3.51	3.44	3.41	3.38	3.34	3.30	3.27	3.23
8	5.32	4.46	4.07	3.84	3.69	3.58	3.50	3.44	3.39	3.35	3.28	3.22	3.15	3.12	3.08	3.04	3.01	2.97	2.93
9	5.12	4.26	3.86	3.63	3.48	3.37	3.29	3.23	3.18	3.14	3.07	3.01	2.94	2.90	2.86	2.83	2.79	2.75	2.71
10	4.96	4.10	3.71	3.48	3.33	3.22	3.14	3.07	3.02	2.98	2.91	2.85	2.77	2.74	2.70	2.66	2.62	2.58	2.54
11	4.84	3.98	3.59	3.36	3.20	3.09	3.01	2.95	2.90	2.85	2.79	2.72	2.65	2.61	2.57	2.53	2.49	2.45	2.40
12	4.75	3.89	3.49	3.26	3.11	3.00	2.91	2.85	2.80	2.75	2.69	2.62	2.54	2.51	2.47	2.43	2.38	2.34	2.30
13	4.67	3.81	3.41	3.18	3.03	2.92	2.83	2.77	2.71	2.67	2.60	2.53	2.46	2.42	2.38	2.34	2.30	2.25	2.21
14	4.60	3.74	3.34	3.11	2.96	2.85	2.76	2.70	2.65	2.60	2.53	2.46	2.39	2.35	2.31	2.27	2.22	2.18	2.13
15	4.54	3.68	3.29	3.06	2.90	2.79	2.71	2.64	2.59	2.54	2.48	2.40	2.33	2.29	2.25	2.20	2.16	2.11	2.07
16	4.49	3.63	3.24	3.01	2.85	2.74	2.66	2.59	2.54	2.49	2.42	2.35	2.28	2.24	2.19	2.15	2.11	2.06	2.01
17	4.45	3.59	3.20	2.96	2.81	2.70	2.61	2.55	2.49	2.45	2.38	2.31	2.23	2.19	2.15	2.10	2.06	2.01	1.96
18	4.41	3.55	3.16	2.93	2.77	2.66	2.58	2.51	2.46	2.41	2.34	2.27	2.19	2.15	2.11	2.06	2.02	1.97	1.92
19	4.38	3.52	3.13	2.90	2.74	2.63	2.54	2.48	2.42	2.38	2.31	2.23	2.16	2.11	2.07	2.03	1.98	1.93	1.88
20	4.35	3.49	3.10	2.87	2.71	2.60	2.51	2.45	2.39	2.35	2.28	2.20	2.12	2.08	2.04	1.99	1.95	1.90	1.84
21	4.32	3.47	3.07	2.84	2.68	2.57	2.49	2.42	2.37	2.32	2.25	2.18	2.10	2.05	2.01	1.96	1.92	1.87	1.81
22	4.30	3.44	3.05	2.82	2.66	2.55	2.46	2.40	2.34	2.30	2.23	2.15	2.07	2.03	1.98	1.94	1.89	1.84	1.78
23	4.28	3.42	3.03	2.80	2.64	2.53	2.44	2.37	2.32	2.27	2.20	2.13	2.05	2.01	1.96	1.91	1.86	1.81	1.76
24	4.26	3.40	3.01	2.78	2.62	2.51	2.42	2.36	2.30	2.25	2.18	2.11	2.03	1.98	1.94	1.89	1.84	1.79	1.73
25	4.24	3.39	2.99	2.76	2.60	2.49	2.40	2.34	2.28	2.24	2.16	2.09	2.01	1.96	1.92	1.87	1.82	1.77	1.71
30	4.17	3.32	2.92	2.69	2.53	2.42	2.33	2.27	2.21	2.16	2.09	2.01	1.93	1.89	1.84	1.79	1.74	1.68	1.62
40	4.08	3.23	2.84	2.61	2.45	2.34	2.25	2.18	2.12	2.08	2.00	1.92	1.84	1.79	1.74	1.69	1.64	1.58	1.51
60	4.00	3.15	2.76	2.53	2.37	2.25	2.17	2.10	2.04	1.99	1.92	1.84	1.75	1.70	1.65	1.59	1.53	1.47	1.39
120	3.92	3.07	2.68	2.45	2.29	2.18	2.09	2.02	1.96	1.91	1.83	1.75	1.66	1.61	1.55	1.50	1.43	1.35	1.25
∞	3.84	3.00	2.60	2.37	2.21	2.10	2.01	1.94	1.88	1.83	1.75	1.67	1.57	1.52	1.46	1.39	1.32	1.22	1.00

Interpolation should be performed using reciprocals of the degrees of freedom.

[1] This table is reproduced with the permission of the Biometrika Trustees from M. Merrington, C. M. Thompson, "Tables of percentage points of the inverted beta (F) distribution," *Biometrika*, vol. 33, p. 73, 1943. Also reprinted in Dixon and Massey, *op. cit.*

Table E-8 F distribution, upper 1% points $(F_{0.99})$.[1]

Degrees of freedom for numerator (columns); degrees of freedom for denominator (rows)

	1	2	3	4	5	6	7	8	9	10	12	15	20	24	30	40	60	120	∞
1	4,052	5,000	5,403	5,625	5,764	5,859	5,928	5,982	6,023	6,056	6,106	6,157	6,209	6,235	6,261	6,287	6,313	6,339	6,366
2	98.5	99.0	99.2	99.2	99.3	99.3	99.4	99.4	99.4	99.4	99.4	99.4	99.4	99.5	99.5	99.5	99.5	99.5	99.5
3	34.1	30.8	29.5	28.7	28.2	27.9	27.7	27.5	27.3	27.2	27.1	26.9	26.7	26.6	26.5	26.4	26.3	26.2	26.1
4	21.2	18.0	16.7	16.0	15.5	15.2	15.0	14.8	14.7	14.5	14.4	14.2	14.0	13.9	13.8	13.7	13.7	13.6	13.5
5	16.3	13.3	12.1	11.4	11.0	10.7	10.5	10.3	10.2	10.1	9.89	9.72	9.55	9.47	9.38	9.29	9.20	9.11	9.02
6	13.7	10.9	9.78	9.15	8.75	8.47	8.26	8.10	7.98	7.87	7.72	7.56	7.40	7.31	7.23	7.14	7.06	6.97	6.88
7	12.2	9.55	8.45	7.85	7.46	7.19	6.99	6.84	6.72	6.62	6.47	6.31	6.16	6.07	5.99	5.91	5.82	5.74	5.65
8	11.3	8.65	7.59	7.01	6.63	6.37	6.18	6.03	5.91	5.81	5.67	5.52	5.36	5.28	5.20	5.12	5.03	4.95	4.86
9	10.6	8.02	6.99	6.42	6.06	5.80	5.61	5.47	5.35	5.26	5.11	4.96	4.81	4.73	4.65	4.57	4.48	4.40	4.31
10	10.0	7.56	6.55	5.99	5.64	5.39	5.20	5.06	4.94	4.85	4.71	4.56	4.41	4.33	4.25	4.17	4.08	4.00	3.91
11	9.65	7.21	6.22	5.67	5.32	5.07	4.89	4.74	4.63	4.54	4.40	4.25	4.10	4.02	3.94	3.86	3.78	3.69	3.60
12	9.33	6.93	5.95	5.41	5.06	4.82	4.64	4.50	4.39	4.30	4.16	4.01	3.86	3.78	3.70	3.62	3.54	3.45	3.36
13	9.07	6.70	5.74	5.21	4.86	4.62	4.44	4.30	4.19	4.10	3.96	3.82	3.66	3.59	3.51	3.43	3.34	3.25	3.17
14	8.86	6.51	5.56	5.04	4.70	4.46	4.28	4.14	4.03	3.94	3.80	3.66	3.51	3.43	3.35	3.27	3.18	3.09	3.00
15	8.68	6.36	5.42	4.89	4.56	4.32	4.14	4.00	3.89	3.80	3.67	3.52	3.37	3.29	3.21	3.13	3.05	2.96	2.87
16	8.53	6.23	5.29	4.77	4.44	4.20	4.03	3.89	3.78	3.69	3.55	3.41	3.26	3.18	3.10	3.02	2.93	2.84	2.75
17	8.40	6.11	5.19	4.67	4.34	4.10	3.93	3.79	3.68	3.59	3.46	3.31	3.16	3.08	3.00	2.92	2.83	2.75	2.65
18	8.29	6.01	5.09	4.58	4.25	4.01	3.84	3.71	3.60	3.51	3.37	3.23	3.08	3.00	2.92	2.84	2.75	2.66	2.57
19	8.19	5.93	5.01	4.50	4.17	3.94	3.77	3.63	3.52	3.43	3.30	3.15	3.00	2.92	2.84	2.76	2.67	2.58	2.49
20	8.10	5.85	4.94	4.43	4.10	3.87	3.70	3.56	3.46	3.37	3.23	3.09	2.94	2.86	2.78	2.69	2.61	2.52	2.42
21	8.02	5.78	4.87	4.37	4.04	3.81	3.64	3.51	3.40	3.31	3.17	3.03	2.88	2.80	2.72	2.64	2.55	2.46	2.36
22	7.95	5.72	4.82	4.31	3.99	3.76	3.59	3.45	3.35	3.26	3.12	2.98	2.83	2.75	2.67	2.58	2.50	2.40	2.31
23	7.88	5.66	4.76	4.26	3.94	3.71	3.54	3.41	3.30	3.21	3.07	2.93	2.78	2.70	2.62	2.54	2.45	2.35	2.26
24	7.82	5.61	4.72	4.22	3.90	3.67	3.50	3.36	3.26	3.17	3.03	2.89	2.74	2.66	2.58	2.49	2.40	2.31	2.21
25	7.77	5.57	4.68	4.18	3.86	3.63	3.46	3.32	3.22	3.13	2.99	2.85	2.70	2.62	2.53	2.45	2.36	2.27	2.17
30	7.56	5.39	4.51	4.02	3.70	3.47	3.30	3.17	3.07	2.98	2.84	2.70	2.55	2.47	2.39	2.30	2.21	2.11	2.01
40	7.31	5.18	4.31	3.83	3.51	3.29	3.12	2.99	2.89	2.80	2.66	2.52	2.37	2.29	2.20	2.11	2.02	1.92	1.80
60	7.08	4.98	4.13	3.65	3.34	3.12	2.95	2.82	2.72	2.63	2.50	2.35	2.20	2.12	2.03	1.94	1.84	1.73	1.60
120	6.85	4.79	3.95	3.48	3.17	2.96	2.79	2.66	2.56	2.47	2.34	2.19	2.03	1.95	1.86	1.76	1.66	1.53	1.38
∞	6.63	4.61	3.78	3.32	3.02	2.80	2.64	2.51	2.41	2.32	2.18	2.04	1.88	1.79	1.70	1.59	1.47	1.32	1.00

Interpolation should be performed using reciprocals of the degrees of freedom.

[1] This table is reproduced with the permission of the Biometrika Trustees from M. Merrington, C. M. Thompson, "Tables of percentage points of the inverted beta (F) distribution," *Biometrika*, vol. 33, p. 73, 1943. Also reprinted in Dixon and Massey, *op. cit.*

INDEX